OPERATING O AND O-27 TRAINS:

A Complete Guide to the Design, Construction and Operation of a Layout for Lionel* Trains.

Distributed by

MDK, Inc.

*LIONEL IS THE REGISTERED TRADE MARK OF THE LIONEL TOY CORPORATION, NEW YORK, NEW YORK.

SOURCES

Pages 7-168 are reproduced from the *Handbook for Model Engineers* (1940).

Pages 169-197, 201-233, 236-238 and 243-245 are Lionel instruction sheets completely reformatted and rewritten by Maury D. Klein.

Pages 198-200 are new material created expressly for this book by Albert C. Ruocchio.

Pages 234-235 and 239-242 are reproduced from *Track Layout and Accessory Manual for Lionel Trains* (1979).

Neither MDK, Inc. or Maury D. Klein are related in any way to the Lionel Toy Corporation or the Lionel Fundimensions division of General Mills Fun Group, Inc. or CPG Products Corp.

K-LINE Stock No K-1
ISBN No. 0-934580-02-2

CONTENTS

6206
6206

How to Begin

Chapter One

In miniature railroading there is an exciting fascination for every boy, whether he is interested in engineering, electricity, mechanics, architecture, showmanship, or in none of these, but is just wholesome Young America pulling at the leash and thrilling to the dramatic action of churning locomotive drive rods, to the hurtling speed of the racing streamliner and to the power, force and tireless energy of the puffing freighter.

This book is written and compiled for boys of all ages, to bring within their reach the essence and spirit of railroading; to enable them to develop around their own sets of train and track, by means of their own handiwork, a complete system on which their models will be able to duplicate everything that real trains do—in the same efficient, business-like, methodical manner.

To begin is the only problem for, once begun, this is an inspiring, absorbing hobby that is never left. The railroad is planned, construction is started, but the system is never finished, for imagination speeds on ahead of the builder to explore new fields for conquest, new branch lines to be added, freight yards to be extended, the main line to be double-tracked, new signal or control systems to be installed, facilities at the locomotive terminal to be improved, a mountain divison, elevated track, bridges, tunnels, lakes, a waterfall! The march ahead is endless but every step of the way brings increased opportunities for train operations and each job finished well delivers special thrill and satisfaction.

To begin a model railroad calls for a set of trains and space where a table or bench may be built and on which track may be fixed permanently. Two things are important. The first is that the track must be raised off the floor on a fixture that brings it to waist-height, at least. The second important thing is that the space provided must be available permanently for the purpose. Operating trains on the floor of a drawing room may be a splendid idea during a holiday, but a week or a month later the drawing room or living room will be required for other purposes and projected ideas of a model empire will be packed away on the shelf with good, old No. 700 and its string of cars and circle of track.

It may not be easy to obtain space for your model, but remember, real railroads once had the same trouble.

If you live in a house, there is the attic and the basement which might be used to solve the space problem. If you live in an apartment, there is "00" gauge, the space-saving, half-size, scale model equipment. A good "00" gauge layout can be built on a ping-pong table and an elaborate, complicated system will fit into a spare room.

This book is written in chapters and the chapters are placed in sequence as each subject might normally arise.

After you have determined to become a full-fledged model railroader and have found suitable space for your project, the next step is to decide which gauge track you will use—"0" gauge which is quarter-inch scale, or "00" gauge which is 5/8-inch scale. In "0" gauge a greater variety of equipment is available. In "00" gauge a much more extensive road can be reproduced in the same given space.

After the question of space and gauge have been settled, get busy at once on a layout and tables for it. From then on you are a model railroader and, before you, the track stretches straight to Wonderland, gleaming with excitement! All-aboard!

PLANNING THE LAYOUT

CHAPTER TWO

IF you enjoy games and puzzles that are a test of skill, imagination and rational deduction, then the planning of a realistic layout will be as interesting and exciting an occupation as the actual construction of the railroad and the operation of the trains—for there are numerous, excellent, gratifying results to be achieved, as well as a number of rules which must be followed.

The first step in the development of a suitable layout is to decide on what you want your trains to do—what kind of show you want them to perform—for, opportunities for switching, reversing, passing, and other movements, must be kept in mind when the track arrangement is designed.

Essentially, there are only three types of track layouts. One is a circle, another a straight line and the third resembles the letter Q. The first is known as the "continuous" layout, being comprised of a circuit of main line around which trains may travel again and again, as on a simple loop or oval. A "point-to-point" layout is the second type. It resembles a real right-of-way most closely in that it has two terminals with a stretch of straight track between them. The third type of track layout is called "home-and-back" and contains only one terminal feeding into a continuous track circuit.

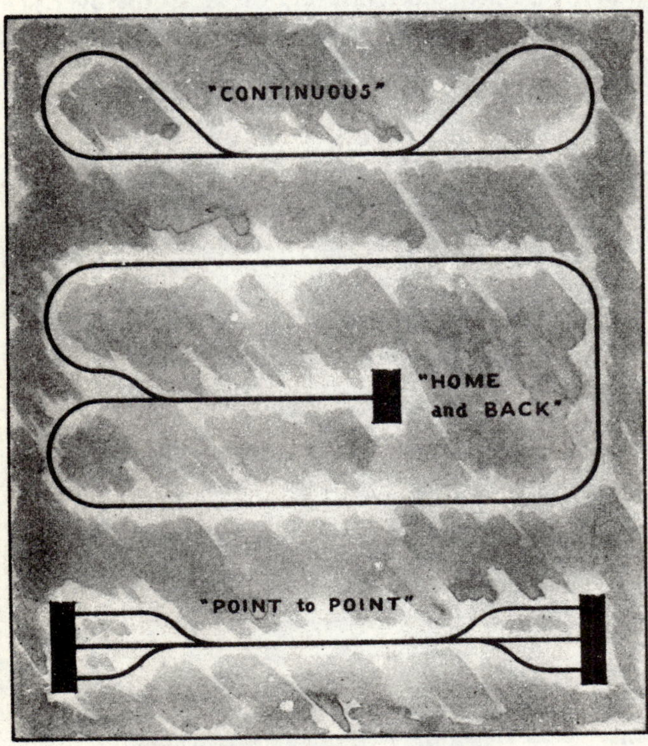

Each of these systems of track has its own advantages. The continuous layout is the easiest to operate. The point-to-point layout is by far the most realistic but at each terminal the train must be uncoupled and the engine turned around and re-coupled. The home-and-back system is actually a combination of the other two with added advantages for a single operator in that all making-up and breaking-up of trains and changing the direction of the engine is done at one point close to the railroad's one set of controls.

Each of these systems provides opportunity for reproducing a different department of real railroading. The continuous layout might be decorated and operated as if it were some central division of a railroad, with the railroad's terminals on beyond in the imagined distance. The point-to-point layout might include stubs, spurs, yards and service tracks and reproduce every manner of shunting action of a busy terminal, but with the line between the terminals so compressed that very little mileage is represented. The home-and-back layout could combine a terminal layout with an extensive line.

On the opposite page are a number of illustrations of track devices which can be included in the whole track pattern to serve definite purposes. A and D indicate methods of building reversing loops. In order to reproduce the shape indicated in the first diagram, without distortion, it is necessary to use a very short piece of straight track cut from a full-length section. Cutting track to any desired length may be done easily by locking the track in a vice and cutting it with a metal hack saw. B shows a crossing and two "O" gauge switches fitted together at intersecting lines. C, E, F and J show turnouts for freight or industrial sidings on a single-track main line. For a double-track siding, J is considered better practice than C. F is a type of industrial siding which offers considerable opportunity for car spotting tricks and engine escapement.

If the model railroad has a single track main line and two or more trains are being operated at the same time, a passing track is an essential device.

Three different types of passing tracks, made with regular "O" gauge sections, are indicated in sketches G, H and I.

Such arrangements also are used on a double-track main line to enable a fast train to pass ahead of a slow train which is held in the siding.

The passing siding is insulated from the rest of the layout so that it can be controlled separately from the control board.

Sketches H and I indicate track arrangements

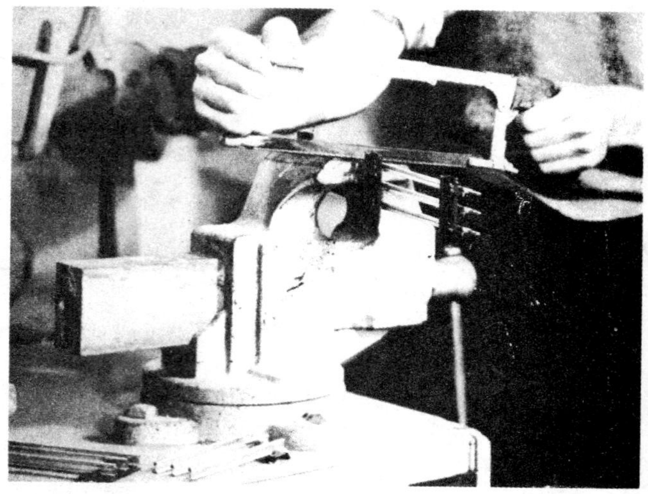

sometimes used to pass one train ahead of the other without stopping either.

Sketch K is known as a wye and may be used in yards or around terminals for reversing the direction of locomotives or trains. A locomotive is run in on one arm of the wye formation, backed out on the other arm of the wye and started ahead across the third side of the triangle, running forwards in the opposite direction from the way it started.

Sketch L indicates a comprehensive switching arrangement on a three-track main line. Switches used in this manner are known as a crossover. The eight switches used on these three main line tracks enable trains travelling in either direction to cross into any other track without reversing.

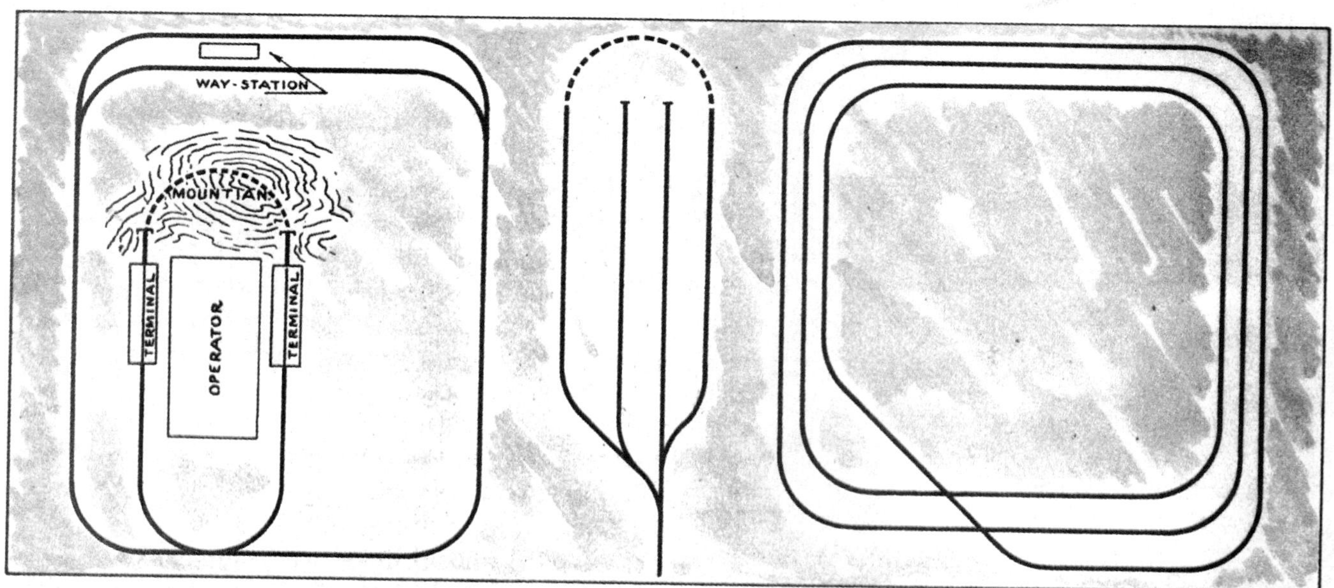

At the left is a modified "home and back" system having a hidden loop to eliminate the necessity of reversing locomotives. In the center is a terminal track loop for reversing the direction of a train. At right is a "continuous" system which looks like a three-track roadway.

ILLINOIS
CENTRAL

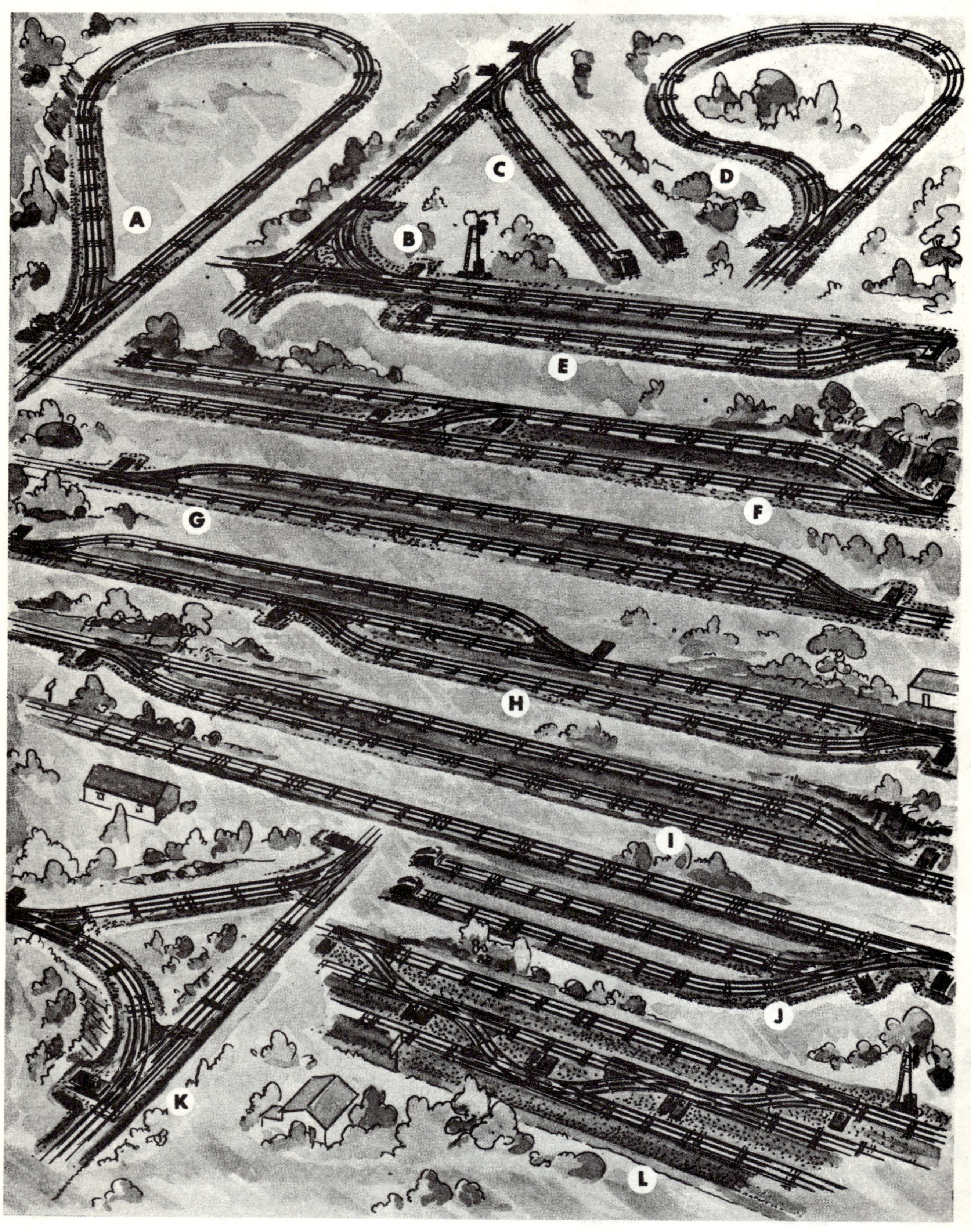
A
B
C
D
E
F
G
H
I
J
K
L

LOOKING AHEAD

CHAPTER THREE

THE miniature railroad system should be planned as a series of steps, each one adding some operating feature or increasing the track mileage over which trains can run. A comprehensive plan should be made which will fill all of the space that is available and which will include every operating feature that is desired, then the layout as a whole is carefully divided into a number of parts, the first loop of track acquired with the original train being the first step in the railroading building project.

Before a single piece of equipment is added, there is a tremendous amount of interesting work to be done. The platform is built and initial landscape effects are added to it, such as the painting of streets and highways and breaking up the flat tabletop with trees, shrubs, boulders and earthworks.

The next step in the extension of a system, such as the one illustrated by the sketches below, is in the addition of a single switch, a few sections of straight track, a bumper and a crossing warning. This addition improves appearances, giving the single station in the layout a through track as well as a waiting track.

The model railroad building program should be divided not only into periods for the acquisition of new trains and equipment but for the handcraft projects as well, with definite dates established for the completion of each and every undertaking.

Later, three more switches are added, more track, another bumper and a coal elevator. On the enlarged layout it is possible to operate both a freight train and a passenger train, holding the passenger train at the station while the freight makes a circuit of the layout, or holding the freight train in the central freight siding.

The system illustrated is so arranged that trains may be reversed to travel in either direction by backing them through the line of track in the center of the layout.

Any of the track layouts to be found among the blueprints in this book may be constructed sectionally in this same manner.

By starting the railroad with a single loop of track rather than to begin at one end of some enormous project, trains may be placed into operation immediately and the fun of operating trains can be mixed with the pleasure of scenic and architectural designing and building. Each will be found to support and sustain the other.

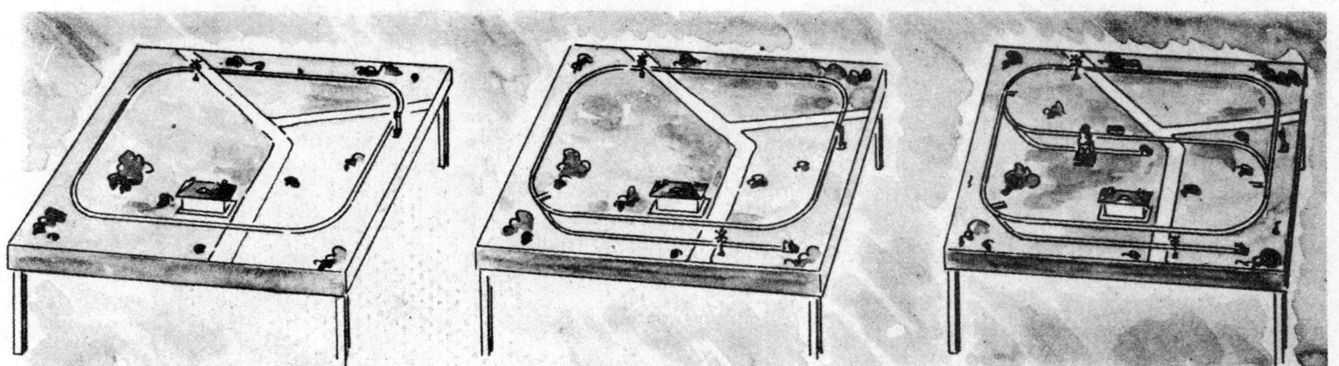

In three installments, a simple railroad system is developed into one which has a number of interesting operating features.

In the illustration below is a more ambitious undertaking than the layout shown on the previous page. It is started, however, with not much more than a simple loop of track and several switches. Before any additional equipment is obtained the embankment for the inclined track is prepared. Then sections of straight and curved track and a pair of switches are obtained and the entire main line is double-tracked. With the double-tracking of the main line, an enormous amount of mileage is provided for the continuous operation of trains.

Between the second and third steps, a large amount of scenic work is done, the embankment is completed and a lake is built in the center of the layout. With the lake completed, the third phase in the project is started. Two loops are added and the main line actually becomes a double-tracked road able to accommodate trains running in either direction.

The final set adds a locomotive service track, turntable, roundhouse and industrial sidings.

The important thing to note, in a study of the railroad project below, is that at each point, A, B, C and D, there is a complete layout. This constant appearance of a finished job is much easier to work with than a long flat bench with only one corner of the job actually finished and the remainder staring you in the face and discouraging you every time you look up.

On the following page are five sketches of a five-year building program. The first four sketches show track only, whereas the scenery and buildings are added piece by piece each step of the way. It might be found cheaper to purchase at one time all of the required lumber for an extensive project, but if it is purchased it should be stored away and only one section of the platform erected at a time, just enough to accommodate the division of the layout that is to be built immediately.

The layout shown is built on an irregular shelf. Below the shelf is plenty of storage space for the trunks and disused furniture with which most attics are cluttered.

These sketches are made not to provide any definite plan which might fit into space that is available, but merely as suggestions of how any plotted system might first be designed in scale on paper, then divided for sectional construction.

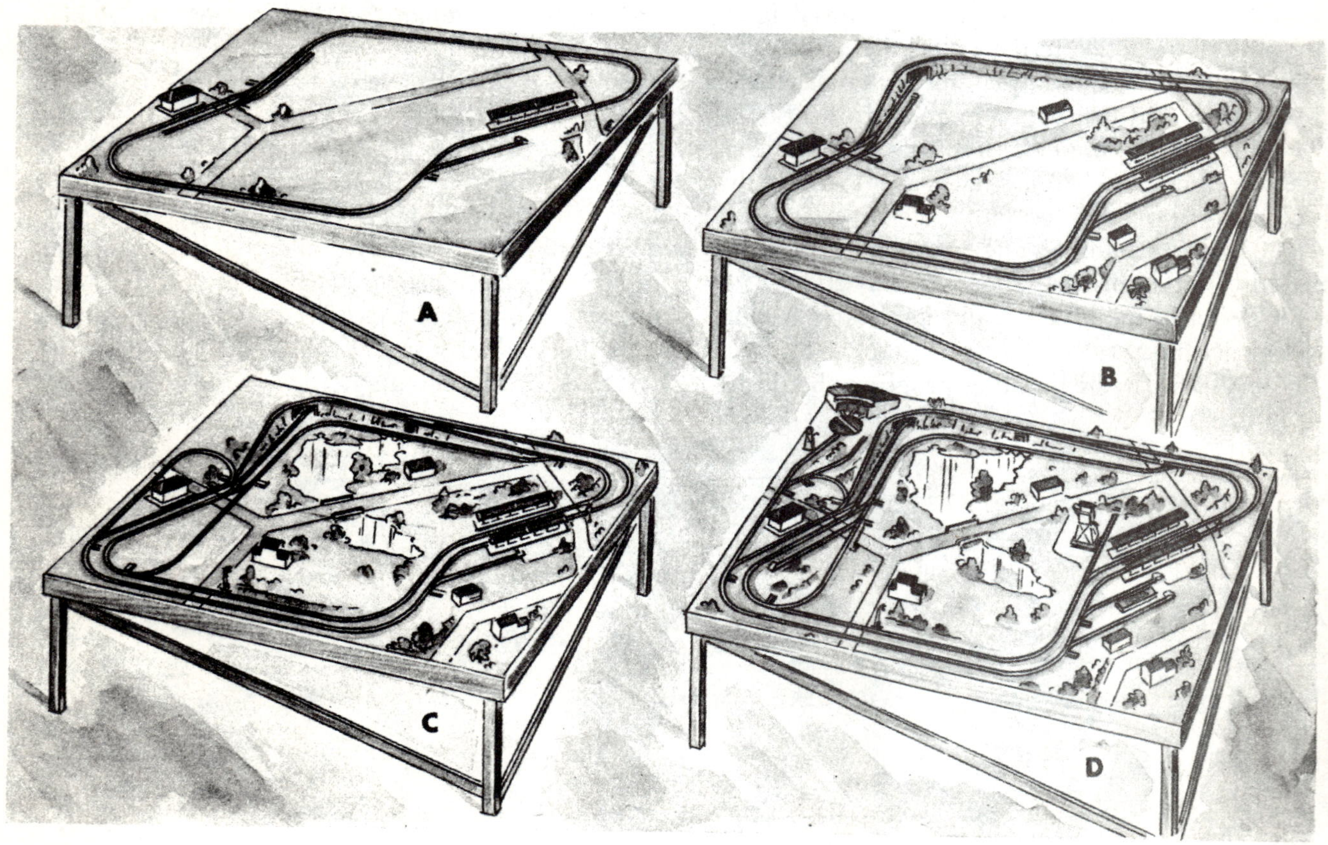

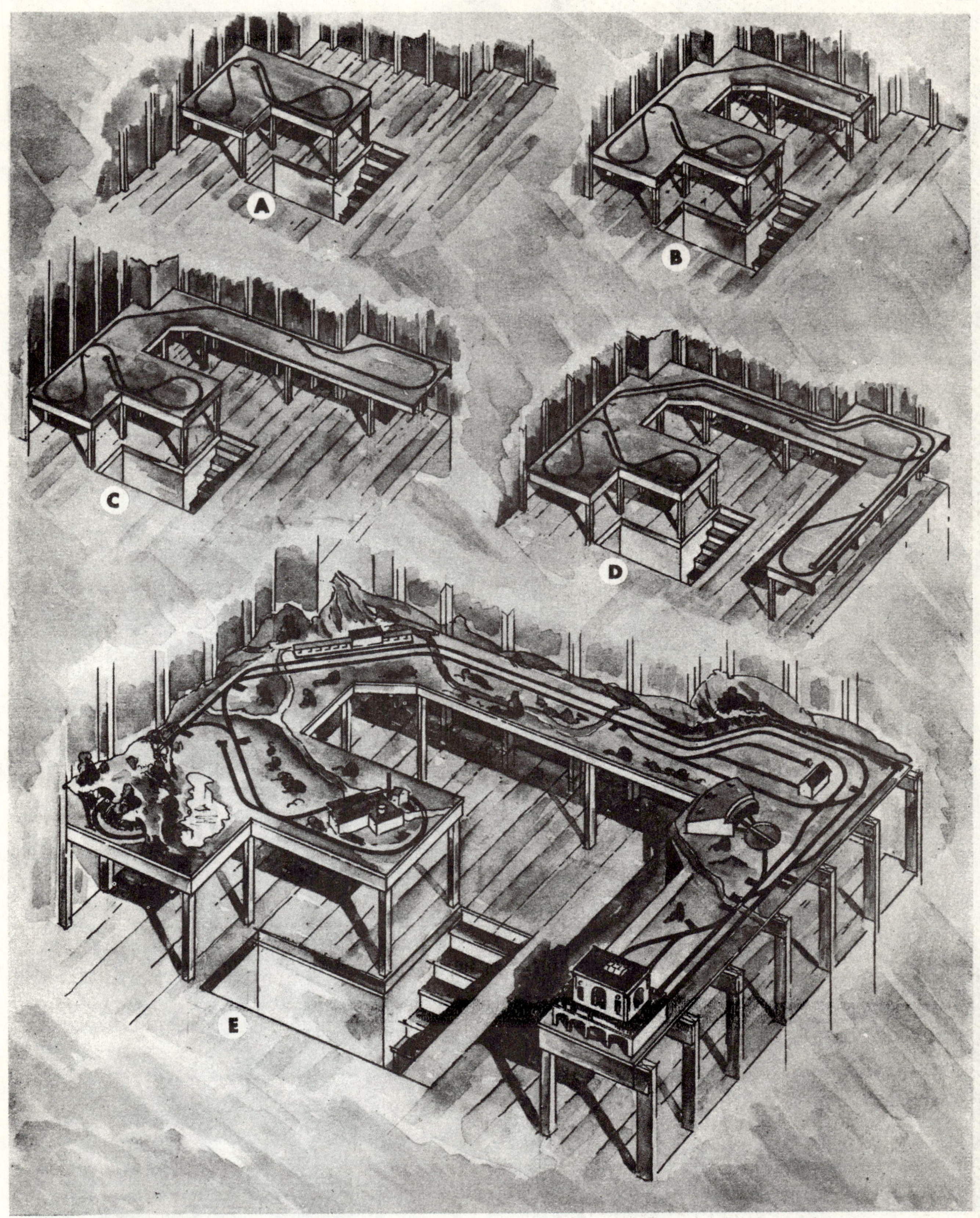
A
B
C
D
E

134

Layout Suggestions

Chapter Four

BEFORE getting out paper and pencil and starting the first rough draft of the trackage for a model railroad system, it is helpful to have a general idea of what a model railroad can be made to look like when it is landscaped and when all auxiliary houses and buildings are in place. For signals, stations, crossing gates, factories and homes are as important to the complete model railroad picture as the number of trains and switches and the amount of track that are being used.

On the following pages are sketches of finished railroad systems which will start your imagination to work. They show layouts using the trains, tracks and accessories which most boys have—but including also the hills, valleys, fields, lakes, rivers and highways—all built by hand—which are able to convert a set of trains into a model railroad project. With most of the plans on following pages, wiring diagrams are indicated which show by what means each road can be controlled from a switchboard.

It is doubtful that any one of the ideas suggested will meet all of the requirements anyone might establish, yet in each design there may be some arrangement of track, location of factory, station, river, or suggestion of some other nature that may be copied or adapted.

An attempt has been made to include plans for a wide variety of floor shapes, and to picture roads on which only one train is used with a few switches and a small amount of track, as well as systems which fill a whole attic and embrace many scale miles of track, alternate routes, large terminals, extensive yards; and provide for the operation of a half dozen trains at a single time.

Spectators in front of a model railroad layout and the operator as well are going to be called upon to imagine that each journey made by a miniature represents the regular scheduled movement of a real train in real railroading. This should be remembered constantly when a track layout is being designed. Everything possible should be done to help in presenting a complete picture. An effort should be made to include station stops and the industrial sidings where a real railroad actually performs its service to the public and collects its revenues.

If your own interests center along the lines of passenger traffic and you own passenger equipment, then the model railroad might be built as a suburban line with a number of small stations and many homes.

If you are interested in one particular industry, your whole railroad layout might present the story of that industry from raw materials to manufactured product and retail distribution, with the model railroad serving as the means of transportation between the different points.

If you want to portray a diversity of activity on your line, then your railroad may be planned to include all of the more important industries that are to be found in real railroading, with a representation of manufacturing in the reproduction of factory buildings and a representation of passenger business in the use of several passenger stations.

The important thing is to provide in the model system not only an excuse for the operation of the trains but evidence that the whole model community is dependent upon its railroad and that the railroad itself is an integral part of community life.

The sketches on the following pages make an attempt to build around the tracks a harmonious country-side in which the model railroad assumes a correctly balanced relationship to all other units.

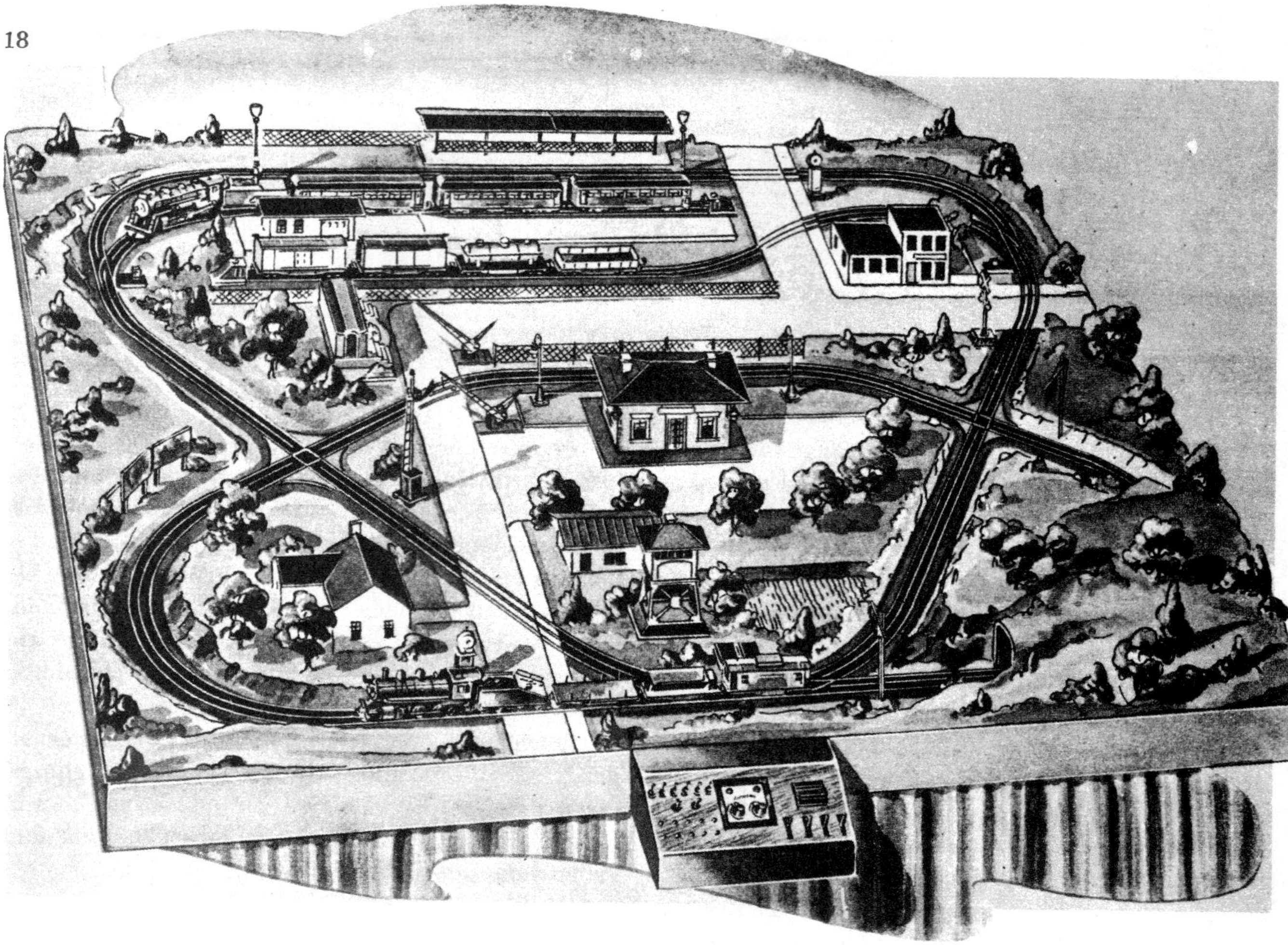

SMALL TWO-TRAIN RAILROAD

TWO pairs of switches and two crossings in this layout provide several alternative routes for the passenger and freight train that this system will accommodate.

The two long sidings shown in the layout plan can be used as passing tracks or for the storage of surplus cars.

The layout can be reproduced with "O-27" equipment as easily as with "O" gauge equipment.

A conveniently located control panel box is shown to one side of the railroad table. This houses all the controls.

The track layout is sectionalized, the main line tracks being broken into four sections, each controlled by a toggle switch. The power for either siding can be cut in or out by two other switches.

This sectionalizing is found useful in the operation of two trains, where one is to be stopped for the benefit of the other.

The track diagram calls for the use of three sections of RCS track, located at the entrance to sidings so that a train can back into a siding and uncouple its cars by electric remote control.

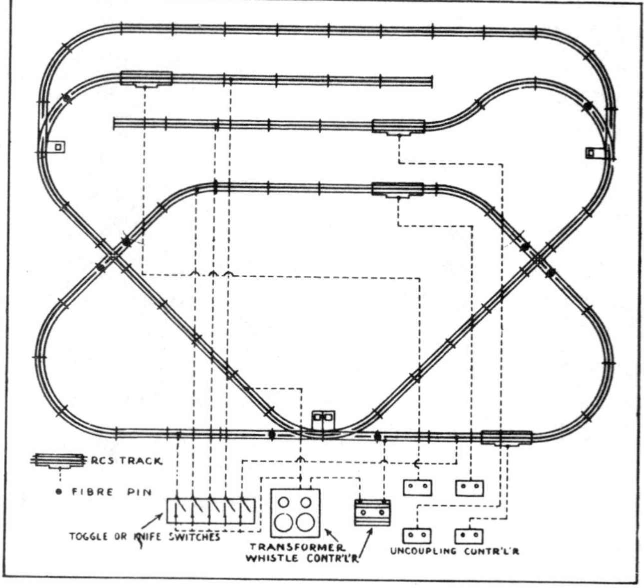

LAYOUT FOR "O-27" TRACK

A SIMPLE loop, double-tracked half way, and two sidings make this an easy plan to reproduce. As it is designed for only one locomotive, no sectionalizing is necessary.

A layout of this type is small enough to be placed on end against a wall when not in use. In this event, the framing of the table top is built strongly and the legs made collapsible. The various accessories such as signals and stations are fastened to the platform.

The tunnel appearing in the background has interesting wooden portals. A picturesque waterfall is simulated with cellophane drawn in tight vertical lines. Streamers are fastened over the cellophane further to portray falling water. The conventional glass over a base of pastel colors gives a good imitation of water for the flat surfaces. Small bits of sandstone are distributed unevenly along the banks of the stream while the scenery is being made. Glue holds them securely in place.

The furrowed field in the center of the layout is made of shreaded, peat moss glued to the table.

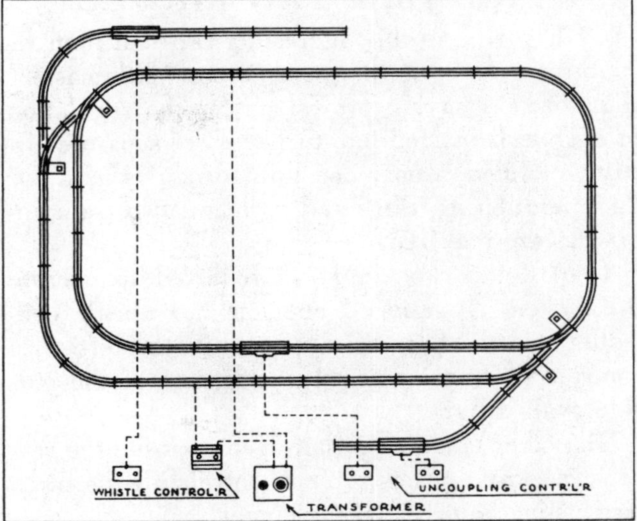

The two sidings are equipped with RCS track for uncoupling cars to be left behind by the rest of the train. RCS track might also be used in front of the coal elevator on the main line for dumping coal into the elevator basin by remote control.

A TRAINMASTER PROJECT

THE wiring in this interesting railroad plan requires one of the new type "trainmaster" transformers having provisions for the regulation of current being fed into two or more separate circuits. Although only one transformer is used for the operation of trains and switches, two train engineers are required.

One of the two engineers required to operate this system is stationed opposite the whistle controller and the two knife switches at the left. He controls the main line which consists of the outside oval of track.

The other engineer is stationed opposite the row of seven knife switches, and controls all the track circuits on the inside of the layout.

This layout will accommodate the simultaneous operation of two trains. One engineer can feed trains into the main line where the second engineer will take over their control. The main line itself is divided into two circuits so it can accommodate two trains whenever it is necessary.

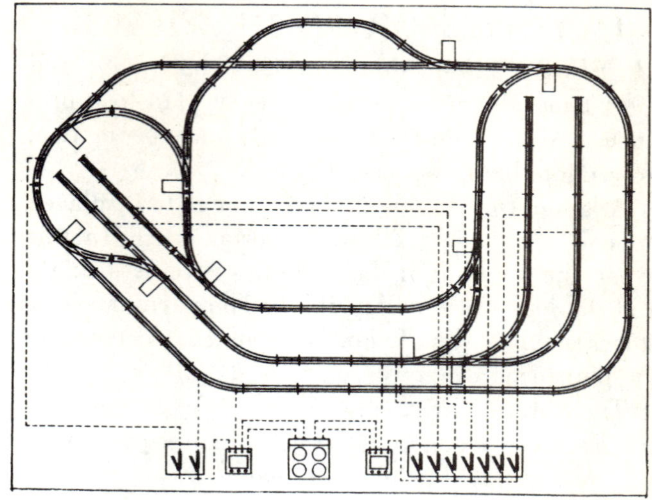

The layout enables trains to be reversed when travelling in either direction. A number of other interesting and railroad-like train movements is also possible. Cars or whole trains may be stored on the long sidings where RCS track should be used, for the uncoupling of the engine which can be accomplished by remote control.

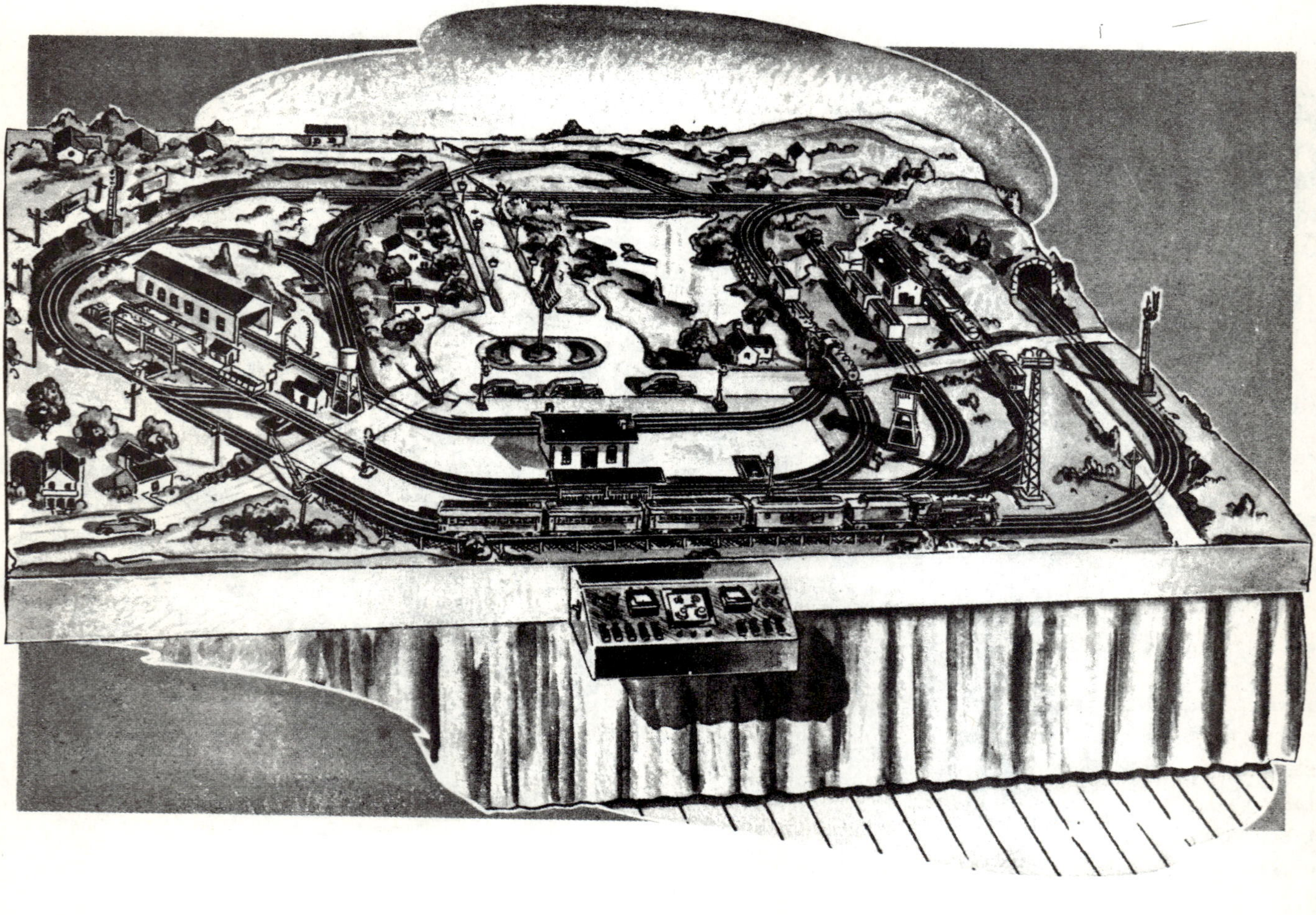

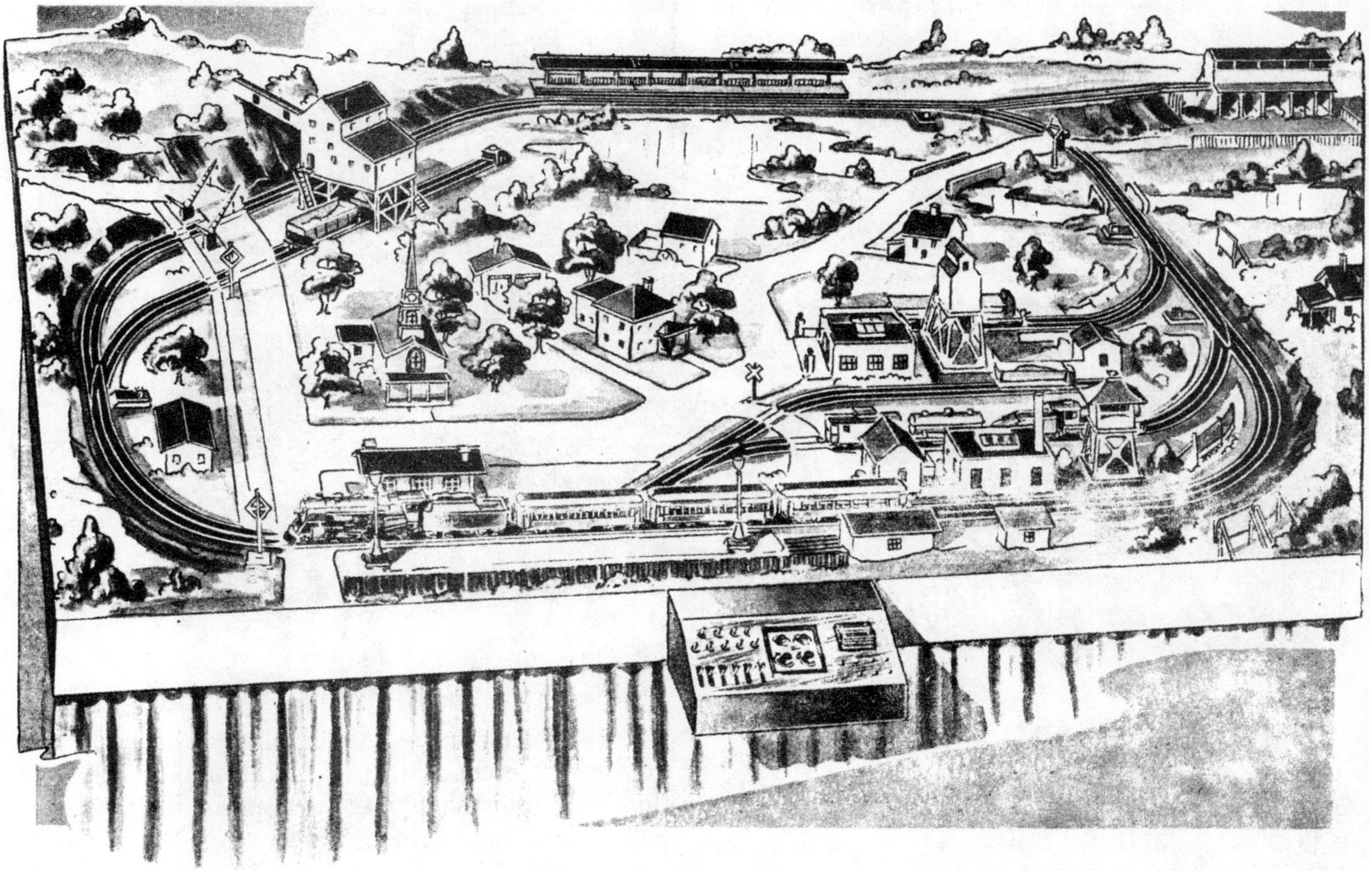

COAL FIELD RAILROAD

THIS system consists of a single track main line with a passing siding and a number of spur sidings. A coal mine head and coal pocket are two of the many interesting miniatures that are indicated in this sketch. They are combined in the plan, appropriately, with the electrically operated coal elevator. Plans for construction of the coal mine are given later in this book.

Station facilities are provided for the passenger business of this prosperous little line which boasts a freight and a passenger train. A small country station is seen in the foreground and a simple, illuminated passenger shed is located in the background.

A stream starts in one corner of the layout, and winds along the countryside, passing beneath the railroad tracks and a highway and widening into a lake of considerable proportions in the center of the layout.

The scene represented by the entire system is that of a small country town which has a church, stores, garage and a few houses and depends for its income on the coal mine.

A small coal yard is located on one of the sidings. Crossing gates, signals, lamp posts and other accessories are included for the sake of action and illumination.

The main line is divided into two track blocks which are wired individually. The passing siding at the lower right, and the industrial spurs are insulated from the rest of the layout.

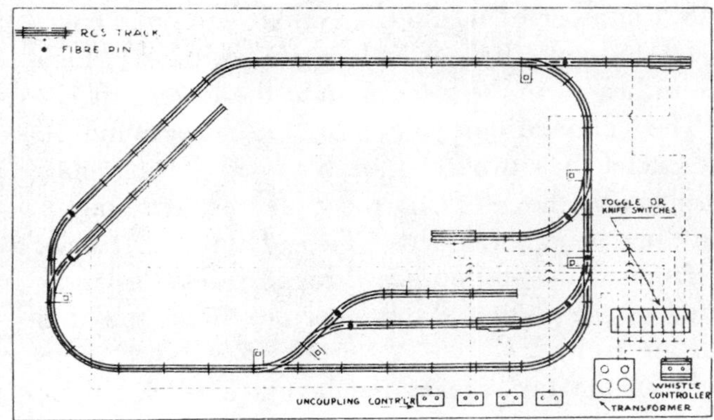

EMPIRE IN THE BASEMENT

A SPACE of only ten feet by twelve feet is required for the outfit in the sketch above yet it is able to represent hundreds of square miles of country-side including a fairly representative little city, a river, a mountain region and a suggestion of industry, with its bulk oil storage tanks and coal elevator.

Most unusual feature of this system is the "sneak-off" circle of track, hidden under the mountain, on which trains may be reversed.

The transformer used with a railroad plan such as this one should be of the "trainmaster" type which provides dial control of a number of circuits. Only one transformer is needed when one or two trains are being used, the main line being divided into a number of insulated sections each one energized individually through knife switches which are indicated in the track plan at the lower left.

The commodious station in the foreground in the sketch has two rows of No. 156 station platforms with the roofs of those nearest the station building being extended. Two of the four tracks in front of the station are through tracks, as indicated by the plan, and the other are track stubs for waiting trains.

From the far side of the layout a track siding extends into the center of the layout and halts in front of a freight platform. On all sidings of this kind RCS track should be used to provide for remote control uncoupling.

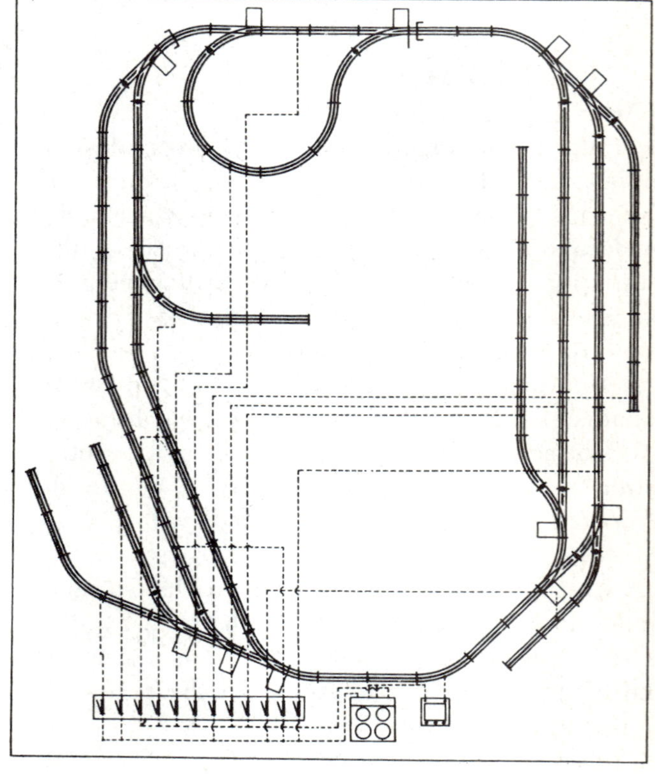

A DOUBLE-TRACKING PLAN

TWO completely independent loops of track enable trains to be operated without collision. On the outer track a short siding is provided and the inner loop has three side tracks. The plan shows two cross-overs and a reversing circle for either loop.

Power in all the sidings may be cut out. The outside mainline loop is divided into three circuits. The inside loop is likewise divided into three sections but only two large sections are controlled by transformer control No. 1. A double throw toggle switch is provided for the third inner section of track connected to the reversing loop. This is done so that either control No. 1 or No. 2 can energize that section, and train reversing can be controlled by either one of the controllers.

A train running "eastbound" on the outer track can be put into the inner loop. When moving over a train from one loop to the next, the two-way toggle switch is set so that control No. 2 energizes

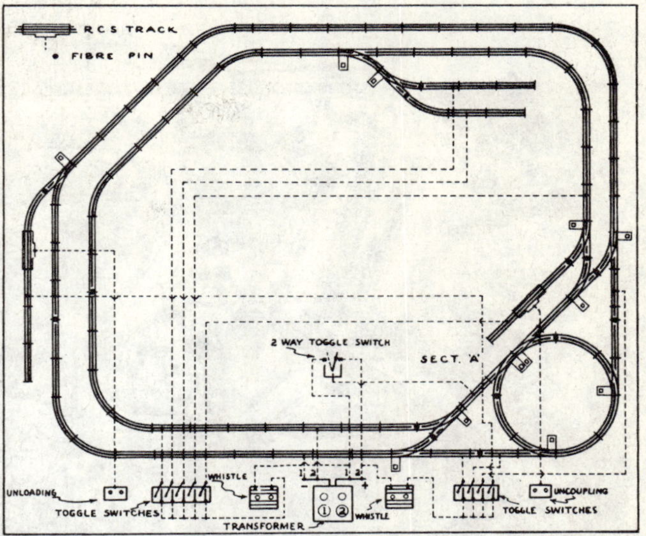

that section of track. When this switching operation is completed, and the train is on the "westbound" inner track, the two-way toggle switch is again thrown back so that control No. 1 is energizing it.

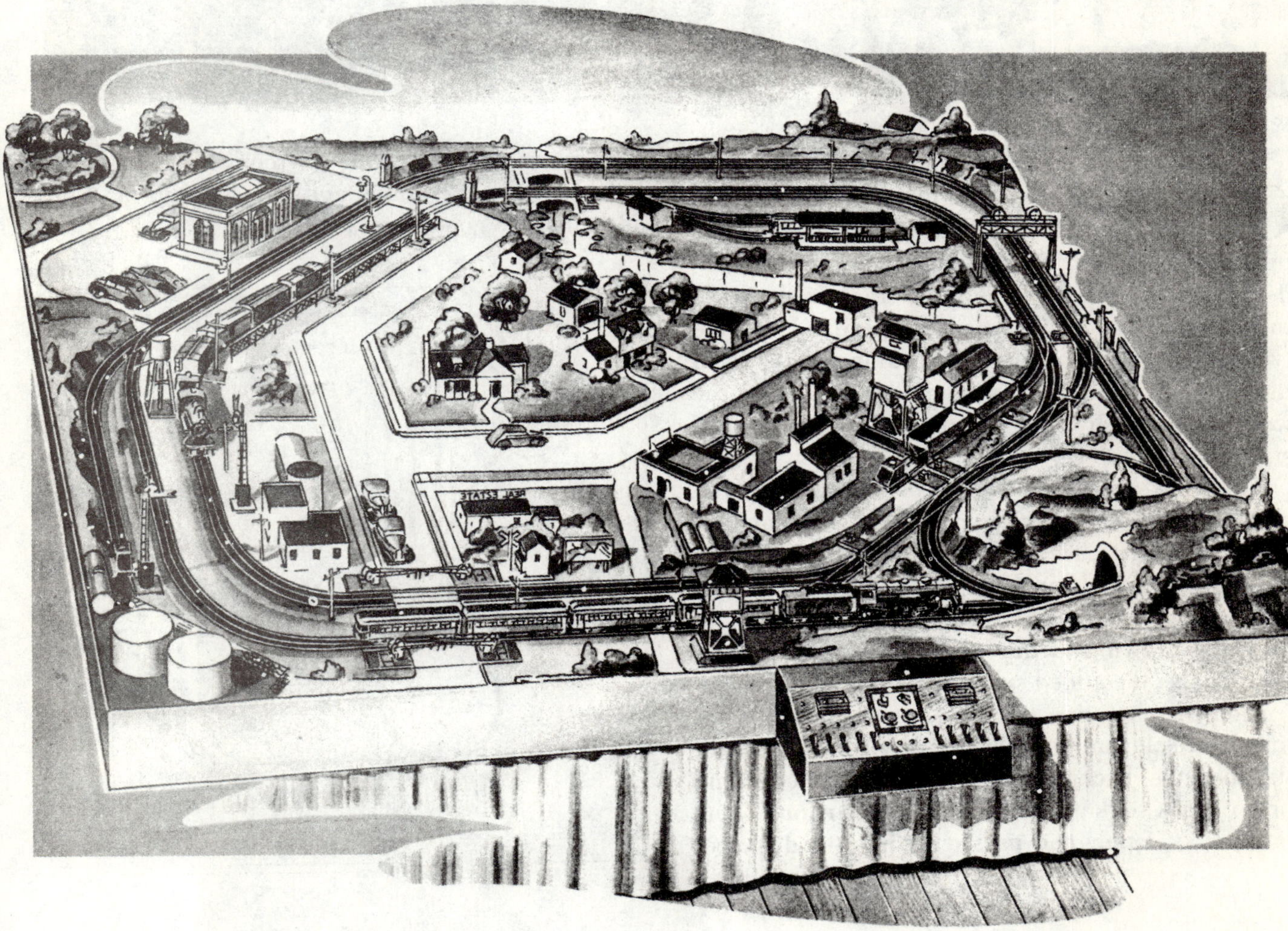

WELL-TYPE ATTIC SYSTEM

ON the opposite page is a plan for an attic system with a well provided in the center for the operators' stations. A similar but somewhat condensed arrangement of the same track is shown in the drawings and plans on this page. Here the two control positions are placed along one side of the railroad table with a complete table top, the well in the center being eliminated and a countryside taking its place.

The track arrangement is of the continuous type but embodies interesting principles of point-to-point operations, as trains may be switched from track to track and can be jockeyed into position to travel over any track in either direction.

In the drawing of the larger layout, on the opposite page, the added space has allowed for an extension of main line track and the inclusion of a timber trestle on the elevated division. In both sketches the background is used to conceal one line of track so that trains will disappear for a short interval as if they had passed off into the distance. Both plans provide plenty of room for locomotive service track operations and car shunting as well as to include good, long main lines.

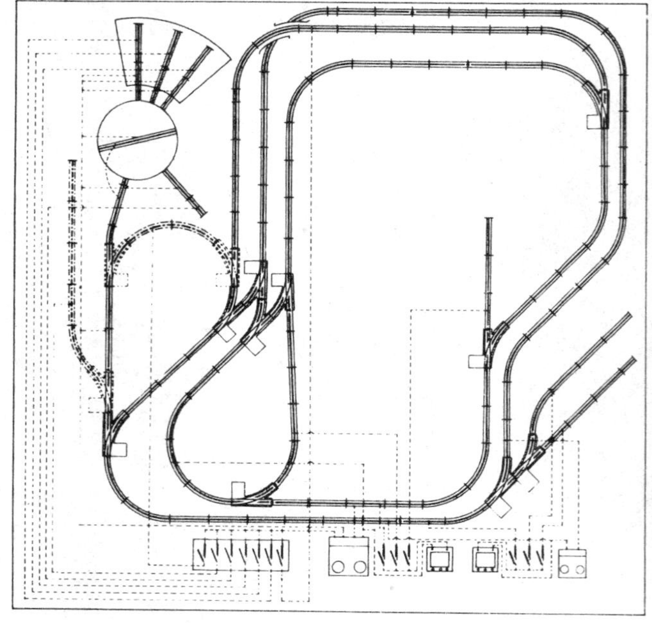

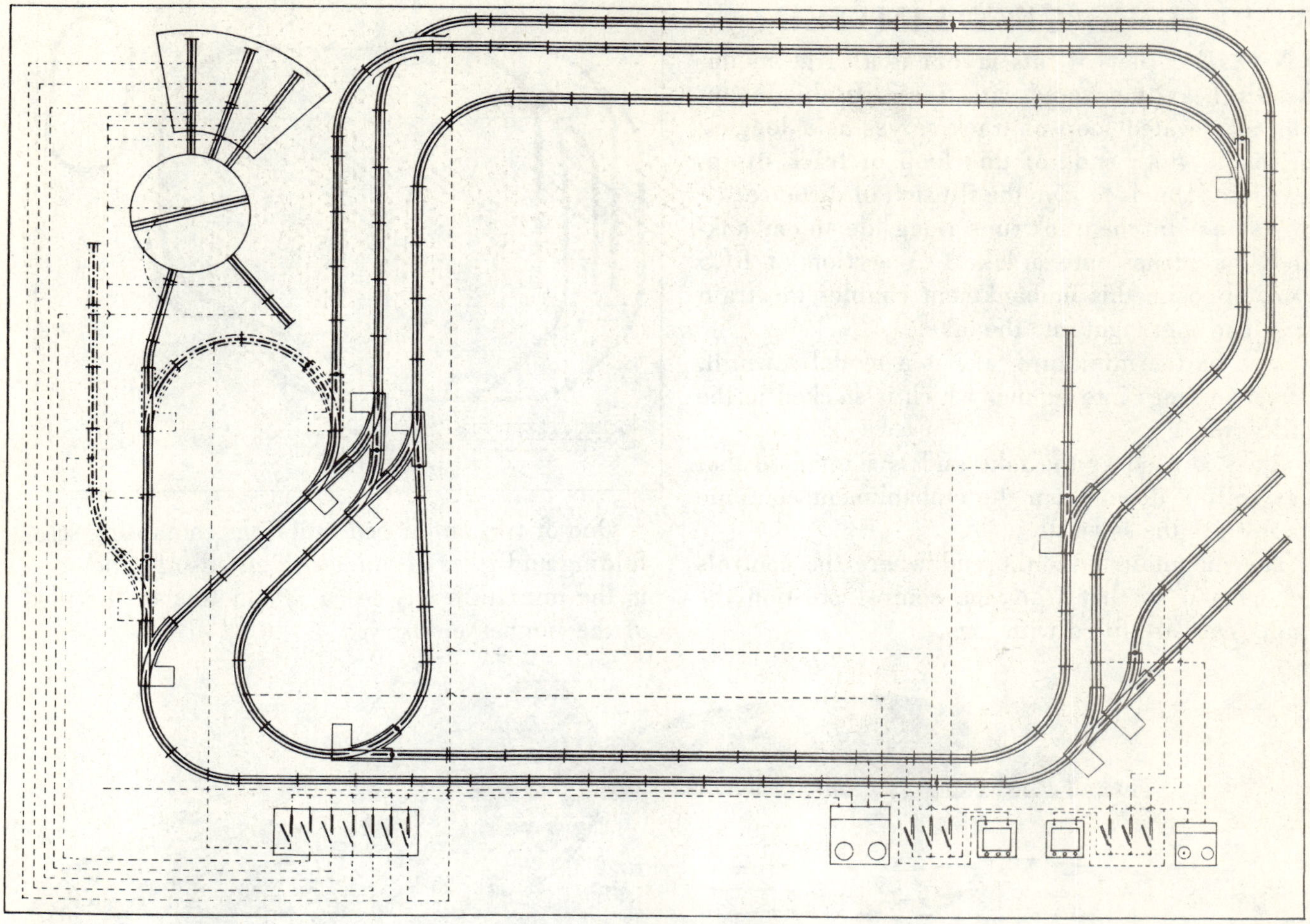

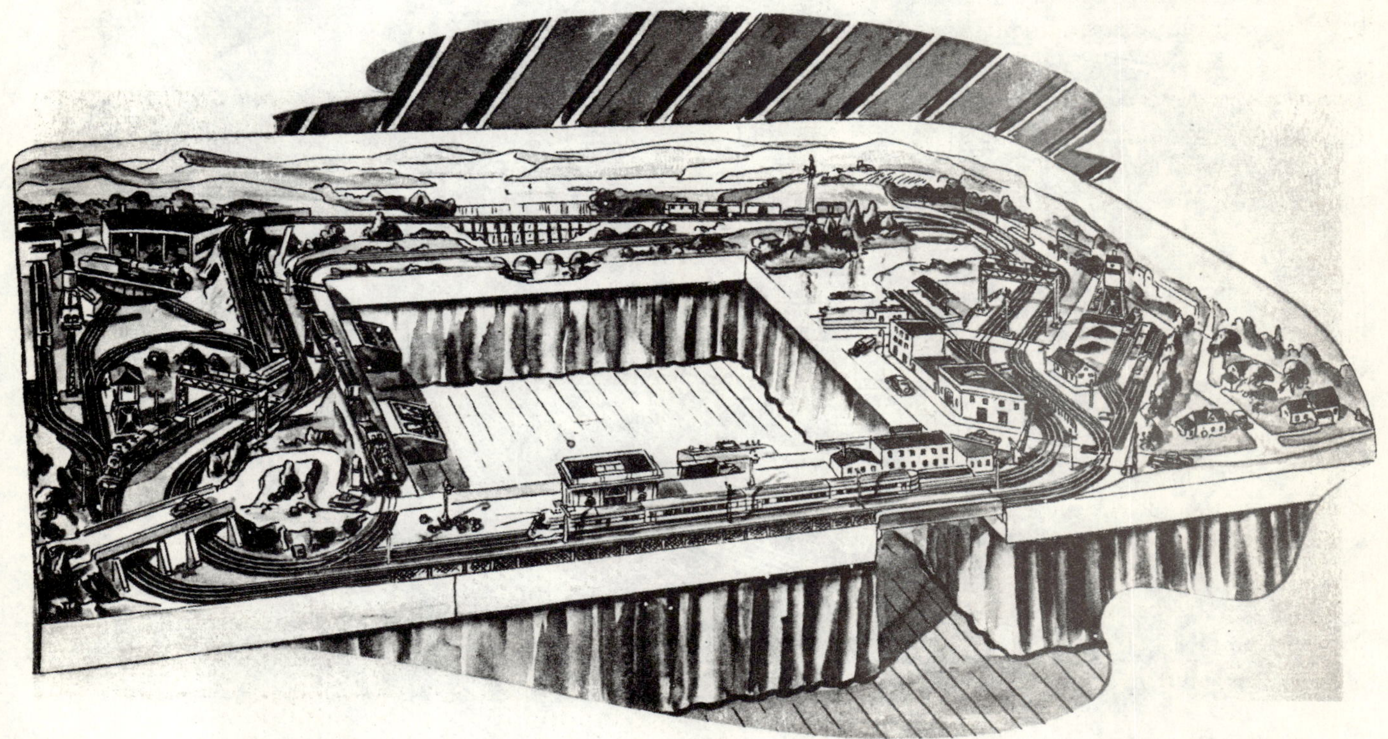

LUMBER CITY LIMITED

IN ONE corner of this layout is a large mountain heavily covered with trees. In this mountain an elevated loop of track serves as a logging railroad. Both ends of this loop of track disappear into tunnels to give the illusion of distance.

At one point the track runs alongside an embankment that drops into a lake. A section of RCS track opposite this embankment enables the train to unload logs right into the lake.

Also on the miniature lake is a model sawmill, converting logs into lumber which is stacked in the mill yard.

Glass is used as the lake and is slanted so that logs rolling down from the embankment continue on down to the sawmill.

The mountain is at the end where the controls are located so that from the control position the empty cars are filled with logs.

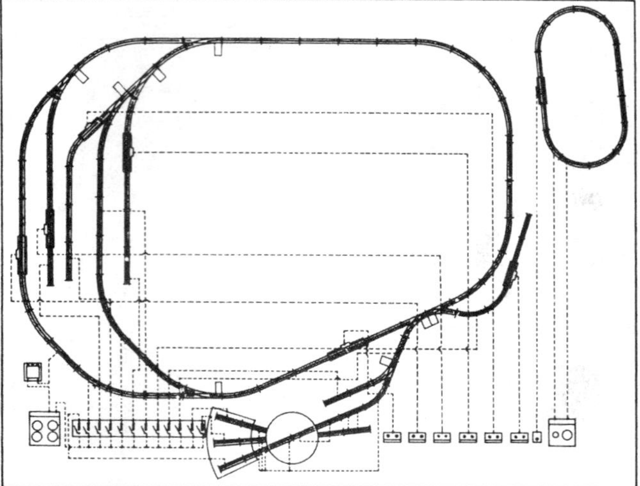

One or two unfinished buildings containing scaffolding and piles of lumber might also be included in the miniature city to carry out further the idea of the lumber industry.

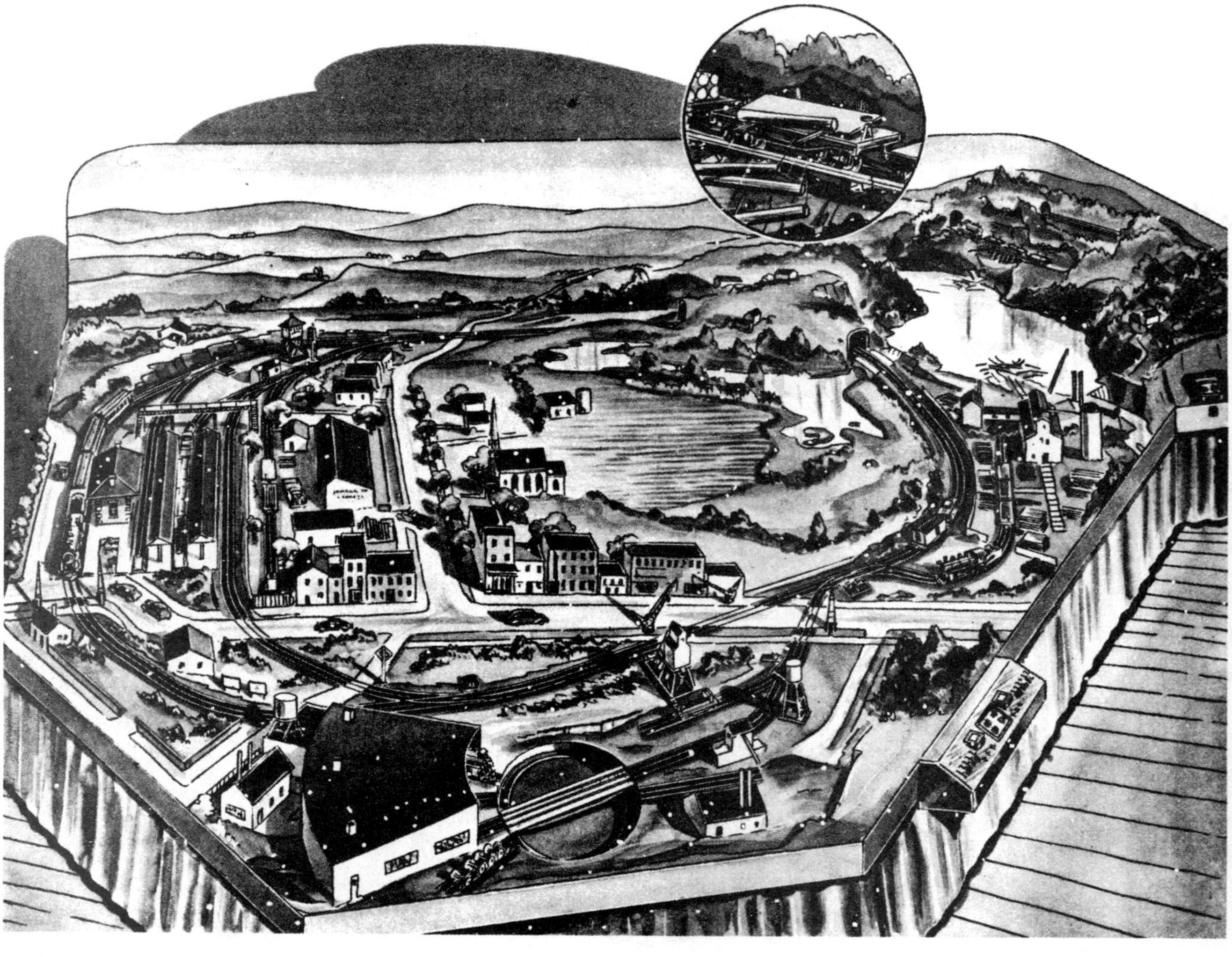

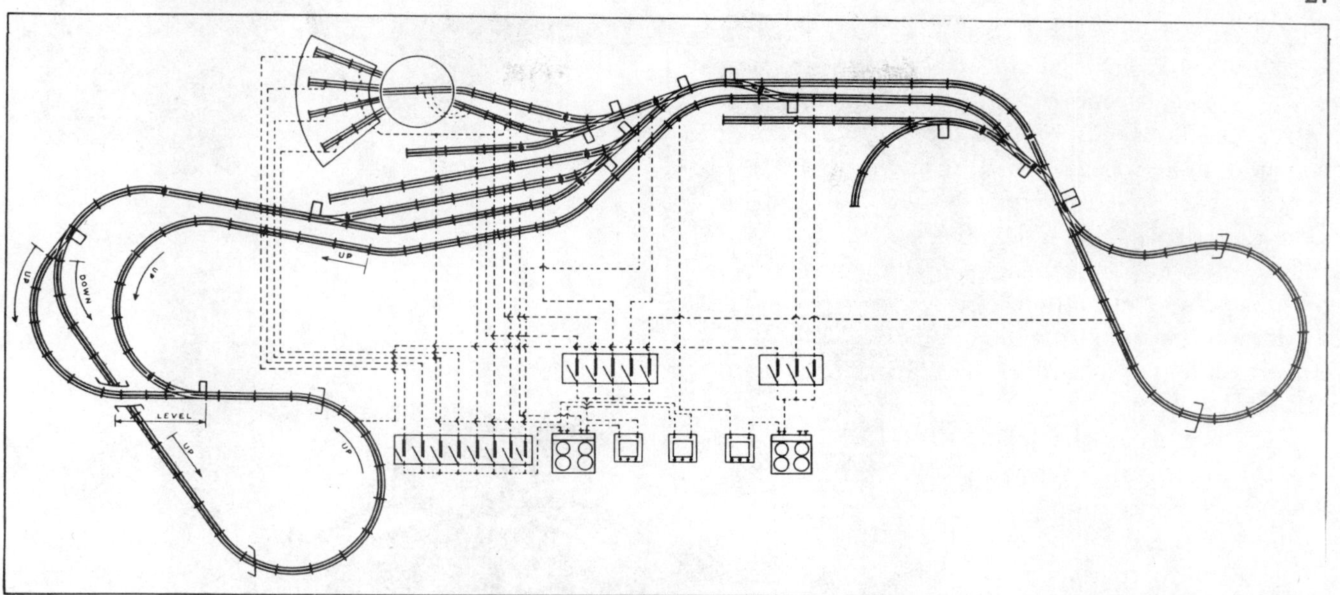

COMPLETE ATTIC ROAD

THIS plan is known as a continuous type but it resembles a system made for point-to-point operation. It is large enough to accommodate three stations, one large one and two small way stations. The finished layout has a roundhouse, turntable, coal pocket and other engine terminal equipment. It has mountains, city districts and factories.

5415

Giant Railroads

Chapter Five

ON two following pages are drawings and layouts of dream roads which put into black and white what happens when the imagination is allowed to travel away into the distance without any restrictions of space, time and expense.

Purely imaginative as these vast systems may appear, they nevertheless are practical and possible. Numerous miniature railroads similar to them have been constructed by individuals, in the course of several years of determined application to the model building project.

Most boys and men, however much they may desire and hope to possess roads as elaborate, do not have enough time, space and equipment to develop such layouts.

For them the miniature railroad club is the ideal solution. The question of work-time is answered by the cooperative effort of all boys in the group. With eight, ten or a dozen members of a club all working together, it is really surprising what can be accomplished in short order. By dividing the membership into small groups of two or three boys, each under a group leader, the entire labor of the whole railroad can be assigned at the very outset. In a club affiliated with a high school, Y.M.C.A., recreation center, church or scouting troop, the question of space is answered for the club by the sponsoring, parent organization. The question of expense is eliminated through the pooling of certain types of equipment, such as track and switches; and by the joint use of other equipment loaned to the club by members, such as locomotives, and passenger and freight cars.

When a railroad like one of those on following pages is to be constructed by a club, it is wise to sub-divide it into three or four steps, with the very first division containing a complete circuit of track, so that the club as a whole is able to operate trains at the earliest possible moment.

In plans for a club-operated railroad, provisions must be made for a number of operating control points, so that meetings devoted to scheduled movement of trains will put every boy to work at equally interesting jobs. This method of wiring divides all of the track of the system into separate electrical circuits or blocks. The transformer supplying current to any block is built into a panel board, which is mounted on the edge of the train table, close enough to the block so that the operator can see any train that may arrive on it.

The freight car classification yard, coach yard, terminals and roundhouse tracks are each controlled from separate switchboards by different boys. From a boy who has earned the temporary title of superintendent or dispatcher, a train order is issued and all operators or towermen at affected points are notified of it.

If the order calls for a passenger train, it is made up in the coach yard and sent into the terminal. If it is a freight train, it is made up in the classification yard and turned over to a road engine.

The order advises the destination of the train and where and when it is to be switched from one track to another, and how. Each operator at his transformer assumes control of the train when it is delivered to him at one end of his block.

With two or three trains running simultaneously according to a regular timetable, interspersed by an "extra" or two ordered out by the superintendent, all operators on a club road are kept busy and on their toes at all times.

For more information concerning the organization of a miniature railroad club, turn to the chapter devoted to that subject.

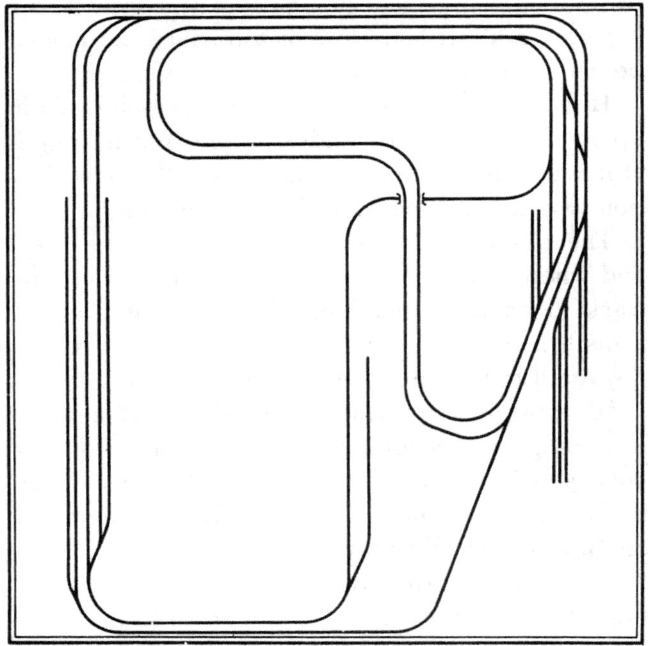

The North York R. R

WHEN the North York Railroad was first built many years ago some of the council members of the town of Greystone did everything they could to stop the trains. A law was passed which said, "When two trains approach each other, both shall stop and neither shall proceed until the other has passed." All trains were stopped in pairs facing each other. Something had to be done.

Finally the North York promised to send a hot shot freight roaring through town, blowing its whistle all of the way every morning except Sundays, at 7:25. In consideration for this unusual "alarm clock" service the law was repealed.

From that day to this no Greystonite has ever been late to work, and the United Employers' Union recently gave a medal for distinguished service to U. R. Wideawake, President of N.Y.R.R.

Eastern Belt Lines

THE Eastern Belt Lines is a dream road, painted with a model railroader's vivid imagination. Notice the slips in which freighters are docked and the warehouses in the foreground.

This pike is built in a lovely spot, landscaped to bring out its beauty. Factories and industrial sidings alike are surrounded by trees and shrubs. A bascule bridge crosses the meandering river at the left and in the distance is a plate girder bridge. Signal bridges, semaphores, powerful floodlights on industrial sidings make this an attractive system for night operations.

The Eastern Belt Line is a busy road. Two locomotives are in the terminal, and several others out on the road. A crane is working on an industrial siding. Car classification and storage tracks are full. Automobiles move along the highways.

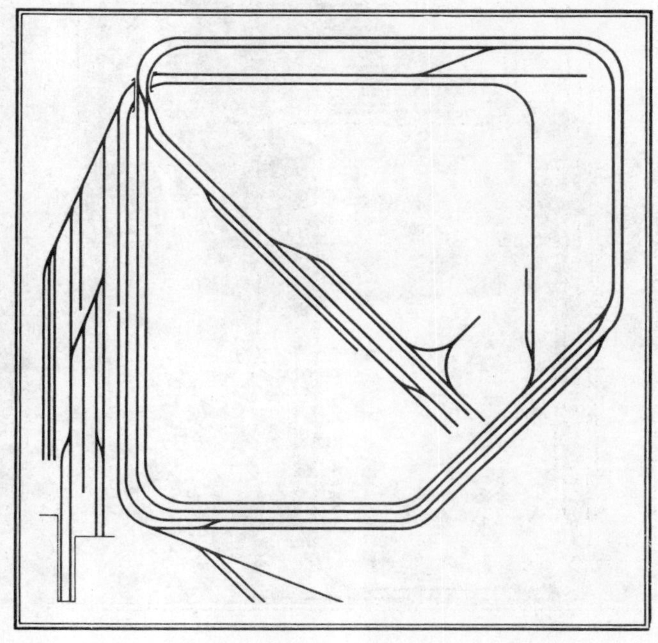

R

LAYOUT PLANS

CHAPTER SIX

ON following pages are blueprints of track layouts for boys who want to select a ready-made system so they can start at once on actual construction work. An attempt has been made to include suggestions in each gauge for every conceivable size and shape. Sections of track are indicated by cross bars. Frequently drawings call for half-sections or pieces of track cut to odd lengths. Track may be cut easily when it is held in a vise and a hack saw is used.

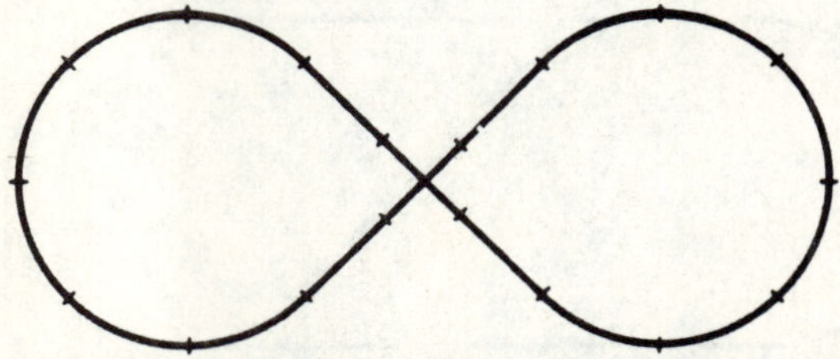

Figure-8 track layout gives the action of a large system in a small space. Two trains can operate on this track. Track cross-overs suggest that this line is in a busy suburban section. Space required is 32" by 72".

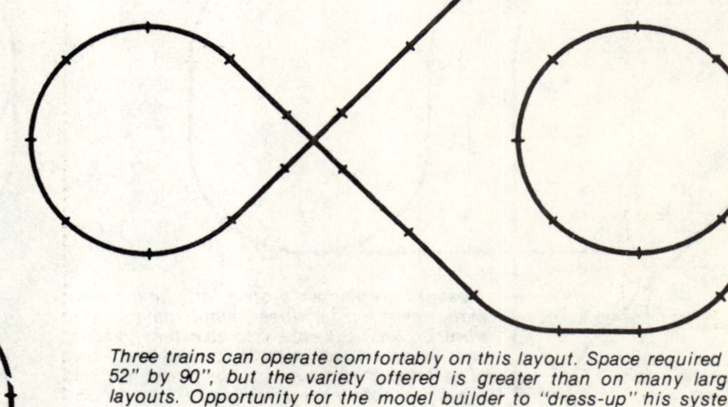

Three trains can operate comfortably on this layout. Space required is 52" by 90", but the variety offered is greater than on many larger layouts. Opportunity for the model builder to "dress-up" his system with scenic additions.

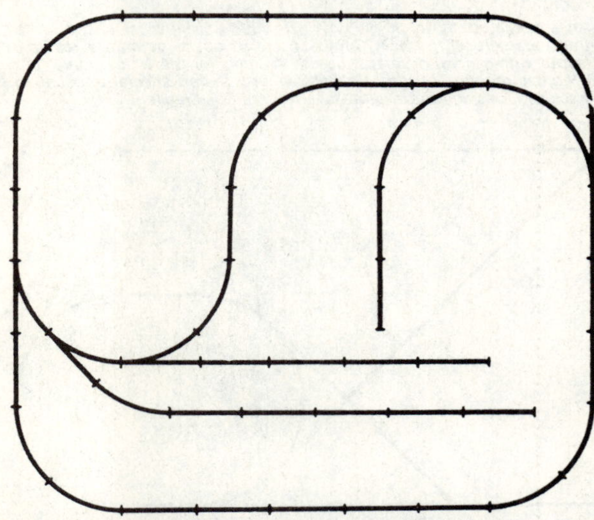

This layout is extremely attractive. Passing and directional reversing facilities are provided and interesting industrial sidings are included. Space required for this road is 82" by 72". Ideal for the boy who likes plenty of movement.

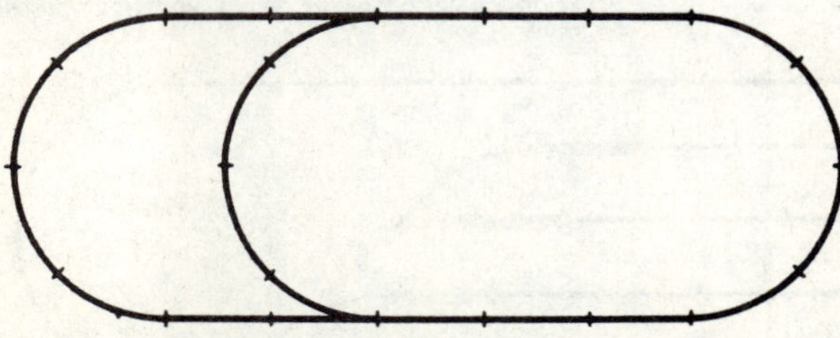

If your layout is built on a shelf, this is a good basic track. Space required is 32" by 82". The track is planned for future expansion and will give your trains plenty of running space. Two trains can be operated on this layout.

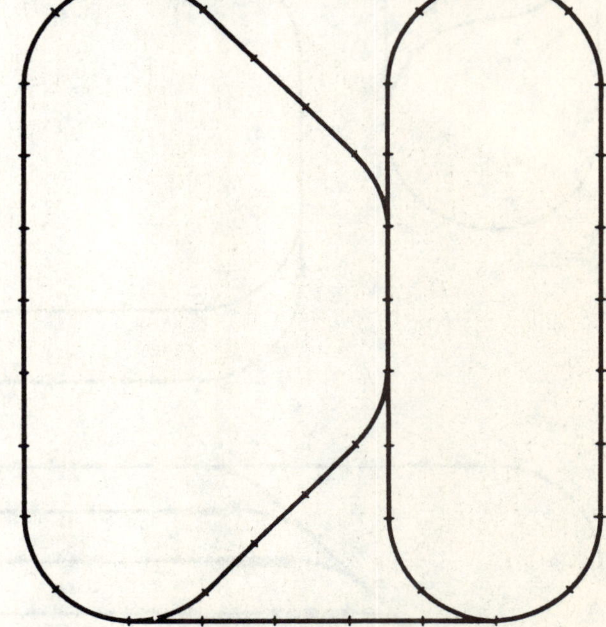

This unconventional layout gets real variety in the system. A mountain division at the left would give a chance for good scenic effects, and the model builder will find room for plenty of railroad structures. Space: 92" by 82".

"O" GAUGE TRACK LAYOUT PLANS

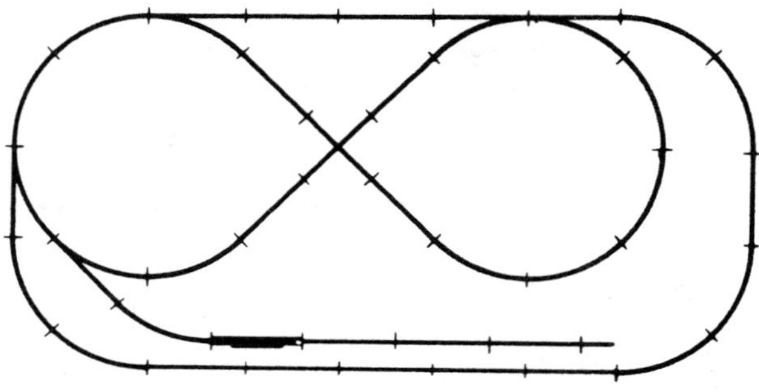

Track oval with a figure-8 reversing loop and a long industrial siding packs plenty of action into a relatively small floor space. Freight trains and passenger cars will both get plenty of operating chances on a system like this. Track-side equipment will help to add realistic details.

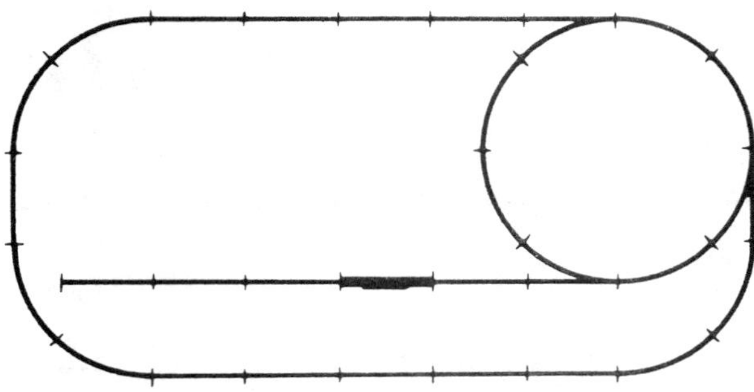

This is a simple track layout which offers an invitation for the model builder to create realistic buildings and scenery for his railroad empire. The reversing loop might partially be concealed by a tunnel and the long industrial siding could pass through a busy manufacturing center.

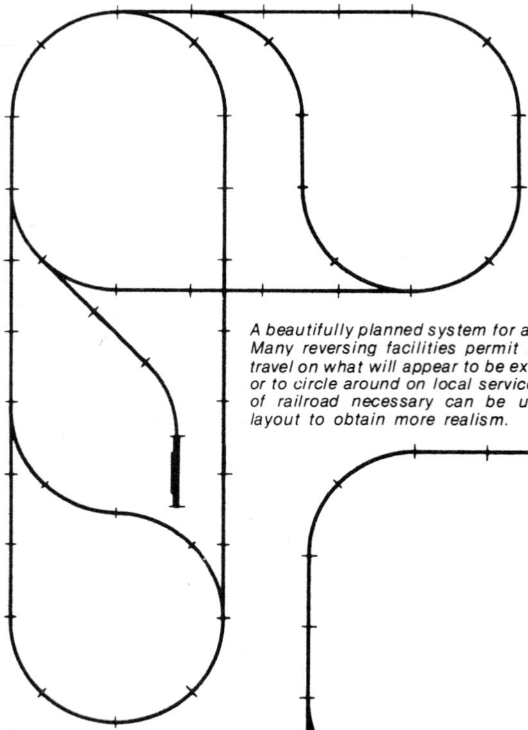

A beautifully planned system for attic or cellar. Many reversing facilities permit the trains to travel on what will appear to be extensive runs, or to circle around on local service. Every type of railroad necessary can be used on this layout to obtain more realism.

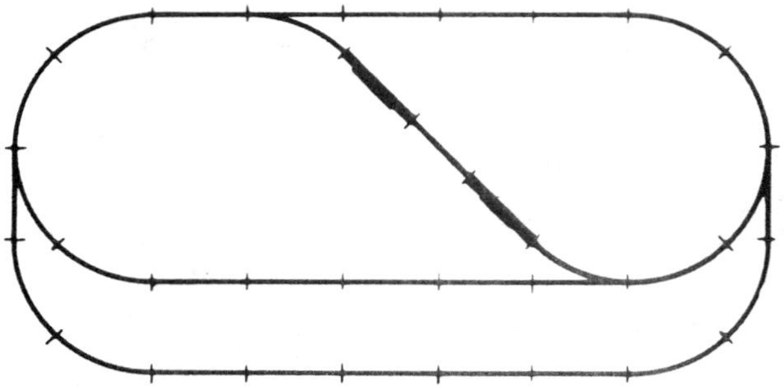

An outer loop of track 82" by 41" with an inner semi-oval with transverse crossing track. Compact use of space permits a realistic layout with several different routes provided for the trains. Only four switches required for this flexible system. Install special uncoupling track sections anywhere in the layout for railroad realism.

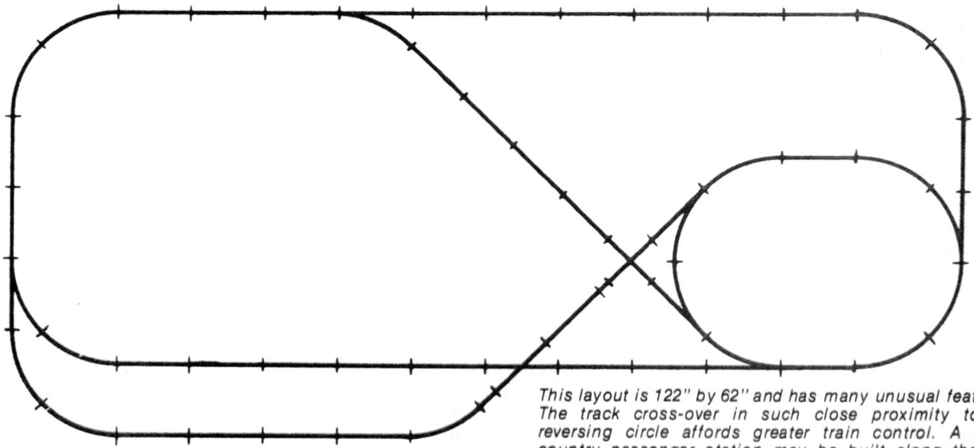

This layout is 122" by 62" and has many unusual features. The track cross-over in such close proximity to the reversing circle affords greater train control. A small country passenger station may be built along the two tracks on the bottom of the layout, and other models may be added.

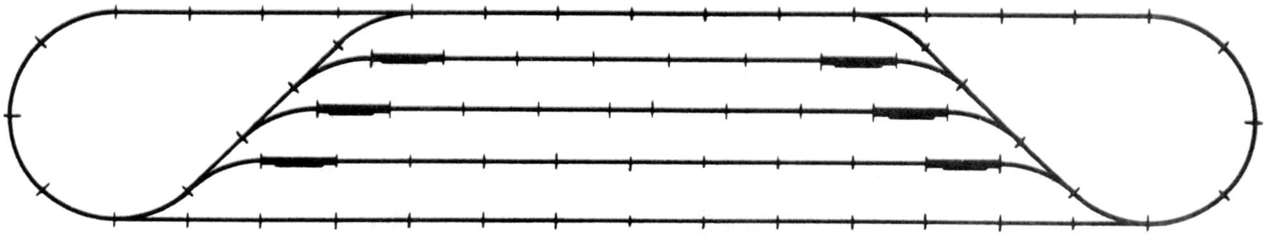

A perfect layout for an industrial division. Long and narrow, this system is 172" by 31". Pear-shaped reversing loops on either end give trains chance to change their route. Parallel streches of side track suggest a real classification yard for loading and unloading, coupling and uncoupling of freight cars.

A most interesting variety of turns and destinations are built into this railroad. Here we have an assurance against monotony. Three reversing loops make the layout an engineer's dream. Sidings shown here are short. Perhaps in building this layout you may wish to add more of them. Large enough to run two trains. System is 62" by 177".

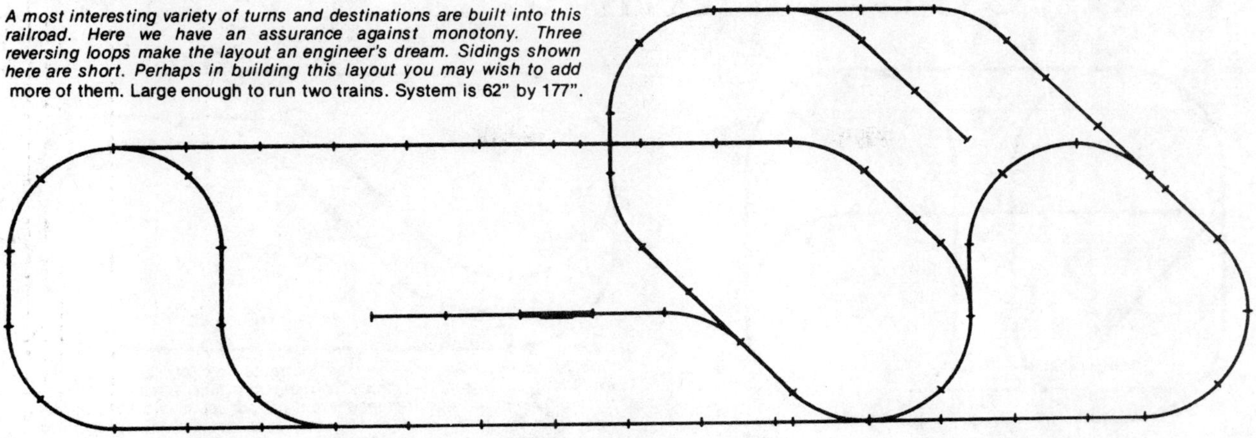

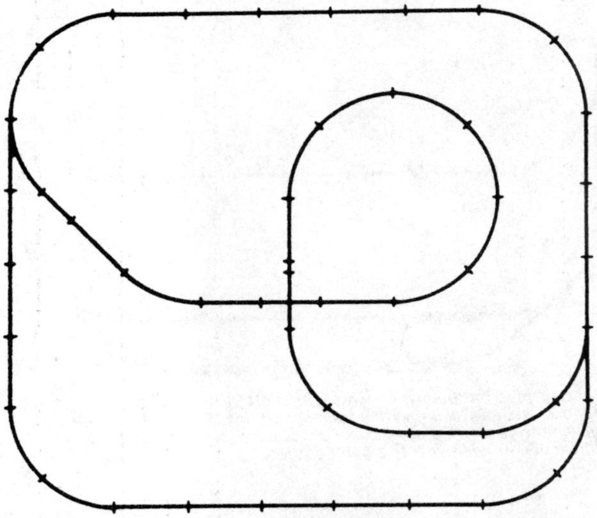

Simple and interesting. This railroad was designed to be inexpensive and still have a great degree of interest value. Dad, this is a fine layout to build for Junior. You can fix a table with little houses, trees, and even a waterfall. Size of layout is 72" by 82".

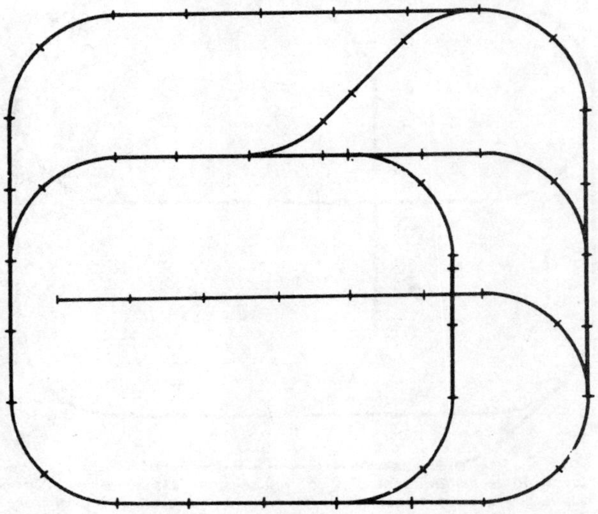

Here is another miniature railroad which will not involve too much money. Notice that the switches are placed to the greatest advantage, resulting in the creation of a life-like system. A switch engine would be a lot of fun on this layout. Requires space 72" by 82".

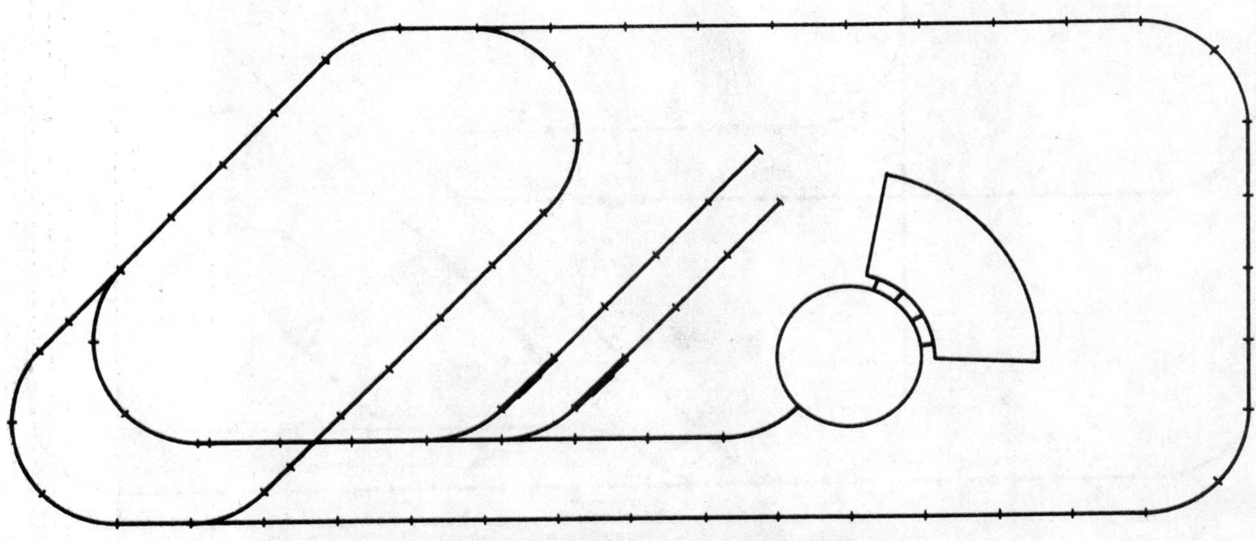

Long straight runs make it possible to open the throttle wide. But don't forget to slow down for the curves. Loops, sidings, a turntable and a roundhouse complete the railroad. Dimensions of the system are 72" by 172".

"O" GAUGE TRACK LAYOUT PLANS

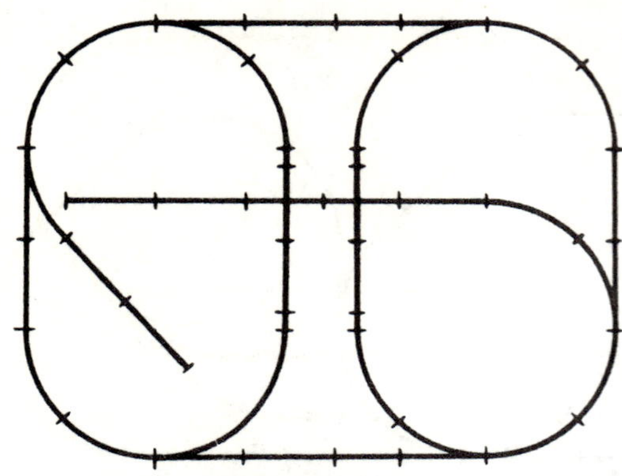

On this "O" gauge system the engineer can guide his train over a variety of routes, making the operation of trains a continuously exciting adventure. Layout area, 52" by 72".

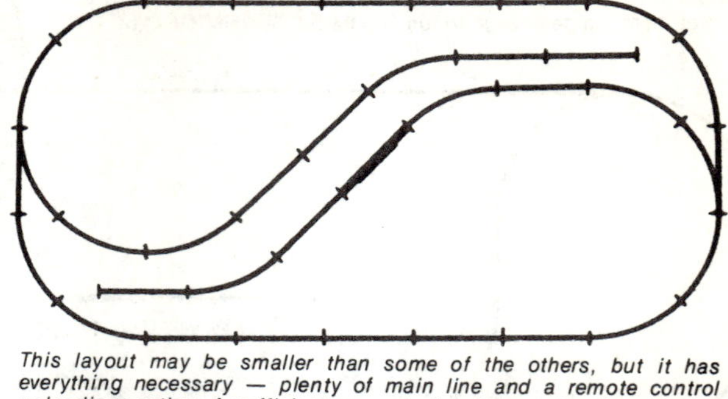

This layout may be smaller than some of the others, but it has everything necessary — plenty of main line and a remote control unloading section. A sufficient amount of yard space is offered in this layout for building the industrial structures that are so necessary to every railroad. The sidings will prove useful for holding excess rolling stock. Total space required for setting up this model railroad is 42" by 80".

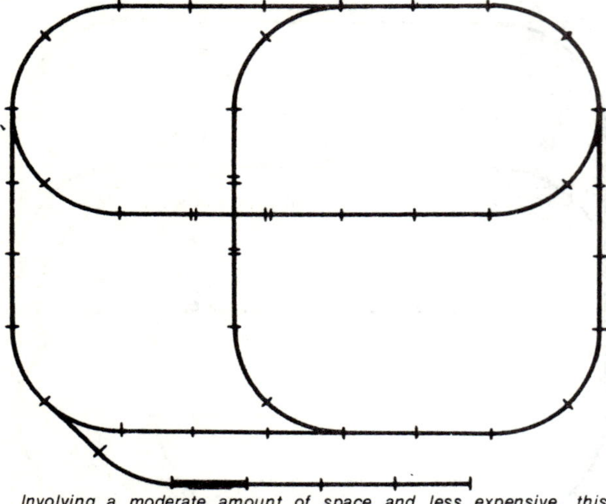

Involving a moderate amount of space and less expensive, this miniature railroad is just about the type for the average model train hobbyist. Notice the variety of routes offered in this system. The siding has a remote control track section which may be used for uncoupling and unloading cars at the touch of a button. System measures 72" by 82".

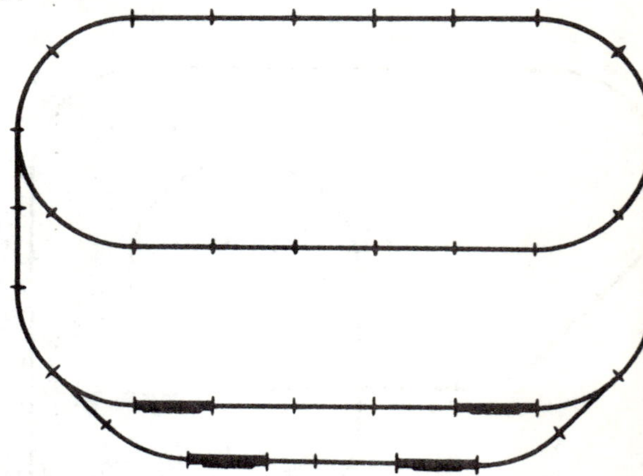

This system is for the person who cannot afford too much space; and for those who desire interesting train operations. Provision is made for four remote control unloading and uncoupling sections. This road has four parallel routes. Only two pairs of switches required. Space 62" by 82".

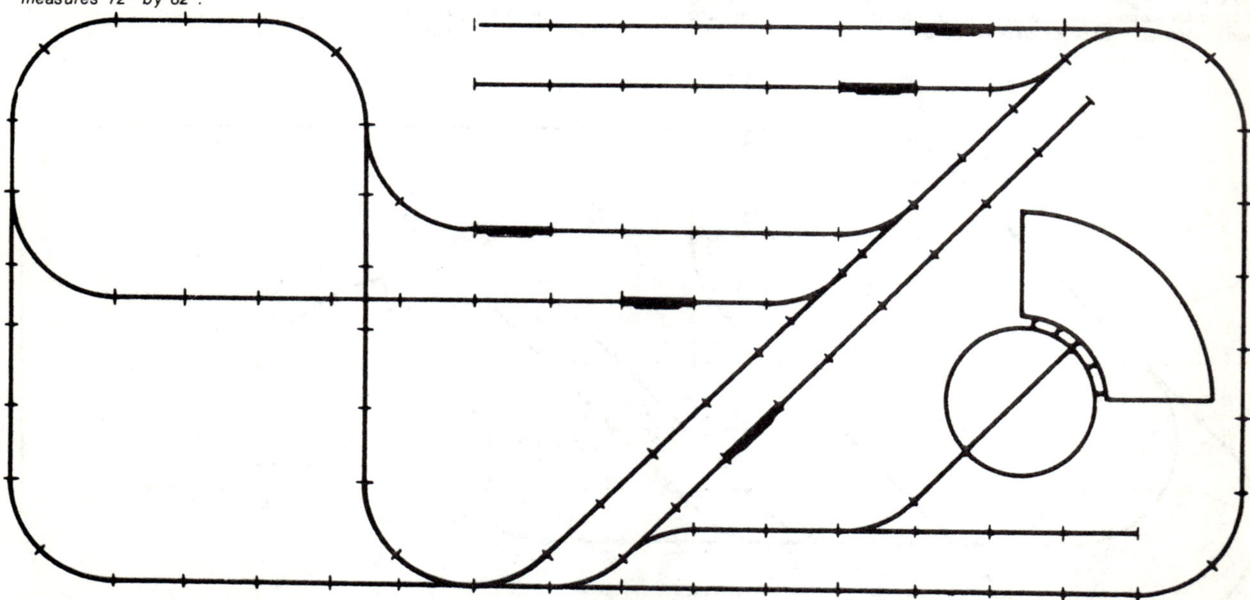

For the more advanced student of modern railroading this "O" gauge railroad is ideal. Turntable, roundhouse, sidings, switches, cross-overs, and plenty of track are combined to form a most thrilling and exciting miniature railroad. Stations, freight platforms, landscaping, highways, signals and houses should be added. Space necessary for construction 87" by 172".

A complete freight yard with facilities for car marshalling. Yard goat breaks up cars and distributes them on parallel classification tracks. This is an excellent unit in a large layout or can be regarded as complete by the boy interested in yardwork above everything else. Area is 170" by 60".

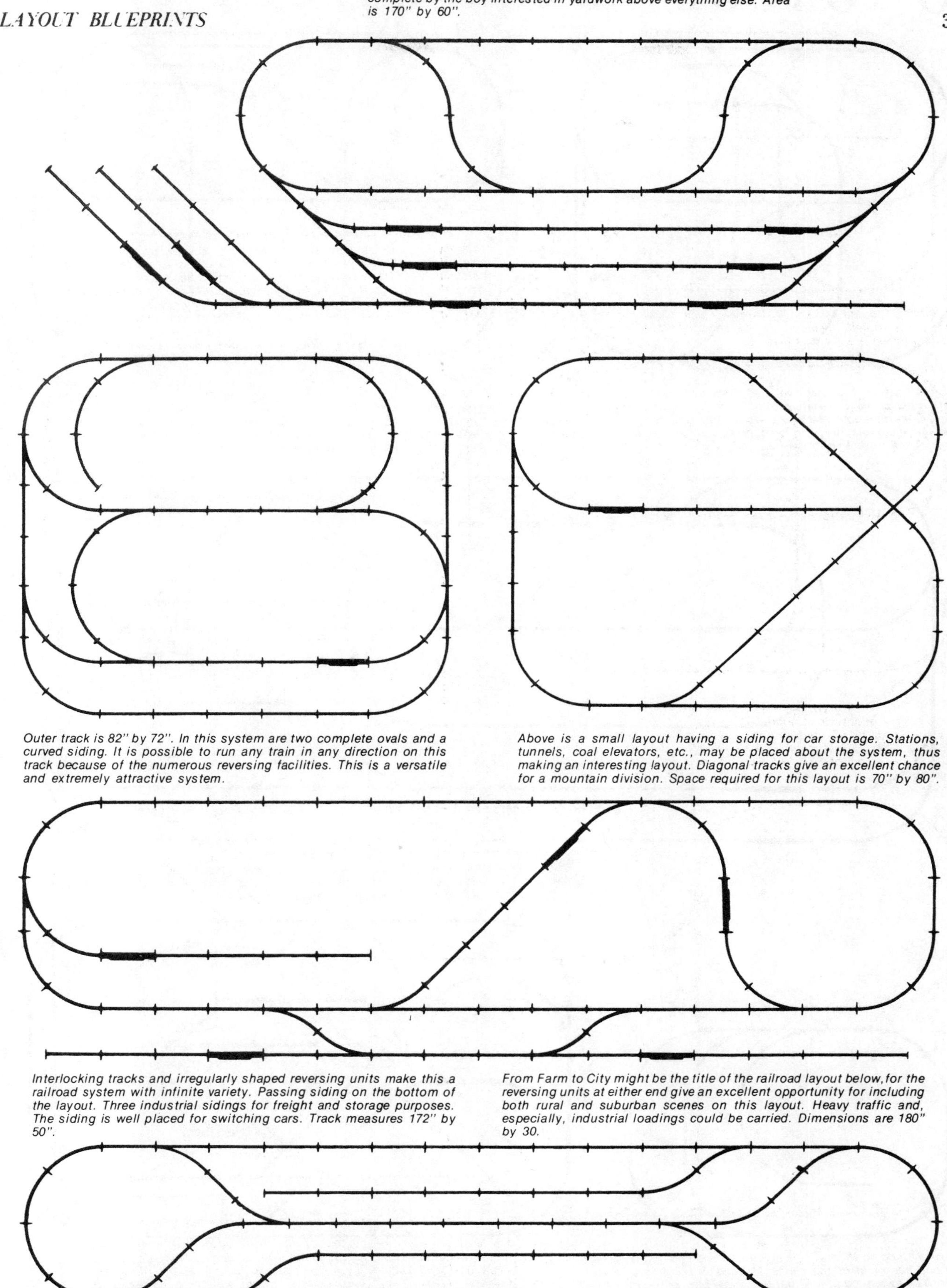

Outer track is 82" by 72". In this system are two complete ovals and a curved siding. It is possible to run any train in any direction on this track because of the numerous reversing facilities. This is a versatile and extremely attractive system.

Above is a small layout having a siding for car storage. Stations, tunnels, coal elevators, etc., may be placed about the system, thus making an interesting layout. Diagonal tracks give an excellent chance for a mountain division. Space required for this layout is 70" by 80".

Interlocking tracks and irregularly shaped reversing units make this a railroad system with infinite variety. Passing siding on the bottom of the layout. Three industrial sidings for freight and storage purposes. The siding is well placed for switching cars. Track measures 172" by 50".

From Farm to City might be the title of the railroad layout below, for the reversing units at either end give an excellent opportunity for including both rural and suburban scenes on this layout. Heavy traffic and, especially, industrial loadings could be carried. Dimensions are 180" by 30.

"O" GAUGE TRACK LAYOUT PLANS

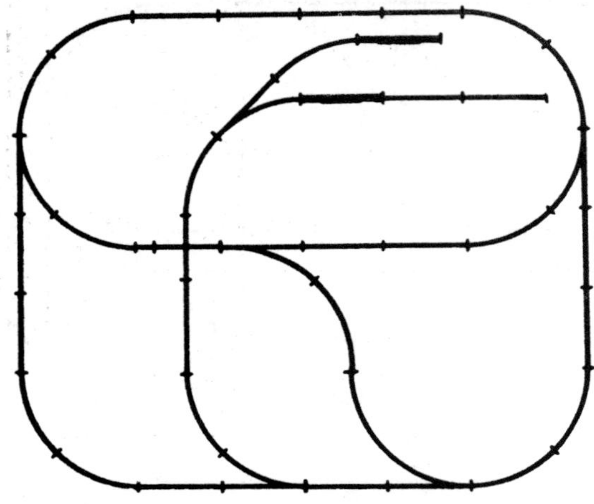

72" by 62" pike with inner oval and S-shaped track connection for direction reversing. Interesting double-track industrial spur. Lumber loader might be erected between two freight sidings. This is a small layout and nearly any boy will have the equipment necessary to use it in making an attractive model railroad.

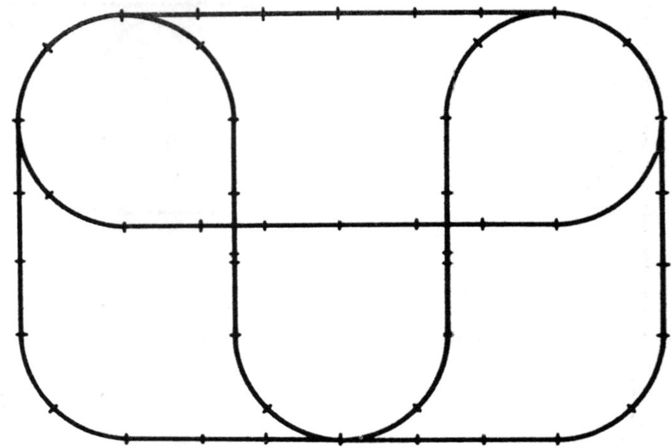

This "hook and eye" railroad layout is imaginative and efficient. Excellent for smooth-running express trains which wind around the track, reversing direction and changing their route. Stations, tunnels, mountains, etc., should provide interesting scenery. The layout is big enough to operate two trains by sectionalizing the track, thus making each train individually controlled.

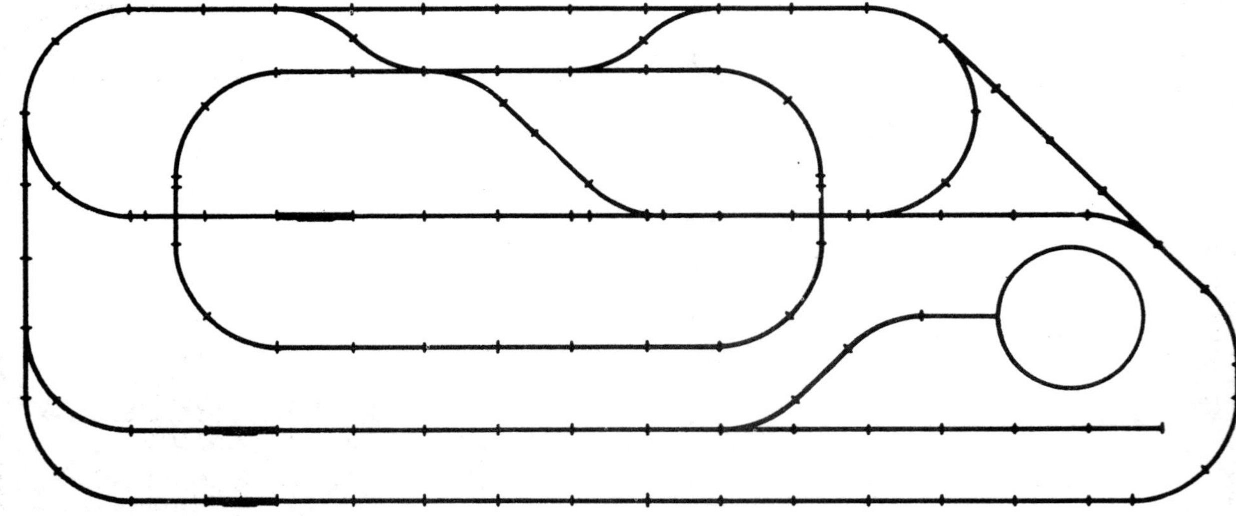

An exciting layout which includes every type of railroad operation. Plenty of reversing loops so that a train can run for a long time without duplicating its route. Excellent for small club.

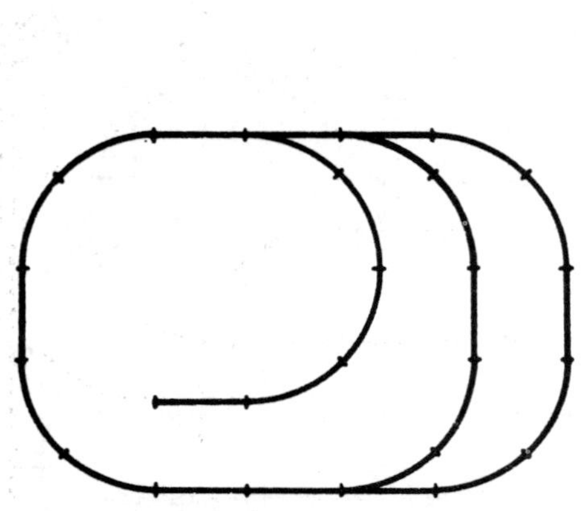

A variation on a standard theme. This layout is the bread-and-butter of railroading and has most of the elements used in building a model railroad. It can be expanded at will, but has a real play value while it is growing.

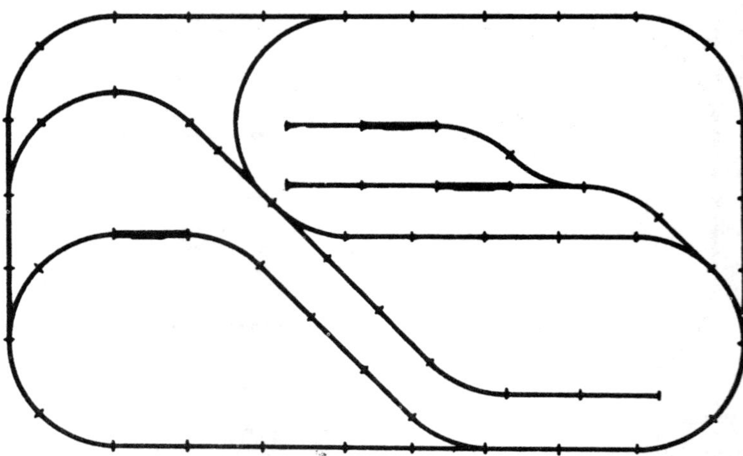

This rectangle of track is nicely intersected to give the maximum action. Industrial sidings could be used in manufacturing areas. Some attractive scenery and realistic model buildings might well be added to the scene.

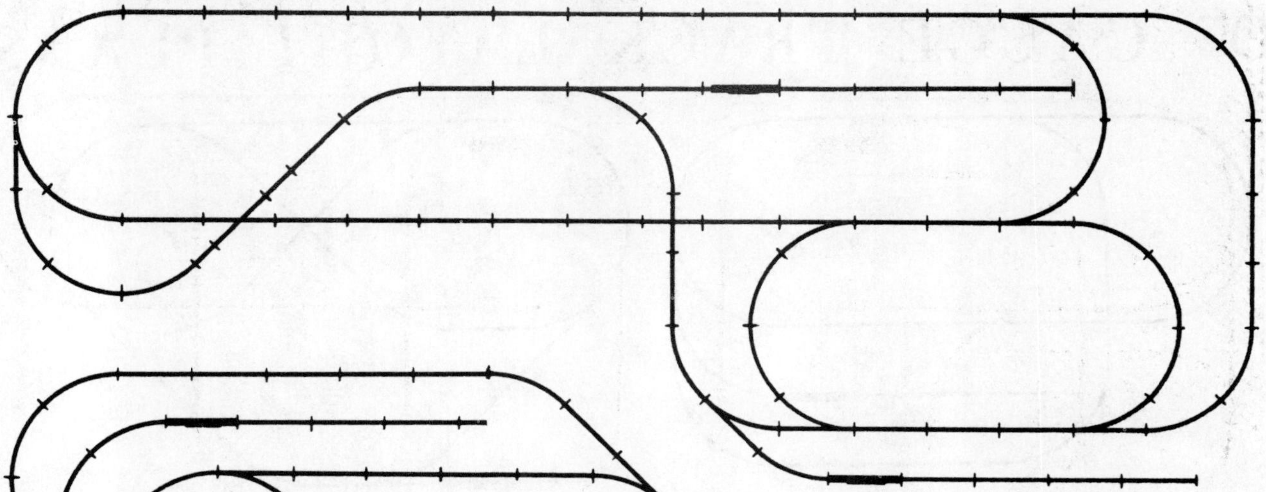

Here's still another for the more advanced students of model railroading. If you have a space in your attic, spare room or cellar, this might fill your requirements. Track system, tunnels, cuts, bridges and fills would all help to make it a spectacular layout. System covers a space 62" by 172".

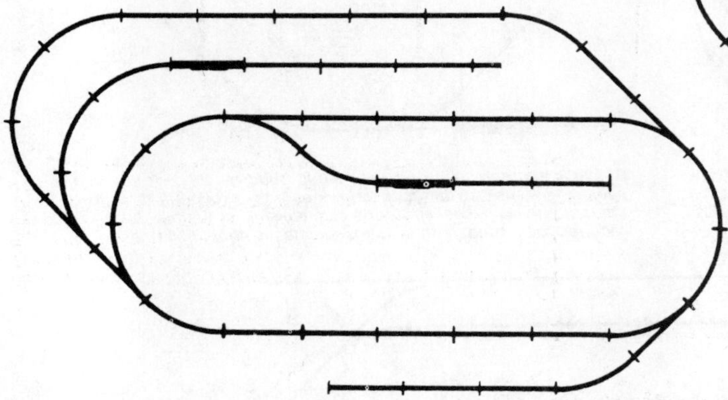

Available space sometimes necessitates a small layout. The one shown above is simple, has one-way operation, but several switches give you something to do. Space: 55" by 97".

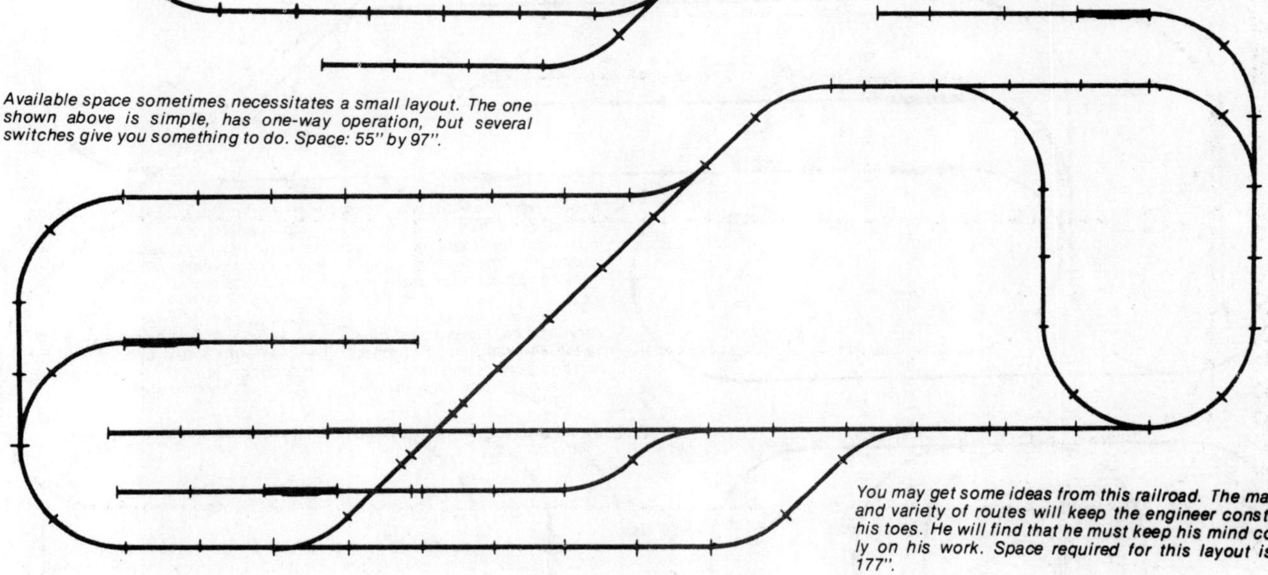

You may get some ideas from this railroad. The many turns and variety of routes will keep the engineer constantly on his toes. He will find that he must keep his mind continually on his work. Space required for this layout is 75" by 177".

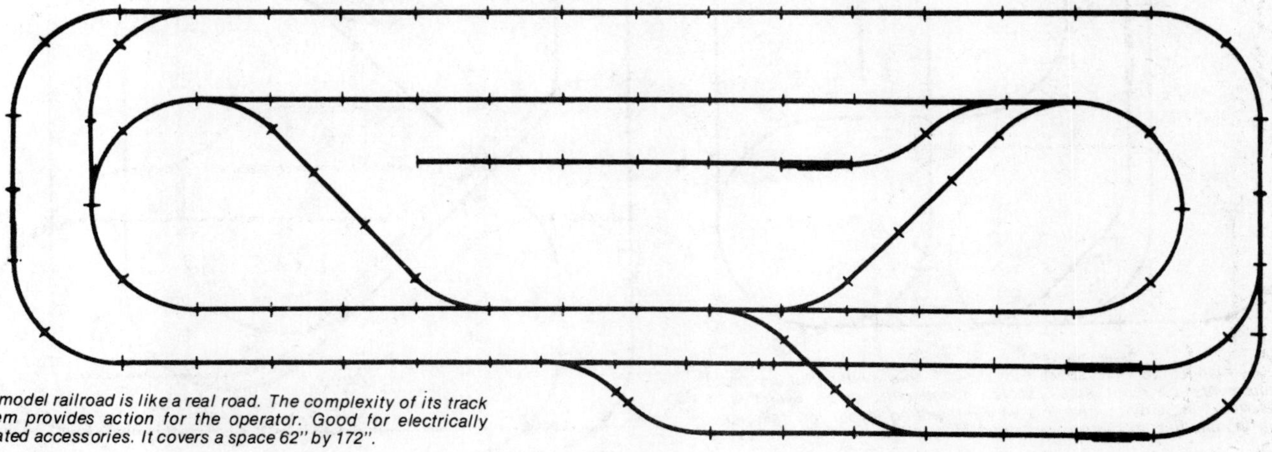

This model railroad is like a real road. The complexity of its track system provides action for the operator. Good for electrically operated accessories. It covers a space 62" by 172".

"O" GAUGE TRACK LAYOUT PLANS

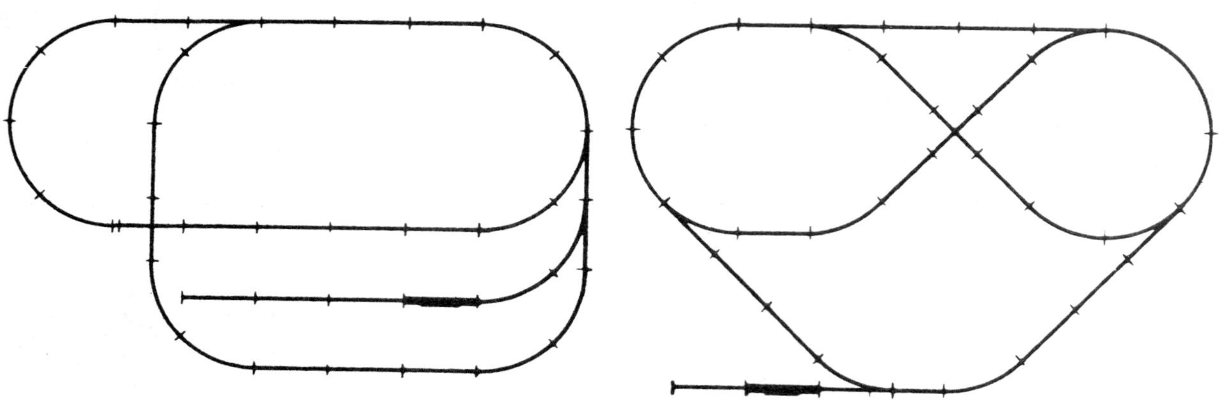

This track layout is not complex or expensive to build yet it offers interesting train operations. Plenty of room for building a model city, freight terminal, and a rural district. Area is 52" by 82", and entire system easily could be built on a portable table 60" by 90".

Above is a simple layout anyone could build quickly. Notice that this system is made so that your train is able to reverse its direction. The short siding is an ideal spot for a coal elevator or lumber loader. Space required for setting up this "O" gauge plan is only 67" by 82".

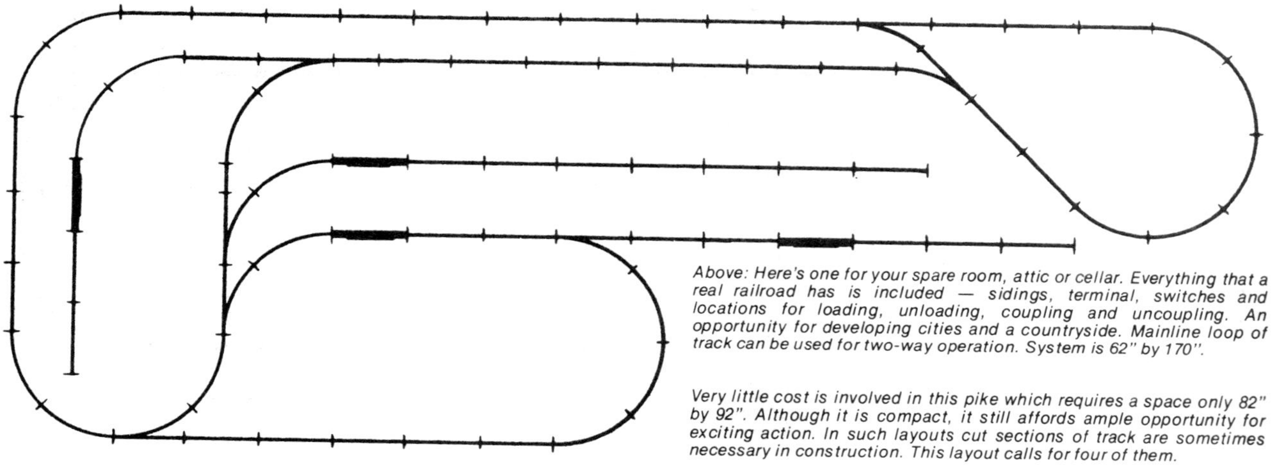

Above: Here's one for your spare room, attic or cellar. Everything that a real railroad has is included — sidings, terminal, switches and locations for loading, unloading, coupling and uncoupling. An opportunity for developing cities and a countryside. Mainline loop of track can be used for two-way operation. System is 62" by 170".

Very little cost is involved in this pike which requires a space only 82" by 92". Although it is compact, it still affords ample opportunity for exciting action. In such layouts cut sections of track are sometimes necessary in construction. This layout calls for four of them.

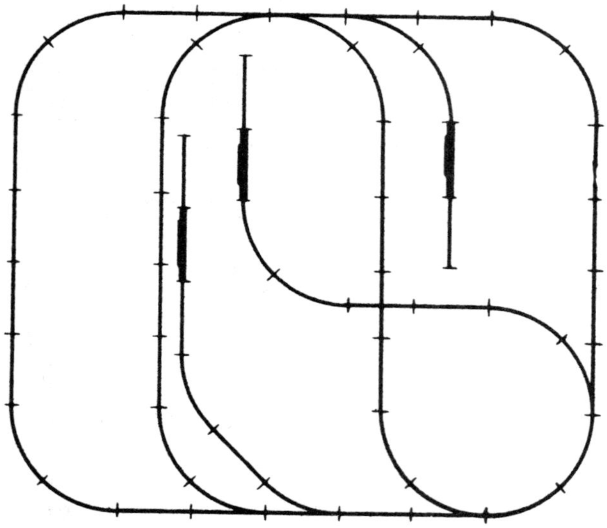

Above: Planned to fit a space 72" by 82", this system fulfills the requirements of most small scale model railroaders. Switches, crossovers, and sidings give this very interesting layout real railroad operating qualities.

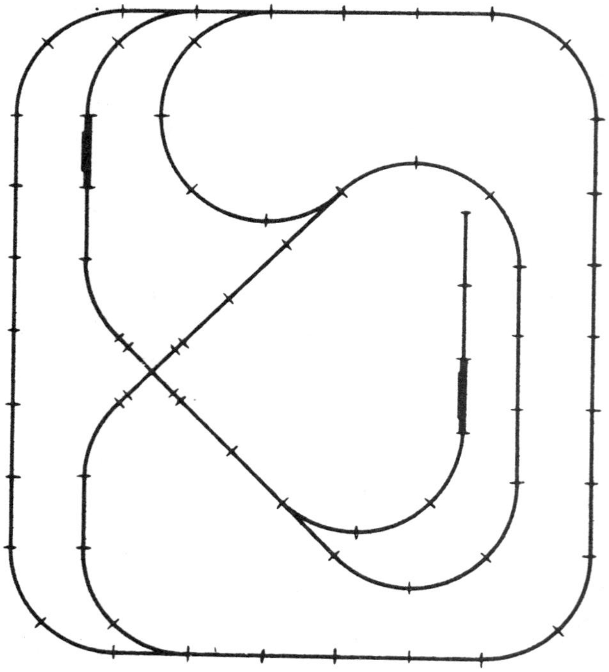

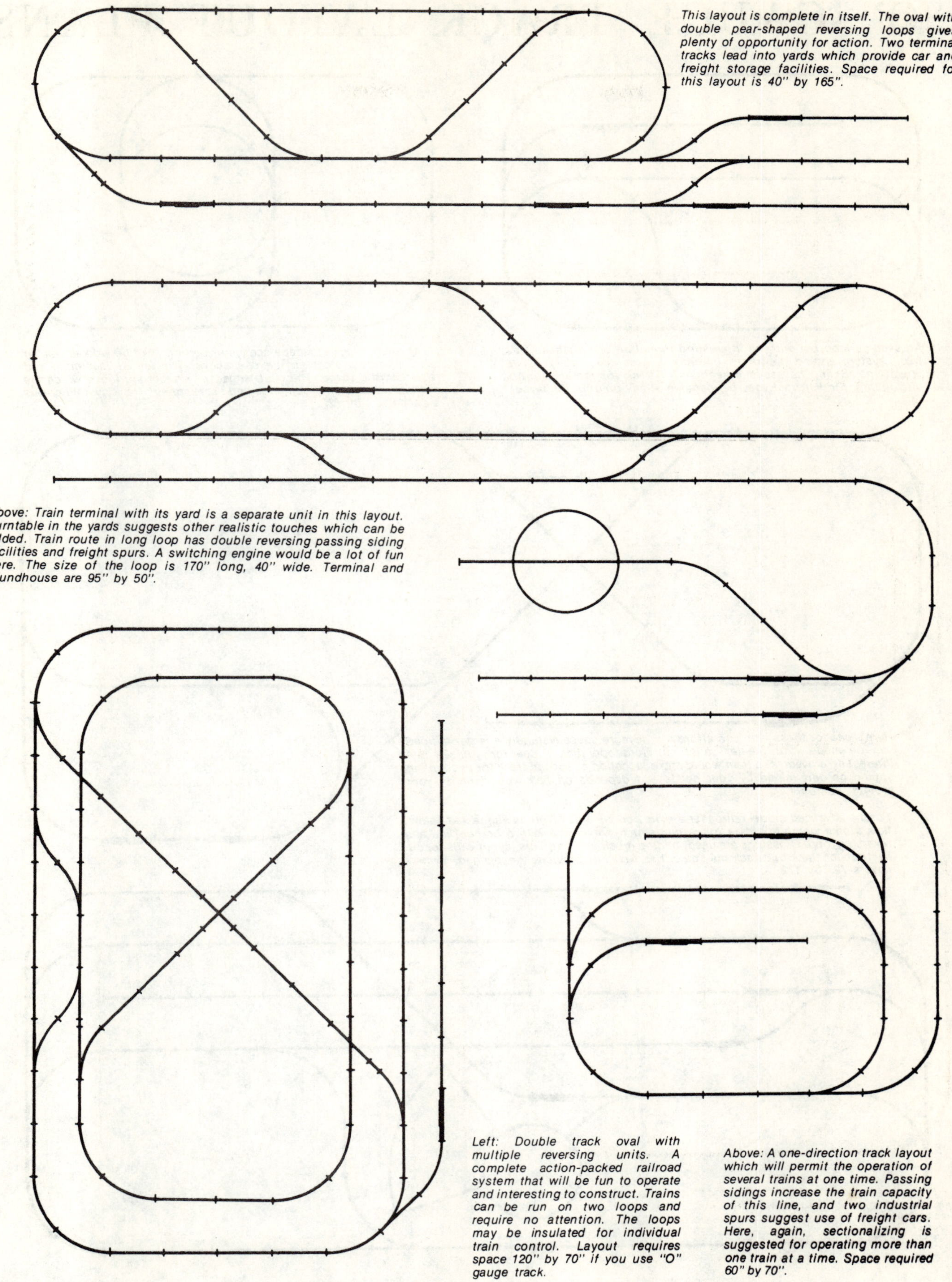

This layout is complete in itself. The oval with double pear-shaped reversing loops gives plenty of opportunity for action. Two terminal tracks lead into yards which provide car and freight storage facilities. Space required for this layout is 40" by 165".

Above: Train terminal with its yard is a separate unit in this layout. Turntable in the yards suggests other realistic touches which can be added. Train route in long loop has double reversing passing siding facilities and freight spurs. A switching engine would be a lot of fun here. The size of the loop is 170" long, 40" wide. Terminal and roundhouse are 95" by 50".

Left: Double track oval with multiple reversing units. A complete action-packed railroad system that will be fun to operate and interesting to construct. Trains can be run on two loops and require no attention. The loops may be insulated for individual train control. Layout requires space 120" by 70" if you use "O" gauge track.

Above: A one-direction track layout which will permit the operation of several trains at one time. Passing sidings increase the train capacity of this line, and two industrial spurs suggest use of freight cars. Here, again, sectionalizing is suggested for operating more than one train at a time. Space required 60" by 70".

"O" GAUGE TRACK LAYOUT PLANS

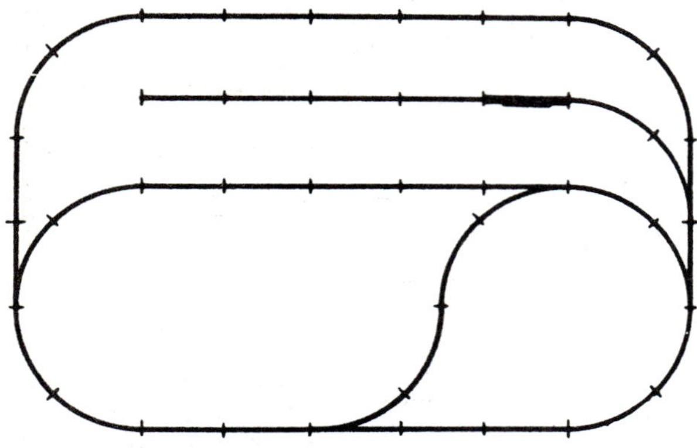

An average loop but with an interesting formation of switches. This track system should be traced in order to see the variety of its operations. Siding has special sections of track for remote control uncoupling. Similar track may be installed at any point in the layout. Space: 52" by 82".

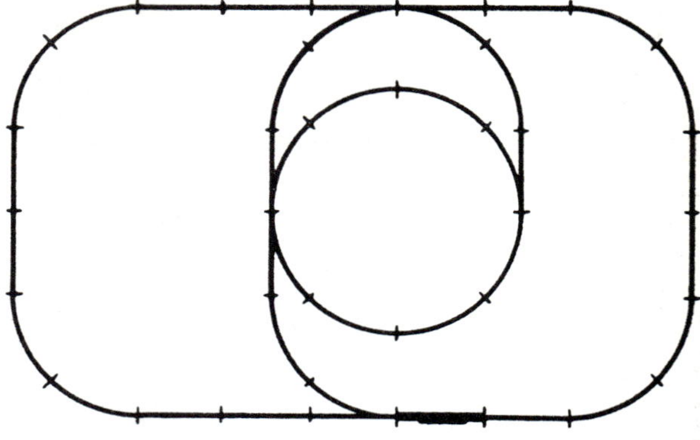

Many interesting landscape scenes or settings can be worked out on such a track system as the one above. The layout is simple and requires little space. The best landscape effects are those which are not too crowded with buildings and accessories. Track system covers a space 52" by 82".

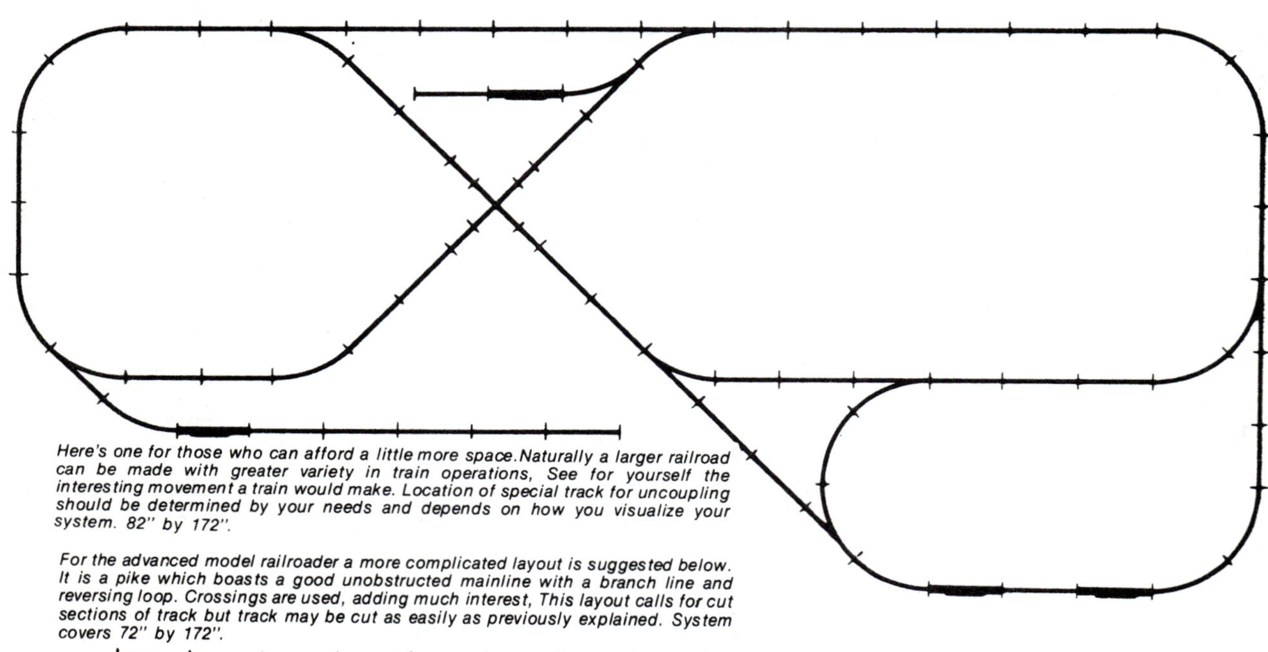

Here's one for those who can afford a little more space. Naturally a larger railroad can be made with greater variety in train operations, See for yourself the interesting movement a train would make. Location of special track for uncoupling should be determined by your needs and depends on how you visualize your system. 82" by 172".

For the advanced model railroader a more complicated layout is suggested below. It is a pike which boasts a good unobstructed mainline with a branch line and reversing loop. Crossings are used, adding much interest, This layout calls for cut sections of track but track may be cut as easily as previously explained. System covers 72" by 172".

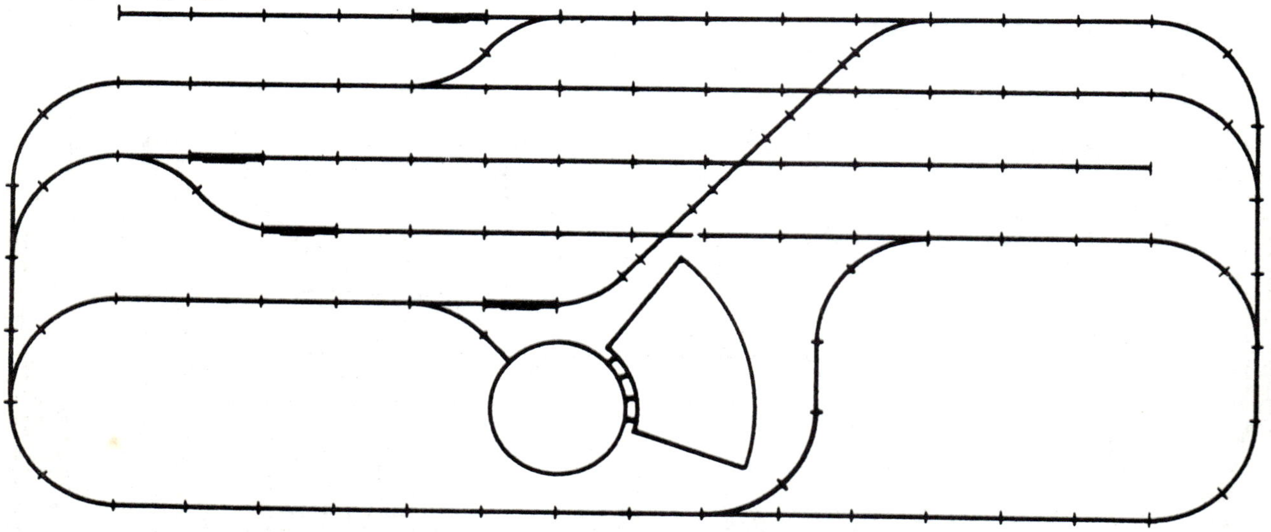

The "O" gauge railroad above has its own unusual qualities. A long straight-away makes it possible for the engineer to operate trains at very high speeds. Two reversing loops create directional control. To build a model railroad such as this would mean a great deal of work, but would provide many hours of fun and entertainment. Space filled by this railroad measures 82" by 172".

Simple and concise, yet the "O" gauge layout below has the basic character of a real railroad. There is quite a bit of space around this layout for the building of mountains, automobile roadways, bridges, tunnels, houses, stations, freight platforms and many other things which all help to make a model system interesting. Track. for this layout covers a space 52" by 72".

A railroad which has an abundance of interesting routes. Unloading stations, terminal, sidings and reversing loops are combined in a much desired manner. Four parallel tracks and three diagonals plus a reversing loop as shown in this system are the features that most boys want. Area required is 122" by 132".

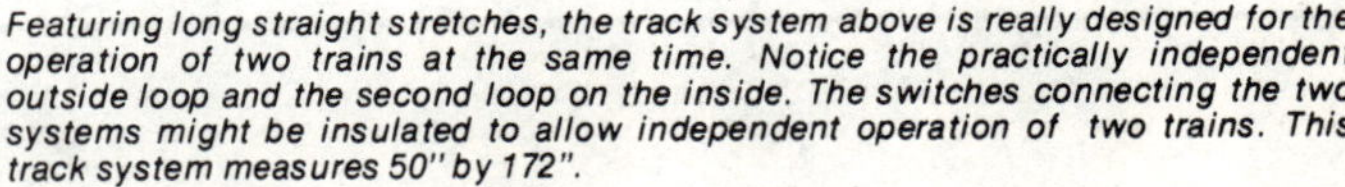

Featuring long straight stretches, the track system above is really designed for the operation of two trains at the same time. Notice the practically independent outside loop and the second loop on the inside. The switches connecting the two systems might be insulated to allow independent operation of two trains. This track system measures 50" by 172".

"O" GAUGE TRACK LAYOUT PLANS

The miniature railroad illustrated at the left is chiefly a system of different routes. Such a layout can be adapted to almost any type of space—cellar, attic or spare room. Whatever your space, one of these plans will meet your needs.

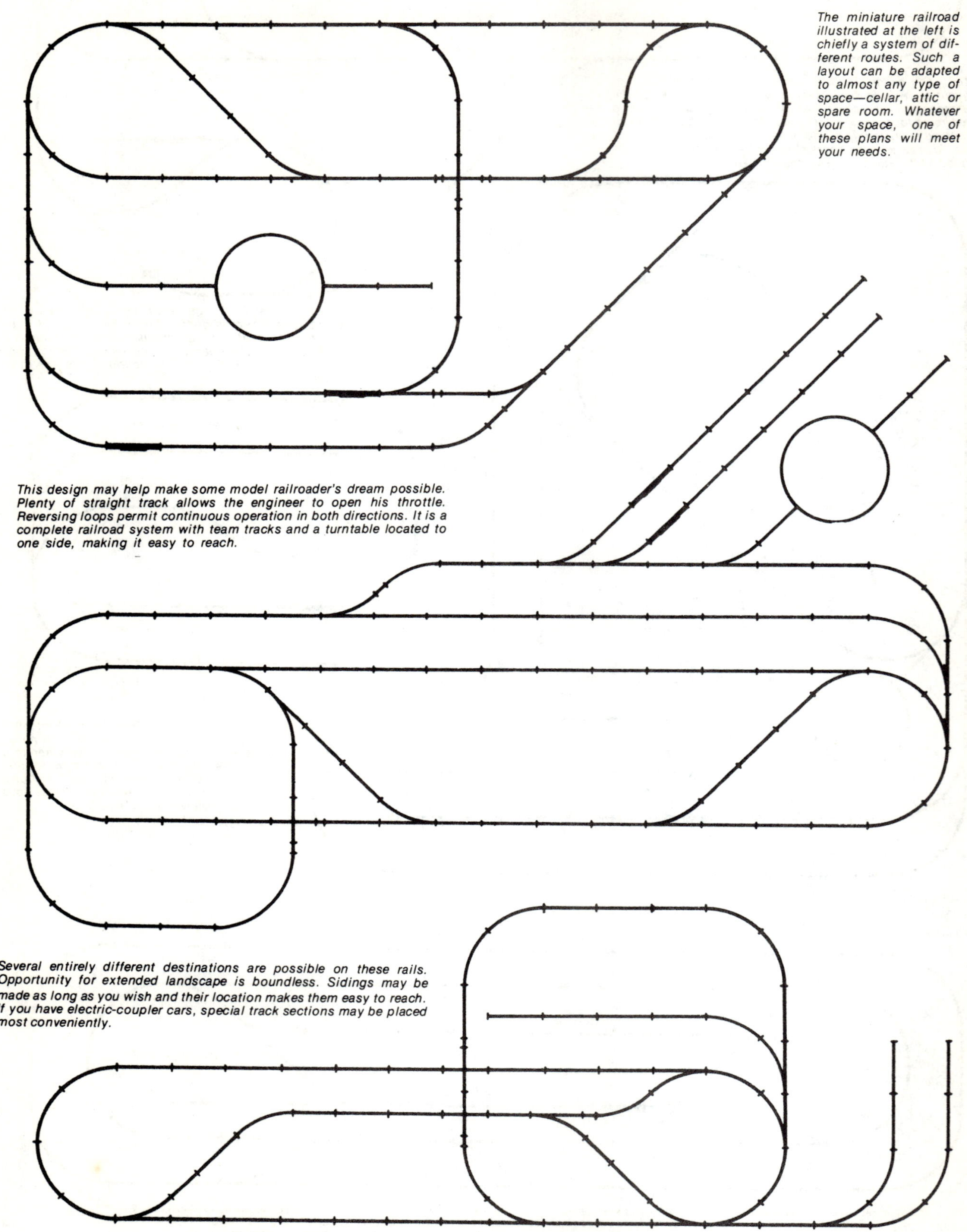

This design may help make some model railroader's dream possible. Plenty of straight track allows the engineer to open his throttle. Reversing loops permit continuous operation in both directions. It is a complete railroad system with team tracks and a turntable located to one side, making it easy to reach.

Several entirely different destinations are possible on these rails. Opportunity for extended landscape is boundless. Sidings may be made as long as you wish and their location makes them easy to reach. If you have electric-coupler cars, special track sections may be placed most conveniently.

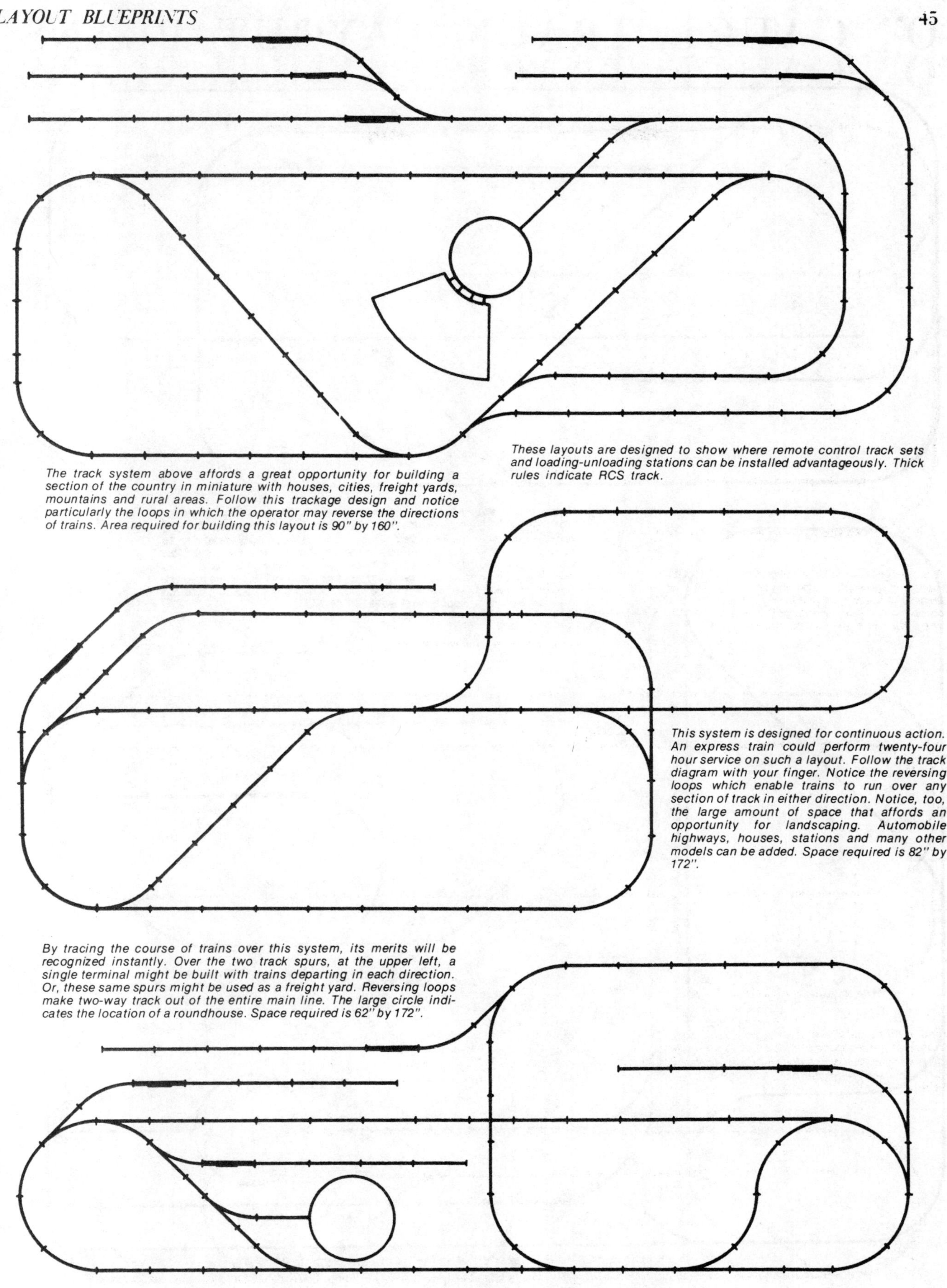

The track system above affords a great opportunity for building a section of the country in miniature with houses, cities, freight yards, mountains and rural areas. Follow this trackage design and notice particularly the loops in which the operator may reverse the directions of trains. Area required for building this layout is 90" by 160".

These layouts are designed to show where remote control track sets and loading-unloading stations can be installed advantageously. Thick rules indicate RCS track.

This system is designed for continuous action. An express train could perform twenty-four hour service on such a layout. Follow the track diagram with your finger. Notice the reversing loops which enable trains to run over any section of track in either direction. Notice, too, the large amount of space that affords an opportunity for landscaping. Automobile highways, houses, stations and many other models can be added. Space required is 82" by 172".

By tracing the course of trains over this system, its merits will be recognized instantly. Over the two track spurs, at the upper left, a single terminal might be built with trains departing in each direction. Or, these same spurs might be used as a freight yard. Reversing loops make two-way track out of the entire main line. The large circle indicates the location of a roundhouse. Space required is 62" by 172".

"O" GAUGE TRACK LAYOUT PLANS

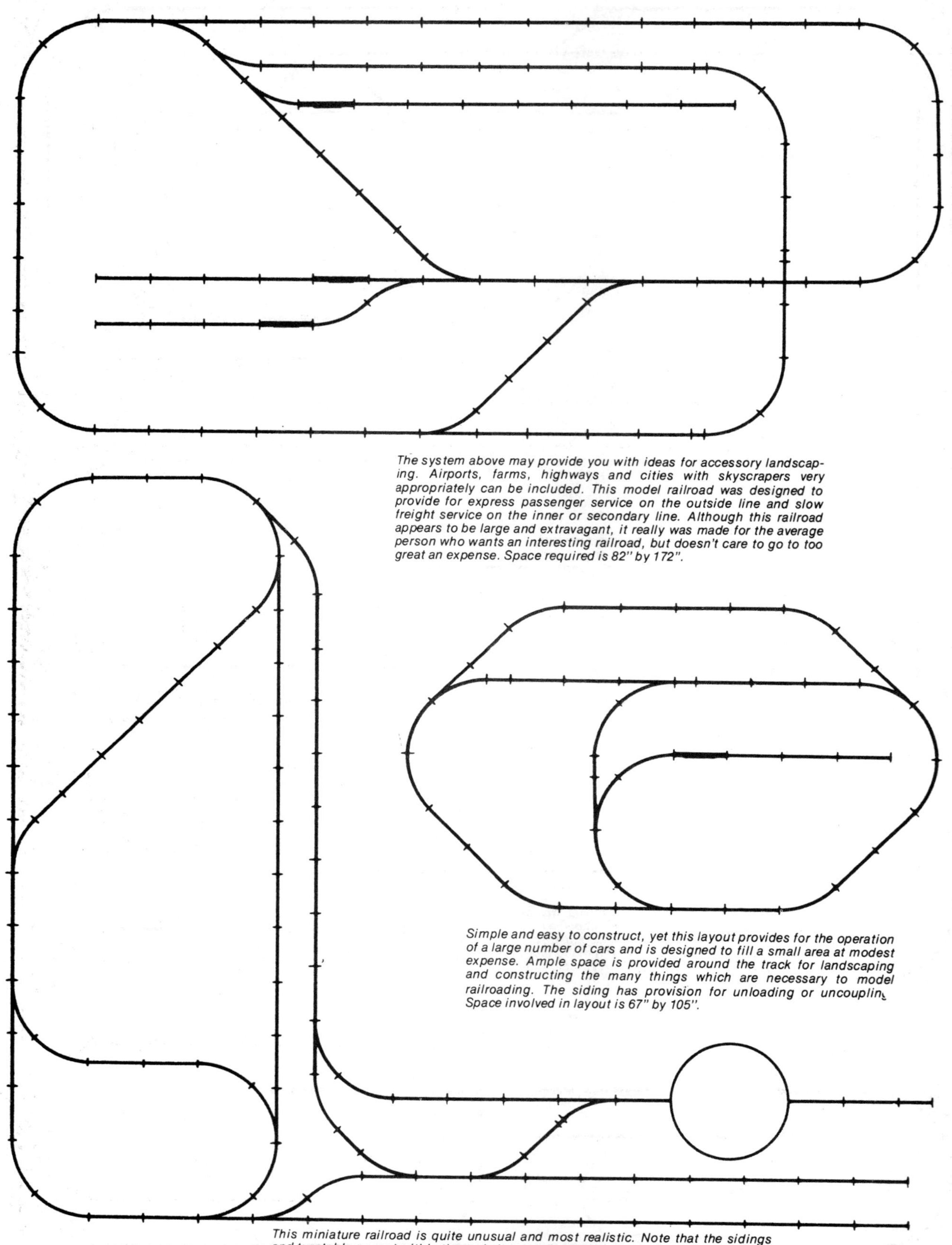

The system above may provide you with ideas for accessory landscaping. Airports, farms, highways and cities with skyscrapers very appropriately can be included. This model railroad was designed to provide for express passenger service on the outside line and slow freight service on the inner or secondary line. Although this railroad appears to be large and extravagant, it really was made for the average person who wants an interesting railroad, but doesn't care to go to too great an expense. Space required is 82" by 172".

Simple and easy to construct, yet this layout provides for the operation of a large number of cars and is designed to fill a small area at modest expense. Ample space is provided around the track for landscaping and constructing the many things which are necessary to model railroading. The siding has provision for unloading or uncoupling. Space involved in layout is 67" by 105".

This miniature railroad is quite unusual and most realistic. Note that the sidings and turntable are not within the main loop, as in most systems, but off to one side, as they are on real railroads. This layout is particularly suitable for an attic space where there are obstructions. Switching off the fast main line are the sidings and turntable to which a round house may be added. Across the main loop this railroad is 58". The width including the sidings and turntable is 175", and the length of the main pike, top to bottom, is 143".

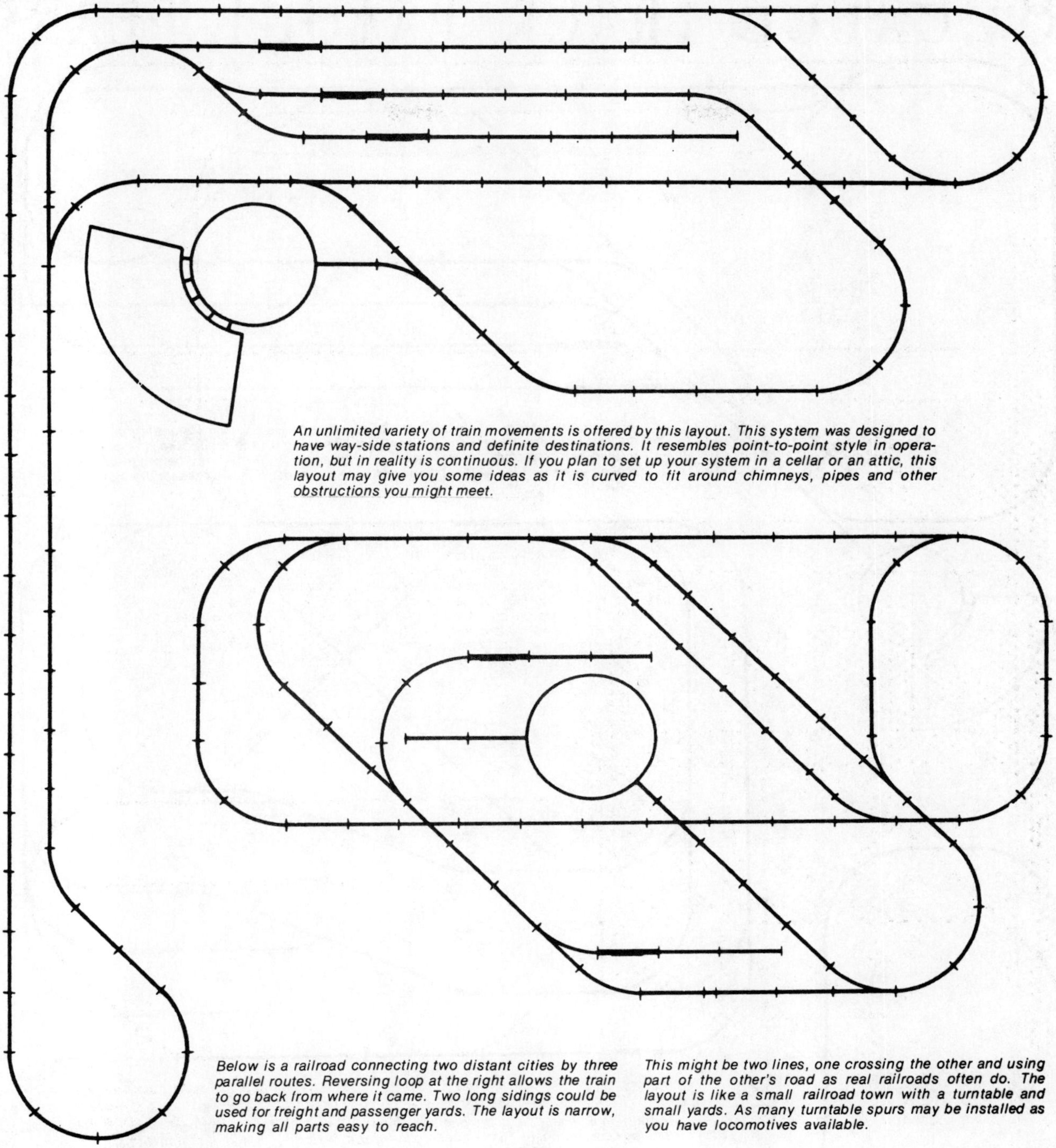

An unlimited variety of train movements is offered by this layout. This system was designed to have way-side stations and definite destinations. It resembles point-to-point style in operation, but in reality is continuous. If you plan to set up your system in a cellar or an attic, this layout may give you some ideas as it is curved to fit around chimneys, pipes and other obstructions you might meet.

Below is a railroad connecting two distant cities by three parallel routes. Reversing loop at the right allows the train to go back from where it came. Two long sidings could be used for freight and passenger yards. The layout is narrow, making all parts easy to reach.

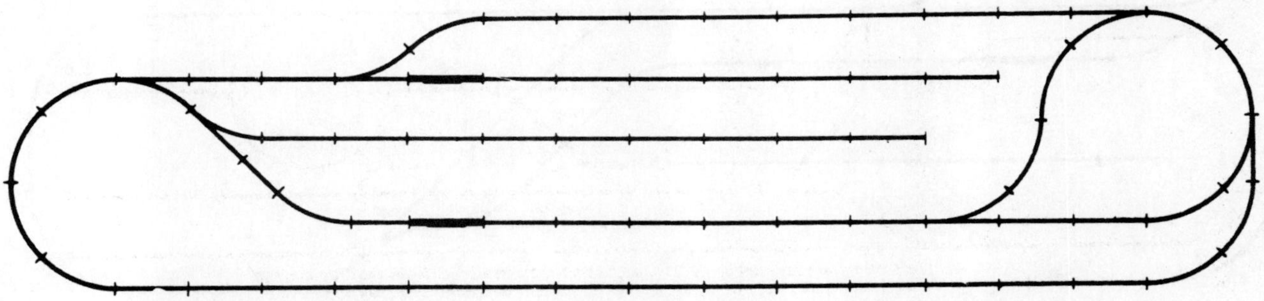

This might be two lines, one crossing the other and using part of the other's road as real railroads often do. The layout is like a small railroad town with a turntable and small yards. As many turntable spurs may be installed as you have locomotives available.

"O" GAUGE TRACK LAYOUT PLANS

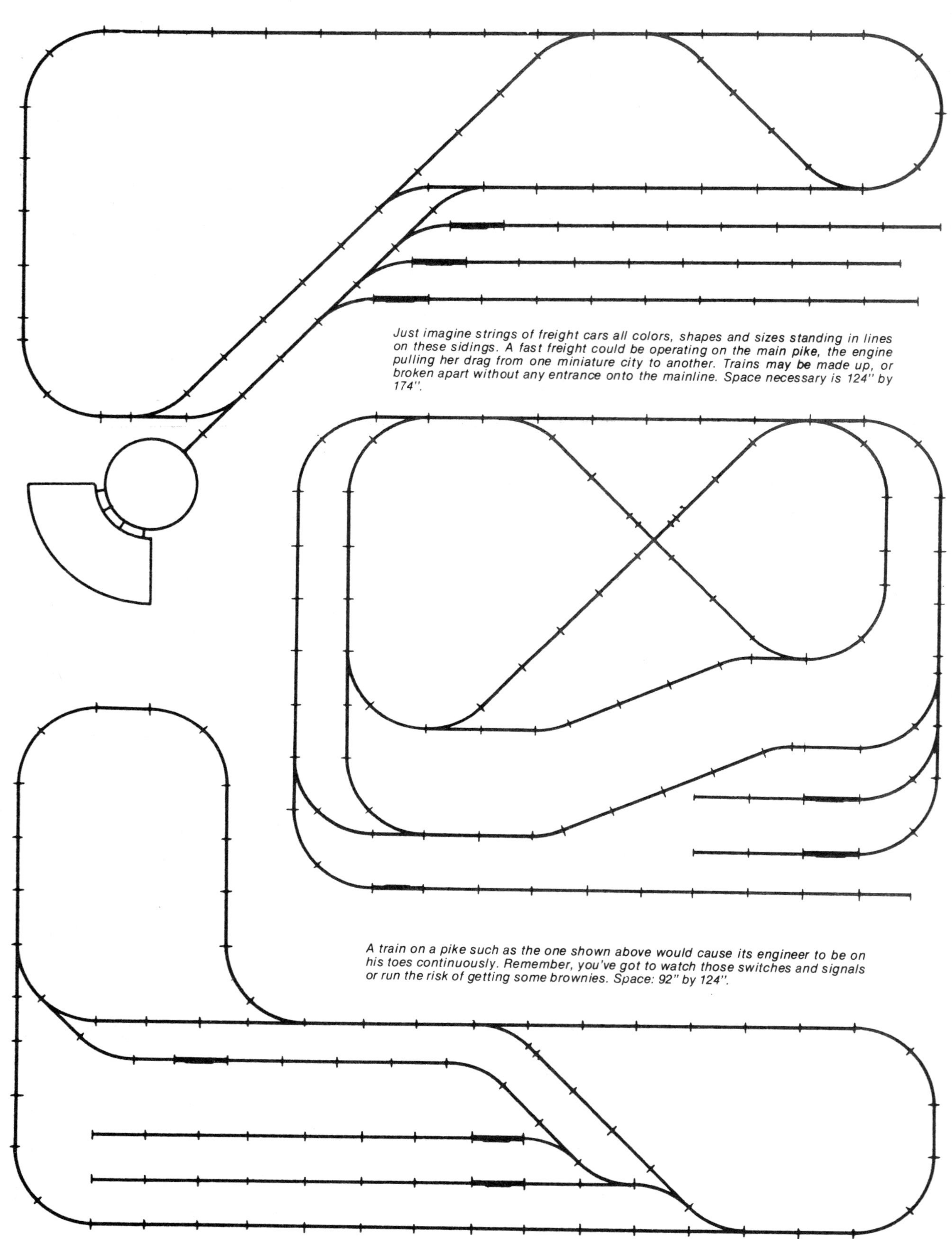

Just imagine strings of freight cars all colors, shapes and sizes standing in lines on these sidings. A fast freight could be operating on the main pike, the engine pulling her drag from one miniature city to another. Trains may be made up, or broken apart without any entrance onto the mainline. Space necessary is 124" by 174".

A train on a pike such as the one shown above would cause its engineer to be on his toes continuously. Remember, you've got to watch those switches and signals or run the risk of getting some brownies. Space: 92" by 124".

Above is a system for a long narrow space such as part of your cellar or attic. It has long sidings, switches, terminal space, and trains may run in either direction. Space required for laying out this railroad is 100" by 174".

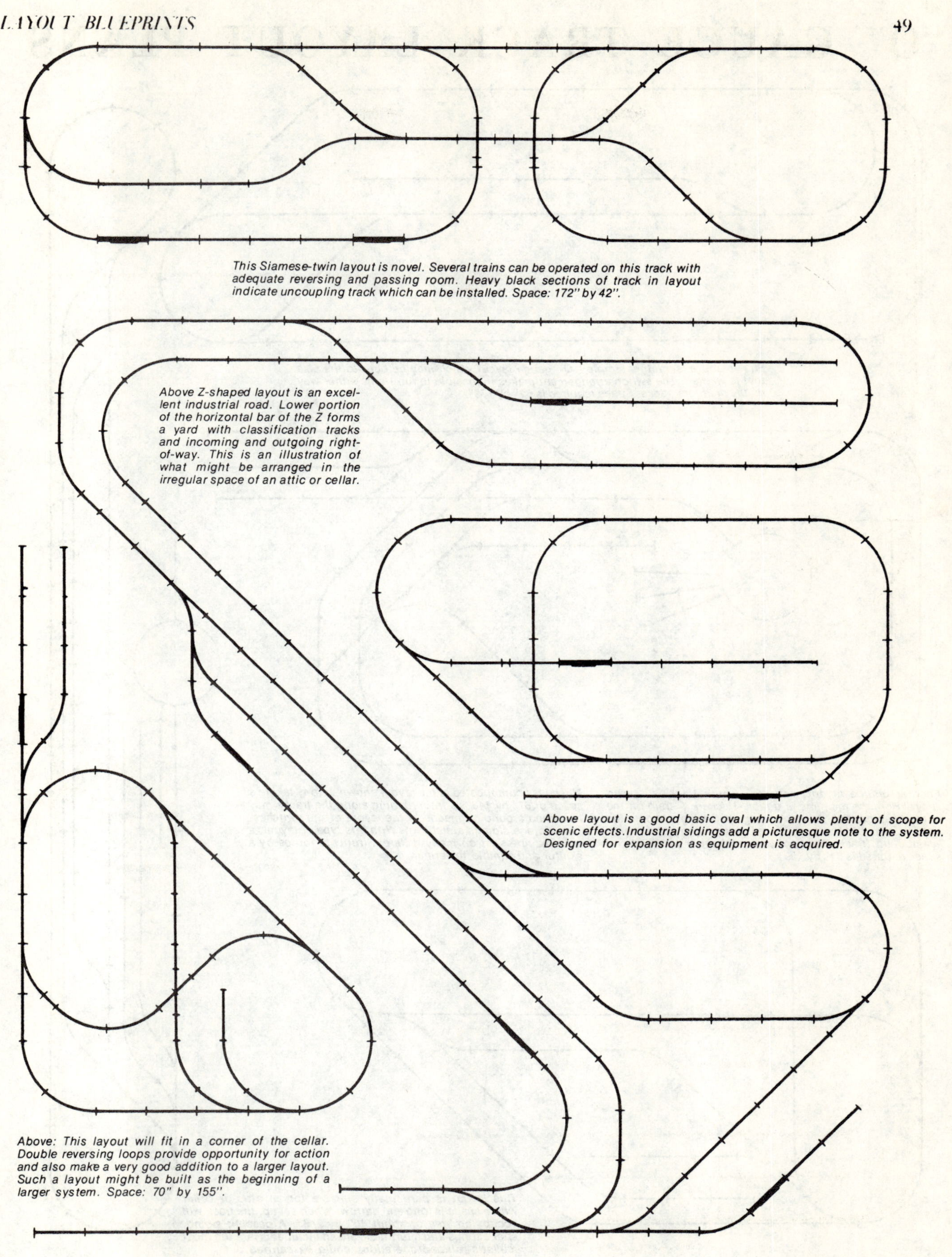

This Siamese-twin layout is novel. Several trains can be operated on this track with adequate reversing and passing room. Heavy black sections of track in layout indicate uncoupling track which can be installed. Space: 172" by 42".

Above Z-shaped layout is an excellent industrial road. Lower portion of the horizontal bar of the Z forms a yard with classification tracks and incoming and outgoing right-of-way. This is an illustration of what might be arranged in the irregular space of an attic or cellar.

Above layout is a good basic oval which allows plenty of scope for scenic effects. Industrial sidings add a picturesque note to the system. Designed for expansion as equipment is acquired.

Above: This layout will fit in a corner of the cellar. Double reversing loops provide opportunity for action and also make a very good addition to a larger layout. Such a layout might be built as the beginning of a larger system. Space: 70" by 155".

"O" GAUGE TRACK LAYOUT PLANS

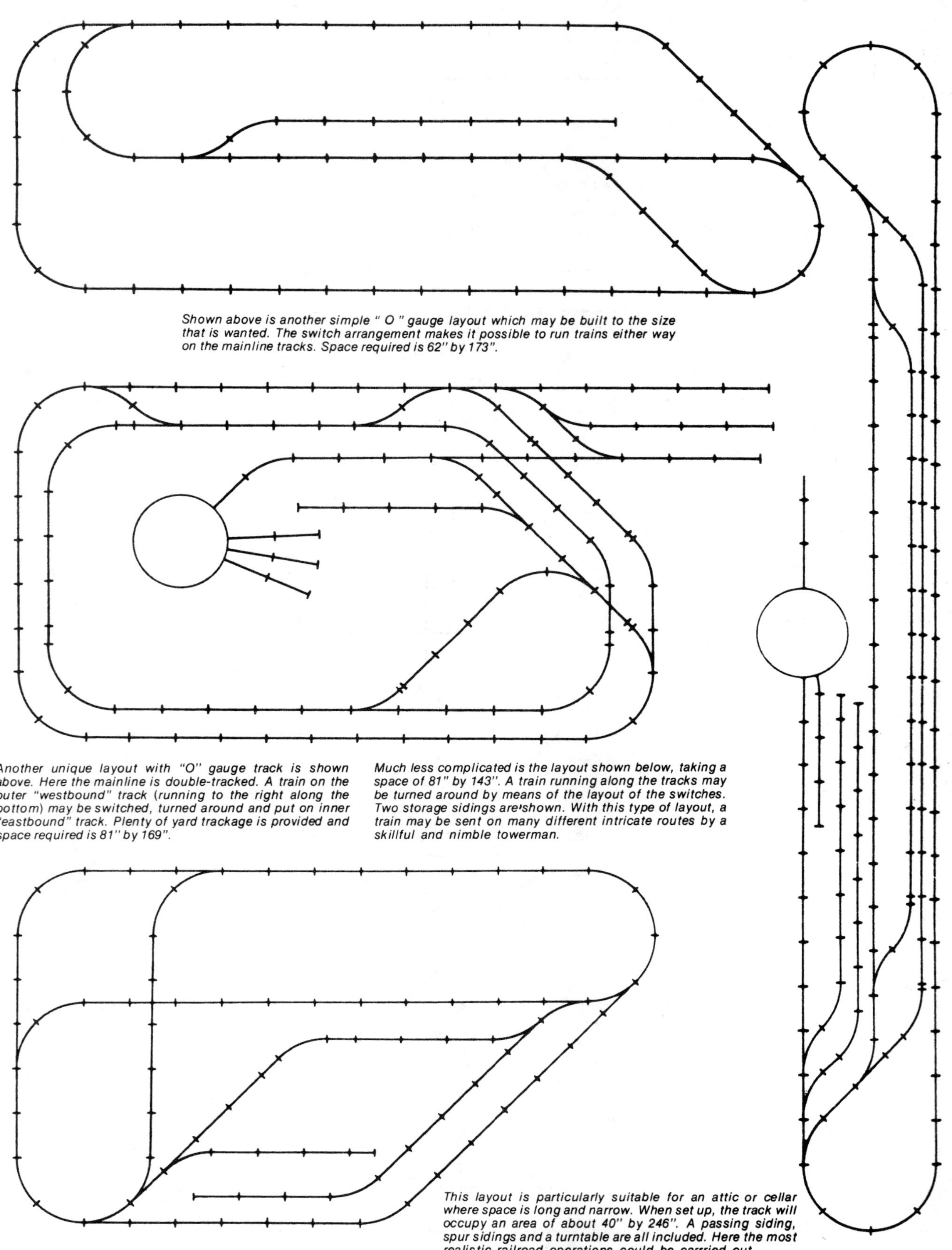

Shown above is another simple " O " gauge layout which may be built to the size that is wanted. The switch arrangement makes it possible to run trains either way on the mainline tracks. Space required is 62" by 173".

Another unique layout with "O" gauge track is shown above. Here the mainline is double-tracked. A train on the outer "westbound" track (running to the right along the bottom) may be switched, turned around and put on inner "eastbound" track. Plenty of yard trackage is provided and space required is 81" by 169".

Much less complicated is the layout shown below, taking a space of 81" by 143". A train running along the tracks may be turned around by means of the layout of the switches. Two storage sidings are shown. With this type of layout, a train may be sent on many different intricate routes by a skillful and nimble towerman.

This layout is particularly suitable for an attic or cellar where space is long and narrow. When set up, the track will occupy an area of about 40" by 246". A passing siding, spur sidings and a turntable are all included. Here the most realistic railroad operations could be carrried out.

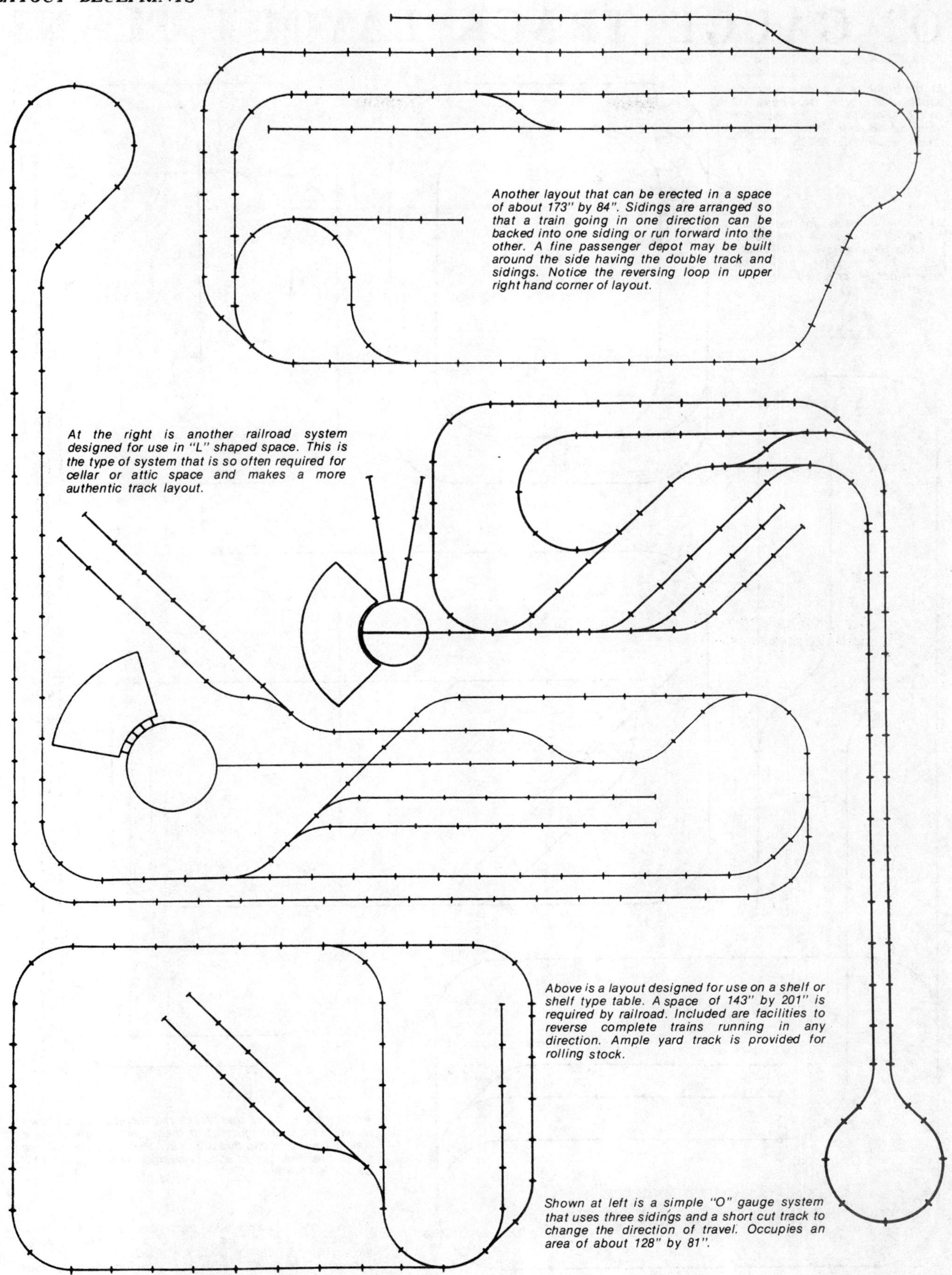

Another layout that can be erected in a space of about 173" by 84". Sidings are arranged so that a train going in one direction can be backed into one siding or run forward into the other. A fine passenger depot may be built around the side having the double track and sidings. Notice the reversing loop in upper right hand corner of layout.

At the right is another railroad system designed for use in "L" shaped space. This is the type of system that is so often required for cellar or attic space and makes a more authentic track layout.

Above is a layout designed for use on a shelf or shelf type table. A space of 143" by 201" is required by railroad. Included are facilities to reverse complete trains running in any direction. Ample yard track is provided for rolling stock.

Shown at left is a simple "O" gauge system that uses three sidings and a short cut track to change the direction of travel. Occupies an area of about 128" by 81".

"O" GAUGE TRACK LAYOUT PLANS

At the right is a simple loop of double track with two pairs of switches, providing cross-overs for trains operating in either direction. Space required is 72" by 92".

At the far right is another small layout for "O" gauge. The space required for this layout is 72" by 92". Two trains may be independently operated on this layout.

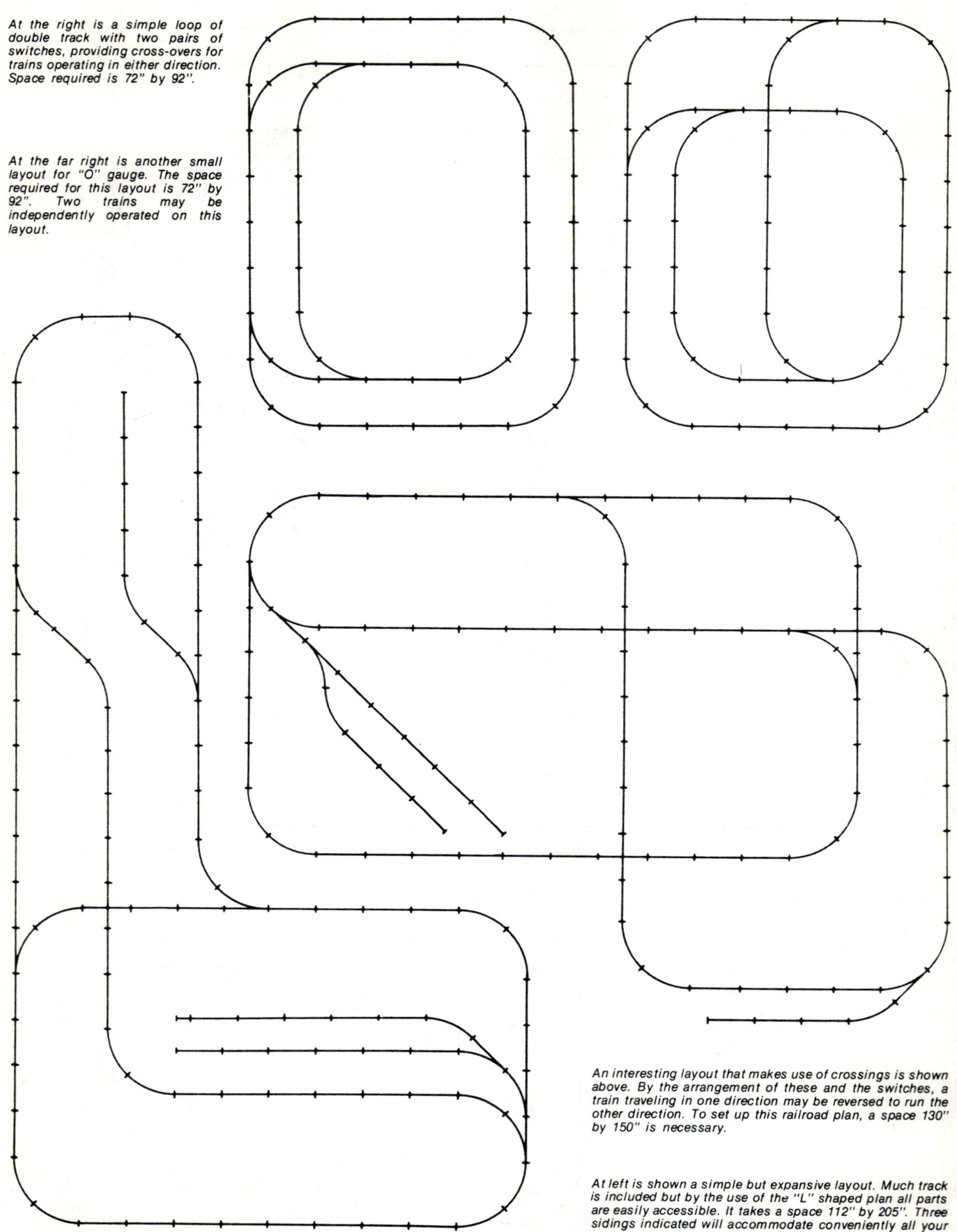

An interesting layout that makes use of crossings is shown above. By the arrangement of these and the switches, a train traveling in one direction may be reversed to run the other direction. To set up this railroad plan, a space 130" by 150" is necessary.

At left is shown a simple but expansive layout. Much track is included but by the use of the "L" shaped plan all parts are easily accessible. It takes a space 112" by 205". Three sidings indicated will accommodate conveniently all your cars.

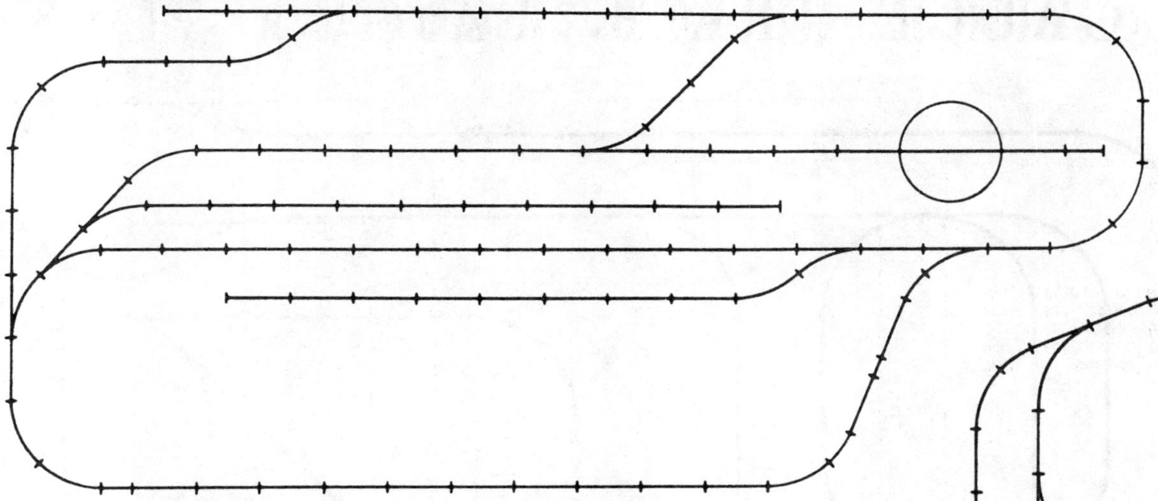

Above is an interesting layout with small but convenient yard trackage. A turntable is included on which your engine may be turned to make a round trip. Two yard lead tracks and two sidings for car storage are included. Space required for this layout is 82" by 183".

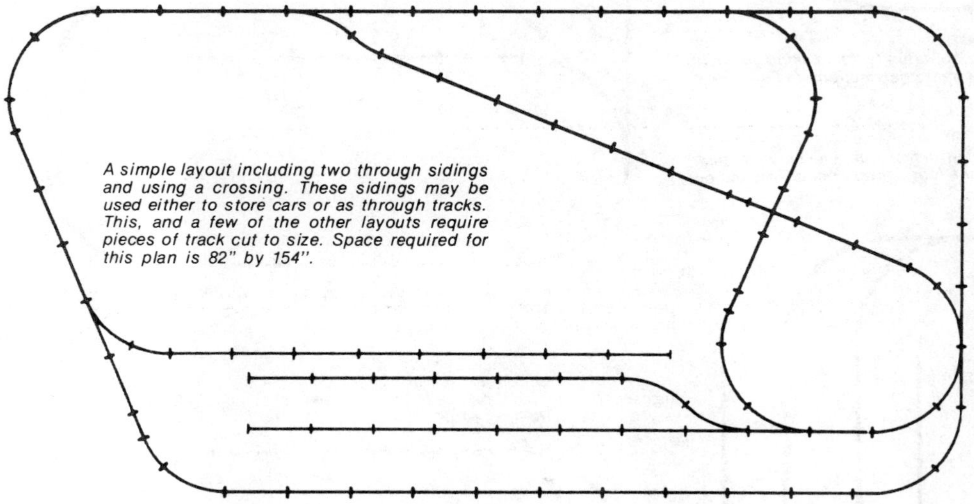

A simple layout including two through sidings and using a crossing. These sidings may be used either to store cars or as through tracks. This, and a few of the other layouts require pieces of track cut to size. Space required for this plan is 82" by 154".

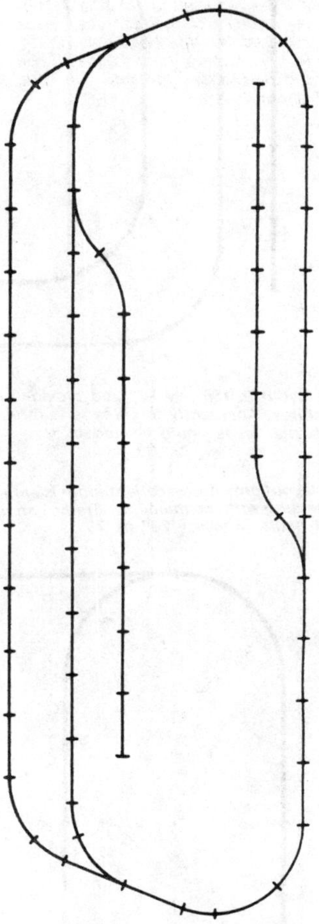

At the right is a small layout with a passing siding and two spur sidings. This track arrangement will fill a space of about 51" by 149". By ommission or addition of straight track on both sides this layout may be enlarged or contracted to fit available space

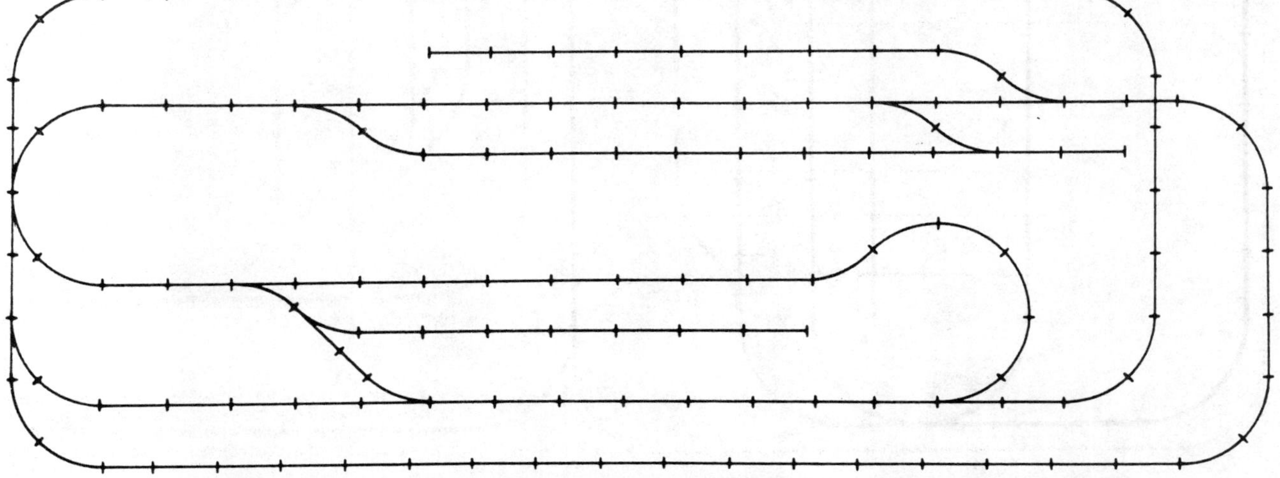

Above is a track layout for a large system. 82" by 205" is the space this layout requires. Ample side trackage is included and several different routes are possible.. A reversing loop is used to reverse a train or locomotive. thus enlarging scope of operations.

"O" GAUGE TRACK LAYOUT PLANS

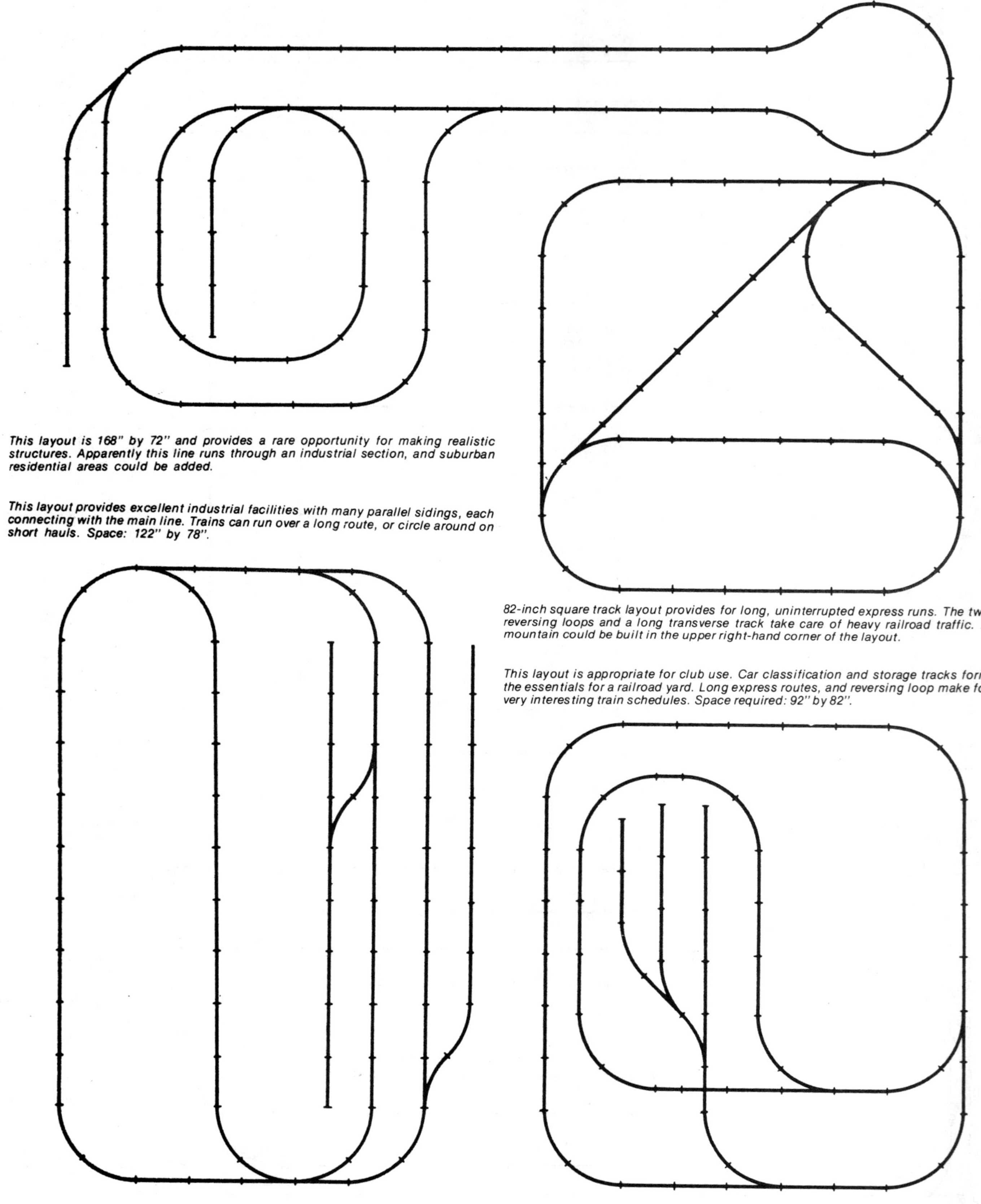

This layout is 168" by 72" and provides a rare opportunity for making realistic structures. Apparently this line runs through an industrial section, and suburban residential areas could be added.

This layout provides excellent industrial facilities with many parallel sidings, each connecting with the main line. Trains can run over a long route, or circle around on short hauls. Space: 122" by 78".

82-inch square track layout provides for long, uninterrupted express runs. The two reversing loops and a long transverse track take care of heavy railroad traffic. A mountain could be built in the upper right-hand corner of the layout.

This layout is appropriate for club use. Car classification and storage tracks form the essentials for a railroad yard. Long express routes, and reversing loop make for very interesting train schedules. Space required: 92" by 82".

"O" PLANS FOR 6 FT. BY 9 FT. AND 9 FT. BY 12 FT. SPACES

The two "O" gauge layouts below are designed to fit on a table 6' by 9'. These are two of many different types. More side trackage could be added or the mainline could be double-tracked. Space is available for model buildings.

The "O" gauge plan below is designed to fit on a table 9' by 12'. This layout might provide a nucleus for your own layout. If you build it on a table, it will provide opportunity for permanent model scenery building.

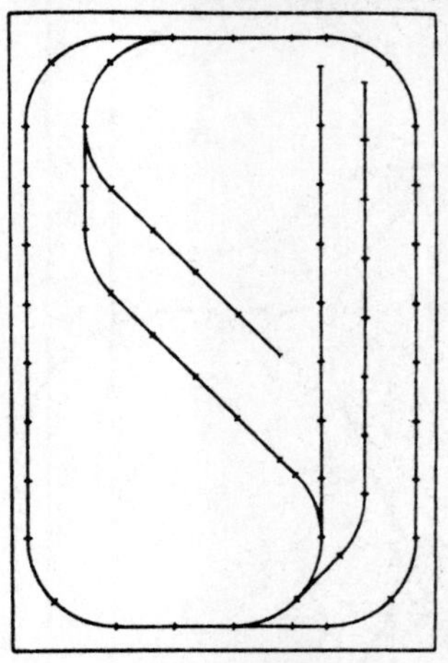

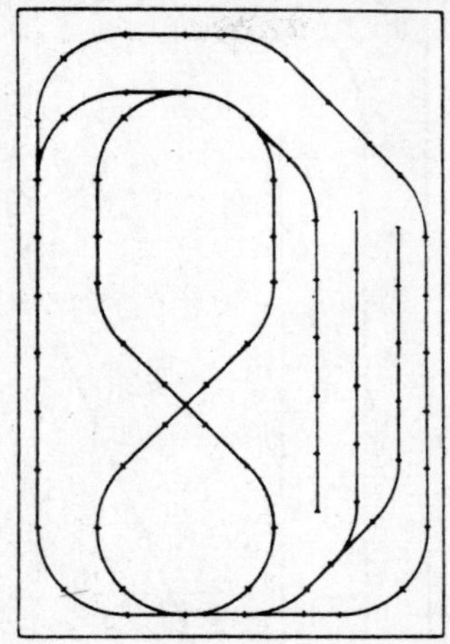

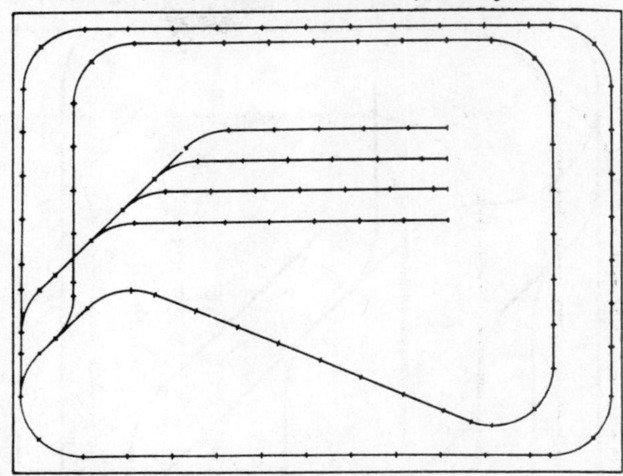

"OO" PLANS FOR SPACES 6 FT. BY 9 FT. AND 9 FT. BY 12 FT.

An "OO" gauge system for a table 9 ft. by 12 ft. This track layout is simple and offers an excellent opportunity for the use of many interesting landscaped effects. Siding space is shown to take care of all of extra cars.

Below are two "OO" gauge layouts for a table 6 ft. by 9 ft. Both are complete and flexible, with siding tracks and reversing loops. Sidings and loops should be planned when the railroad system is originally designed.

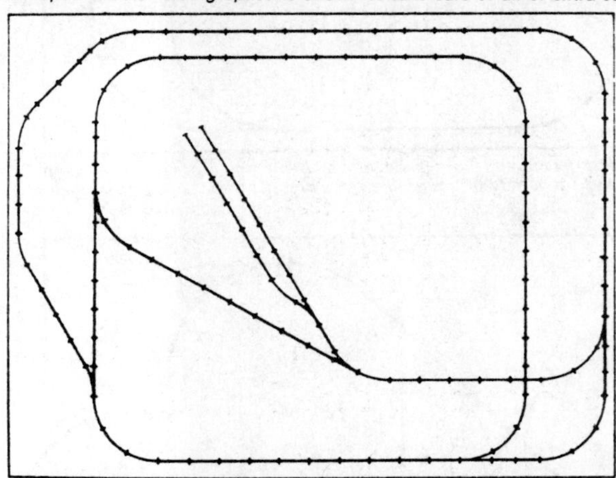

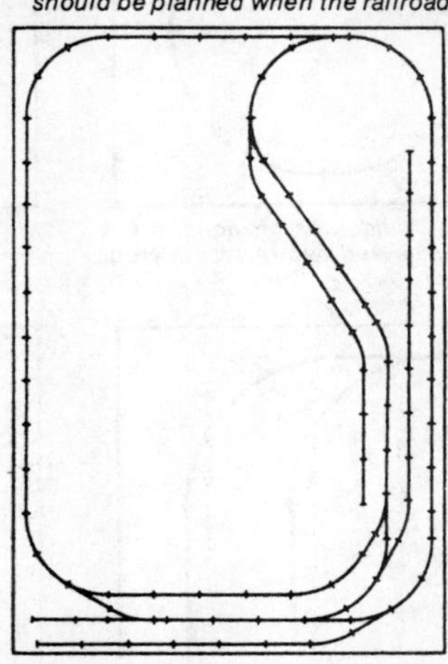

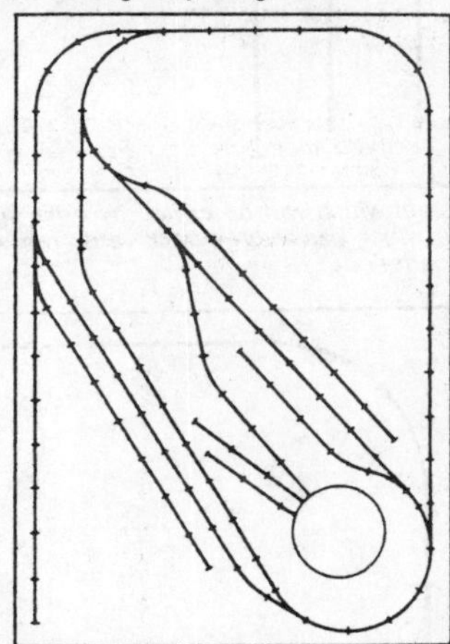

"O-72" GAUGE LAYOUTS FOR 9 FT. BY 12 FT. SPACE.

The layout below is for wide-radius track and includes a turntable. It is planned to fit a space 9 ft. by 12 ft. Any area much smaller will not be sufficient for wide-radius track. This plan makes excellent use of the limited space allotted.

Another wide radius "O" gauge track layout for a table 9 ft. by 12 ft. It will be noticed that by the use of curved tracks in the sidings more trackage can be obtained. More sidings can be added conveniently in this layout if wanted.

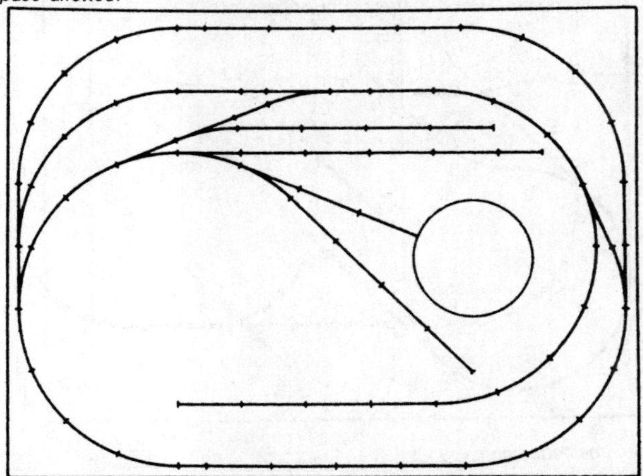

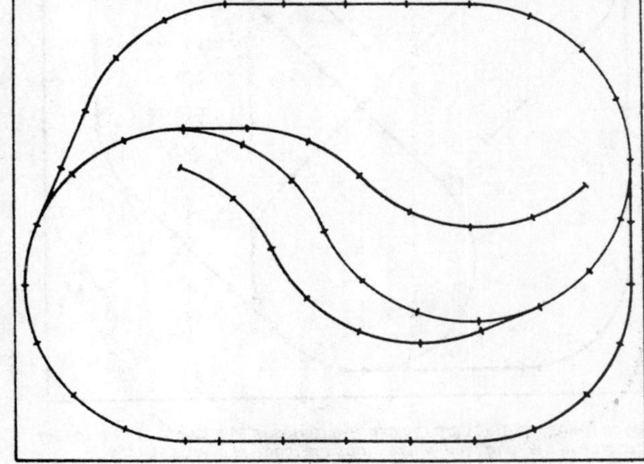

"O" GAUGE TRACK LAYOUT PLANS

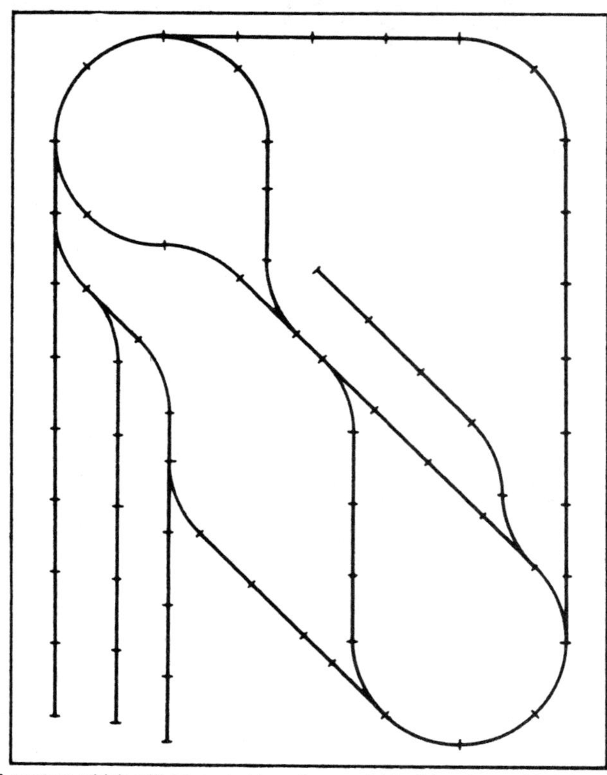

A system which will be envied by other model builders is provided in this layout which has a three-track yard. Ten switches and two reversing loops lend variety.

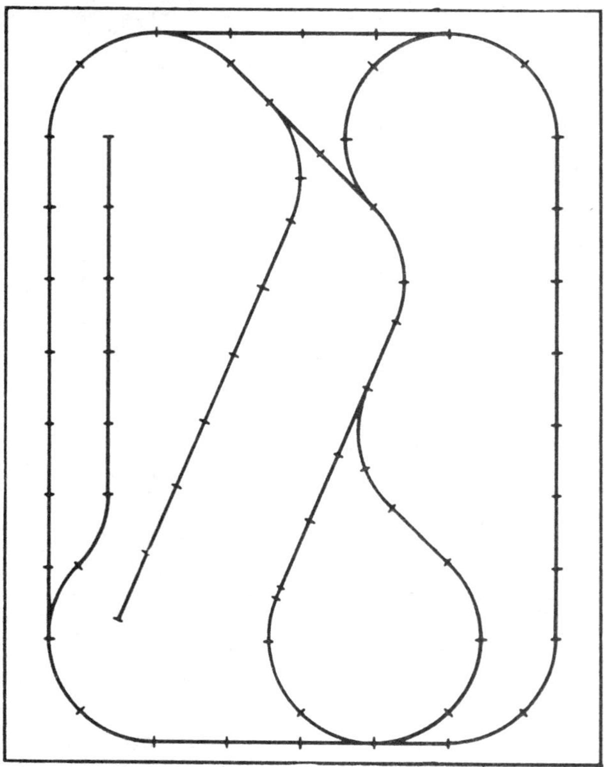

This miniature railroad layout is ideal for a six-by-nine-foot space. Notice the possibilities for variety of train routes that are afforded by use of the center loop.

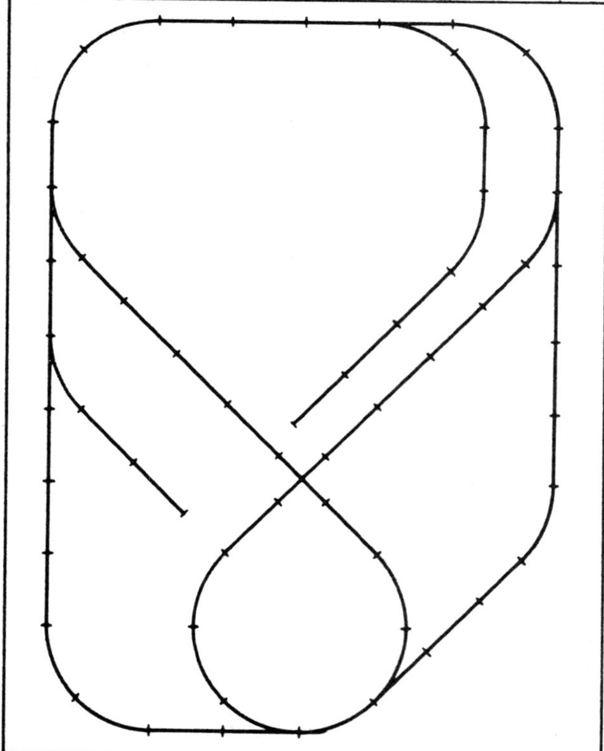

The diagonal lines of track are the express routes in this layout. The track on the outer side is the long haul where stops are made at every small town.

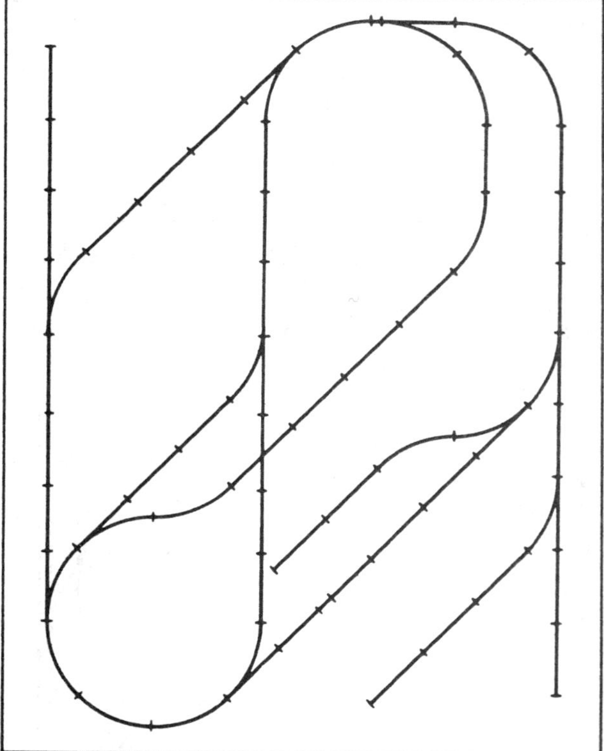

Opportunity for building cities, villages, mountains and a variety of landscaping is offered in a system of this type, which also permits two-way train operation.

DESIGNED FOR 6 FT. BY 9 FT. TABLE

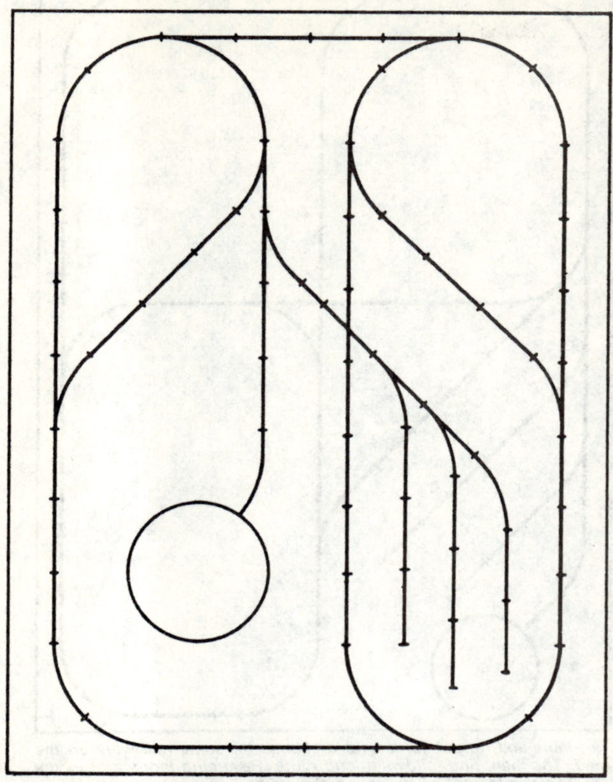

Double reversing loops vary train routes. Turntable and yards serve the terminal and make a railroad which hums with action. A well planned layout.

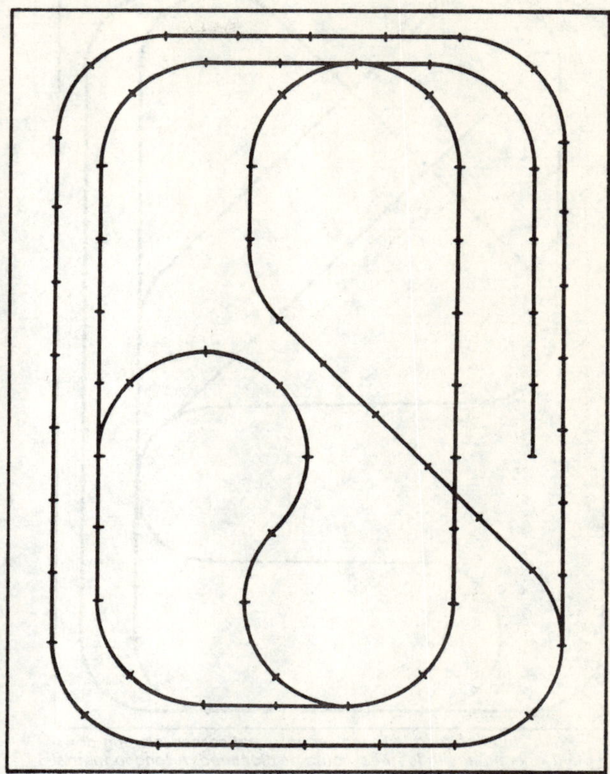

For the boy who wants his trains to follow a long and interesting road. One spur track connects outer and inner ovals. Several switches and crossovers are used.

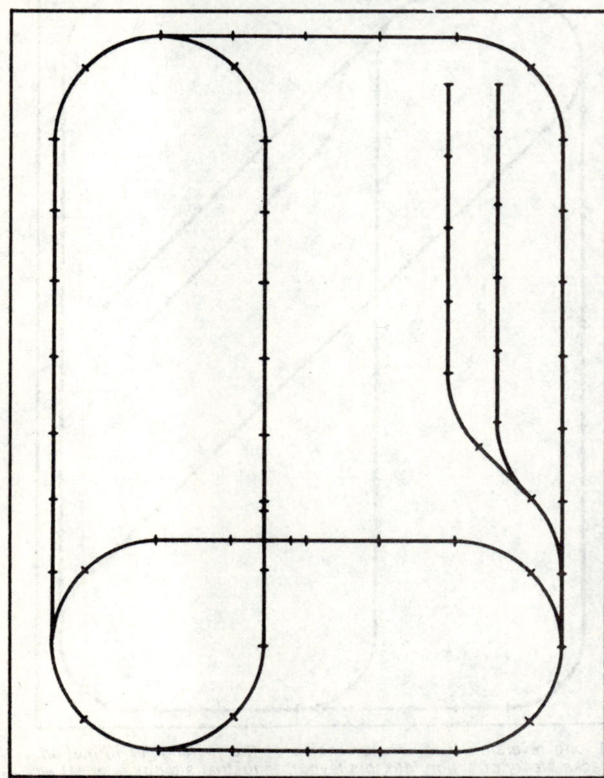

This layout permits the simultaneous operation of several trains. Freight sidings and a junction break the regularity of the layout in an attractive fashion.

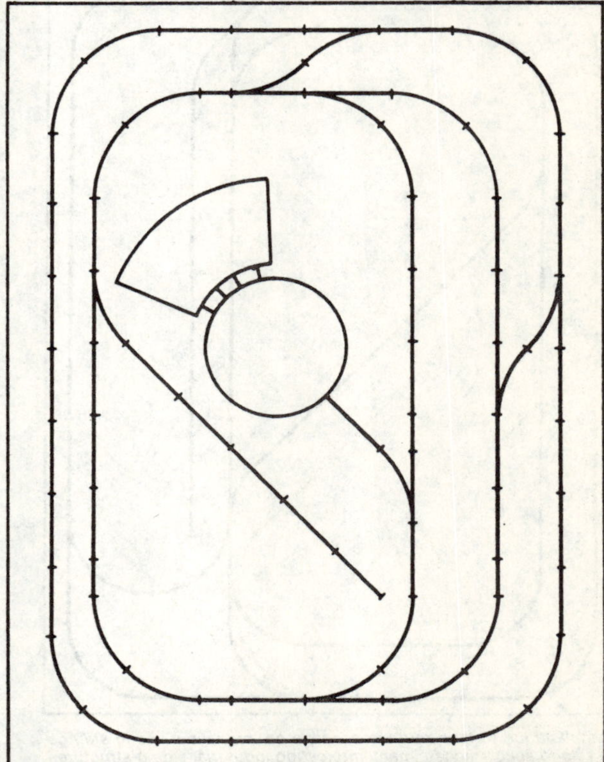

Roundhouse has tracks for locomotives. Several trains could run on this exceptional layout. Look at the facilities for passing and the double track.

"O" GAUGE TRACK LAYOUT PLANS

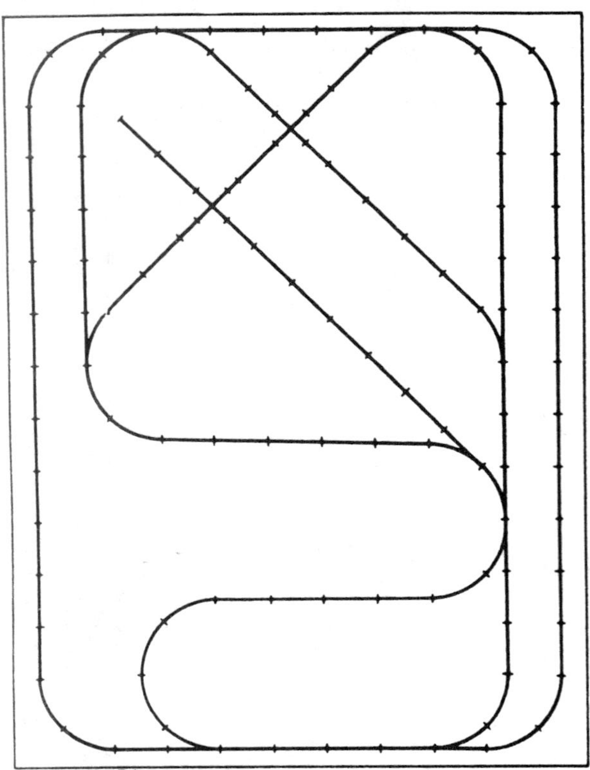

A mountain could be built in the lower left-hand corner, sloping down to a plain where many industries would be clustered. A long industrial spur indicates a commercial section.

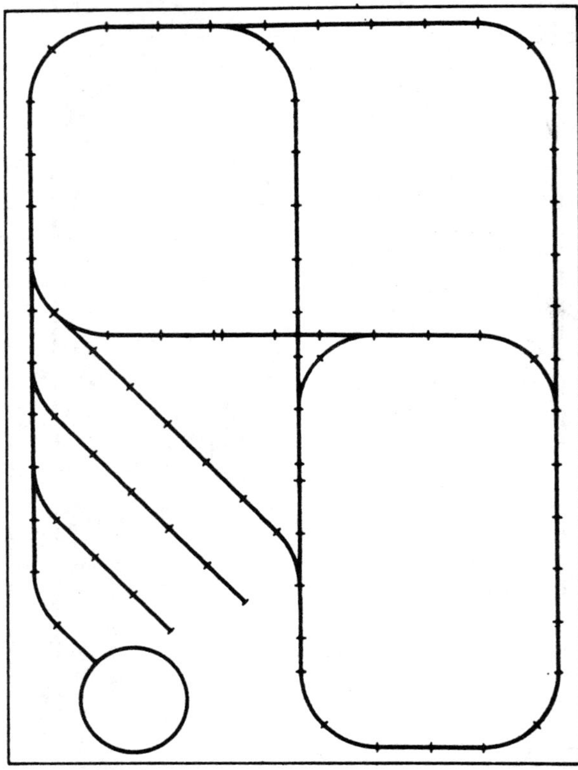

Turntable and freight yards give a chance for some real work on the road. The main line follows a long route. Reversing loops add to the fun and excitement of operating the trains.

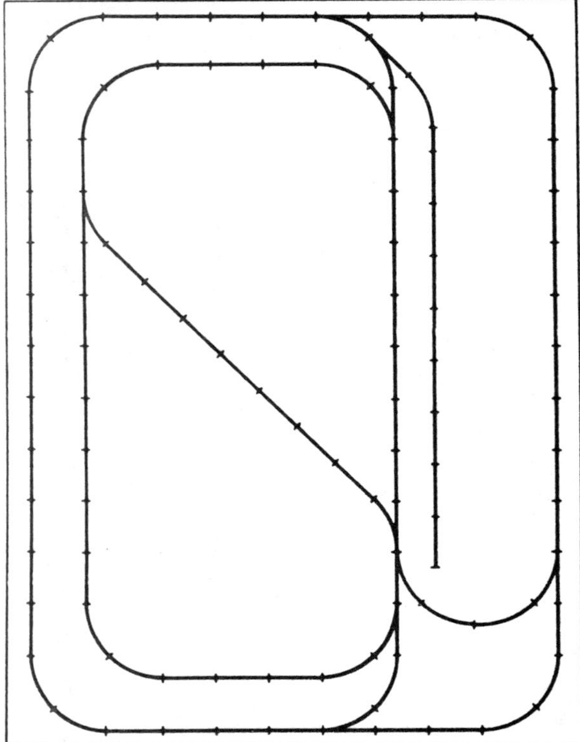

Great variation in train route is possible on this layout. Long sidings are able to accommodate many interesting industrial siding structures such as coal elevator, crane or lumber loader.

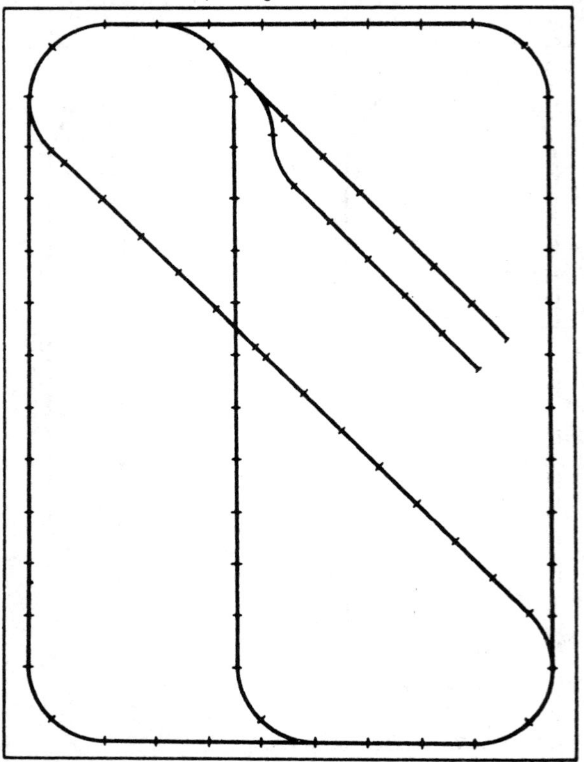

A long reversing loop, on the inside of the rectangular formation, packs plenty of action into this layout. Industrial sidings suggest an appropriate location for several model factories.

DESIGNED FOR 9 FT. BY 12 FT. TABLE

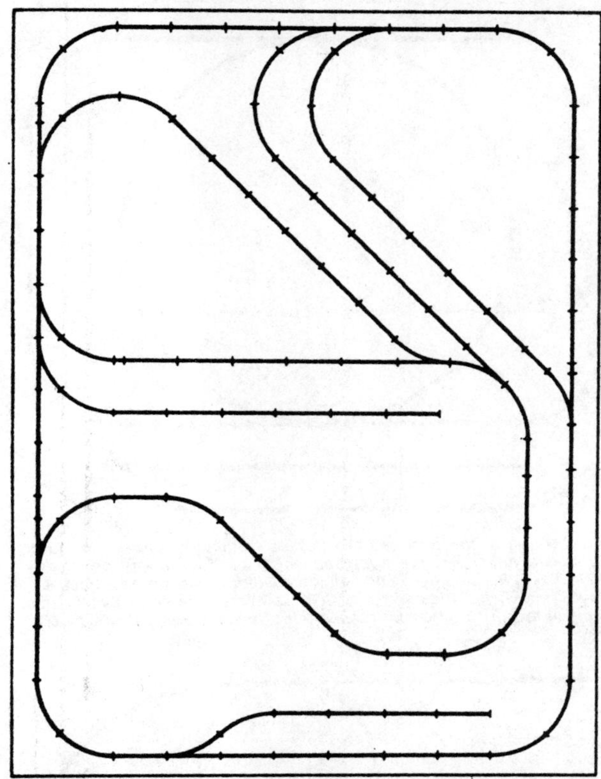

Factory buildings, oil refineries and industrial structures could be erected on this layout. Tracks criss-crossing the platform suggest a busy commercial landscape and terminals.

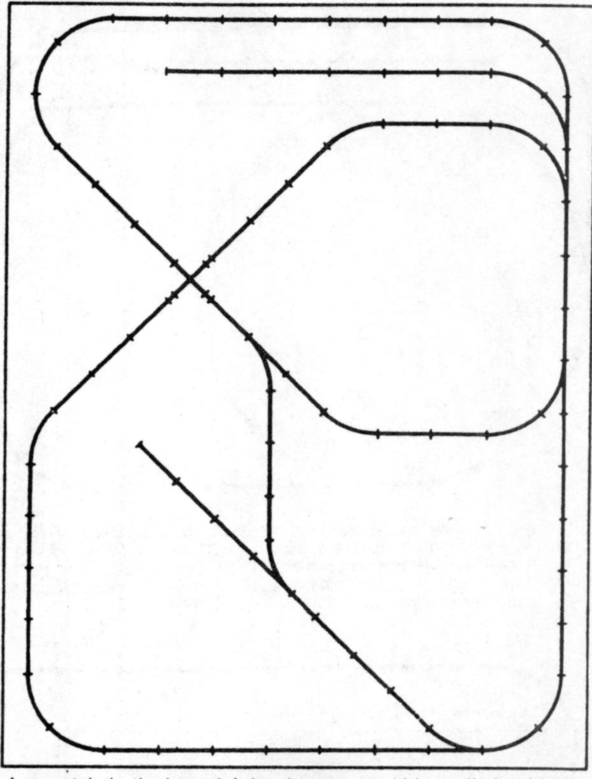

A mountain in the lower left-hand corner would be realistic with the train coming out of a tunnel as it starts up the cross-bar of the x-shaped section of track in this layout.

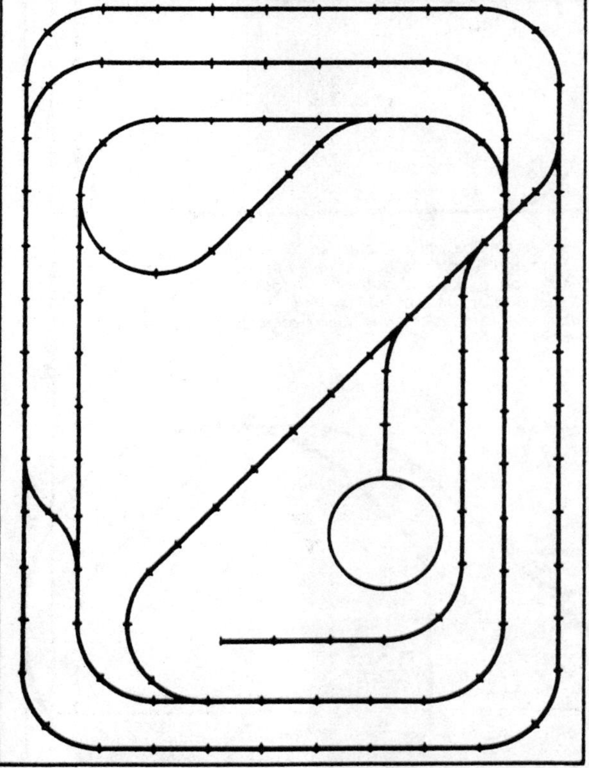

A complete railroad system with opportunities for operating your yard engines and express trains. Railroading is never monotonous on a layout with so much opportunity for variety.

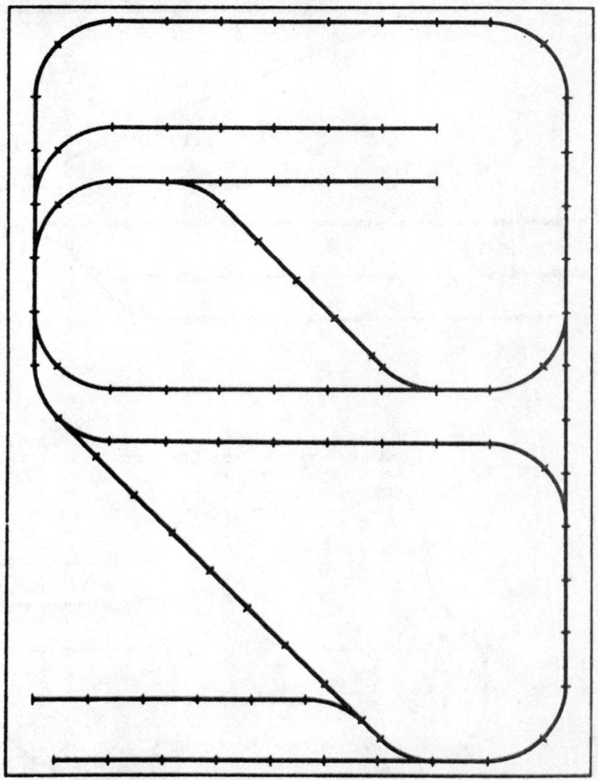

The rectangular formation at the loop could be a complete system. Later, the bottom section could be added, thereby increasing the number of different routes a train could take.

"O" AND "O-72" TRACK PLANS

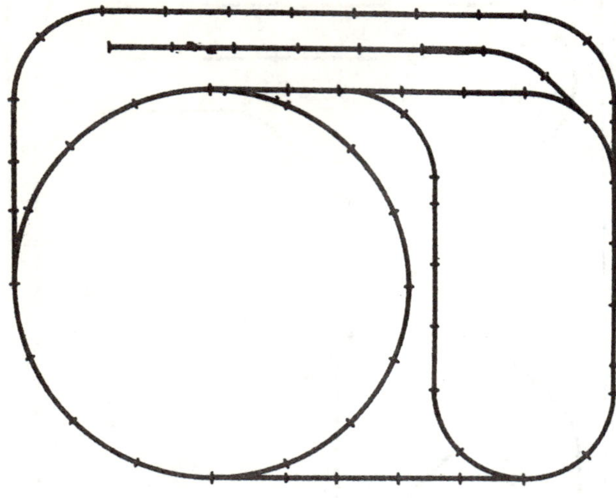

Plenty of passing track and several reversing loops provide for a constantly changing scene. Wide radius "O-72" curved track and three "O-72" switches are combined with "O" gauge. "O-72" series trains cannot be operated on this type of system as they cannot negotiate "O" gauge curves which are 30" in diameter. Space 100" by 80".

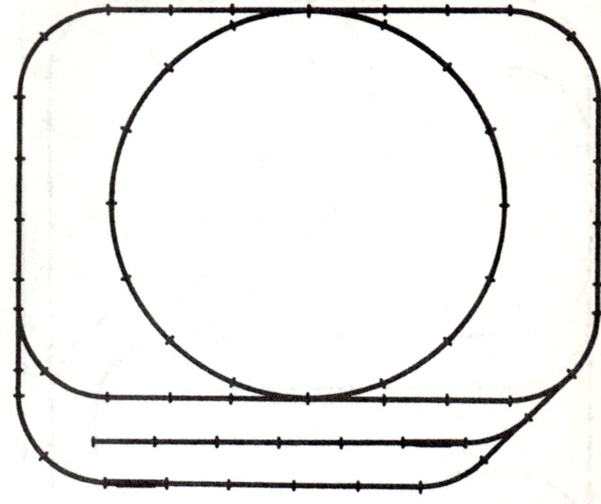

If a section of the circular track passes through a tunnel and skirts around a mountain, the apparent length of the run will be greatly increased. Passing track and industrial siding make this an attractive layout. "O-72" circle and four "O-72" switches are combined in this unique layout for interesting operation. Space required is 90" by 80".

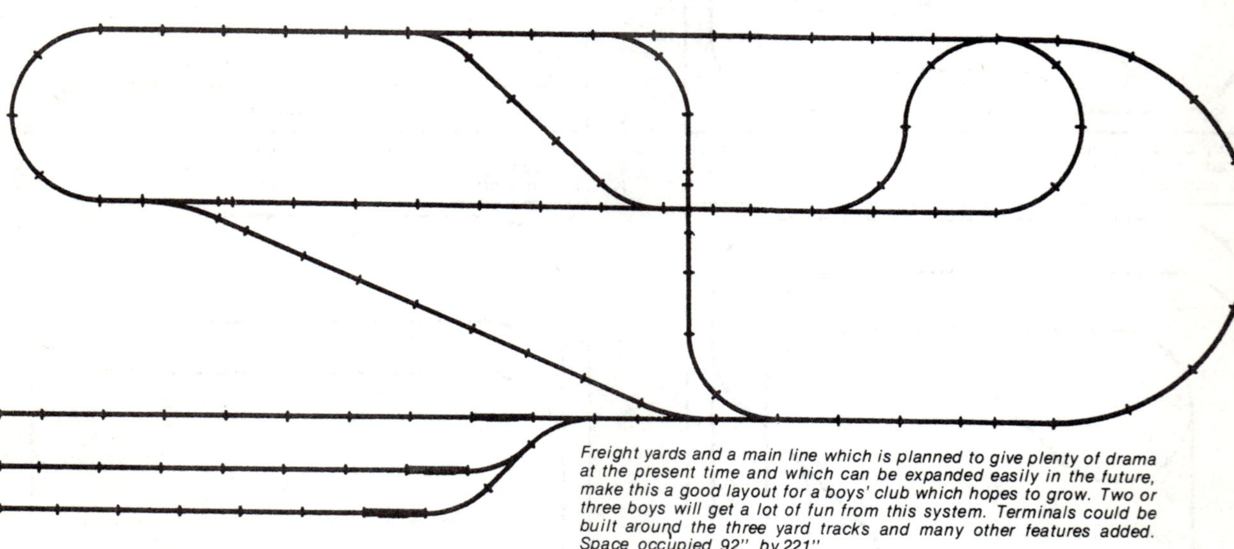

Freight yards and a main line which is planned to give plenty of drama at the present time and which can be expanded easily in the future, make this a good layout for a boys' club which hopes to grow. Two or three boys will get a lot of fun from this system. Terminals could be built around the three yard tracks and many other features added. Space occupied 92" by 221".

This is a layout with an eye to future progress. It is extremely well-planned and has a small car yard and enough looping track so that trains can vary their route. Wide radius "O-72" curves and switches make trains round courves more gracefully and true to life. Special uncoupling sections may be located where needed. Space 72" by 221".

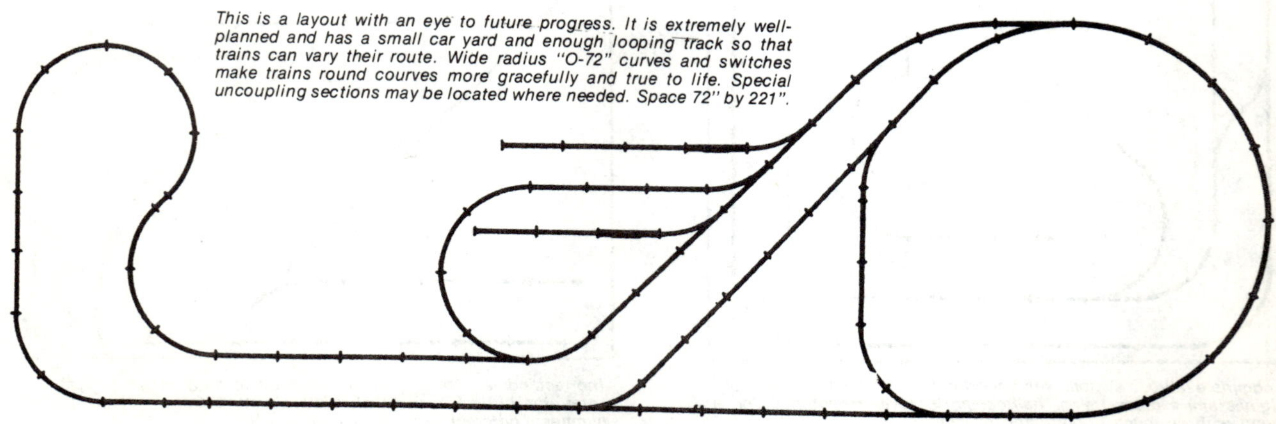

U-shaped layout has plenty of work space so that the system can be repaired or changed as the need arises. Many reversing loops make this an exciting system to operate. Siding at the left could lead to the repair bench. Right hand loop uses wide radius curves. This is an interesting combination of "O" gauge and "O-72" gauge track. Space: 110" by 211".

Freight and car yards make good use of your yard goats. The main line is a double reversing loop. The left-hand loop uses wide radius curved track. All switches are "O" gauge, and no "O-72" straight track is used in this entire layout. This is a good industrial system and gives a chance for some realistic model building. Space: 72" by 211".

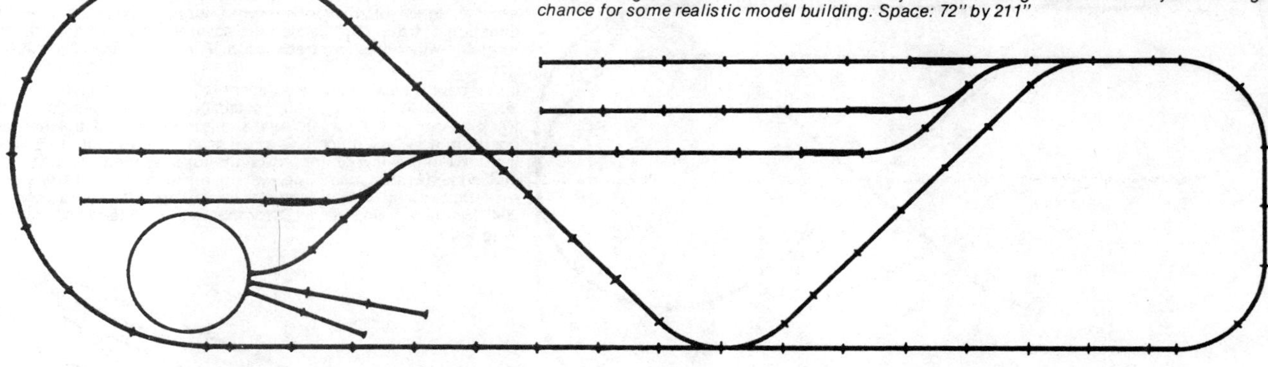

Plenty of thrills can be packed into this layout with its hairpin curves and winding route. Several trains can be operated at the same time by using the passing track. Curved track in outer loop is regular "O" gauge; inner loop, "O-72" series. Space for layout: 90" by 90".

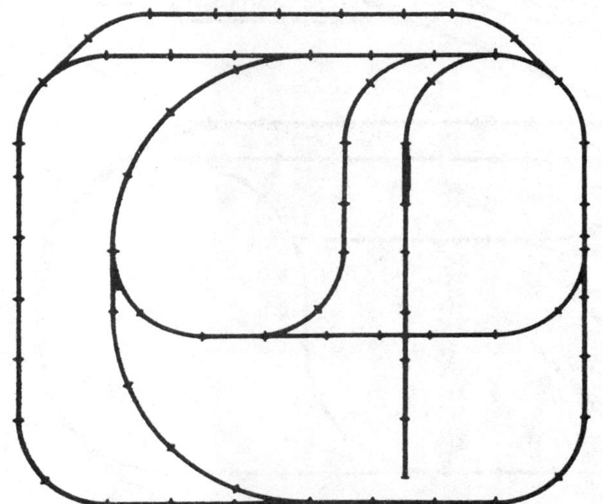

Another variation on the conventional rectangular layout. This track set-up suggests some of the many effective engineering twists which can increase the fun on your road. Main line is composed of "O" gauge track. Several sections of track are cut to fit. Space: 85" by 96".

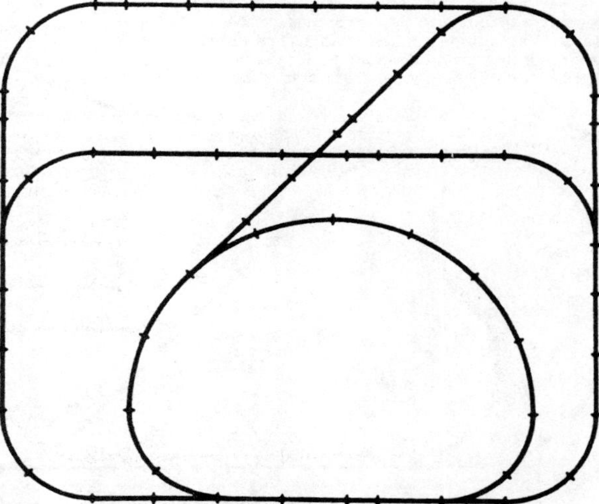

"O-72" GAUGE TRACK LAYOUT IDEAS

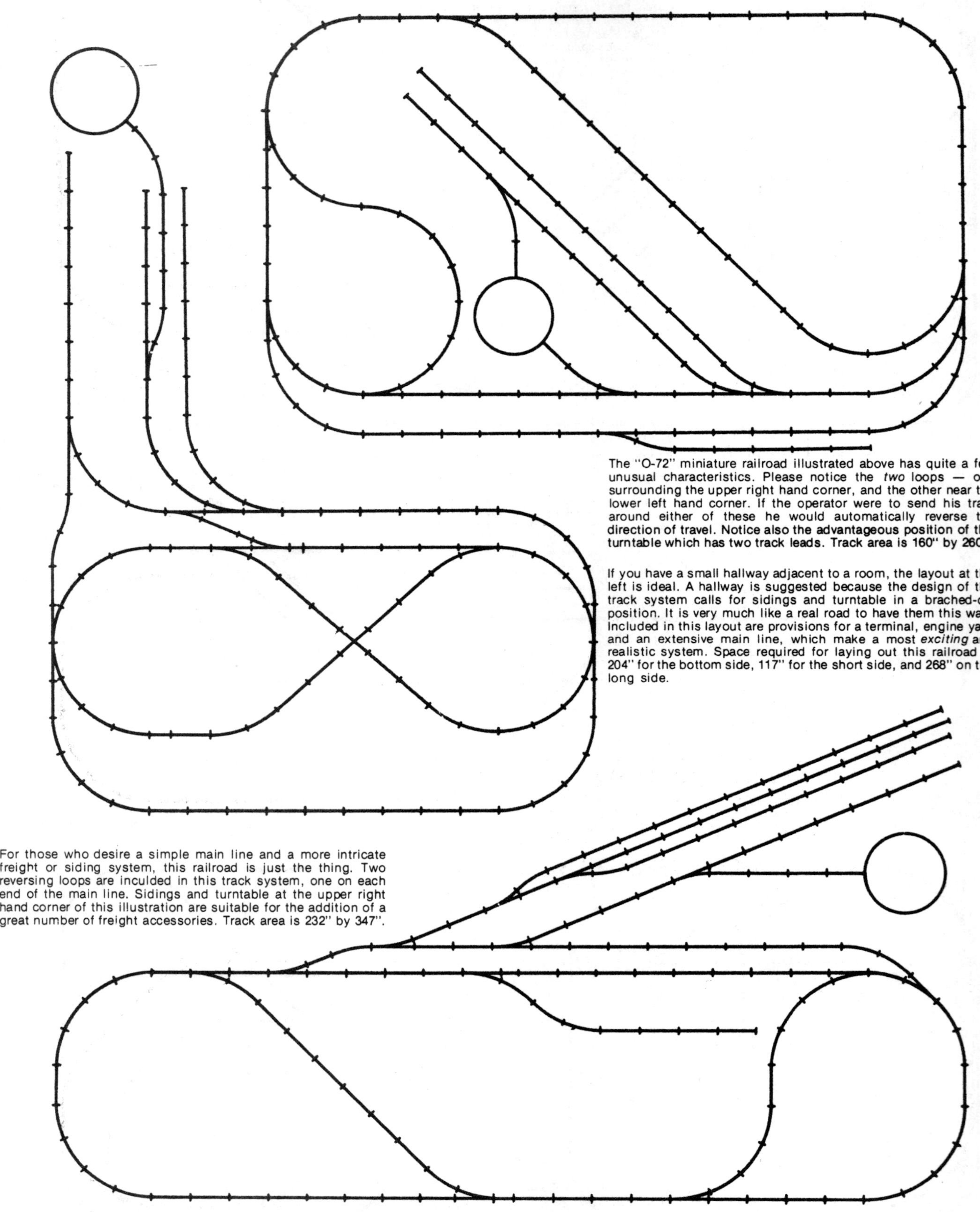

The "O-72" miniature railroad illustrated above has quite a few unusual characteristics. Please notice the *two* loops — one surrounding the upper right hand corner, and the other near the lower left hand corner. If the operator were to send his train around either of these he would automatically reverse the direction of travel. Notice also the advantageous position of the turntable which has two track leads. Track area is 160" by 260".

If you have a small hallway adjacent to a room, the layout at the left is ideal. A hallway is suggested because the design of the track system calls for sidings and turntable in a brached-off position. It is very much like a real road to have them this way. Included in this layout are provisions for a terminal, engine yard and an extensive main line, which make a most *exciting* and realistic system. Space required for laying out this railroad is 204" for the bottom side, 117" for the short side, and 268" on the long side.

For those who desire a simple main line and a more intricate freight or siding system, this railroad is just the thing. Two reversing loops are inculded in this track system, one on each end of the main line. Sidings and turntable at the upper right hand corner of this illustration are suitable for the addition of a great number of freight accessories. Track area is 232" by 347".

Long spurs of track give an opportunity for local stops for passenger and freight loading. Some variety of route is gained by the passing track. A layout large enough for two trains. Requires space 162" by 147".

A reversing loop and a passing siding are for trains running on the mainline of this interesting small layout. A system that may be beautifully landscaped with mountains and low lands. Space 147" by 162".

Above: Two track cross-overs on this layout give the appearance of a railroad network probably in suburban surroundings. Double reversing routes permit trains to change direction. Space: 352" by 134".

A turntable and roundhouse with four tracks is the most interesting item of this layout. Notice freight yards in industrial area and excellent train reversing facilities. Space required is 352" by 134".

"O-72" GAUGE TRACK LAYOUT IDEAS

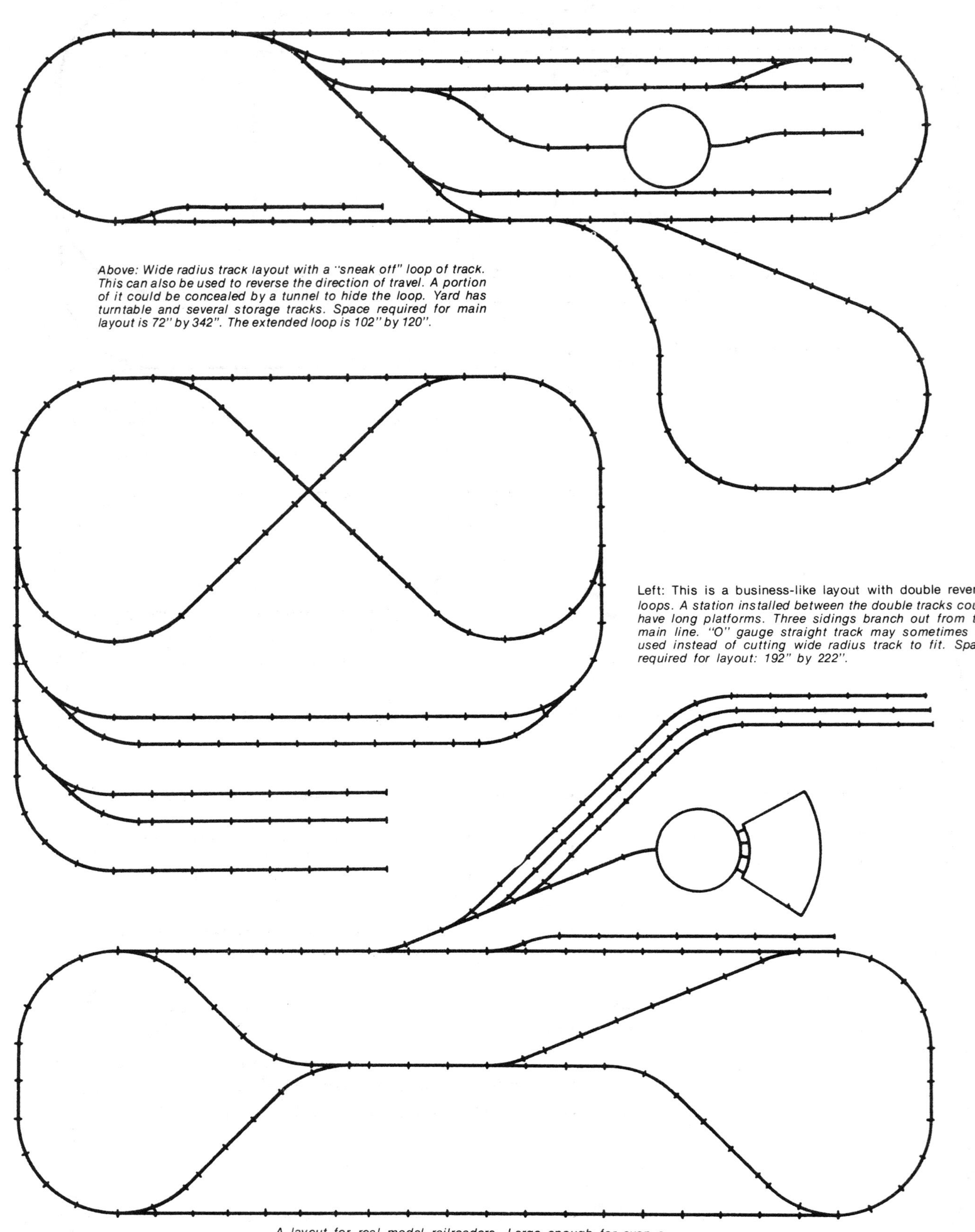

Above: Wide radius track layout with a "sneak off" loop of track. This can also be used to reverse the direction of travel. A portion of it could be concealed by a tunnel to hide the loop. Yard has turntable and several storage tracks. Space required for main layout is 72" by 342". The extended loop is 102" by 120".

Left: *This is a business-like layout with double reverse loops. A station installed between the double tracks could have long platforms. Three sidings branch out from the main line. "O" gauge straight track may sometimes be used instead of cutting wide radius track to fit. Space required for layout: 192" by 222".*

A layout for real model railroaders. Large enough for even a serious model railroad club. Mainline track has two elaborate reversing loops. A series of yard tracks branch off from the mainline. Also notice the roundhouse and turntable. Passenger and freight cars can be stored in the yards, and the equipment for yard work included in the railroad panorama. 342" by 196".

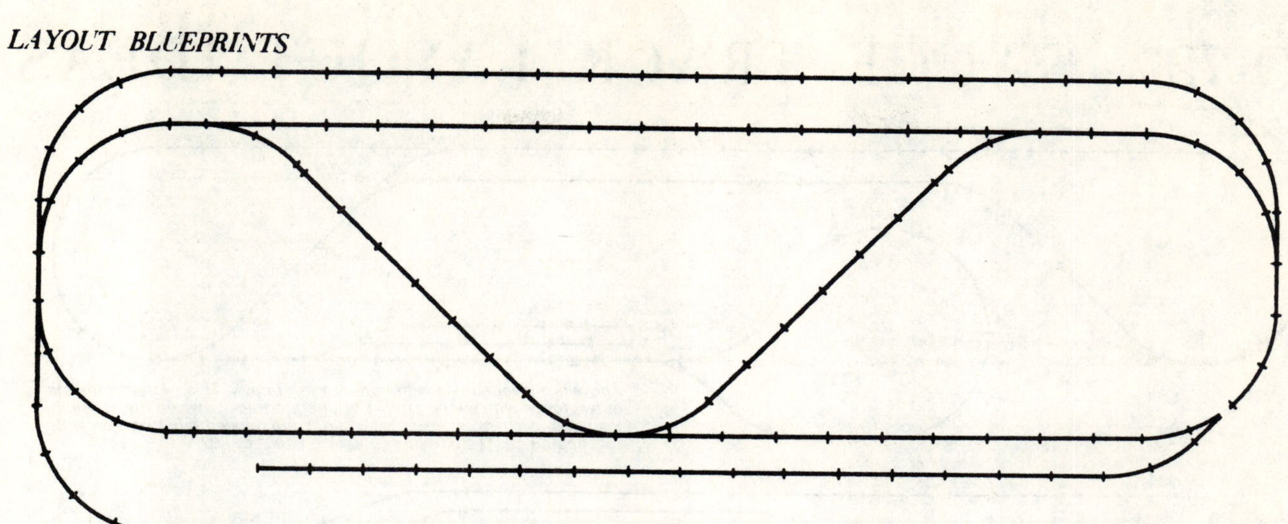

For the model railroader wanting a layout suitable for fast express service, this track arrangement is ideal. Long straight and without interruptions, it is designed particularly for those who like to keep the throttle wide open. The lower side of the layout has two long sidings with one long approach track. The size is 132" by 340".

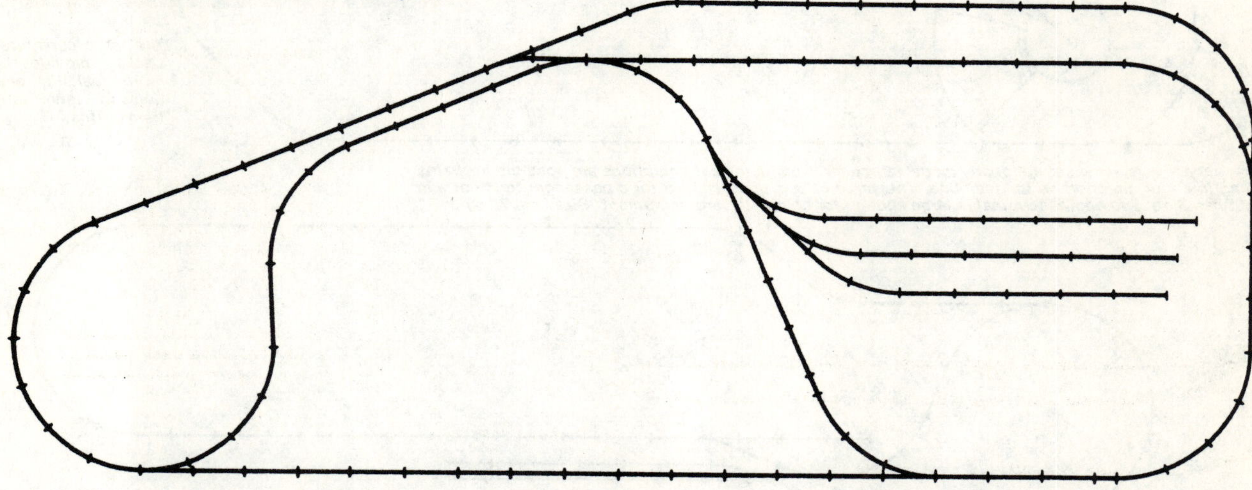

Above is a miniature system which is reasonably simple but embodies many characteristics of a real railroad. The three spur tracks may be employed as a passenger or freight car yard or terminal. Provision is made for two-way operation by the use of reversing loops. 132" by 337".

Shown below is a system designed for the operation of two trains entirely under separate control. Notice the reversing loops at both ends of the layout. The switches joining the inner and outer loops might be insulated so that each mainline could be controlled individually. Size 132" by 337".

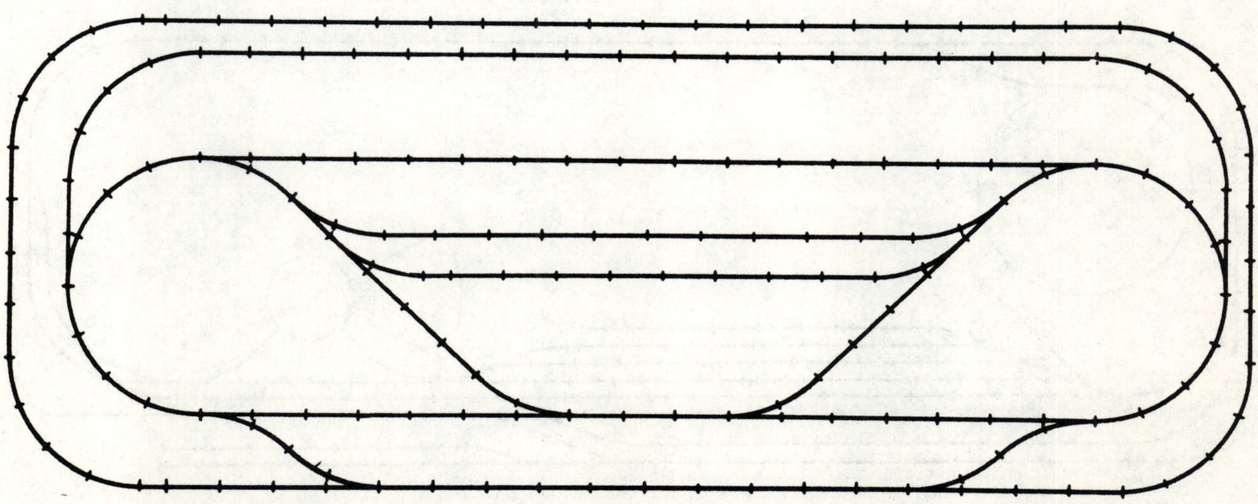

"O-72" GAUGE TRACK LAYOUT IDEAS

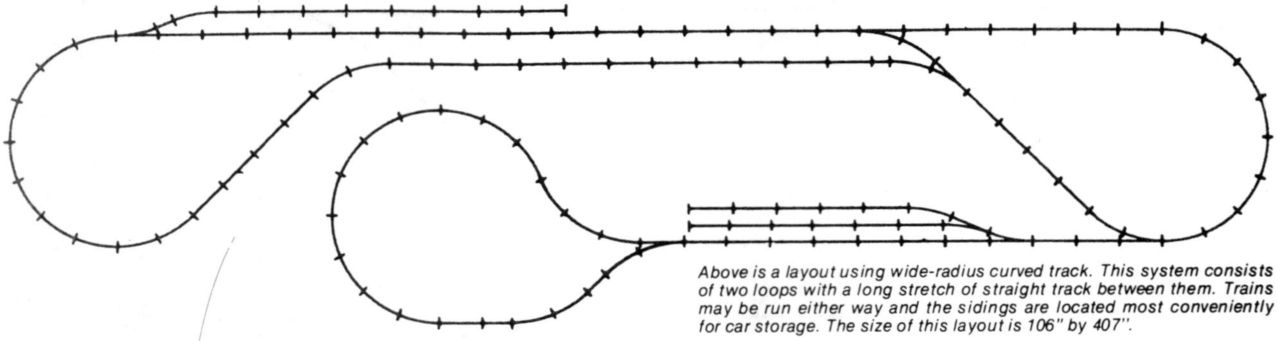

Above is a layout using wide-radius curved track. This system consists of two loops with a long stretch of straight track between them. Trains may be run either way and the sidings are located most conveniently for car storage. The size of this layout is 106" by 407".

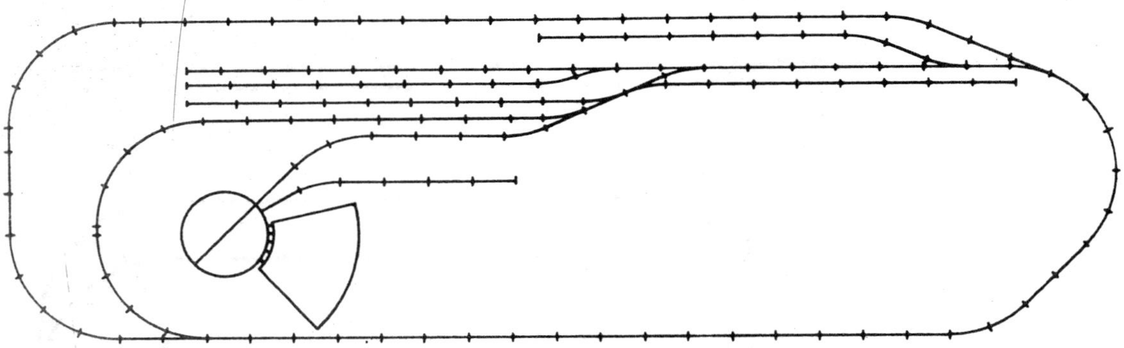

The large curvature of tracks provides for more realistic operation of long freight train outfits.

The layout above is a fine set-up for any model railroader. Complete yard operations are possible for trains running in either direction on the mainline. The yards offer a good chance for a passenger terminal and freight handling. The engine terminal is large enough for complete yard equipment. Size is 107" by 367".

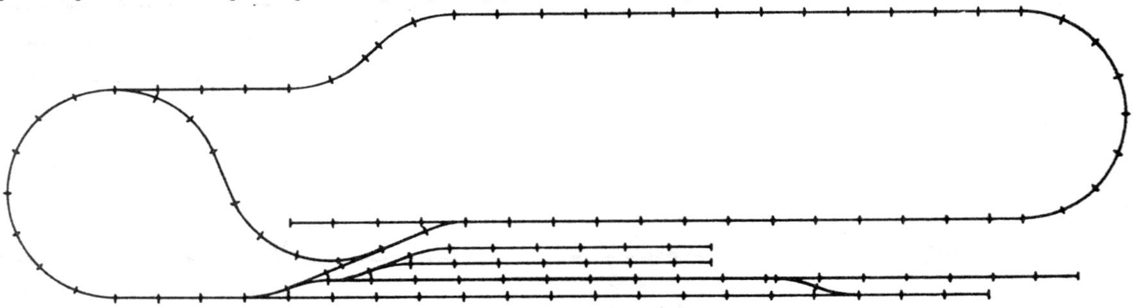

Below: Large layout having a real classification yard for freight, rolling stock and a turntable roundhouse with two lead-in tracks. The circular track in upper left corner may be concealed beneath a tunnel and used as a sneak-off, so the same train is not continuously seen. Area 135" by 417".

Above: Another wide radius track layout having a single tracked mainline with a short-cut track for reversing. A large amount of yard trackage is shown. The bottom two sidings would make an ideal location for a terminal where trains may be relayed by means of a cross-over. Size 98" by 374".

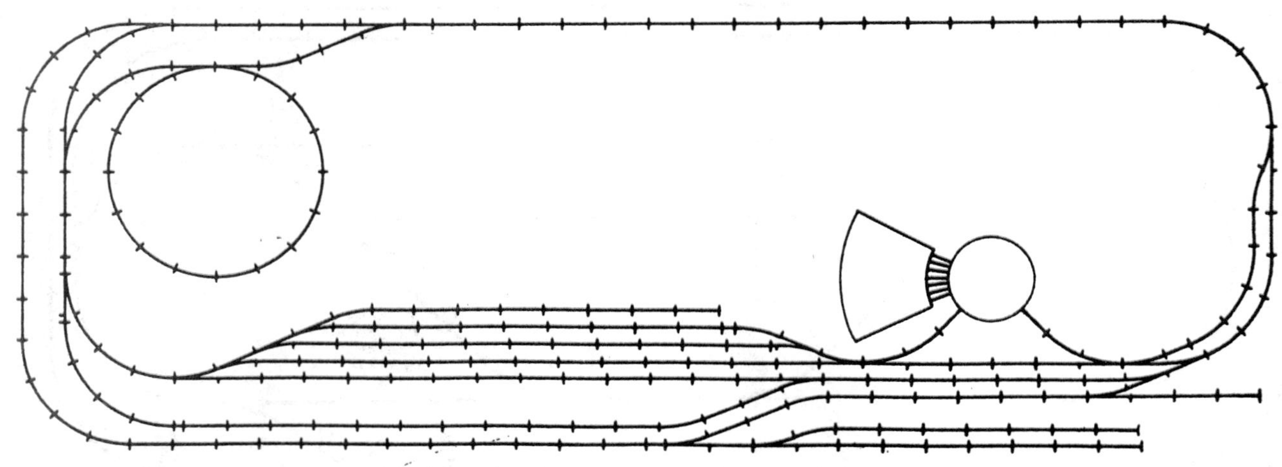

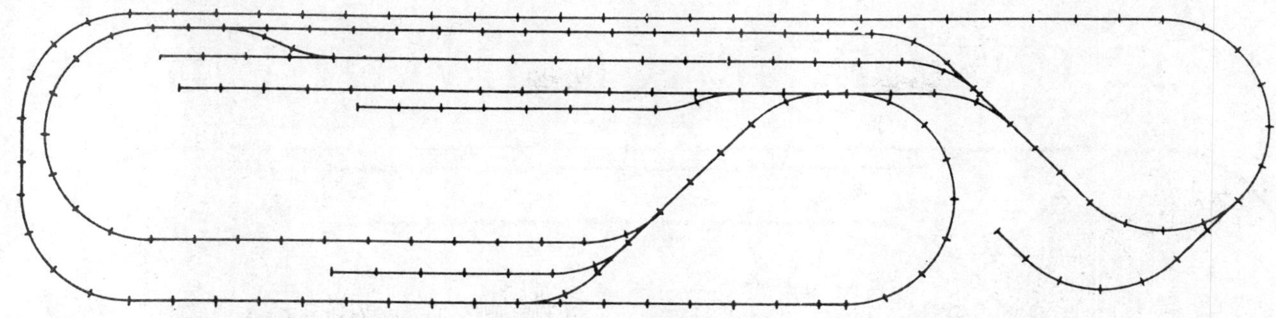

Imagine your "Broadway Limited" roaring around a layout such as this. Sidings may be used for car storage, terminal, and industrial use. The size of layouts on these pages is easily altered by subtracting or adding sections of straight track. This one takes a space of 97" by 417". Regular "O" gauge and 1/2"O" gauge sections have been used in these layouts to save cutting.

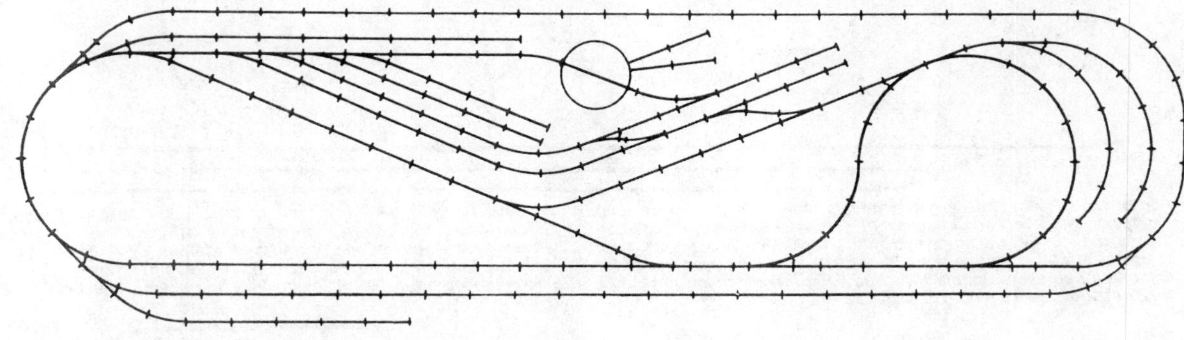

This layout has been designed so that a small number of switches give great variety of yard movements. Trains running either way may enter these yards or depart from them. You can relay your trains just as real railroads do. This track set-up occupies 87" by 390". Sidings are provided on which you could build industrial sidings. Separate sidings for passenger and freight equipment are desirable to follow actual railroad practice. A turntable is built in the layout for greater realism and operating action.

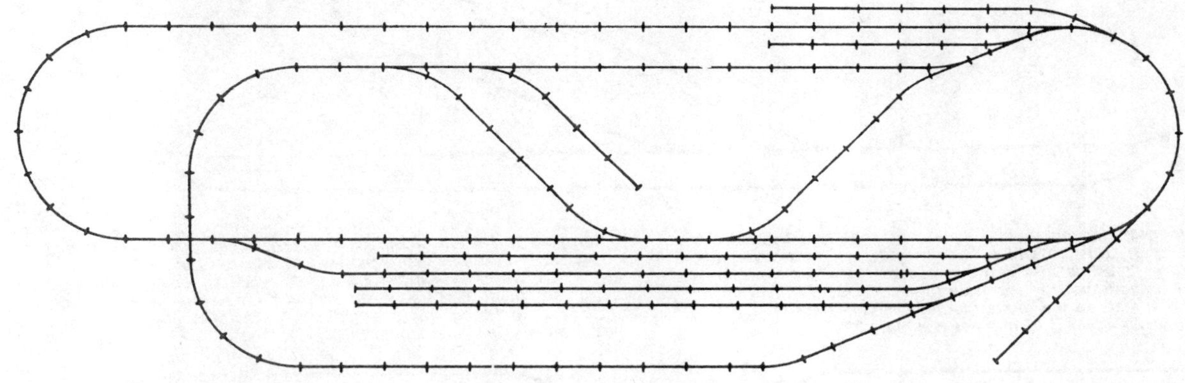

The layout above may provide you with an idea for helping you meet your own requirements. Long sidings as shown in all layouts on this page are excellent for through-stations. Space required is 113" by 390". Notice the two separate routes that can be used for many exciting railroad operations.

A double track wide radius railroad such as that shown below is an excellent one for continuous operation. This naturally would be an expensive system to create, but at the finish you would become master of a fine railroad with great opportunity for scenic additions. Space occupied is 44" by 417".

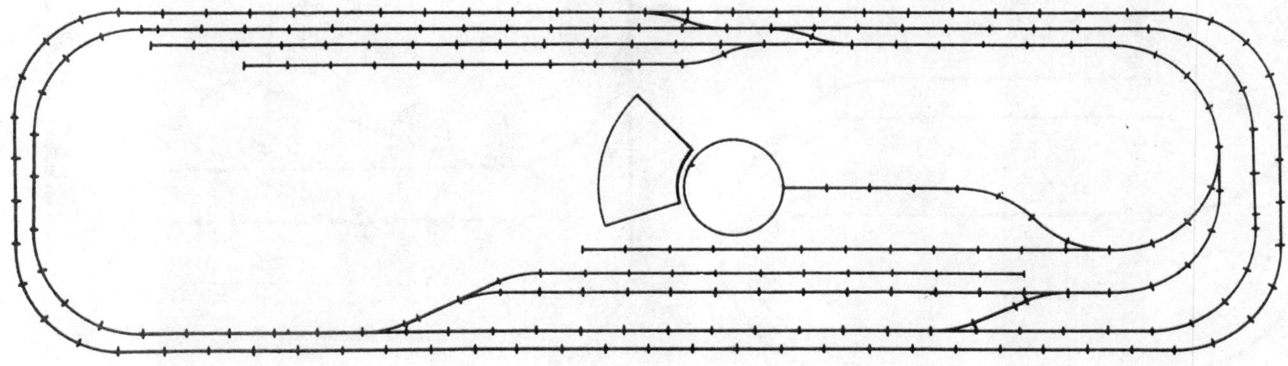

"O-72" GAUGE TRACK LAYOUT IDEAS

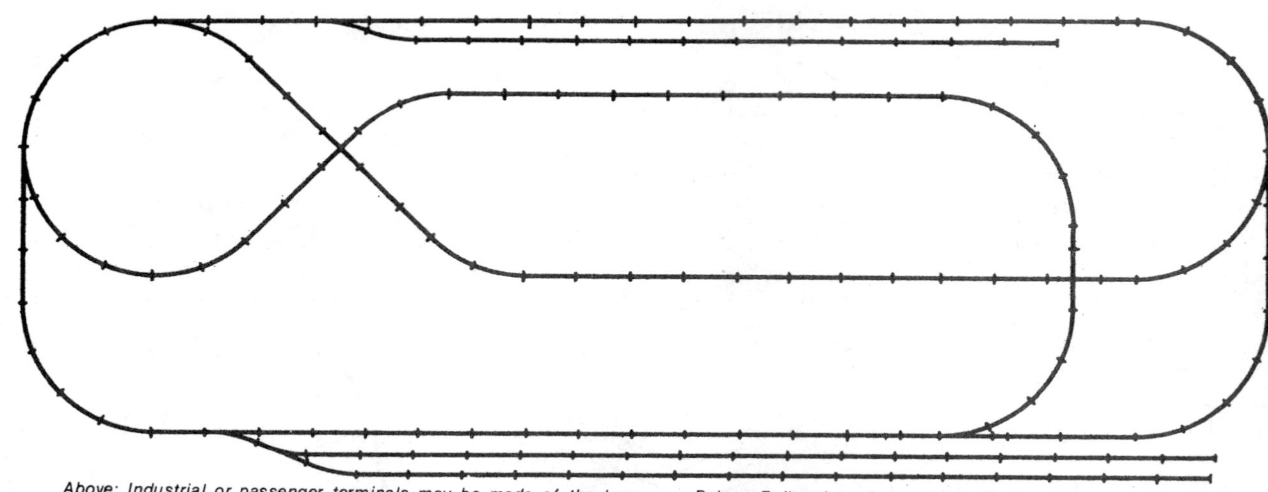

Above: Industrial or passenger terminals may be made of the long sidings on the lower part of this layout. One extra siding is included on the top and may be built at the end of this track. This layout, with room to spare for scenic additions, is the type that can be used nicely for exhibition purposes. Double reversing loops permit trains to change their direction. Space required is 132" by 342".

Below: Railroad yard complete with turntable, reversing loops and sidings, provides action and excitement in this layout. Long double-track accommodates heavy traffic. A station might be used at that point. For even greater realism, an engine service track and roundhouse may also be built into the system. Area used: 342" by 100".

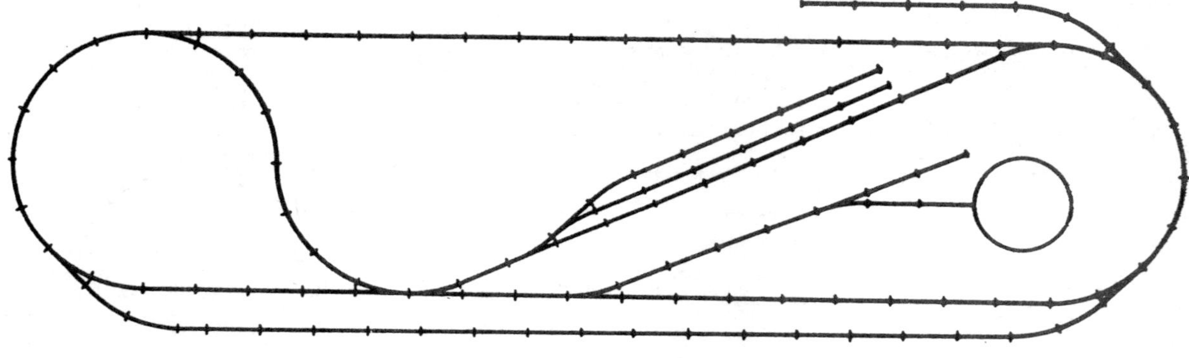

This simple, nearly-square layout requires a space 147" by 162" and has three sidings, Coal elevators, lumber loaders or other automatic accessories might be installed between sidings. Here is an opportunity for lots of fun and things for your train to do. A good basic layout for the boy who intends to add to his railroad system. Stations, tunnels, scenery,etc., will all help to make it complete.

A turntable which permits a locomotive and tender to be turned around and faced in the opposite direction is a most interesting feature of this layout. While this system has no double reversing loop, engines can be turned around and trains can always be run either way. A single track loop, and long industrial sidings for factories and warehouses add interest. Space occupied is 147" by 162".

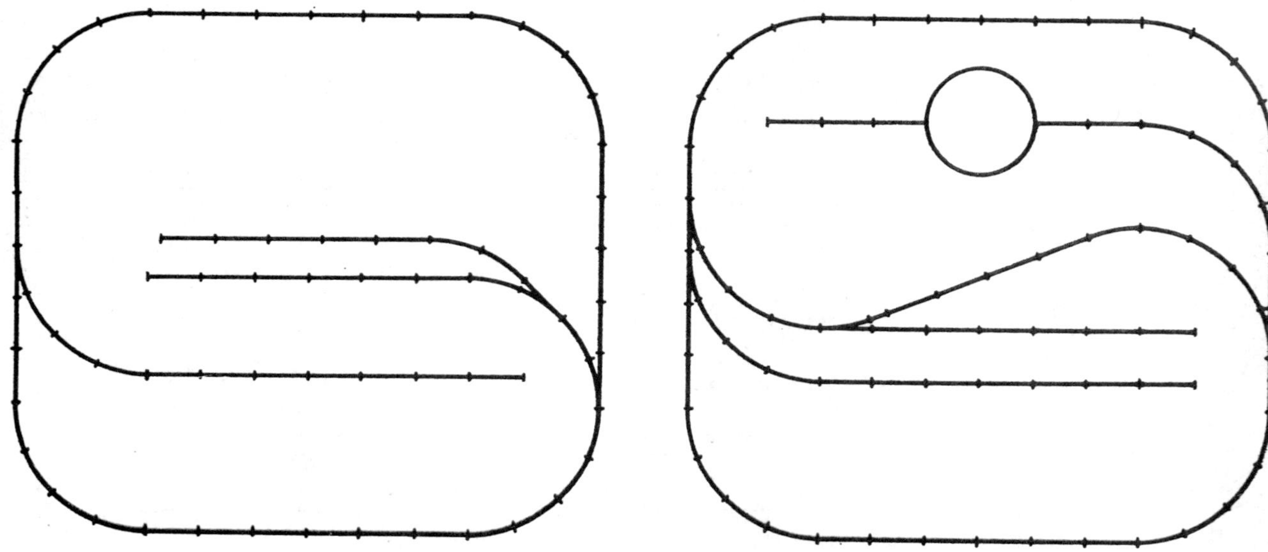

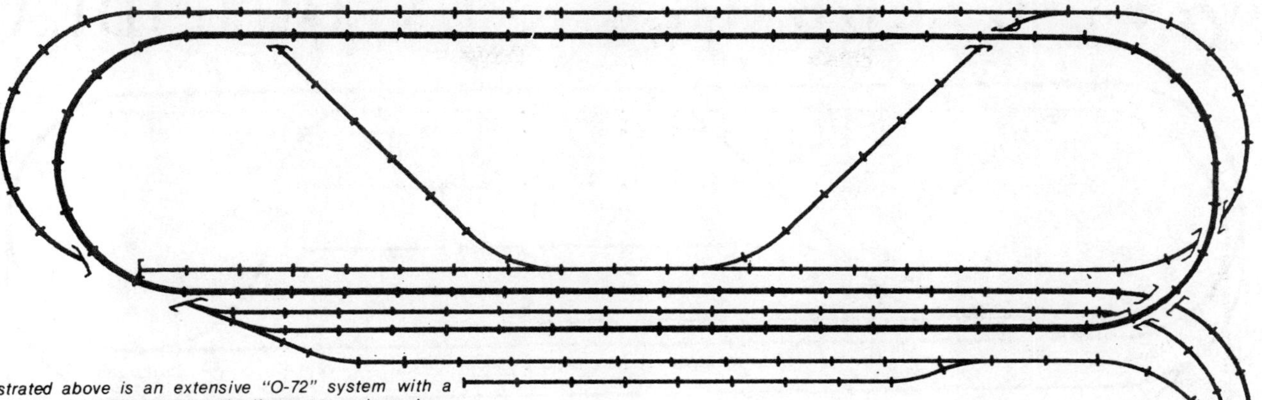

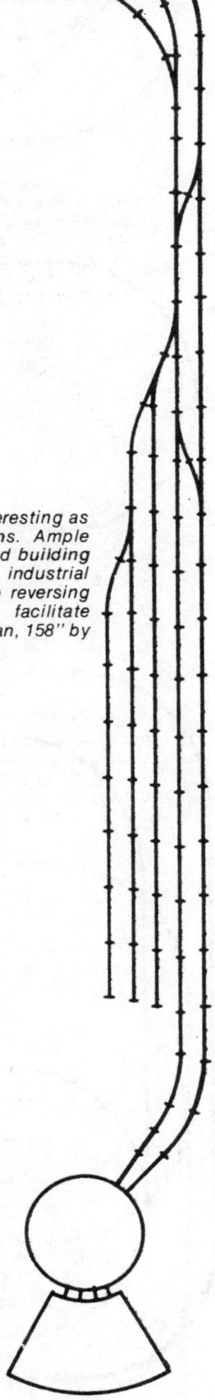

Illustrated above is an extensive "O-72" system with a mountain division, a long main line, cut yards and an engine terminal with long, realistic leads. Elevated track is shown by thicker lines. Railroad covers a space of 345" by 128". The lead track and terminal extend an additional 360".

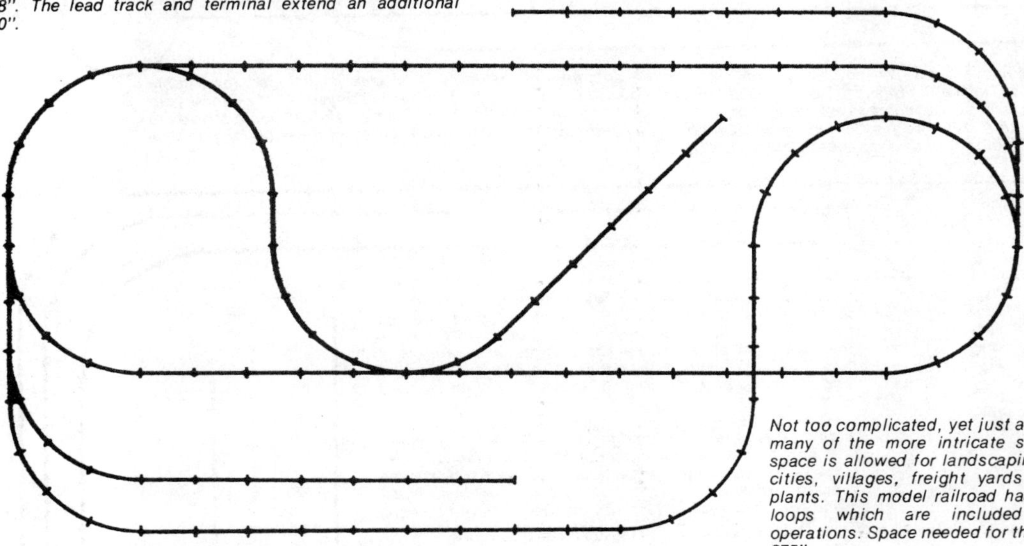

Not too complicated, yet just as interesting as many of the more intricate systems. Ample space is allowed for landscaping and building cities, villages, freight yards and industrial plants. This model railroad has two reversing loops which are included to facilitate operations. Space needed for this plan, 158" by 275".

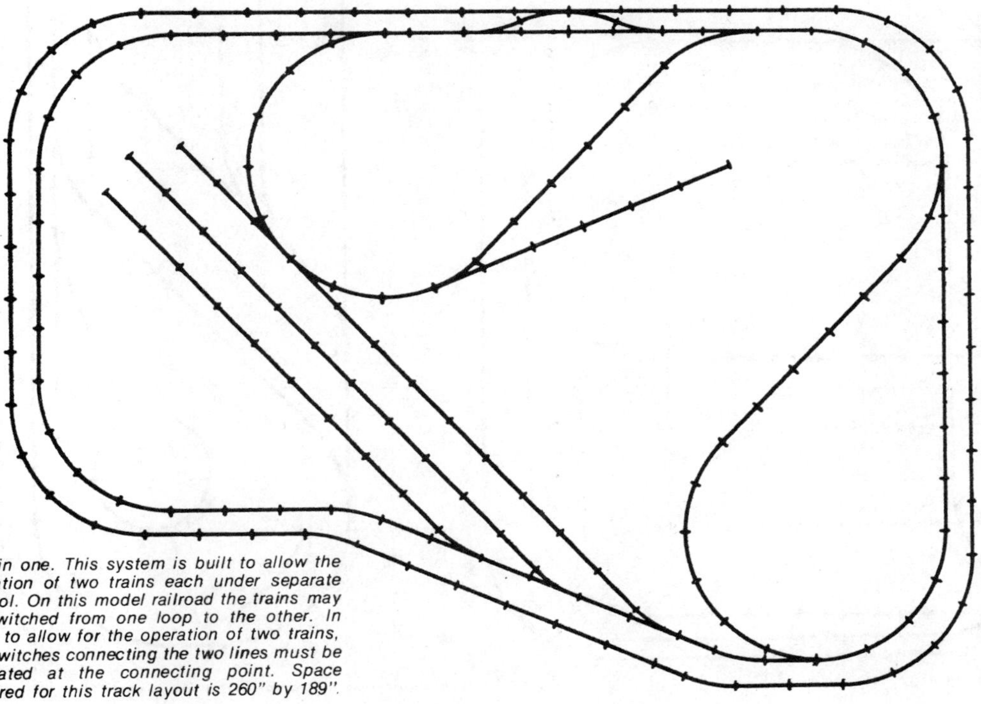

Two in one. This system is built to allow the operation of two trains each under separate control. On this model railroad the trains may be switched from one loop to the other. In order to allow for the operation of two trains, the switches connecting the two lines must be insulated at the connecting point. Space required for this track layout is 260" by 189".

"O-72" GAUGE TRACK LAYOUT IDEAS

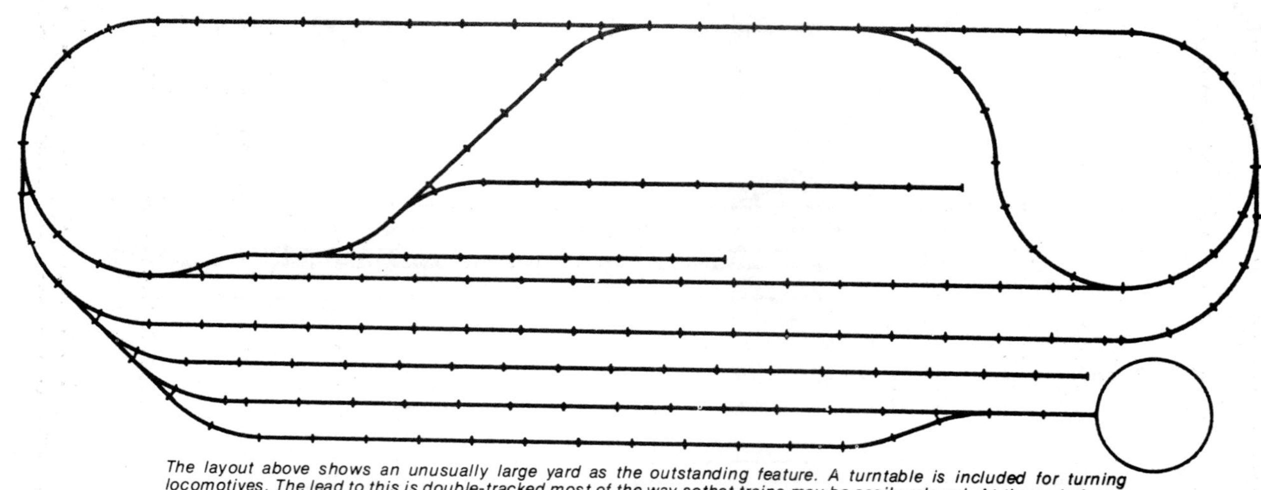

The layout above shows an unusually large yard as the outstanding feature. A turntable is included for turning locomotives. The lead to this is double-tracked most of the way sothat trains may be easily relayed. At the end of your train run, uncouple the locomotive here, turn it, and couple it into the other end of the same train and you are ready to start the return run. The main line is nicely broken up with double reversing loops and industrial sidings for the addition of factories and warehouses. Space: 132" by 332".

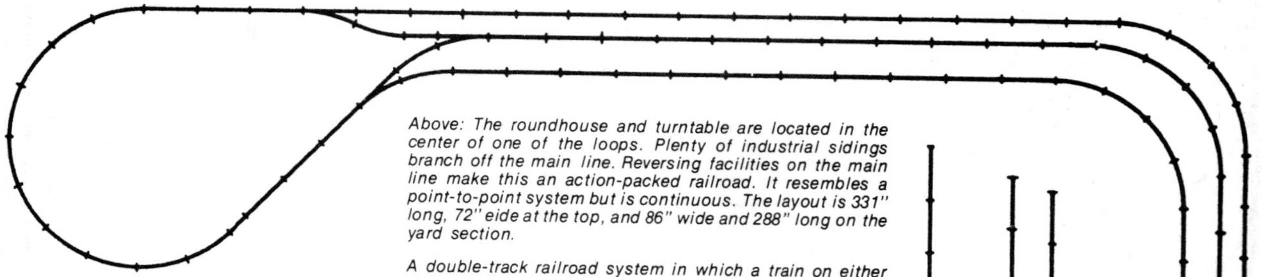

Above: The roundhouse and turntable are located in the center of one of the loops. Plenty of industrial sidings branch off the main line. Reversing facilities on the main line make this an action-packed railroad. It resembles a point-to-point system but is continuous. The layout is 331" long, 72" eide at the top, and 86" wide and 288" long on the yard section.

A double-track railroad system in which a train on either loop may be reversed to run in the opposite direction. Two cross-overs, one on top and one on the lower side may be used to switch a train form one loop to the other. A car storage track is shown. This spur otherwise might be used as an industrial siding. System requires space 217" by 117".

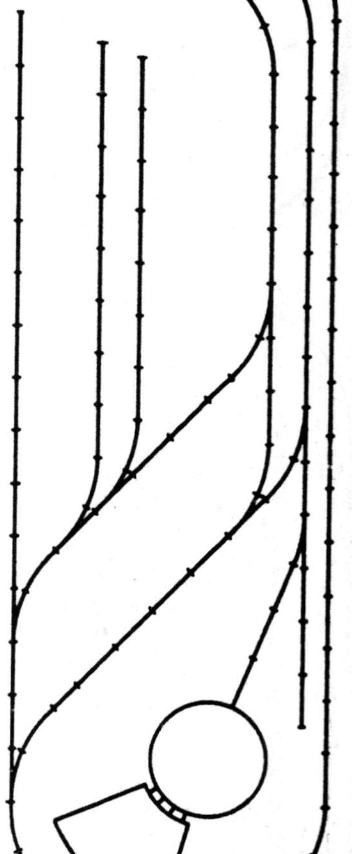

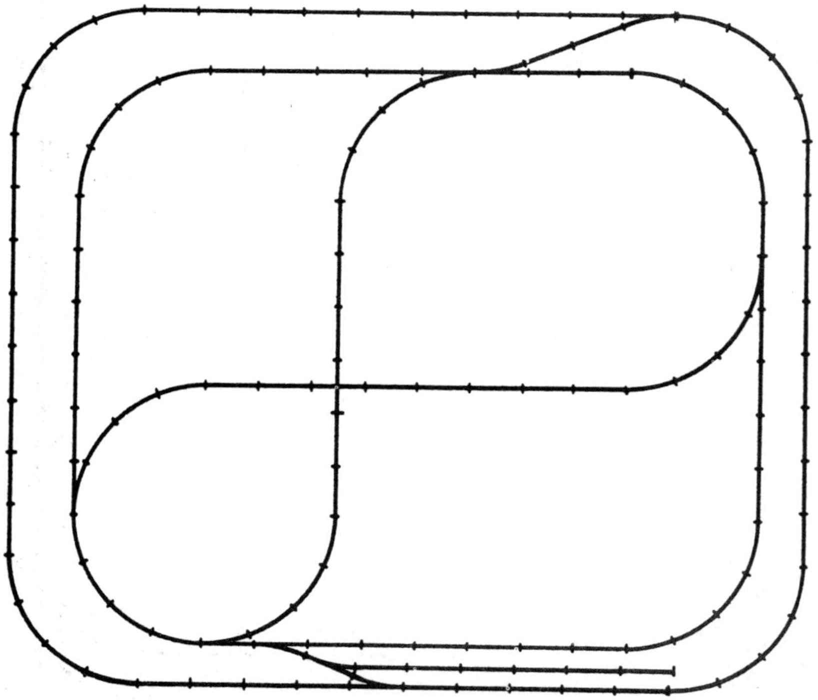

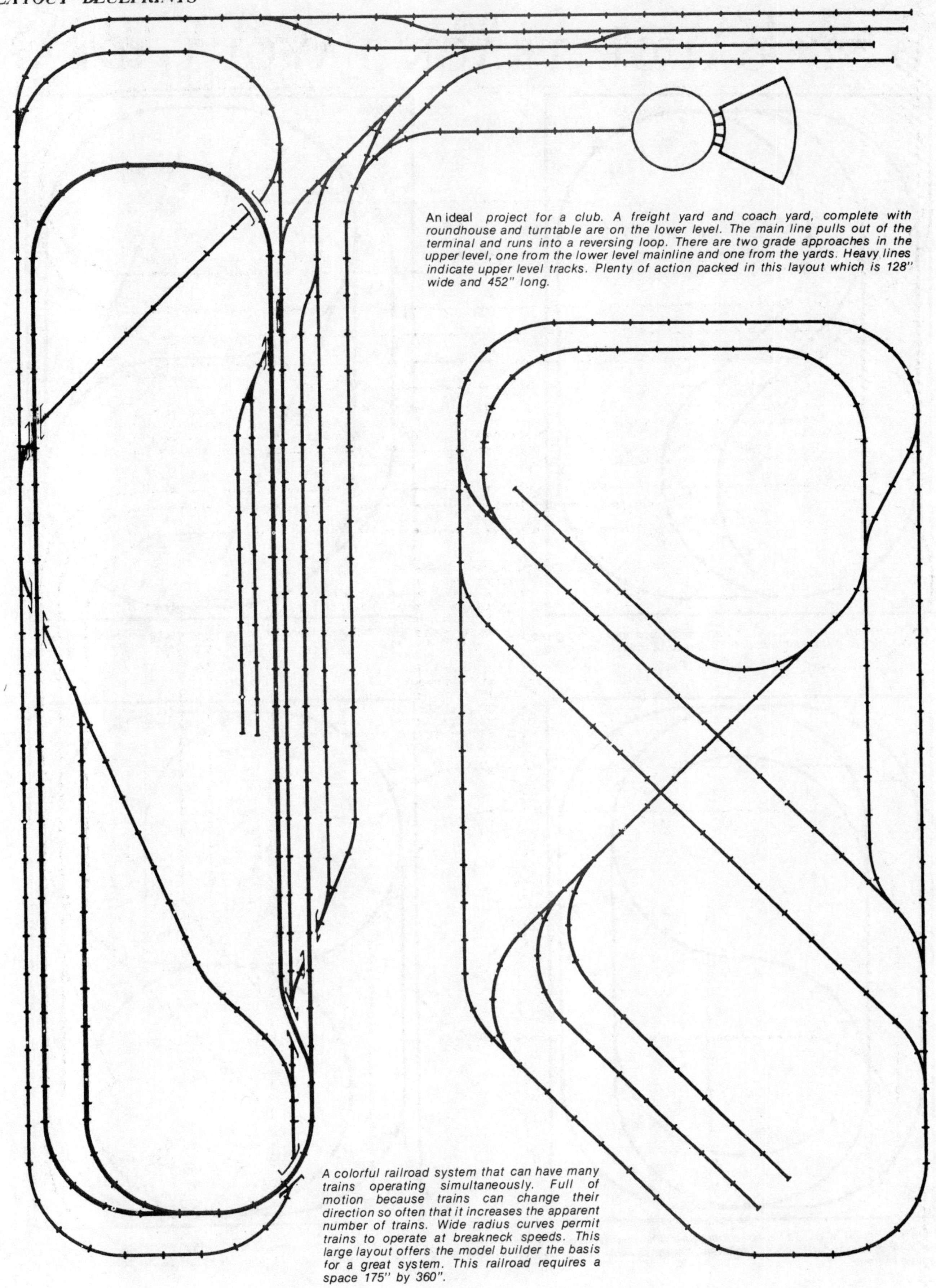

An ideal project for a club. A freight yard and coach yard, complete with roundhouse and turntable are on the lower level. The main line pulls out of the terminal and runs into a reversing loop. There are two grade approaches in the upper level, one from the lower level mainline and one from the yards. Heavy lines indicate upper level tracks. Plenty of action packed in this layout which is 128" wide and 452" long.

A colorful railroad system that can have many trains operating simultaneously. Full of motion because trains can change their direction so often that it increases the apparent number of trains. Wide radius curves permit trains to operate at breakneck speeds. This large layout offers the model builder the basis for a great system. This railroad requires a space 175" by 360".

"O-72" GAUGE TRACK LAYOUT IDEAS

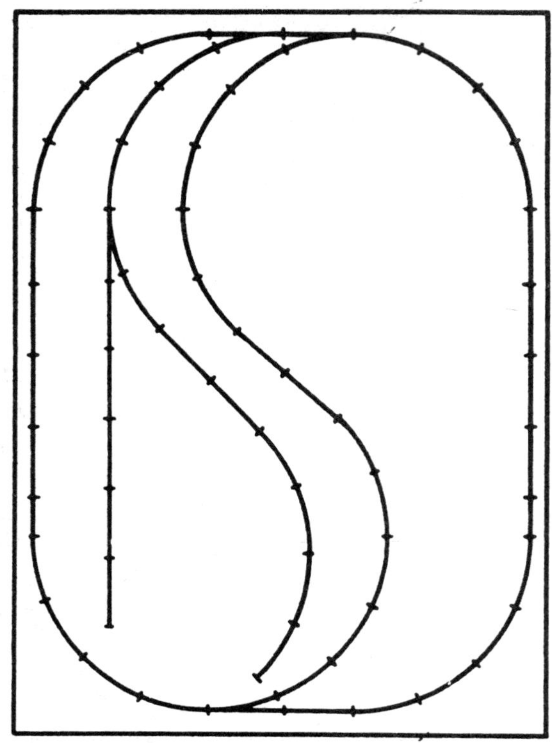

This is a variation on the oval layout. Junction of two spur tracks gives an opportunity to the model builder for using some realistic structures.

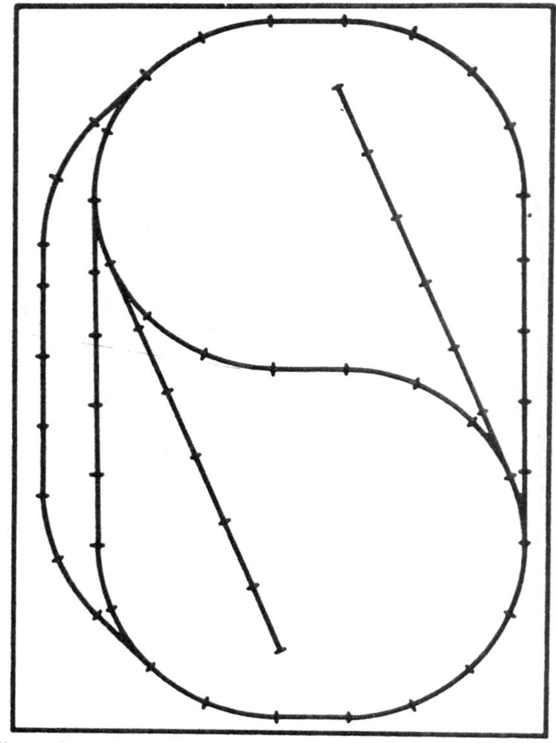

Plenty of action is packed in the passing tracks and reversing loops of this model railroad. An excellent layout for freight and passenger trains.

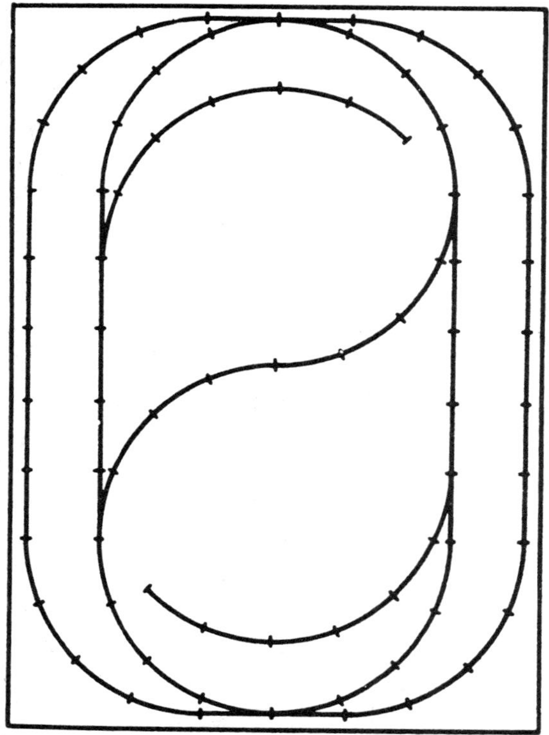

Double track oval with S-shaped connecting line and twin curved sidings. A symmetrical track arrangement for those who like a well balanced railroad.

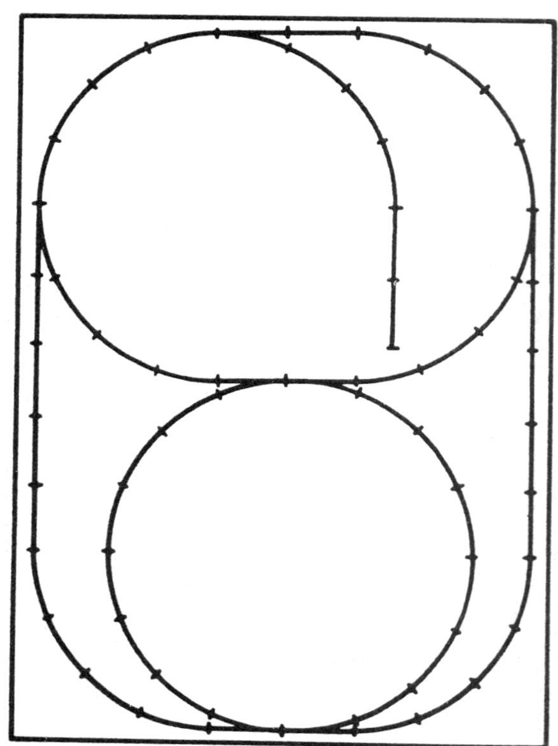

This plan will provide a railroad for the boy who wants to run his trains on a simple timetable. Double reversing loops add variety to the layout.

DESIGNED FOR 9 FT. BY 12 FT. TABLE

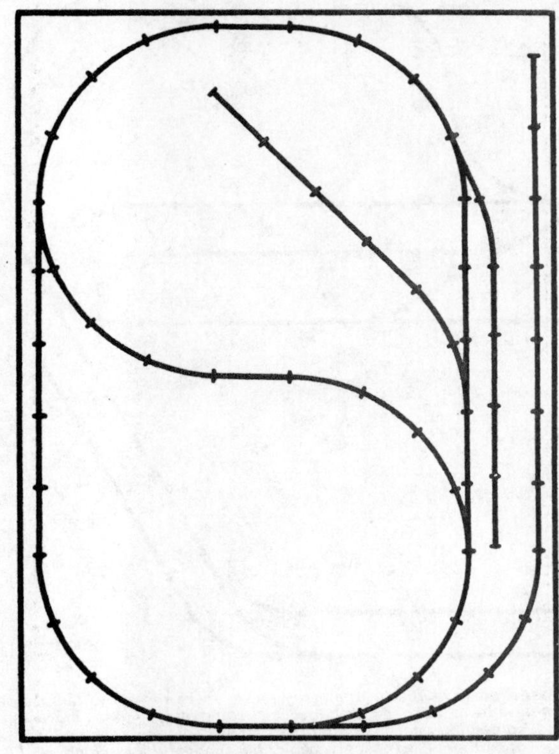

A simple layout whose interest lies in the three industrial sidings. This is a good freight road with some opportunity for variation in route.

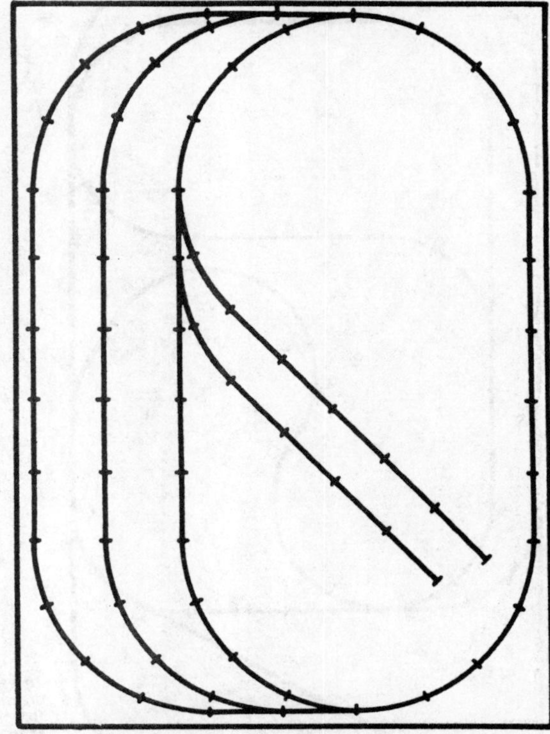

Three trains operate on this oval—an express, a passenger local, and a freight. Track spurs give opportunity for loading and unloading cars.

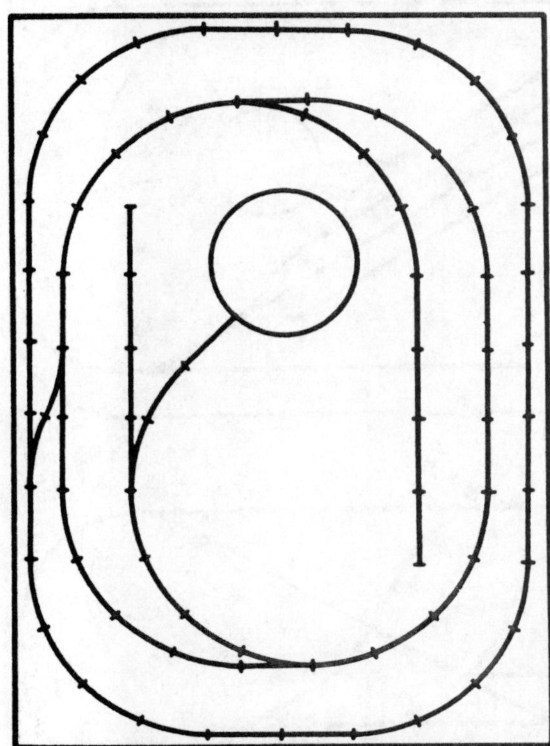

A layout with possibilities for yard work and continuous self-reversing operation. A system with a generous cross-sampling of railroad work.

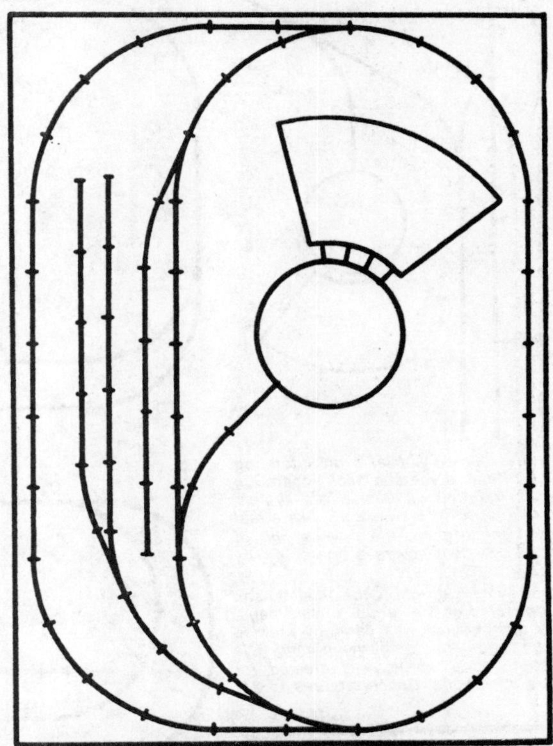

Freight and coach yard facilities dominate this layout. It is a good yard unit of a larger layout, but is also a complete layout as it stands.

TRACK LAYOUTS FOR "OO" GAUGE

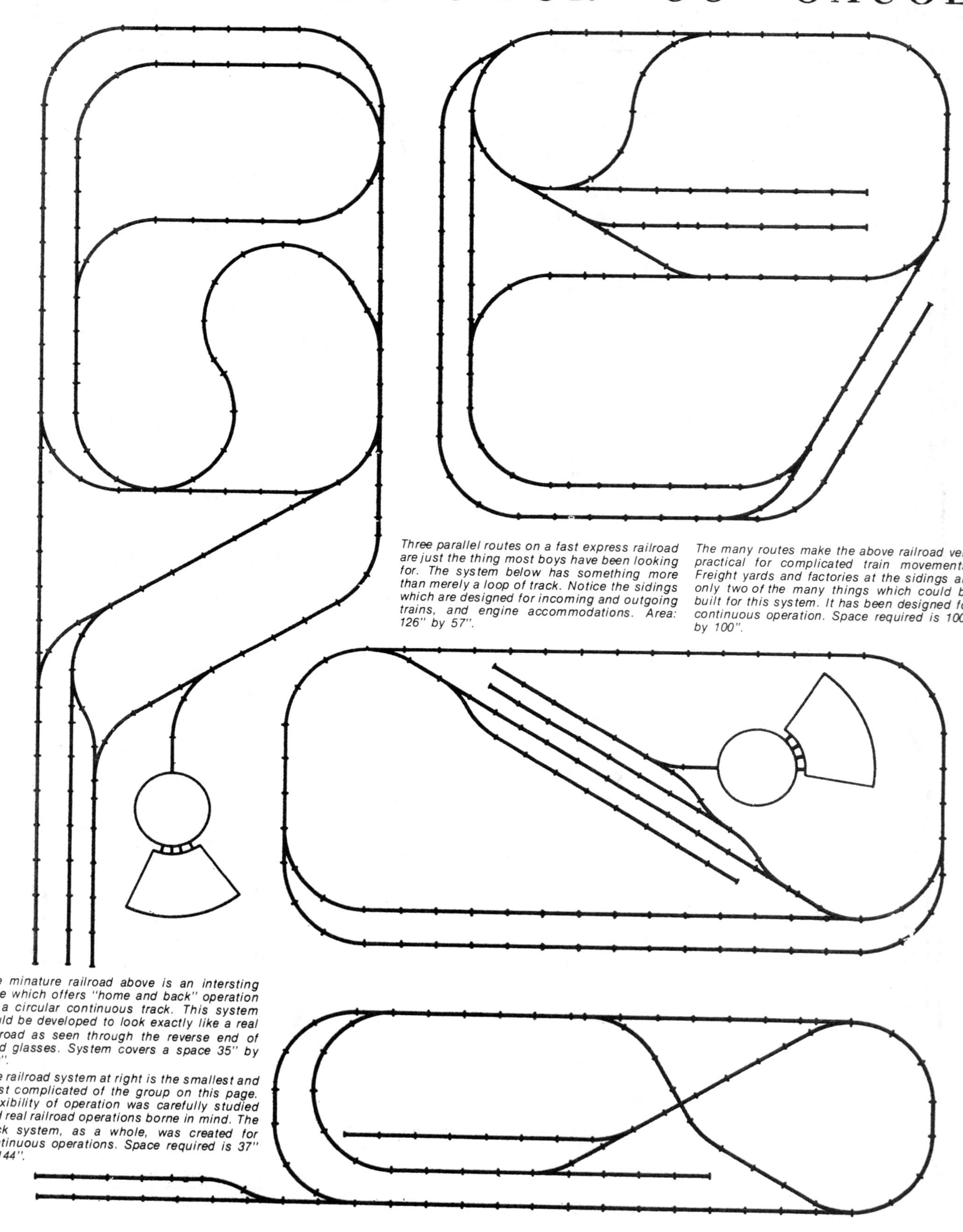

Three parallel routes on a fast express railroad are just the thing most boys have been looking for. The system below has something more than merely a loop of track. Notice the sidings which are designed for incoming and outgoing trains, and engine accommodations. Area: 126" by 57".

The many routes make the above railroad very practical for complicated train movements. Freight yards and factories at the sidings are only two of the many things which could be built for this system. It has been designed for continuous operation. Space required is 100" by 100".

The minature railroad above is an intersting type which offers "home and back" operation on a circular continuous track. This system could be developed to look exactly like a real railroad as seen through the reverse end of field glasses. System covers a space 35" by 170".

The railroad system at right is the smallest and least complicated of the group on this page. Flexibility of operation was carefully studied and real railroad operations borne in mind. The track system, as a whole, was created for continuous operations. Space required is 37" by 144".

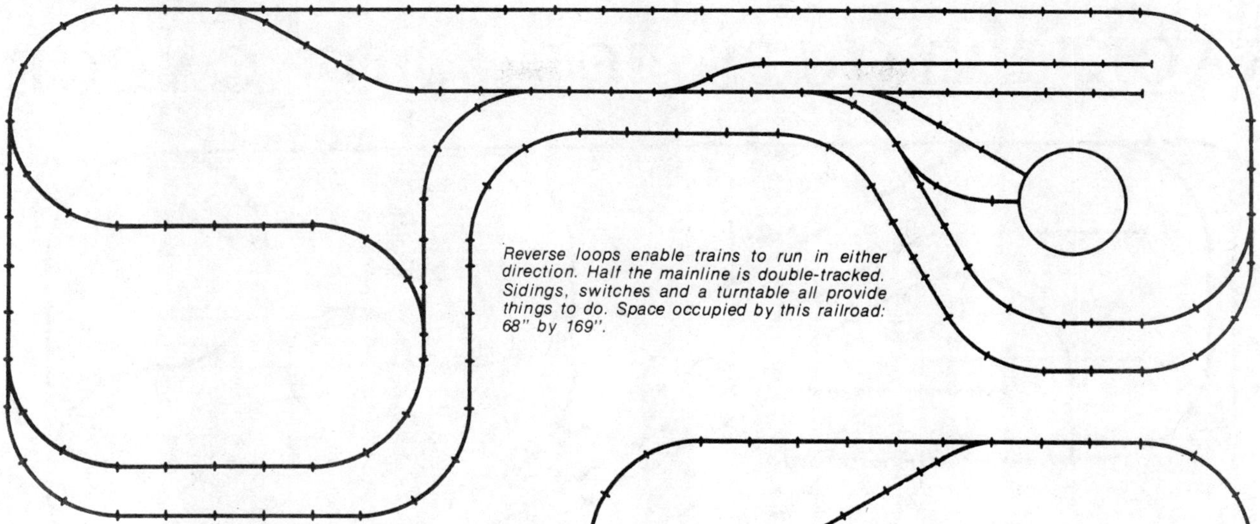

Reverse loops enable trains to run in either direction. Half the mainline is double-tracked. Sidings, switches and a turntable all provide things to do. Space occupied by this railroad: 68" by 169".

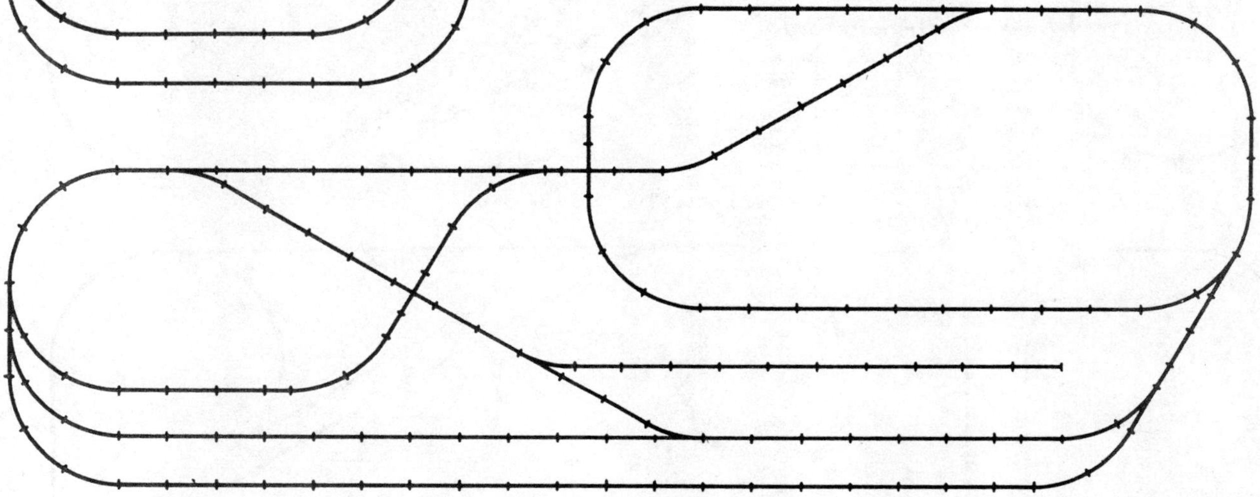

Above: "OO" gauge layout, 2-in-1 style. Two distinct loops that can be used separately or combined. Reversing loops and a long passing siding are included. Set this up, add scenery and you will understand the popularity of model railroads. System requires a space 169" by 72".

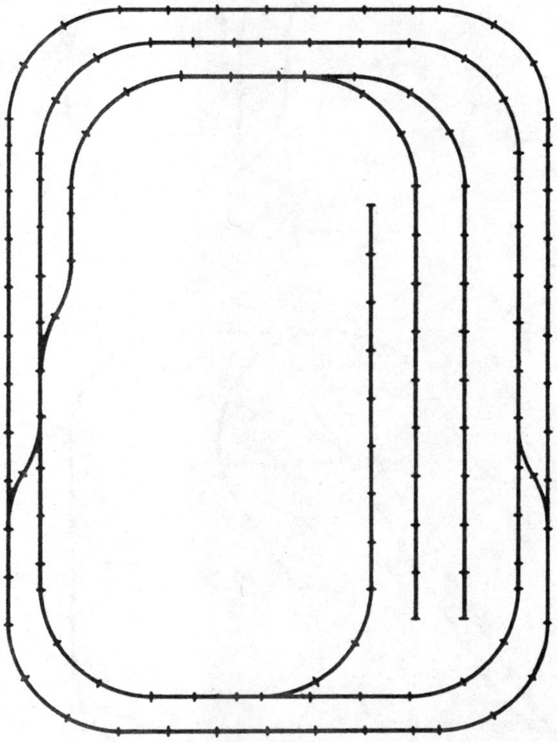

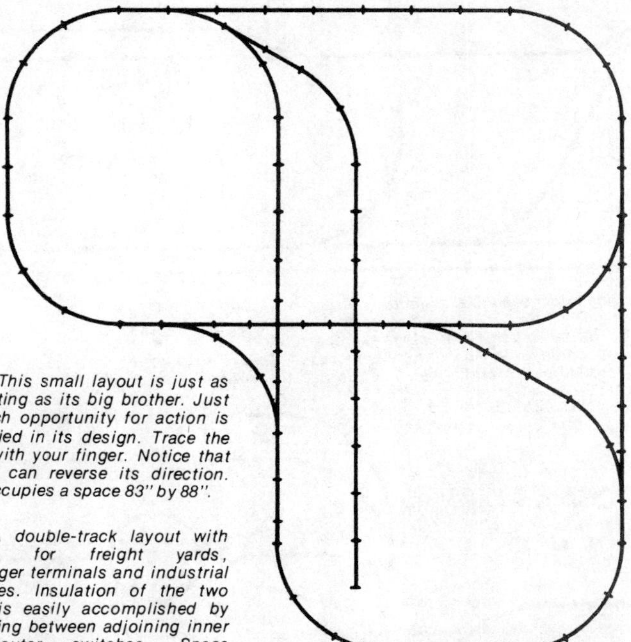

Right: This small layout is just as interesting as its big brother. Just as much opportunity for action is embodied in its design. Trace the route with your finger. Notice that a train can reverse its direction. Plan occupies a space 83" by 88".

Left: A double-track layout with sidings for freight yards, passenger terminals and industrial purposes. Insulation of the two loops is easily accomplished by insulating between adjoining inner and outer switches. Space required: 97" by 64".

TRACK LAYOUTS FOR "OO" GAUGE

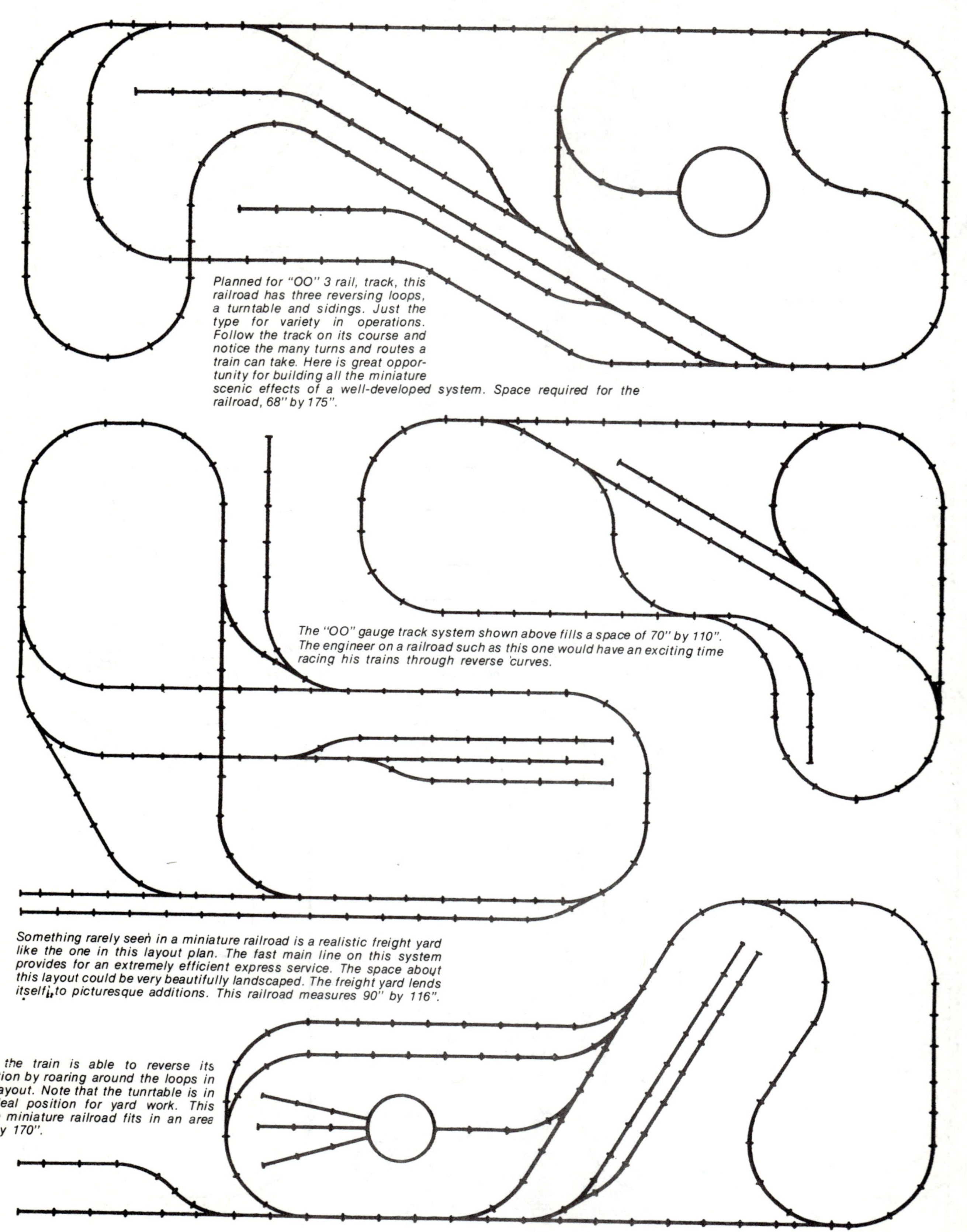

Planned for "OO" 3 rail, track, this railroad has three reversing loops, a turntable and sidings. Just the type for variety in operations. Follow the track on its course and notice the many turns and routes a train can take. Here is great opportunity for building all the miniature scenic effects of a well-developed system. Space required for the railroad, 68" by 175".

The "OO" gauge track system shown above fills a space of 70" by 110". The engineer on a railroad such as this one would have an exciting time racing his trains through reverse curves.

Something rarely seen in a miniature railroad is a realistic freight yard like the one in this layout plan. The fast main line on this system provides for an extremely efficient express service. The space about this layout could be very beautifully landscaped. The freight yard lends itself to picturesque additions. This railroad measures 90" by 116".

Here the train is able to reverse its direction by roaring around the loops in this layout. Note that the tunrtable is in an ideal position for yard work. This entire miniature railroad fits in an aree 57" by 170".

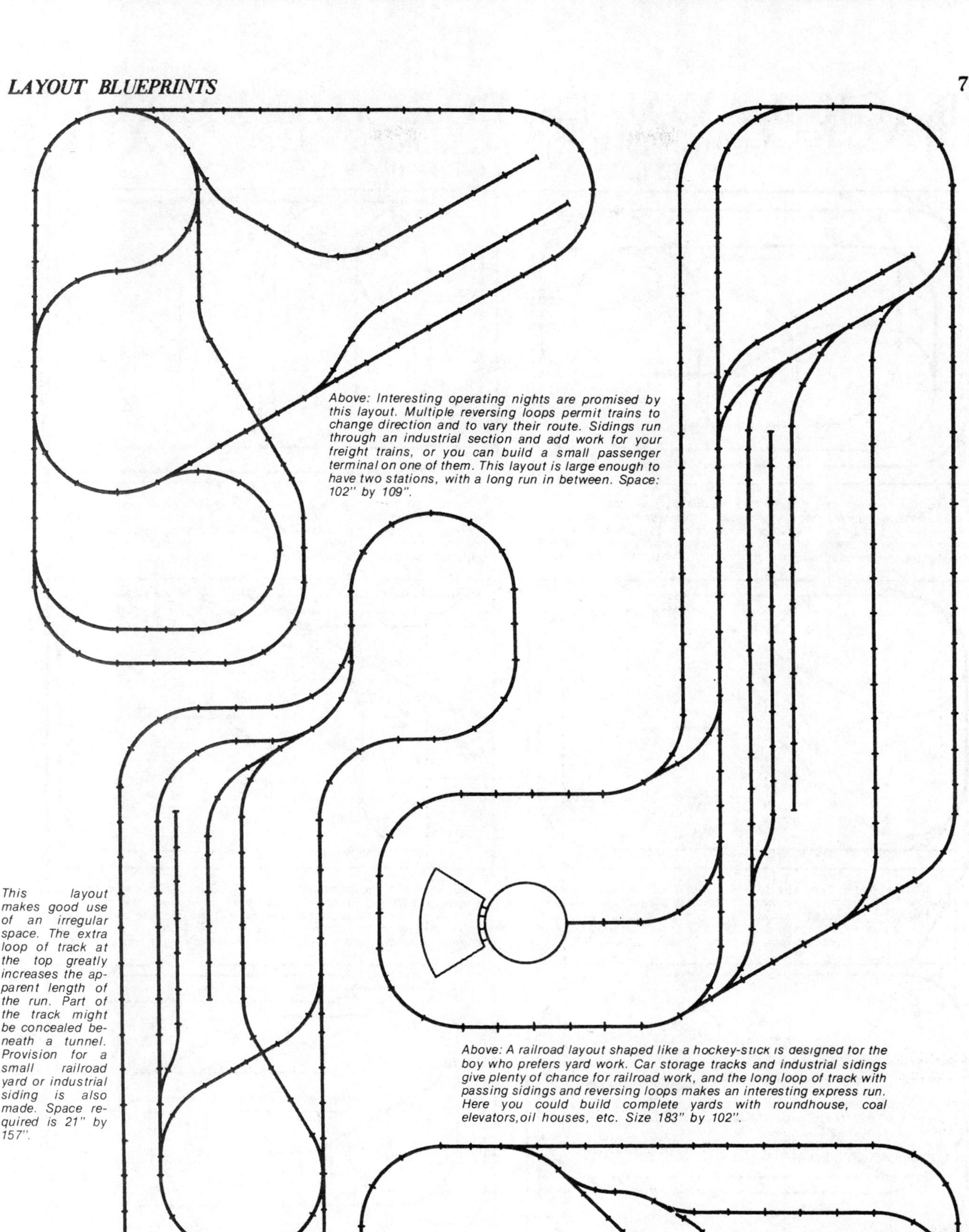

Above: Interesting operating nights are promised by this layout. Multiple reversing loops permit trains to change direction and to vary their route. Sidings run through an industrial section and add work for your freight trains, or you can build a small passenger terminal on one of them. This layout is large enough to have two stations, with a long run in between. Space: 102" by 109".

This layout makes good use of an irregular space. The extra loop of track at the top greatly increases the apparent length of the run. Part of the track might be concealed beneath a tunnel. Provision for a small railroad yard or industrial siding is also made. Space required is 21" by 157".

Above: A railroad layout shaped like a hockey-stick is designed for the boy who prefers yard work. Car storage tracks and industrial sidings give plenty of chance for railroad work, and the long loop of track with passing sidings and reversing loops makes an interesting express run. Here you could build complete yards with roundhouse, coal elevators, oil houses, etc. Size 183" by 102".

This layout looks different. It is compact, and has lots of play value because the trains can reverse direction and choose alternating routes. There is a siding for loading and unloading. A good layout for a spare room. Size is 125" by 41".

TRACK LAYOUTS FOR "OO" GAUGE

BUILD A PERMANENT RAILROAD SYSTEM TO FIT A TABLE 6 FT. BY 9 FT.

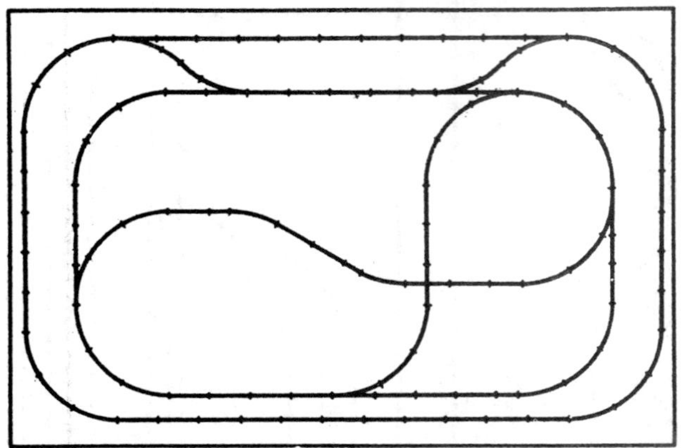

This compact system crowds a lot of railroading action into a relatively small space. Eight switches and one track cross-over give a maximum of flexibility to this road. Two loops of track forming a double-tracked main line may be insulated from each other for individual control. Track may be sectionalized for the operation of more than one train.

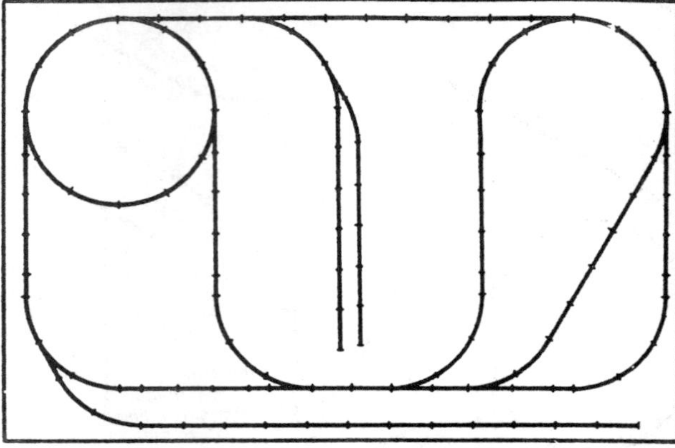

Circular section of track could surround a densely populated area and the model builder could plan a city with houses, streets and parks. Or the track could be partly concealed in a tunnel. Freight trains will make good use of the industrial spurs. Circle and loop make for excellent direction reversing facilities and the planning of many train operations.

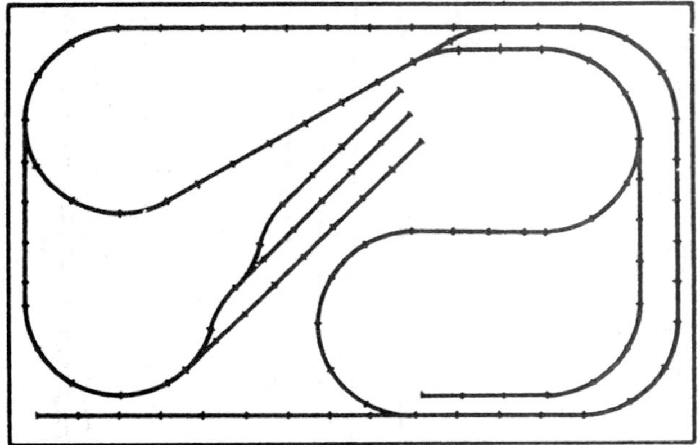

This layout embodies two extremely long spurs. A coal mine might be situated at the end of one, and a lumber camp at the end of the other. Main line winds around an unusual route and ends in a yard with card classification tracks. A system such as this one will increase the fun and excitement of operating trains on many different routes.

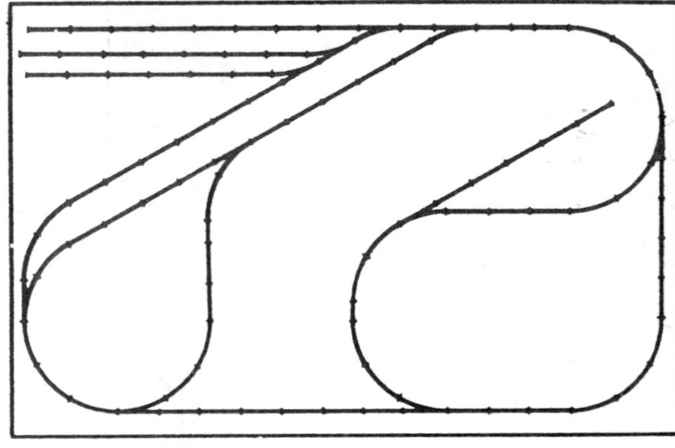

Realistic yard layout with main line having good passing and direction-reversing features. Excellent opportunity for making the landscape appealing. A terminal could be built around the three side tracks in the upper left corner. Long straight stretches of track give good chance to display railroad structures and many other interesting scenic effects.

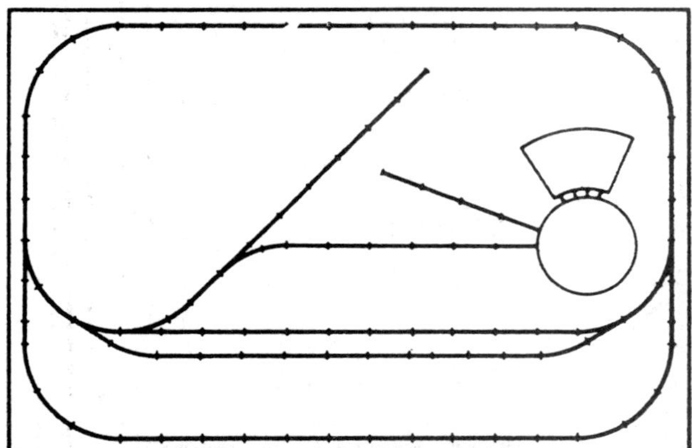

Good passing tracks and interesting industrial sidings. Layout combines simplicity of track plan with drama-packed operation. A roundhouse and turntable are the heart of the railroad yard. Unobstructed straight tracks are splendid for fast train schedules. This layout is large enough to operate two or three trains. Better control of trains is easily procured by track sectionalizing. In laying tracks on a table, don't run them so close to the edge that derailment might cause cars to crash to the floor.

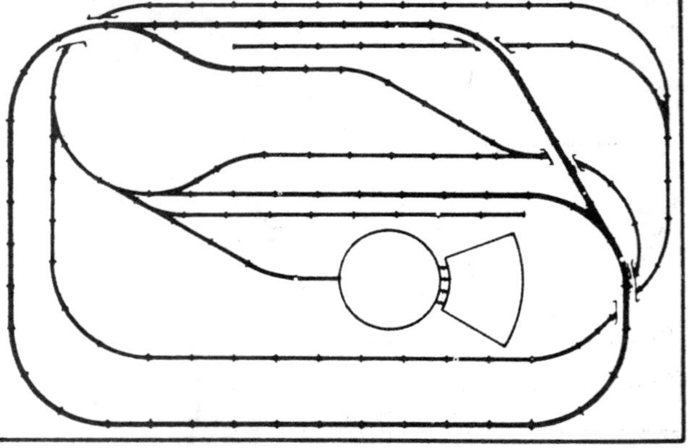

Four overhead track crossings are indicated on this layout. Obviously located in a metropolitan center, the railroads cross and recross each other's right-of-way. Excellent opportunity for the model builder to install trestle or plate girder bridges. Upper and lower level each may be used separately or as pairs of the same circuit. Heavy lines indicate upper-level tracks. There are two connecting tracks between upper and lower level. Note the convenient position of turntable and roundhouse.

TRACK LAYOUTS FOR "OO" GAUGE

DESIGNED FOR A TABLE 8 FT. BY 10 FT.

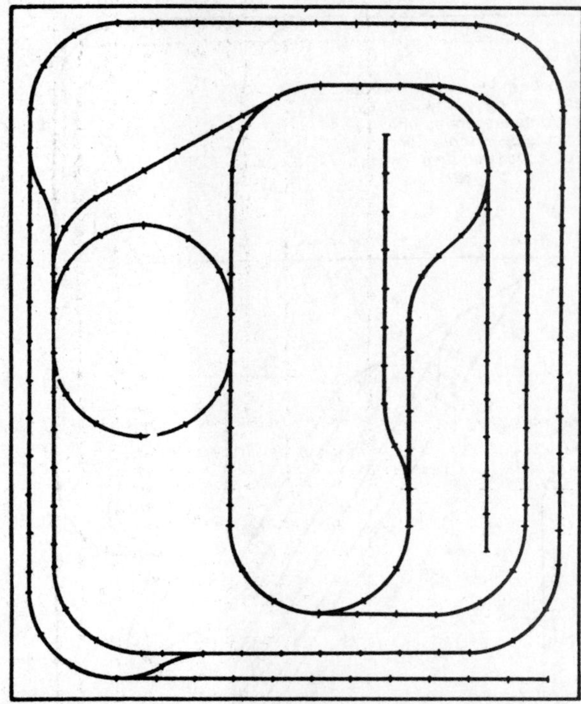

This layout is extremely attractive for intricate operation of trains. Long spurs give a chance for local color and an attractive up-to-date station can be planned for the main line, possibly on the lower side where the siding track is conveniently located for such an addition.

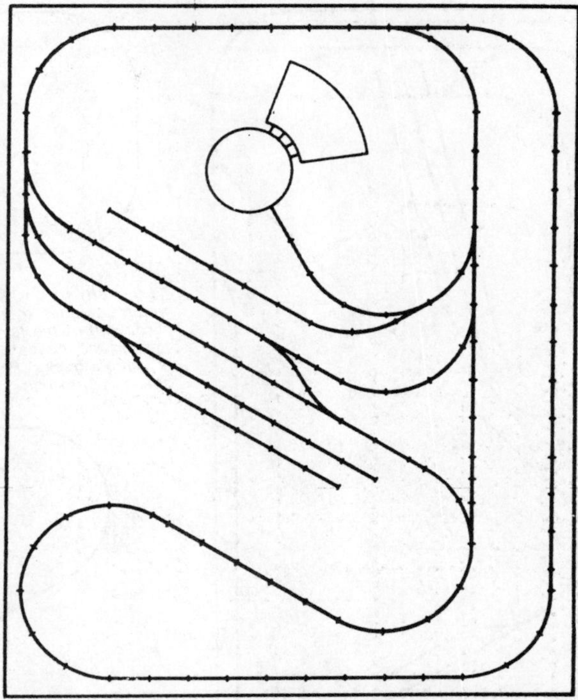

The center of interest in this layout is in the yards. Freight and coach yards are provided, and incoming and outgoing terminal tracks run through them. Here is a system packed with action and having a long mainline run. Plenty of opportunity for many real railroad operations.

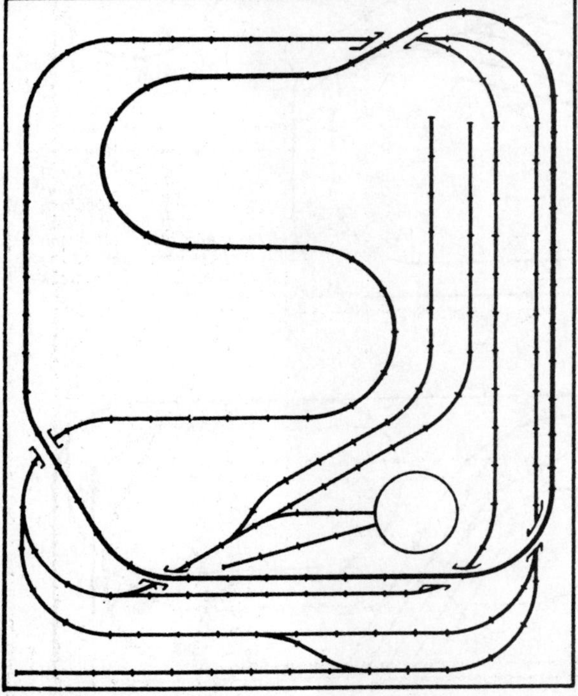

Two track elevations are used in this layout. Heavy line indicates inclined track. Tracks may be built on a trestle structure, and then on a fill when the ground level can be raised to the track's height. The lower tracks will pass through a cut. In five places the elevated line crosses the street-level line, providing an action packed layout.

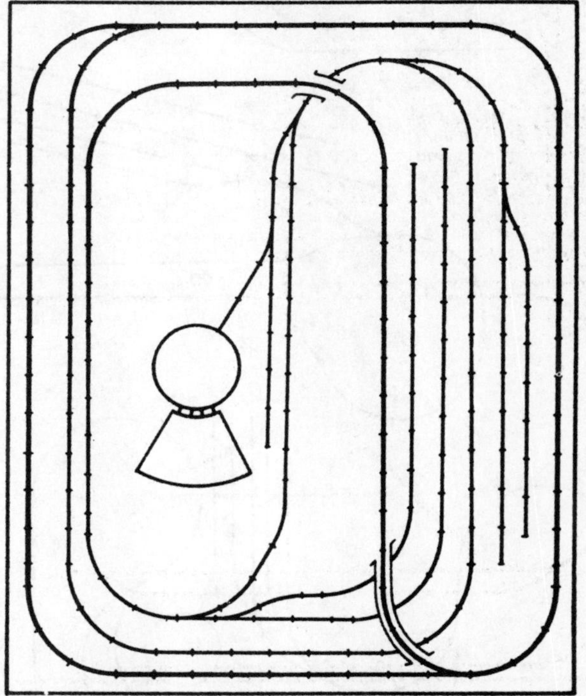

A very attractive layout with complete yard facilities and an elevated track section. A viaduct is indicated where the elevated crosses three yard sidings. Here is an opportunity for some beautiful scenic work with cuts, fills, trestles, bridges, valleys and mountains. This layout is large enough to provide ample space for the operation of three trains.

TRACK LAYOUTS FOR "OO" GAUGE

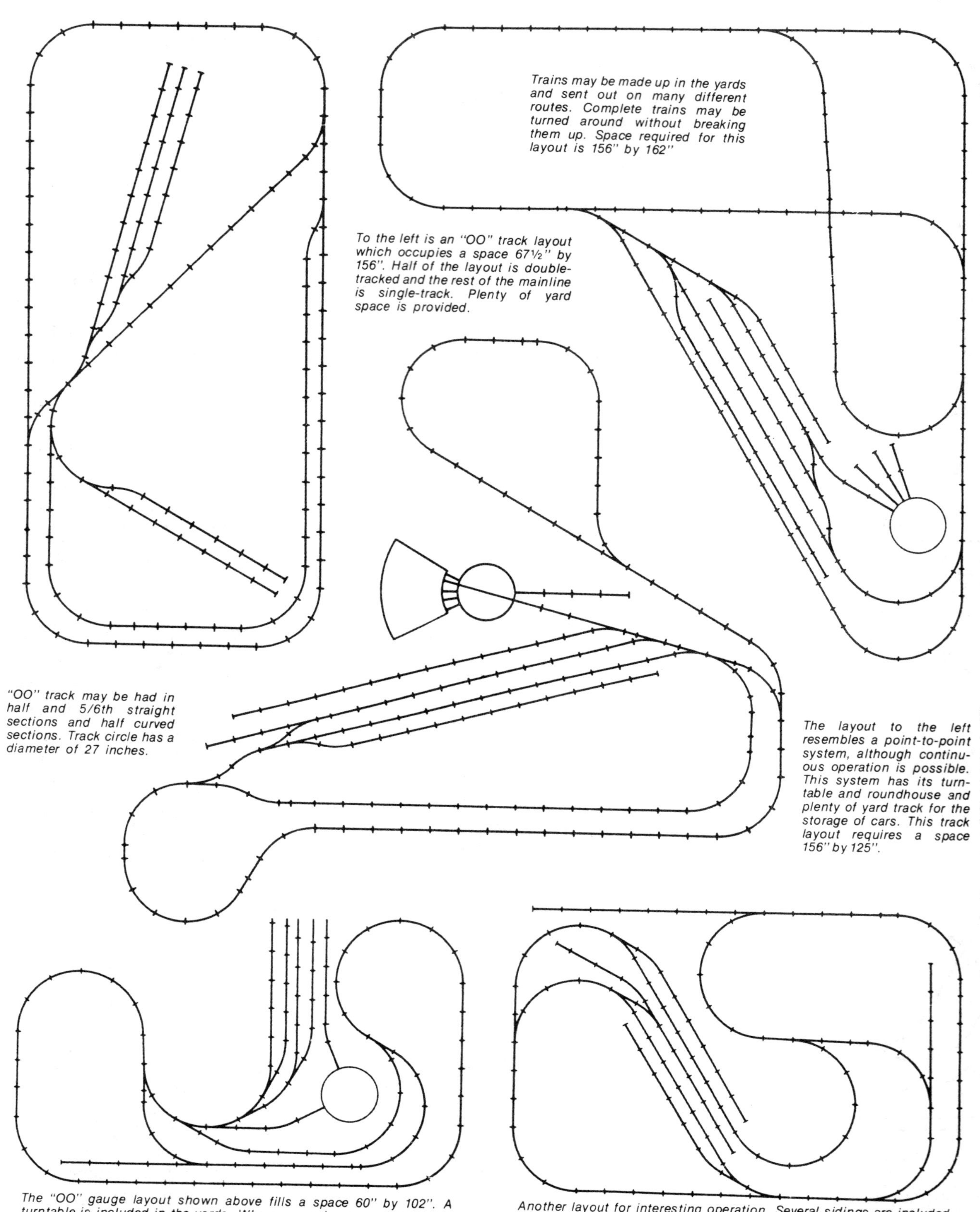

Trains may be made up in the yards and sent out on many different routes. Complete trains may be turned around without breaking them up. Space required for this layout is 156" by 162"

To the left is an "OO" track layout which occupies a space 67½" by 156". Half of the layout is double-tracked and the rest of the mainline is single-track. Plenty of yard space is provided.

"OO" track may be had in half and 5/6th straight sections and half curved sections. Track circle has a diameter of 27 inches.

The layout to the left resembles a point-to-point system, although continuous operation is possible. This system has its turntable and roundhouse and plenty of yard track for the storage of cars. This track layout requires a space 156" by 125".

The "OO" gauge layout shown above fills a space 60" by 102". A turntable is included in the yards. Where space is at a premium, the use of curves produces some interesting track layouts. A storage yard of four tracks branches off from the yard "make up" track.

Another layout for interesting operation. Several sidings are included so that yard tracks will not be crowded and switching operations can be carried out without congestion. Space is 64" by 102". Here again the use of curved track provides a much longer mainline.

Tables and Benches

Chapter Seven

After the track design has been selected, a platform of the necessary shape is planned before materials are purchased or construction started. Much depends upon the available location and the size of the system. In most homes a cellar or attic is found available and suitable.

Many private roads are built on platforms supported with two-by-two or two-by-four lumber as legs. This results in sturdy construction, but in many cases it may be unnecessarily so. If the layout is large and on a table centrally located in the room so that it cannot be fastened to the building, and if the railroad is subject to frequent public display, it is wise to build a heavy and sturdy structure to support the tracks.

Cellar layouts can be of the round-the-wall shelf type or the central-table type. In either case, considerable extra bracing of legs is eliminated if the structure is fastened to the wall or columns at several places. The elimination of bracing reduces expense, and anchoring to walls increases the rigidity of the fixture.

In Figure D is a bracket which is suitable for holding a narrow line. A narrow roadbed is sometimes required for passing between furnace and wall. This type of support is clear of the floor. It is fastened with two screws and plugs to the cellar masonry. It is completely assembled before being attached to the wall.

The masonry is drilled with a stone drill and hammer. Fibre or patented plugs measuring about one inch long are inserted in the drilled hole. An ordinary two-inch wood screw with a flat head is used to hold the bracket to the wall.

The choice of material for the top of the platform depends upon the size and shape of the layout and the type and amount of the scenery that is contemplated. Plywood one-fourth-inch thick has certain advantages when the platform is wide and long. Plywood requires little cutting and fitting, and a plywood platform has few seams to open from shrinkage. Plywood is not expensive and it is easy to handle.

White pine dressed on all sides has certain advantages where the roadbed varies in width, becomes very narrow in parts, or is irregular in shape. Being sturdier than plywood it requires fewer supports and cross frames. Being quite solid, tracks and other objects are attached by small nails. Pine shrinks if installed in a dry, warm place before it is thoroughly seasoned.

When plans call for a platform wide enough to permit the use of several parallel tracks and a large amount of scenery, the method of support show in Figure B is appropriate. It has the advantage of simplicity and rigidity without the need for any bracing of the legs. Attachment to the wall prevents motion away from the wall while the material used on the top of the platform prevents motion or swaying in a parallel direction.

When pine boards are used for the top of the platform they are screwed to each cross frame with two-inch flat head screws to prevent warping.

An open attic makes construction such as that shown in Figure B a simple task. Where the roof beams and the joists are exposed, the cross frame is nailed to them.

The type of construction shown in Figure F is suitable for platforms, placed in the center of a room, which must be entirely self-supporting.

For a platform like this one, the legs made from two-by-two lumber and the cross frames are made from either three-by-one or four-by-one lumber. Legs are located at the intersection of the two cross frames and are screwed to each of them.

Legs spaced three to four feet apart afford ample support for this type of construction. If the area is large, the central portion of the table is left open and used as an operating position.

Elevated track is one of the most interesting features which can be built in a model railroad. Changes in track elevations are accomplished by small supports screwed to the main frames as shown in figure C. Lateral planks placed across the tops of these high-track supports serve as the base for the track roadbed. If these high-track supports are used intelligently throughout the system to obtain a slight but constant variation in the track levels, the model road will become more realistic in appearance.

These high-track supports are also used to elevate a right-of-way gradually up to a height where it is possible to use a timber trestle or a high bridge with the unusual effects they provide. Additional cross frames are added to the foundation of the layout when required for holding additional high-track supports.

After these high-track supports are erected and the track boards are attached to them, it is possible to economize on the use of plywood or other table-top material by attaching wire screen to the edges of the track boards and draping it down irregularly to the edge of the platform. After the screen is draped, plaster is used to fill it. It is then painted to represent a countryside.

Few people agree on the height above the floor that is most practical for a model railroad platform. For adult use, forty inches is suggested; and for seven or eight-year-olds, about twenty-six inches. In cases where the model railroad is to be used jointly by father and son, it is possible to construct a narrow, six-inch step to take care of the junior partner.

Wide shelves can be used to build a railroad such as this one.

There are numerous advocates of very high tables and shelves. They reason with considerable justification that a real railroad is seldom viewed from an elevation comparable to that of our normal eye-level when standing near by and looking down on a platform thirty-six inches high.

These realists recommended the operation of trains at or only slightly below the operators' and spectators' eye-level.

When the shelves are about four feet wide this is possible and practical. However, when shelves of greater width are used, an elevation of this kind destroys the effect of any detail built in the center of the layouts; a good, general view of it is shut off by all hills, mountains and tall buildings.

Framework being used in the construction of an attic system.

Sturdy shelf construction for a layout erected in a basement.

A
B
C
D
E
F
G
H

CUTS AND FILLS

CHAPTER EIGHT

REAL railroads would rejoice if it were possible to build real roadbeds over land as smooth and flat as the top of a table. For fills and cuts thus would be eliminated, and fills and cuts are a major operation in the building of any line. However, the reverse is true on the miniature system. There, every effort is made to break up the monotony of a flat table or bench, and to obtain the appearance of rolling countryside or hilly, rocky terraine.

To do this most successfully, the table or bench is built several inches lower than the average level of the roadbed and the track itself is elevated slightly over most of its course, so that it is possible to build valleys below the level of the right-of-way, as well as hills and mountains that tower above it.

The railroad term "cut" is given to the excavated channel through a short hilltop which is made so that the right-of-way may continue across it without the necessity of a gradient. The railroad term "fill" is used to describe an embankment constructed for a right-of-way so that it may continue across a valley without a change in track elevation.

In the flat plains of the Middle-West and parts of the South-West a right-of-way might continue for hundreds of miles on an absolute level and without the necessty of either cut or embankment. However, there is something inspiring in watching a train round a hillside, travel through a cut and out over an interesting valley on a high embankment, and the time and effort necessary to obtain such an effect on a miniature road is well rewarded.

On a real railroad, fills usually are made out of the earth or rock excavated from a cut. On a miniature line, the long flat board holding track is supported on wooden forms as shown in the series of drawings on Page 89. From the edge of the trackboard, hardware mesh or chicken-wire is draped and then filled with a coating of plaster. The first coating of plaster is allowed to dry overnight and then a second layer is applied. Before this second layer has set and hardened, it is sprinkled with dirt, tiny rocks and pebbles. When the plaster has dried, it is painted with a coating of dark, ground color.

For increased realism, a small drainage ditch is impressed into the plaster, on each side of the roadbed, as shown in illustrations C and F. At the lowest level in the valley, a stream is indicated, which passes the right-of-way through a box type culvert built into the embankment.

One of the most impressive pictures seen from the windows of a passenger train are the jagged edges of colorful rock where railroad cuts have been broken through or blasted away in order to build the right-of-way straight ahead in a true and level course. There are two types of cuts. One is the rock cut and the other is a cut through soft earth. Both are interesting and colorful when reproduced in miniature.

Three types of rock are to be considered for the model railroad cut. The first is hard rock such as granite which has many sharp angles and is generally gray in color. The second is soft rock such as sandstone and limestone with edges worn round by weathering. The color of this rock might range from blue-gray to strong red. The third type is the crumbling rock known as shale which appears in thin layers or strata tilted at various angles. Rock of this type generally is very dark brown.

To make a rock cut a wooden frame work is erected on each side of the track and over this a fine chicken wire mesh is spread and carefully molded into the desired shape. On top of the mesh a coating of plaster is applied. After this is thoroughly dry, a stiffer and much thicker mixture is added. When the second layer of plaster has dried the strata lines are indicated by using a kitchen knife or pocket knife, the end of which is kept moist. Hundreds of fine, shallow lines are required to represent the grain in the rock. The grain may be horizontal or at any inclination, but is uniformly in one direction. Wide crevices between the rock are imitated by inserting the knife blade between formations of plaster resembling individual stones, and gently pushing the plaster apart.

In making a cut through shales, very few angles are allowed in the chicken wire netting. The face of a shale cut resembles the side of a stack of pancakes. Broken strata is indicated by opening the plaster with a knife blade in cracks which are nearly perpendicular. The strata lines are thrown out of gear so they do not match on opposite sides.

This makes it appear as if the whole section of the formation had cracked and one part had settled.

Earth cuts are created in a different manner. The wood form which is set beneath the edges of the hill slopes gradually where the cut is to appear. Strong open mesh cloth is used instead of chicken wire. This is tacked to the frame in irregular waves so that it will form many folds which will resemble erosion gullies in the finished work. The cloth is dampened and a very thin mixture of plaster is applied. When this has dried, a second and a third thin coating are added.

A rock cut made out of plaster with engraved strata and fissure lines.

Soft dirt cut formed over an open-mesh cloth foundation.

For rock cuts the plaster is dyed or stained to the suitable color. A very thin wash of flat color is used and allowed to spread as it soaks in. A bold band of strong color in stratified rock adds interest. A second coat of wash is applied later and allowed to settle into the cracks and fissures. If a sandstone cut is being built, a streak of deep, dark carmin help the realism of the scene. For the cut through dirt the paint consists of a mixture of white, burnt sienna and a slight touch of black. The color of the bare dirt is made several shades lighter than the color of the surrounding ground area.

In the sketches on the following page A shows a single-track, shallow cut in a gently sloping hill. B shows a rock cut in the side of a hill where one side of the right-of-way is supported by a fill. C is a long, high fill or embankment. D is an embankment showing two different types of retaining walls. At the bottom is a common concrete retaining wall and at the top a reinforced wall. A deep hard-rock cut is illustrated in sketch E. A long, shallow two track embankment is shown in sketch F.

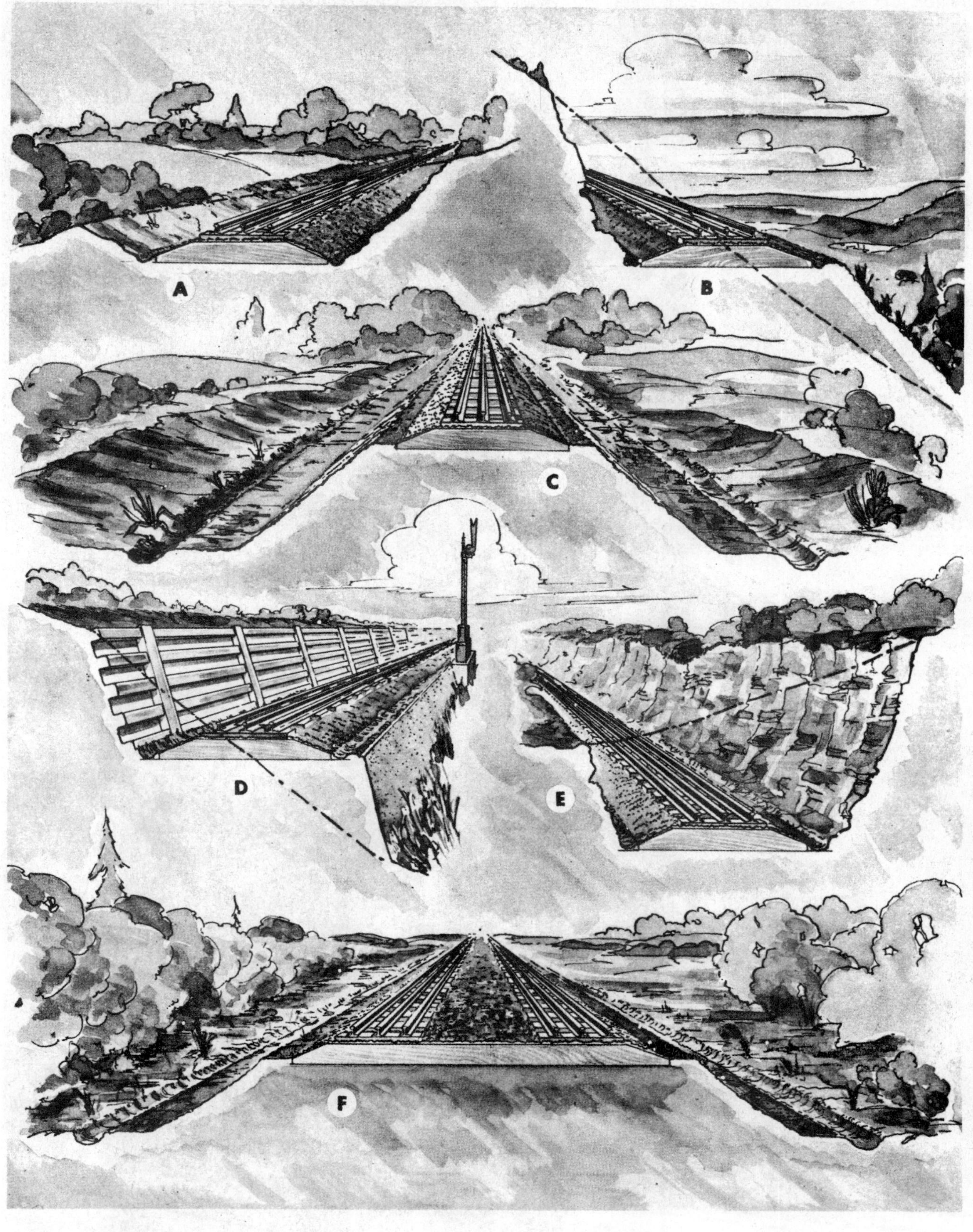
A
B
C
D
E
F

1928

GRADES AND ELEVATIONS

CHAPTER NINE

WHEN planning the construction of a real railroad, the one thing engineers fight to overcome is grade. For track elevation is the arch enemy of rail transportation, requiring heavier motive power, restricting loads and costing hundreds of thousands of dollars each year in added fuel expense.

To eliminate costly grade, or gradient as it is more properly called, railroads are willing to spend millions of dollars to bore through tunnels, to blast away the top of a hill or excavate a channel cut, and will haul fill for miles to erect embankments that will bring the roadbed up to the level of adjoining track.

Yet, the elevating of track is the dream of all model railroaders, for there is a great, proud thrill in watching a powerful locomotive puff and pant and strain itself to snake a long string of cars up a stiff incline.

In a series of sketches opposite the following page is a number of railroad settings which are possible when one line of track is inclined sufficiently to clear another. Jacking up the track with piles of books, old cigar boxes and anything else that happens to be handy is the first, simple step in obtaining the desired results.

But when a permanent model system is being constructed and the model locomotive is to pull heavy trains up-grade, the track must be supported firmly and the climb must not be too severe. The simplest and best way to build a mountain division is to fasten all the elevated portion of the track on wooden boards supported at regular intervals by short blocks as illustrated by sketch C.

Another illustration of this method of elevating track is shown in the photograph of a basement railroad printed on the top of Page 90.

One way for finding the rate of incline for the elevated track is by trial and error, by building a temporary incline and trying out the heaviest equipment on it.

When the right spacing for the blocks is found, the test track is removed and the supports are nailed firmly to the top of the shelf or table. To attach the uprights to the railroad table or bench, small right-angle braces will be found useful.

The roadbed for the level stretches of elevated track is made in the same way, except that the supporting blocks are all of the same height.

This same plan of constructing a mountain division is used if the outfit is erected on a table, on wall shelves, or even if it must, unfortunately, be used on the floor. By using wider boards a two-track elevation is made.

Any thickness of board from one-quarter inch to one-inch is used for this construction. Yellow

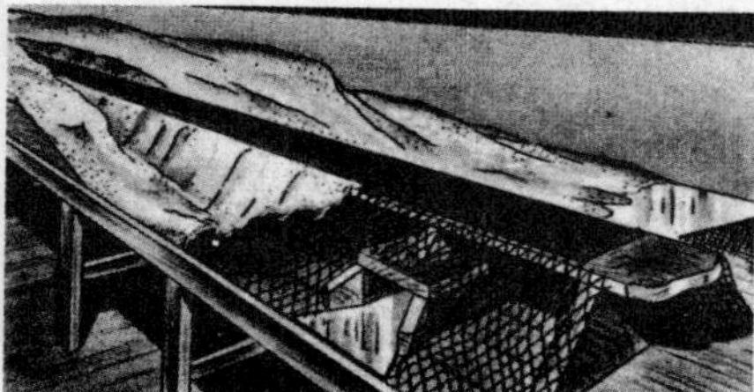

Three stages in the construction of an embankment or track elevation. Notice the supports used under the track boards.

Notice the gradual elevation of the track in this model railroad.

pine siding boards, which are about three-quarters of an inch thick are suitable and can be obtained from any lumber yard at surprisingly low cost.

To determine the rate of incline according to real railroad practice is a long process entailing the determination of tractive effort of model locomotives, engine and train resistance and the weight of the engine and train. The formula is too long and unstable in its application to models to be of much practical value.

Railroad grades are always expressed in percentages such as 1% or 1.5%. To many a young engineer this is often puzzling.

Perhaps the easiest way to explain what it means is by picturing a hill 100 feet long and one foot high, the length being measured horizontally. The percentage of grade is obtained by dividing the height by the length—thus if the elevation is 1/100, giving .01, it is called a 1% grade. As another example, a grade two inches high and 200 inches long is also a 1% grade.

To get down to the practical point for model engineers, if seven sections of "O" gauge track are fastened together, the length is 7 x 10 inches or 70 inches. If one end is lifted 1.4 inches off the floor the resulting grade is $\frac{1.4}{70}$ or 2%.

A 2% grade is not much of a hill but real railroad engineers consider a 2% grade as rather a tough climb and a 3% grade as terrible.

Unfortunately, many model engineers construct grades without a knowledge of their engines' capacity for up-grade work. The result is often disappointing and the model railroader finds after hours of painstaking construction that the grade is too steep and that it causes trains to stall. Careful experiments must be made with the most sluggish engine in the roundhouse at the head of the longest train of cars it will ever be required to haul, before the maximum grade can be determined. In no case should it be allowed to exceed 4%. Wherever possible, curved track sections should be avoided on grades as curved track increases the strain on the locomotive.

If the elevated portion of the right-of-way is allowed to disappear from the scene occasionally, the glamor of two-level railroading is intensified. One method for doing this is to conceal a section of the elevated track behind a mountain partition, as shown in sketch E, bringing it back to view by arranging the mountain scenery in such a way that it imparts the effect of the right-of-way emerging from behind a cliff.

The photograph below shows how the sides of an inclined embankment are treated for greatest realism. From the track board to the top of the table or shelf, fine hardware screening is draped in rolling folds. On top of this, two layers of plaster are applied, the second being moulded and carved. The final touch of realism is added by painting the embankment a ground color, working several small rocks into the hardening plaster and adding bushes and scrub growth.

Method of elevating track when the bench is an open framework.

A
B
C
D
E
F

5212

LAKES AND WATERWAYS

CHAPTER TEN

WHETHER available space and facilities are the finest or limited to a small room, it is possible to have a river in the model railroad scene. For no special devices are necessary and no water is involved. Rocks, cellophane, cement and varnish are the only ingredients.

The lake, river or stream is planned for the lowest ground level in its immediate vicinity. Banks are raised on each side by tacking down an irregular framework of baby chick wire or hardware mesh and covering it with burlap which later is painted. If a river is to be situated among hills, they are sloped gently to the water level; if on a plane, only a slight descent is necessary; if in a rocky ravine, the sides of the mountain are steep.

It is possible to build a waterfall and rushing stream like this.

When plotting the course of the river, it is reduced in width as it travels away from the front of the bench, to accentuate perspective.

So that it will not end abruptly at the wall, the river may have a falls with painted scenery above them, or its ending may be camouflaged by having it disappear behind a mountain.

For rapids, one section of the river is raised a few inches higher than the rest. Rocks, varying in size from about an inch to boulders of four or five inches, are placed at the base of the falls, and cover the place where the rapids are wanted. A few rocks are placed haphazardly in the river if the surrounding land suggests them.

When everything is arranged, the boards of the river bed are painted, using a pale blue in the center, over which a thin streaked film of aluminum paint is used. A muddy brown, blended in near the banks, suggests shallows.

The appearance of water is obtained by the use of clear celophane. Several sheets of cellophane are moistened and crumpled in the palm of the hand and then halfway straightened.

To give the suggestion of current, several long strips of varying width and shape are stretched, placed in position and pressed down firmly. Several sheets that have been wet and crumpled are used to cover the whole surface of the river from bank to bank. These sheets are not bumpy but made to lie as flat as possible.

Rocks in the stream break the current and send it around either side. The wrinkles in the cellophane likewise are curved around the rocks.

As a last touch, objects in the path of the water are made to appear wet by varnishing.

Culverts, Bridges, Trestles

Chapter Eleven

WHEN a real railroad right-of-way is constructed below the level of surrounding land, it becomes a canal that collects and carries flood waters. When built on the side of a hill or mountain, the road obstructs the free passage of water on its down hill course. When the road is raised as an embankment bi-secting a valley it becomes a dam. In each instance, the flow of storm water after thaws and during rainy seasons would play havoc with the roadbed. No matter how well built, the road would be subject to such abuse that it soon would be undermined and washed away.

To overcome this problem, railroads do not fight the tendencies of water but they adapt the right-of-way to conform to them. Instead of attempting to construct great steel and concrete structures capable of withstanding water pressure and preventing erosion and wear, they build a roadbed that is porous and use numerous culverts under the track to allow water to pass through. A drainage system for the entire line is developed and placed into operation. This system consists of lateral ditches which catch water, before it reaches the roadbed, and carry it along to the culverts. On the high side of the right-of-way, these ditches are wide and deep and graded so they cannot turn into stagnant pools.

The only difference between a culvert and a bridge is that one is small and the other is large. A culvert usually is used in connection with a small manufactured drainage system. A bridge usually is used to carry the right-of-way across a natural waterway, a canal or canyon.

On a model railroad, a culvert is an easily built and effective accessory. Every model pike with a countryside of hills and valleys and with a right-of-way built on an embankment should have several small culverts as well as a couple of bridges in order to show that proper consideration has been given to the serious problem of drainage.

Real railroad culverts range in size from a single corrugated steel pipe of three-foot diameter to a series of stone or concrete works with openings six or seven feet wide. The size of the culvert to be used at any particular spot is, of course, determined by the amount of storm water anticipated, predicted upon the area drained, its slope and the nature of the ground.

In the illustration on the following page are three culverts which are common types found in use by nearly all railroads throughout the country. Identified by the letters A, B and C, they are, respectively, pipe, box and arch types.

One of the engineering rules in the construction of a culvert is that there should be not less than three feet of earthwork and ballast between the top of the culvert and the track ties. Another rule is that the culvert must be placed at the lowest possible ground level in its immediate vicinity and all of the ground around the culvert be graded, tamped down and prepared for rapid discharge of water.

Bridges are divided into two groups—those which are fixed or stationary and those which have movable spans designed to revolve or lift open to permit navigation. The No. 314 through girder and the No. 315 truss bridges are fixed types. The No. 313 electric bascule or jack-knife bridge is a moveable type.

These three bridges can be used in any layout with striking effect. They are so made that they may be placed under track on a flat table or on the floor without the necessity of inclines.

Two methods for obtaining even greater realism are available, however. The first is to build the table top so that it has a depressed area which can be painted and decorated to resemble a river or stream, and to use one of these bridges over this waterway. The most gratifying realism for a railroad bridge scene can be obtained on a layout which is landscaped with hills and valleys and where the track has been arranged to run through cuts and over fills.

On such a system the high hills are gradually sloped to the valley river located at the lowest point in the layout. The track issues from a tunnel, travels for a short distance through a cut, then out over a fill and onto the bridgeworks. On such a system it is possible to combine several types of bridge spans into one long structure and to include all of the sub-structures and concrete work which make the bridge scene come to life.

Abutments are sub-structures designed for the end support of spans. All bridge abutments contain a seat on which the end of the bridge superstructure is rested. The central portion of the abutment containing the seat is called the breast. The breast acts as a retaining wall for the fill or earthwork behind it. Most abutments also have wings to prevent the retained material from working its way around on either side of the breast.

There are five common types. These are known as arch, wing, breast, "T" and "U". The common types which can be adapted most readily and most effectively for a model railroad, are illustrated on the following page.

The bridge pier is also known as a sub-structure. Sometimes it is made of creosoted timber, sometimes of stone but most often of reinforced concrete. The reinforced concrete pier is the easiest type to construct in miniature. Several piers are illustrated in the drawing on the following page.

The dotted lines in all these drawings indicate the manner in which the bridge is supported by pier or abutment.

In the engineering of real railroad bridges, the location of piers is determined for even distribution of the weight of the super-structure and so that the center of gravity of bridge loads coincides with the center line of the pier.

Some bridge piers are square, some rounded, while still others are pointed at the up-stream edge. In real railroad bridge building such things as ice flow, type of water traffic and flood pressure of the stream are the considerations in the selecting of one type of pier or another.

Sub-structures for bridges on the model railroad consist of blocks of wood which serve as actual supports of the weight of the bridge and passing train. Around these crude blocks of wood, carefully detailed, accurately shaped cardboard piers and abutments are constructed. The cardboard piers and abutments are then painted gray to resemble concrete.

The timber trestle is another type of railroad bridge that finds a warm welcome among enthusiasts in the field of model railroading.

There was a time when railroads would not attempt to bridge a river used for navigation. One railroad would take its passengers to the edge of a river and discharge them. There they would have to take a boat to get across the river and board a train of another line on the other side. Then a few timber bridges were built. They were a success and soon timber bridges and timber trestles were constructed for all types of crossings all over the country. For the lightweight trains of that

Roadbed, embankments and bridge abutments all ready and waiting for the installation of the large, steel superstructure.

A
B
C
D
E
F
G
H
I

A huge, impressive timber trestle is being used effectively for a single track line, to span a natural gulley, on this outdoor railroad.

day, timber was adequate. But trains grew heavier and speeds were increased. The result has been that nearly all bridges on heavy-traffic lines today are made of steel and reinforced concrete. Timber trestles will be found most frequently, today, on branch lines and on small roads having light traffic.

Nevertheless the timber trestle remains the most admired and the most desired structure in the realm of model railroading.

The timber trestle consists of horizontal spans, vertical bents and diagonal braces. The vertical bents usually are erected on concrete footings. The timber trestle may be made of small square sticks throughout as illustrated by the photographs at the right and above. It also may be made of small dowels to represent round poles, with flat sticks used for sway braces, as illustrated by the photograph at the beginning of this chapter.

Technically, there are two types of trestles, one being known as a pile trestle with its upright members entering the ground, the other being known as the frame trestle with its upright members secured to a transverse base beam which in turn is rested on concrete foundation blocks. At the top of each bent is another transverse member, connecting each one of the uprights, which is known as the cap. Resting on the caps are the longitudinal stringers which, in turn support long, heavy, closely spaced track ties.

Of the two types of timber trestles, the frame trestle is probably the easiest to reproduce.

In building a frame trestle, the bents are made individually with their transverse base and cap beams and cross bracing. On a single-track line, where five upright posts are used, the base of the bent is about twice the width of the top, with the top of the bent twice or three times as wide as the track gauge.

When all bents are finished they are fastened

to small blocks of wood representing concrete foundations. Stringers with track mounted on them are then glued on top of the bents. The longitudinal members are added to each side of the row of bents. The diagonal sway braces running from bent to bent are the last pieces applied.

In the construction of a pile type trestle, the method of construction found most practical is to use a base board at least as wide and as long as the intended trestle. This board becomes the water-level foundation under the trestle. This board is drilled with accurately spaced holes in the exact locations where the piles are wanted. Dowels or square sticks are then forced into the holes, making certain, first, that they are of the correct length to furnish a perfectly flat top. Cross braces and longitudinal members are then added. If a graduated slope of ground down to the center of the trestle is desired, it can be built around the bents and between the piles. This is done by making a crude, wooden framework of the approximate shape required and nailing it to the floor boards around the trestle. Wire mesh is spread over the top of the framework and nailed in place. Over the mesh, plaster is applied and later painted.

In building a trestle of either type it is always a good plan to have all track attached to stringers before the stringers are attached to the top framework of the bents, in order to avoid hammering on the top of the trestle. Creosote finish for timber is applied before actual construction is started.

Model timber trestle and concrete abutment, under construction.

Trackwork and Ballast

Chapter Twelve

NOTHING improves the appearance of a model railroad more than realistic track work. Every model railroader wants to obtain a trim appearance for his right-of-way, just as real railroads do. How this can be done is illustrated by the photographs on the following pages.

Of the track that can be bought, "OO", with two rails, is the most realistic.

In this track, actual steel rails are laid on a molded bakelite base which includes correctly spaced ties and the general shape of the roadbed. Ballast is not represented but must be added.

In building a realistic, ballasted "OO" gauge roadbed, the sections of track first are mounted on a board in long sections. If the track can be laid out where it will not have to be taken up, the job is made much easier. If the roadbed will have to be taken up from time to time, six or seven pieces of track are fastened down on one board and regarded as one unit. The sections of track are attached to the boards with small screws.

Surrounding groundwork on the track boards is built of plaster or papier-mache. The only other thing that must then be done to complete the model track is to obtain finely sifted ballast from a roofing company and apply it between the ties. This may be done in two ways; using glue, shellac, varnish, or any other adhesive, the base between the ties is painted with a fine brush; or the fluid is dropped into the desired space by using a small eye dropper. While still wet, the ballast is sprinkled over the track base. Two coats sometimes are required as the first does not always completely cover the base. Any glue and ballast that gets on the rail or ties is scraped off with a small knife or razor blade. The ditches on the side of the track are modelled and painted with dull greys and browns.

Three-rail "OO" gauge track is shown in the same illustration. This is treated in a similar manner. Motor housings of switches sometimes are covered with landscape effects or an occasional building such as a section house or handcar house. The main point is to try to make the entire scene look as natural and life-like as possible.

In this chapter, wide-radius "O" gauge track is shown which has been ballasted for more realism. This track has solid steel T-shaped rails just like real rail. They are mounted on cast crossties

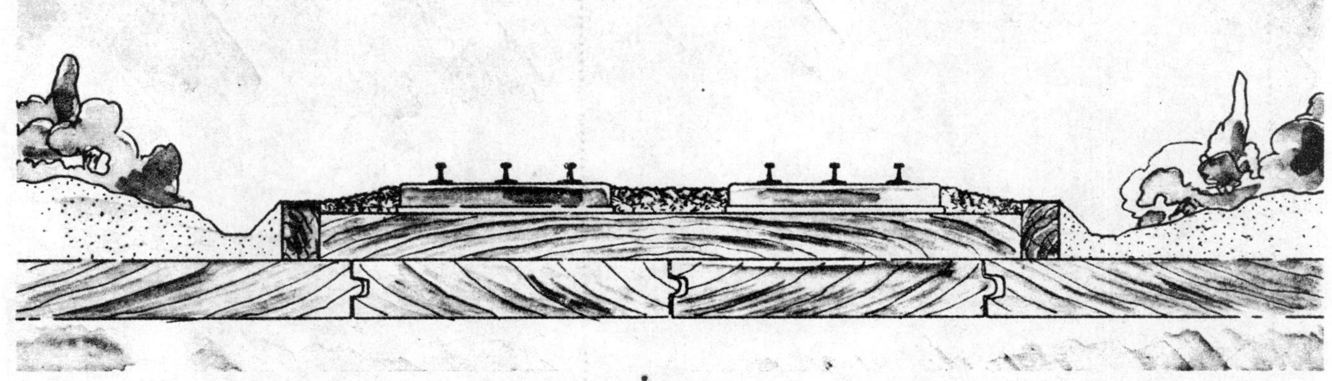

Cross section of double-track main line showing table boards, track boards and strips of wood used to retain loose ballast in position.

Ballasted "00" gauge two-rail and three-rail track.

which are used sometimes on real railroads. As far as appearance of these models is concerned, they can represent conventional wood crossties as well.

The first step in fixing up this track is to mount it on a piece of half-inch or quarter-inch shelving. This forms a suitable base and lengths of four to six feet are made. On each piece, the solid-rail track is squarely attached with screws or nails. Care is exercised that all rail is mounted so that it is straight and true. These sections of track are joined by tiny nuts and bolts and rail joint bars. The result is that from four to seven sections of track are mounted on one board

If the model railroad system calls for double-tracking, with part of the roadbed on tangents or straight sections, the centers of the two tracks should be not less than 3½ inches for "O" gauge, or 2 1/16 inches for "OO" gauge. Curved, double-trackage should be widened out a little so that plenty of clearance is provided.

Ties are cut out of wood so that one may be inserted between each crosstie to make the tie spacing resemble more closely that of a real roadway. These ties are made the same size as the metal ones on the track and are painted a dull black before being put in place. The ties are dipped in a thin

"0-72" track ballasted with water glass, above, and with glue, below.

Solid rail "0-72" track.

watery solution of black paint.

The last step is to apply the ballast. The best way to obtain the most realism is to lay the ballast loosely. That is, to use no glue, water glass or other adhesive. If this is done, the adjoining scenery will have to have a slightly raised edge to hold the ballast in place.

Another way to ballast is by painting the roadbed a grey color, the same as that of the ballast, and then sprinkling the ballast on while the paint is still wet. This may require two coats of paint for the best results. The ballast may be soaked in a solution of water glass and, when this has dried, it keeps the ballast in place.

Switch motors are covered with scenery. A small building is used occasionally and one or two switch motors sometimes are left exposed.

Shown on these pages are illustrations of ordinary tubular track. This is fixed in exactly the same way as the solid-rail track and with the same procedure. All ties are painted black and are the same size. For the most realism in all cases, the ballast is brought to within 1/16-inch of the tops of the ties. Sometimes real track looks rather rusty, and this rusty appearance is copied.

Laying wooden ties between metal ones is a simple job as the wooden ties are produced on a power saw and all of them are painted at one time by dipping them into a thin mixture of black paint.

The few steps of this job are accomplished by more or less mass-production methods. When the ballast is put down great care is exercised that it is not placed into the switch points, as it would foul the switches and make it necessary to take them up, clean them, and replace them in the layout and do the ballasting job all over again.

The illustration shows two methods of applying ballast permanently—by waterglass and with paint.

Regular "0" gauge track with extra ties.

Signals

Chapter Thirteen

SIGNALS are the nerve system of a railroad. They are the reins of the great iron horse telling her where and when to go or commanding her to stop.

On real railroads there are two general classes

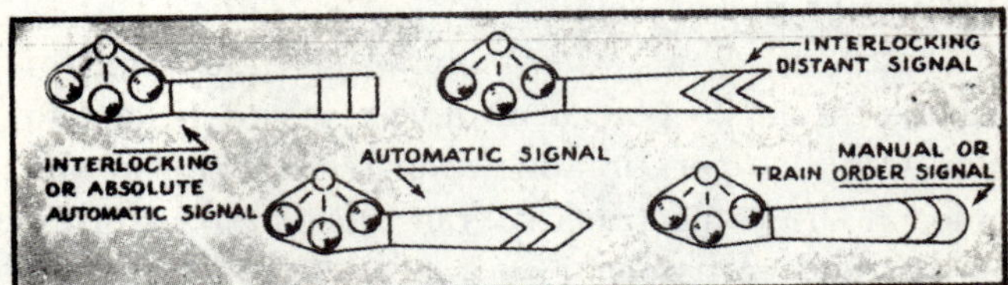

of signals. One is the automatic signal and the other the manually controlled signal.

Automatic signals usually are found on open stretches of the road, where there are no complicated switches and crossovers. The trains themselves operate them.

Automatic signals are built in three common classes—the semaphore signal, the color light signal and the position light signal.

The automatic semaphore was developed from the manual semaphore. It consists of a movable signal arm painted red and yellow, so it will be visible clearly. It has a yellow and red lens—and sometimes a green lens—mounted in the pivot end of the arm. At night a white light, which burns in the semaphore, is covered by the red, yellow or green lens, depending upon the position at which the signal is set. By day the engineer gets signals from the position of the arm.

The color light signal consists of a red, green and sometimes a yellow lens. Each is illuminated by a separate electric lamp. The beam thrown by one of these lamps is much more powerful than the old type signal light and will pierce the most stubborn weather. Lenses are covered with a shield at the top to protect them from reflection of the sun and from accumulation of snow.

But railroad officials found that occasionally an accident was caused because some member of the train crew developed color blindness and misread a signal. So a still more modern signal was devised.

It is called the light position signal because it uses a light but does not depend on the color of the beams for signaling.

All the lenses of this type are yellow, because

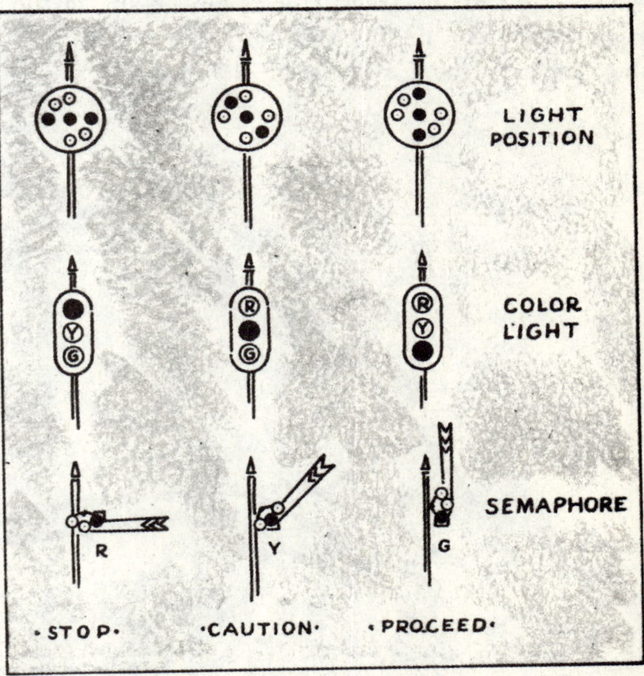

color experts have found that yellow will penetrate a mist better than any other color.

The light position signal has seven lenses, mounted on a black background, or sometimes on an open-pipe framework. Three lights are lit at one time. The position of these three lights imitates the position of the semaphore. In other words, the three lights may be in a line straight across, like a semaphore which is horizontal, or they may be in a line straight up and down, or at an angle.

As in the color light signal, illumination during both day and night is required for the position light signal.

Semaphore arms bobbing and colored lights blinking add so much glamor and excitement to the miniature road that most boys place their signals haphazardly along the line, just to get them into action and without heed to railroad practice.

Yet, real railroad signal practice is a very serious part of train operation and is governed by many rules and conventions. Some of the simple rules of elementary signalling might be followed on the model road merely for the sake of realism as nothing can be added in performance.

The most important of these rules is that the signal must be free from obstructions and so placed that the engineer can see it in time to bring his train to a halt before over-running it. Another rule is that the semaphore must be placed on the engineer' side of the track (the engineer sits in the right hand seat in the locomotive cab) and that the arm must hang away from the track.

In the drawing on the following page, sketches A and B show the right and wrong locations.

Signals are placed where they serve a definite purpose. First there is the location of a switch or crossing which always calls for a signal. One is also needed where a single track is spread into a double track, as illustrated by sketch C.

When traffic flows in the reverse direction, as shown by sketch D, two signals are needed. Where traffic moves in both directions over a similar track arrangement, as shown by E, two signals are also required and are placed as illustrated.

In the next illustration, if traffic moves only in the direction shown, only two signals are needed. If flowing in both directions, four would be required.

A good terminal layout with a "throat" signal is shown in sketch G. This system allows a train to run in on one track and out on another without backing or uncoupling.

Sketch H shows where No. 153 block control signals might be placed on an extensive system to facilitate the operation of two or three trains at one time on the same track layout without possibility of rear-end collisions.

At the bottom of this page is another illustration of a complete model system with signals correctly placed and using the No. 440 signal bridge.

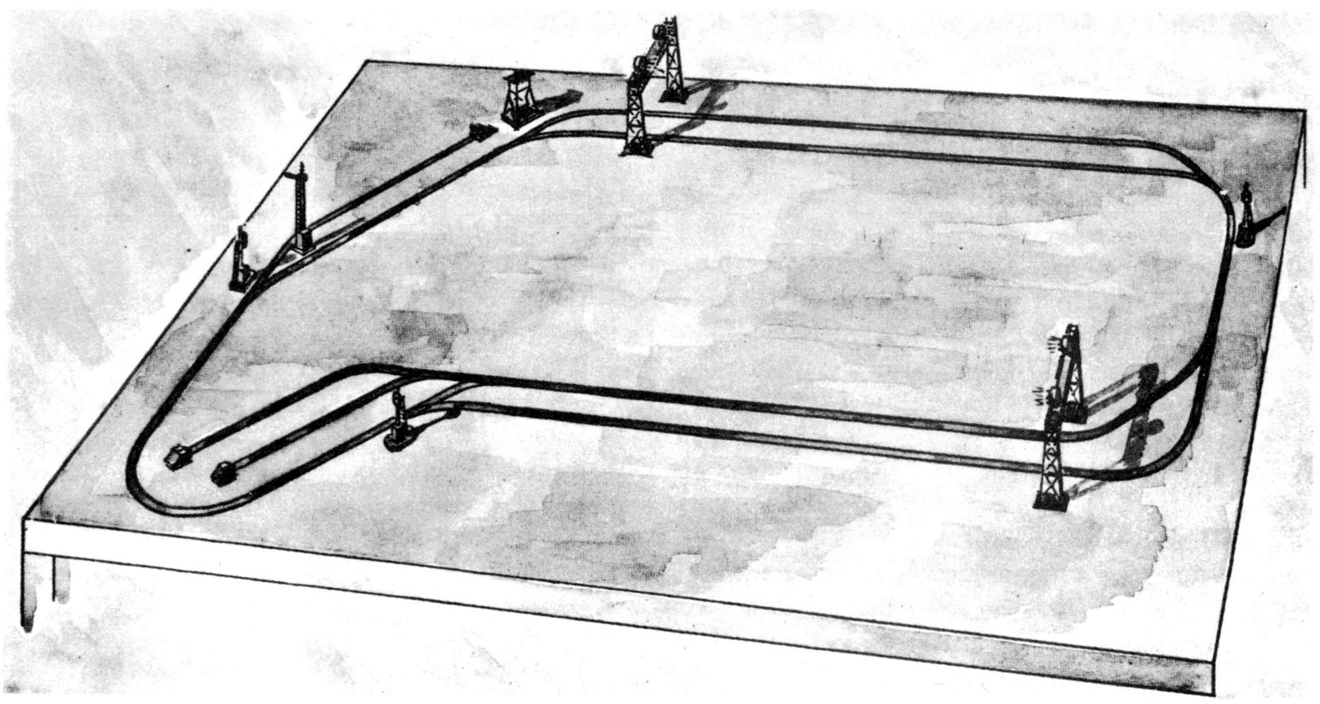

A model railroad project showing where signals might be used in accordance with real railroad practice.

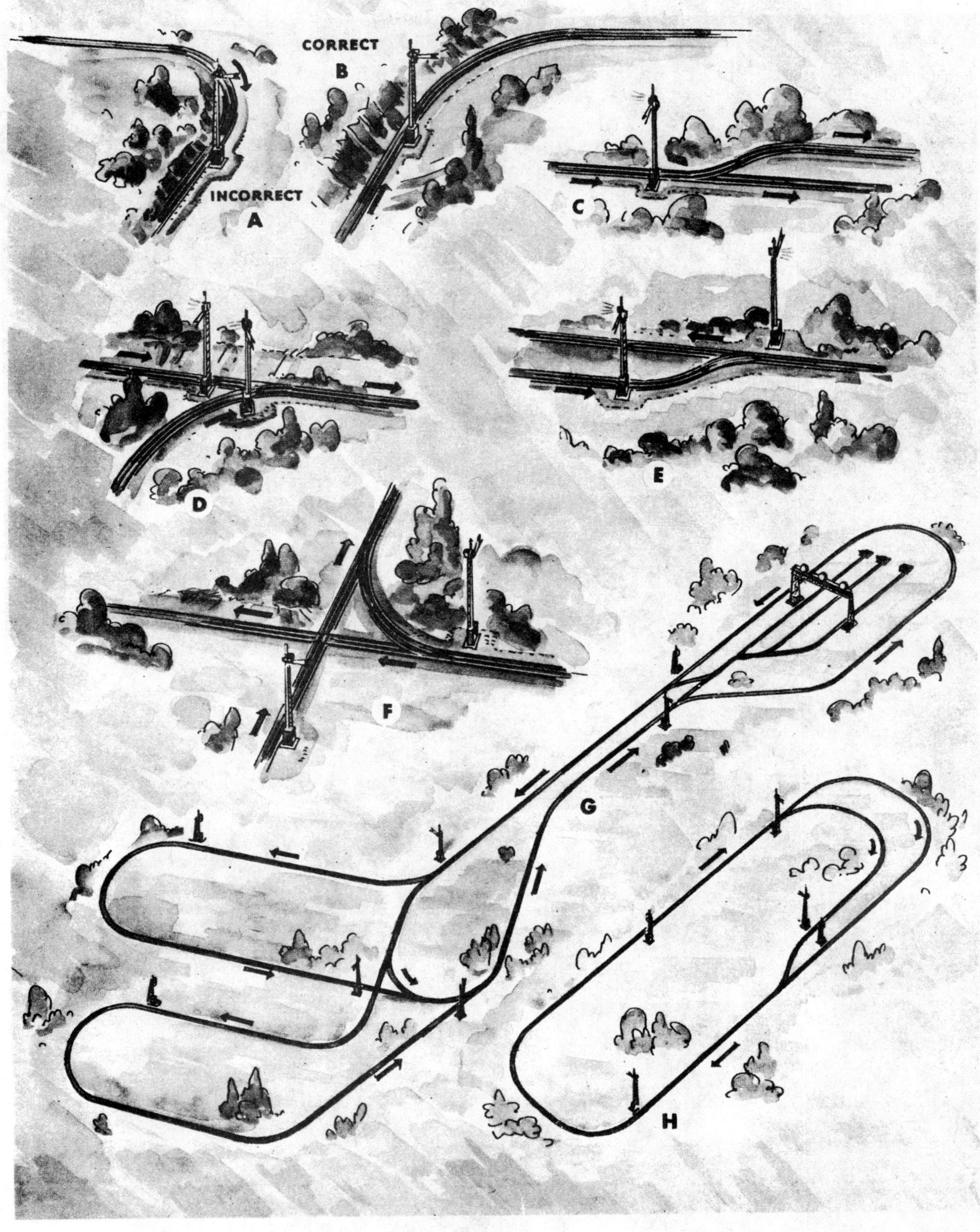
CORRECT
B
INCORRECT
A
C
D
E
F
G
H

4413

Lineside Scenery

Chapter Fourteen

RIGHT-OF-WAY is not only the roadbed and track over which trains operate but includes all of the property adjacent to the track which is owned and used by the railroad together with the signals, stations and all other fixtures and buildings that are on it.

This chapter is devoted to the incidental equipment and lineside scenery that belongs to no other category and is of intrinsic importance to the final, finished appearance of the miniature main tracks and right-of-way.

Every mile of main line on prototype roads contains some small lineside fixture which can be reproduced on the model road, such as a transformer box attached to a power line post, a snow fence, an emergency spare rail support holding one or two rails, a neatly arranged pile of wooden ties.

Look for these items every time you take a trip on a train. Make a quick mental note of all details, then build models and you will be delighted at the extent to which they will enhance the appearance of your road.

The section foreman's house is one building which will be found repeated often on a real right-of-way.

This house usually is not much more than a simple, unpainted shack that can be made out of pieces of cardboard.

The section crew camp frequently will be found with the foreman's shack. Often this may be an out-moded box car from which the running gear has been removed.

The car is jacked up on cross ties and is fitted with rows of bunks and a wood stove.

A second out-moded car may be placed next to the bunkhouse and used as a cookhouse and mess car.

The section foreman's house and the section crew's camp usually will be situated in the center of the track section they are charged with maintaining and keeping in perfect order. Nearby will be the tool house and hand car house.

Other pieces of lineside equipment which will be found easy to make and effective are the locomotive water columns which might be carved out of wood, the elevated shack for the crossing gateman and a highway bridge over the railroad tracks.

Where the right-of-way runs along in a deep cut in a hilltop, an excellent opportunity is presented for building a highway or country road through the hill and have it cross the railroad tracks on bridge. For a modern highway lined with white posts and a cable fence, an up-to-date, manufactured plate girder bridge might be used, or the new truss bridges that are illuminated with a red beacon light. If the road is little more than a country trail, a wooden, hand-made bridge might be sufficient.

The snow fence is another interesting piece of lineside scenery. Sometimes these fences are permanent, year-'round fixtures on the right-of-way and sometimes they are portable. They are used to break the wind that drives snow into drifts and are needed most in railroad cuts where snow is most likely to collect. A permanent snow fence is built as long and as high as conditions require and usually consists of posts imbeded deeply in the ground supporting stout, one-inch lateral boards.

On following pages are several additional lineside fixtures that will be found easy to reproduce, most impressive being an icing platform which might be used on a track siding or in a freight car yard.

A pair of regular No. 47 crossing gates, with sidewalks and roadways built around them.

GRADE CROSSING PROTECTION

AS the miniature city grows and develops, it will acquire paved streets and highways and, with the help of the dime store, a parade of toy automobiles, trucks and buses probably will make its appearance. Traffic problems will be created and the model railroad company eventually will be called upon for better safety devices at grade crossings.

How grade crossings on the model system can be protected in a thoroughly modern and up-to-date fashion is illustrated in the photograph above.

Two sets of No. 47 automatic, illuminated gates are obtained. Each set consists of two gates with sidewalk extensions. When attached to the track, the gates are lowered automatically at approach of a train, and tiny lanters are illuminated. When the train has passed, the gates rise. To increase the realism of the gates, the extension arms may be painted, as shown in the photographs.

A sheet of cardboard, about $\frac{1}{8}$-inch thick and as wide as the base of the No. 47 accessory, is used to represent the highway and to form a foundation for the sidewalks.

Pieces of cardboard also are cut, scored and inserted between rails of the track.

Corners are notched out of the sheet of cardboard that is used as a highway so that it fits snugly over the enamel base of the accessory.

Sidewalks on each side of highway are made of layers of cardboard which are built up to the height of sidewalks on the accessory. Sidewalks and highway are painted to simulate concrete.

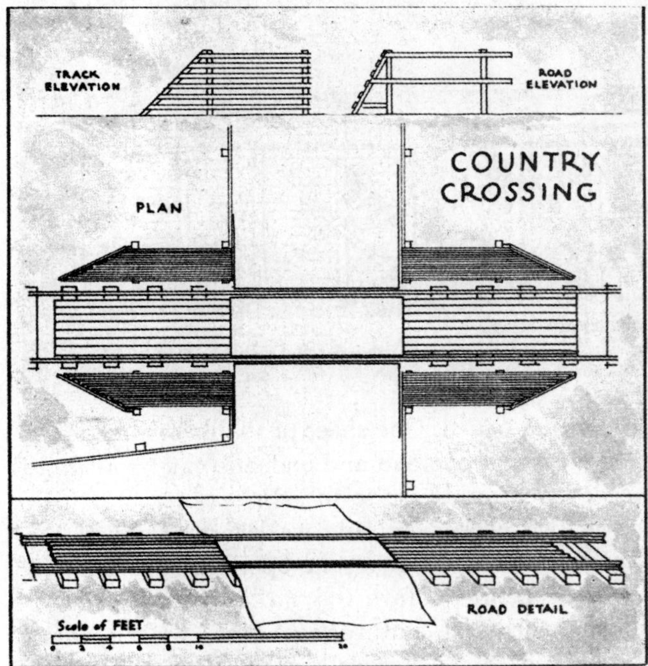

COUNTRY GRADE CROSSING

OUT on some single-track section of every model railroad is an excellent location for constructing a rural dirt road grade crossing and bringing a high degree of realism to a spot which otherwise would be relegated to background obscurity. A white fence along the road stands out among the green fields. The dirt road is rutted as if it had remained uncared for during many years of service. The cattle guards give the final realistic touch to the crossing picture.

Eight A-shaped fence supports are made out of small square sticks. At the track side, the guard fences are inclined as shown in the photographs. The bottom of each fence is placed close to the track. Each fence has five rails which are glued or cemented to the A-shaped supports.

The triangular strips of wood between rails on each side of the road prevent cattle from straying onto the right-of-way. These strips are made of corrugated paper, painted weatherbeaten grey. On real railroads, these strips of wood are about six feet long. Their edges are sharp and uncomfortable for cloven-hoof animals. Cattle being driven down the roadway automatically turn away from the triangles and thus are kept off the tracks.

The road level is raised on each side of the crossing to the top of the rails. Between the rails blocks of wood are tacked, with allowances made next to each running rail for passage of the wheel flanges. The tops of these blocks of wood are painted a neutral dark color and sprinkled with dirt to match the road.

A square strip of wood also is attached to the extension of the ties on the outsides of the running rail. One piece is used on each side of the track. Cemented on top of these pieces of wood and extending away from the track are bands of heavy brown paper as wide as the intended road, as indicated in the plan at the left. The bands of paper act as a base for the dirt, gravel or sand that is used to form the road.

The photograph and drawings represent a project which might be made for "00" gauge two-rail track. For three-rail track an allowance must be made for the inside third rail to run through the corrugated cattle guards as well as through the road board.

The inclined cattle fences and highway fence are painted white. The picture is completed by the acquisition of a number of figures from the dime store. These may include cattle, farmers, farm tractors and even a hitched hay rack.

Country highway crossing with white cattle guards.

TRACK · ELEVATION · SCALE of ACTUAL FEET · PLATFORM · END · EL.

MID-WAY ICING PLATFORM

REFRIGERATOR cars are one of the miracles of modern railroading. These huge, moving ice boxes carry perishable foodstuffs across the continent to feed a nation with out-of-season foods.

Refrigerator cars are built like tremendous ice boxes with a compartment on each end into which ice is lowered through roof hatches. These pockets of ice cool the car so that its contents are kept at an even, low temperature.

Railroads store ice in ice houses, and load the cars from them. This loading is done rapidly to prevent ice loss. Complete refrigerator trains can be iced en route while the engine is being serviced.

The model ice house pictured here is a small type adapted for use on the average model railroad and is built easily of wood and cardboard.

The four sides of the buildings are laid out on illustration board. One sheet probably will be large enough so that one end and one side can be a single piece, scored and bent to shape.

The two clearstory side walls are made of the same material and the vent openings are cut out from the inside before the walls are applied.

The horizontal and vertical lines of the doors are scribed. Strap hinges are cut from thin cardboard and cemented to the door.

The four sections of the roof are cut out of sandpaper and cemented on, to simulate an asphalt roof. The clearstory roof is cut from one piece, and bent to the roof lines after it has been scored.

The sides and roofs are cemented together and wood sticks are glued into the corners as reinforcements.

The footings for the low platform are cut from strips of pine wood and the floor from a sheet of thin wood or illustration board.

Icing platforms like this model are used by real railroads to repack refrigerator cars.

INCIDENTAL EQUIPMENT

SOME of the numerous little pieces of equipment that can be built alongside the right-of-way are illustrated in the two pictures on this page.

In the photograph above is another handcar and tool house, large enough to accommodate two vehicles. Between the two tracks is a swinging water column and an old-fashioned ball type signal.

A handcar made from regular car trucks.

The water column in the illustration was made of metal parts but a very representative model might be carved out of wood with a pocket knife.

Ball signal towers like the one illustrated are a quaint and colorful remnant from the days of wood-burning locomotives and passenger coaches that were upholstered in red plush and decorated with gilt. From it came the word "highball" which is one of the most common expressions in the vocabulary of the railroader. Reproduction of a ball signal tower in a miniature railroad would be a fit and suitable tribute to the pioneering years of railroading.

A green ball hoisted to the top of the tower is the clear indication signal and a red ball at the top is the stop indication. Sometimes one ball is used on each side, one painted green and the other red. By night, red or green lanterns are hoisted to the top by means of pulleys.

The construction of this signal is simple, as most of it can be made of wood. The signal post is a square wooden shaft, about twenty feet high. The signal balls are either cut and whittled from pieces of dowel and attached to black thread, or small, colored beads are used.

STATIONS

CHAPTER FIFTEEN

IN general there are only two types of stations: terminals and passing stations. Terminals mark the beginning and the end of a railroad system or the end of a branch line. Passing stations are the big-city stations and small-town stations and unimportant little way-stations between two terminals.

If the model railroad track layout is of the continuous type, passing stations which are sometimes called through stations are used and no terminals are required. If the system is of the point-to-point variety, two terminals must be planned and several way stations should be added for time-card operations. If the layout is a home-and-back system, only one terminal is needed with several through stations added to give some purpose to the operation of passenger trains.

The track arrangement, train sheds and station house on a continuous type layout can be made just as elaborate and as complex as they might be at any terminal. The through type station may have its spurs, track throat, interlocked switches and signals and associated engine and coach storage yards. It can, if desired, have all of the features and the appearance of a terminal, with the added advantage of continuous train movement.

Many model railroaders, however, have no desire to curtail the long procedure of switching and shunting, coupling and uncoupling cars and making-up and breaking-up trains for the sake of continuous train movement and greater action on the main line. They look upon the activity of switching jacks in the terminal as the high point in the hobby of railroading.

The activity of a stub-track station or terminal follows a very definite course on all roads and some model railroaders adhere to it as a ritual. A train leaves the main track at what is known as the throat. The engine pulls its train up to its appointed platform and is uncoupled. A switching engine pulls up behind the train and is coupled to the last car. After all passengers have left the cars, the switching engine takes the train out of the terminal and into nearby coach yards. There the cars are cleaned and washed, filled with fresh water, packed with fresh ice and inspected for their next run. At the proper time, a switching engine returns them to a platform track and is uncoupled. A road engine follows the train into the platform track from the engine yard, where it likewise has been put through a servicing routine. It backs into the train, tender first. When coupled, it is ready for the highball that will send it out on its scheduled run.

Opposite the following page are a number of sketches of model railroad stations. In the drawings, four types are represented, and with each a track arrangement is suggested. At the top of the page is a plan for a combination station. It is called a combination station because it combines through tracks with stub tracks. A double-track main line is indicated and at the approach to the station, a double crossover undoubtedly would be used. The station is planned, for use with either "0" gauge regular or wide-radius track, so that the building itself covers a right-angle corner in the track layout. A regular No. 116 station is used on top of a train shed structure built out of fibre board, reinforced by wooden braces.

At the letter B is another combination station, this one being the most simple. It has an island platform and a single hold-over track stub. The steel station is surrounded by platforms made out of sheets of fibre board, appropriately painted. A series of lamps is used on the platforms.

The sketch identified by the letter C is a typical through station on a double-track main line. The station and the illuminated platforms are all regularly catalogued items but they are connected by means of one large continuous platform cut out of fibre board. The station and platform roofs are joined by a central roof made out of cardboard to match.

The station set is finished when station and platforms are repainted in harmonizing colors.

At the bottom of the opposite page is a plan for a small, four-track terminal on a home-and-back type layout. Here again regularly catalogued equipment is used with a number of hand-made additions.

The station has been landscaped and has acquired two wings and a long concourse which joins the station proper and the train sheds.

In the track layout for this system the throat might be rearranged with a ladder track and a single-track wye so that trains leaving the terminal could proceed onto the main line headed in either direction.

At the bottom of the layout a turntable is indicated by a circle. Two tracks are shown leading to the terminal which might be used for refueling and engine service work. Opposite the turntable, at the top of the layout are two spurs which might be used as a coach and car-service yard or as a freight depot.

TRUNKS AND LUGGAGE

TRUNKS are made from light cardboard medicine boxes or from blocks of soft white pine. The attractive fittings and colorings can be noted at a trunk store. The various dimensions are measured in order to make them to scale. A wardrobe trunk three feet high should be less than an inch high on the station platform. Usual size of a wardrobe trunk is about three-quarters of an inch square. Some have rounded tops, others flat. Sample cases are usually odd sizes and generally larger than personal luggage. The trunks are covered with the lightest-weight broadcloth in colors to match the trunks copied. Thin, enameled paper, also in the desired colors, cemented neatly at the corners, looks like trunk binding. Bits of the same paper looped loosely at the ends represent the straps. Bits of colored paper pasted on the personal luggage represent travel stickers. For greater interest, they may be lettered with the names of distant or foreign cities or resorts. The fibre trunks are covered with red paper of the desired dull tone.

Hand luggage of various styles is also cut from wood. Some bags are made with reddish brown coverings, others of light tan, still others of dull and enameled papers.

A
B
C
D

BAGGAGE AND EXPRESS

A BAGGAGE room relieves the traveller of the responsibility of caring for his belongings during a trip, no matter how many changes in trains may be entailed.

The photograph shows a baggage room built to be used with a manufactured main station. The three walls are cut from one piece of cardboard. A base of thicker stone is represented by cementing a strip of wood at the bottom of the wall. The roof is cut from the end of an apple box. A number of cardboard strips are cemented horizontally around the walls and cut off wherever door or window openings are encountered. The cornice, made from small picture-frame moulding, is nailed to the wall.

Flat white filler as a base, mixed with drops of black from a tube of oil paint, secures the desired shade of gray to match the main building. When dry, vertical lines are drawn in to mark the joints of the stones. Random stones are painted a darker or lighter shade to add naturalness.

Doors may be added to the openings or omitted. Showing one door open and one closed gives a casual appearance to the building. The door is cut from cardboard to fit the height and half the width of the opening, allowing extra width for gluing behind the wall. A panel for glass is cut out in the upper part of the door. The heavy braces are represented by cutting out a second cardboard the size of the door, drawing in the design of the braces and cutting them out with a sharp knife or razor blade. This is cemented to the door. The door is

painted a mahogany brown by using some burnt sienna, toned with a little white filler.

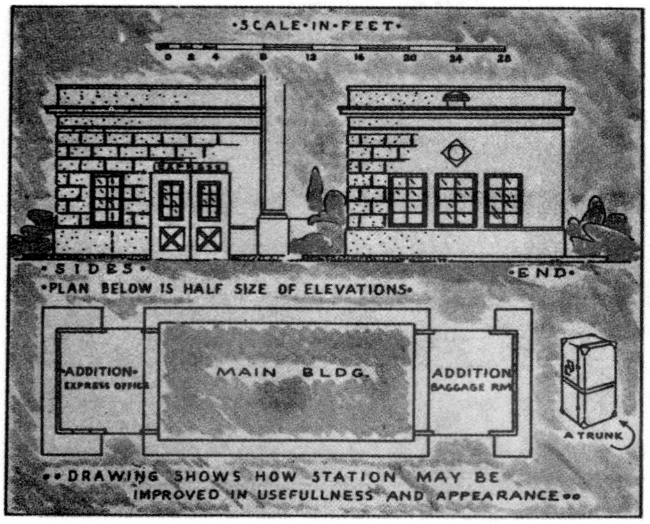

With black ink the window sash is marked off on a piece of tracing paper and cemented behind the three little windows in the end wall. The roof is painted black and sprinkled with sand while still wet to secure a gravelled effect. A ventilator made of two short lengths of dowel rod are fastened to the center of the roof.

On the other side of the station a railway express office is built to balance the baggage room. Its construction is similar to the baggage room. For variety, a smoke stack is made from a small metal pipe and braced against the wind by small wires running down from the stack to the roof. The collar is cut from a thin piece of tin and the three brace wires are hooked over it. The stack is inserted in a hole in the roof and the wires run through small holes in the roof and bent over underneath.

There is a counter across two of the doors for the service of the public, the remaining door being used for company trucks.

The trade-marked sign of the Railway Express Agency, printed in color, is cut out of some advertising folder and cemented over the doors and on the end wall of the building.

Appropriately used in connection with both the baggage and express offices are the two trucks on the following page and the luggage previously described.

TWO-WHEEL BAGGAGE TRUCK

THE making of a baggage truck of this type calls for steady hands and patience because a number of tiny parts must be cut and assembled carefully. Cigar-box wood is used for the heavy members of the frame and strips of cardboard or model airplane balsa are used for the slats.

The X-shape frame is made by notching halfway through the sticks so that they are flush when glued together. The two X's are fastened by cementing small sticks from frame to frame.

The wheels are obtained from a ten-cent store toy. They are nailed to the ends of a slender stick which is glued in place as shown.

The remainder of the truck consists of thin slats glued over the cross members. A more finished appearance is obtained by rounding off the ends of the slats with sandpaper before they are glued in place.

A number of these trucks are seen at all big stations.

On real trucks of this type the body usually is painted battleship gray and the wheels black.

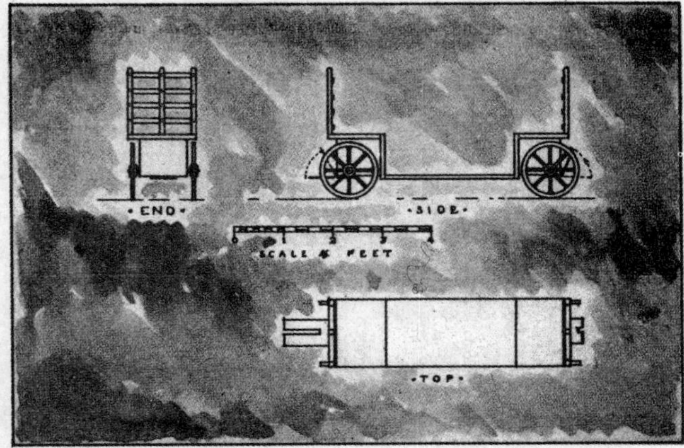

ELECTRIC BAGGAGE TRUCK

ELECTRICALLY operated baggage trucks will be found frequently at terminals and large city stations where platforms are elevated to the height of car floors.

Sometimes these baggage trucks are owned and operated by the Railway Express Agency and sometimes they are owned by the railroad itself and are used to carry luggage and trunks from the baggage room to the trains. They are operated by means of large, self-contained storage batteries.

At each end of the truck a step projects for the operator to stand on. It is hinged so that it may be folded out of the way when not in use.

A steering handle and electric controller are provided at both ends.

The body parts are glued together and the battery boxes are attached after the wheels and platforms are in place.

The uprights of the end stakes are made of square wood with the tops slightly tapered. The cross slats are very thin wood glued in position.

The two motor covers and battery boxes are solid blocks of wood to which the wheels are nailed so that they nearly touch the under side of the truck body.

The small steering handle is a piece of wire bent to shape and inserted in the ends of the truck floor.

The wheels and battery boxes are painted a brilliant red, the body green and the folding platforms and steering handles black.

A Railway Express emblem is cut from an advertisement and cemented in position.

This truck is operated by storage batteries.

YARDS

CHAPTER SIXTEEN

A RAILROAD yard is an arrangement of tracks off the main line for loading and unloading freight cars; or for making-up and breaking-up freight trains, which is called freight car classification; or for storage of empty freight cars that are ready to be used when needed; or for cleaning and storage of passenger cars between trips; or for servicing locomotives before and after each run. These five kinds of yards are called freight yards, classification yards, storage yards, coach yards, and engine yards.

The locomotive service yard is such an interesting subject that a whole chapter in this book has been devoted to it.

Many model railroaders find little reason for incorporating in the model system a passenger car service yard or a coach yard, as it is more commonly known. On a large system operating two or three passenger trains and having one or two stub-track terminals, a single hold-over track or through siding usually is found sufficient for all storage purposes.

Every model railroad with a freight business, however, should have a freight station, team tracks and freight yards. Only by the use of this group is it possible to effect delivery of freight shipments to businesses, stores and factories which do not have their own spur sidings. What a small freight yard looks like is shown at the letter C in the illustration below. Two other small freight yard suggestions for model roads appear on the following page.

Team tracks are stubs in the freight yard with space enough between each track so that trucks or wagons can back up to box cars and load or unload them. The small freight yard also includes a freight station or depot, usually placed between two stub tracks and with long platforms on a level with car floors. The entire freight yard is frequently enclosed within a high cyclone fence with gates at the entrance track.

The miniature railroad system having an extensive freight business should also have a classification yard. There are two types of classification yards. One is a "hump" yard with freight cars sorted by means of gravity. The other classification yard is an engine-manned yard with busy switching engines shunting cars from track to track.

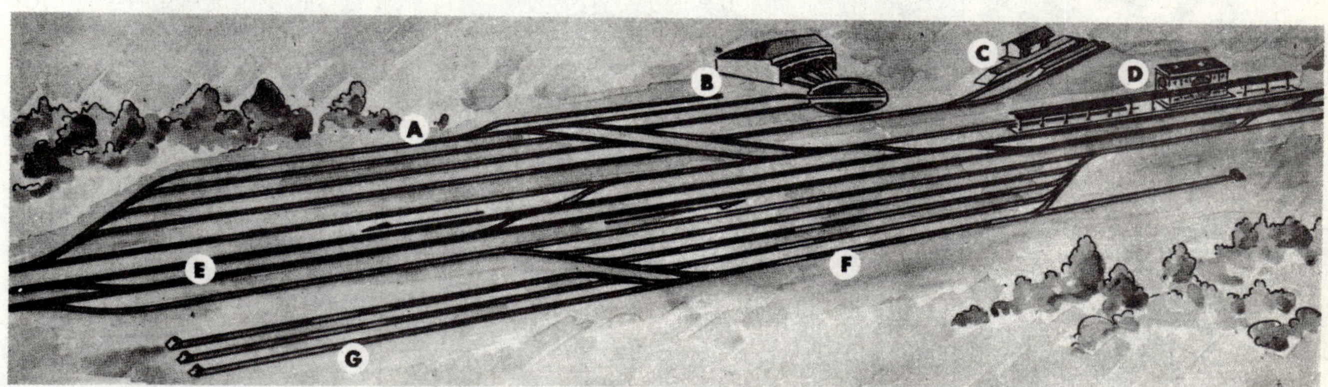

Five yards jammed into one. A, the coach yard. B, the engine service tracks. C, a small freight station yard. D, a through type station with a hold-over track. E, the main line. F, a small classification yard. G, a freight car storage yard.

Six freight yard suggestions suitable for use on the model railroad are illustrated on the following page. They represent an effort to condense real yard trackage for real yard activity into the smallest possible space. In each sketch sections of RCS track are indicated by means of which cars can be uncoupled by electric, remote control. This remote control operation makes the shunting, switching and classifying of cars a realistic and exciting performance.

In sketch A, the lead track from the main line is open at both ends and the double-track main line contains crossovers so that made-up trains may depart in either direction and the yard may be entered by cars coming from either way. The turntable and engine yard are shown with a special cut-over to the lead track for the rapid handling of road engines.

In sketch B is a simple yard arrangement with a loop, indicated by dotted lines, on which the direction of locomotives might be reversed when available space does not allow for the use of a turntable.

At the letter C is a plan which might be bent or turned to fit any table shape that is available. Included are freight station and platforms, team tracks, engine service track, turntable and radial engine tracks and a little classification yard which should be adequate for a model system having ten or twelve freight cars.

At D are four stub tracks on a single track main line into which a wye has been built for reversing purposes.

E shows a track plan that might be used for a hump, with the hump placed at the direction arrow in the lower left-hand corner. If used as a gravity yard, only one section of RCS track would be needed and that one would be placed at the crest of the hump.

F is a yard suggestion on which two alternate freight stations are shown, one a single-track siding which is the most simple form, and the other having two additional team tracks for direct loading or unloading of cars into trucks and wagons.

A large hump or gravity type classification yard is actually two yards in one. There is a set of tracks devoted to receiving and another to outgoing trains. Between the receiving and outgoing fan-shaped track arrangements is the hump or track elevation. Cars are pushed up the hump and released. As they roll down hill by gravity, they are switched from a control tower into one body track or another to couple into their proper trains. The speed of the rolling cars is regulated by track device known as a car retarder, also controlled from the tower. The retarder acts as a brake in pinching the wheel flanges against the rails.

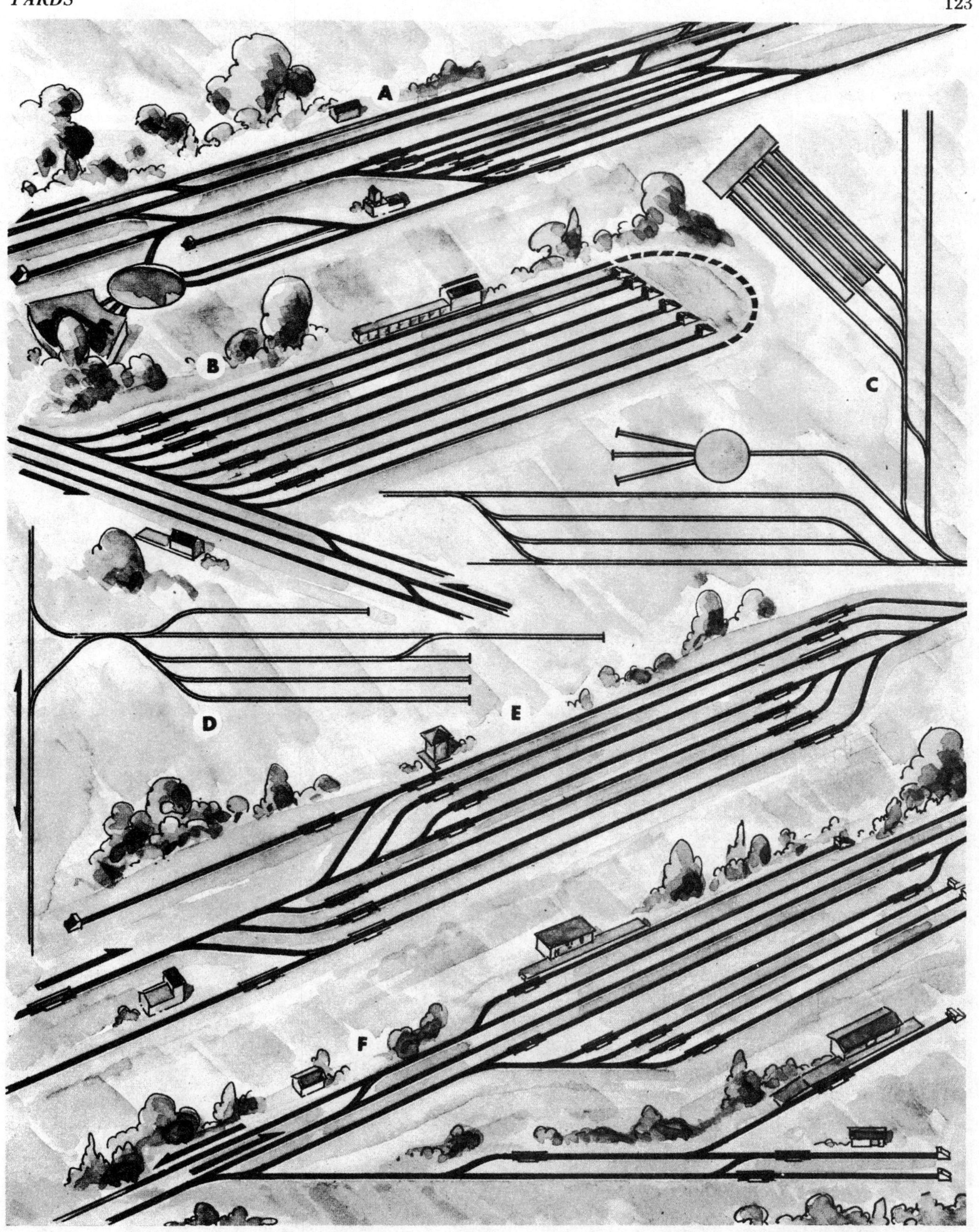
A
B
C
D
E
F

1513

ENGINE TERMINALS

CHAPTER SEVENTEEN

STRONG, swift monsters that they are, locomotives require constant care and a great deal of attention. A trip of 150 to 200 miles between division points is a normal run for an engine and its crew. When a train is to continue further, the locomotive and its crew are changed.

At division points where trains are relayed, roundhouses and extensive engine service yards are situated. The locomotive which has just completed its run is taken into the yard by engine hostlers and passes through a strictly supervised routine of inspection, preening and re-fueling. Ash pans are dumped. Grates are cleaned of ashes and clinkers. The dust and grime of the road which has adhered to the exterior of the engine is washed off by the use of a high-pressure spray. The boiler is cleaned. Fresh sand is put in the sand dome and the supply of fuel and water in the tender is replenished. Skilled mechanics examine the running gear, pumps and instruments and controls in the cab, making adjustments and minor repairs. Before the engine is ready for another trip, it has been attended by many men and thoroughly checked and re-checked. It is not within the province of miniature railroading to duplicate the interesting activity of a real railroad engine terminal, yet all of the glamour of a busy yard can be reproduced in a model system by installation of the many, closely grouped and distinctive buildings for which the engine terminal is noted.

On following pages are plans and photographs for the reproduction of many of the important structures used on engine service tracks. The electrically operated coal elevator is a manufactured accessory which can be used in the locomotive terminal with effective results.

In the sketch below is a practical arrangement of units of the roundhouse group, with an associated series of tracks for light repairs of engines or cars and employing a transfer table to be seen at the top center in the sketch. The track layout suggested is one that might be used on a model railroad having both an in-bound and an out-bound track and two auxiliaries.

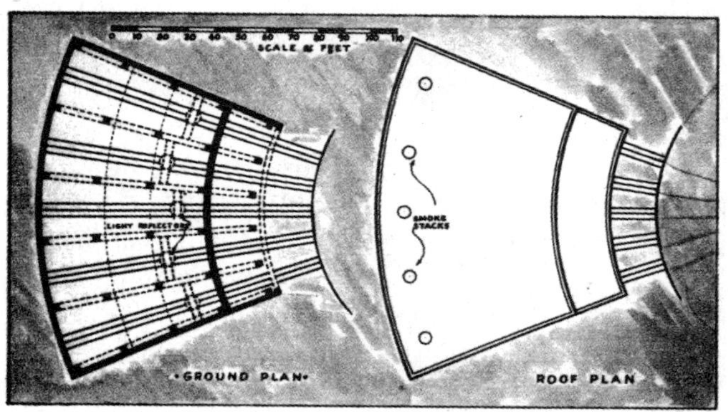

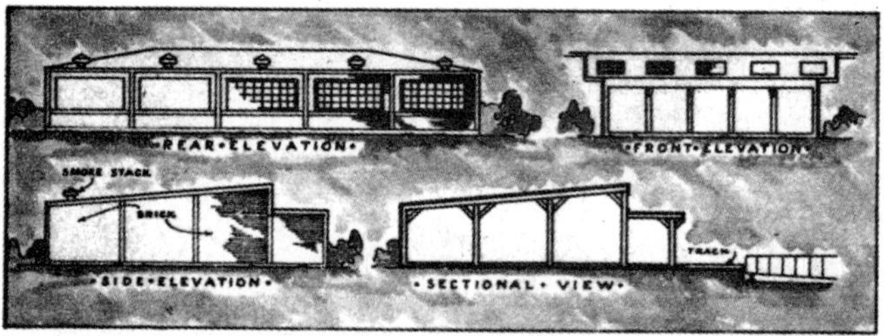

A MODEL ROUNDHOUSE

OF all miniature buildings that can be built for a model railroad, the roundhouse is best able to impart true railroading atmosphere for there is no industrial structure bearing even the remotest resemblance to it.

A roundhouse is used by a locomotive as its home. There it remains at all times when not in use. Hostlers in the roundhouse service locomotives brought in, make minor repairs and adjustments and maintain a head of steam in the boilers. In the roundhouse are tracks radiating from the turntable and between the tracks are working pits.

There are roundhouses of all sizes on real railroads. The model shown is one of the smallest, being able to accommodate only five engines. It will be found sufficiently large, however, for nearly all model systems. Where more stalls are wanted, they may be added by extending the width of the structure. The entire construction is explained in the photographs and diagrams.

The scale of feet printed with the ground plan at the left shows the size of the prototype from which this model was copied. All dimensions measured by this foot rule must necessarily be reduced to the scale of your miniature railroad, 1/48th the size for "O" gauge or 1/76th for "OO" gauge.

The floor is cut from plywood and the diagram illustrated is drawn on it with a pencil. The solid squares in the ground plan show the position of the pillars. Wherever one is shown, a hole is drilled into the plywood base. Through these holes the nails that hold the posts are inserted.

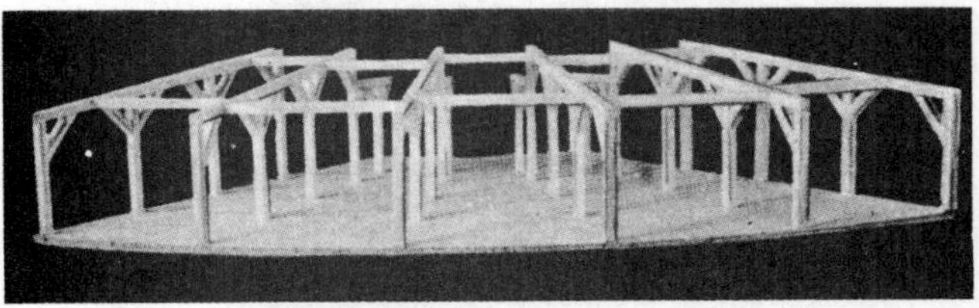

The posts are cut from square strip wood and the tops are beveled to fit the slanting roof. Nails and glue are used to hold the posts securely in place.

After the posts have been attached to the base, the roof beams are attached to the posts. Six beams are used on top of the six rows of posts from front to back. In addition, two rows of cross-beams are tacked and cemented in place. For further support, braces are attached at an angle between posts and beams as indicated in the photographs.

The strips at the top of the side walls extend over the roof. The diagram shows the small edging that goes around the top of the small roof. This is made of strips of cardboard and applied with cement.

Celluloid or cellophane is cut to fit the windows and strips of black paper are glued in place to form the framework.

The roof is cut to fit the inside the extended strips of the walls, and is flush with the outside of the side walls.

The insides of the roof are painted white to reflect the light. The outside walls are covered with brick paper, which is made by ruling writing paper and painting it with water color. Charcoal is used for shading the brick.

Several small sockets might be attached behind the posts inside the roundhouse for interior illumination. To illuminate the turntable in front of the roundhouse several lamp fixtures from floodlight towers are attached to the roof of the roundhouse, with connecting wires carried on the inside of the roof.

This roundhouse is designed for use with the turntable described elsewhere. It is very important that the radial lines of each wall or row of pillars be determined accurately from the center of the turntable.

LOCOMOTIVE TURNTABLE

THE turntable is a device used for changing the direction of a locomotive. The model illustrated on this page is a relatively simple design which can be used on the floor or on a flat table.

This turntable is built in two pieces—the turntable itself and the platform on which it revolves. The platform should be constructed first.

The two square sheets cut for the platform are six inches larger all around than the turntable is long and are identical. The center of the board is used as a guide and on one piece of plywood a circle is drawn with the diameter of the turntable.

Both sheets of plywood are tacked together temporarily and a hole is drilled in the center for the turntable shaft. After the hole is drilled, the sheets are separated but marked so they can be put together again with the same adjoining sides.

From tin or other sheet metal a piece about two inches square is cut and a hole is drilled in the center for the shaft. This is nailed in place directly over the hole in the baseboard. A means for electrical connections is provided by soldering to the metal plate a wire extending over the platform.

An old lamp shade, with a base the same diameter as the distance between the metal plates on the bottom of the turntable, is fastened to the lower piece of plywood, for the turntable to swing around on. The ring is placed on the base board with the bearing hole of the turntable in the exact center and a line is traced around it on the board.

Six or seven evenly spaced screws are put in flush with the top of the board around the circle. The wire ring is soldered to the screws. It is important to get this ring very close to the wood base so the tracks are the same height as an ordinary track.

The other wire for the electric connections is soldered to the ring and extended out to the edge of the base board.

The two sections of the platform are joined with wood screws and protruding ends are cut off with a hack saw and filed down even with the bottom.

The turntable consists of two sides and the floor. The floor is cut from two-ply plywood like that used for the platform. It is about a quarter of an inch wider on each side than the largest locomotive. A hole is drilled in the center for a good-sized nail

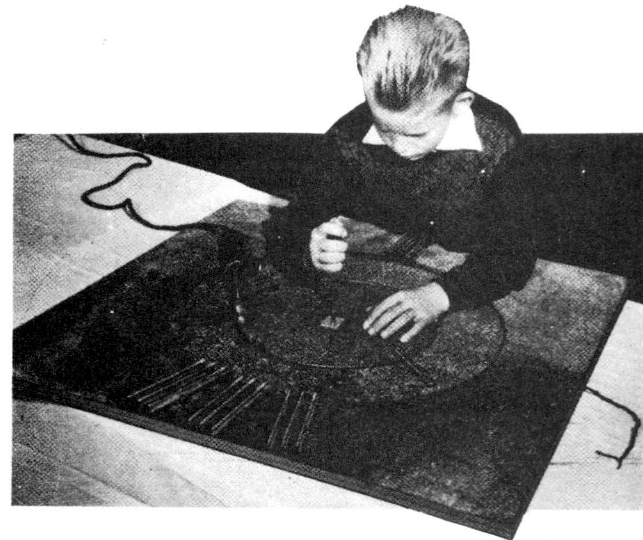

which acts as the shaft.

The two sides of the turntable are cut out and the upper ends are planed into curves and sandpapered smooth. The sides are nailed to the floor and a little glue or cement is added for strength.

Strips for the vertical divisions are cut from pieces of cardboard about one-sixteenth of an inch wide. To duplicate the plate girder, a piece of cardboard is cut about one-eighth of an inch wider than the sides and long enough to extend up one end, across the top and down the other end. It is bent to shape and cemented in place with a sixteenth of an inch overhang on each side of the girder.

The ties are removed from a couple of old pieces of straight track, and the rail is spiked to the turntable floor.

The third rail is soldered over the shaft. A square piece of tin, with a hole drilled in the center to admit the shaft, supports it. A small tension spring soldered to the bottom of the plate is adjusted so it makes a light contact with the plate in the center of the turntable pit.

For runners, two pieces of tin about one-and-a-half inches wide and slightly shorter than the width of the turnable are put in place on the bottom of the turntable with small brads. A wire from one of these tin plates is soldered to one of the running rails on top of the turntable.

The framework which supports the electric pole is made from two pieces of square pine and glued in place. The top horizontal pieces are wider and a small hole is drilled to receive the electric pole. Two diagonal braces are added to support this structure.

The two wires of the turntable are connected to a "live" track in some other part of the layout so that current flows into the turntable and the locomotives move on and off under their own power.

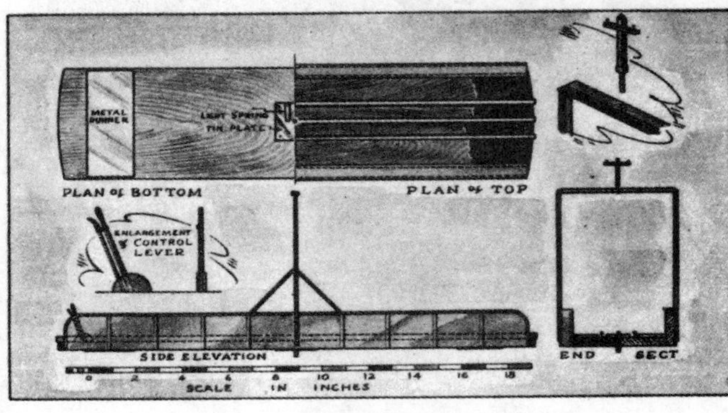

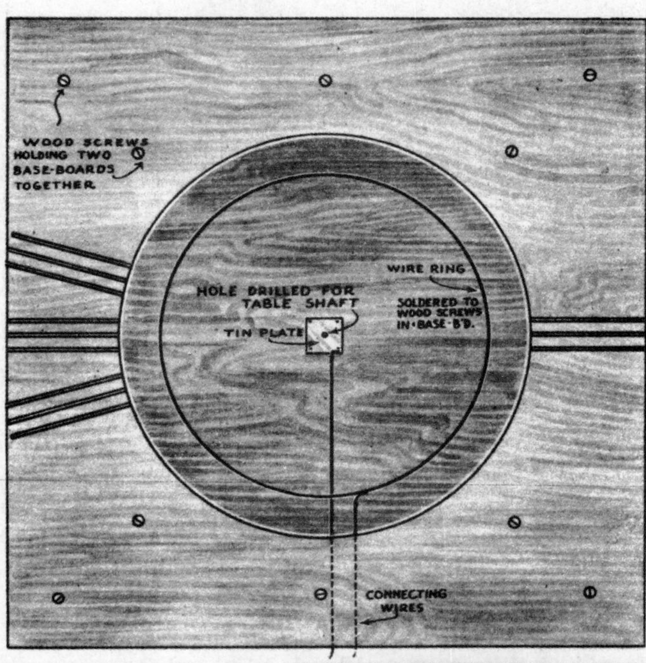

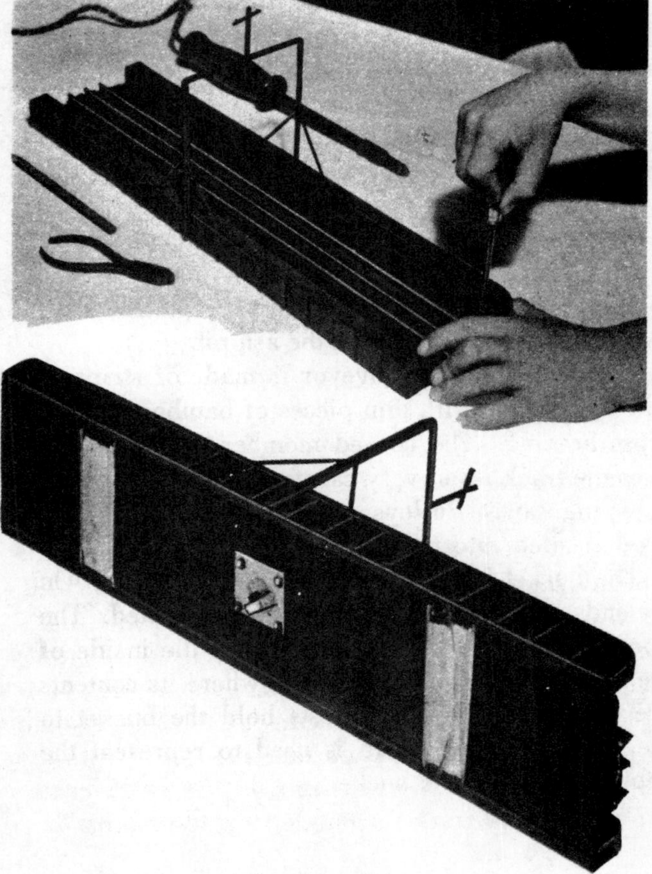

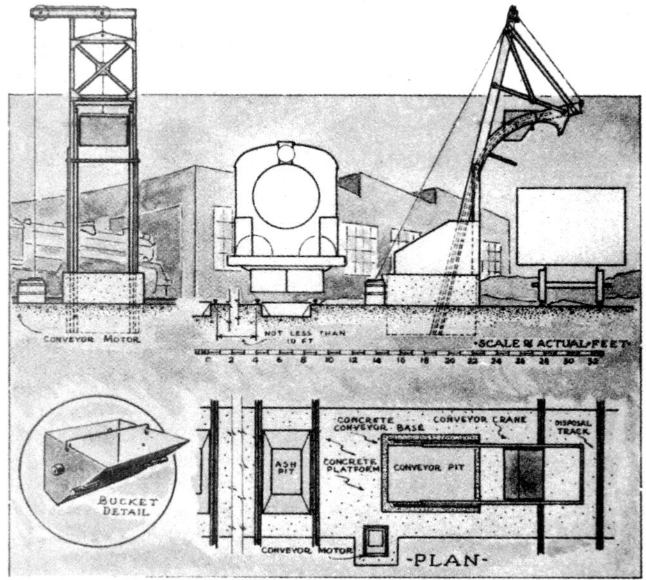

CINDER PIT AND CONVEYOR

A LOCOMOTIVE brought into the engine yards for servicing is wheeled over the ash pit. Its ashes are cleaned out and fall through openings in the track to the ash pit beneath. Once or twice each day the cinders in the pit are lifted out by a conveyor and loaded into a hopper car. The hopper car carries the cinders off to some location where they are used as fill.

The original of this cinder conveyor is a modern piece of railroad equipment and is of steel construction.

The first step in constructing this model is to select the base board. The track is fastened down on the board and the ash pit and platforms are built around it. A hole is cut in the platform between the track to represent the ash pit.

The frame of the conveyor is made of strips of soft white pine, with thin pieces of bamboo used as cross bracing. The curved member extending out over the track is cut very carefully out of pine with a coping saw. Pulleys are pieces of dowel with grooves filed into them.

The bucket itself is made out of cardboard. On the ends of the bucket tiny posts are cemented. The bucket runs along in two grooves on the inside of the frame and out over the track where its contents are dumped. The guide posts hold the bucket to the frame. Black thread is used to represent the cable attached to the bucket.

The foundation for the ash removal machine is built up so that there is a deep pit beneath. Alongside a real ash pit on its concrete platform is a hose for washing cinders out from under the engine.

A hose like this is made from a piece of wire covered with cloth.

The straight side vertical bars are cut from a piece of pine. These extend down into the pit and are cemented rigidly in place. The cross-piece on the top of the structure is put in place and two very thin strips of wood (bamboo is obtained from a model supplier for this purpose) are cemented on each side of the cross-bar to form the flanges of the I-beams. A flange is also cemented on each side as shown.

A pulley is made by filing grooves in a dowel and cutting between the grooves to make pulleys of the required thickness.

The cinder bucket is made from thin wood, cardboard or metal. It runs along in a groove inside the vertical beams and out over the car where its contents are dumped.

A heavy rug thread is used for hoisting the bucket and is inserted after painting. It runs through the pulleys and down the side of the machine to the electric motor.

Ashes are raised from pit, and dumped into waiting car.

MODEL GANTRY CRANE

A GANTRY crane is a common implement in modern railroading. It is used to hoist and transfer heavy objects. Sometimes it is used to shift these heavy objects from one freight car to another. It may also be employed on a team track to load or unload auto trucks. When equipped with a grab scoop or bucket, the gantry crane is used to lift and transfer bulk materials.

The crane photographed here is situated in a model engine terminal. It is used for scooping cinders out of a cinder pit and loading them into a gondola car to be hauled away and used as fill.

Some of the required materials which can be purchased for a few cents are a dowel, a tube of cement, some pieces of balsa wood. Some of the things that can be found around the house consist of an empty can, an old round pencil stub, a piece of bell wire, nine small nails from the lids of cigar boxes, and a handful of white sand. Work

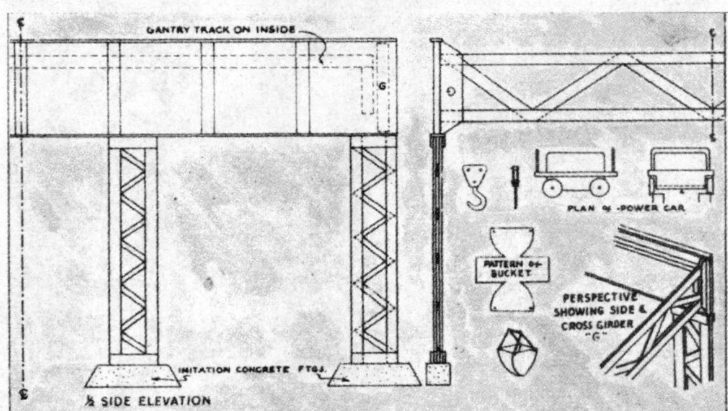

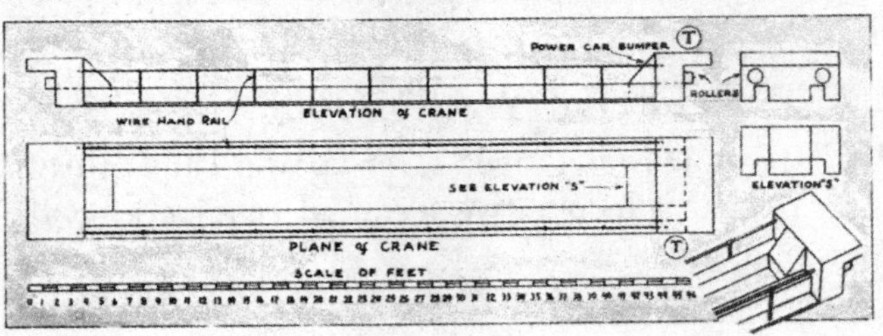

bench materials include a small piece of acid core solder, a small amount of flat black paint and white or gray paint. The only tools required are a single-edge razor blade, scissors for cutting tin, paint brush and alcohol soldering lamp.

The balsa can be purchased at any hobbycraft or model airplane store or in any toy department selling model airplanes.

Construction of the crane is very simple because most of the materials come in the proper thicknesses and widths. It is necessary to cut only the balsa to required lengths and cement is used in all cases to hold pieces of balsa together.

POWER HOUSE FOR WASHOUTS

THE numerous needs for power and steam around a locomotive terminal require a small power plant.

This one is typical of such houses to be found at small engine terminals and can be made in a couple of evenings.

The baseboard is cut from a plank and the walls are cut from stiff cardboard. Openings are cut into the walls for the windows. The walls are cemented and nailed to the baseboard and painted with a flat paint.

The window sash is cut from thin, stiff cardboard and cemented behind the window openings. The complicated-looking roof is made by following the cuts and bends shown in the photograph. Ventilators are cut out and slats are cemented in place. The roof is cemented to the sides.

Holes are cut in the roof for smoke stacks made from round sticks long enough to extend high above the roof. A whistle is made by wrapping electric tape around the upper part of a nail.

The large coal hopper is made of cardboard, cut as shown in the photograph. This unit is painted dull black and fastened to the house.

Locomotive boilers, as almost all model railroaders know, are filled with tubes through which heat from the fire box travels on its way to the smoke stack. These tubes change water into steam very quickly when clean, but a scale forms in the tubes which retards the desired quick steaming.

The scale must be periodically removed. Most locomotive terminals are equipped with a boiler washout system which is nothing but large tanks holding compound and hot water and small tanks acting as reservoirs of air pressure.

The washout system shown in the photograph is just behind the powerhouse and is located near the roundhouse where the hot compound is piped underground to the repair pits.

The tanks are made from mailing tubes with rounded wooden plugs inserted in each end.

The concrete saddles to support the tanks are made from boards cut and shaped as shown in the photograph. They are then glued firmly to the tanks. The three vertical air reservoirs are cut from a shade roller, rounded slightly on each end.

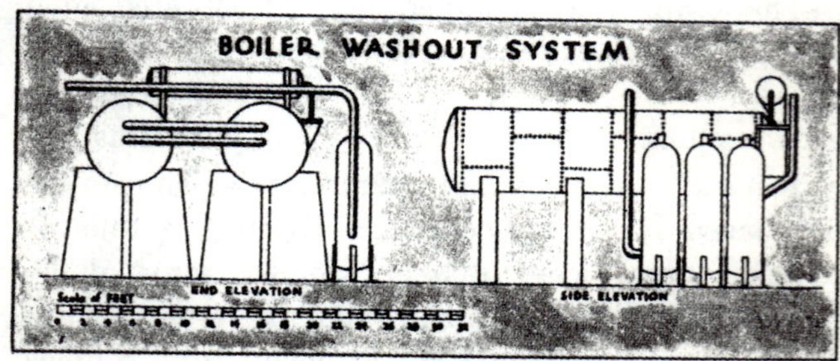

A bit of heavy wire is inserted in a hole at the top of each tank. The three tanks are then nailed upright to a small baseboard so that they stand about a half inch off the baseboard. Small strips of cardboard are cut, scored and cemented to the bottoms of the tanks so that they appear to be right-angle, band type legs.

All of the tanks are painted dull black. The saddles and baseboards are painted a yellowish grey to represent concrete. Heavy wires are used between the tanks and the roundhouse to represent high-pressure pipes.

LOCOMOTIVE WASH RACKS

WHEN a locomotive has completed its run, it is taken into the service yard and stopped over a wash rack where it is cleaned of all road dust and grime. To do this, a heavy mist of cleaning oil mixed with hot water is sprayed over the running gear, under heavy pressure, from a triple nozzle. Three lines of hose feed the nozzle. One of these hose lines contains oil, the second contains hot water and the third air under heavy pressure. The air pressure creates the mist.

Examination of the picture on this page will reveal the tripple nozzle gun and the three hoses in a holder on each side of the track.

These hoses and nozzles are made by bending common soft iron wire over the gratings and soldering them together at the ends. A heavier wire is inserted upright in the grating as shown, and over this the nozzles are rested. The nozzles are painted yellow to represent brass and the lines of hose are painted black, green and red.

The photograph and diagrams indicate the manner in which the gratings are built. The model wash rack in the photograph is large enough to handle a Hudson type locomotive.

The framework of each rack is made of square wooden sticks cemented and nailed together. Cardboard is fitted as a floor inside each frame and painted. Square match sticks are cut to fit and glued to the top of the cardboard.

A tank for containing the oil usually will be found close to the wash racks. The model tank is made out of a piece of shade roller, rounded at the ends. It is painted dull black, mounted on carved blocks of wood which are painted to represent concrete. A lean-to is built to protect the oil tank. The roof is made from a small piece of thin wood. The walls are painted cardboard. A square post is nailed into position to hold up the roof. The lean-to is painted a dull grey, streaked with black to indicate the dirt and grime that is inherent in all the locomotive yards.

Sand is poured through pipe into locomotive sand dome.

LOCOMOTIVE SAND TOWER

WHEN track is slippery, locomotive wheels spin and fail to grip the rails. When wheels spin in this way it becomes difficult for the engineer to drive his locomotive forward and to stop it.

The usual way for a real engineer to overcome the danger of slippery rails is to sprinkle sand on them. A supply of free-running sand is stored in one of the domes seen on the tops of all locomotive boilers. The heat at this point keeps it dry, making it able to flow through pipes to the rails.

The sand domes on locomotives are examined after each trip and fresh sand is added to replace that which may have been used.

There are many different devices used to clean, dry and raise the sand to an elevation so that it will run by gravity into the dome. The prototype of the little sand house, yard and tower in the photograph is in actual use on one of the big railroads.

The tower is square. Its construction is started with the four square sticks which support the elevated bin. These are re-inforced with cross bracing.

Two walls are cut out and two corner posts cemented to each so that the posts will be on the outside. Next the block for the floor is cut out and the corners notched for the posts. This is cemented between the two walls. A block of the same size for the top is cemented between the two walls just below the point where the eaves of the roof will come. The two remaining side walls are then cemented between the other walls and to the two blocks.

The lower half of the bin has the planking on the outside of the posts. Squares of cardboard are cemented around the four sides and on the outside of the posts.

The horizontal and diagonal bracing is made of square sticks cut and cemented in position.

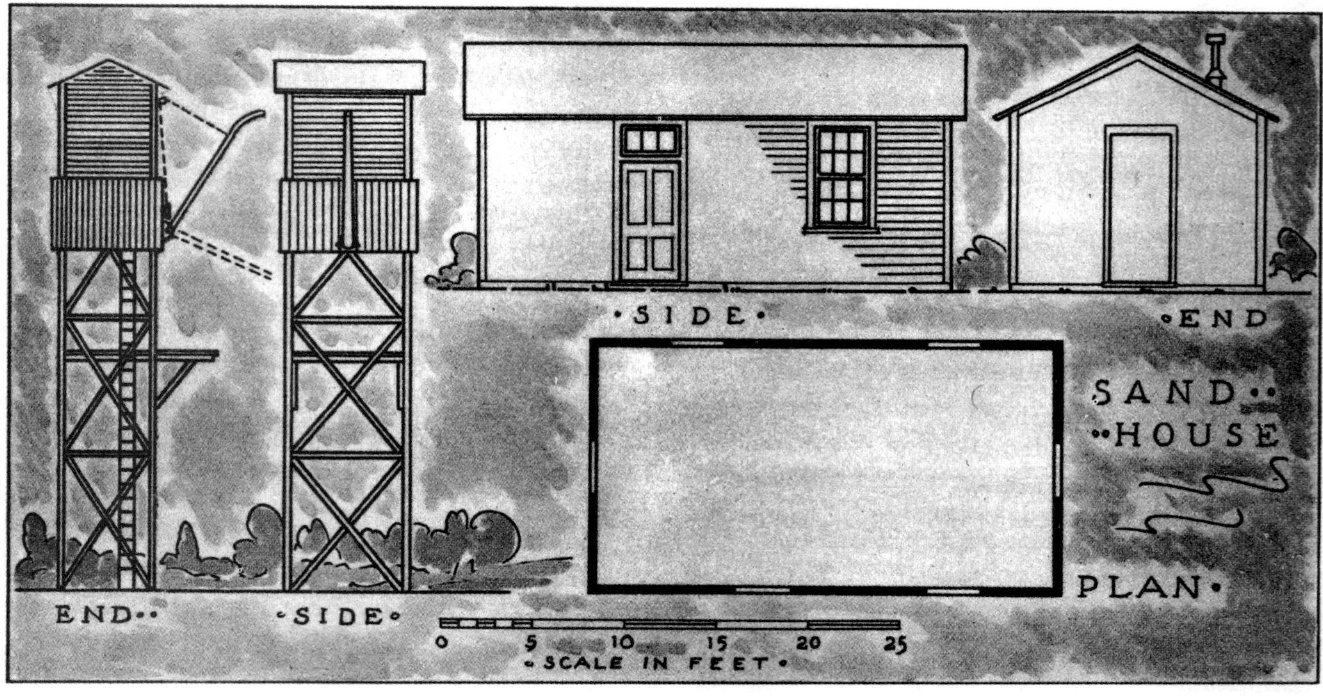

Storage bin for dry sand is mounted on the drying house.

ANOTHER SAND HOUSE PLAN

THE sand house illustrated on this page, although essentially the same as the one previously described, is easier and cheaper to make and requires less space. The economy in space is obtained by placement of the elevated bin on the roof of the drying room.

A piece of plywood or heavy cardboard is used as the base. The solid walls of the wet-sand bin, the walls and roof of the drying room and of the elevated storage bin all are made of heavy cardboard which is cemented over a framework of small square sticks.

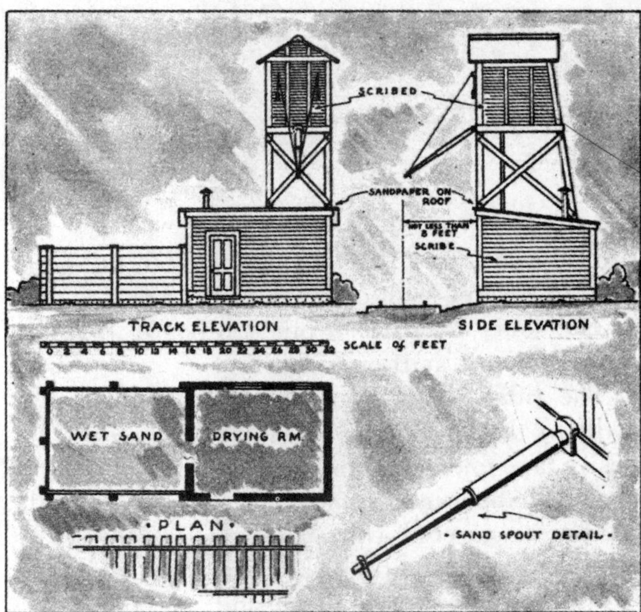

The doors are made of cardboard and cemented into place. To get the paneled effect, strips of thin bristol board are used to form the raised portions of the door. The head of a pin is used for the door knob. The windows are cut from heavy cellophane or celluloid. The muntins or cross-bars of the window sashes are painted the same color as the trim. The trim is cut from bristol board.

In assembling the elevated storage bin, square wood sticks are used as corner supports inside the walls. These same sticks extend through the bottom to form the posts of the supporting timber work.

Looking down into the wet sand yard connected to drying house.

Particular pains are taken to cut them exactly right so that the storage bin is set straight and squarely on the roof of the building below. Ample cement is used to hold it in place and it is allowed to dry thoroughly before the cross bracing of the timber and other details are applied. The cross bracing is cut from illustration board. A definite sharp edge is made with a sharp, single-edged razor blade.

The sand spout is shown in detail. It is made from a lolly-pop stick. A piece of metal tubing is slipped over the stick and it is held in place with a drop of cement on the inside of the tube. A hole is drilled in the one end of the tube and a pin is inserted to act as a hinge for the spout.

LOCOMOTIVE REPAIR SHOPS

RAILROAD ENGINES, like all other intricate machines, need frequent routine maintenance service. Occasionally worn parts must be replaced and moving members re-aligned or adjusted. As one example, brake shoes wear out and must be replaced. The complete brake system must be inspected and adjusted.

Work of this kind is done usually in a building erected close to one of the railroad's engine terminals. Real locomotive and car shops are long enough to contain two or three locomotives on a track and have three or four tracks, but they vary in size according to the amount of work that is expected.

The photograph shows a model shop which can be started and finished in the same evening.

Two end boards are cut to shape out of laminated wood. They are then connected by means of long, square sticks. In all, nine of these sticks are used, one along the base of each side wall and one at each corner of the wall and roof.

For a strong, rigid structure these long supporting sticks are reinforced, at the center of the building, by cross braces.

The long walls and roof of the building are made of heavy cardboard with windows carefully cut out with a razor blade. Walls and roof are then cemented and tacked to the framework. For improved appearance, the wooden ends of the building are covered with cardboard cut to fit.

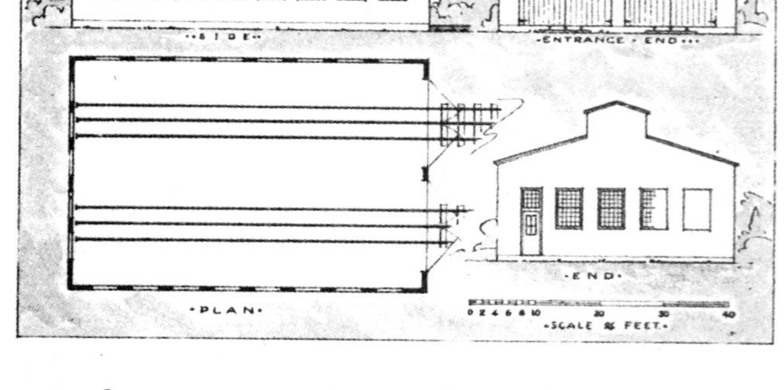

The doors are parts of this cardboard which are scored to open as if on hinges.

The ridge of the roof and corners formed by walls of the building are covered by strips of adhesive tape to obtain a more finished job.

All of the windows may be glazed with cellophane, or covered with hardware mesh wire as shown in the photograph.

Doors are painted black, inside and out. Walls may be any dull, dark color. A gravel roof is simulated by applying large sheets of sand paper.

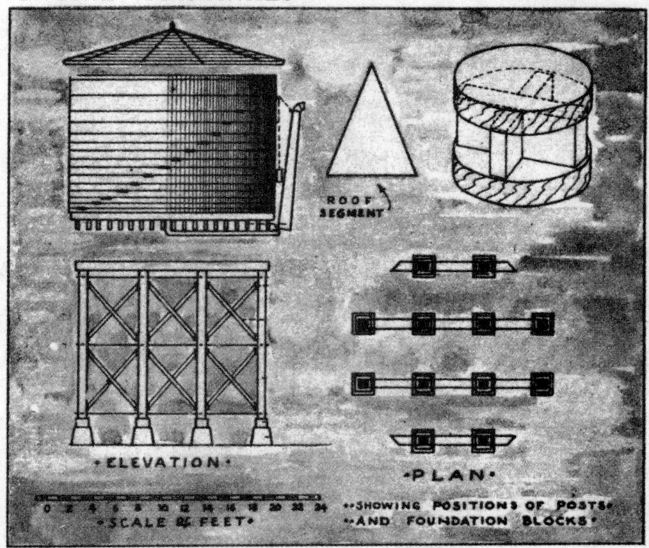

LOCOMOTIVE WATER TANK

OF all the structures that can be reproduced for a model road, an accurate, well-built, correctly placed locomotive water tank will reward the builder with the greatest satisfaction.

The photograph on this page shows a scale model of a typical railroad tank having a water capacity of about 30,000 gallons.

The unusual feature of this reproduction is the wall of the tank which is comprised of numerous tiny staves cemented to two round drums.

The drums are cut in a perfect circle, out of one-inch soft pine, by the use of scroll saw. The edges of the drums are brought to a smooth finish with files and sandpaper and then are attached to spacer blocks, as shown in the diagram.

Thin strips of wood to be used as staves are purchased from a model airpline supply store. They are cut to the proper length and attached with several coats of cement.

After the staves are all in place and the cement has dried, the wire hoops are drawn firmly around the tank.

Ends of the wires are twisted together with a pair of pliers.

The wires are spaced closely at the bottom of the tank, with the distance gradually widening toward the top.

The roof of the tank is made by cutting eight segments of cardboard.

These are cemented to a small supporting block in the center of the tank, as well as to rim of the wall.

Particular care is taken in construction of the supports for the tank. The upright posts and cross beams are square lumber. The posts rest on square blocks which have a concrete foundation. The foundation blocks are cut to shape out of wood and painted grey to represent concrete. The rest of the structure is painted in a brownish black with burnt sienna used to impart a weathered appearance.

Thirty-thousand gallons of water are held by its prototype.

SUPERINTENDENT'S OFFICE

A LOCOMOTIVE service yard is a busy place. Its headquarters are in the yard superintendent's office where the engineers and firemen report and where mechanics and hostlers obtain orders.

A small-size yard superintendent's office is illustrated on this page.

It would be appropriate for a yard handling eight or ten locomotives a day.

All four walls are one single piece of cardboard, scored and folded at the corners and with windows and doors cut out.

The window sash is made from thin but stiff cardboard.

Cellophane is cemented behind the window sash to represent glass.

At the top of each window and behind the cellophane small separators are attached.

On these separators the window shades are hung.

The window shades are bits of green or yellow blotting paper.

Small blocks of wood are placed under the building to represent pedestal foundations. The blocks are painted brick red and mortar lines are drawn with a white pencil.

The roof is a single piece of cardboard scored and folded at the center. It is painted a dark flat gray and striped with black ink to look like tar-paper roofing.

A block of wood serves as the brick chimney. It is cut to the proper size, painted, grooved to fit the incline of the roof and glued in place. The steps and platform are made from blocks of wood or built up with thin sticks and cardboard.

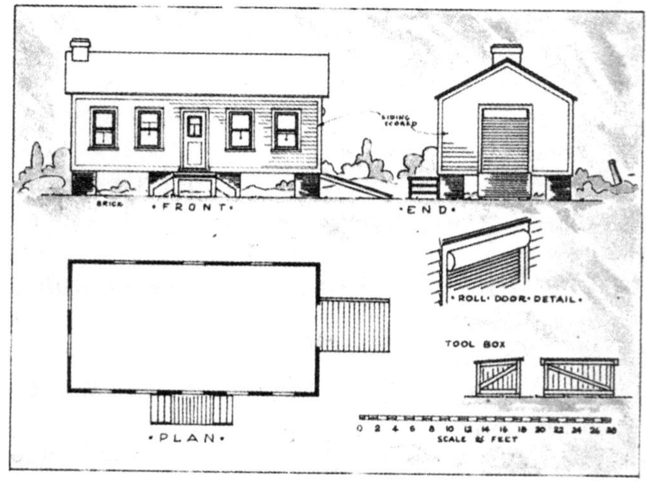

BLACKSMITH'S FORGE

ONE building in a locomotive terminal or repair yard which doesn't appear to follow any predetermined pattern is the blacksmith shop or forge. It is one of the most important departments of the service yard, for, in larger establishments, the giant driving wheels of the locomotive must be shrunken on or off, giant cylinder block castings must be welded and the side frames of trucks must be rebuilt. The smaller work, such as the forming of hand rails, pilot beams, brake rods and coil springs, is done in a small shop like the one pictured on this page.

The walls of the shop are made from a single piece of heavy cardboard. Doors are not cut out but are scored in the cardboard and bent open. Small strips of thin cardboard are pasted to the doors to represent battens and braces. The walls are cardboard, reinforced by strips of wood.

The base of the forge is a block of wood painted to resemble brickwork. The chimney is cardboard pasted over a long block of wood and also painted.

The spreading base of the chimney is made from two blocks of wood cut in the shape of steps. The hood is carved from a block of wood or shaped out of cardboard. It is painted black. Chimney, hood and forge are assembled with cement. On the forge, finely ground coke or slate is mixed with chips of orange and amber to resemble a glowing fire.

The tub, electric blower and benches are details which are simple to build or may be eliminated.

The roof is a piece of heavy cardboard, scored at the center, and with wide shed extensions on each side held up by square corner posts.

Old wheels and spare parts from a box of odds and ends are scattered around the shop.

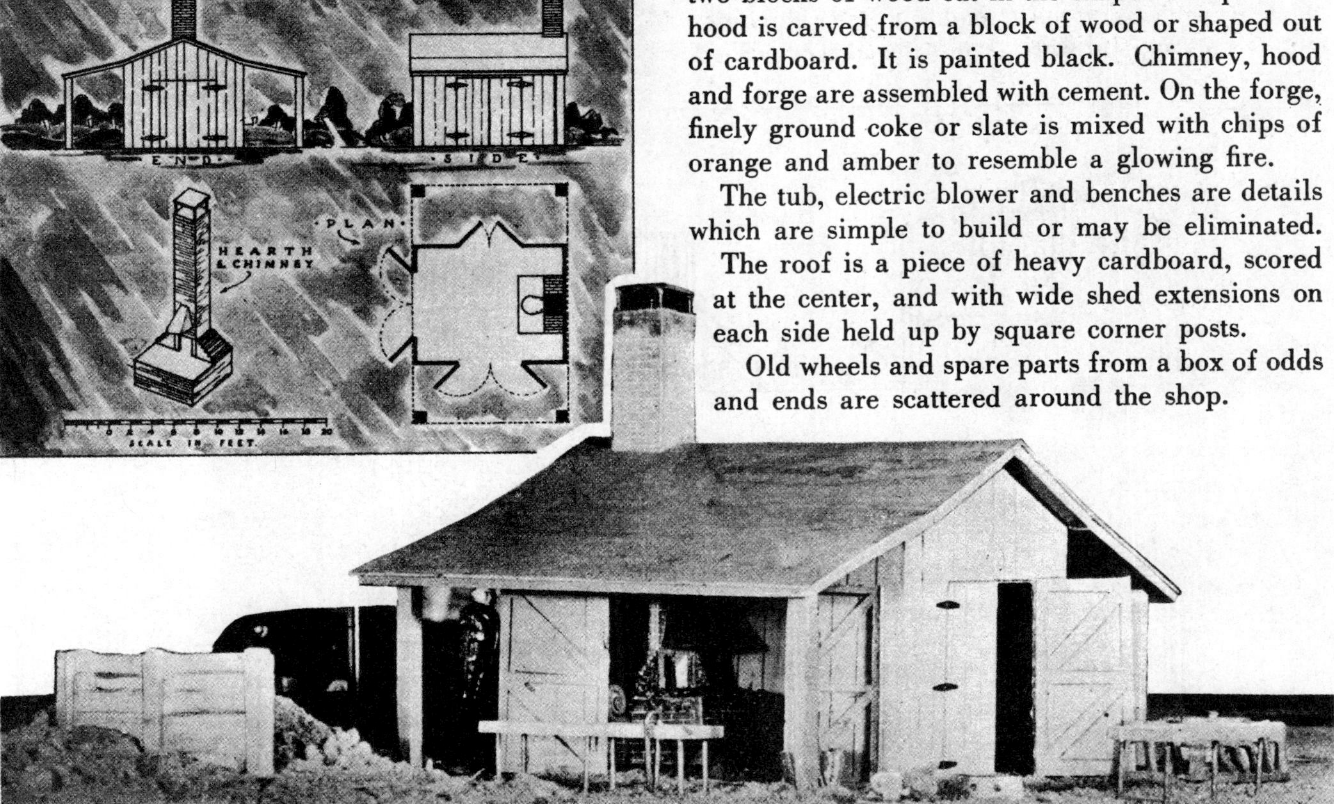

FREIGHT CAR REPAIR SHOPS

CARS in need of small repairs are consigned to the "rip track." This is a track or group of tracks where cars are repaired and restored to service. It may be only a single spur track where a few cars are shunted for minor repairs, or it may be an elaborate collection of specialized buildings where cars are rebuilt completely, from the wheels up.

Freight car repair shops are not a part of a locomotive roundhouse group, but are kindred and should be situated on a model railroad somewhere in the same general vicinity.

The track running through the building in the photograph carries a car along from place to place much the same as on the assembling line of an automobile factory, and work progresses as it is pushed along. Repairs to running gears are made outside or at a wheel repair pit.

The walls and ends of the building are cut out of thick cardboard, in the ornamental shape indicated in the photograph. The trim, battens and ventilator slats are pieces of thin cardboard cemented in position.

The posts are square sticks that are cemented and tacked into position. Strips of light wood are used inside the ends and walls to stiffen and reinforce the structure. The cardboard roof also helps to make the building more rigid if it is cemented and tacked to the wooden framework.

The suspended platform or scaffold on the inside of the shop is used by workmen repairing the walls or roofs of freight cars. It is made from strips of cigar box wood and held up by stiff wires which are painted black.

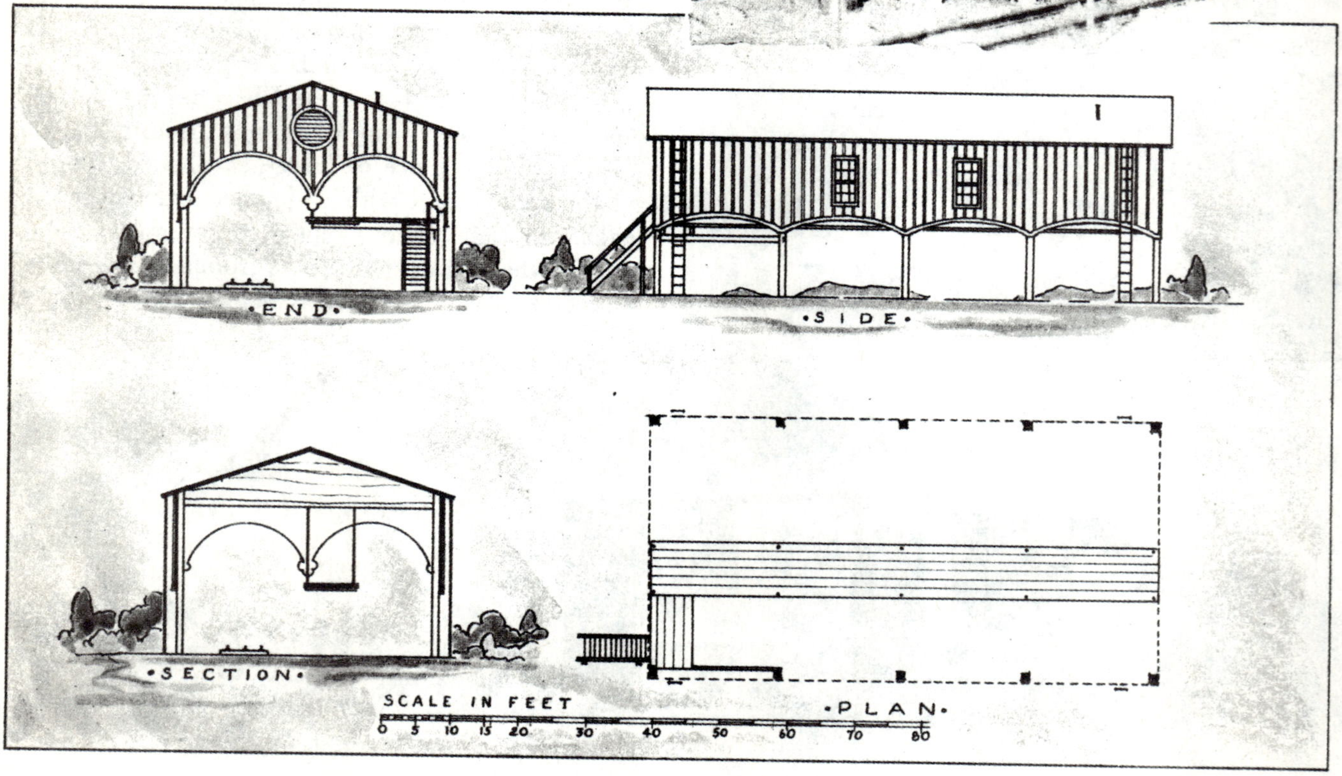

•END• •SIDE•

•SECTION• •PLAN•

SCALE IN FEET

0 5 10 15 20 30 40 50 60 70 80

WHEEL PIT AND LATHE

IN AN extensive yard where, in addition to the routine servicing of locomotives, minor car and engine repairs are also made, one of the most interesting little groups of buildings is the wheel repair pit and lathe.

The photograph shows a repair pit with shelter buildings, storage tracks, a wheel lathe where new treads are ground, a portable welding unit for broken springs, bolsters, truck sides, etc.

The main building is made from cardboard with square posts and framing. The roof is cut from cardboard and rafters are glued to the under side.

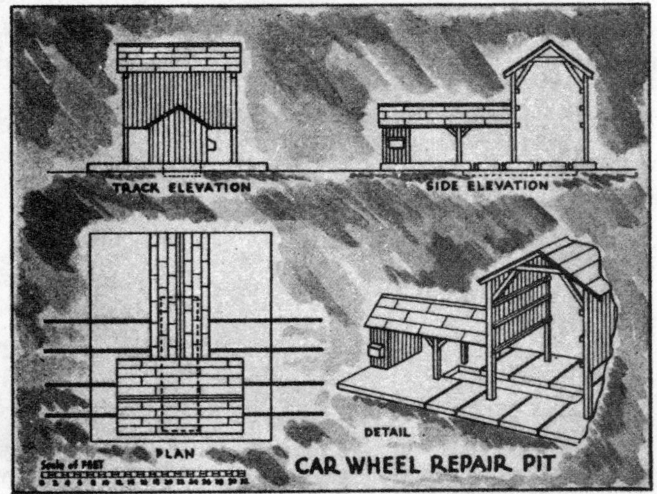

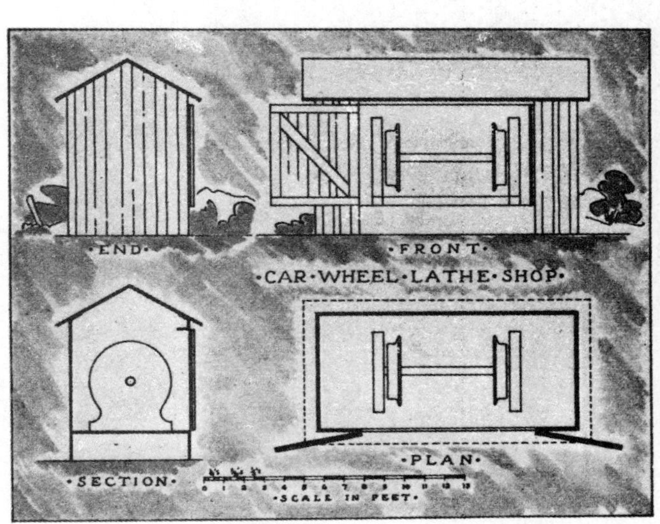

Blocks of wood are fashioned to fit beneath the roof and to the sides of the walls so that the building may be firmly cemented together. The diagonal bracing shown in the photograph is made from sticks cemented into place.

The lathe shop is a simple structure with cardboard walls and roof and with ends cut out of half-inch lumber.

The lathe inside the shop consists of head and tail stocks which are whittled out of blocks of wood or cut to shape with a coping saw. A hole is drilled into the center of the head and tail stocks to receive the axle. The bottom of the lathe is a square piece of wood to which the blocks are nailed.

REAL ESTATE IMPROVEMENTS

CHAPTER EIGHTEEN

THE breath of life is blown into a miniature railroad project when it acquires evidence of the communities that it serves, when factories are erected alongside track spurs, when stores surround the main terminal and when houses, buildings, farms and highways are used to eliminate the monotony of a plain countryside.

On the pages which follow are photographs and plans for the reproduction of a number of typical structures. Most of them may be made with household tools, out of cardboard, small sticks of wood, cement, brads and paint.

If the initial train outfit consists of freight cars, an individual industrial building may be erected to symbolize the service performed by each car. For the cattle car, both ends of the train trip are represented in the farm from which the cattle are shipped, and in the stockyard pens or corrals of the slaughter house where cattle are unloaded. For the coal or hopper car, there is the coal mine and tipple built on the side of a hill. For the lumber car, there is the retail lumber yard. For the tank car a representation of the entire oil industry can be included in a single railroad layout.

By following instructions given for making an oil derrick, a whole oil field of many wells can be reproduced and will add color and interest to some otherwise drab hillside in the layout. From the wells, crude oil often is shipped to refineries in oil tank cars. A refinery in a miniature railroad system always wins admiration and praise from everyone who sees it. The refinery is an extensive, impressive collection of oddly shaped tanks and queer buildings which are connected by a web of pipes; yet the tanks and each one of the buildings are simple to make, a twelve-year-old boy being able to reproduce the whole group without difficulty. From the refinery, gasoline, oil and other petroleum products are shipped to wholesalers' establishments, known as bulk oil depots. Here again tank cars are called upon for shipping, the bulk oil depot being situated on a track siding for convenient unloading of tank cars that arrive from the refinery. The last phase in the distribution of petroleum products is represented by the corner service station. The service station suggested on a following page may be situated on a city building lot or, with slight changes to the curbing, may be used appropriately on a country highway.

Coal, oil, lumber, meat—they are the fundamental industries—the big four that account for millions of tons of freight on railroads. They likewise are the four cars which appear most frequently in miniature train outfits. With each car symbolized by miniature loading and unloading points, the operation of the model railroad actually becomes functional. The services of a real road are then re-enacted in miniature. Empty cars are spotted on industrial sidings and loaded cars are picked up, taken to the classification yards, made up into new trains and hauled to their proper destinations. The model road comes alive with activity and realism. It looks the part and the operator of the system is able to make it act the part, as well.

All of the instructions given on the following pages are for full-scale, three-dimensional reproductions. This type of building is required on tables and benches which can be viewed for all sides, as distinguished from the diorama which is built against the wall. The scales included in each drawing give dimensions of real buildings and must be reduced to agree with the scale of the railroad equipment being used; 1/48th size for "O" gauge, 1/76th for "OO".

COAL MINE AND TIPPLE

IT is necessary to have a hill or mountain before building a mine head of this kind. For this reason a suitable location in the layout should be found for the hill before the mine is started.

The list of necessary materials consists of two sheets of white poster board, corrugated board, cellophane, cardboard, sandpaper, square strips of wood, glue, poultry mesh wire and cement.

Vertical supports for framework of the building are cut from wood stock, rear ones and those supporting the chute being of different lengths.

Vertical and horizontal beams are cemented and nailed together. Diagonal braces are cut out of poster board and cemented in place. The bases are applied to the bottom of each post. After the sides are made, the structure is assembled.

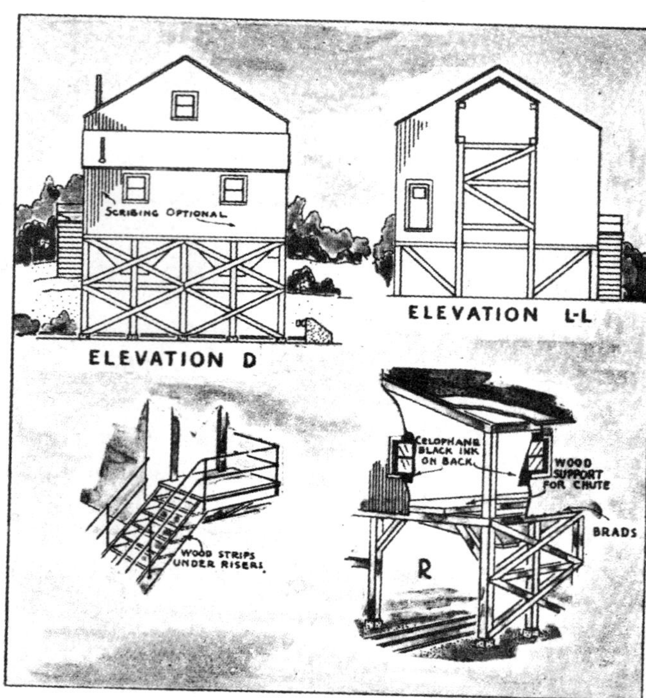

Sides and ends are cut out of poster board and vertical planking is indicated with pencil marks.

Pieces of poster board used for the gabled roof is scored with a dull instrument so that it will fold easily. Sandpaper is cemented to the roof.

The sides of the conveyor house are cut out of corrugated board, glued together and attached to the beams and supports with brads.

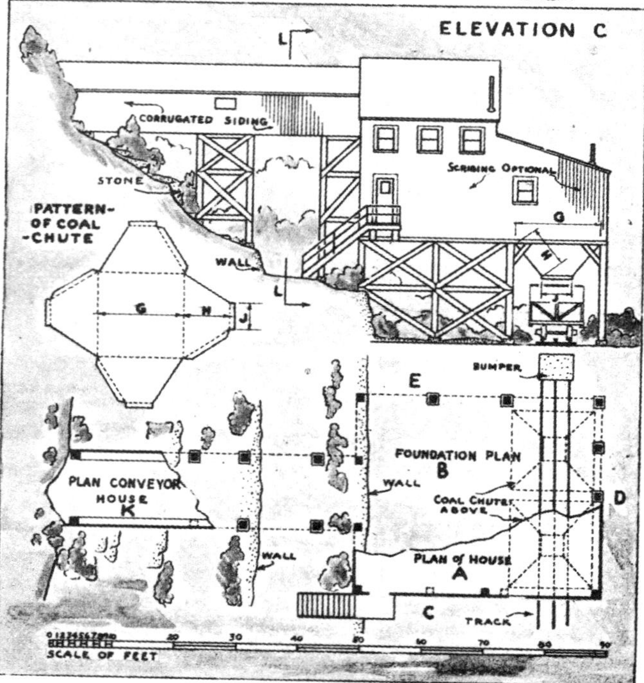

LIVESTOCK CORRALS

THE general features of all corrals used for livestock are similar but seldom are two corrals exactly alike. There are small, meanly-built enclosures found alongside track on private ranch property in the cattle country, some of them made of quartered logs and others being poles of young pine cutting. On prosperous ranches and at thriving cattle-collecting centers, trim, neatly-built, whitewashed corrals may be seen. In large stock yards, such as at Chicago, Omaha, Kansas City, Fort Worth, stock pens are made of wide and heavy planks which are bolted to sturdy, square posts.

A model railroad may include both the corral for cattle which is waiting to be shipped to market, and the stockyard pens into which cattle are driven from the stock cars. The model shown here is of the latter type, with accompanying barns, runways, ramps and a water tank for fire protection as well as to keep water troughs in every corral full, fresh and inviting.

The base of the yards is a piece of ply-wood. Planks are strips of cardboard which are cemented to square sticks used as posts. The assemblage is painted the color of weathered boards. The plan shows where the stock yard might be located on a single track siding with cleated ramps leading from a raised platform to the pens.

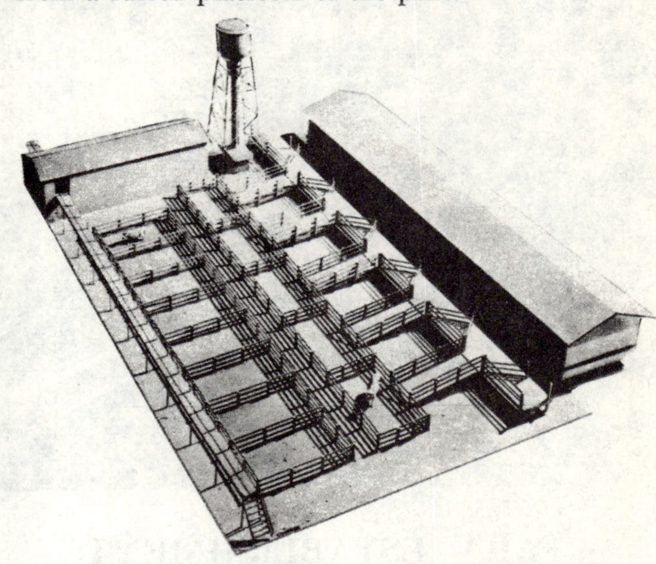

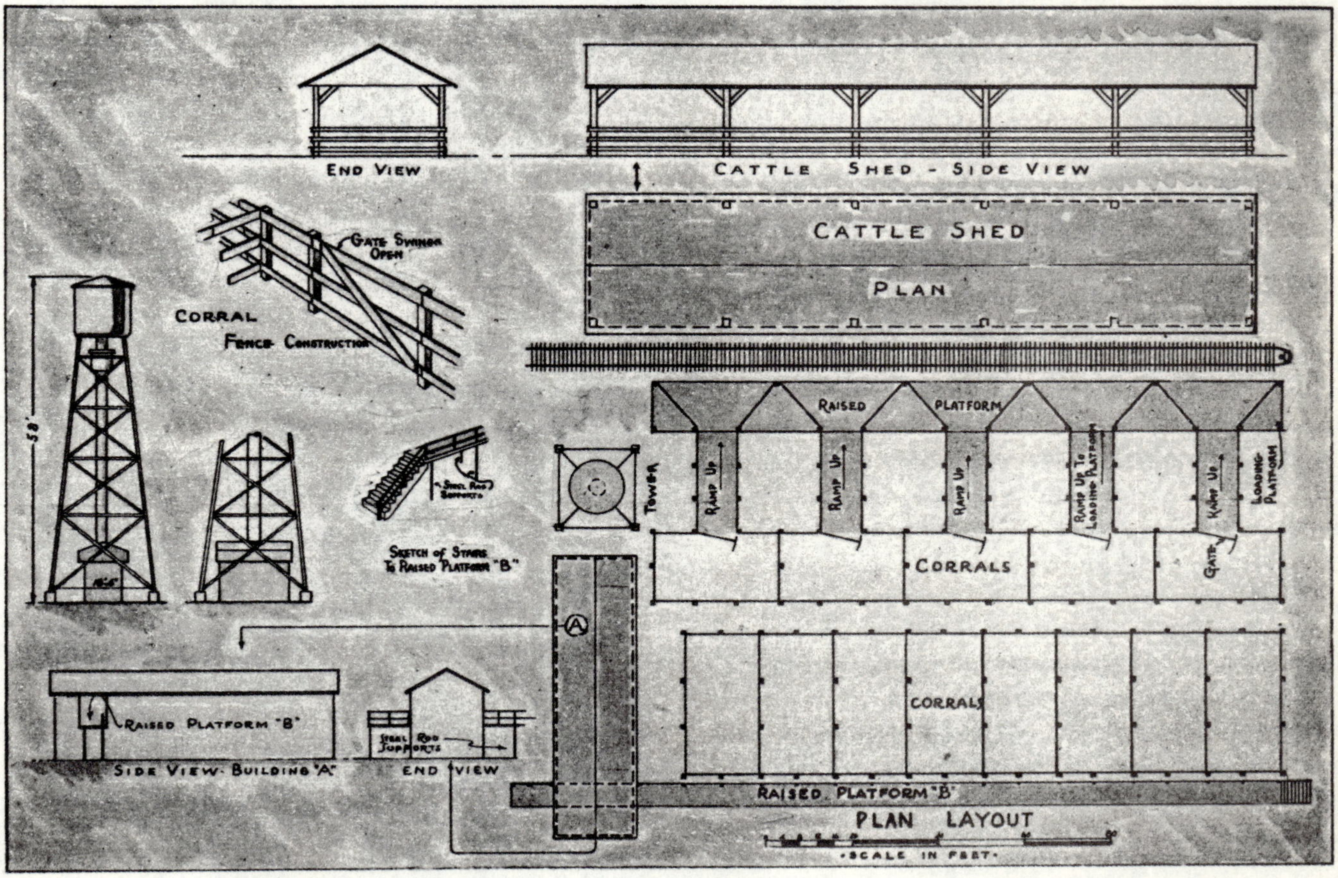

END VIEW
CATTLE SHED - SIDE VIEW
CATTLE SHED
PLAN
GATE SWINGS OPEN
CORRAL
FENCE CONSTRUCTION
58'
TOWER
RAISED PLATFORM
RAMP UP
RAMP UP TO LOADING PLATFORM
LOADING PLATFORM
GATE
CORRALS
SKETCH OF STAIRS TO RAISED PLATFORM "B"
STEEL ROD SUPPORTS
A
RAISED PLATFORM "B"
SIDE VIEW - BUILDING "A"
END VIEW
CORRALS
RAISED PLATFORM "B"
PLAN LAYOUT
SCALE IN FEET

A FARM ESTABLISHMENT

FARM houses and barns are always an important part of any broad model railroad scene. Some farms may be large, impressive and prosperous establishments like the one pictured here while other models may consist of a modest house, a small barn or two and a few acres of ground.

The farm in the picture is about as complete as any model should be, yet its construction is not a difficult task.

The house is a one-floor plan of semi-modern style with bath, kitchen, living room and two bedrooms. There is a stairway to the attic which is semi-finished for sleeping quarters when additional hired help is taken on during the harvesting season. Paneled doors are made with two or three thicknesses of bristol board. All of the windows have real curtains and blinds.

The house is made out of cardboard, with one piece used for two walls, being scored and folded at the corners. A framework of quarter-inch wooden sticks is cemented to the insides of the cardboard to make the structure rigid and sturdy. Cardboard is used also for the roof, and is scribed to represent a shingled roof. The chimney is a block of wood with one end cut at an angle to match the slope of the roof, and cemented in place. The porch roof is a piece of cardboard reinforced on the inside by strips of wood. It is glued to the wall and supported by square wooden posts which are painted white.

The farmhouse in the photograph was covered with brick paper but a brick or fieldstone finish might also be obtained by painting as described for the construction of the drug store and the model

Silo attached to the barn, and an actual working windmill.

church.

Around the farmhouse lot and down the side of the country road is a fence that is made by cementing long strips of cardboard to square, upright posts which first are tacked into the plywood base on which the entire farm establishment is built. The fences are painted in a dirty, weather-beaten grey.

Finely shredded peat moss is glued to the base all around the group of buildings in irregular hills. It is painted in various shades of green and brown.

The silo is a 3-inch mailing tube, strengthened by correctly spaced bands of wire. On the top of it is a lightning rod. A granary, not far away, has an elevator for hoisting and distributing grain.

It has doors on both ends making it a through drive and is completely finished inside, with walls, bins, etc. The building is made of cardboard.

Moonlight, accomplished by circular cutout in the backdrop.

The shape of the barn is typical of the Mid-West. All doors are suspended on tiny wire hangers. The rollers for the doors are carved out of wood so that the doors slide open.

The pig pen, or single row farrowing house, has four stalls with a skylight over each. Pigs wallowing in the mud are moulded out of clay. A barbed wire fence parallels the track.

The background is chalked on brown wrapping paper.

The windmill is made from the ribs of an umbrella. Small sticks and black thread form the bracing. Quarter-inch mesh wire painted black forms the ladder.

The windmill spins and the tail turns on a rod or wire.

The chicken run is a fine hair net glued to a small wooden framework. The woman is a lead cast figure. Chickens are made by drawing outlines on bristol board, glueing little tufts of cotton to each side and then painting in wings, bills, eyes and tail feathers.

The hay rake is made with toy cannon wheels. Evenly spaced holes are drilled in the strip of wood between wheels and short pieces of wire are inserted to make it look like a rake. The tongue seat and bracing is of wood and cardboard glued together. The stick for raising the rake after a load is gathered is a hairpin.

House, barn and all out-buildings are made of cardboard cemented to wooden frames. Brick paper purchased at a model supply store is used on the dwelling. Other buildings are painted and lined to indicate planking. Battens, angle stiffeners and frames are strips of cardboard.

Hay hangs out of the doors of the model barn's loft.

Complete panoramic view of the railside Avalon Farm with the fields at the left being painted on the backdrop.

OIL FIELD DERRICKS

AN OIL field in miniature is built very easily. The oil well itself is only a hole in the ground. The derrick, however, is extremely picturesque. An oil derrick is used only during the drilling and casing operations. The machinery located in the sheds near the base of the derrick is used in the drilling and casing operation, too, but in some instances it is used to pump the well if it is not free-flowing.

In the cable tool drilling method the string of drilling tools, about 40 feet long and weighing 4000 to 6000 pounds, is suspended by a wire cable from the end of the walking beam. The walking beam is made to rock by the crank on the opposite end and as it rocks the drilling tools rise and fall, drilling deeper and deeper.

The cable clamp is adjustable and more of the drill line allowed to go into the well as it deepens.

A derrick of the wooden type is made of square sticks for the legs and thin strips of wood glued in place for the bracing. A ladder runs from the ground to the top of the derrick. The bull wheel is usually mounted between two of the derrick legs. Between the two wheels is a drum for winding up the drill line.

Oil derricks make this look like a part of Oklahoma.

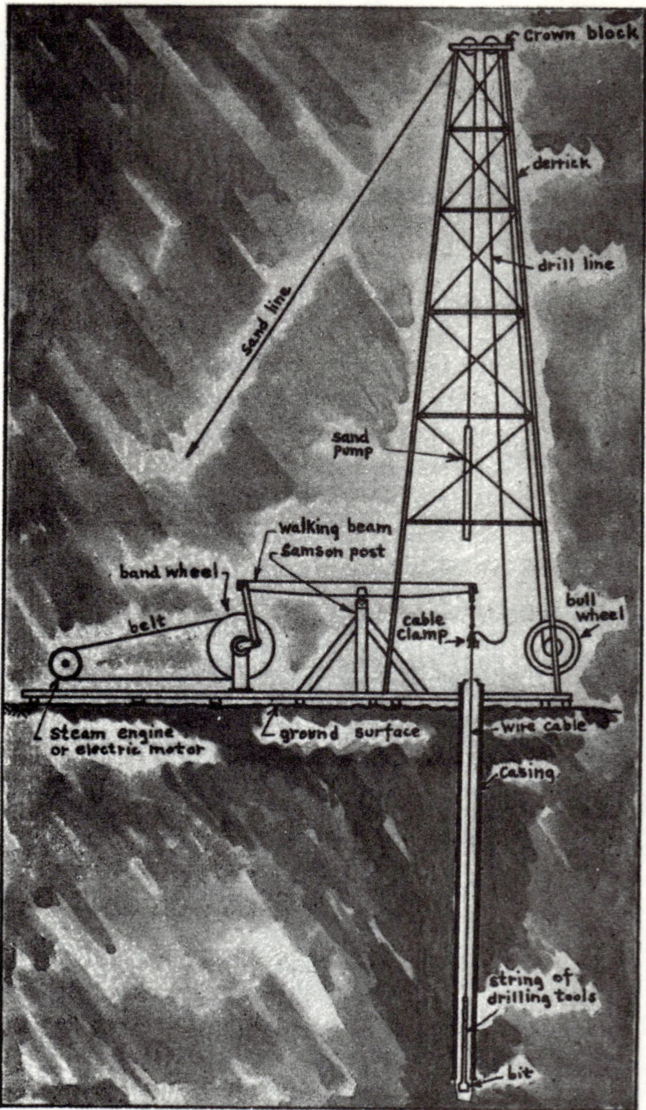

The walking beam and Samson post are fashioned of wood.

In case the well produces a mixture of gas and oil it is conducted through pipes from the top of the well to separator or gas trap, in which the gas containing gasoline vapor separates, then passes through gas pipes to an absorption plant. The oil is then conducted to storage tanks for measurement.

Several derricks, tanks, tool buildings, storage racks for pipe, etc., are needed to complete a comprehensive model oil field.

OIL REFINERY

AN oil refinery is a group of building and tanks that are very impressive in miniature because they appear complicated when, actually, they are so simple that any boy can put them together.

First to build is the base on which the refinery is erected. This is either a platform made from scrap material or a large sheet of plywood. The platform is painted dull gray and sprinkled with sand or sawdust while it is still wet.

The refinery is more easily built when sections are completed and cemented in place, one at a time. The topping unit is the name of the section consisting of five towers with a heater in front of each, at the extreme left in the photograph. The base is of wood. The steps and walks along the top are made of wood or cardboard and applied.

The heater platform is fastened next to adjoining platforms. The overhang on the top is a piece of cardboard cemented on. The units (half round units in front of each fractionating tower) are made of a piece of wood cut in half to form a circle and nailed in place. They can also be made of cardboard.

The tops of the towers are cut roughly to shape, by using files, and are finished with sandpaper. The towers are cemented and nailed in place. The pipes in back of them and the pipe across the top of the heater are dowels. The curved pipe from the top of the tower straight down the side is copper tubing. The large pipe across the top of the towers is a dowel and the rest of the pipes are wires or brass rods. Where these pipes meet the large ones they are just pushed into the dowels.

The large tank in the center of the picture is called the stabilizer. In the foreground are storage and mixing tanks and, behind them, tanks of the cracking unit. The building at the left with the tall stack is the clay plant.

All of the houses are built of poster board reinforced at the four corners by sticks of wood. The windows are cut out and cellophane is pasted to the inside. The doors in all cases are cut out. The roof ventilators are made of wood. Coping is put at the top of walls, the sills of windows and steps.

The platform for the towers is pinkish gray imitating concrete. The pipes, heaters and towers are aluminum.

Most of the buildings are painted concrete gray with a dark medium gray roof. The roof fixtures are flat black.

BULK OIL DEPOT

PARTICULARLY on the fringes of metropolitan cities, the colorful, giant tanks of a bulk oil depot are a familiar and fascinating sight. To these depots go the products of the refinery and, from them, gasoline is delivered to service stations.

Tank cars arriving at a bulk oil depot are spotted for unloading. The gasoline, kerosene or fuel oil is pumped from the cars to the storage tanks. The pipes through which the oil flows run along the ground and are often painted various colors so that any possible leakage can be detected easily.

The photograph on this page shows a small, complete bulk oil depot. The only units in this group which are unusual are the car unloading platform and the truck loading racks. The other buildings are very simple to reproduce. Large tin cans painted aluminum serve as the tanks.

The roof and the steps of the truck loading rack are made of cardboard and wood for uprights. The valve wheels of pipe are taken from ten-cent store toys. Entire structure is painted black.

The car unloading rack has a sinking platform which is hinged so that it may be lowered to the top of a tank car. The framework is wood. The floors and braces are strips of cardboard. The small pipes which run to the tanks are connected to a swinging pipe which is extended over the car. String is used to support the pipe on the end of the post. The pipes are strands of wire.

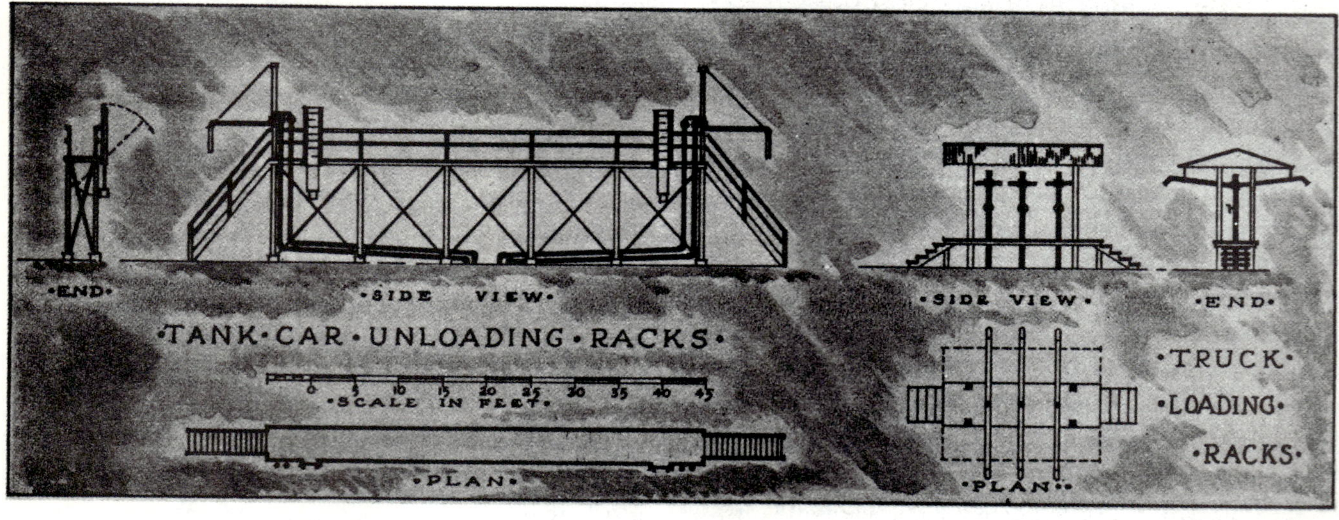

SERVICE STATION

ON preceding pages, instructions for building an oil well, a refinery, and a bulk oil depot have been given. The next step in the production and distribution of petroleum products is the familiar service station.

With all four of these units in the miniature layout, all the phases of the industry are represented and a real purpose is given to the use of a number of oil tank cars.

In nearly all service stations there are the cut-away curbing; paved driveways; island platform containing gasoline pumps; conspicuous racks for crank-case oil; and the service station building itself which is usually divided into two parts, one containing the office and the rest rooms and the other containing a drive-in lubritorium.

The largest piece of equipment in the service station is the lift in the lubritorium. When an automobile is driven onto this lift, the station operator touches a button, and by hydraulic pressure, car, platform and all are elevated so that an attendant can walk underneath to drain oil or to grease the car.

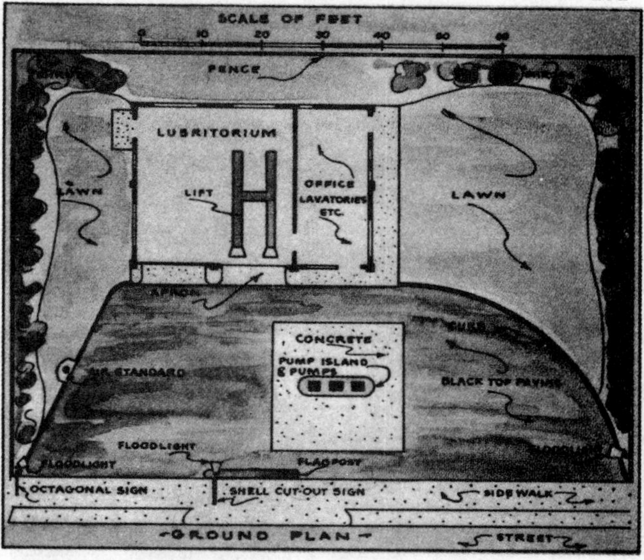

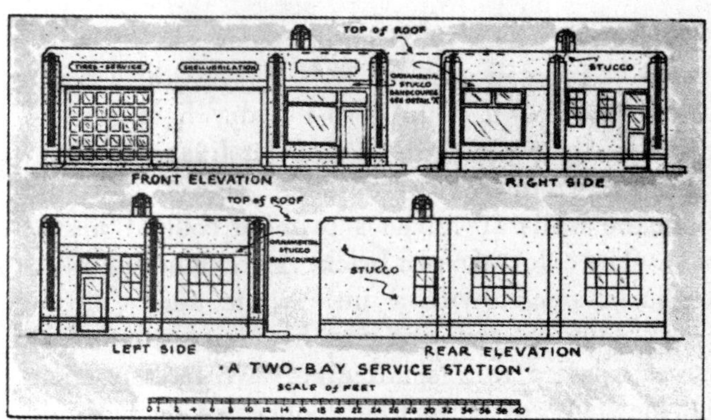

The service station itself is made of heavy cardboard. The pilasters and vertical ornamental pillars are assembled strips of cardboard.

The windows of the station are cut out and cellophane or celluloid is used for the panes.

The roof of the building is sunk below the sides of the walls. Sandpaper is cemented to the roof and painted black to represent roofing paper.

The inside of the building is reinforced with small square sticks of wood.

The building is painted the color of the favorite local station or in a neutral cream color.

For the sake of appearance, it is best to erect the dividing wall on the inside of the building.

A block of wood is used as the base for the pumps. The pumps, themselves, are made of solid blocks of wood carved to shape and painted.

A BUSY CORNER DRUG STORE

THE corner druggist is a smart merchant. His success depends upon a large volume of pedestrian traffic. Therefore he picks the busiest corner he can find for his establishment.

In plans for a complete model city, a corner should be set aside for a drug store. The large display windows of a modern drug store will furnish an excellent opportunity for adding color and interest to the miniature scene and, when illuminated, will attract considerable attention.

The building illustrated on this page is of a type that is common throughout the country. On the second floor are apartments with bay windows. On each street are doorways, one leading to the apartments, and the other being a service entrance.

Buildings of this type can be made of pressed wood. Essentially, there are four walls, a roof and a floor. The bay windows are made of fine sandpaper to represent stucco. The sandpaper is reinforced by cardboard and applied to the wall with glue. The short tile roofs extending over the second-floor windows are made of corrugated board. Show windows and apartment windows are glazed by cementing pieces of clear cellophane to the inside walls.

When cutting the pressed wood for the walls, allowance is made for the corner door. The door itself is cardboard. A toothpick painted aluminum and cemented across each door looks like a chromium push bar.

The lower part of each door is painted with gilt to resemble a brass kick plate. The large sidewalk sign is cut out of pressed wood, carefully lettered and hung with wires.

In order to obtain the brick effect on the walls, they are painted with a priming coat of white filler. After this has dried thoroughly, the walls are painted in the color of the brick desired, usually some shade of brown which is obtained by mixing burnt sienna with a slight amount of white and black. While the second coat of paint is still wet a nail or some other sharply pointed instrument is used to scratch through the brown paint to the white below it. These scratched lines are ruled in horizontally and vertically to represent the white mortar between the bricks.

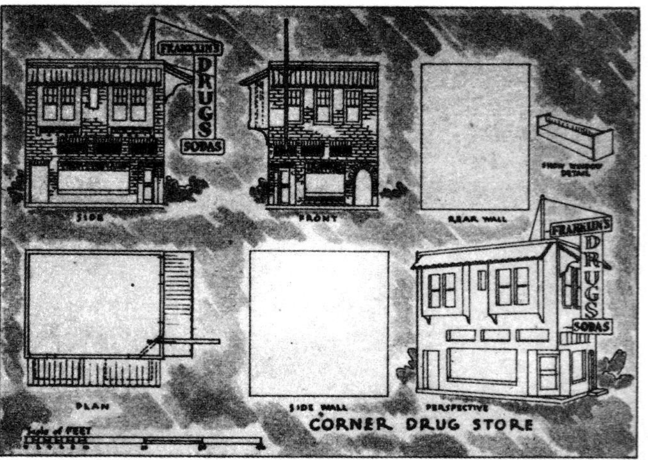

Only one section of the wall should be painted with the finishing coat at a time so that the brown paint does not dry before it is ready for the scribing of the mortar lines.

Before windows or any other details are applied, the walls are given a priming coat of white paint. The color of worn bricks is obtained by mixing burnt sienna with a little white and a little black. After the priming coat has dried, this mixture is applied to a small area. While it is still wet, the shape of the bricks is obtained by scoring through the white paint, with the point of a nail.

A MODEL LUMBER YARD

THE enterprising model railroader can increase his freight business handsomely by helping in the construction of a lumber yard to meet the constant demands for lumber that exist in every community. The yard is a very simple undertaking and is made very quickly.

The shed floor is a thin board with seven square sticks nailed crosswise on the bottom side for foundation posts. The two walls are cut from ten-ply cardboard and cemented to each end of the floor board. The roof is cut from the same material and cemented to the ends so it projects over each end and each side.

The shed is divided lengthwise into six equal parts by studs and joists. Since the second floor is only for stacking lumber it is an open grid. The joists are cut so that they project on each side to form a walkway. Each joist is cemented crosswise of the shed, to a pair of studs above the lower floor.

Three lengthwise beams are laid, one in the middle and one on each side just inside the row of studding, and fastened with cement. Planking is laid down on each side and fastened to the protruding joists to form walkways.

The framework and insides of end walls are stained to give them a weathered appearance. The roof is stained with thicker black and the ends painted. Balsa sticks of various thicknesses are used as scale-sized lumber.

The office, a plain frame building, is made by folding and cementing cardboard around a thin block of wood which serves as the floor. The doors and windows are cut out with a knife. The cardboard roof projects over three walls and the building is mounted on blocks so it stands against the end of the shed.

The steps are made by cementing thin strips of wood across sawtooth stringers and are cemented to the doorway. The fence is built of posts and boards or a solid strip of cardboard.

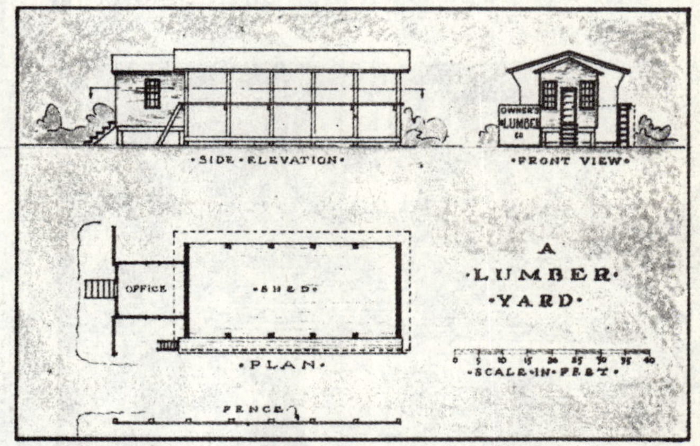

One of the buildings found most often on its own track spur is the retail lumber shed and yard, an excellent model to use with the new, electric log loader.

PROSPEROUS CITY BANK

AS the model city grows and expands, new stores and business houses will be opened and the day will come when modern banking facilities will be required.

The photographs show an easily-made but impressive home for the local bank. It is a four-story limestone and brick building with two floors of doctor and dentist offices.

The floor, roof and four sides of the building are made of tempered, pressed wood. The recessed effect at the front of the building is obtained by cutting out the pressed wood and inserting a second wall behind the first one.

Windows and doors are cut out of the pressed wood. Grills at the lower windows are made of mesh wire. The wire is cut to fit and bent over on all four edges. The projecting wires are pushed into holes and bent down where they protrude on the inside of the wall.

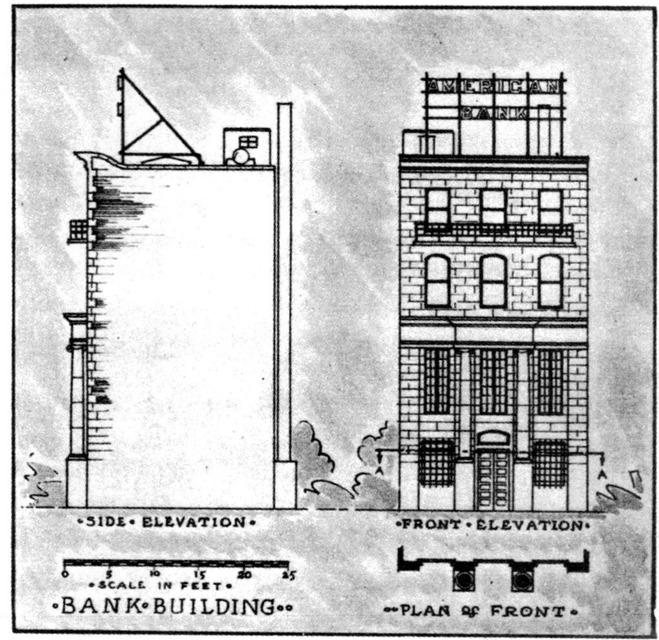

Four-story bank in the center of a model city block.

The ornamental windows have two vertical strips of balsa wood and one horizontal strip of the same size glued behind the openings. Smaller mullins are represented by stretching thin linen thread or cord horizontally and vertically across the opening and glueing it down. Cellophane cemented behind the whole row of windows represents glass.

The window sashes of the upper windows are cut out of cardboard. They are painted green, tan, white, or any appropriate color. Some green or yellow paper glued to a thin block of wood, which is in turn glued above each window, represents window shades. When window assemblies are ready, they are cemented to the window openings. Some picture moulding nailed across the top of the wall completes the front.

The walls are painted a cold, light, flat gray into which just a little blue has been added. The stone joints are made with India ink. The base of the building, looking like a polished black marble, is actually a high-gloss, black enamel.

The roof is covered with emery paper to imitate tar roofing. The ladder is a strip cut from mesh wire. The steam pipe began life as a candy stick. The smoke stack rising from the furnace room in the basement is a dowel rod.

AN ILLUMINATED CHURCH

SPACIOUS lawns, trim plantings and several costly, leaded-glass memorial windows imply that this scale model church has a large and prosperous congregation. The tall, imposing belfry is of the type housing Westminster chimes that fill the air with musical chords every Sunday morning. On Sunday nights, the church is illuminated brilliantly, lighting the numerous, colorful windows.

The model is not difficult to construct. Walls and roof are tempered pressed-wood. The arched windows are cut out with a jig saw.

Windows are glazed with translucent paper which is ruled into diamond-shaped panes and painted with water colors.

Shingles cemented on the roof are irregular in color. They are made of heavy paper cut in strips from a large manila envelope.

The stone effect for the walls is obtained by giving the pressed-wood a prime coat of white paint. After this has dried a coat of stone-color paint is applied.

When still wet it is scored with a sharp point so that the white paints shows through.

Aglow with lights, the church exhibits its colorful windows.

STONE · CHURCH ·

· PLAN ·

· SCALE · IN · FEET ·

- SCALE - THIS SKETCH - ONLY -

LANDSCAPES

CHAPTER NINETEEN

ONE of the things which make scale model railroading such an absorbing hobby is the astonishingly different viewpoints with which the model railroader approaches this subject. As with thumbprints, it is doubtful that the views of any two model railroaders are alike.

For example, there is a school of thought which believes no model railroad can represent adequately a four-track trunk line; that being confined to the limitations of basement, attic or spare room, the model can duplicate but a mile or two of track and, for this reason, that it is better to plan every model system as a branch line.

Opponents to this group set forth that such a conception is needlessly confining; that cleverly planned track, a little legitimate deception and trickery in handling scenes may, with imagination, create a life-like section of a Class I railroad.

There is one basement railroad where a whole main-line division is represented and operated as if the trains enter the division at one city and leave at another, a hundred miles away. Yet the owner of this particular railroad has but one station. The track loops and spirals three times around a modest room and terminates at the same point from which it started. Over this division from point to point, the owner operates his trains by actual time card. That is imagination!

We must use our imagination. With it we may recreate the world; without it, we are like a locomotive without its tender or a freight train without a caboose.

But imagination needs help. We may look at a mountain and imagine the green valleys beyond,

The picture above shows a combination of painted backdrops, flats, perspective models and full scale reproductions.

This is the picture on Page 157 seen from an angle.

or tread a city street and sense unseen buildings, traffic and activities around the corner. In this same way, we must use our imagination in model railroading.

A railroad needs population—gobs of it—in big and little groups. Population represents revenue in the form of passengers, baggage, express and mail. It also provides a reason for the flow of freight from factories to jobbers, retailers, offices and homes. Therefore, population must be represented in any layout where an attempt is being made to portray the story of transportation. To be complete, it should include the leisurely life of the village as well as the hustle and bustle of the metropolis.

On a model system built on shelves or benches around the walls of a room, towns and cities require very little space. They may be tucked away into the trackage in a room of average size, and the walls themselves used to portray most of the picture.

The whole effort in the landscaping of the model railroad is to transport the spectator from within four walls of a room to the broad expanses of the country-side or city represented by the miniature system—much in the same way a scenic designer lifts his audience out of their seats in a theatre and makes them feel they are a part of the set on the stage.

In order that buildings may have an appearance of depth, the principles of perspective drawing are brought into use. These are few and easily followed. The horizon on the back drop is created at the level of the eye. A mark at the center of the scene and located on the horizon is called the vanishing point. All building lines, streets and fence lines that run back into the distance lead to this point and vanish.

Should a store or other object be below the horizon, the lines run upward to the point; if above the horizon line, they run downward.

Getting rid of a road by sending it under a viaduct.

Because objects appear to diminish in size as they recede from the eye, the scale of all buildings gradually and uniformly is reduced the farther they are from the front of the train bench.

There are four ways in which to create buildings for the model railroad and all four can be combined with good effect. First, full-scale buildings with all dimensions in correct relationship to each other. Second, perspective buildings consisting of cardboard fronts with sides drawn in perspective and folded back. Third, flat cut outs drawn on cardboard and mounted on strips of wood, to hold them upright, and used in series in front of each other. Fourth, the painted wall.

For the most part, it is advisable to paint on the walls and on flats only those buildings which may be seen from a corner so that both side and front are shown. As the front row of buildings hide all but the tops of the houses which are behind them, it is necessary to draw and paint only the portion that will be seen.

The corners of a room fight every effort made to obtain a broad panoramic scene and consequently they must be eliminated. This may be done by tacking large sheets of cardboard into the corners, from one wall to the other, in order to obtain the appearance of a round room. The more gradual the curvature of this false wall, the more deceiving will be the results obtained.

In reproducing an area of many acres on a shelf only four or five feet wide, the most important task is to trick the eye into seeing greater depth than really exists. Consequently no streets running directly into the back wall are shown as their shallowness would be apparent and the illusion of depth would be destroyed. Streets are planned to run back at various angles and hide themselves eventually behind foreground buildings.

Perspective buildings unmasked.

The eye is tricked further by the coloring of the buildings. Strong colors and sharply defined details are used in the foreground, lighter tones in the middle distance and pale tones and hazy detail definition in the background.

This is the way that relief, or perspective buildings appear when placed against a backdrop and viewed from the proper angle.

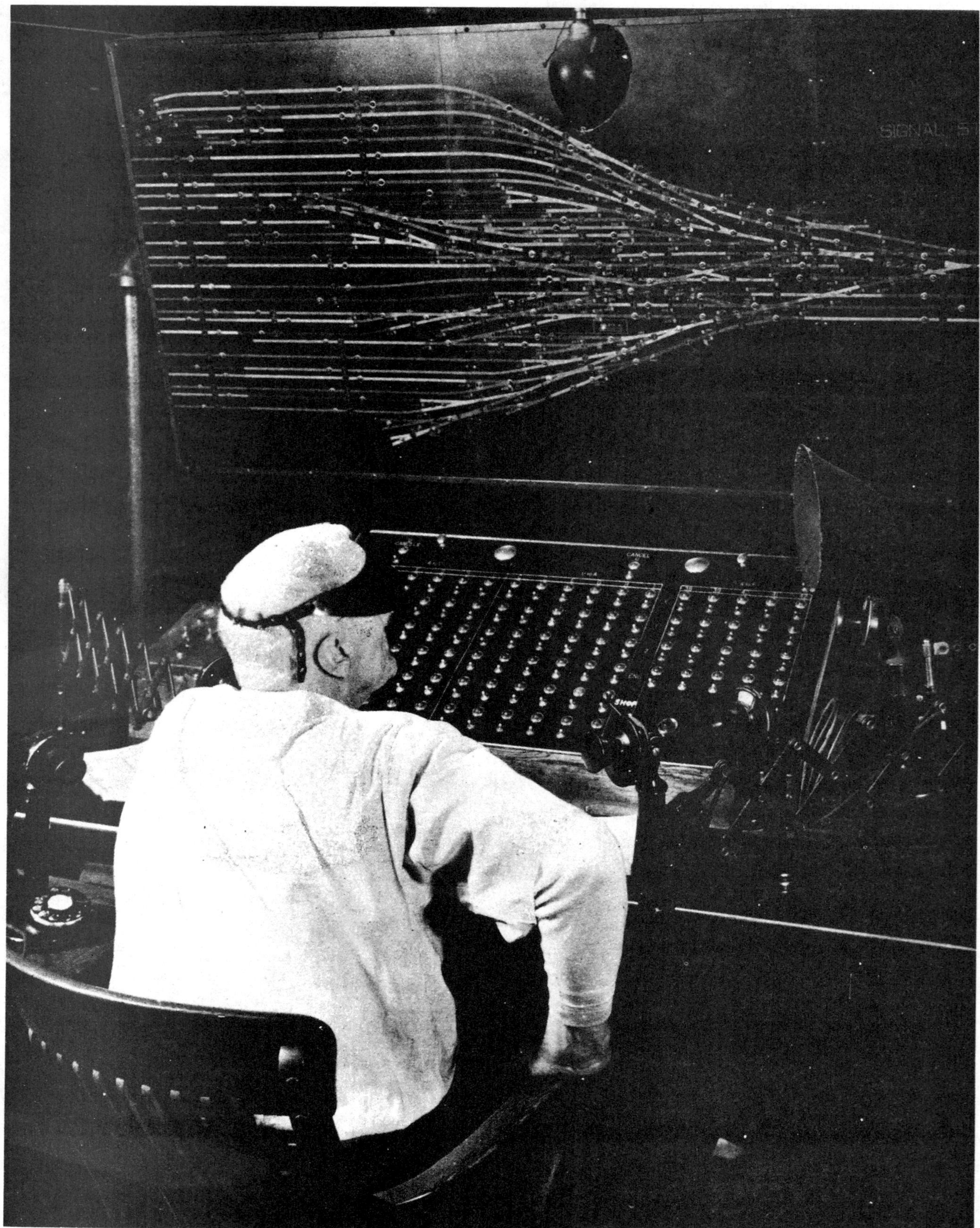
SIGNAL

ELECTRICITY AND CONTROL

CHAPTER TWENTY

THE first thing to learn about electricity is how it is measured. Comparing it with water flowing a pipe helps to understand it. If water is flowing in a pipe it is difficult to tell what can be done with it without knowing what its pressure is and how much water is flowing. The same is true with electricity.

If the faucet is turned on at the end of the pipe and the water flows out slowly, the pressure is low. If it rushes out, the pressure is high. Gages that tell what the water pressure is are marked in pounds. Electrical pressure, the "push" behind an electrical current, is measured in volts.

The volume of water flowing in a pipe depends upon the size of the pipe and the pressure behind it. At the same pressure, a larger pipe will give a greater flow of water. The volume of electric current flowing through a wire is measured in amperes. It is roughly like the number of cubic feet of water flowing in a pipe.

The voltage (or pressure of an electric current) and amperage (or quantity of flow) have a definite relationship to each other just as do the pressure and volume of water flowing through a pipe. The way in which voltage and amperage affect each other is controlled by other things about the electrical circuit.

The simplest form of electrical pressure is a battery. If a piece of zinc and a piece of carbon are put in a glass containing water to which almost any kind of salt or acid has been added, the chemical action immediately produces an electrical pressure or voltage between zinc and carbon. Strength of the voltage depends on the kind of acid or salt used. If the water contains sal-ammoniac (ammonium chloride) one and one-half volts will be generated. If four or five sal-ammoniac cells are connected with the zinc of one cell wired to the carbon of the next so that the voltages add up, it will run a motor. The battery from a flashlight is nothing but a sal-ammoniac cell with the liquid soaked up by blotting paper. Ordinary door bell batteries are made the same way.

The storage battery also produces electrical voltage by chemical action. It differs from the sal-ammoniac cell only in that the chemical action in a storage battery is reversible, which means that it can be recharged by forcing current through it in the reverse direction and thus re-form the chemical to produce electricity.

All the electrical voltage or pressure that forces current through the light bulbs in a house and that runs big electric trains is made by dynamos. A dynamo is, in theory, nothing but a huge machine built along the same lines as the motor in an electric locomotive. These big dynamos are run by steam turbines or water wheels. If the wheels of a locomotive were turned fast enough by hand the motor would become a dynamo and produce electrical voltage or pressure—not much, because it isn't designed for that service. The alternating current transformer which runs trains delivers electrical pressure or voltage between its binding posts.

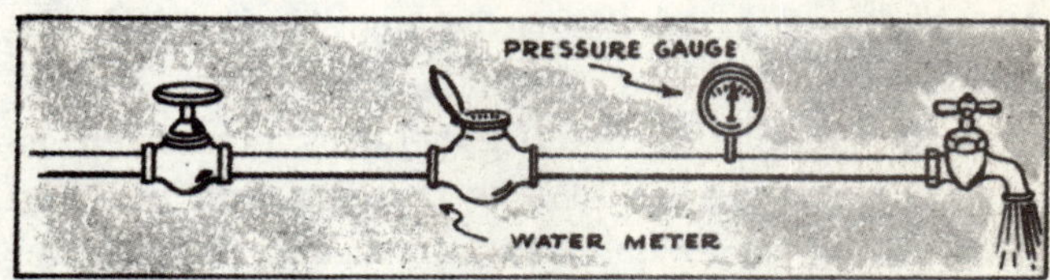

The points to remember now are, first, that electrical current, which is measured in amperes, flows through a wire because of its electrical pressure which is measured in volts; second, that electrical pressure or voltage can be produced in a number of ways, and third that the voltage is always between two points and that the current flows between these points on any metallic path that is provided for it. Voltage is developed at terminals of the

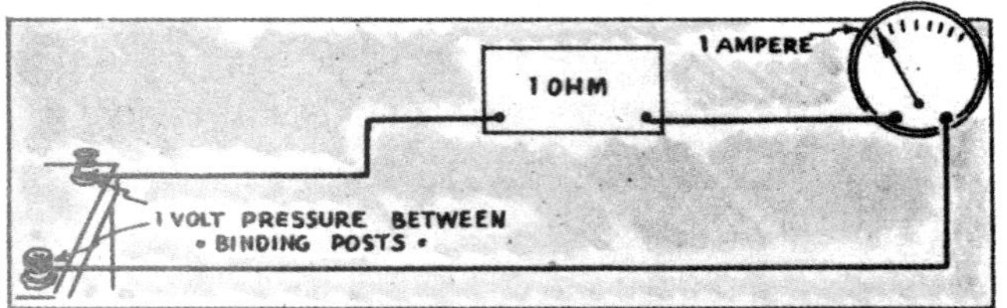

transformer and flows between them by way of two wires leading to the track. As the third rail is insulated from running rails this current flow must be through the locomotive.

When a long stretch of track is laid down the hall and into the room at the other end of the house, it takes more "juice"—higher electrical voltage—to make the locomotive run as fast when it is at the far end of the track.

That is because the long stretch of track adds electrical resistance to the circuit. Resistance is much the same as friction in machinery.

If a bicycle did not have ball bearings to cut down friction, it would pedal a lot harder, and if oil was not put on bearings of a locomotive it would not run so fast or pull so many cars.

Whenever friction in any piece of machinery is increased it takes more "push" to run. The same thing is true of electricity. The higher the electrical friction or resistance, the more electrical "push" is needed to make the current flow.

Electrical friction or resistance is measured in ohms. An ohm is the amount of resistance which will let one ampere flow when pressure is one volt.

If the relation between volts and amperes and ohms is memorized all sorts of interesting calculations in electricity can be made. For example, if the voltage is doubled, the current flow also will be doubled; or if the resistance is doubled, the current flow will be cut in half.

Two twelve-volt headlight bulbs connected so that the current has to flow through first one and then the other, in its circuit from one transformer binding post to the other, require twenty-four volts in order to make the bulbs as bright as usual. The resistance of two bulbs is added together and it takes twice as much pressure or voltage to cause the same current to flow.

Christmas tree lighting outfits operate on this principle. Each of eight bulbs in a string requires fifteen volts as they are connected one to the next; that makes eight times fifteen volts, or 120, which is the house supply voltage.

Every time a train is slowed down by moving a rheostat knob the effect of increasing the resistance or ohms on current flow is demonstrated.

Every kind of metal conducts electric current, but all do not conduct it with equal ease. Some metals have more electrical resistance than others. Silver is the best conductor known, copper comes next. That is why electric wire is made of copper. Some alloys or mixtures of different metals have a higher resistance than that of any of the metals used in the alloy. Wire made of such alloys is used in rheostats because it takes so much less of it to get the desired resistance.

The size of wire and the metal of which it is made determines its resistance. The smaller and longer the wire, the greater the resistance.

1 AMPERE ×1 VOLT =1 WATT
2 AMPERES×2 VOLTS=4 WATTS

If the pressure or voltage were two instead of one, then it would be a two-watt current. Or if the current were two amperes instead of one it would be a two-watt current. The wattage is always the voltage multiplied by the amperage. A 115 watt current might be one ampere flowing at 115 volts, or two amperes flowing at 57½ volts, or 115 amperes at a pressure of one volt.

Knowing what watts are makes it easy to figure how many amperes a transformer will deliver.

The real fun in learning about electricity is in using this knowledge to improve the train operations. There is a real thrill in figuring out the result wanted and then finding it really works.

Ohm's Law is used to make trains run better. Suppose, for example, that a track layout runs around one room, down the hall and loops around in another room. When the train runs over such a track, the locomotive seems to run much faster in the room where the transformer is located.

Ohm's Law explains why the locomotive acts this way. It takes a certain flow of electric current in amperes to run the locomotive at a certain speed. If it slows down in the other room it is certain that not so much current is flowing when it is there. The flow of current is controlled by voltage or electrical pressure and by resistance. Since there is no change in the voltage it must be that the resistance is greater.

The only place this extra resistance could be is in the extra long track, and the first place to look for the extra resistance is in a poor connection between sections of track. Perhaps one or more of the connecting pins is loose. When loose ones are tightened the train may speed up but won't run

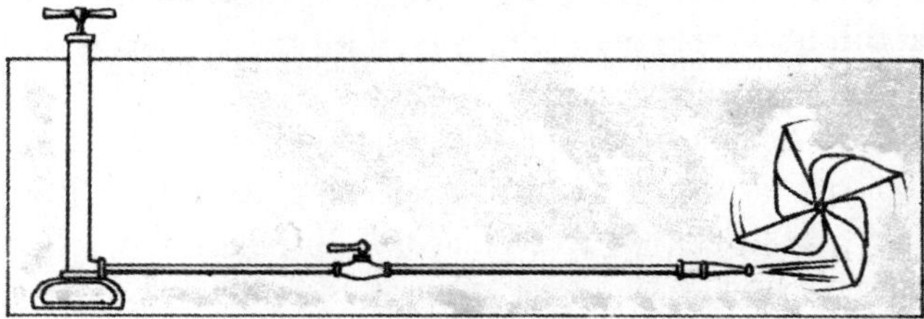

the same at both ends of the layout.

Electric resistance depends on the size of wire and its length, as well as the kind of metal of which it is made. Things should be fixed so the current won't find any more resistance in its path when it flows to the locomotive at the far end of the track than it does when the train passes close to the transformer.

A simple way to do that is to take two pieces of ordinary bell wire and run one of them from the transformer to the far end of the track, connecting it there to the running rails; and run the other from the transformer to the third rail at the far end of the track.

These two extra wires provide an extra path for the electric current and the effect is the same as though heavier track had been laid and all the joints between the sections soldered. The train will run better at the far end of the track after these extra wires are put in.

When a train runs poorly and the commutator of the motor is found to be dirty and the track is covered with a gummy dirt, the real trouble is electrical, not mechanical. Wheels roll on dirty tracks as easily as they do on clean tracks. The dirty commutator seems to turn just as easily before cleaning as after the dirt has been removed. It must, however, be remembered that electricity travels by a metallic path and dirt keeps the brushes from making a good contact with the commutator and a dirty track lets the wheels touch the track only in tiny spots.

Here is where Ohm's Law comes in again, for the flow of electric current depends on the size of the path. Small contacts can not let as much current flow as large ones.

Electricity controlled and regulated to just the right amount is what makes the wheels of a locomotive go around.

A horseshoe magnet is a piece of magnetizer steel bent in a U and usually painted bright red except at the ends which are called the poles.

Scientists do not know what magnetism really is, but they have learned why one piece of steel is magnetic and another is not. They say that all the tiny particles in any piece of steel or iron really are little magnets. The only reason that all pieces of steel or iron do not attract each other is because the particles in ordinary iron are turned every which way so that the pull of each little particle is balanced by other particles pulling in the opposite direction.

One of the interesting things about electricity is that when it flows through a wire it produces a magnetic pull on any piece of steel or iron that is near it.

A careful examination of a locomotive motor shows how this is done. The stationary piece of iron called the field magnet is made of a number of thin pieces of iron, shaped like a horseshoe. There is a coil of wire around its middle and another coil of wire around each of the three poles of the armature, the part that turns around within the ends of the field magnet.

The motor runs and drives the wheels because the poles of the armature are pulled by the magnetism toward the ends of the stationary field magnet. The commutator, the flat disc made of three sections of copper on which the brushes slide, keeps changing the flow of current so that the magnet pull always keeps just ahead of the poles that are coming together, like a horse walking up a treadmill and never getting to the top.

LOCOMOTIVE REVERSING

A TRAIN may be made to reverse wherever and whenever desired. This action is accomplished by making certain changes to a whistling locomotive. The automatic whistle feature in the engine is sacrificed but the whistle itself is used by concealing it in a station and wiring it via a push button, direct to the track circuit.

The whistle unit is removed from the tender or electric engine. The relay is separated from the whistle and blower motor by removing the one holding bolt and disconnecting the two wires connecting the contacts to the motor and the one wire connecting the relay to the ground.

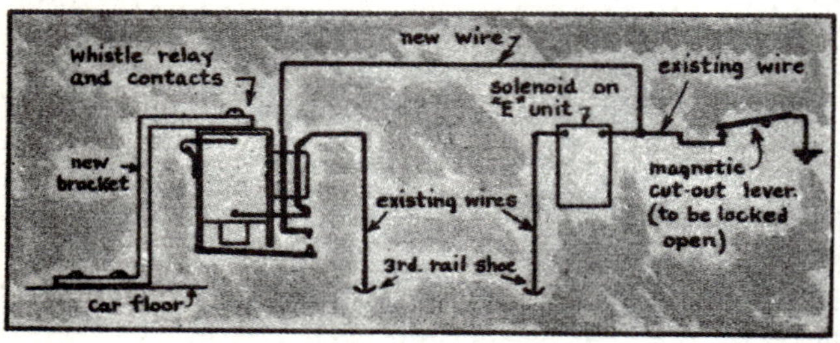

The wire from the relay contact (a ground wire when relay is closed) is run to the reversing mechanism solenoid coil in the engine and connected to that coil lead which is grounded when the magnetic cutout lever arm closes its own contact. The cutout lever is removed or made inoperative.

The tender and engine covers are reassembled and the train run under power, in the normal way. To reverse the engine, instead of opening the power circuit as done previously, the reversing mechanism will respond when the whistle control button is pressed, providing the third rail is drawing power.

AUTOMATIC CROSSING CONTROL

THE various methods for preventing two trains colliding at a crossing involve the following general principle.

Referring to the diagram, note first that the direction of traffic on each track is indicated by an arrow. The control will function properly only when traffic is in the direction shown.

On one side of the crossing the outside rail is insulated for a length of three or four sections by use of fibre pins. Special insulated track sections are used here. On the lower left track in the crossing the third rail is isolated in a similar manner for a length of about three sections. (Special track is not required here.)

The relay used consists of an electric magnet and a single contact which remains closed when the magnet is not energized. If a high resistance magnet or relay suitable for operation on about 17 to 25 volts alternating current is obtained, it is wired directly to the third rail as shown.

If no such a relay is obtained an ordinary electric buzzer from a hardware or 5-and-10-cent store is used. Buzzers of this type will operate on one or two dry batteries, therefore wire is shown in the alternate scheme.

Be sure to note where the batteries are located and that wires connect to the two outside rails when batteries are used.

The operation depends upon the first train reaching the crossing at A, completing a circuit that energizes the relay. When this happens the relay contact opens and cuts off power to the third rail section at B. The second train approaching at B will come to a stop, lacking power until the first train has made the crossing and left section A.

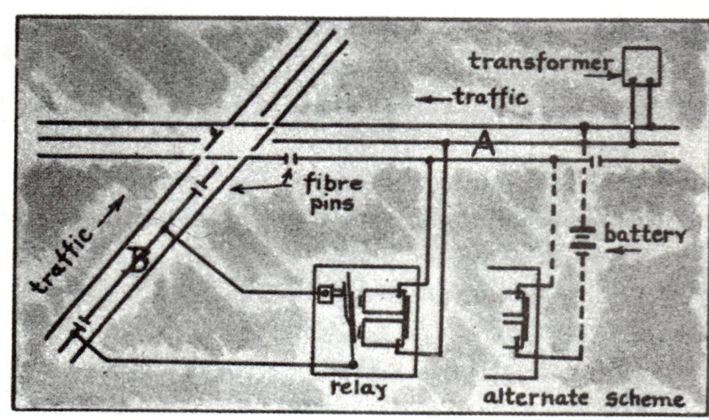

The success of this scheme depends upon the first train reaching section A in advance of the second train reaching B. Should the reverse be the case, the train on track B might be halfway over the crossing when train on track A hits it.

The latter predicament can be overcome merely by using two relays and duplicating the entire scheme. This means one outside rail opposite B must be insulated and a section of third rail A.

When this is done the first train to reach control section A or B will stop the second train.

PANEL BOARD CONTROL

As a model railroad grows with the addition of switches, remote control accessories and illuminated buildings, the opportunity comes to group all of the accumulated levers, pushbuttons and knobs on one central operating panel which will have the well-organized, business-like appearance of a real railroad towerman's station. A well-planned control panel will, in fact, reduce hazards in the manipulation of a complex model system, and will bring a greater measure of fun and satisfaction to the train operator.

A neat and workable control panel can be made by screwing your controllers and transformers to a board. However that arrangement is not so practical nor good-looking as the control box pictured on these pages.

The type of control box illustrated gives a chance to centralize many different contact switches used in track sectionalizing and train control, and controlling the illumination of buildings and other accessories. All wiring is out of the way, and the various controllers of different sizes and shapes can be completely concealed. At the same time they are brought together so that the complete railroad system can be operated from one central point.

If a railroad system has grown haphazardly, the addition of a central control switch board will bring order into the confusion. When such a panel is added the operator's station assumes a business-like and efficient aspect, and the whole railroad is engineered from this central point.

The first step in constructing the box is to decide how the controls and transformers are to be arranged on the panel board. Allowance should be made for controls that may be added in the future as the system grows.

In a large system where the trains cannot be seen all the time, it is a good idea to have a track diagram on the same switch board which includes the various switch controls and sectionalizing toggle switches. This type of control panel is similar to that used in real railroad practice and gives a professional appearance to the layout.

The construction of the box and the panel board that fits over it comes first. The drawings and photos accompanying this article are of a particular box designed to meet the requirements of a specific model railroad. Each control panel must be adapted to the requirements of the system for which it is intended.

The wood for the box should be new and well-seasoned. Good kiln-dried wood can be obtained at a lumber yard. Plain pine shelving is the best material and a few knots are not objectionable. Enough $\frac{1}{2}$-by-2-inch wood stripping to form the inside braces and supports for the controls and the base around the bottom of the box will also be required. A piece of masonite may be used for the panel board on top of the control box. This is a hard material made of wood pulp. Plywood might be substituted but is much more difficult to work with and requires more time and patience. Two or three-ply plywood is satisfactory.

When building the box, the inclined top is cut at

the same angle as the top of the trainmaster transformer.

The box is assembled with finishing nails that are afterwards counter-sunk. Triangular braces are added on the four bottom corners for greater strength. Round-head screws are used as indicated on the top and sides of the box. The nails are not driven in all the way until the whole box is put together. In case some part does not go together squarely, it is then easy to take the box apart and make the necessary corrections.

The base of the control box is cut out and the edges beveled with a plane and scandpapered until they are smooth. The two corners are mitered joints. This base need only be on the front and two sides.

The rear of the control box is drilled for the various wires before the box is assembled. Binding

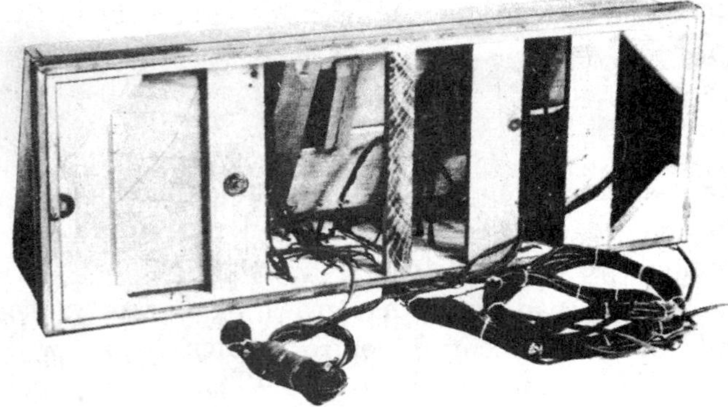

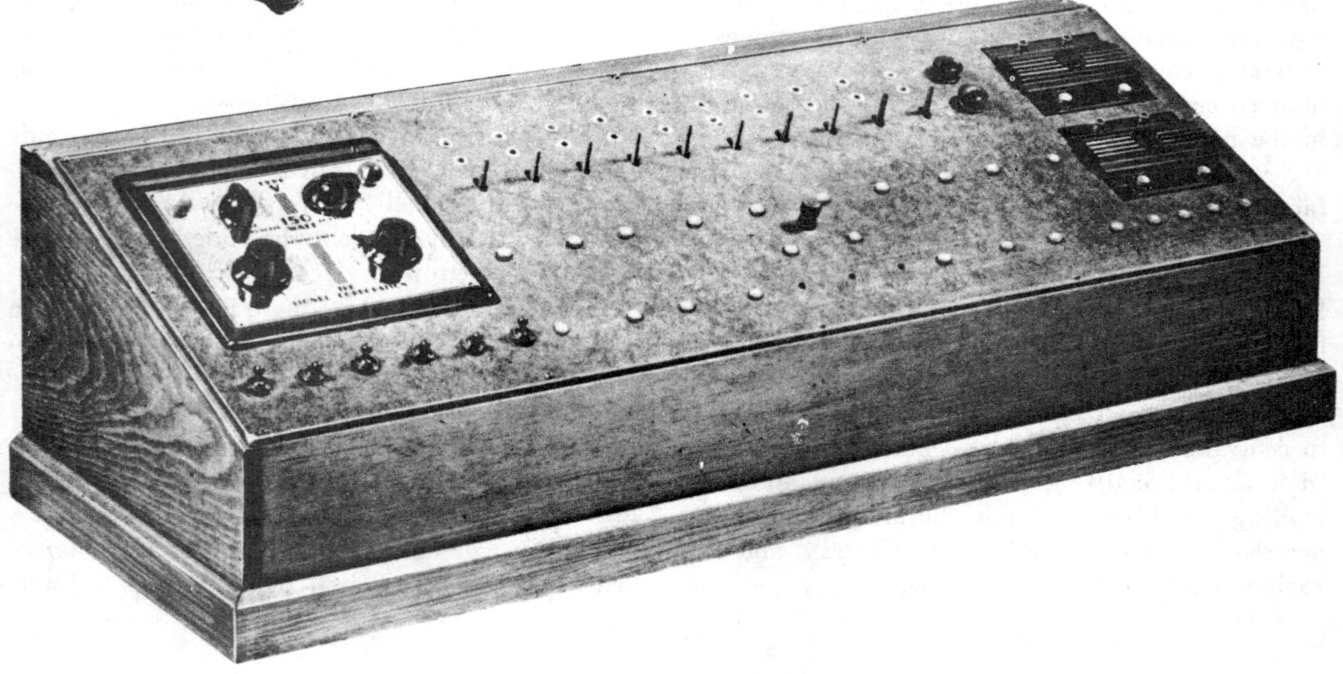

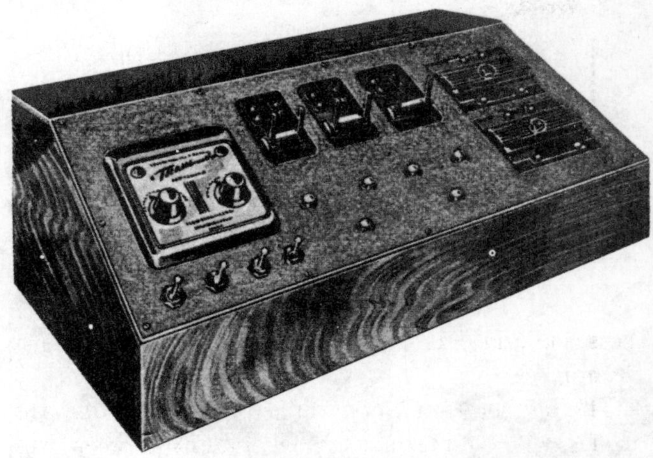

posts may be used instead of running the wires through the holes. This is advisable if the control box is to be used in a layout that is to be picked up and put down again. Having the wires come through holes in the back is suitable on a permanent system but the wires would soon break if the system were moved frequently.

The masonite top is made according to the following directions. The measurements of the top of the box where the panel board is to go are marked out on the masonite. The places for the controllers are carefully marked for their positions. The panel is cut out one-eighth of an inch oversize on each side. This is later planed down to the line and the bevel made on the edges. Great care is taken in laying out the holes for the controls and the work is done accurately as any scored mark that is a mistake cannot be removed easily.

If a trainmaster transformer is used, the top and bottom of the opening must be filed to correspond to the contour of the transformer. This type of transformer looks the best if the face rises a half or three-quarters of an inch above the top surface of the panel board.

Old square type transformers may be mounted with or without the face showing. Whistle controllers and other controls are mounted flush with the top of the panel board. Holes for the push buttons and whistle controllers are drilled very accurately as an untidy job would spoil the appearance. Small, rat-tail files are very useful in making the parts fit. These are used to enlarge the holes if the drills are not exactly the right size.

Colored lights placed on the top of the board indicate the position of each switch. Holes for the colored discs are drilled directly above the indication lights which are provided on the switch controllers. Pilot light jewels, obtained at radio stores, are ideal for this purpose. As a less expensive substitute, small washers are cemented over red or green pieces of cellophane or celluloid and they in turn are cemented over the pilot light hole in the panel board. The holes in the panel board are one-eighth of an inch smaller than the outside diameter of the washers so that a surface is provided on which to cement. These are also slightly countersunk, so that the top surface of the washers will be flush with the panel board.

Toggle switches, rheostats and turn buttons are fitted on the board. Care is taken when these controlls are being put on so that they are not scratched and their appearance marred.

Small screw holes are drilled along the outer edges for attaching the panel board to the box. Small nickel-plated or chromium-plated roundhead screws are used for this purpose.

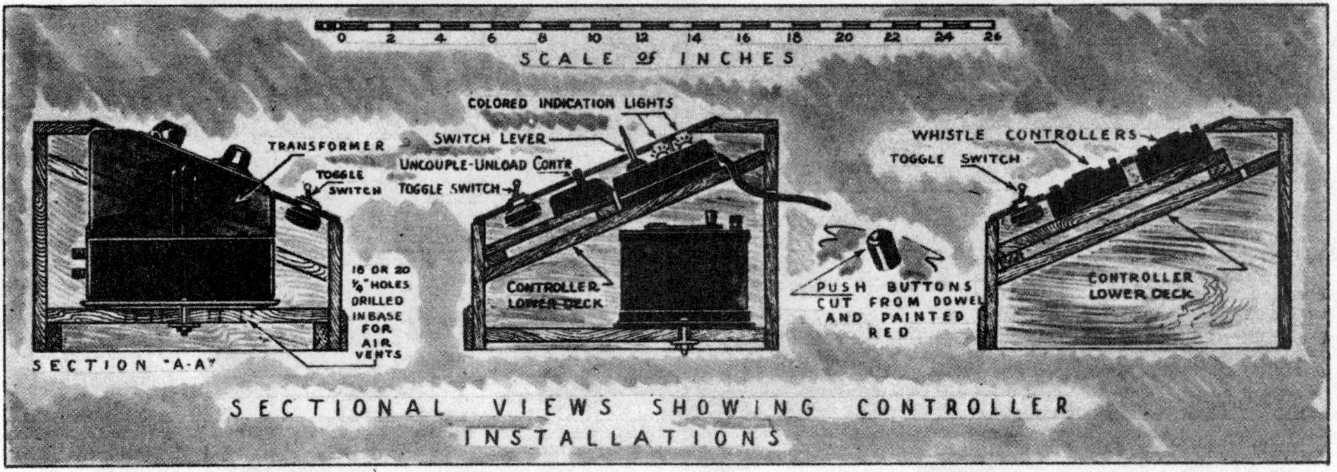

SECTIONAL VIEWS SHOWING CONTROLLER INSTALLATIONS

IMPORTANT FACTS

If an automobile is operated without lubrication, it will soon be damaged seriously. If operated without being cleaned, it will lose its shiny, appearance.

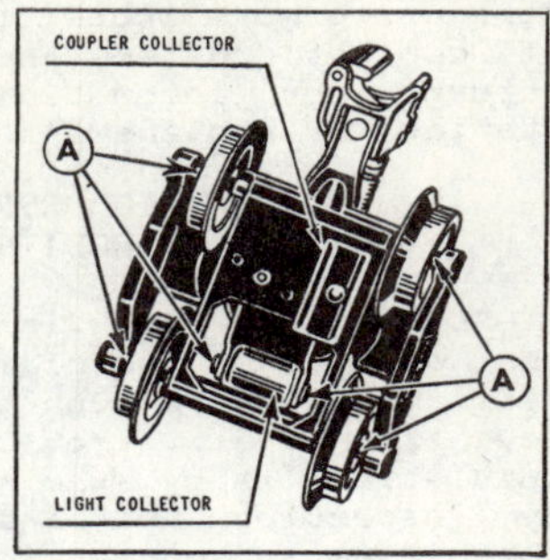

Figure 37

The same is true with Lionel Electric Trains. If they are cleaned and lubricated with Lionel Train Lubricant, there is no limit to the time they will last and the long service they will give.

In order to maintain the brilliance of the enameled finish of cars and equipment, wipe with a moistened cloth, followed by a dry cloth.

Other parts of of your outfit that should be cleaned are: tires of wheels, rollers of contact shoes, track and the commutator.

CLEANING WHEELS AND CONTACT SHOES

The tires of wheels and the roller contact shoes of your locomotive and cars must be kept clean to insure proper contact with track. Dampen a clean cloth with benzine, or other household cleaning fluid, run it over the surface to be cleaned, and then wipe dry with a clean cloth.

CLEANING TRACK AND COMMUTATOR

Clean your track as described above. This will permit a perfect contact between the locomotive and cars with the track. It will also do away with uneven speed and sluggishness

If your locomotive has a slider-type shoe, it may be lubricated. This follows the practice in real railroading, where the third rail must be lubricated to decrease friction and diminish wear. With this type of shoe a thin film of lubricant will not impair the contact. As a safety precaution when cleaning track with benzine, make certain that current is turned off.

The commutator is that part of the armature on which the brushes make contact. A dirty commutator will retard the speed of the motor and reduce the life of the brushes. If locomotive is operating much slower than it did previously on the same voltage, disconnect the two wires connected to the transformer, turn the locomotive upside down, touch one of the wires to any unpainted part of the motor frame and the other wire to the contact shoe. The motor will run, see Figure 41.

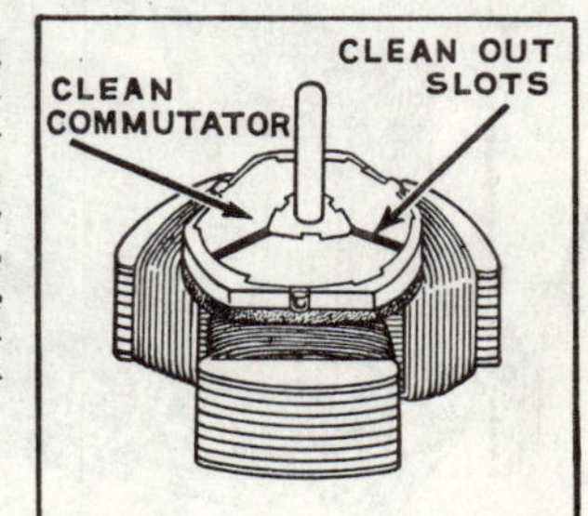

Figure 38

While motor is running, press a piece of very fine sandpaper ("OO"size or finer) against the armature commutator as it rotates. Then, with a pointed tool, scrape the slots between the segments of the commutator.

What Parts of Your Train to Lubricate

Lionel Train Lubricant has been developed after years of laboratory tests, to replace ordinary oil. When using oil as a lubricant, the locomotive must be oiled at the end of every two or three hours of operation. Proper use of Lionel Train Lubricant, on the other hand, will assure efficient operation for a considerably longer time and will increase the life of all working parts.

Always lubricate your equipment before using it. If the train is noisy or loses speed, lubrication will probably restore its quiet, smooth operation.

The following parts of your train should be lubricated; both ends of armature shafts; all gears; all axle bearings; in brief, all points shown in Figures 37, 39 and 40.

Periodic cleaning and servicing of equipment should be done at your experienced local Lionel-Approved Service Station.

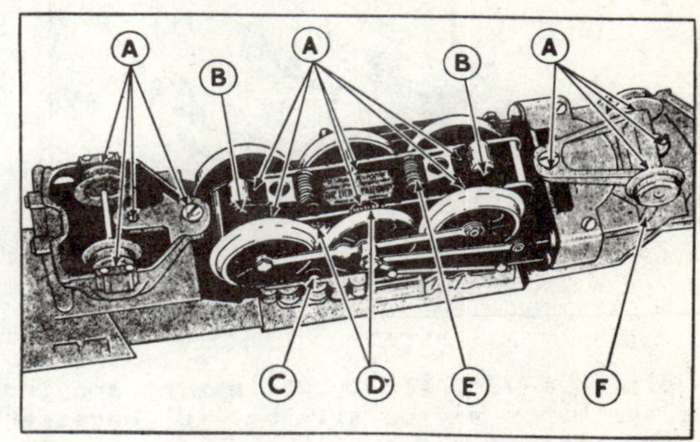

Figure 39

PROPER CARE LIONEL MOTORS

Figure 40 shows the bottom of a Lionel Scale Switching locomotive. Lubricate all points indicated by arrows at "A". Remove screws "B" to lubcricate center and end bearings. Screws retaining roller collector shoe assemblies indicated by "C". Do not remove these screws. Be sure to keep the wheels and track free of any lubricant, since this may cause the driving wheels of your locomotive to slip.

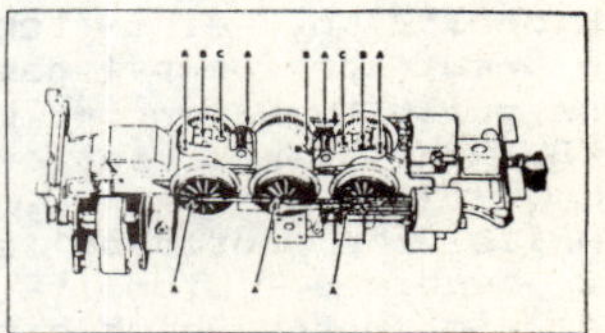

Figure 40

Lionel locomotives No. 671, 703, 726, and 2020 are equipped with single bearing motors with sealed oil-retaining bearings. These motors do not require lubrication at the commutator end. Periodically clean commutator slots (See Figure 38) thru the hole in the brush plate using a tooth pick to remove any accumulation of carbon.

HOW YOU CAN TEST THE MOTOR

If your train refuses to run, first make sure the current is on and that you are getting the correct voltage. Then see that all connections on transformers and track are correct and firmly fastened. See that there are three steel pins inserted at the end each section of track.

If train still does not run, disconnect the two wires from the track but leave the other ends of wires connected to transformer. Turn locomotive upside down, as illustrated in Figure 41, and touch one of these wires to any unpainted part of the motor frame. With the other wire touch the contact shoe which collects the current from the rail of track. If motor does not operate, it may be that the reversing unit is in a neutal position.

When the reversing unit is in a neutral position, the locomotive will not run although the headlights will be on as all car lights. Place the locomotive in an upright position, again touch wires as described above, and try with different adjustments of the reversing unit lever.

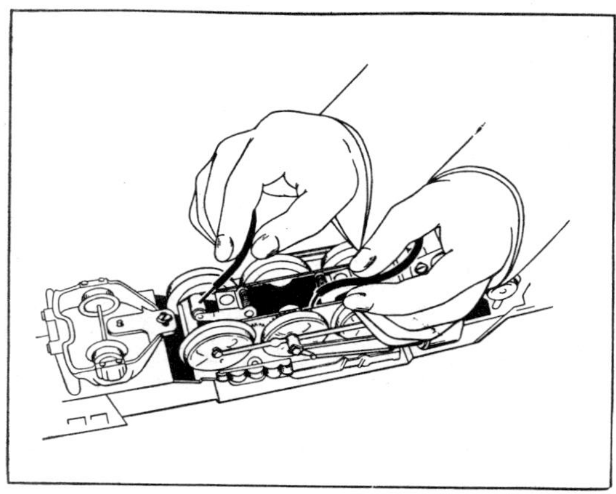

Figure 41

If wheels move very slowly, cleaning and lubricating the motor may be all that is necessary to restore original power.

If motor starts and stops or if wheels do not revolve, look for loose connections. See if brushes make good contact with commutator.

If wheels revolve freely there is nothing wrong with the locomotive. The trouble may be that the contact shoe rollers do not have enough tension to make proper contact with center rail. If contact rollers appear to be badly worn, return your locomotive to the nearest Service Station for replacement.

HOW TO REPAIR SHORT-CIRCUITED TRACK

A section of track is short-circuited because one or more of the clamps that hold the center rail have cut through the insulating fiber and touch the metal. You can easily see where this insulation is by examining a section of track. By inspecting the insulating material under these clamps, you can locate the one causing the short circuit and repair it by releasing the pressure on the insulation so as not to make contact with the metal.

FINDING SHORT CIRCUITS ON TRACK

Remove the train and all other equipment from the track and make sure that a piece of metal or Christmas Tree tinsel is not touching the rails. See that all sections of track fit tightly. Then connect one wire from trans-former to an outside rail and brush the end of the other wire across the center rail. If the track is perfectly insulated, not a spark will be visible at the place where the wire touches the rail, but if it is short-circuited, sparks will appear.

To locate the short-circuited section, disconnect one section of track at a time and apply the wires to the remaining sections as explained above. When the defective section is removed, the sparking will stop.

NO. 308

LIONEL No. 41 GAS TURBINE SWITCHER

Lionel's No. 41 switcher is a scale model of the new experimental gas turbine switching engine built by Davenport Locomotive Works for the U. S. Army Transportation Corps.

While the prototype is powered by two Boeing gas turbines, Lionel's model is driven by an electric motor which has an operating voltage range of 9 to 16 volts. Since the top speed of the Davenport locomotive is only 35 miles per hour, Lionel No. 41 switcher is also designed to be considerably slower than the speedy road locomotives. Like its prototype it is intended for relatively light yard switching duties and should not be expected top pull more than 34 freight cars.

Figure 1—No. 41 Gas Turbine Switcher

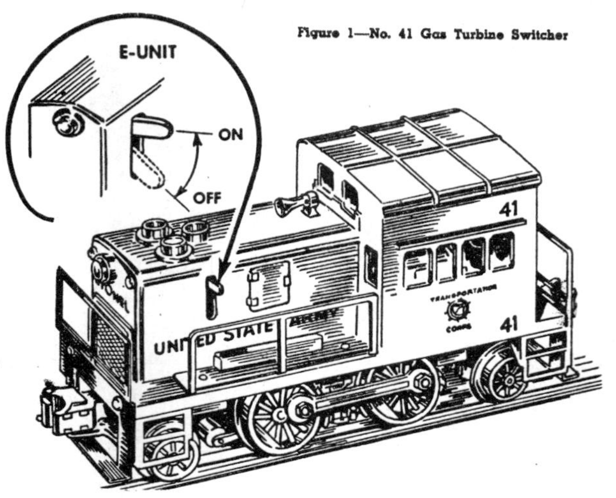

REVERSING THE LOCOMOTIVE

No. 41 Switcher is equipped with a standard Lionel threeposition reversing unit which makes it possible to stop, start and reverse the direction of the locomotive by remote control. The reversing unit works in sequence: Forward, Neutral, Reverse, Neutral. To stop a moving locomotive operate the "Direction" control on the transformer once; to change the direction of the locomotive operate the "Direction" control twice. Because the reversing unit is activated by interruptions of track current it will also be tripped to its next step by turning the transformer voltage to "off" position or whenever power to the track is interrupted by a short circuit, a loose wire, etc.

LIONEL NO. 60 TROLLY

Lionel No. 60 Trolly is made to run on regular "027" or "0" track. It can be operated in conjuction with a lionel trian outfit or on a seperate line or siding as a town or interurban trolly.

The trolley is powered with an electric motor which operates on 8-16 volts using a regular Lionel transformer. It is equipped with a reversing mechanism is which changes the direction of the car's motion whenever its foward bumper strikes an obstruction or whenever it is moved by hand. The reversing mechanism is connected to the trolley pole on top of the car causing it to swing in the opposite direction whenever the trolley changes direction. A "neutral" position in which the trolley will stop although the track is energized is half-way between the extreme positions of the bumper. the reversing mechanism can be set in "neutral" position either by hand or by striking the bumper just hard enough.

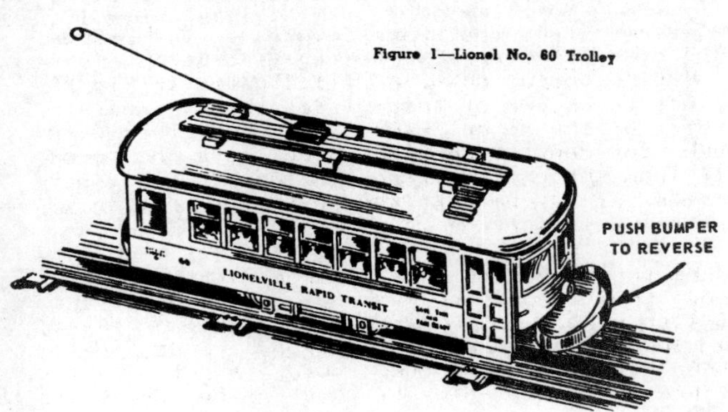

Figure 1—Lionel No. 60 Trolley

DISASSEMBLING THE TROLLEY

To disassemble the trolley for lubrication of the motor or for replacement of a burned out lamp, (Lionel No. L53) remove the body in the following manner.

1. Take off the trolley pole assembly by pulling the base straight up.
2. Remove the screw on the bottom of the car.
3. Lift the body up at the unscrewed end and slide it foward.

To replace the body reverse the procedure:

1. Line up the car body so that the vertical post holding the trolley pole assembly is in line with the hole in the roof.
2. Insert the front of the body first so that the projections on the frame fits into the supports on the body.
3. Lower the other end of the body in place making sure that the vertical post projects through the hole.
4. Replace the screw on the bottom of the car.
5. Mount the trolley pole assembly on the vertical post.

No. 400 & 404 RDC RAIL DIESEL CARS

Lionel Rail Diesel Cars are modeled on several types of commuter cars made by Budd for short-run service on many railroads. These cars are generally self-powered and may be used either singly, or combined with non-powered units into short trains, according to the requirements of the service.

Lionel's models of these cars are built to run on all types of Lionel track. The powered models are equipped with a single worm-drive motor driving two magne-traction axles. These axles enclose permanent Alnico magnet which magnetize the wheels in order to grip the track rails and enable the car to climb steep grades without slipping on the track. Be careful not to let pins, paper clips, carpet tacks or other small iron objects come in contact with the magnetized wheels and axles or they may jam the gears and interfere with the action of the mechanism. NOTE: "Magne-Traction" is not effective on aluminum, brass or other non-magnetic rails.

COUPLING AND UNCOUPLING

Both ends of these cars are equipped with operating knuckle couplers, so that two cars can be coupled or uncoupled by remote control. To open a closed coupler move the car to a remote control track section so that the coupler trigger disc is just above the track electro-magnet, then press the "Uncouple" button. The coupler can also be opened while the car is in motion by pressing the button at right moment.

To couple the car to another car push or run them together until the couplers meet and latch. This can be done along any straight stretch of track as long as at least one of the mating couplers is open.

HOW TO REVERSE

RDC cars are stopped, started and reversed by means of the reversing "E-Unit" located inside the car. The E-Unit is three-position sequence relay which trips whenever current to the motor is interrupted. This can be done by operating the "direction" control on the transformer, or by moving the transformer voltage control to the OFF position. The sequence of its operation is Forward, Stop, Reverse, etc. In other words, if the car is in motion, operate the "Direction" control once to stop it and twice to reverse it.

If you want to operate the car in one direction only, which is necessary if you have automatic stations or insulated blocks in your layout, you must disconnect the E-Unit. This is done by moving the E-Unit lever, which projects from the bottom of the car just in front of the battery cover, to its OFF position, or toward the right side of the locomotive. See Figure 1.

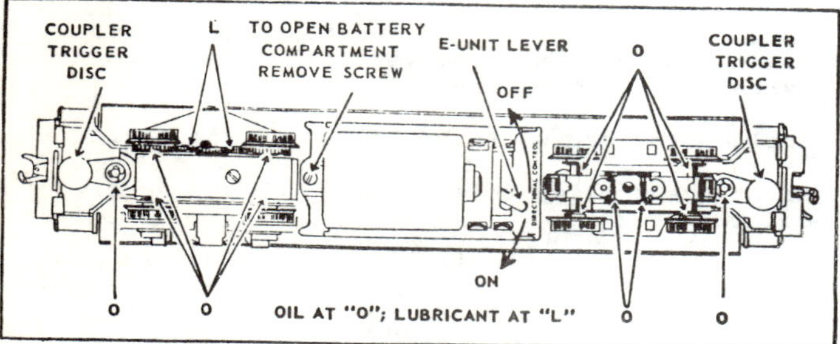

Figure 1—Underside of Rail Diesel Car Showing Location of E-Unit Lever

Make sure the car is moving in the desired direction, stop it without operating the "Direction" control (Either turn off the power or hold the car with your hand) then move the E-Unit lever to OFF. If the reversing unit is disconnected while it is in its Stop position the car will not run at all. Also because the E-Unit works partly by gravity it will not operate properly if the car is held on its side or upside down.

HOW TO INSERT HORN BATTERY

RDC cars are equipped with a warning horn which is powered by a flashlight battery remotely controlled, like a regular Lionel train whistle, by a built-in relay and the "Whistle" control on your Multi-Control transformer.

The battery supplied with the car must be inserted into its position before the horn can be sounded. Remove the screw holding the battery housing in the bottom of the car.

Insert the front of the battery but leave the back of the battery resting on the bottom of the car exactly as shown in the illustration on the right. Don't finish inserting the battery into place just yet.

Place the cover on the battery keeping the front of the cover close to the car bottom in order to get it under the wheels. Then push the cover forward, keeping the front down. After the hook enters the slot in the cover push the back down. The battery and the cover snap into place at the same time.

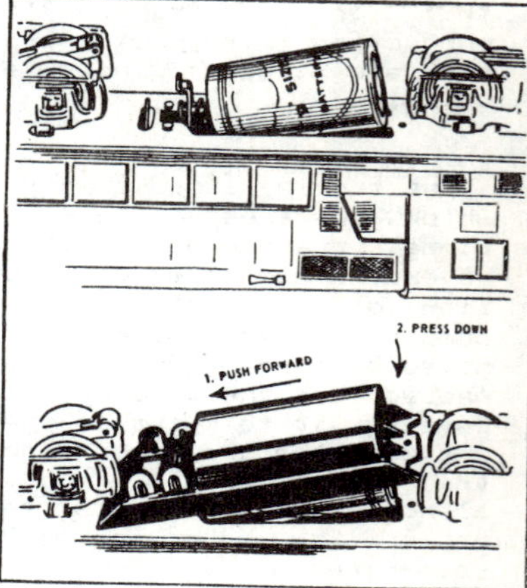

Fig. 2—How to Insert Battery

The horn will sound whenever the car is tilted to the side or placed upside down, because in these positions the relay will close through its own weight. For this reason take out the battery whenever the car is to be transported. The battery should also be removed before the car is stored away, to protect the car against possible battery leaks, particularly if the storage place is damp or unheated.

The battery will last a long time, but will, of course, eventually wear out even if it is not used. Replace with any good quality, nationally known size "D" battery, preferably of the "leak-proof" type.

"600" SERIES DIESEL SWITCHERS

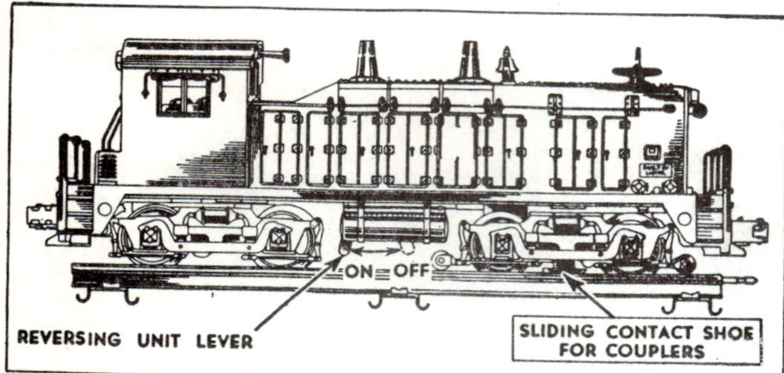

Figure 1—Location of Reversing Unit Lever on Lionel Diesel Switcher

Lionel Diesel Switching Locomotives are equipped with remote control electromagnetic operating couplers front and back. To open these couplers run the locomotive onto any Remote Control Track Section so that the sliding contact shoes ride up on the control rails and then push the "Uncouple" button.

To couple the locomotive to any car simply run it slowly up to the car until their couplers mate and lock. This operation can be done along any straight stretch of track but at least one of the couplers should be in open position for the coupling to take place.

LIONEL "MAGNE-TRACTION"

Lionel Diesel Switchers are "Magne-Traction" locomotives, which means that their driving wheels are magnetized to grip the track more securely and to enable the locomotive to pull heavier loads and to climb steeper grades without slipping on the track. Be careful not to let pins, paper clips, screws, carpet tacks or other small iron objects to come in contact with the locomotive or they will be attracted to the magnetized wheels and gears and may interfere with the action of the locomotive.

Note: "Magne-Traction" is not effective on aluminum, brass, or other non-ferrous rails.

REVERSING THE LOCOMOTIVE

Like all Lionel locomotives the Diesel Switchers are equipped with a three-position reversing unit which makes it possible to stop, start and reverse the locomotives by remote control.

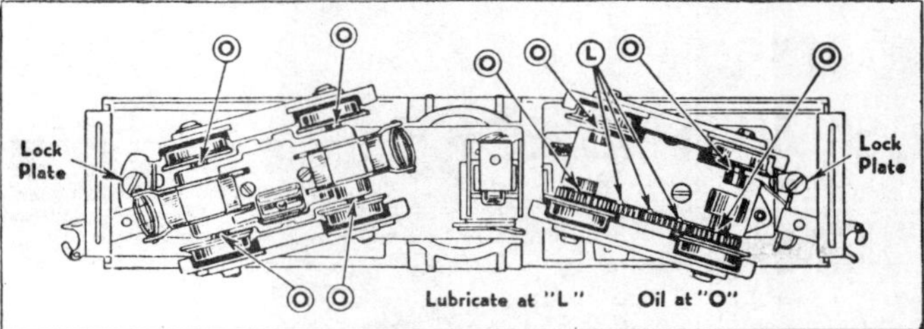

Figure 2—Bottom View of the Diesel Switcher Showing Lubricating Points

HOW TO DISCONNECT REVERSING UNIT

The reversing unit can be disconnected by moving the lever on the bottom of the locomotive forward. (See Figure 1.) When the reversing unit is disconnected the locomotive cannot change its direction, but will continue to run in the same direction. This is useful when operating a layout with an automatic stop station or insulated track blocks. The reversing unit is disconnected in the following way: Get the locomotive to run in the desired direction. Stop it *without operating the reversing unit.* (Either stop the locomotive with your hand, or turn off the track voltage.) Then while the locomotive is standing on the track move the reversing unit lever forward. If the reversing unit is disconnected while the locomotive is standing in neutral, it will stay in that position and will not run at all even when power is re-applied. Because the reversing unit works partly by gravity it will not operate properly if the locomotive is held upside down.

LUBRICATING THE LOCOMOTIVE

The life and performance of the locomotive depend to a considerable degree upon proper lubrication of the motor and other moving parts. Since your locomotive might have been stored on the dealer's shelves for some time, it's a good idea to lubricate it before running it for the first time. Follow the lubricating chart in Figure 3, using a small dab of Lionel Lubricant at all points marked "L" and a drop or two of light machine oil at points "O". Lubricate thoroughly but never to excess. Be careful not to get any oil or lubricant on the running surfaces of the wheels or the locomotive will lose traction. Also do not lubricate the locomotive rollers.

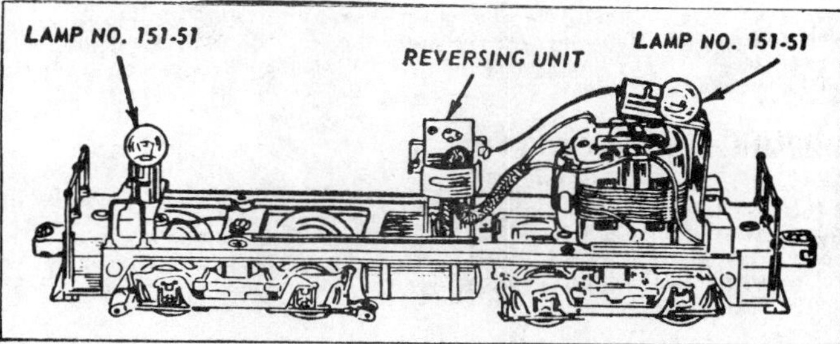

Figure 3—Lionel Diesel Switcher with Body Removed

No. 773 HUDSON-TYPE LOCOMOTIVE For "O" Gauge Track

Lionel No. 773 locomotive is a close replica of the famous "Hudson" type locomotive used by the New York Central and other railroads, and conforms in many respects to the rigid specifications for 1/48 scale model locomotive.

While this locomotive has been designed to operate on "0" gauge track layouts, its scale proportions will be displayed to best advantage if wide radius "072" track is used on curves when possible. Like a real locomotive, the 773 will not operate successfully over poorly laid track. Remember that a displacement of a 1/16" in any direction is equivalent to a displacement of 3 inches on a real railroad track.

No. 773 locomotive may be operated either on Alternating or Direct Current. On Alternating Current, supplied by a step-down transformer, 10 volts will be sufficient to operate the locomotive and tender alone. With additional cars, voltage up to 20 volts may be required. On Direct Current used by some model railroaders, its operating voltage will vary from 6 to 16 volts under the same conditions.

LIONEL "MAGNE-TRACTION"

Like all modern Lionel locomotives, the 773 "Hudson" is equipped with **"Magne-Traction"**, which means that its driving wheels are held to the rails by magnetic attraction and enable the locomotive to pull heavier loads and climb steeper grades without slipping on the track.

NOTE: "Magne-Traction" is not effective on aluminum, brass or other non-ferrous rails.

LIONEL SMOKE GENERATOR

No. 773 locomotive is equipped with a smoke generator which produces realistic appearing smoke. Simply drop an SP Smoke Pellet into the smoke stack and turn on the track power. Smoke is produced in a few seconds, as soon as the heating element in the generator melts the pellet, and is blown out of the stack in puffs timed by the locomotive driving wheels.

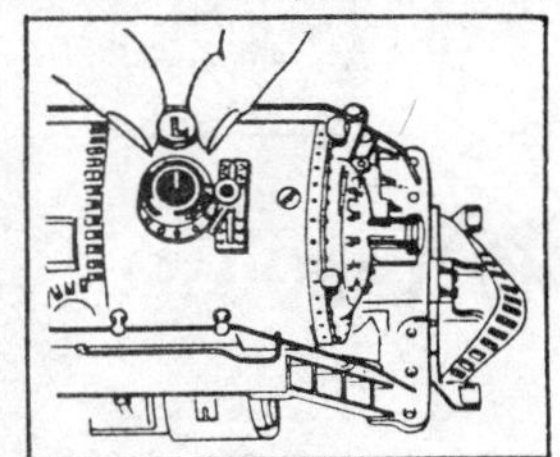

Figure 1–Smoke Pellet

HOW TO CLEAN SMOKE GENERATOR

Smoke pellets are consumed without leaving any ash. After several hours of operation some white powdery material will accumulate in the smokestack. This is all smoke material and should be pushed back into the generator with the wooden tamper provided. Do not use any sharp instrument or you may dmage the delicate heater element.

If the generator has been clogged up by too much smoke material and fails to produce enough smoke, raise the track power slightly and let the locomotive stand neutral a few minutes until all the smoke material in the generator melts. Then lift up the locomotive slightly and let the wheels turn rapidly for a few moments to blow out the excess smoke material. The whitish deposit which may be formed on a locomotive body after a long period of operation may be cleaned off with a little Lionel lubricant-applied with a soft cloth.

REVERSING THE LOCOMOTIVE

The locomotive is reversed by means of its built-in "E-Unit". The "E-Unit" is a sequence switch which trips whenever current to the locomotive is interrupted. This is done by operating the "Direction" control on your transformer or by turning the transformer voltage to OFF, or through any interruption of track current, intentional or otherwise.

The "E-Unit" has three positions which follow each other in sequence: Forward, Stop, Reverse, Stop, etc. In other words, if the locomotive is in motion, operate the "Direction" control **once** to stop it and **twice** to reverse it. If you want to operate the train in one direction only, which is necessary if you have automatic stations or insulated blocks in your layouts, you must disconnect the "E-Unit". This is done by pulling out the "E-Unit" plug out of the right hand socket "A" and inserting it instead into the left hand socket "B". (see Figure 2) Make sure the locomotive is moving in the desired direction, stop it with one hand (without operating the "E-Unit" mechanism) and pull out the "E-Unit" plug with the other.

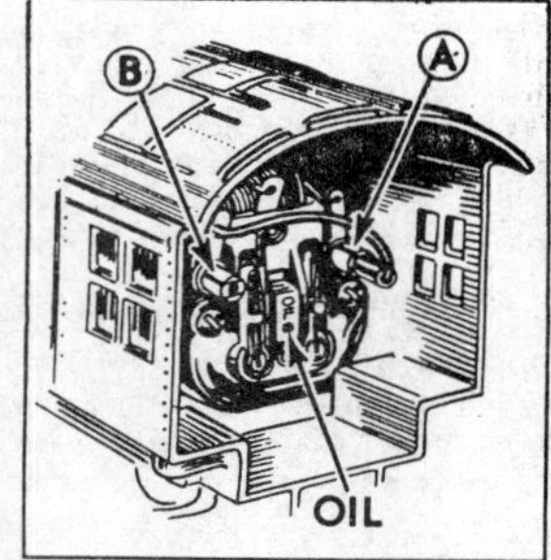

Figure 2–"E-Unit" Connection

HOW TO REPLACE HEADLIGHT

For its headlight No. 773 locomotive uses an 18 volt miniature screw-base lamp, Lionel No. 1447-300. To reach the lamp swing open the hinged locomotive boiler front. Before assuming that the lamp is burned out check to see that it is tight in its socket.

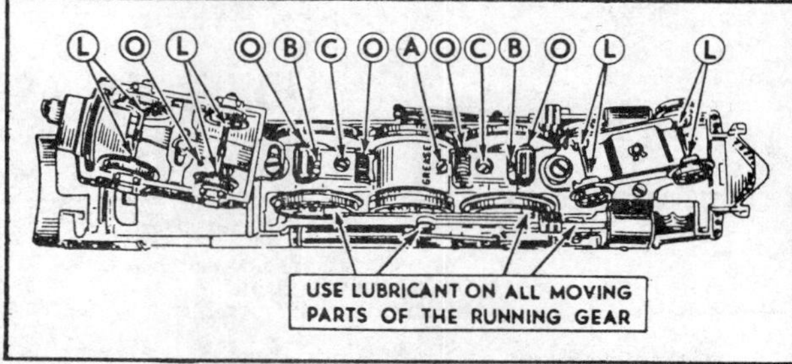

Figure 3–How to Lubricate No. 773 Locomotive

HOW TO LUBRICATE LOCOMOTIVE

The life and performance of the 773 locomotive depend to a considerable degree upon proper lubrication. Adequate sealed-in lubrication has been provided for the motor, reduction gears, and other important parts, but the grease reservoirs which are capped by screws "A" and "B" (Figure 3) may be filled occasionally. In order to get at screws "B", however, the two contact roller brackets must be taken off by removing screws "C". Use Lionel Lubricant for lubricant reservoirs and other lubricating points marked "L". Use light machine oil for points marked "O". Lubrication of the motor armature is maintained by means of an oil wick (see Figure 2), which should be replenished occasionally with a few drops of oil applied with a dropper, toothpick or other pointed tool.

To minimize the drag on the locomotive don't neglect to lubricate all wheel axles on the tender and the other cars in the train. Avoid flooding the points of friction with oil or lubricant or the excess will get on the track rails and cause locomotive to lose traction.

LIONEL LOCOMOTIVES WITH SMOKE

READ INSTRUCTIONS CAREFULLY

Locomotives bearing Catalog No's. 2020, 671, 726, or 703 are equipped with smoke producing devices.

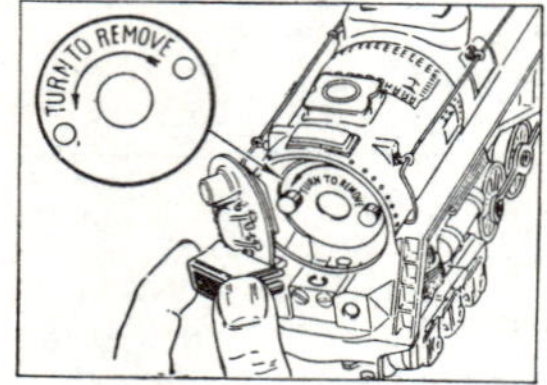

Figure 14

Smoke is generated when a Lionel smoke pellet is dropped into the smoke stack of the locomotive and is activated by the heat of a special lamp, which is also the locomotive headlight, provided for the purpose. This lamp has a small cup-shaped depression located just below the stack in which the pellet rests.

In about one minute the heat from the lamp liquidfies the pellet, smoke is generated and blown out in synchronized puffs by a flapper plate at the bottom of the smoke chamber directly linked to the driving wheels.

While all of the pellet in contact with the bulb is consumed without residue, there will be some fine dust-like accumulation in the stack and the interior smoke chamber. Before inserting a fresh pellet, brush out stack with the special brush provided for this purpose.

After one hour of operation (5 or 10 pellets), the boiler front should be removed in the 2020 or 671 locomotive (see figure 14) or swung open in the 726--703 locomotives (see illustration figure 15) and the smoke box cover removed. The interior of the smoke box should be brushed thoroughly clean. Be careful not to bend or damage the flapper plate at the bottom of the chamber.

To remove smoke box cover, turn the cover slightly in the direction indicated by the arrow. Theis movement will unhook the cover which is then pushed out by the lamp contact spring placed in the rear of the smoke box. Before replacing the assembly, brush off any accumulation on the lamp holder, smokebox cover, and transparent window in the center of the cover.

Replace lamp assembly by pushing it in as far as the locking ears in cover will permit and "lock" by turning the assembly slightly in the opposite to that shown by the arrow. When bulb is burned out, replace with type called for in lamp chart, page 32, being careful to replace with pellet bowl in upward position.

When cleaning out smoke box, turn wheels of locomotive and observe movement of flapper plate. A movement of about 3/16" indicates that it is free. A stuck flapper will cause the puffing to cease.

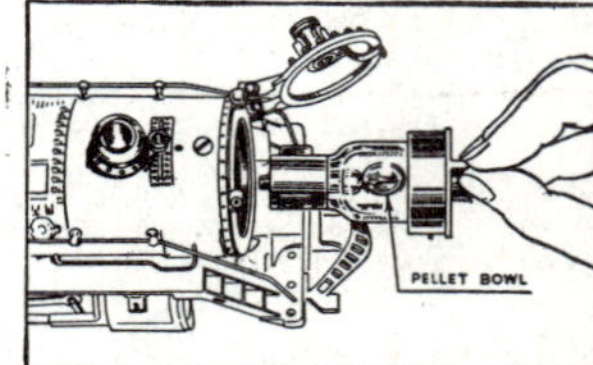

Figure 15

The pellet bowl has ample capacity to hold one smoke pellet but will overflow if more than one is dropped at one time or before the previous pellet is entirely consumed.

The amount of smoke produced does not depend on the amount of material. In fact, it will increase somewhat as the pellet is cosumed. Therefore, add pellet only after smoking has practically ceased.

LIONEL No. 6557 SMOKING CABOOSE

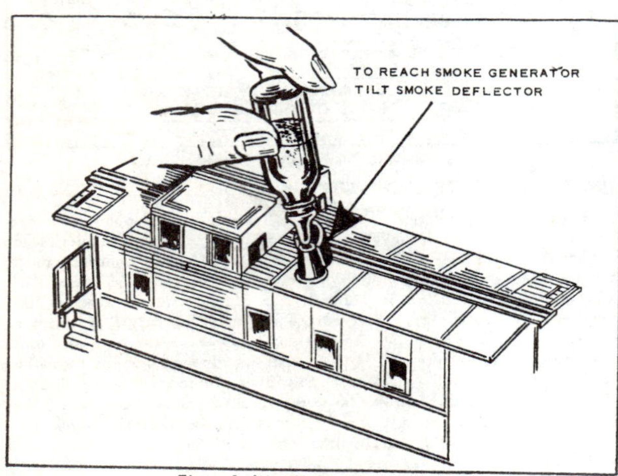

Figure 1 - No. 6557 Smoking Caboose

The last car on every freight train is the caboose, also called conductor's car or cabin. The caboose is the home, office and tool shed for the train crew and contains all the facilities for the crew's comfort including a coal or oil stove for heat and cooking.

Lionel's No. 6557 Caboose is equipped with a smoke generator so that smoke will actually rise from the caboose stove pipe. The smoke generator is designed to be used with Lionel No. 909 Smoke Liquid, a container of which is furnished with the caboose.

To produce smoke, place the caboose on an energized track, turn up the smoke deflector and squeeze 6-8 drops of smoke liquid into the smoke stack. The caboose will not produce much smoke while the train is in motion because most of it will be blown away. To produce a larger volume stop the train in neutral (with track energized) and raise the track voltage slightly. Do not use too much smoke liquid or you will cool down the heating element within the generator and actually decrease the amount of smoke.

The caboose lamp is part of the smoke generator circuit and must be on. If it is missing, broken or burned out no smoke can be produced. To reach the lamp take out the two screws in the ends of the caboose, remove the smoke deflector by springing it out and lift off the caboose body. For replacement use only Lamp No. L55.

LIONEL No.2321 DIESEL LOCOMOTIVE

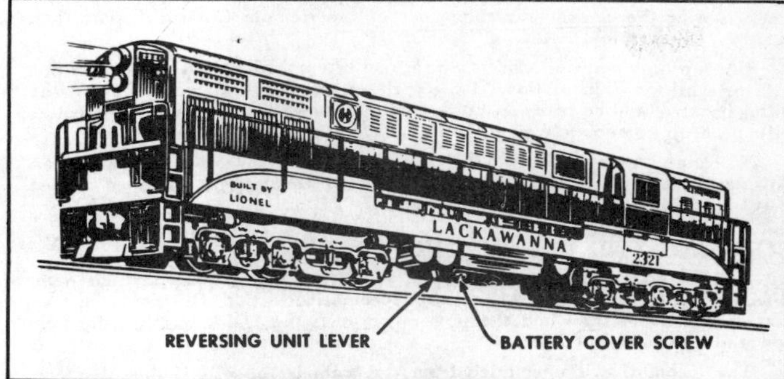

Figure 1 - No. 2321 Fairbanks-Morse Diesel Locomotive

Lionel No. 2321 Diesel Locomotive is a replica of the Fairbanks-Morse 2600 horse power "Trainmaster" locomotive, used by the Lackawanna Railroad for both freight and passenger service.

Lionel model of this locomotive is designed for "0" track but its appearance will be improved even more by the use of the wide "072" curves. Although No. 2321 locomotive will clear the "027" track curves it will interfere with the "027" track switches, and for this reason its use with "027" track is not recommended.

No. 2321 locomotive is powered by two motors which enable it to pull as many as 24 cars along a straight section of the track. On regular "0" curves the number of cars should be limited to about half that number to avoid derailment. The operating voltage of this locomotive is from 9 to 15 volts depending on the train load.

LIONEL "MAGNE-TRACTION"

This locomotive is equipped with "Magne-Traction" which means that its driving wheels are magnetized by powerful Alnico magnets inserted in the driving axles in order to grip the track and enable the locomotive to pull heavier loads and climb steeper grades without slipping on the track. Be careful not to let pins, paper clips, carpet tacks or other small iron objects come in contact with the locomotive or they will be attracted to the wheels, gears, or axles and interfere with the action of the locomotive. NOTE: "Magne-Traction" is not effective on aluminum, brass or other non-magnetic rails.

COUPLING AND UNCOUPLING

Both ends of this locomotive are provided with operating knuckle-type couplers, so that the train can be coupled to the locomotive from either end. The locomotive can be coupled to the train along any straight stretch of track provided that at least one of the mating couplers is open. The locomotive couplers are of the "electro-magnetic" type which are opened by the central electromagnet of a Remote Control Track Section. To open the coupler move the locomotive to the remote control section so that its front steps are in line with the track electromagnet; then press "Uncouple" button. The coupler can also be opened while the locomotive is in motion by pressing the button at the right moment.

If you uncouple the locomotive from the train while the train is in motion, keep one hand on the voltage control of your transformer and be ready to cut down the voltage since the locomotive will speed up immediately when its train load is released.

REVERSING LOCOMOTIVE

The locomotive is stopped, started and reversed by means of the reversing "E-Unit" located inside the locomotive. The E-Unit is three-position sequence relay, which trips whenever current to the locomotive is interrupted. This can be done by operating the "direction" control on the transformer, or by moving the transformer voltage control to the OFF position. The sequence of its operation is Forward, Stop, Reverse, Stop, etc. In other words, if the locomotive is in motion, operate the "Direction" control once to stop it; and twice to reverse it.

If you want to operate the train in one direction only, which is necessary if you have automatic stations or insulated blocks in your layout, you must disconnect the E-Unit. This is done by moving the E-Unit lever, which projects from the bottom of the locomotive just in front of the battery cover, to its OFF position, or toward the right side of the locomotive. See Figure 2. Make sure the locomotive is moving in the desired direction, stop it without operating the "Direction" control (Either turn off the power or hold the locomotive with your hand) then move the E-Unit lever to OFF. If the reversing unit is disconnected while it is in its Stop position the locomotive will not run at all. Also because the E-Unit works partly by gravity it will not operate properly if the locomotive is held on its side or upside down.

HOW TO BLOW HORN.

No. 2321 Locomotive is equipped with a warning horn which is powered by a flashlight battery and remotely controlled, like a regular Lionel train whistle, by a built-in relay and the "Whistle" control on your Multi-Control transformer.

The battery supplied with the locomotive must be inserted into its position before the horn can be sounded. Loosen the thumb screw "A", holding the round cover in the bottom of the locomotive, insert the battery into the space provided for it and reclose the bottom cover. The horn will sound whenever the car is tilted to the side or placed upside down, because in these positions the relay will close through its own weight. For this reason take out the battery whenever the locomotive is to be transported. The battery should also be removed before the locomotive is stored away, to protect the locomotive against possible battery leaks, particularly if the storage place is damp or unheated.

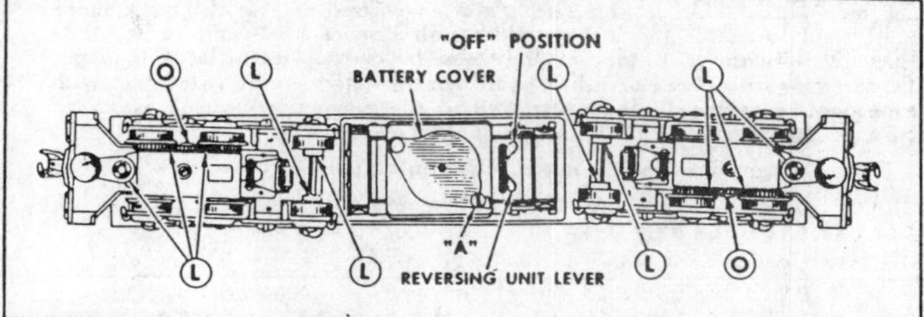

Figure 2 - Lubricating Chart for No. 2321 Locomotive. Use Oil at Points "O," Lubricant at "L"

The battery will last a long time, but will, of course, eventually wear out even if it is not used. Replace with any good quality, nationally known size "D" battery, preferably of the "leak-proof" type.

SERVICE INFORMATION

The life and performance of the locomotive depend to a considerable extent upon proper care and lubrication of the motor and other moving parts. Since your locomotive might have been stored on the dealer's shelves for some time, be sure to lubricate it according to the lubrication chart in Figure 2 before running it for the first time. Put a small dab of Lionel Lubricant at all points marked 'L'. Using the point of a pin or a thin wire put a drop of Lionel Oil at points marked 'O'. Lubricate carefully but *never to excess.* A small amount of oil or lubricant, properly applied, goes a long way. Be careful not to get any oil or lubricant on the running surfaces of the wheels or on the rails, or your locomotive will lose traction and do not lubricate locomotive rollers.

The motors of this locomotive are lubricated by means of a felt oil wick which should be replenished occasionally with a few drops of light machine oil. To get at the motors the locomotive body must first be removed by removing the two screws in the ends of the locomotive.

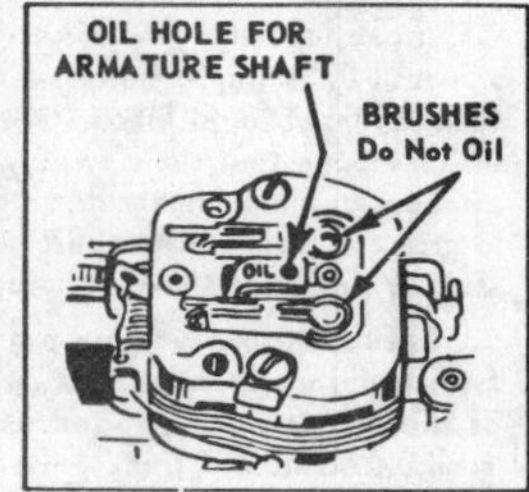

Figure 3 - Lubricating Motor

This locomotive has front and rear headlights which are illuminated by 12-16 volt miniature, bayonet-base lamps No. L57. To reach the lamps take off the locomotive body. To take out a lamp from its socket press it into the socket and turn it slightly to the left.

Note: When replacing locomotive body be sure to fit the locomotive cab over the horn. Otherwise it will sound somewhat muffled.

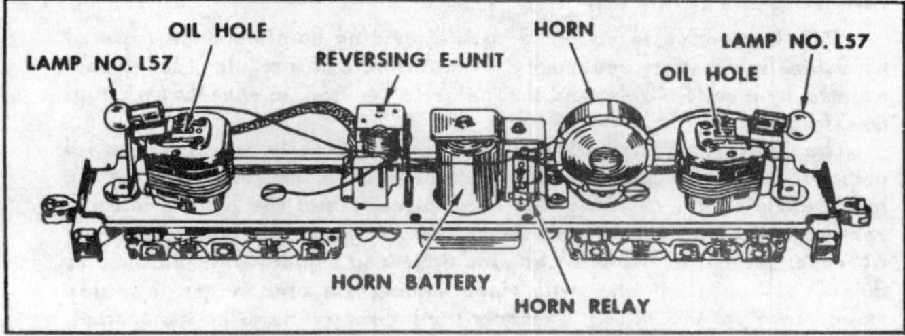

Figure 4 - No. 2321 Locomotive with Body Removed

LIONEL No. 2343 and 2344 TWIN DIESEL LOCOMOTIVES

This Lionel Twin Diesel locomotive is modeled on the 1500 horse-power freight locomotives built by the American Locomotive Company. The Lionel version of this locomotive consists of two "A" sections coupled together. One of the sections, the power car, contains the motor, the reversing "E-Unit", and the warning horn together with its controlling relay and dry cell. The other section is non-powered. The outer ends of both sections are equipped with headlights and operating remote control knuckle couplers. The couplers at the inner ends are non-operating.

These locomotives are designed especially to operate on the sharp-curved Lionel "027" track, but will run as well on "O" track, or any track measuring $1\frac{1}{4}''$ between the outside rails. The operating voltage of this locomotive ranges from 9 to 14 volts, depending on the load.

LIONEL MAGNE-TRACTION

The powered units of the twin diesels are equipped with "Magne-Traction", which means that their driving wheels are magnetized to grip the track more securely and to enable the locomotive to pull heavier loads and to negotiate steeper grades without slipping on the track. Be careful not to let pins, paper clips, screws, carpet tacks or other small iron objects to come in contact with the locomotive or they will be attracted to the magnetized wheels, gears or axles and may interfere with the action of the locomotive.

NOTE: "Magne-Traction" is not effective on aluminum, brass, or other non-ferrous rails.

COUPLING AND UNCOUPLING

Because both sections are equipped with operating couplers at their outer ends, the train can be coupled to either locomotive section. However, the traction is slightly better when the power car pulls the train, pushing the non-powered unit ahead of itself.

The locomotive is uncoupled from the train by opening either the locomotive coupler or the coupler of the car joined to it. To open the locomotive coupler wait until the sliding contact shoe on the bottom of the locomotive rides up on one of the control rails of the Remote Control Track; then push the "Uncouple" button of the controller. To open the car coupler wait until the car truck is over the central electro-magnet of the Remote Control Track; then push the "Uncouple" button.

Uncoupling operation can be performed either while the train is standing still, or while it is in motion. If the train is moving, keep one hand on the voltage control and be ready to cut down the track voltage, since the locomotive will speed up immediately when its train load is released.

To couple the locomotive to the train simply push it against the mating car. This can be done anywhere along a straight stretch of track, provided that at least one of the mating couplers is open.

Nos. 2350, 2351, 2352, and 2358 RECTIFIER TYPE ELECTRIC LOCOMOTIVES

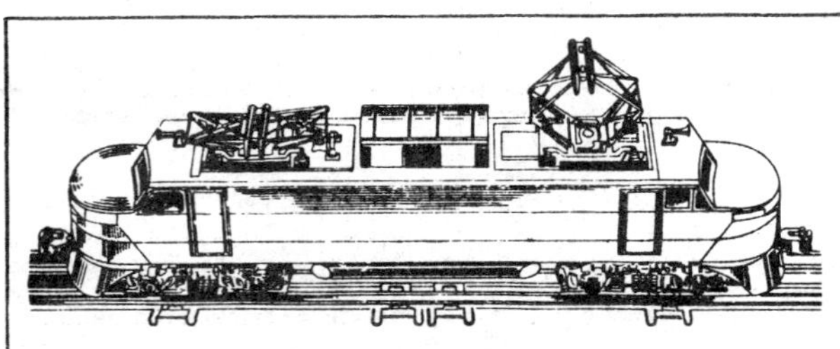

Lionel locomotives described are modeled on the new rectifier-type electric locomotive originally built by General Electric Corporation for the New Haven Railroad for fast commuter service on the electrified New York-New Haven run, but made by Lionel with markings of several other railroads using similar locomotives.

These locomotives are designed to operate on all Lionel track and are powered by a single motor worm-geared directly to two driving axles. Like most modern Lionel locomotives, they are equipped with "magne-traction" which means that their driving wheels are magnetized by powerful Alnico magnets enclosed in the driving axles. This enables the locomotive wheels to grip the rails more securely so that it can pull heavier loads and climb steeper grades without slipping on the track.

These locomotives are provided with operating remote control knuckle-type couplers at both ends so that the train can be coupled to either end of the locomotive. The locomotive can be coupled to the train along any straight stretch of track provided that at least one of the mating couplers is open. Simply run the locomotive to the train until the mating couplers mate and latch.

REVERSING THE LOCOMOTIVE

The locomotive is stopped, started and reversed by means of the reversing "E-Unit" located inside the locomotive. The E-Unit is a three position sequence relay which trips whenever current to the locomotive is interrupted.

HOW TO BLOW HORN

This locomotive is equipped with a warning horn which is powered by a flashlight battery and remotely controlled, like a regular Lionel train whistle, by a built-in relay and the "Whistle" control on your Multi-Control transformer.

The battery supplied with the locomotive must be inserted into its position before the horn can be sounded. Loosen the screw holding the round cover in the bottom of the locomotive, insert the battery into the space provided for it and reclose the bottom cover. The horn will sound whenever the car is tilted to the side or placed upside down, because in these positions the relay will close through its own weight. For this reason take out the battery whenever the locomotive is to be transported. The battery should also be removed before the locomotive is stored away, to protect the locomotive against possible battery leaks, particularly if the storage place is damp or unheated.

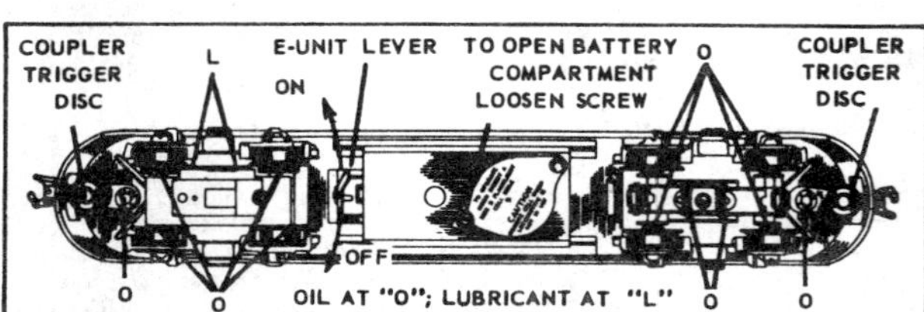

Figure 2 - Bottom View of Locomotive

PANTOGRAPH OPERATION

Although this locomotive is wired to operate on a three-rail track it is equipped with operating pantograph collectors which can be wired into the power circuit by any model railroader who wants to operate with a catenary or overhead power line.

To convert to this type of operation, unsolder and tape up the wire that leads from the collector roller to the E-Unit terminal panel, and replace it with a wire leading from the two solder lugs provided inside the locomotive body.

Figure 3 - Mounting Pantograph

Lionel does not make catenary poles or wires but "Erect-A-Wire" components for such a system, suitable for permanent mounting on a train table, are manufactured by Pittman Electric Developments Company in Sellersville, Pa. and are generally available in hobby stores.

The pantographs are held in place by a spring catch and can be removed simply by pulling the base frame upward. This is an important safety feature as it prevents damage to the pantograph in the event of derailment or catching on some overhead obstruction. To replace, open the pantograph and snap it into place by pushing in the center as shown in Figure 3.

NOTE: Because the pantographs are desinged to provide adequate pressure against a catenary, their height in fully extended position is too great to clear under Lionel No. 110 Trestle, No. 920 Tunnel Portals, and several other Lionel accessories.

The motors of this locomotive are lubricated by means of a felt oil wick which should be replenished occasionally with a few drops of light machine oil as shown in Figure 4. To get at the motors the locomotive body must first be removed by removing the two screws in the ends of the locomotive.

This locomotive has front and rear headlights which are illuminated by 12-16 volt miniature, bayonet-base lamps No. L57,

To reach the lamps take off the locomotive body. To take out a lamp from its socket press it into the socket and turn it slightly to the left.

No. 3356 & 3366 HORSE CARS

Figure 1 - Car and Corral

These sets consist of an operating car, a corral, a package of nine miniature horses, No. 364C Controller, and No. 36 Remote Control Blade which can be used in any straight section of "Super-O" track. An OTC contactor is also furnished so that the car may be used with "O" or "O27" track. The corral platforms are shipped set up for "Super-O" and "O27" track. If you have "O" track, you will have to raise the corral to the proper height by removing the rubber feet at the four corners of the corral base and replacing them upside down. They can be removed most easily with a screwdriver or large nail. You will also have to raise the control rails of the OTC contactor by inserting the wire adapters, as shown in Figure 3.

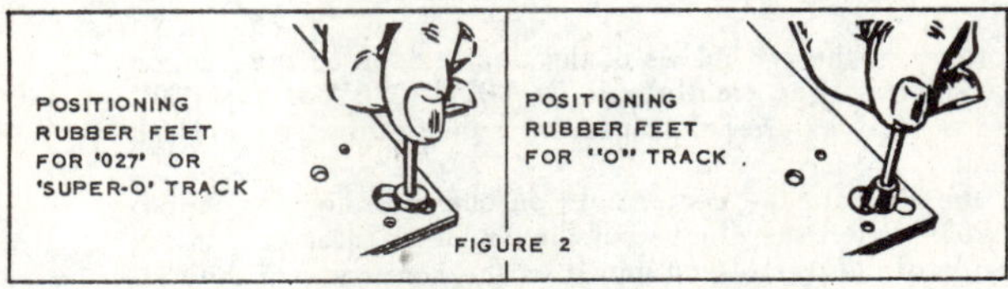

FIGURE 2

The corral and the No. 36 Control Blade which supplies power to the horse car are wired together to No. 364C controller and to transformer terminals. The car and the corral operate within the range of 11 to 14 volts but usually require fine voltage control to obtain best operation. For this reason it is usually advisable to connect them to the same variable voltage posts which are used to supply the track current. Figure 5 which shows these connections also shows the fixed voltage posts which may also be suitable.

INSTALLATION

The Corral can be placed anywhere along a straight stretch of track at least two track sections in length. The track fits into the hinged locating arms pivoted from the bottom of the corral.

If you have "O27" track it's a good idea to cover the bottom of the OTC contactor with a piece of tape to avoid possible 'shorts' against the metal locating arms.

Figure 3 - OTC Contactor

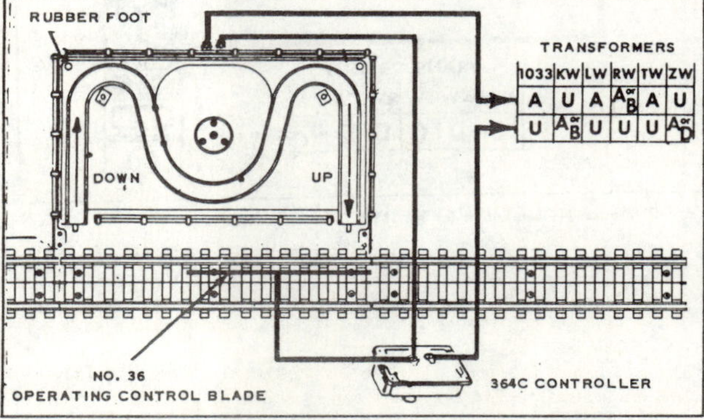

Figure 4 - Installation and Wiring of Horse Corral for "SUPER-O" Track

OPERATION

Stop the car in front of the corral so that its operating drop doors face the corral and the sliding contact shoe under one truck rides up on the "Super-O" control blade or the OTC contactor. If the car is facing the wrong way the shoe will not touch the blade and the car will not operate. Line up the miniature horses in the corral passage in the direction shown by arrows in Figure 4. To provide clear passage from one ramp to the other, the gate leading to the area around the drinking trough should be closed. Before the car can be operated, the center door *facing* the corral must be opened. (It opens about half-way). This closes an internal switch and permits current from the energized control blade or contactor to reach the car mechanism. When this door is closed, the car cannot be operated even on energized control rails. When you energize the corral and the control rails by pushing the switch of the 364C controller, the car doors drop down to meet the corral ramps and the horses troop up the ramp and enter the car. If the center door on the side facing *away* from the corral is closed the horses will pass right through the car and come out the other door. If the center door of the car is left open the horses will remain inside the car. The vibration of the corral platform can be regulated by an adjustment screw in the center of the bottom.

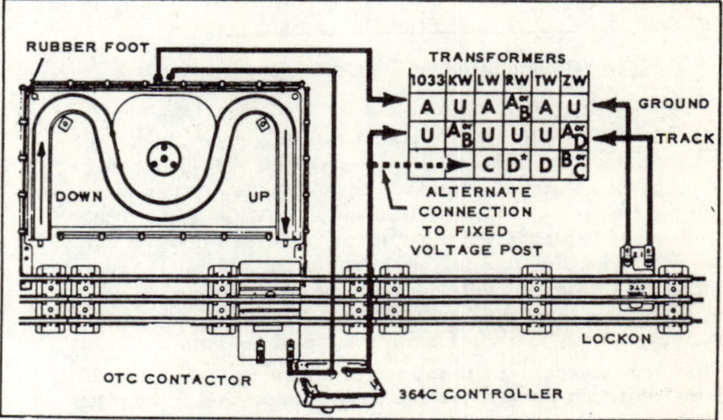

Figure 5 - Installation and Wiring of Horse Corral for "027" and "0" Track.

NOTE

When used with "Super-O" the unit may energize (operate) each time the train passes the corral. If this should happen bend the No. 36 Control Blade toward the center rail.

PLEASE NOTE

Due to the handling during shipment and the tendency of certain materials to deaden vibration in the horse corral, it may be necessary to make an adjustment in order to obtain maximum operating efficiency.

Adjust as follows:

1–If any section of the corral center section has come into contact with the outer fence (see Figure 1) bend it away slightly as this could dampen the vibrations required for the "High Spirited" action of the horses.

2–With the corral set in position on your layout place a horse in the path and adjust the screw underneath the base for the desired speed.

No. 3357 COP & HOBO CAR

Figure 1—Operation of the Cop and Hobo Car.

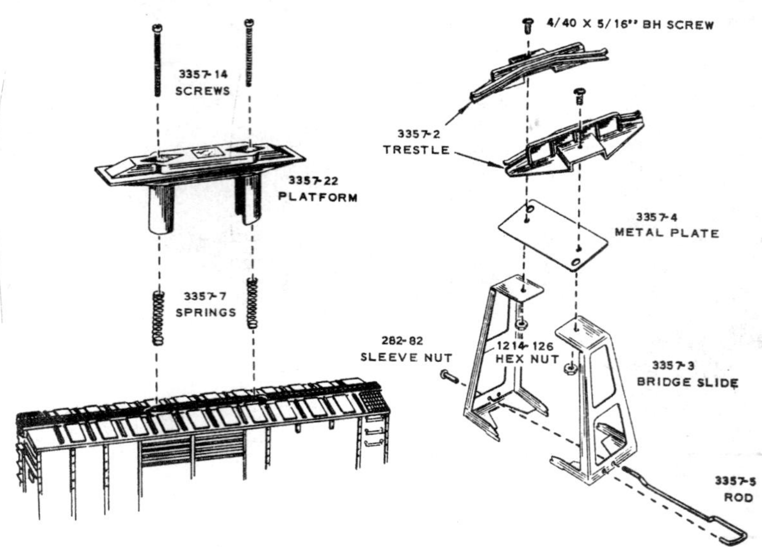

Figure 3—Assembly of the Trestle.

No. 3357 Cop and Hobo Car enacts an exciting chase involving a railroad policeman and a hobo. As the car, with the hobo riding on the top, passes under a trestle, a railroad cop who has been waiting on the trestle hops to the top of the car. At the same time, however, the hobo jumps off the car to the trestle. When the car again passes under the trestle the situation is reversed – the policeman jumps off and the hobo jumps back on.

Before the car can be operated you must assemble the trestle to the track and the special platform to the top of the car.

The platform is assembled to the top of the car by means of two long screws which go through the two long springs and screw into the car roof.

The two halves of the trestle are held across the tops by a metal plate and two plastic guides fastened to the trestle halves by two screws and nuts.

The bottoms of the two halves of the trestle hook on the flanges of the track rails. (The trestle will fit "027", "0" or Super"0" track). The two halves are held together on the bottom by a rod and a sleeve nut.

Insert the rod into the center hole on one side hooking it into the other hole. Insert the sleeve nut through the center hole in the opposite side of the trestle and spin it on the screw end of the rod.

No. 3359 TWIN-BIN DUMP CAR

No. 3359 Dump Car is equipped with two bins which operate individually and in sequence so that the dump car can be unloaded in two distinct steps into the same track-side storage receptacle, or carry two different kinds of load which can be unloaded at two different stations.

Because of its length and its novel design, this car cannot be operated by centering it on a standard remote control track section, like other operating cars, but requires the use of OTC contactors, two of which are furnished with each No. 3359 Dump Car.

OTC CONTACTORS

OTC contactors snap onto the track just like ordinary track lockons. They are equipped with two short auxiliary control rails which can be energized by means of a push button switch furnished with the car. Either track voltage or fixed voltage may be used as shown in Figure 2.

OTC contactors can be used with either "027" or "0" track, but when used with "0" track the height of the OTC control rails must be increased by inserting the brass rail clips as shown in Figure 1.

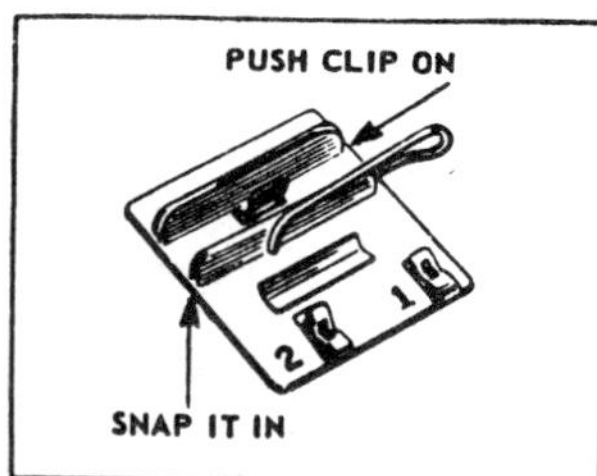

Figure 1—Adjusting Rail Height of OTC Contactor

1033	KW	LW	RW	TW	ZW
C	D	C	D	D	B or C

Figure 2—Installation for No. 3359 Twin-Bin Dump Car

INSTALLING OTC CONTACTORS

If both sides of the dump car carry the same freight and are to be unloaded into the same receptacle, the car has to be moved about half of its length after the first bin has been unloaded, so that the second bin can be dumped into the same place. For this reason the two OTC Contactors have to be clipped to the track about 13" apart, so that one of the car's sliding shoes will be on a control rail in both of its operating positions.

No. 3361 LUMBER CAR

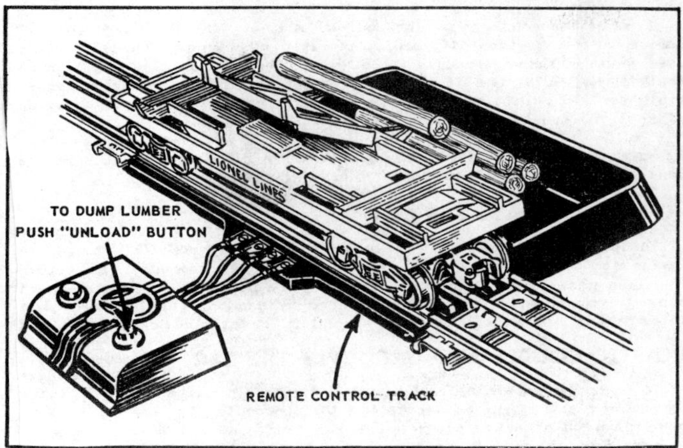

Fig. 1—No. 3361 Lumber Car in Operating Position on UCS Track Section.

To operate Lionel remote control unloading cars a special section of track is required. The special section used with "O" track is known as the UCS; the section matching "027" track is No. 6019.

A remote control section is inserted in the track layout as any other section of track but to make coupling and uncoupling easier, at least one regular straight section should be placed on both sides of the remote control section.

One remote control section is packed with every Lionel set. Additional sections may be purchased from your dealer. Since these sections do not consume any power except when actually used, any number of them can be installed in a layout without overloading the transformer. If other operating cars are added to the outfit, they can all be operated from the same remote control section.

UNLOADING THE CAR

To unload No. 3361 Lumber Car, position the car on the remote control track so that the car's sliding contact shoes ride up on the control rails. Then press the "Unload" button several times. Each time you press the button the dumping ribs of the car will rise a notch until the logs roll off the car. After reaching their highest elevation, the dumping mechanism drops back to normal position.

The mechanism of this car operates on 12-16 volts. If you are running the train slowly and track voltage is low you may have to increase it when unloading to get a snappier dumping action.

Nos. 3376 & 3386 GIRAFFE CARS

The Giraffe being transported in this box car has his head protruding through the roof hatch. When warned by a "low-bridge" signal, the Giraffe lowers his head to avoid the obstruction. After passing, the Giraffe rises again.

This action takes place as car passes over a cam plate which is placed along side of a straight section of track (or on the INSIDE of a straight and curved section).

INSTALLING TELL-TALES TO POLE

- Slide the twelve Tell-Tales onto the Extension Rod.
- Insert the knurled end of the Extension Rod into the hole in the horizontal brace of the Pole - pressing it fully in place (see illustration).

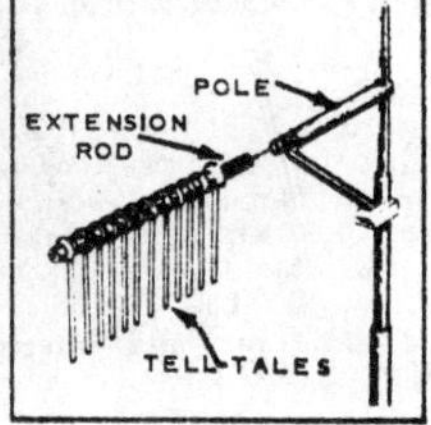

CLAMPING SIGNAL BASE TO TRACK

The Signal Base may be clamped to any straight track. If placed next to a curved track, it must be faced so that the Pole is on the INSIDE of the curve.

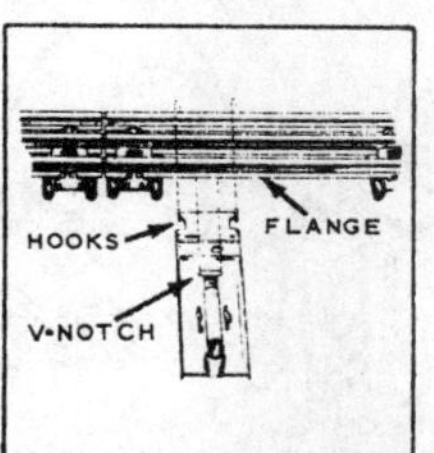

- Place Signal Base under the track with the Flange of the outer rail against V-Notch.
- Hold the track and press the Signal Base inward until the Hooks are clear to clamp the Flange of the opposite track rail.

CAM PLATE TO SIGNAL BASE

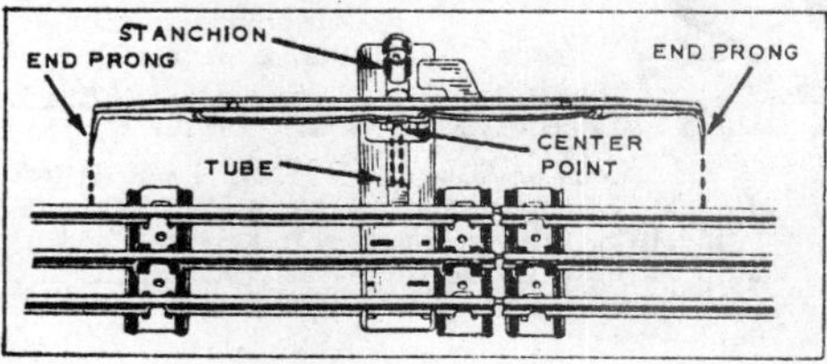

- Place Cam Plate centered over the Signal Base with the End Prongs faced inward toward the track rail.
- Put End Prongs against side of track rail and press the center of the Cam Plate inward allowing the Center Point to lock in the Tube of the Signal Base.
- Insert the Pole into the Stanchion with the Tell-Tales hanging over the track.

- Giraffe is packed in a "locked - down" position. To unlock, push Hook with finger.
- To lock, push giraffe head down.

No. 3464 OPERATING BOX CAR

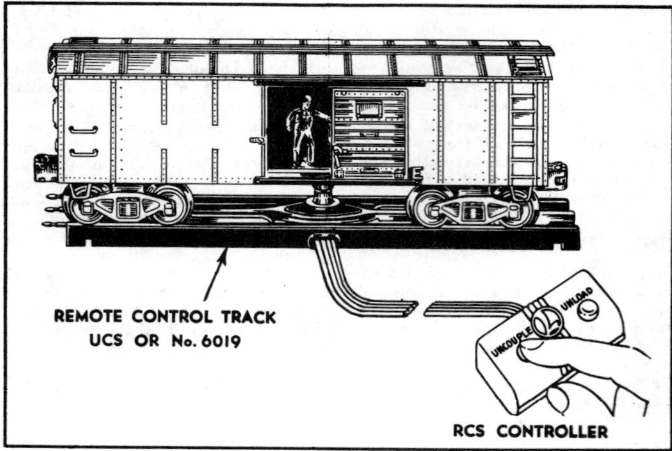

Figure 1 - No. 3464 Box Car Positioned for Opening Door

To open the couplers or the door of the No. 3464 Box Car a special Remote Control Section of track is required. The Remote Control Section used with '0' Gauge track is the UCS; the section matching '027' Gauge track is No. 6019. One of these sections is included with every Lionel train set. To permit operation in various places in the layout additional sections can be purchased from your dealer.

Note: This car cannot be operated by the old RCS and No. 1019 Remote Control Sections which have no central electromagnets.

HOW TO OPERATE THE CAR

To open the door and make the crewman appear position the plunger in the bottom of the car directly over the track electromagnet (See Figure 1). Then press the 'Uncouple' button. Once opened, the door does not close automatically but must be closed by hand. Slide the door shut to move the man back into the car and to reset the mechanism.

HOW TO COUPLE AND UNCOUPLE THE CAR

To uncouple cars the front wheels of either truck must be directly above the electromagnet. Pressing the 'Uncouple' button will pull down the iron armature plate under the truck and allow the coupler to snap open. To couple cars simply push them together.

No. 3472 AUTOMATIC MILK CAR

WITH UNLOADING PLATFORM

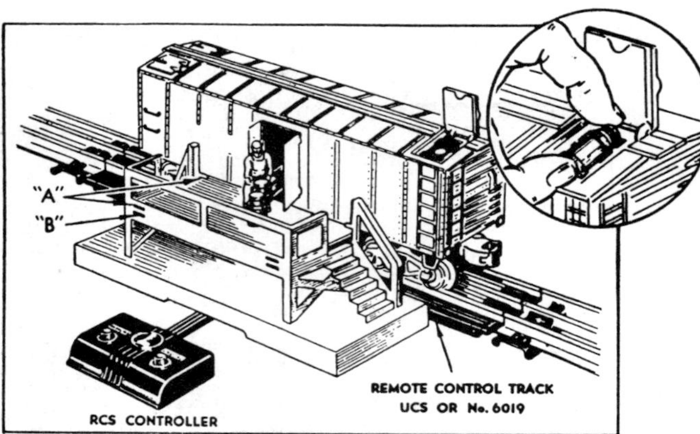

Figure 1—Installation for Automatic Milk Car

To operate Lionel Automatic Milk Car No. 3472 a special five-rail Remote Control Section of track is required. The Remote Control Section used with "O" track is known as the UCS. The Remote Control Section which matches the "027" track is known as No. 6019. The previously manufactured No. 1019 and RCS Remote Control Sections cannot be used with this car, which is equipped with magnetic couplers.

One Remote Control Section together with its controller is packed with every Lionel train set, but as many more as desired can be purchased from your dealer and used in your layout. Remote Control Sections are inserted into the layout as any ordinary sections of track and are used to uncouple cars equipped with automatic knuckle-type couplers and to operate Lionel automatic unloading cars.

In order to align the couplers and make coupling and uncoupling easier it is advisable to include at least one straight section of track on either side of the Remote Control Section.

HOW TO INSTALL UNLOADING PLATFORM

The unloading platform provided with Lionel Automatic Milk Car must be installed next to the Remote Control Section. Insert the Controller through the opening in the base of the platform so that controller cable runs under the platform and the Remote Control Section rests on the platform base and in front of the platform. See Figure 1. After that is done, insert the Remote Control Section and the unloading platform in the desired place in the layout.

When used with "O" track, the floor of the loading platform should be inserted into the top slots of the platform framework ("A" in Figure 1) in order to compensate for the greater height of the "O" track. When used with "027" track the floor should fit into the bottom slots ("B" in Figure 1.) This changeover is done simply by pulling out the platform floor and inserting it into the proper slots in the framework. Be sure to insert the platform floor into a matching pair of slots on the side of the framework facing the track.

When used with "027" track layouts, the **action of the milk car can be greatly improved by making sure that No. 6019 Remote Control Section is located as close as possible to the platform.** The play which exists because of the width of the slot in the base of the platform (Figure 2) can be eliminated by wedging a small spacer between the Remote Control Track and the back of the platform base.

SLOT

Figure 2—Bottom View of 6019 Section Properly Located on Platform Base

OPERATING THE MILK CAR

A set of miniature milk cans is furnished with each milk car. These are loaded into the car through an opening in the roof of the car shown in Figure 1. They can go into the opening in only one way—with the top of the can toward the center of the car. The unloading chute of the milk car holds five cans. Do not try to force any more than that into the car.

To unload, maneuver the car so that the sliding contacts of both car trucks are on the Remote Control Section in front of the unloading platform. Then push the controller button marked "Unload." Each time the button is pushed the doors of the car open and the milkman pushes a can out into the platform. Adjust your track voltage until the milkman unloads the cans without knocking them over. You will notice that a small magnet has been inserted into the bottom of each can to help keep it upright on the platform.

To uncouple the car, maneuver it so that the coupler you wish opened is over the center electromagnet of the Remote Control Section, then press the controller button marked "Uncouple."

The cars can be coupled anywhere along the track provided that at least one of the mating couplers is open. If both are closed move one of the cars to the Remote Control Section and push the "Uncouple" button or open coupler by hand by pulling down armature plate under the truck.

After assembling the platform floor to the framework, bend the two tabs down to hold the floor in place. (See Figure 3) Make sure to make a neat, sharp bend by using a screwdriver or some other tool so that the floor is kept from slipping out and interfering with the Milk Car doors.

Figure 3—After Inserting Floor Bend Down Tabs As Shown

No. 3520 SEARCHLIGHT CAR

WITH ROTATING SEARCHLIGHT

No. 3520 Rotating Searchlight Car is equipped with a fixed searchlight lamp and a rotating searchlight housing which is turned by a driving coil. The searchlight housing is loose and is packed separately. To assemble the car for operation, lower the housing over the lamp so that it rests on the special rubber washer cemented to the top of the driving coil. See Figure 1.

CAUTION: Do not remove this washer or disturb the little rubber 'fingers' on the washer surface. It is the main driving element of the searchlight and the searchlight housing will not turn without it. If you should lose it replace with Lionel Part No. 3520-16

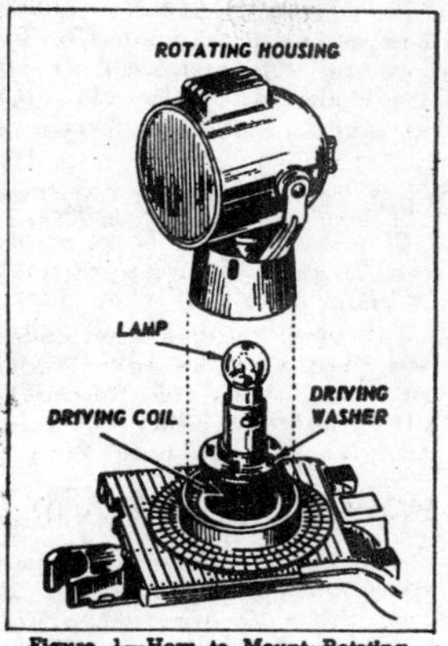

Figure 1—How to Mount Rotating Housing

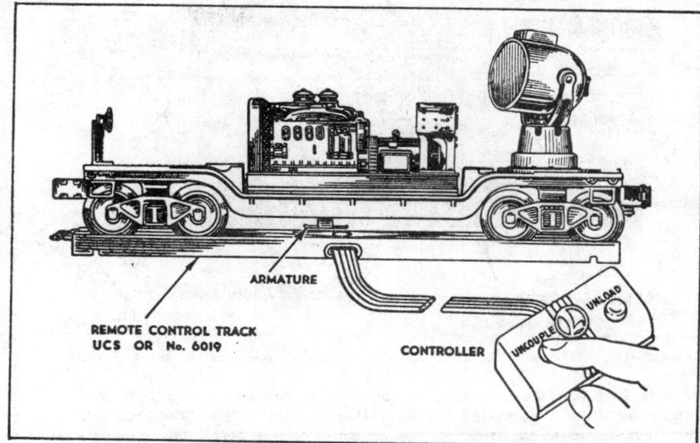

Figure 2—No. 3520 Searchlight Car in Position for Switching on the Searchlight

HOW TO CONTROL SEARCHLIGHT

The searchlight lamp and the motion of the rotating housing are switched on and off by means of a UCS, No. 6019 or No. 6009 Remote Control Track Set, one of which is supplied with every Lionel Train outfit. *Note:* This car *cannot* be operated by the old RCS and No. 1019 Remote Control Track Sections which have no central electro magnet.

LIONEL No. 3562 BARREL CAR

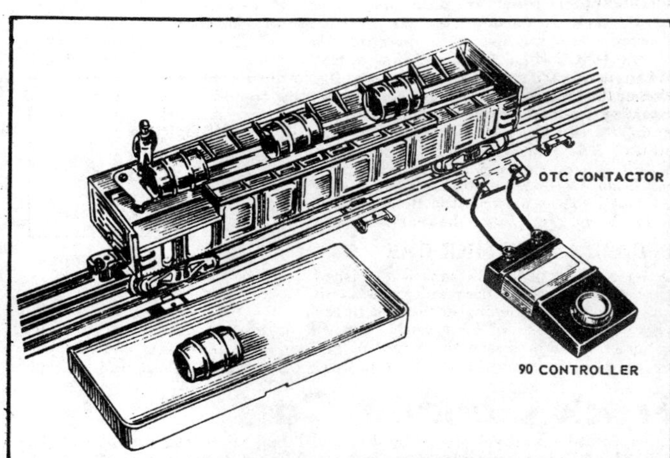

Figure 1—Installation for Operating No. 3562 Barrel Car

Lionel No. 3562 Barrel Car is usually operated by means of the special OTC track contactor furnished with the car and illustrated in Figure 2. The OTC contactor can be clipped on any straight track section in the same manner as a track lockon and is connected by a pair of wires to a No. 90 push-button controller. The Barrel Car is positioned on the OTC contactor so that either one of the contact sliders rides up on a control rail of the OTC contactor. Pushing the controller button will now connect track power to the contactor rails and energize the cars mechanism causing the barrels to move along the car until they reach the end and roll off.

Note: The Barrel Car can also be operated on any regular remote control section by positioning one of its sliding shoes on the right-hand side of the remote control section and pushing the "Unload" button of the controller. Care must be taken, however, not to locate both sliding shoes on remote control rails, because pushing the "Unload" button under these conditions will cause a "short". While the car will also operate if "Uncouple" button is pressed this is not recommended because continuous pressure on the "Uncouple" button energizes the track electro-magnet causing it to overheat.

Figure 2—Adjusting Rail Height of OTC Contactor

The OTC Controller can be used with either "027" or "O" track, but when used with "O" track the height of its control rails must be increased by inserting the brass rail clips which are furnished with the Barrel Car outfit. Figure 2 illustrates how this is done.

INSTALLATION WITH NO. 362 BARREL LOADER

If you wish to use No 3562 Barrel Car together with No. 362 Barrel Loader make this installation:

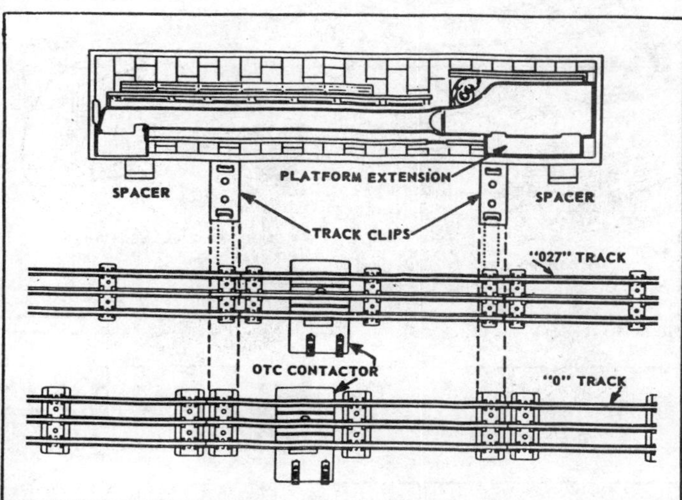

Figure 3 - How to Install No. 362 Barrel Loader for Use with No. 3562 Barrel Car

Join three sections of straight track and set them against the Barrel Loader so that the center section fits on the loader track clips. If you have "0" track the section will just fit on the clips. If you have "027" track, which is a little shorter, the loader clips will accommodate a full section plus a track tie of the of the next section. See Figure 3.

The rubber spacers furnished with this outfit and shown in Figure 3 are not absolutely necessary in most cases but they will help to align the track and keep it the proper distance away from the loader. Figure 4 shows in cross section how the spacers fit the track. If your track is "027" mount the spacers as shown. If the track is "0" reverse the spacer so that the higher slot in the spacer fits the higher rail flange of "0" track.

Figure 4 - Position of Track Spacer

The OTC track contactor is clipped next to the center track tie of the middle track section. The idea is to locate the OTC contactor at the center of the loader so that one of the car's contact sliders will ride on the contactor control rails whether the car is positioned for loading or for unloading. See Figures 5 and 6.

A little metal platform extension is clipped on the lower end of the loader platform as shown in Figure 3 so that the barrels unloaded from the car will roll down the platform extension to the loader.

ELECTRICAL CONNECTIONS

Normally the only electrical connection needed for operating the Barrel Car is accomplished by connecting the two spring clips of the OTC contactor to the binding posts of the 96C controller, as shown in Figure 1. In some cases, however,

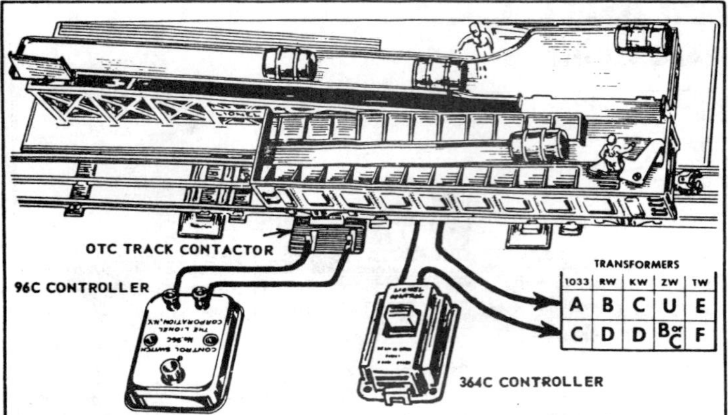

Figure 5 - No. 3562 Barrel Car Positioned for Unloading into No. 362 Barrel Loader

you may find that the operation is improved if you make it independent of track voltage by using a so-called "fixed voltage" post of your transformer. This has the effect of providing power for the operation of the barrel car even though track power may be turned off entirely. The installation using "fixed voltage" is illustrated in Figure 6.

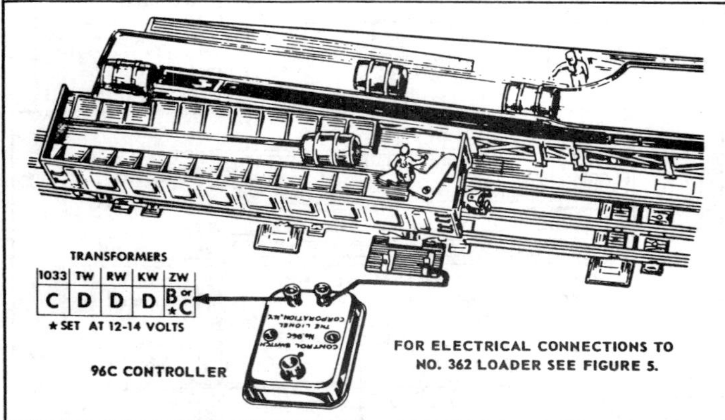

Figure 6 - Loading the Barrel Car. The Fixed Voltage Connection Shown Is Optional

HOW TO UNLOAD BARRELS FROM CAR TO LOADER

To move the barrels from the loaded car to the loader platform locate the car so that its chute is against the loader platform extension, as shown in Figure 5. (If your installation has been properly made, the slide shoe of the left-hand truck will be on one of the control rails of the OTC contactor). Press the button of the 96C controller to energize the control rails and the barrels will move from the car to the loader. As the barrels roll onto the loader platform operate the loader in short spurts to move the barrels along the loader.

HOW TO MOVE BARRELS FROM THE LOADER TO THE CAR

To move the barrels from the loader to the empty car position the car so that it is under the chute of the loader. In this position, the slide shoe of the right-hand truck will be on the control rail of the OTC contactor.

By operating the 364C controller you move the barrels from the lower platform up toward the loader chute where they will roll down into the waiting empty barrel car. By pressing the No. 90 controller button you will be able to move the barrel along the car to make room for the next barrel as it comes rolling down from the loader chute. To keep the barrels from rolling off the end of the car while you are trying to load it, swing the metal platform which holds the figure of the man all the way back and hook the bent part in the back of the catch provided in the car surface. (See Fig. 7) Don't forget to unhook it when you are ready to unload, or else it won't allow the barrels to move off the car.

Figure 7—How to Keep the Barrels from Being Unloaded Accidentally

HOW TO COUPLE AND UNCOUPLE BARREL CAR

The barrel car is provided with regular Lionel remote-control magnetic knuckle couplers which are uncoupled on either the 6019 or the UCS Remote Control Track. To uncouple the car move it to the remote control track so that the truck you want opened is directly over the center electro-magnet. Then push the UNCOUPLE button of the controller. To couple the car you simply move it over to the mating car or locomotive until the couplers mate and latch. This can be done on any straight stretch of track provided that at least one of the mating couplers is open.

LIONEL No. 3927 Track Cleaning Car

FOR "0" AND "027" TRACK

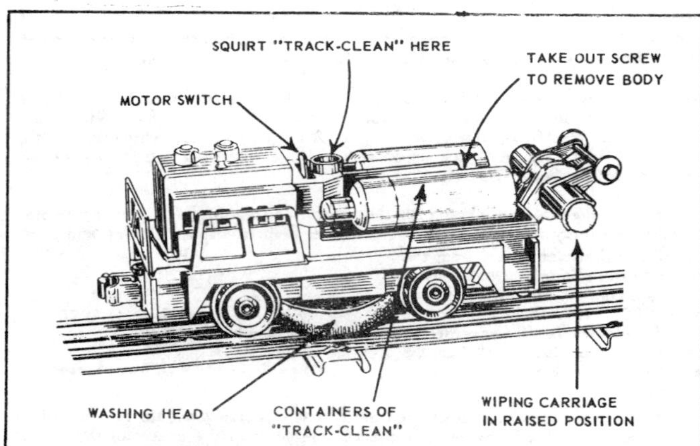

Figure 1 - No. 3927 Track Cleaning Car

Lionel No. 3927 Track Cleaning Car has been designed to clean and condition the track rails in order to restore their appearance and to improve locomotive traction.

To do an effective job of track cleaning, the accumulated dirt and grease are first scrubbed off the rails by means of a motor-driven rotating plastic sponge "washing head" saturated with Lionel's special "Track-Clean" fluid. Then the dissolved dirt and grime are wiped off the rails by means of an absorbent cotton cylinder pressed to the track by means of a spring-loaded "wiping carriage".

To clean the rails couple the Track Cleaning Car to a locomotive or a work train. Squirt a little "Track Clean" from the plastic squeeze containers into the well on top of the car. Switch on the washing head motor and let the locomotive pull the Track Cleaning Car slowly around the track several times. If you have grades in your layout and find that your locomotive has trouble in pulling the heavy track cleaning car, couple the car to the front of the locomotive, or back the locomotive up the grade pushing the Track Cleaning Car ahead of it. The wetting action of "Track-Clean" will improve the locomotive traction immediately.

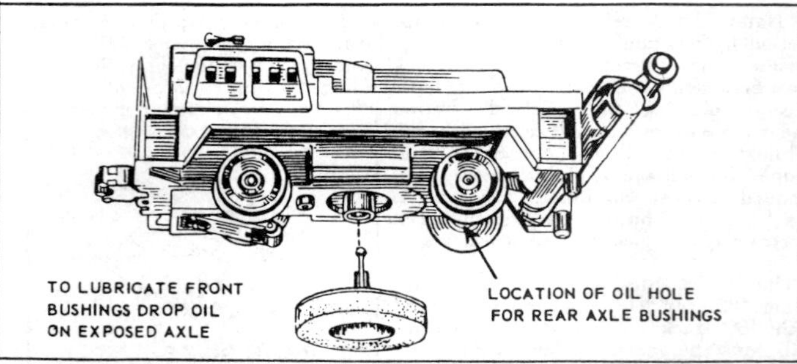

Figure 2 - Bottom View of Track Cleaning Car Showing Mounting of Washing Head Assembly

After several circuits of the track, switch off the motor, pull out the washing head, lower the wiping carriage loaded with a cotton cylinder over the rails and let the car make several more turns to wipe the track clean. In exceptional cases where the track is very dirty the washing and wiping action can be done at the same time, so that some of the dissolved dirt and grease can be picked up off the rails immediately.

When the sponge washing head becomes saturated with dirt or grease it can be washed out with Lionel "Track-Clean". The washing head will last a very long time, but when it finally wears out through long use it can be easily replaced. To remove the sponge with its metal backing from the washing head shaft squeeze the two plastic catches (See Figure 4). The new part snaps right on. The sponge and metal back assembly is Part No. 3927-47

Fig. 3
Wiping Carriage in Lowered Position

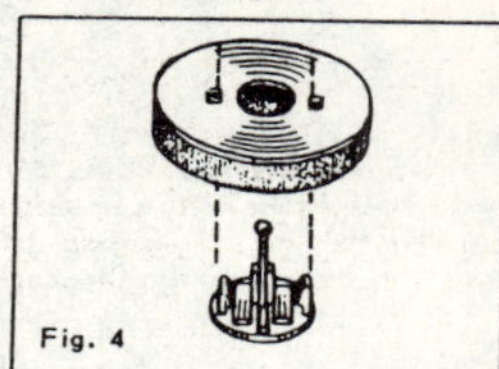
Fig. 4
How to Replace Washing Sponge

A generous supply of Lionel "Track-Clean" fluid and of cotton wiping cylinders is furnished with the car.

Fig. 5
No. 3927-75 "Track-Clean"

WARNING: Lionel No. 3927-75 "Track-Clean" has been specially compounded for use with No. 3927 Track Cleaning Car. It is non-toxic, non-flammable and non-corrosive and will greatly improve your locomotive traction.

No. 3656 STOCK CAR OUTFIT

FOR "027" and "O" GAUGE TRACK

What Is Included In the Outfit

Check these items:

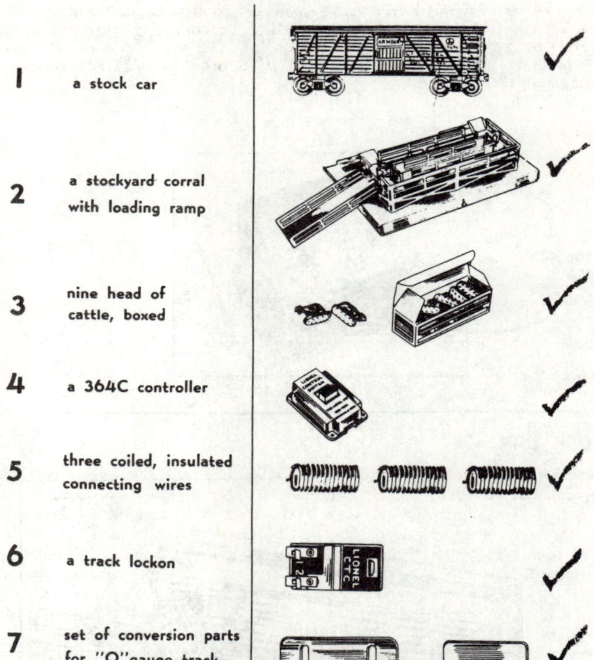

1 a stock car

2 a stockyard corral with loading ramp

3 nine head of cattle, boxed

4 a 364C controller

5 three coiled, insulated connecting wires

6 a track lockon

7 set of conversion parts for "O" gauge track

ground clip — power blade

Here's the easiest way to do this job!
use both hands --- do one side at a time

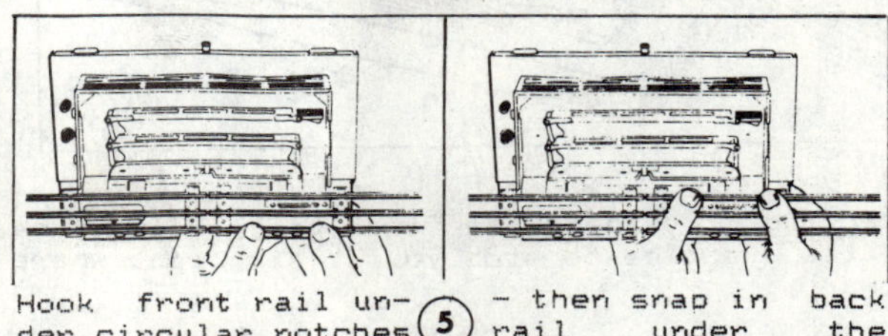

(5) Hook front rail under circular notches -- top for "O" gauge, bottom for "027" gauge track - — then snap in back rail under the corresponding back notches squeezing the track slightly.

How to Install Corral Platform In the Layout

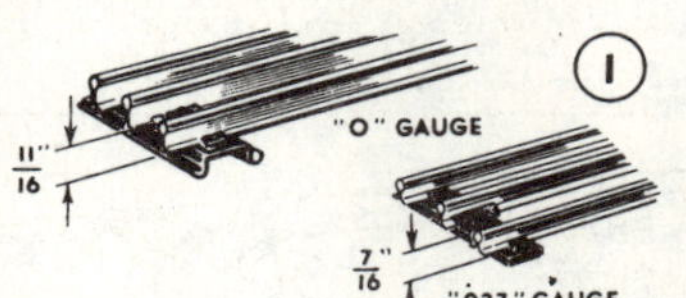

Important!
This platform comes assembled for '027' track. If your track is '027' continue reading. If it is 'O', first read page 7.

Quickest way to tell the difference is by shape of track ties.

(2)

First, assemble two-sections of track on the platform base with track joint in the center, but don't try to fit it in place yet. First read below.

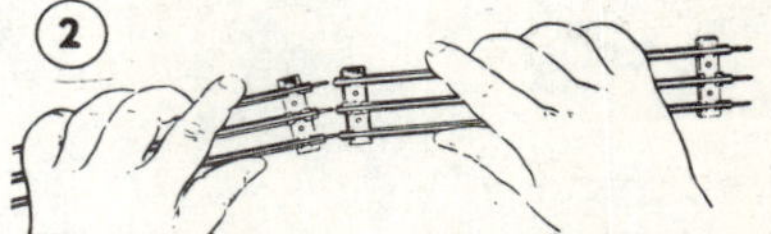

Put this two-section track on the platform base with track joint in the center, but don't try to fit it in place yet. First read below.

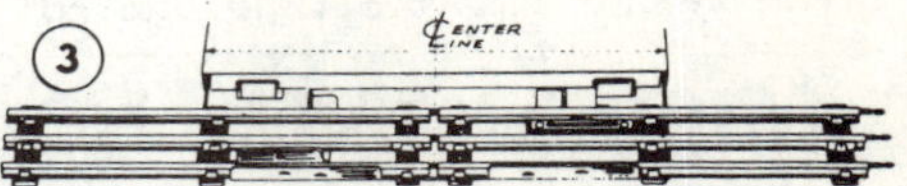

(4) The track in the picture is "027" and fits under the bottom notches. The top notches are for "O" gauge track which is higher (See Fig. 1).

Make sure the track fits under all four corresponding notches or the car will be tilted and will not operate properly.

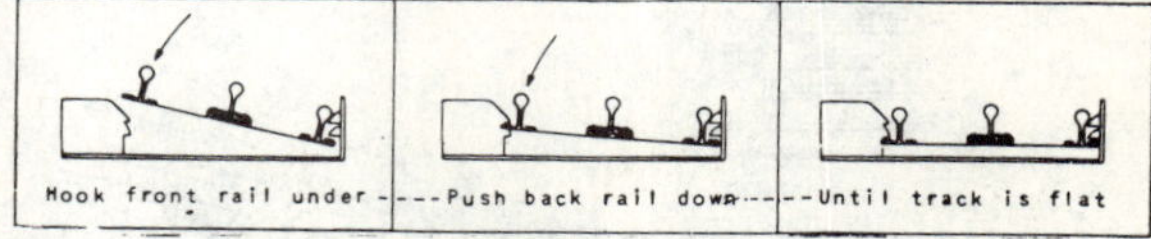

(6) After the two-section track and the platform are assembled together, fit them to the rest of the layout. You can put on the loading ramp or leave it off. It's not needed for operation of the outfit.

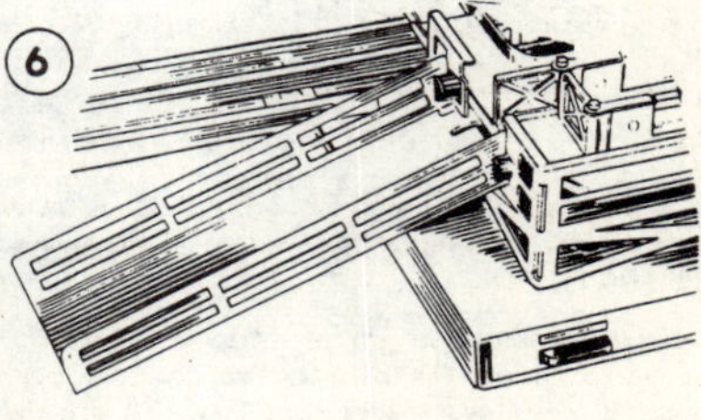

THESE ARE THE WIRE CONNECTIONS

* Lockon clip No. 2 to plain binding post
* Insulated post (with the black fibre washer) to either control screw
* Lockon clip No. 1 to remaining controller screw

HOW TO MAKE ELECTRICAL CONNECTIONS

First snap the lockon onto the track next to your corral platform.

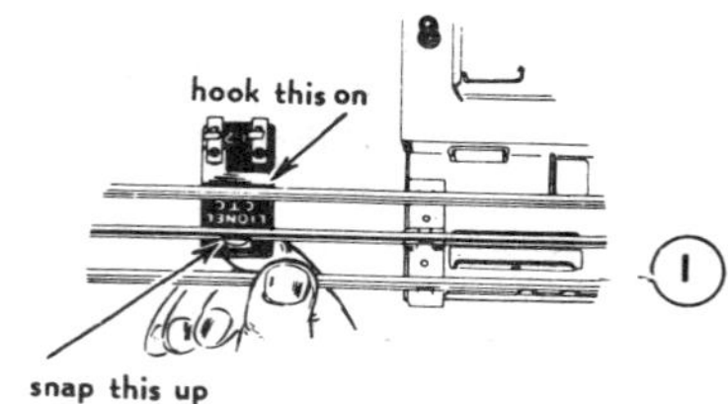

Don't forget to clean off the insulation from the ends of the wires.

Either side of track and of platform will do. but this spot is the most convenient.

Press down clip.
Slip wire into loop.

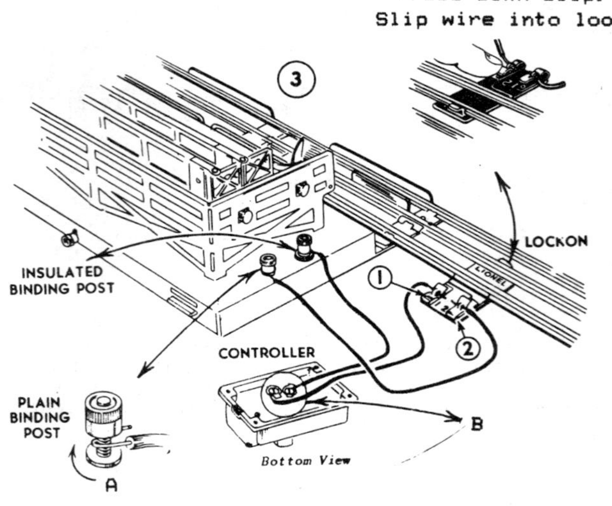

The trick here is NOT TO CUT THE WIRES. Wrap the wire around your index finger. Rest the wire on a solid surface. Place the knife edge firmly on the wire. Pull the wire toward you.

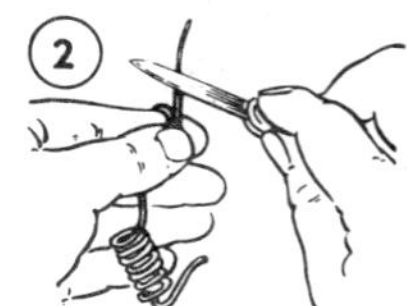

A If you wrap wire around post clockwise (as arrow), it won't slip out as you tighten the nut.

B You'll have to use a screw-driver to tighten these. Disregard the letters on the bottom.

Connected in this way the car and the platform get the same voltage as the train. To raise or lower the voltage to obtain better action move the transformer voltage control handle.

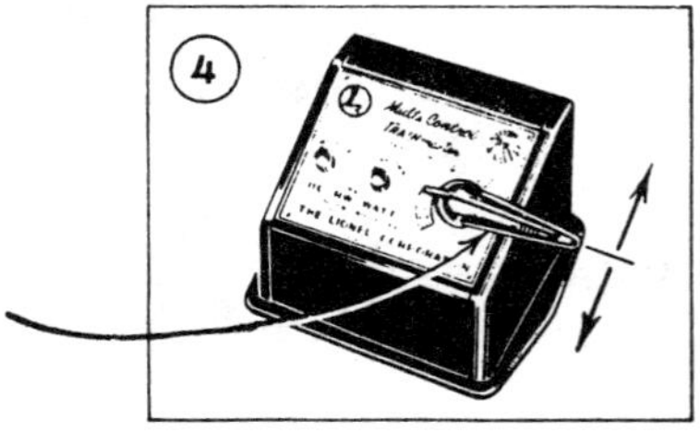

HOW TO OPERATE THE STOCK CAR

Line up five head of cattle (all the car will hold) with their heads away from the ramp. Use any passage you wish. Open proper gates.

LINE UP THE CAR IN FRONT OF THE PLATFORM ACCURATELY. THE OVERHEAD DOORS MUST LINE UP WITH THE EDGES OF THE PLATFORM.

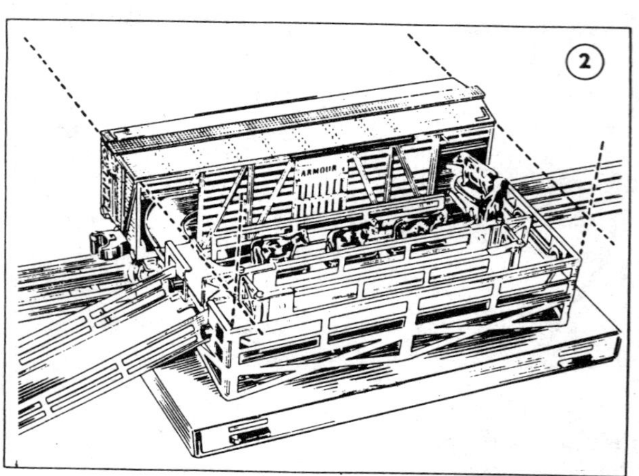

Better do it by hand the first time -- It takes a little practice to stop your train right where you want it.

IS YOUR TRANSFORMER CONNECTED TO THE TRACK?

IS IT PLUGGED IN THE WALL SOCKET?

IS THE TRANSFORMER VOLTAGE TURNED ON?

YES? THEN SLIDE THE CONTROLLER SWITCH:

The overhead car doors will rise. Platform ramps will drop to meet the car and the vibrations of the platform and the cattle track in the car will send the cattle trooping along the corral passage and into the car.

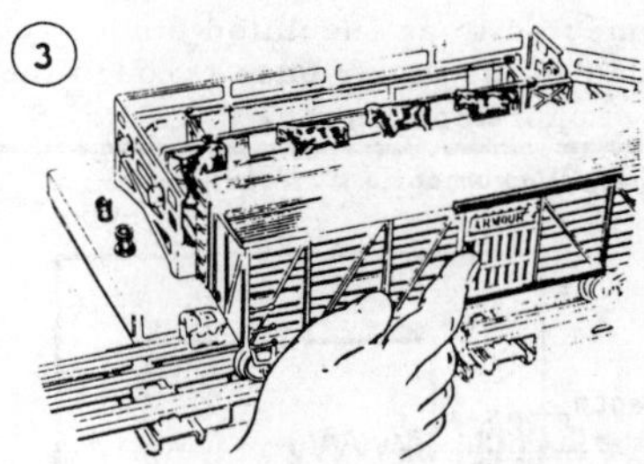

If you want the cattle to pass right through the car and back of the car. If you want them to stay in the car slide the back door shut.

When sliding door is closed, the stop inside the car. Opening the door moves the stop out of the way and lets the cattle out of the car.

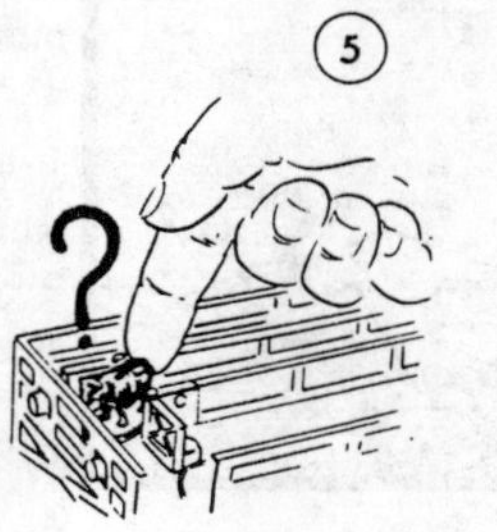

If your "steers" get balky - just like real cattle do - and refuse to turn a corner give them a "helping hand" and raise the voltage. A thin film of Lionel lubricant along the edge of the base helps them slide around corners more easily.

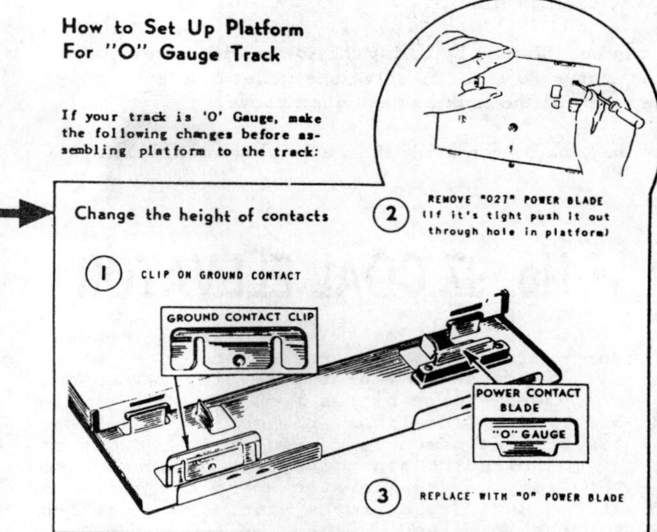

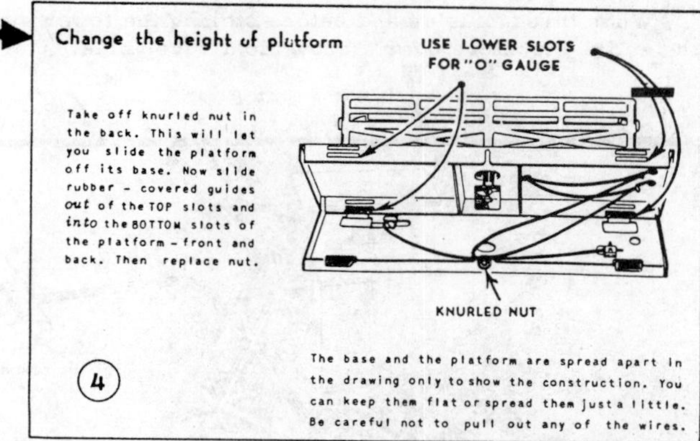

How to Take Care Of Your Stock Car Outfit

This outfit has been thoroughly tested at the Factory and should be in perfect operating condition. If you give it a little care it will last you a long time.

Don't bend or force anything. If you distort the platform or the base they may not work properly.

Don't destroy or alter the little 'fingers' on the bottom of the miniature animals. These fingers cause the animal to move and turn.

Don't let the contact blades get rusty. Polish the edges with fine sand paper and cover with a light coat of Lionel lubricant to keep from rusting. If your track is '027' do the same thing for edge of platform used as 'ground,'

keep these edges clean

OPERATING ACCESSORIES

No. 30 & No. 38 WATER TOWER

The No. 30 Water Tower and No. 38 Pumping Water Tower are both wired either to a pair of fixed voltage terminals of the transformer or directly to track by means of a Lockon (see Figure). To operate the Water Tower press No. 96C Controller button. The spout will drop to "fill" the water tank in the tender. When the button is released, the spout will lift. If operation of water tower is sluggish, raise track voltage slightly before pushing button. Normal operation requires 12-16 volts.

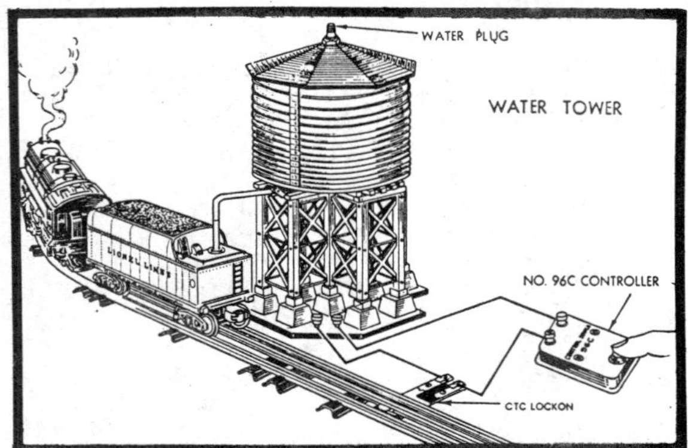

The movement of the water spout is accomplished by a coil-and-solenoid mechanism linked to a push rod which bears against the bottom of the water spout. In its normal non-operating position the water spout is kept in upright position by a coiled spring located in the back of the solenoid plunger tube. When the solenoid is energized the plunger moves back into the tube drawing the push rod with it and allowing the water spout to lower itself by gravity.

One side of the coil is connected to an insulated binding post while the other side is grounded to the tower base through the coil mounting plate and the metal supporting column.

Wiring Diagram of No. 30 Water Tower

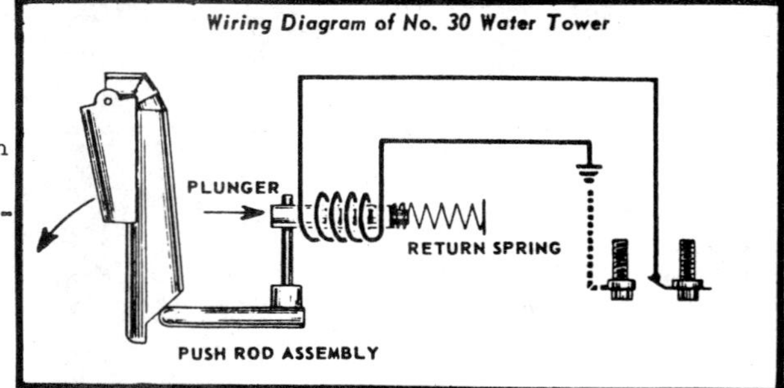

To prepare the No. 38 Pumping Water Tower for operation remove the water plug from the center of the roof, and using a funnel, pour very slowly 7 ounces (slightly less than a glassful) of clean cold water into the transparent plastic tank. Do not fill beyond the No. 1 graduation of the scale at the side of the tank or the water will overflow. Replace the water plug.

To operate, press No. 96C Controller button. The spout will drop to horizontal position for apparent "filling" the water tank in the tender and at the same time, a concealed motor-driven pump will transfer the water from the outer transparent tank to a second tank concealed under the tower roof. When the outer tank appears empty, release the Controller button, the tank spout will lift, and the outer tank will slowly "refill" itself.

While plain water may be used, a much more striking effect can be obtained by filling the tower with water colored by means of one of No. 38-70 Color Tablets supplied with the Water Tower. Dissolve one tablet in a few spoonfuls of hot water, add cold water to make up the required 7 ounces and fill the tank as described above.

When through using and before storing the tower away, empty the tank by removing the water plug and inverting the entire structure over a convenient receptacle.

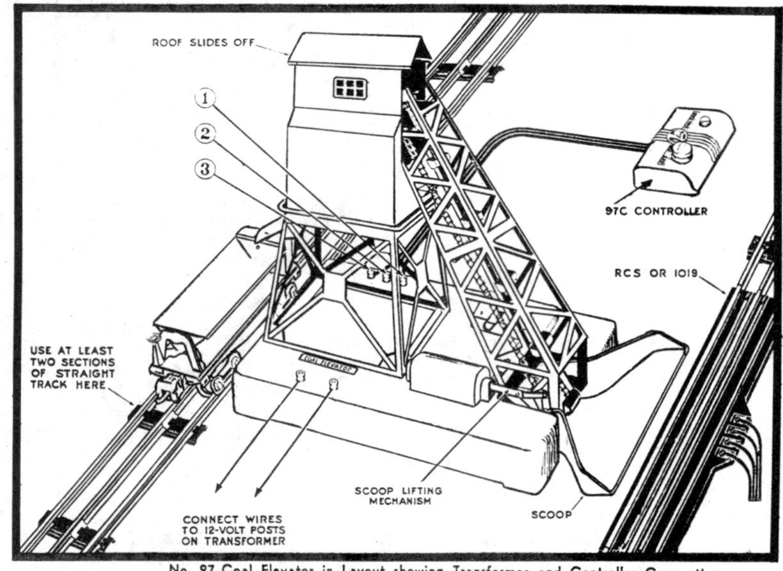

No. 97 Coal Elevator in Layout showing Transformer and Controller Connections.

No. 97 COAL ELEVATOR

The No. 97 Coal Elevator is a remote-controlled, motor-operated accessory which will increase many times the play value and enjoyment to be gained from a Lionel Train Set. Artificial coal placed in the automatic tilting scoop is picked up by buckets on a motorized chain conveyor and carried to the loft of the Elevator where the coal is stored until ready to be used. By pushing the button marked "unload" on the cotroller, the gate in the loft is opened and the coal is delivered by gravity down the chute. The flow of the coal will continueas long as the button is held down.

HOW TO CONNECT CONTROLLER

Attach the three conductors on the No. 97C Controller Cable from left to right to the binding posts numbered 1, 2, and 3 on the base of the Coal Elevator, as shown in Figure 1. Be sure that the cable is flat and untwisted when connections are made.

HOW TO CONNECT COAL ELEVATOR TO TRANSFORMER

Attach one wire to each of the two binding posts on the base of Elevator marked "Connect to transformer". Approximately 12 to 14 volts are required to operate the Elevator. Therefore, connect two wires from the Elevator to the two post on your Lionel Transformer which give a Fixed Voltage in this range.

The No. 97C Controller has controls: the knob to start and stop the motor-driven buckets and the red push button marked "unload", to control the gate or coal-releasein the loft of the Elevator.

OPERATING NOTES

Although Lionel Remote Control Dump Cars are not necessary in order to use the No. 97 Coal Elevator, a layout such as that illustrated in Figure 1, with the Coal Elevator located between parallel tracks and using Lionel Dump Cars will enhance considerably the fun to be had from the No. 97. In such a layout the Dump Cars can unload directly into the scoop and can be loaded directly into the scoop and can be loaded merely by routing the empty cars to the other track. This provides cotinuous remote control operation and does not necessitate handling the coal by hand at any stage, or even use of Unloading Bins unless desired. Any layout measuring approximately 14 3/4 inches between center rails of parallel tracks may be used in like manner.

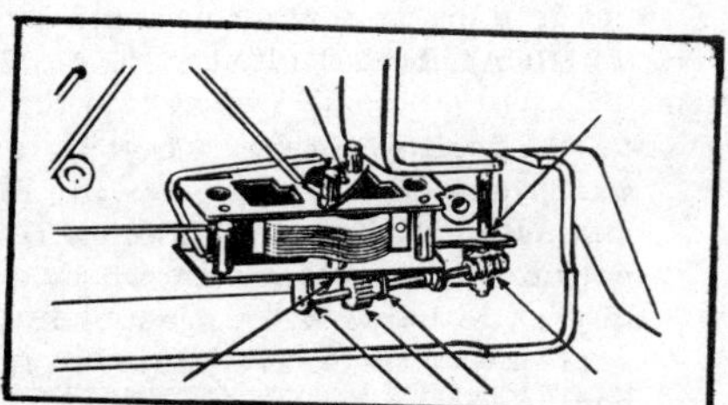

Figure 2—Lubricate points indicated by arrows.

Do not overload the Elevator by attempting to use too much coal so that the scoop does not lift or the surplus coal spills from the loft. If the gate at any time should jam, the loft may be cleared by removing the sliding roof.

The working mechanism, motor, shafts, and other points indicated in Figure 2 should be kept clean at all times. Lubricate lightly with Lionel No. 925 Lubricant. Do not lubricate the gate mechanism nor the chain and sprocket at this may cause it to jam.

No. 110 & No. 111 TRESTLE SETS

No. 110 Trestle Set consists of 12 pairs of graduated trestle piers or "bents" which are designed to elevate the track from ground level to a height of approximately five inches, which is the clearance reqiired for an overpass. The bents should be placed one full track section apart so that each bent supports the joint between two track sections. The difference in the heights of most adjacent bents is 1/2 inch, allowing the train to rise that amount per section. However, in order to provide a smooth transition between level and graded portion of the track, the heights of the three top and two bottom bents vary less than 1/2 inch. The bents are lettered in sequence from "A" to "L" with "A" being the highest, "B" the next and so on. The "L" bents are included in the envelope with the channels and screws.

The trestle can be used in a great many different ways to give added realism and interest to your railroad. Some of the typical layouts which can be made with one Trestle Set and within a limited space are illustrated. To extend the elevatedportion of the railroad auxiliary No. 111 Trestle Set, consisting of ten "A" size bents and the necessary track mounting hardware, is available.

HOW TO MOUNT THE TRACK

Earlier Models -- In order to hold the track firmly to the top of the trestle two types of track clamps are provided: one to fit over the ties of "O27" track; the other to hold "O" and other types of track.

To mount the track to the trestle, the track sections are first assembled together firmly. The "tee" nut is slipped into the channel on top of the trestle bent (see Figure 1). The track clamp is fitted over the track ties and then screwed down to the "tee" nut by means of the screws provided. To avoid distorting the track clamp do not screw down the screw too tightly. Figure 1 shows how the track clamps are used for different types of track.

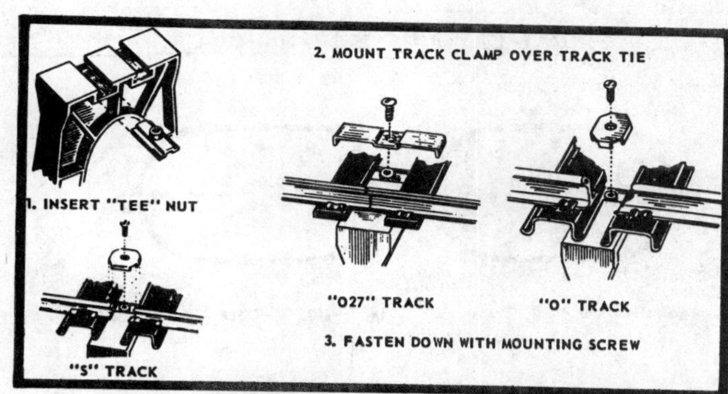

Figure 1 - How to Mount Various Types of Track on No. 110 Trestle

Later Models -- Later model trestle sets No. 110 and 111 mount the track differenlty from those described above. As shown in Figure 2(above) a tie channel is slipped into the grooves on top of each bent. The four holes in the tie channel are so placed that at least one diagonally opposite pair will line up with the holes in the track ties when the joint is placed at the center of the bent. A pair of #4 x 1/2 sheet metal screws are inserted through the track ties and screwed into the tie channel. Again, remember not to screw down too tightly.

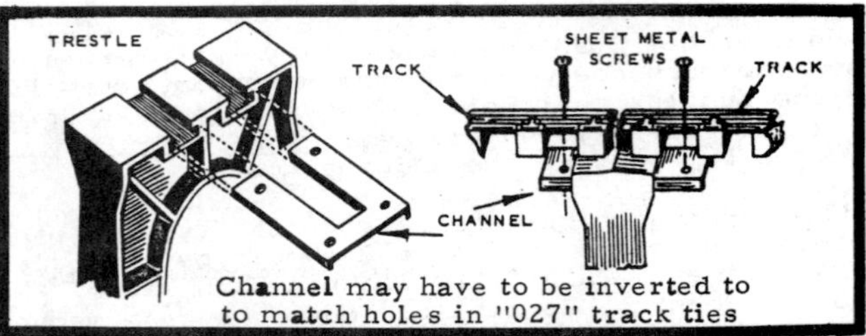

Figure 2 - Positioning of Tie Channel and Track On Trestle Bent

After the track system is mounted to the bents, the assembled trestle is ready to be fastened to a level platform or table by means of No. 5 or No. 6 wood screws passed through the slots in the base of each bent.

TRAIN OPERATION

The grade provided by No. 110 Trestle Set can be climbed by all modern Lionel Magne-Traction locomotives pulling 5 or 6 light freight cars, but some steam-type locomotives require careful control of speed on the downgrade to avoid derailment, particularly if the downgrade includes a sharp curve. To effect automatic control, downgrade sections of track can be insulated from the rest of the road and powered separately, with about 8 volts so that the train speed is automatically moderated on the downgrade. A grade which is used for two-way traffic will, of course, require a switching arrangement to provide full power for climbing. Twin-motored locomotives will usually be able to climb and descend the grade at the same voltage.

For very heavy locomotives such as the GG-1 Pennsylvania electric it is advisable to reinforce the track curves with additional bents supporting the center of each curved section to prevent the track from bending under the weight of the engine.

TYPICAL LAYOUTS USING No. 110 & No. 111 TRESTLES

The following track layouts are the most economical which can be made, occupying the least amount of space and using the least number of track sections. Graded postions of track are shown by heavy line and position of trestle bents by corresponding letters. Notice that 12 sections of track are required for upgrade and an equal number for downgrade. It is best to use only full track sections between adjacent trestle bents.

The layouts are designed so that the underpass in most cases fits between a pair of "A" trestles which provide clearance for all Lionel rolling stock except electric locomotives with raised pantographs and No. 3424 Brakeman Car with the man in upright position.

"O" and "O27" layouts are similar, but "O" layouts will occupy approximately 10% more space. "Super-O" layouts have to be somewhat different because the track circles, which measure 38" across, are made up of 12 instead of 8 curved sections (compare Layouts 5 & 6). Each straight section of "Super-O" track is 9" long.

TYPICAL LAYOUTS USING No. 110 GRADUATED TRESTLE SETS & No. 111 ELEVATED TRESTLE SETS

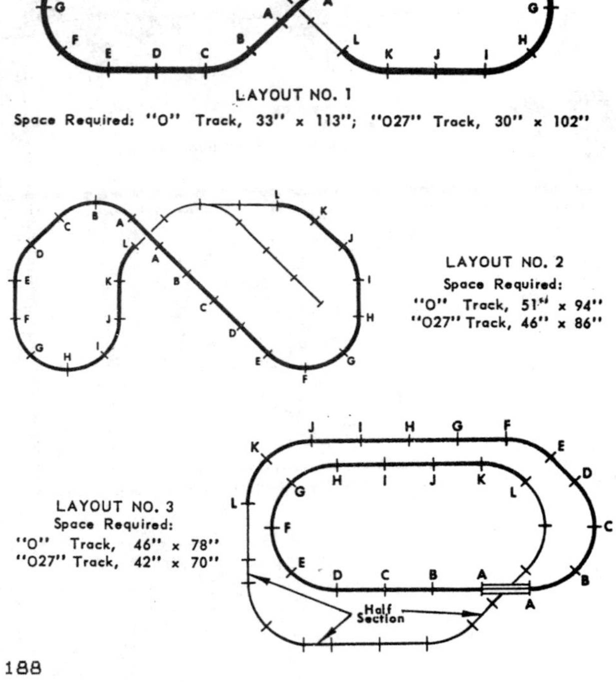

LAYOUT NO. 1
Space Required: "O" Track, 33" x 113"; "027" Track, 30" x 102"

LAYOUT NO. 2
Space Required:
"O" Track, 51" x 94"
"027" Track, 46" x 86"

LAYOUT NO. 3
Space Required:
"O" Track, 46" x 78"
"027" Track, 42" x 70"

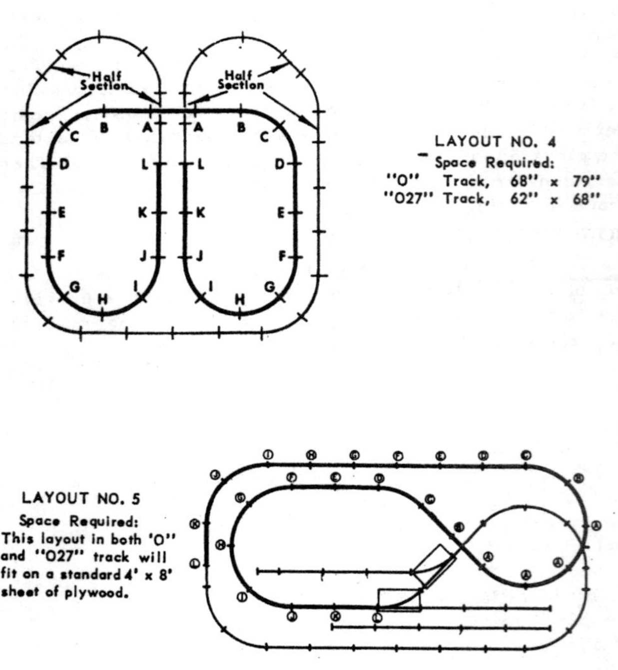

LAYOUT NO. 4
Space Required:
"O" Track, 68" x 79"
"027" Track, 62" x 68"

LAYOUT NO. 5
Space Required:
This layout in both 'O" and "027" track will fit on a standard 4' x 8' sheet of plywood.

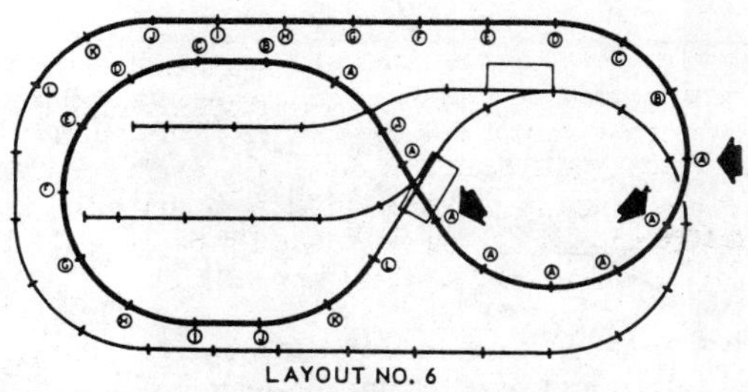

This layout is similar to Layout No. 5 but is in "Super-O" track which requires wider curves and so does not leave enough room for a separate trolley line as in Layout No. 5. Space Required: 4' x 8'. NOTE: You may have to use only one tie channel screw at the points indicated by arrows so that you can pivot the bents to clear the lower track.

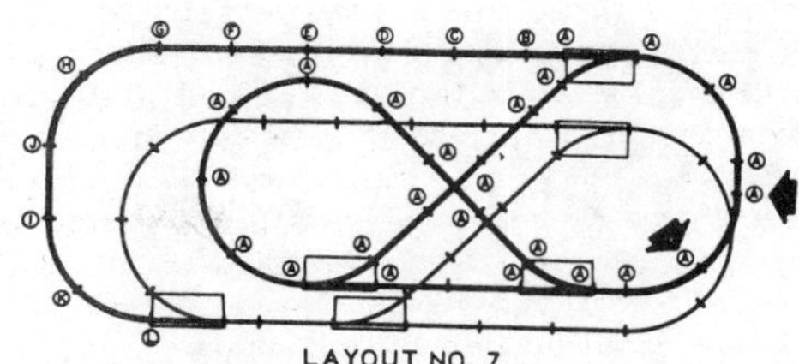

This compact two level layout is designed for two-train operation and will fit on a 4' x 8' board in either "O" or "O27" track. Note that only one-half of a standard No. 110 Trestle Set is used in this layout since the train uses the same graded portion of track to go from one level to the other. The entire upper level is supported by size "A" bents. See note above about turning bents for track clearance.

No. 114 NEWSSTAND with Electric Horn

No. 114 Newsstand is suitable for installation in any layout, but is particularly useful if your train does not have a built-in warning horn. The bottom of the station has four terminal clips. Two of these are for lighting the lamp inside the newsstand and are connected to a track lockon, or directly to transformer terminals giving about 14 volts. The other two terminals lead to the built-in horn and are connected to No. 90 Controller.

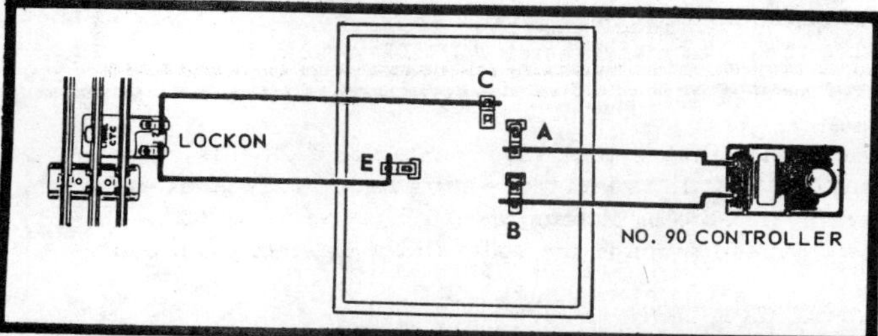

Fig. 1 - Bottom View of No. 114 Newsstand Showing Wiring Connections

Fig. 2 - Location of Dry Cell

The horn is powered by a flashlight cell (size "D") which must be inserted into its position inside the building, as shown in Figure 2. After the dry cell is in place, and the controller is connected, the horn will sound whenever you push the controller button.

If desired the horn can be controlled automatically by the train itself. To do this you must replace the No. 90 Controller with a No. 145C pressure contactor (see 145C CONTACTOR) which is then placed under the track and operated by the weight of the train.

LAMP REPLACEMENT -- The Newsstand uses lamp No. L53.

No. 125 WHISTLING STATION

No. 125 Whistling Station can be installed anywhere in the layout. It can be operated on either AC or DC low voltage (10-14 volts) and is especially useful in communities where the household power supply is less than 40 cycles so that the regular built-in remote control train whistle cannot be used.

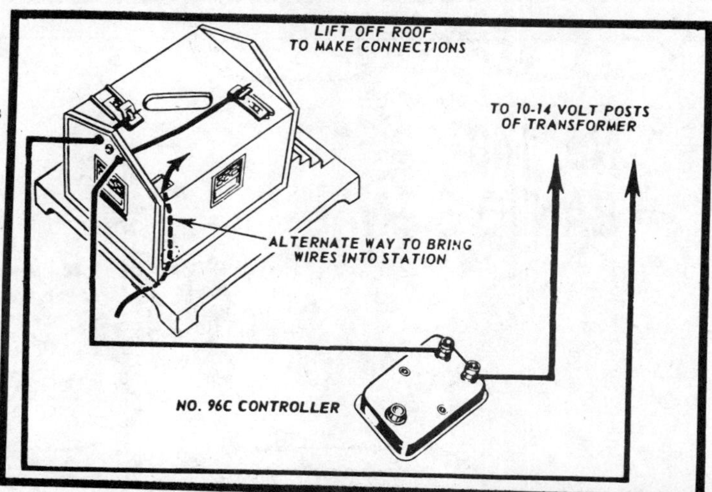

The electrical wiring connections to the Whistling Station are made by means of the two clips which are reached by lifting off the roof of the Station shack. The two wires can be led into the shack either through the hole in the bottom, or throuth the openings in the wall.

The Whistling Station should be connected directly to the proper binding posts on the transformer. A No. 96C push-button controller is inserted into one of the transformer leads in order to blow the whistle when desired.

By installing a 145C or a 153C Contactor, instead of the 96C Controller, the whistle can be sounded automatically whenever the train reaches a pre-determined spot in the track.

NOTE: If you operate your layout on a rug, it is advisable to place a piece of paper underneath the Station or the sound of the whistle may be muffled by the nap of the rug.

No. 128 ANIMATED NEWSSTAND

Figure 1 - No. 128 Animated Newsstand--Electrical Connections

No.128 Animated Newsstand is powered by a vibrator motor (see No. 464 LUMBER MILL). The moving figures are linked to the motor through a series of racks and pinions as illustrated in the schematic diagram below. The proper operating range should by 11-13 volts. Excessively high voltage will cause the mechanism to chatter and may also throw the drive line off its pulley.

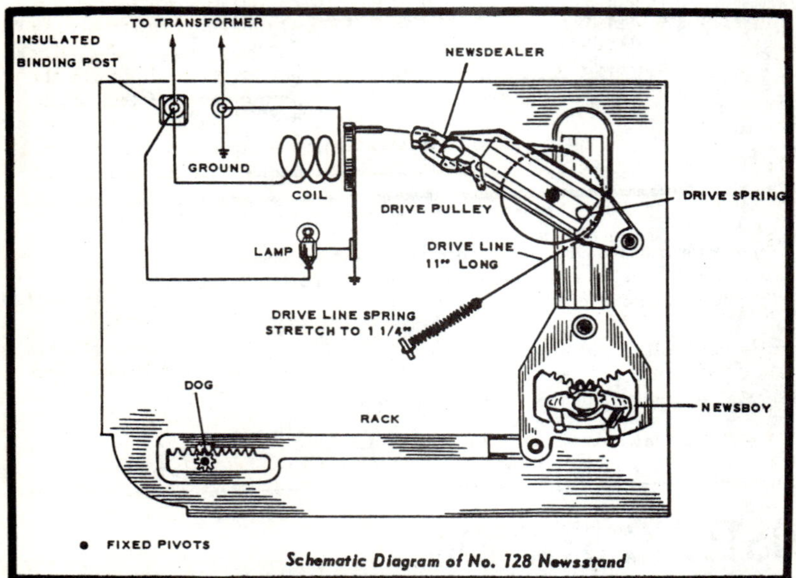

Schematic Diagram of No. 128 Newsstand

SERVICE NOTES

If the animated figures do not move when power is applied, but the lantern lights and a hum is heard, the vertical drive spring on the drive pulley is probably disengaged from the mechanism. Relocate the spring within the slotted arms. The arm and spring are both flexible and can be simply snapped in place. The movement of the mechanism may be slowed down if the base of the dog mounting bracket rubs against the side of the hole in which it is located. This can be remedied either by straightening the pin or by making the hole on the platform larger.

No. 140 BANJO SIGNAL

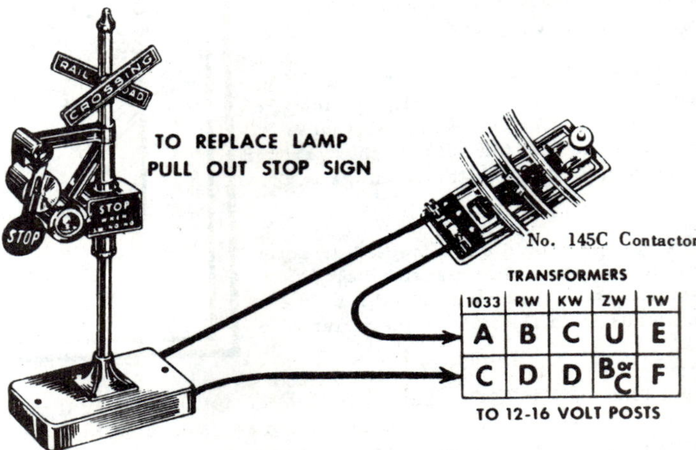

1033	RW	KW	ZW	TW
A	B	C	U	E
C	D	D	B or C	F

TO 12-16 VOLT POSTS

Figure 1 - Electrical Connections for No. 140 Banjo Signal

No. 145 AUTOMATIC GATEMAN

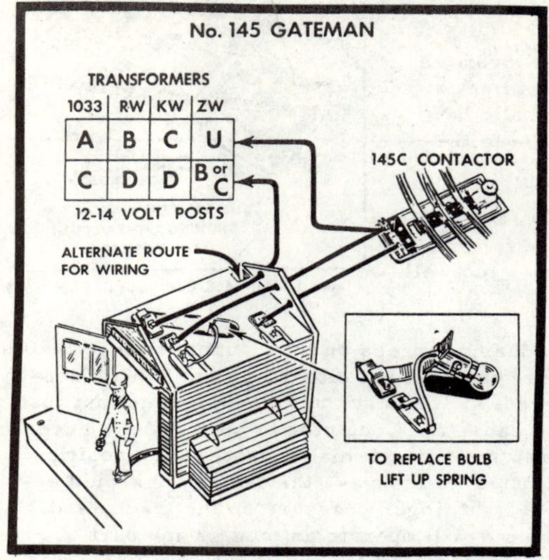

No. 145 Automatic Gateman is operated by a solenoid-and-plunger mechanism which is usually activated by the weight of a train passing over a 145C Contactor. When the solenoid is energized the plunger moves a pivoted gear segment upon which is mounted the figure of the gateman and which meshes with a plastic pinion gear fixed on the bottom of the door. Movement of the gear segment simultaneously opens the door of the shack and moves the figure of the gateman out of the shack. The return movement of the mechanism is accomplished by a coil spring stretched between the gear segment and the base of the shack.

The shack is illuminated by means of a steadily burning 14 volt bayonet-base lamp which is fitted in a spring-mounted socket on top of the shack. Electrical connections to the gateman are made through clips which are reached by lifting off the roof of the shack. The wires can be introduced into the shack either through the three holes in the rear wall or through the holes in the ceiling and bottom of the shack.

The wiring diagram below illustrates the mechanism and the electrical circuit of the Automatic Gateman as well as the electrical connections needed for its operation.

SERVICE NOTES

Sluggish operation of the Gateman mechanism may be caused by any of the following: improper tension of the return spring; excessive friction between the gear segment and metal base of the shack; sticky plunger; or distorted coil spool.

To eliminate excessive friction apply a light coat of lubricant to the bottom surface of the base where it bears against the upturned fingers of the moving gear segment. Adjust the tension of the return coil spring either by stretching the spring slightly to enable the door to open more easily, or by taking off a few more turns to increase the return force. After a long period of operation the plunger and the hole in the coil spool may become dirty and sticky and should be cleaned off. If the coil spool has been overheated it may become distorted. Occasionally the coil will return to normal after it has been allowed to cool off. If the distortion is permanent, however, the coil assembly should be replaced.

In cases where the figure of the gateman rubs against the base, Washer RCS-40 (Lionel No.) may be inserted as a spacer between the gear segment and the figure mounting stud.

LAMP REPLACEMENT -- use lamp No. L53.

Wiring Diagram of No. 145 Automatic Gateman

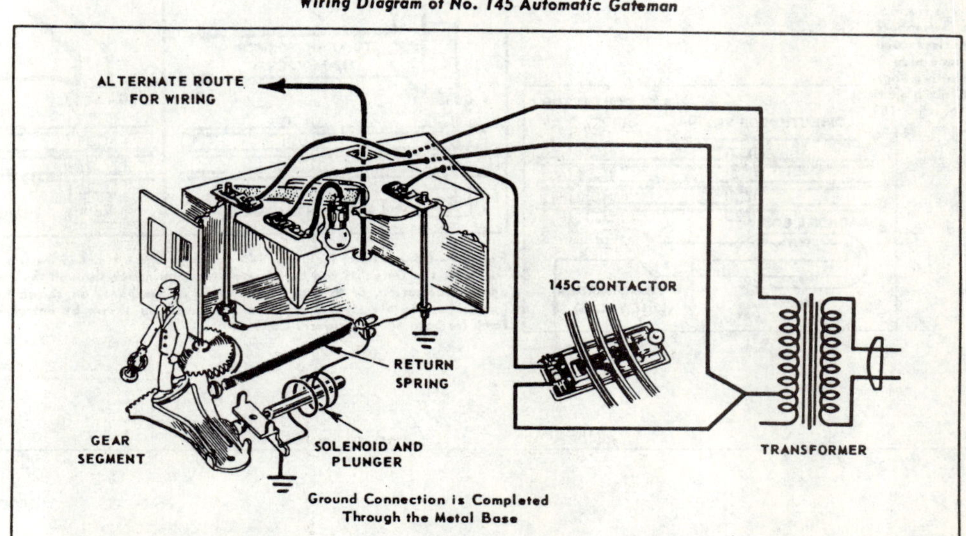

No. 145C CONTACTOR

No. 145C Contactor is an 'ON and OFF' electrical switch which is operated by the weight of a passing train. Normally, that is when there is no weight on the lever plate of the Contactor, the switch is open, or OFF. When the lever plate is pressed down the switch is closed, or ON.

Figure 1--No. 145C Contactor in Position

Slide the Contactor underneath the track so that one of the track ties fits over the lever plate of the Contactor. The Contactor can be placed either under a straight or a curved piece of track, but when placed under a curve the adjustment nut should be toward the center of the curve. The track tie should fit as close as possible to the adjustment nut.

If your layout is mounted on a board do not fasten the track down for several sections on either side of the Contactor. The track must remain sufficiently flexible to bend under the weight of the train. For the same reason the Contactor may not work too well if placed next to a switch.

The Contactor has no electrical connections to the track itself; it acts only as a switch. After it is located in the layout it must be connected to the transformer and to the accessory it operates. Connections are made by inserting bare ends of wires into the spring clips on either side of the Contactor.

After the connections are made and the transformer current is on, the Contactor must be adjusted so that the accessory will operate only at the proper time. First, stop the train several sections away from the Contactor so that the train does not press on the Contactor lever plate. Turn the adjustment nut either way until the accessory operates. Then back up the adjustment nut just enough to cause the Contactor to open and the accessory to return to its normal non-operating position. When adjusted in this way, the Contactor should respond to a light finger pressure on the track, and the accessory will operate as long as any part of the train is passing on the track over the Contactor.

See examples below for use of 145C Contactor.

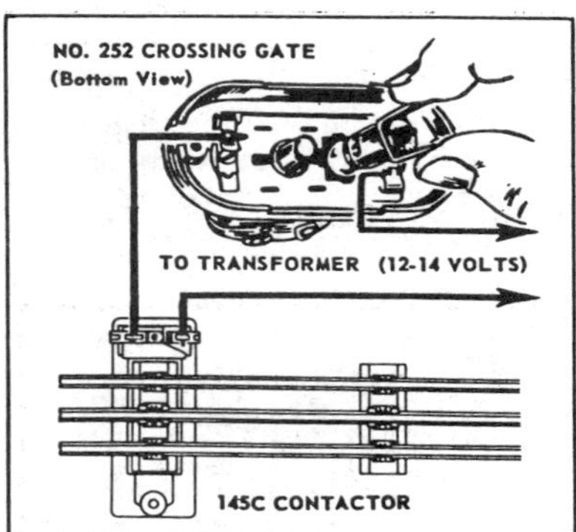

Figure 2---Connections for a No. 252 Crossing Gate. The bottom view of the Crossing Gate also shows how its illuminating lamp can be removed for replacement. The replacement lamp is L363.

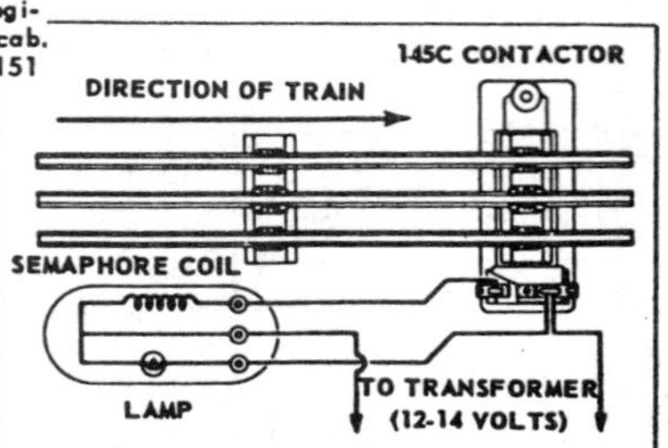

Figure 3---Connections for a No. 151 Semaphore. Note that the Semaphore, as well as other track signals, is usually placed on the right hand side of the track so that the locomotive engineer has a clear view of it from his cab. The replacement lamp for No. 151 Semaphore is L53.

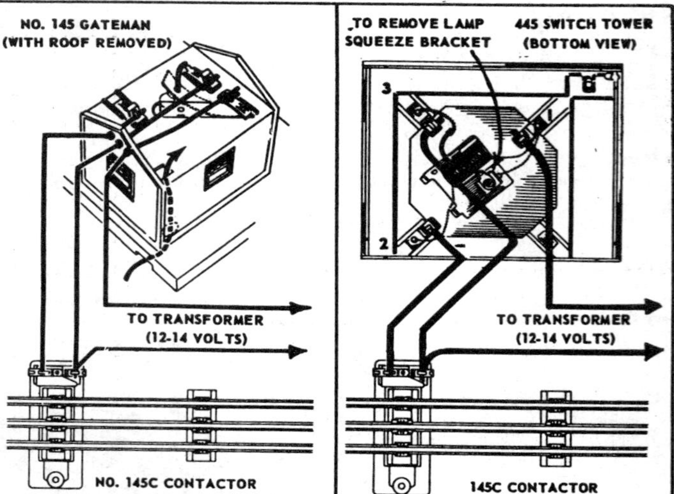

Figure 4--Connections for a No. 145 Gateman and a No. 445 Switch Tower. The connecting wires for the Gateman can be inserted into the shack through the openings in the rear wall, as in illustration, or through the opening in the base, as shown by arrow. To remove the lamp, the flexible lamp bracket is bent back as shown by dotted lines. The replacement lamp for both accessories is L363.

No. 151 SEMAPHORE

No. 151 Semaphore is modeled on the automatic two-indication signal of the type frequently used along stretches of open track without complicated switches or crossovers. It is operated by the train itself. No. 151 Semaphore is equipped with a steadily burning lamp which shines either through a green or a red lens, depending on the position of the indicating arm. Normally, the arm is held in upright or 'clear' position by a compressed coil spring inside the top of the Semaphore post, so that the light shines through the green lens. To indicate 'danger' the solenoid in the base of the Semaphore is energized and the arm is moved by a rack and pinion mechanism to horizontal position causing the light to shine through the red lens.

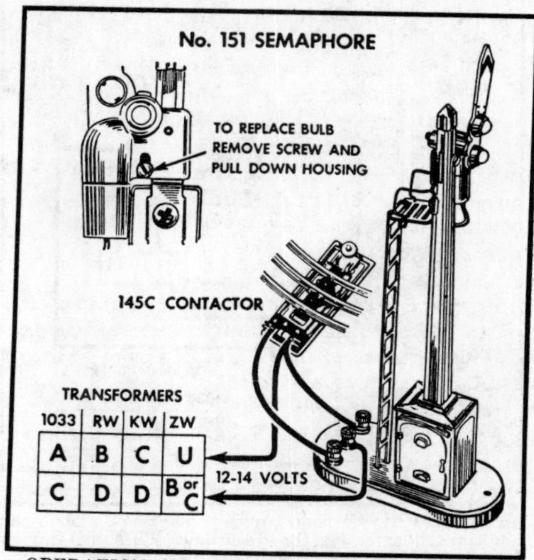

OPERATION: Normally light shows green and the semaphore arm is up. As the contactor is actuated by a passing train current flows through solenoid. Semaphore arm goes down and light shows red.

As shown in the schematic diagram below (Figure 1), the lamp and the solenoid coil are each connected to the outer insulated binding posts, and are grounded through the structure of the Semaphore to the center post.

When checking the electrical circuit of the Semaphore see that the 'high' leads of both the lamp and the coil are properly soldered to the outer binding posts. Also, check the soldered 'ground' connection of the coil to the bottom bracket. Occasionally an apparent open circuit may be caused by a loose center ground binding post.

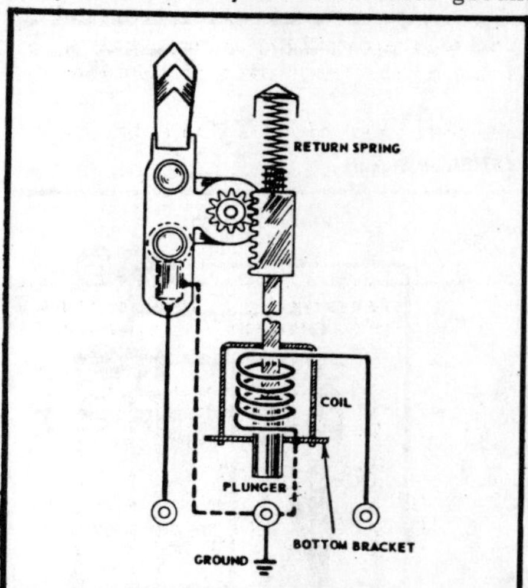

Figure 1 - Diagram of No. 151 Semaphore

SERVICE NOTES

Among mechanical troubles may be the following:

Arm does not come all the way down. Coil positioned too low. Tap bottom bracket to force coil upward slightly. Pinion and rack not in correct relation. When arm is in upright position its pinion should engage between the second and third tooth of the rack. Remove shoulder screw and reassemble Semaphore arm and pinion in proper relation.

Arm does not return to vertical position. Return spring too weak. Increase tension by stretching spring, or replace. Improper alignment between rack pinion caused by loose or twisted post. Square post with a pair of pliers, adjust housing into line with a screwdriver (see Figure 2). If the coil had been overheated, trouble may be caused by a sticky, waxy coating on the plunger and inside the plunger tube. Remove plunger by opening fingers in bottom of plunger tube and clean plunger and tube with alcohol.

Figure 2 - Adjusting Alignment of Rack and Pinion

Arm vibrates within horizontal position. Return spring too strong. Decrease tension by compressing spring, or replace spring.

Loose Semaphore post. Place tension on ladder -- bend platform upward.

NOTE: When removing bottom bracket from the Semaphore base in order to work on the coil, lamp lead, etc., do not disturb the riveted projections cast in the base, but simply bend the bottom bracket until it slides out.

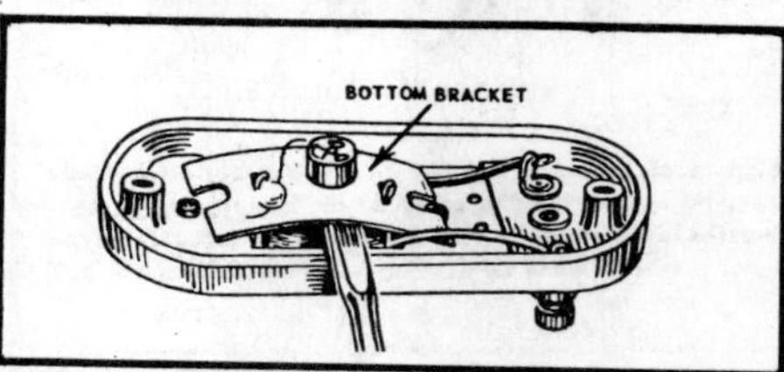

Figure 3 - How to Remove Bottom Bracket

No. 153 BLOCK SIGNAL

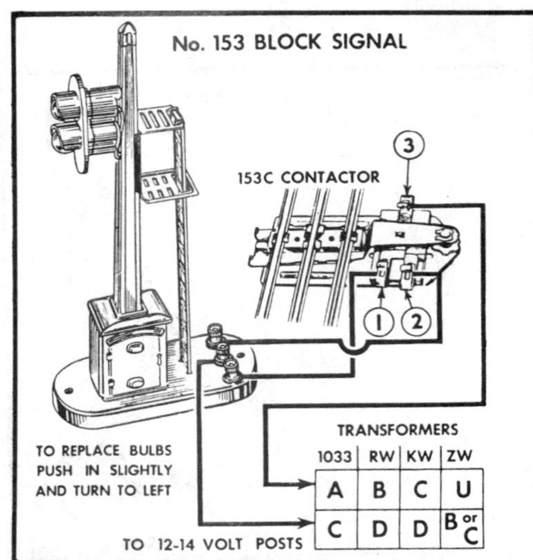

OPERATION: Normally current runs from contactor clip 3 to clip 1 illuminating the green light. When contactor is depressed current runs from clip 3 to clip 2, illuminating red light.

No. 153 Block Signal is an adaptation of one of several types of railroad color position light signals used to govern trains entering and using a track block. The 153 Block Signal is usually operated automatically by means of a 153C Contactor (see 153C CONTACTOR), which is a single-pole, double-throw switch inserted underneath a track tie and activated by the weight of the train passing over it.

In large permanent layouts or displays, the No. 153 Signal is often operated through special insulated rails, relays, or by being connected to other equipment such as No. 022 Switches or No. 132 Automatic Passenger Stations.

No. 153 Block Signals can be connected simply to indicate the passage of a train past a given point in the track, in which case it operates as a 'permissive' signal. The No. 153 Block Signal can also be interconnected with an insulated block so that it becomes an 'absolute' block signal.

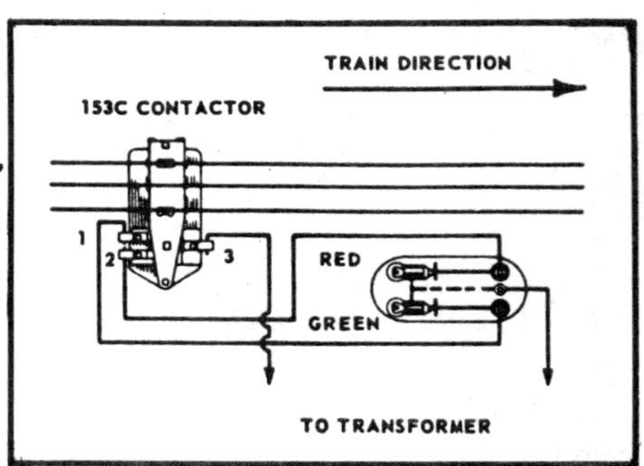

153 Block Signal Installed as a 'Permissive' Signal

No. 153 Block Signals made prior to 1950 used 6-8 volt screw-base lamps 50-301 (red) and 50-302 (green) in series with a 40-ohm voltage-dropping resistor 153-17. In later production the resistor was eliminated and the lamps were replaced by 14-volt bayonet-base lamps 363-301 (red) and 363-302 (green). At the same time target 153-11 made to accommodate screw-base lamps was replaced by a target 153-46 made to suit bayonet-base lamps.

Schematic Diagram of No. 153 Block Signals

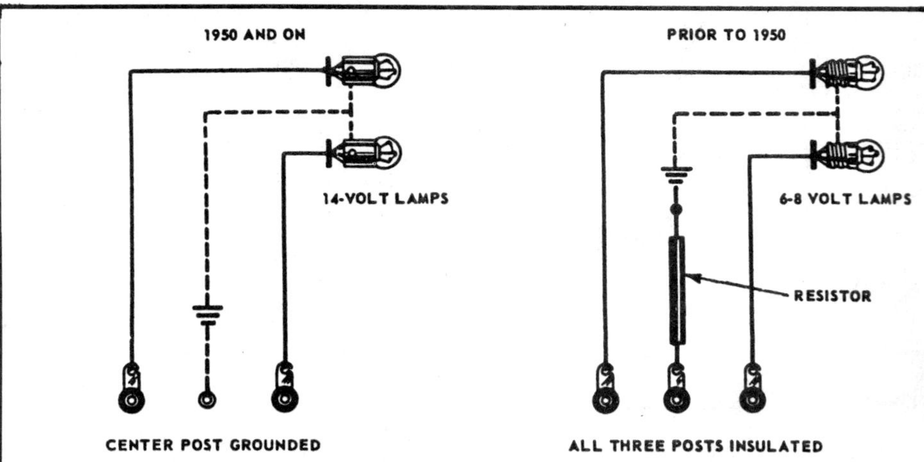

When interconnected with insulated blocks the 153 Block Signals of the older design may, under certain circumstances, show a simultaneous red and green indication. To correct this condition the older Block Signals can be converted to the later design by 'jumping' the resistor and replacing the low voltage lamps with 12 or 14 volt screw type lamps. Suitable red lamps are 45-76 or 154-18 (1449-301). A green lamp can be made by dipping a clear 616-13 (1449-300) in green nail polish.

No. 153C CONTACTOR

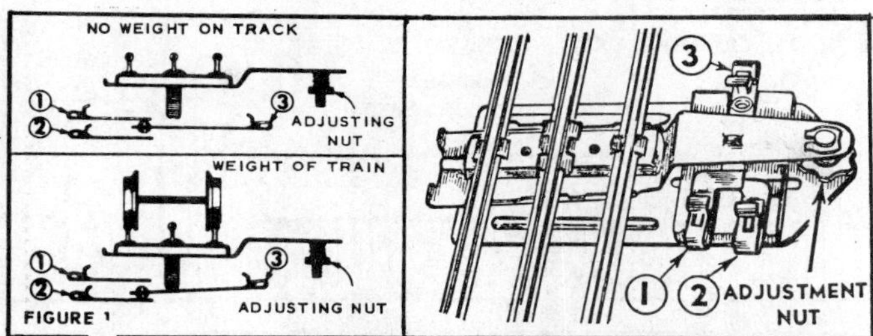

Figure 2—153C Contactor Placed Under the Track

No. 153C Contactor is an electrical switch of the "single pole, double throw" type designed to be operated by the weight of a passing train. The contactor is placed underneath the track as shown in Figure 2. The diagram in Figure 1 shows its electrical operation. When there is no weight on the track above the contactor, its terminal clip No. 3 makes electrical contact with terminal clip No. 1. When the weight of a passing train depresses the track, clip No. 3 breaks contact with clip No. 1 and makes contact with clip No. 2 instead.

This action of 153C Contactors is used for automatic operation of No. 151 Semaphores, No. 153 & No. 163 Block Signals, No. 353 Control Signals, No. 452 Gantry Signals and for controlling power going to insulated train blocks in order to prevent collision between two trains running on the same track.

INSTALLING THE CONTACTOR

Slide the contactor beneath the track so that one of the track ties rests firmly upon the top pressure plate. If your layout is fastened to a board or platform, loosen several sections on either side of the contactor. The track must be sufficiently flexible to bend under the weight of the train. For the same reason the contactor may not work satisfactorily when placed next to a track switch. Note: With "Super-O" track locate the pressure plate under any two plastic ties which are slotted. It will not fit under metal ties.

ADJUSTING THE CONTACTOR

After all the connections are made and transformer current is on, the contactor must be adjusted so that the signal or control operates properly. Stop the train several sections away from the contactor so that it does not press on the contactor plate. Turn the adjustment nut either up or down until the red light goes on. Then back up the adjustment nut just enough to cause the red light to go out and the green light to go on instead. When properly adjusted, the contactor will respond to a light finger pressure on the track and the red light will stay on as long as any part of the train is passing over the contactor plate. If the action of the two lights is reversed interchange the connection to the two outside posts.

CONNECTIONS FOR No. 151 SEMAPHORE

To connect No. 151 Semaphores follow the wiring in Figure 3. When the contactor is correctly adjusted the semaphore arm should lower when the train is passing over the contactor. The Semaphore light, however, will remain on all the time, shining either through the red or green lens depending on the position of the Semaphore arm. If more convenient in your layout, No. 1 terminal of the Semaphore may be connected directly to the transformer instead of the No. 3 Contactor clip. The Semaphore works best at 12-14 volts.

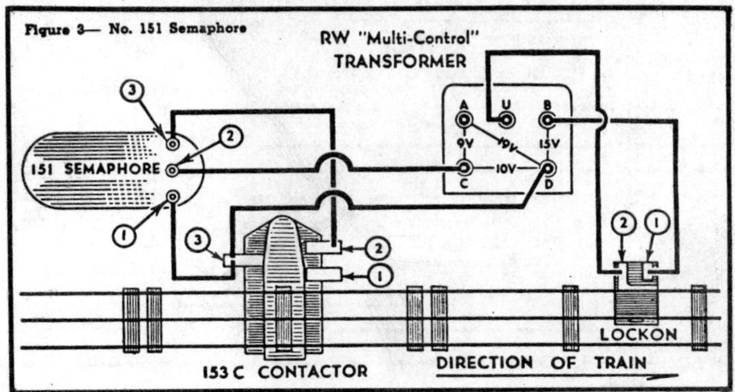
Figure 3— No. 151 Semaphore

CONNECTIONS FOR No. 153 BLOCK SIGNAL

Wire No. 153 Block Signal as shown in Figure 4. With the train stopped on track some distance from the contactor, turn adjustment screw down as far as it will go. If green light in the Block Signal is on, no further adjustment is required. If red light is on, turn the adjustment nut up until the light just changes to green. When the No. 153 Block Signal is properly connected and adjusted its green light will change to red as the train goes over the contactor and then back to green when the train has passed.

The Block Signal in itself does not have any control over the movement of the train, but simply gives a visual indication of the passage of the train past a given point in the layout. However, the Block Signal as well as the No. 151 Semaphore can be also used in conjunction with an insulated track block to show whether the block is 'dead' or 'alive'.

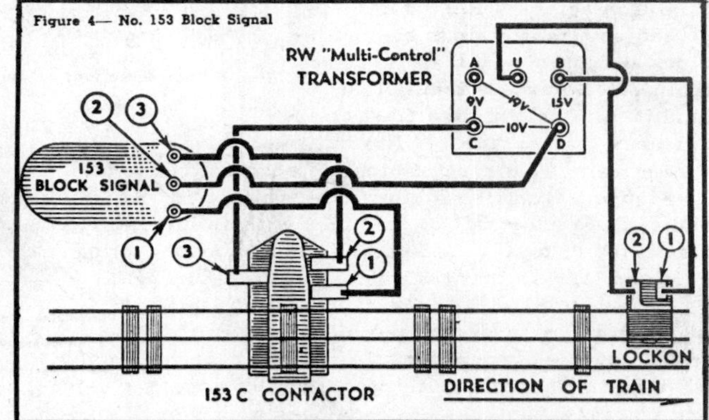
Figure 4— No. 153 Block Signal

CONNECTIONS FOR No. 152 CROSSING GATE

With the No. 152 Crossing Gate wired as shown in Figure 5 the contactor acts as a simple "off and on" switch. When the contactor is depressed by the weight of the passing train it will switch on the accessory circuit. Note that the Crossing Gate has no electrical connection to the track, but operates on a separate circuit. In this way the accessory can be supplied with a fixed voltage nore suitable for its operation than the variable track voltage. 10-12 volts is best for No. 152.

CONNECTIONS FOR Nos. 163, 353 & 452 SIGNALS

When the 153C Contactor is used, make the connections shown in Figures 6 & 7. No. 3 contactor clip and the center post of the signal are wired for 12-14 volts.

CONTINUED

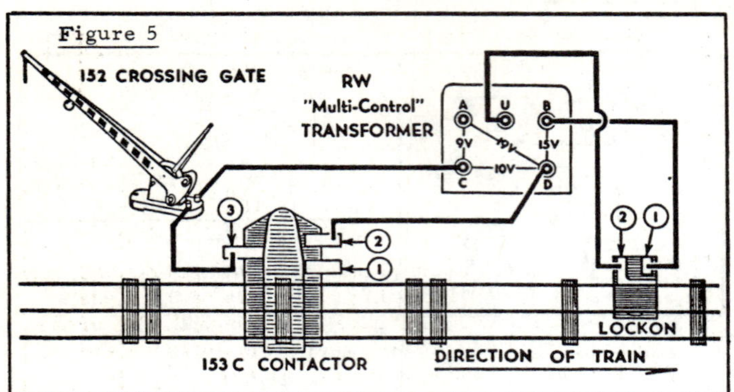

1044	KW	LW	SW	ZW
A	C	A	U	U
C	D	C	C	BorC

Figure 7 -- No. 452 GANTRY SIGNAL

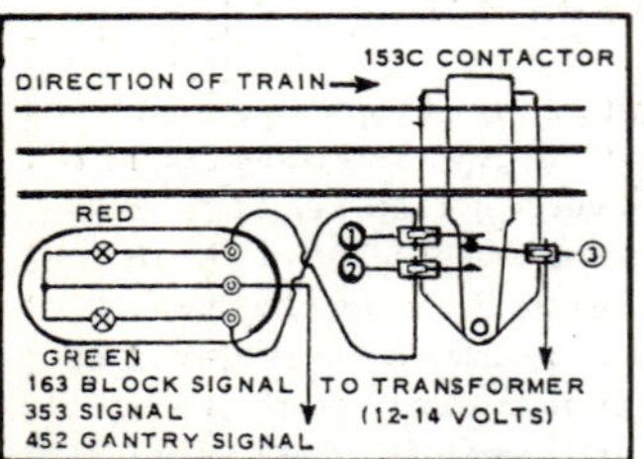

Fig. 6 - No. 153 Block Signal Connected to Show Passage of Train

No. 452 Gantry Signal is designed to act as a direct overhead signal which can be connected to control two trains on the same track. The Gantry Signal is provided with a red and green illuminated signal which can be faced in either direction on the structure (see insert in Figure 7 above).

Figure 7 illustrates the basic wiring which can be used so that the signal lights will blink red and green as the train passes through.

AUTOMATIC BLOCK SYSTEMS for TWO TRAIN OPERATION

If you wish to operate two or more trains on the same track, your layout should be designed to prevent a train from overtaking and colliding with the one ahead. This is done by arranging one or more insulated track "blocks" and connecting each one to the power supply with a 153C Contactor. The contactor is placed several sections beyond the block it controls so that the first train will delay any train close behind it. By the time the first train releases the contactor it has built up a safe lead. This type of block is normally "live".

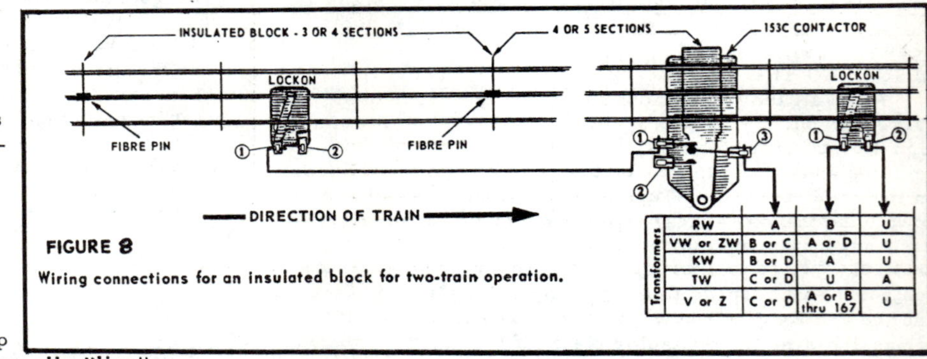

Transformers	A	B	U
RW	A	B	U
VW or ZW	B or C	A or D	U
KW	B or D	A	U
TW	C or D	U	A
V or Z	C or D	A or B thru 167	U

FIGURE 8

Wiring connections for an insulated block for two-train operation.

Figure 8 illustrates a basic block system. An insulated block is prepared by replacing the metal connector at each end of the center rail of the block with an insulating pin or clip. Different size pins are needed for "O" and "O27" track; for "Super-O" a special clip of nonconducting material is used. The block should be at least three or four track sections long so that trains cannot coast through it.

In a medium-sized layout where there may be only one or two insulated blocks, a waiting train may need a quicker start than it can get when main line voltage is only 9 or 10 volts, and you may want to feed the blocks with 2 or 3 volts more than the main line. This is done, as shown in figure 8, with two different transformer circuits having a common ground post. Of course, if the road consists entirely of a series of blocks, this precaution is unnecessary because a train will always be protected from the rear.

It is important that the two trains operate on approximately the same voltage, or the faster train will tend to catch up with the slower train and collide with it before reaching the insulated block. Some of the variation in the speeds of the two locomotives may be compensated for by loading down the speedier train in order to slow it down.

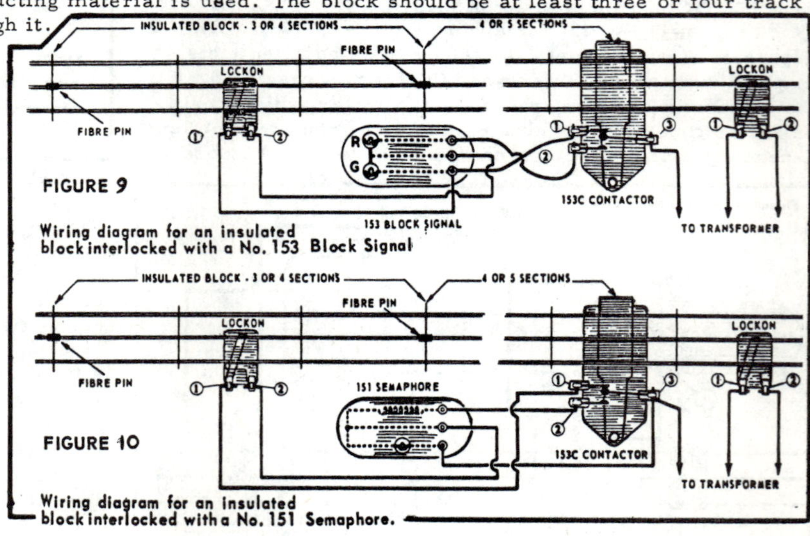

FIGURE 9

Wiring diagram for an insulated block interlocked with a No. 153 Block Signal

FIGURE 10

Wiring diagram for an insulated block interlocked with a No. 151 Semaphore.

To operate two trains with a No. 151 Semaphore, connections are made as indicated in Figure 10 on the previous page. The sequence of train operation will be the same as before and a clear track will be indicated by the lifting of the Semaphore Arm and a flashing of the green Semaphore light.

Figure 11 to the right illustrates insulated block wiring for "Super-O" track. No. 163 & No. 353 Signals are shown, but any of the signals previously discussed may be used.

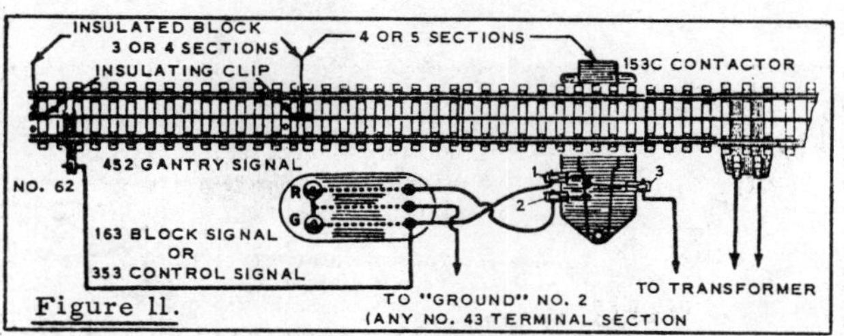

Figure 11.

TWO - TRAIN LAYOUTS

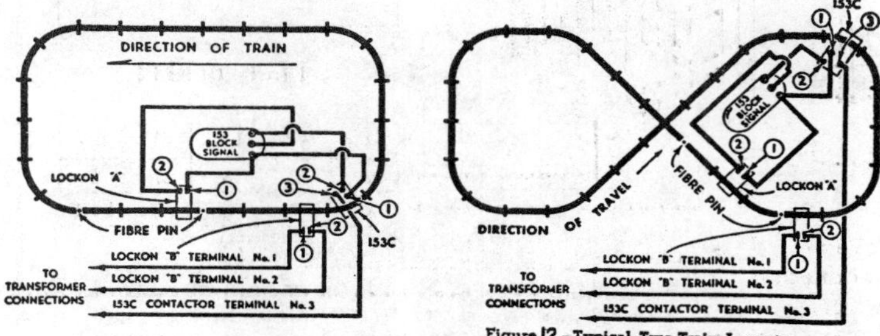

Figure 12 – Typical Two-Train Layouts

Transformer Type	Lockon "B" Terminal No. 1	Lockon "B" Terminal No. 2	153 Contactor Terminal No. 3
1032, 1033, 1034 1041, 1042, "RW"	U	B	A
"VW" and "ZW"	U	A or D	B or C
"S"	A or B	U	C
"R"	A or B through 167	C	F
"V" and "Z"	U	C or D through 167	B or C

Figure 13—Chart showing transformer connections for two-train operation.

Two of the many possible layouts using 153C Contactors for operating two trains of the same track are shown in Figure 12 to the left. The proper connections to various Lionel transformers are listed in the chart following, Figure 13.

DISCONNECTING REVERSING UNIT

When trains are operated in a block system their reversing units must be disconnected so that the trains will resume forward progress after being stopped. To do this, stop the train while it is moving forward, either by holding it or by shutting off track power, and move the E-Unit lever to the "off" position. (If you stop the locomotive my means of the transformer direction, it will go into neutral)

REPLACEMENT LAMPS

No. 151 Semaphore has bayonet base lamp No. L53
No. 163 Block Signal has pin base lamps. To remove do not twist--pull straight out. They are L19(R) Red Lamp and L19(G) Green Lamp.
No. 353 Control Signal -- same as No. 163 above.
No. 452 Gantry Signal uses L53(G) Green and L53(R) Red Lamps.
No. 153 Block Signal uses different types. See section on No. 153 BLOCK SIGNAL.

MULTI–TRAIN OPERATION

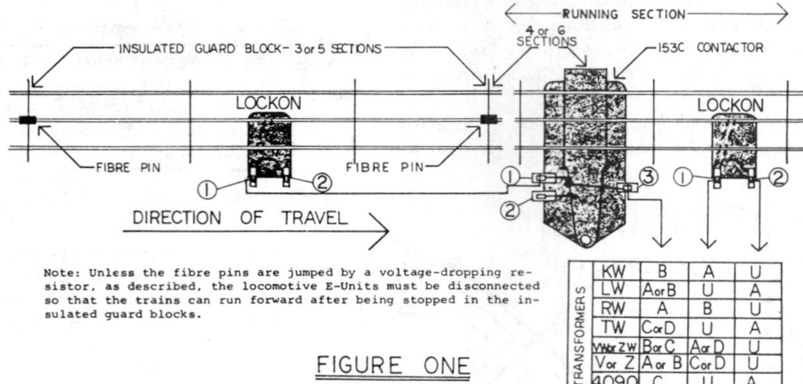

Note: Unless the fibre pins are jumped by a voltage-dropping resistor, as described, the locomotive E-Units must be disconnected so that the trains can run forward after being stopped in the insulated guard blocks.

TRANSFORMERS			
KW	B	A	U
LW	A or B	U	A
RW	A	B	U
TW	C or D	U	A
VW or ZW	B or C	A or D	U
V or Z	A or B	C or D	U
4090	C	U	A

FIGURE ONE

MORE THAN ONE TRAIN ON A SINGLE LOOP

When operating more than one train on the same track, precautions must be added to your railroad to prevent rear end crashes, just like on real railroads. The methods to be described are applicable directly to 027, O, and "Super O" track operation. However with some thought the advanced Standard Gauge operator can apply the same techniques to his larger size railroad. It is really advantageious to consider operation Standard Gauge this way as they are large and running multiple trains on a single loop helps solve the space problem.

ONE TRACK WITH INSULATED SECTIONS

The simplest method uses one track and depending on the length of the loop and the length of the trains, could operate many trains at once. The voltage to the insulated Gaurd Block is connected through a 153C contactor. The Running Section is connected with lockons. The basic arrangement is shown in Figure 1.

The concept of Insulated Guard Blocks and Running Sections is quite simple and fully automatic. Assume a train passes through a Insulated Guard Block Section without requiring a stop. It now enters the Running Section. As it passes into the voltage to the Insulated Guard Block Section. Now, a second train (#2) leaves it's Running Section and is stalled safely in the Insulated Guard Block Section (due to train #1 being in the adjacent Running Section). As soon as train #1 is a safe distance from the Insulated Gaurd Block (where train #2 is stalled) train #2 will move foward to the Running Section formly occupied by train #1.

If the loop is small, train #1 may stall in the same Insulated Guard Block that just held train #2. However, this type of operation usually has enough space to avoid this back to back situation.

In order that the status of each Insulated Guard Block Section be visible, it is conveniet and dynamic to add indicators to your layout. This will allow you and your observing guest to know what is happening. Such indicators include a 450 Signal Bridge (or a Marx 1434 Signal Bridge), a 151 Semaphore, a 148 Dwarf Signal, a 153 Automatic Block, a 163 Single Block Signal, a 253 Automatic Block Signal, a 353 Trackside Signal, and a 2163 Automatic Block Signal. All of these can be connected to the 153C Contactor and will indicate whether the train will stop or move through the Insulated Guard Section.

INSULATED GUARD BLOCK SECTION

An Insulated Gaurd Block Section should be 3 to 5 sections of track long with its center of power rail insulated from the adjacent Running Section with fibre or nylon insulated track pins. Those using Standard Gauge will find that "O" Gauge insulated pins will very well. The 153C contactor in the Running Section should not be too close to the Insulated Guard Block Section as the weight of the train waiting in the block might cause it not to start again. Thus a collision would be created due to an unitentionally stalled train being in the block. It has been found that putting the contactor 4 to 6 sections away from a block should be sufficient.

The Insulated Guard Block Section should be long enough so that your heaviest and best rolling engines will not roll through the Block and start up again in the Running Section already operating a train near the Insulated Guard Block.

If you run your F-3 ABA's with the dummies preceeding the powered unit, you must consider this when placing the 153C Contactor in the running section. Although this is a preferred operation for F-3's, you should consider reversing it for block operation. The choice is yours. Change the block length, or change the position of the powered unit.

In medium sized layouts where only a few blocks are used, it is recommened to set the voltage to the 153C Contactor (and thus the voltage to the Insulated Guard Block Section) at 2 or 3 volts above the voltage of the Running Section. This will enable the stalled train to get a good, fast start and will keep the trains moving on a medium sized loop.

This is easy to accomplish as the larger transformers have a common ground which you tie to lockon terminal #2. The first variable tap can can be set for the Running Section, and the second tap for the Insulated Guard Block Section through the 153C Contactor.

It is important that if you operate the trains with the Insulated Guard Block Section approach that the trains run nearly the same speed for the same voltage setting. If not, the faster engine will overtake the slower one before it reaches the block section. The faster train can be slowed down by adding heavier cars until the two trains are running at about the same speed.

When operating trains this way, the engines should be set to run foward only. To do this, disconnect the E-Unit when the engine has running forward and it will remain in the foward mode until you re-connect and cycle the E-Unit.

FIGURE TWO

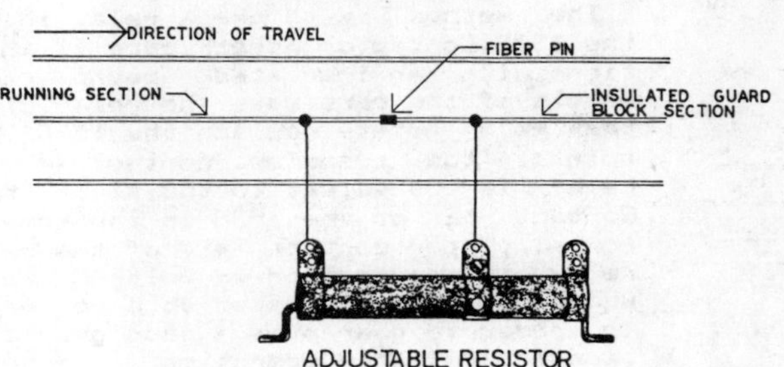

FIGURE THREE

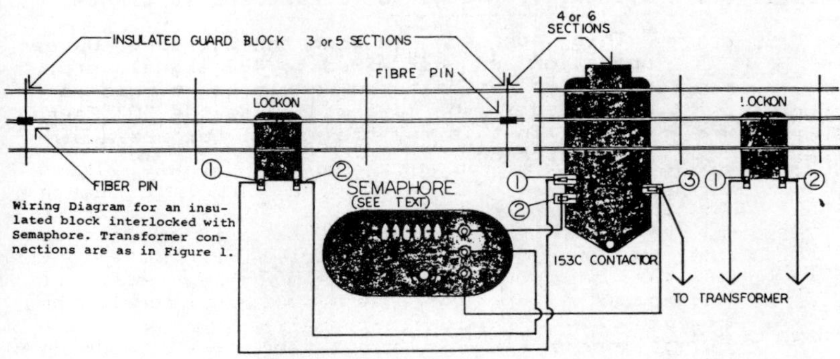

Wiring Diagram for an insulated block interlocked with Semaphore. Transformer connections are as in Figure 1.

FIGURE FOUR

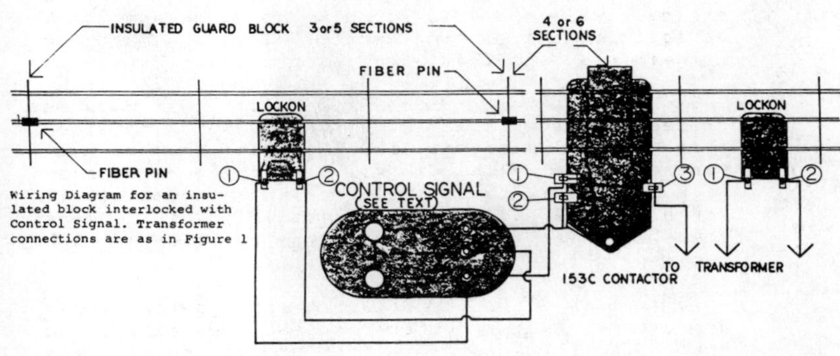

Wiring Diagram for an insulated block interlocked with Control Signal. Transformer connections are as in Figure 1

FIGURE FIVE

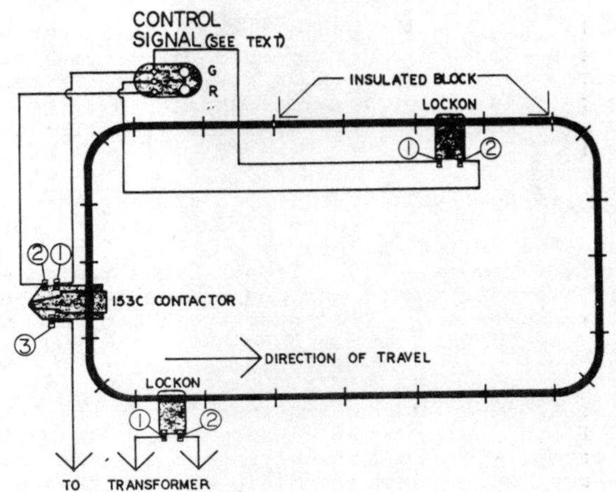

If you desire to continue to use the E-Unit for switching, or alignment and use of accessories, etc., Figure 2 shows the jumpering of the Running Section to the Insulated Guard Block Section through a 5-Ohm, 25 Watt variable resistor. The resistor, aviailable through eletronic supply houses is adjusted so that the engine stalls as planned, but there is enough sneak path current to keep the E-Unit from cycling. When used this way, the block should be longer than 5 sections, as the sneak current helps the engine roll and possibly pass through the block.

This type of operation requires testing of the resistor setting for your engines and block length. The key to success here is patience and care in recording your results for each engine and then making the best compromise selection.

Figure 3 shows the connections for using a Semaphore as an indicator of the selection and Figure 4 shows a control signal. Key to remember for any indicator is that you want it to show Green (or clear) when the block is live, and Red when the block is dead. Using this rule of thumb, you can connect the indicators for Standard Gauge as well as for "O" or O-27.

In Figure 5 you see a diagramatic loop that could be implemented in any shape and is shown here to give understanding to the concept. The Insulated Block is normally live and the indicator Green. Both trains will operate without stopping until train #2 gets to close to train #1. At this point train #2 will stop in the Block and wait for train #1 to clear the contactor. Then train #2 will resume continuous operation until again overtaking train #1.

The "Figure 8" layout (Figure 6) depicts the reverse use of the loop. The block is normally dead, stopping the train (either one) in front of the crossing waiting for the other train to cross. When the track is then clear, the stopped train can proceed across the intersection.

Many operators do not like the 153C Contactor as it must be adjusted to the weight of the passing cars. This could be difficult if a mixture of 1950 and 1970 trains are run on the same loop. It can, with patience, be adjusted, but there is another way which can be used for "O", O-27, "Super-O", and Standard Gauge.

FIGURE SIX

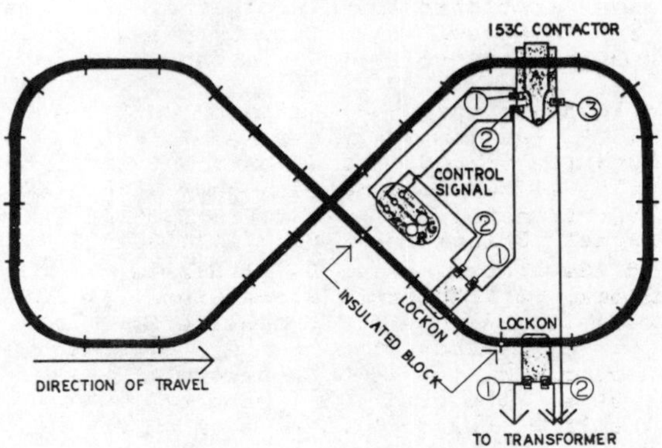

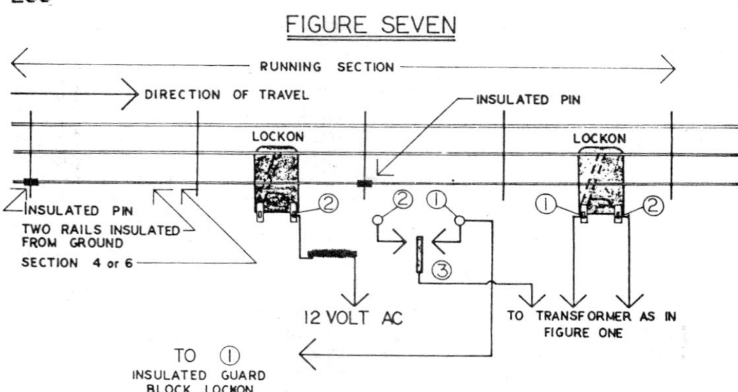

The method is to use a relay in place of the 153C Contactor (see Figure 7) in combination with an insulated ground rail. The wheels of the cars make the relay circuit and the relay points replace the 153C Contactor points. the transfer contact (#3) of the relay is equivalent to the #1 of the 153C. Contact #2 of the 153C is the same as the normally open contact (#2) of the relay. The relay is any common 12 volt AC relay coil whose contacts are rated at 5 to 10 ampheres. In order to guarantee a good ground connection for reliable operation, two sections of track should be insulated. It is easy to insulate the ground rail with either Fish Paper or plastic insulated tape. It should be noted that insulated ground rails were avilable in "Super O" curves and straights.

This approach is good for Standard Gauge operation and when wired to #82 signals etc., the time out features should be turned off and used in the same manner as the "O" Gauge type. In this way the signal becomes a simple indicator.

NO. 154 HIGHWAY FLASHER

No. 154 Crossing Signal can be placed at any grade crossing in your model railroad to give warning when a train is approaching the crossing. The signal consists of two warning lights which flash alternately as the train goes past the crossing. The Highway Signal is operated by means of the 154C Contactor which is clamped to the track and then wired to the Signal.

Attach the 154C Contactor to any section of straight track as shown in the inset of Figure 1. Press down spring lever. Slide contactor under the rail so that clip 'A' grips the flange of the outside rail. Snap spring clip 'B' over center rail by pressing upward. Then release spring lever so that the contact plate lies flat on top of outside rail.

WIRING NOTES: No. 1 clip of the 154C Contactor makes contact with the center or "power" track rail, while clips 2 and 3 are connected to a pair of contact plates which are insulated from each other and from the outside track rail upon which they rest. As the train passes over the contact plates they are alternately grounded to the opposite outside track rail through the train wheels and axles, thus causing the warning lamps to light.

For good operation it is important that the top surface of the contact plates is clean and that the insulating material on the bottom surface of the plates is unbroken.

LAMPS: No. 154 Signals made prior to 1950 were made to accommodate screw-base lamps; those made in 1950 and thereafter use bayonet-base lamps.

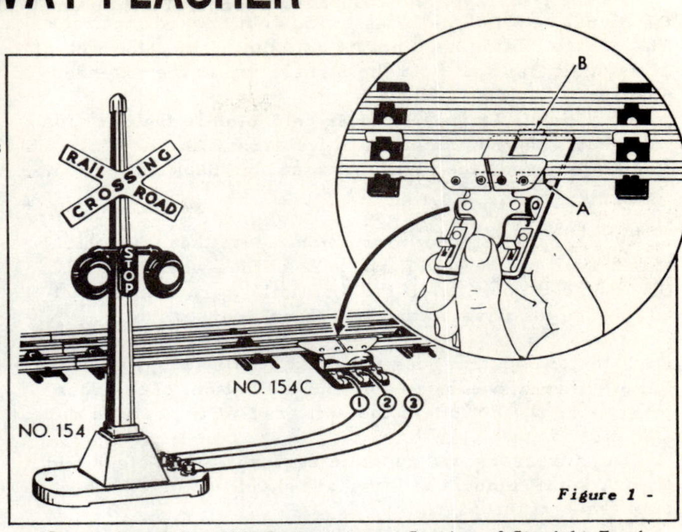

Figure 1 - (Inset) Attach No. 154C Contactor to a Section of Straight Track (Below) Connect Signal to Contactor by Three Wires.

No. 161 MAIL PICKUP SET

Completely be remote control -- at the touch of a button -- the mail bag Signal Arm swings close to the side of the approaching train. The No. 161 Mail Bag Pickup Set is designed to be operated on 10-14 volts A.C. The post which is seated on the plunger of the solenoid coil, is raised by the energized plunger. A cam action between the post and link swings the sweep arm out and the flag is lowered by the weight of the rod.

The magnet which is cemented to the side of a car lifts the magnetized mail bag from the extended Signal Arm. Any Lionel freight or passenger car may carry the "Pick-up Magnet". However, this car must be the widest car in the train.

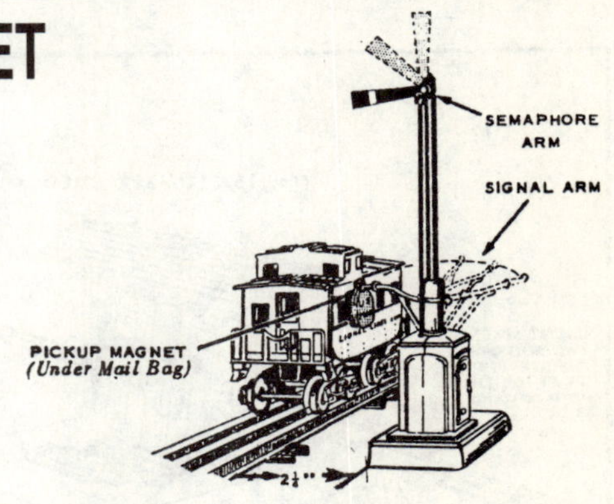

CEMENTING MAGNET TO CAR SIDE

The Pickup Magnet may be cemented to the side of a boxcar, a passenger car or a caboose. However, this magnet must be exactly located so that it will be in line with the Mail Bag on the Signal Arm.

1. Place the car on the track and locate the Signal about 2 1/4" away from the nearest track rail.
2. Put the Mail Bag on the Signal Arm with magnet side facing outward.
3. Pickup Magnet must be placed against the Mail Bag magnet.
4. Push down on the Semaphore Arm to swing the Mail Bag and Pickup Magnet against the side of the car -- move the car until the magnet rests on a smooth surface.
5. Outline the position of the Pickup Magnet on the car side.
6. Cut tip from cement capsule and apply cement to the full surface of the Pickup Magnet.
7. Place cement covered magnet directly over the pencil outline on the side of the car. Allow approximately 2 hours for cement to dry.

PLACING SIGNAL ON TRACK-SIDE

The mail-bag must be located at a definite distance from the track. To do this place the Signal about 2 1/4" from the nearest track rail and swing pickup arm fully out to meet the magnet on the car side. The operation will be more efficient if the signal is fastened down -- using the holes provided.

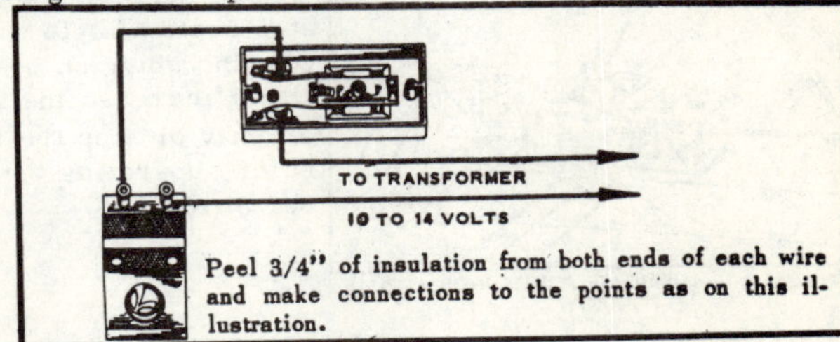

Peel 3/4" of insulation from both ends of each wire and make connections to the points as on this illustration.

OPERATING PROCEDURE

Reduce speed of the train before attempting "Mail Bag Pickup". Place the Mail Bag on the end of the Signal Arm so that the magnet side faces outward.

As the train approaches,press the control button until the Signal with the Mail Bag swings out toward the track. The control button need not be held down since the weight of the Mail Bag will hold the Signal Arm in the extended position.

The Pickup Magnet which is cemented to the car side will snatch the bag from the Signal Arm. As the Mail Bag is removed, the Signal Arm swings back away from the train.

SERVICE NOTES: The instructions state that the control button need not be held down to keep the sweep arm in the extended position. If the arm fails to remain extended, wedge the base so that the signal leans slightly.

If the sweep arm does not make a full swing, decrease the distance between the coil and the bottom of the post by striking the bottom of the coil bracket to position the coil higher.

The accessory will function best when kept clean and dry. A small amount of lubricant should be placed in the cam track on the post.

ASSEMBLING PROCEDURE: for post & arm assembly

1. Post adapter is cemented to the top of the base assembly with the shorter slot corresponding with the key-way in the base.
2. Drop the return spring through the top of the post & insert the post through the bottom of the base & adapter with the key-way on the post fitting in the long slot on the adapter.
3. Place coil assembly into the bottom of the base allowing the post to seat itself into the coil core.
4. The coil bracket is retained by two speednuts, one of which also holds the bushing.
5. Slide link over the post and install it so that the link pins engage the cam-track on the post.
6. The adapter cap snap-locks to the adapter and stabilizes the link;if locks are broken, the cap can be carefully cemented to the adapter.
7. The straight end of the rod is to be inserted into the hole at the top of the base. The hook end of the rod must face toward the post.
8. The flag is assembled with the short side of its pivot shank against the post.
9. Hook the rod to the flag so that the hook is between the flag and post.
10. The pivot pin is inserted through the flag and into the post by squeezing it with a vise.

NO. 164 LUMBER LOADER

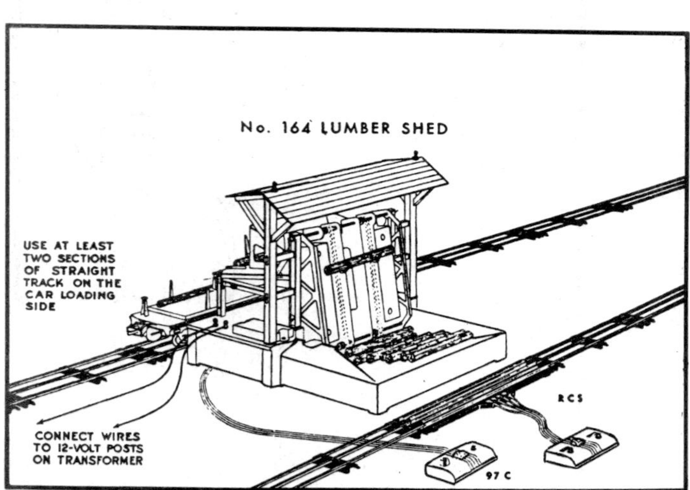

FIGURE 1 — PLACE AND CONNECT LUMBER SHED AS SHOWN ABOVE.

The No.164 Lumber Loader is similar in operation to the No. 97 Coal Elevator (see No. 97 COAL ELEVATOR). The Lumber Loader shown in figure 1 to the left can be placed in any layout measuring approximately 14 3/4" between center rails of parallel tracks (also see figure 3 below).

No. 164 Lumber Loader is especially appropiate for use with Lionel remote control Lumber Cars. These cars will unload lumber into the bin on one side of the loader. The lumber is then picked up by the conveyor chain and transported to the upper loading platform. The conveyor is activated by the start-stop button on the 97C Controller included with the accessory.

After the lumber has been transported to the upper loading platform, pressing the "unload" button on the 97C Controller releases the stored lumber into waiting lumber cars below. Each touch of the button will release two logs

FIGURE 2 — LUBRICATE POINTS INDICATED BY ARROWS.

The Lumber Shed operates best on 12-14 volts. If you find sluggish operation either increase the voltage slightly or stop the train before operating the Lumber Shed.

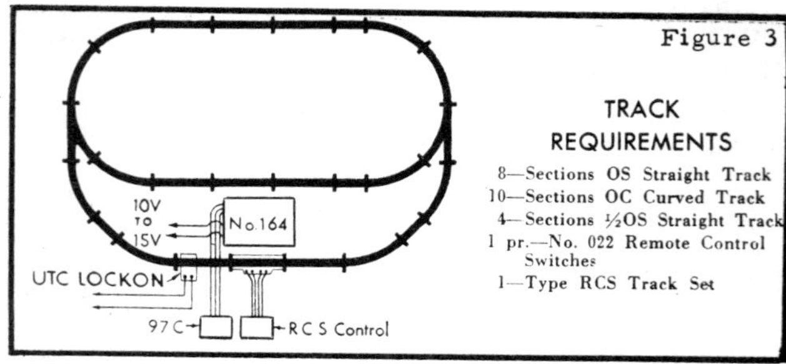

No. 167C WHISTLE CONTROLLER

The patented Lionel Whistle together with the remote Whistle Controller represent one of the most ingenious delelopments ever made in model railroading. The whistle itself is mounted within the locomotive tender so that it can be sounded any place on the track by means of the Whistle Controller which is connected between the transformer and the track at any convenient distance from the layout (see WHISTLE).

The No. 167C Whistle Controller has two control buttons: one button blows the whistle; the other controls the direction of the train.

NOTE: The Whistle Controller can be used only with alternating current having a frequency greater than 40 cycles.

To protect it against being damaged by accidental "short circuits" on the track, particularly when using large transformers capable of delivering heavy current for long periods of time, the controller is provided with a built-in therman circuit breaker. The breaker opens whenever the current exceeds a safe limit. After a few seconds the breaker resets automatically, but will keep on reopening until the cause of the short circuit has been removed.

When using the 167C Whistle Controller in conjunction with a heavy duty transformer, such as Type "V" or "Z", you will find that the whistle controller circuit breaker will open faster than the transformer circuit breaker, so that the red warning signal in the transformer will cease to operate. In this case you will be able to detect short circuits by the dimming and blinking of the track and locomotive lights.

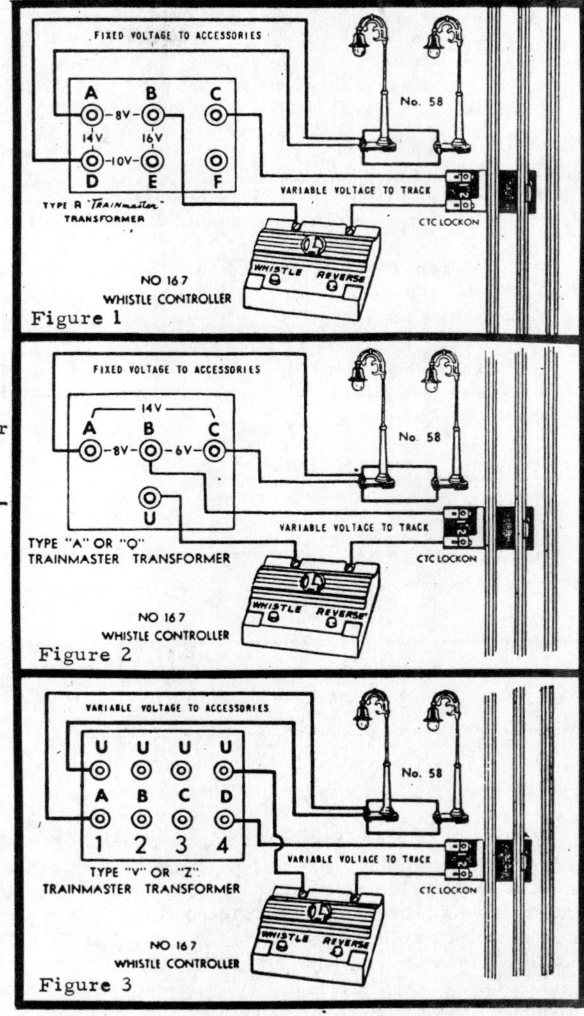

Figure 1
Figure 2
Figure 3

HOW TO CONNECT WHISTLE CONTROLLER

Select the two variable voltage transformer terminals that will properly operate your outfit. You will find that outfits using the whistle controller require from 2 to 3 volts more than those without it because of the voltage losses in the controller itself. Then merely connect the whistle controller in series with the transformer and track. Figures 1,2 and 3 to the right give several examples.

HOW TO OPERATE THE WHISTLE

By pressing the controller button marked "Whistle" you can make your train sound any railroad signal: long, loud whistles or sharp, quick blasts. The whistle will blow as long as the button is held down. Press the button all the way down. Frequently your train will tend to slow down when the whistle is blown. This is normal, because additional power must be supplied by the transformer to operate the whistle motor. You can minimize this effect by keeping one hand on the voltage control of the transformer so that you can increase the voltage slightly as you blow the whistle and decrease it when you stop.

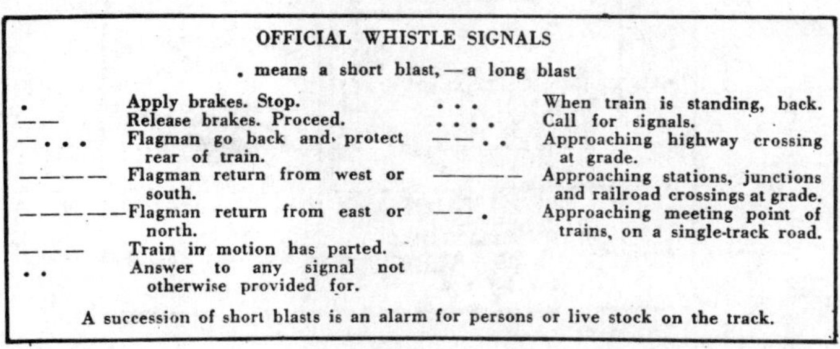

OFFICIAL WHISTLE SIGNALS

. means a short blast, — a long blast

.	Apply brakes. Stop.	. . .	When train is standing, back.
— —	Release brakes. Proceed.	. . . .	Call for signals.
— . . .	Flagman go back and protect rear of train.	— — . .	Approaching highway crossing at grade.
— — — —	Flagman return from west or south.	— — — — —	Approaching stations, junctions and railroad crossings at grade.
— — — — — —	Flagman return from east or north.	— — .	Approaching meeting point of trains, on a single-track road.
— — —	Train in motion has parted.		
. .	Answer to any signal not otherwise provided for.		

A succession of short blasts is an alarm for persons or live stock on the track.

WARNING: Never attempt to blow the whistle while a short circuit exists in the layout as this may result in permanent damage to your controller.

REVERSING DIRECTION OF THE TRAIN

By pressing the "Reverse" button, you can make the train stop, start, and change direction without cutting the power from your other accessories. The reversing unit, contained in the locomotive, has three positions: forward, neutral and reverse. If the train is moving forward, pressing the button once will make it stop; this is the neutral position. Pressing the button again will reverse the train. Now in order to make the train go forward again the button must be pressed two more times -- once into neutral, again into "forward".

Some locomotives have only forward and reverse (no neutral position) and will alternate between the two positions each time the button is pressed.

You can operate the train in one direction only by disconnecting the reversing E-Unit in the locomotive. As the train is going in the desired direction, stop it with your hand and move the lever located on locomotive boiler to opposite direction.

HOW TO OPERATE TWO TRAINS

The diagram below (Figure 4) shows a typical layout running two trains independently. In order to operate two trains in this way, the layout must first be sectionalized, that is, one loop insulated from the other by fibre pins. In this layout, the inside loop is insulated from the outside loop by the fibre pins indicated by the black dots.

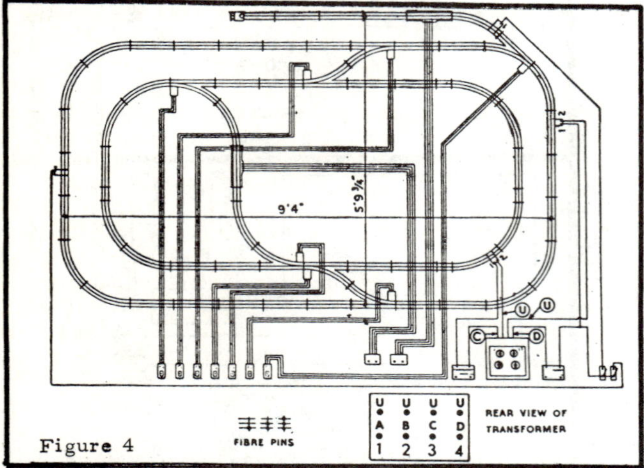

Figure 4

The transformer can be either Type "V" or "Z". The wire connections to the binding posts are shown by the letters "C", "D" and "U" which correspond to the markings on the back of the transformer. Each loop of this layout is controlled by a separate control knob on the transformer, leaving two knobs for accessories.

Two whistle controllers for blowing the two whistles independently are shown on either side of the transformer. You will find that under certain conditions both whistles will blow when one of the controllers is pressed. This may be partially overcome by pressing the "Whistle" controller buttons rapidly.

In the lower right hand corner of the diagram two knife switches are shown. The purpose of the left hand switch is to cut the current in or out of the siding as desired. The other knife switch will be found convenient when you want to stop a train on the outside loop to enable the second train on the inner loop to crossover to the outer loop. This knife switch sectionalizes one-half of the outer loop.

ELECTRICAL DESCRIPTION

The Lionel Whistle is controlled by a d-c relay mounted in the tender together with the whistle mechanism. This relay acts as a switch for the whistle motor which drives a stream of air into the whistle chambers making the characteristic whistling sound. The whistle relay does not respond to alternating current and should remain open even at the highest a-c voltages supplied by the transformers. But, it is sensitive to direct current and is adjusted to close whenever a small amount of d-c voltage is fed to the track. This d-c voltage is supplied by the WHISTLE CONTROLLER whenever you press the whistle button. The whistle controller is connected in 'series' with the transformer and rectifies enough of the transformer output to operate the whistle relay. Actually, as you push the whistle button, two d-c voltages are supplied by the controllers: a momentary 3-4 volt 'pick-up' surge to close the whistle relay, then a steady 'holding' voltage of at least .8 volts to keep the relay closed. These voltages are obtained when a current of one more ampere passes through the controller. Higher currents will result in higher d-c voltages, so that the whistle will work more positively with bigger outfits, or with some added track lights or accessories.

Whistle controllers are built either as a separate accessory unit, as Nos. 167 and 167C Whistle Controllers, or are incorporated in the transformer itself, as in the case of "Multi-Control" such as Types 1033, LW, KW, and ZW.

The controllers consist of a copper oxide rectifier disc, a length of resistance wire (approx. 1.6 ohms) which is automatically shunted across the rectifier to obtain the 'holding' voltage, and some means of compensating for the voltage drop across the rectifier which occurs when the whistle is blown and which would cause the train to slow down or stop altogether.

In the Nos. 167 and 167C Whistle Controllers this voltage compensation is accomplished by means of a choke coil with an impedance approximating that of the rectifier and resistor assembly. The choke coil is normally in the circuit. As you blow the whistle you automatically substitute the rectifier for the choke coil, thus keeping the track voltage at approximately the same level.

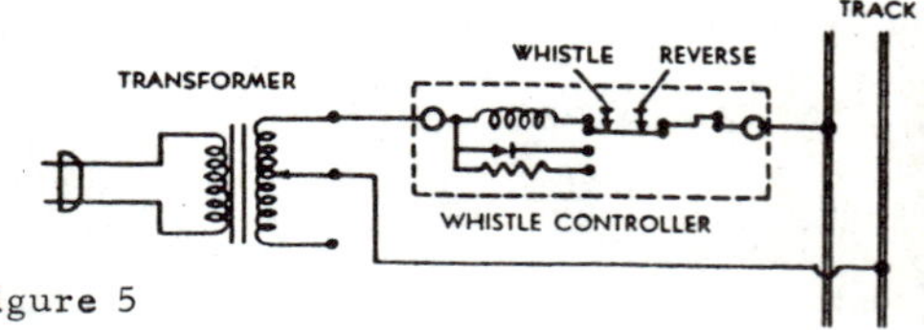

Figure 5

Since the controller is connected in series with the transformer and track, (see Figure 5 above) it is evident that a short circuit on the track will cause a heavy current to pass through the choke coil. The colis are made to withstand a current of 6 amperes, but the heavier short circuit will overheat and eventually burn out the coil. To prevent this damage the 167C Controller has a thermal circuit breaker which opens the circuit when the current through the controller exceeds the 6 ampere limit.

A schematic diagram of No. 167C Whistle Controller is shown in Figure 6 below.

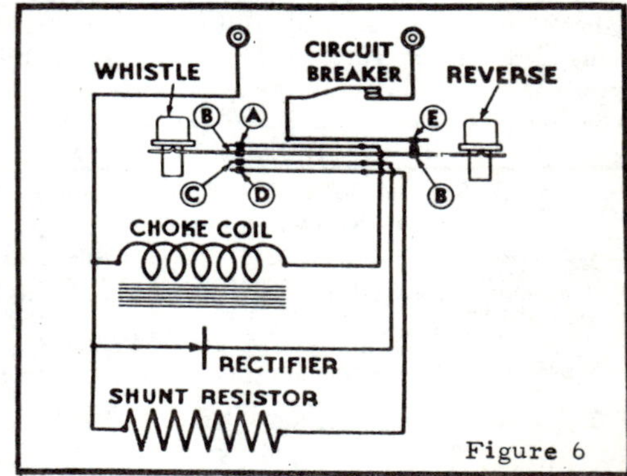

Figure 6

Two push buttons appear on the panel of the 167 and 167C Controllers: one to blow the whistle, the other to reverse the locomotive. The 'Whistle' button operates a pile-up sequence switch to make proper electrical connections among the several controller elements. The 'Reverse' button is a make-and-break switch used to interrupt the track power momentarily in order to operate the locomotive reversing E-Unit.

The sketches below illustrate the action of the sequence switch as the Whistle is blown:

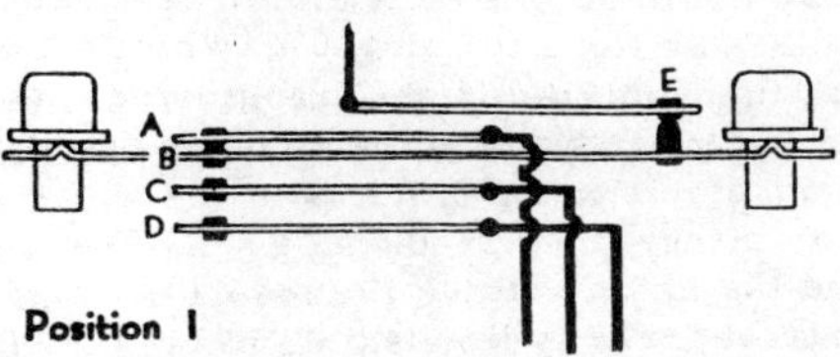

Position 1

Position 1 -- Normal operation of train. Contacts B and A must be normally closed so that the current from the transformer passes through the choke coil to the track. If either 'A' or 'E' fail to touch 'B', you will have an open circuit and no power will reach the track.

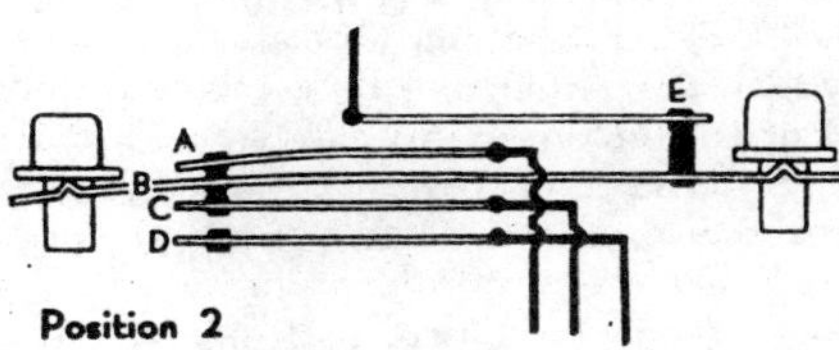

Position 2

Position 2 -- As the whistle button is pressed, 'B' moves down to contact 'C'. 'A' follows through maintaining contact with 'B'. If 'B' breaks with 'A' before touching 'C', the current to the track will be momentarily interrupted and cause the train to reverse.

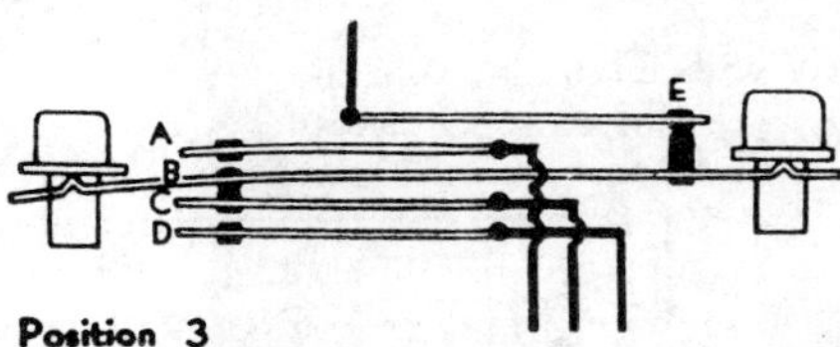

Position 3

Position 3 -- 'B' makes full contact with 'C' and breaks with 'A'. At this moment the full transformer voltage is applied across the rectifier resulting in a high d-c 'pick-up' surge.

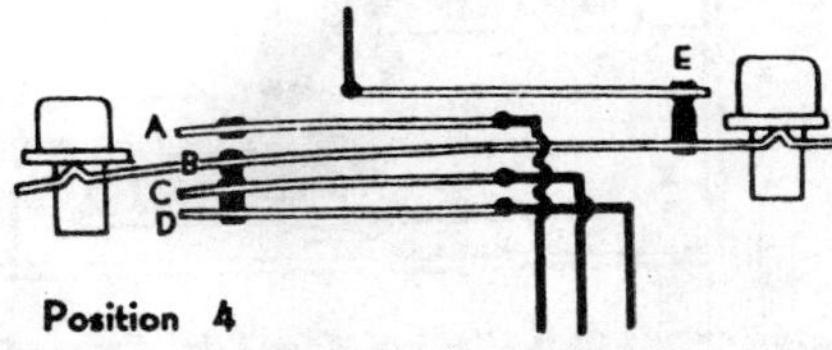

Position 4

Position 4 -- The whistle button at the bottom of its stroke. 'B' and 'C' contact 'D', connecting the resistor across the rectifier. This reduces the 'pick-up' voltage to the 'holding' voltage needed to keep the whistle relay closed. Unless this contact is made, continuous application of the relatively higher 'pick-up' voltage will overheat and eventually damage the rectifier disc while the train will slow down or even stop because of insufficient current flow through the controller.

SERVICING WHISTLE CONTROLLER

Lionel whistle equipment is designed to work at line frequencies of 50-60 cycles. It is not suited for direct current power supply since under this condition the whistle relay would remain closed and the whistle would blow continually. At frequencies appreciably higher than 60 cycles the impedance of the choke coil becomes so high that not enough voltage will be supplied to the track to operate the trains.

Trouble is sometimes encountered when the whistle controllers are used in unusually large layouts which draw large currents for their trains and accessories.

When too large a current is drawn through the controller, its choke coil will overheat. The voltage drop across it will increase, slowing up the train and the coil itself will eventually deteriorate and burn out.

The most frequent cause of breakdown of No. 167 Whistle Controllers, which, unlike the later No. 167C Controllers, are not equipped with protective circuit breakers, is a burned-out choke coil. If the insulation is burned off and the wiring is shorted, the coil will lose its voltage compensating action so that the train will stop whenever you blow the whistle. If the coil is open, the track, naturally will get no power at all.

Another source of trouble common to all whistle controllers is a ruptured rectifier disc, so that the controller loses its ability to furnish d-c voltage. If you try to blow the whistle with a short circuit on the track you will force the rectifier to carry an excessive amount of current. This will overheat the disc and cause it to lose its rectifying ability. Copper oxide rectifiers have shown a remarkable resistance to overloads and will generally regain their rectifying ability after cooling down, but if abused continually they may become permanently damaged.

TROUBLE SHOOTING PROCEDURE

1. Check the Whistle Controller with a whistle which is known to be in good condition to make sure that it is the controller and not the whistle relay which is at fault.
2. Check the operation and the appearance of the contact points to make sure that they are in good condition and make contact in proper sequence. Don't forget to see that 'E' makes contact with 'B' in the normal operating position or no current will be delivered to the track.
3. Make sure that all internal wiring is properly soldered and free of corrosion and rust. See that none of the turns of the resistance wire wound on the rectifier sub-assembly is shorted by touching adjacent turns or the metal plate.
4. Exchange the rectifier disc by prying up 'speed nut' off the bolt holding the disc to the metal plate. Note that the disc is placed with the copper oxide (silvered) side next to the plate. The points of the speed nut should make firm contact with the copper face of the disc. Do not bend or distort the rectifier disc as that may puncture the oxide surface and short out the rectifier.
5. If you have occasion to take apart the pile-up to replace contacts be sure to reassemble the spacers between the contacts in their proper order. They are of two different thicknesses (see Figure 7 next page).

Figure 7 -- Trouble Shooting Procedure # 5

BATTERY OPERATION OF WHISTLE

To operate the shistle under extremely heavy load conditions, or in localities where the line frequency is greater than 60 cycles, the whistle controller can be replaced by an ordinary 1.5 volt No. 6 dry cell. The dry cell is connected in the circuit through a fast-acting single pole double-throw snap switch, as shown below (Figure 8). When switch is in its normal position

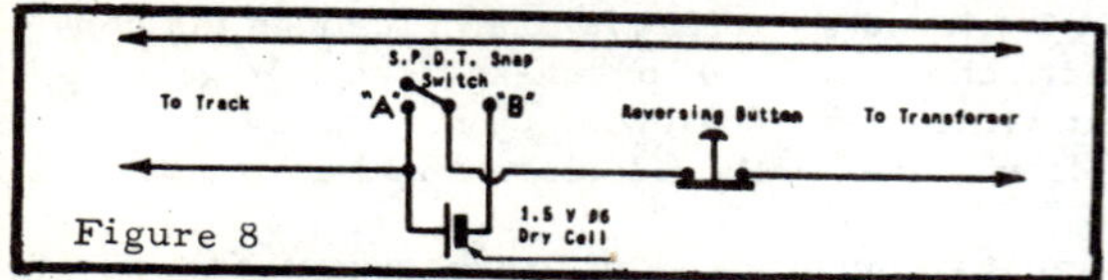

Figure 8

at 'A', the cell is out of the circuit; when switch is snapped to 'B' the dry cell is thrown into the power circuit and picks up the whistle relay. The switch must be fast enough to keep the locomotive reversing E-Unit from tripping while the switch is being snapped.

In exceptional cases where very large currents are used it may be advisable to use two dry cells in parallel to reduce the a-c voltage drop across them.

NO. 167S WHISTLE CONTROLLER

Because lamp-type smoke generators, used in 1946 models of smoke locomotives, drew a relatively large amount of current, these locomotives tended to slow down as the whistle was blown. Te eliminate this difficulty, these smoke outfits were provided with No.167S Whistle Controllers, in which the value of the shunt resistor was decreased from 1.6 ohms to 1 ohm (Approximately one turn of wire less).

When changing from lamp-type to heater type smoke generator (see 671 Locomotive), you may find that the whistle relay gets insufficient d-c 'holding' voltage and drops out, particularly when the locomotive is standing still. To prevent this either add a couple of lights to the outfit to increase current through the Whistle Controller, or add a turn of resistance wire to the shunt resistor.

USE OF 167 WHISTLE CONTROLLER WITH TWIN-MOTORED LOCOMOTIVE

The voltage drop produced by the compensating choke coil in the 167 whistle controller depends directly on the amount of current which passes through it on the way to the track. Since No.167 Whistle Controller was originally intended to be used with single-motored steam-type locomotoves its choke coil is engineered to produce the correct voltage drop when track current is about 1-1/2 amperes, which is the amount normally taken by a single-motored locomotive.

However, if the whistle controller is used with a twin-motored locomotive the track current passing through the choke coil to the track is 3 to 3-1/2 amps and the initial voltage drop produced by the choke coil is doubled and the track voltage is frequently depressed down to a point where it is impossible to obtain satisfactory train operation even at full transformer voltage.

Under these conditions it is necessary to lower the impedance of the choke coil in order to eliminate excessive initial voltage drop produced by it. This is done by removing some of the iron laminations from within the coil. For operating a twin-motored diesel the removal of 10-12 laminations will give satisfactory results, but where the situation is complicated by the use of several different types of locos some experimentation may be required to determine the best possible compromise for the operation of both whistles & horns.

To reach and lift out the choke coil unscrew the bottom of the whistle control case and unsolder the wire leading from the coil to the solder lug attached to the circuit breaker metal strip. To experiment with the whistle controller while the choke coil is out of the case connect a wire jumper from the end of the coil to the solder lug. To prevent buzzing noise after some of the laminations have been removed, the empty space should be filled tightly with cardboard strips.

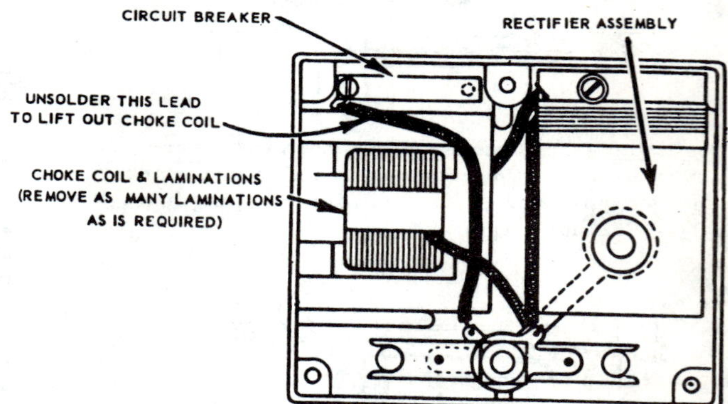

Bottom View of No. 167 Whistle Controller with Base Plate Removed

No. 175 ROCKET LAUNCHER

The No. 175 Rocket Launcher is a replica of the test sites used for defense missiles and space research rockets. Like its prototype it should be given a special area of its own, away from main lines and settled areas. If you plan to transport missiles on a No. 6175 Missile Car, you will of course need a spur track at the site.

INSTALLING THE PLATFORM

Locate the platform on a smooth level area next to the siding as shown in the illustration below. The gantry rail extension is packed with the controller. Install as shown by sliding the rail flanges under the tabs on the

CONTINUED

platform. With the two wires furnished in the package, connect the binding posts on the platform to a 10-14 volt transformer source. Set the gantry structure on its rails with the servicing platform facing the launching pad as shown. Fit the lug on the base of the gantry over the drive pin protruding from the slot in the platform. Prepare the crane for use by raising its mast to the vertical position so that it is caught by the spring latch.

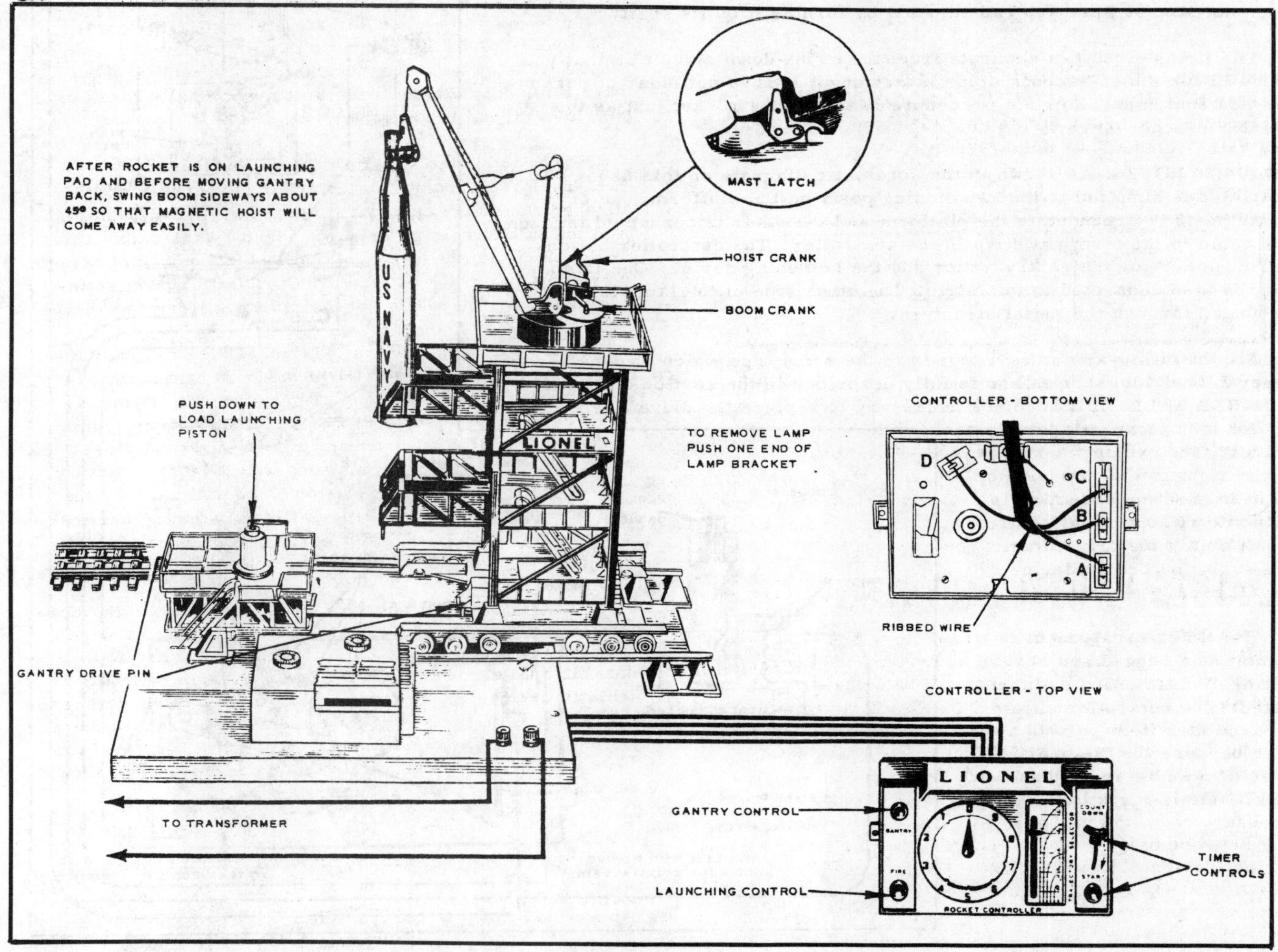

CONTROLLER

Connect the wires of the contro cable to the terminals on the bottom of the controller as shown. Note that one of the outside wires on the cable has ribbed insulation. This wire is connected to terminal B, the next to C, the next to A, and the last to D.

SETTING UP THE ROCKET

Press the "Gantry" button on the controller for a few seconds so that the gantry moves back and forth on its rails. If the motor makes a harsh buzzing sound, the voltage is probably a little too high and should be reduced.

The two cranks on the crane control the hoist line and the boom angle. The magnet on the hoist line picks up the rocket by the metal band on the nose cone. By a combination of winching and swinging movements and gantry travel, the rocket is swung into an upright position, cradled in the service platforms, and moved into position over the launching pad. Arm the launching device by pushing the plunger down until it catches before lowering the rocket into place.

LAMP REPLACEMENT

The socket which holds the L53 pilot lamp snaps into a rectangular hole in the bottom of the controller . Remove the socket by grasping one tab of the spring and pulling sideways toward the other tab.

If you try to squeeze both tabs at once, the socket may pop into the hole and you will have to remove the bottom plate to get it out.

CONTINUED

LAUNCHING PROCEDURE

Check out the count-down timer by pulling the three-cornered reset knob toward you and then pressing the "Start" button. If the pointer does not stop at Zero you can adjust it by turning it on its shaft.

The firing circuit is separate from the count-down circuit so that you can call for a last-second "hold" if the target area is not clear of personnel and equipment. Normal procedure is to fire the rocket just as the pointer reaches Zero.

SERVICE NOTES: As shown in the schematic diagram on this page, 9-12 volts a-c is supplied to the two binding posts on the platform: one of these posts is grounded to the platform and the other is connected through the cable to the terminal strip in the controller. The controller buttons select power for the gantry motor and the launching device. One lamp lead is also connected to this strip. The other side of the lamp is grounded through the metal structure.

The vibrating-armature motor is of the same type which powers several other Lionel accessories and is fully described in the section on No. 464 LUMBER MILL. If it becomes necessary to replace the drive line eyelet, solder it in place using acid core solder. The eyelet must be perfectly tight and the swaging operation used in production is difficult without power tools. Don't crimp the drive line in the eyelet before soldering or it will melt.

The timer escapement is simple and rugged and should not be disassembled or lubricated. The controller should be used on a firm smooth surface because the "flapper" is seated in a hole in the base and can be slowed or stopped by pressure from the nap of a rug or the like.

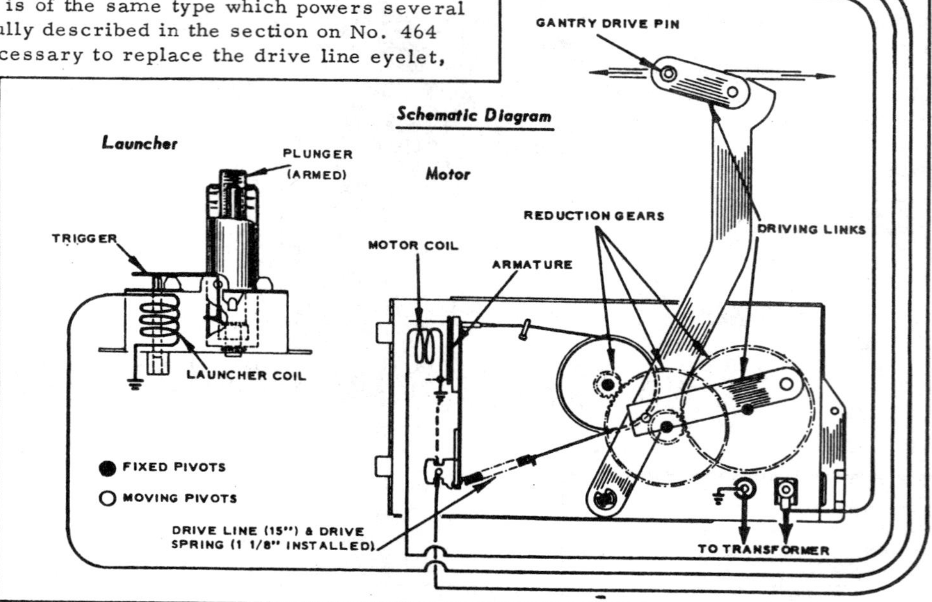

No. 182 ELECTROMAGNETIC CRANE

The No. 182 Electromagnetic Crane performs all of the operations of a real crane, picking up loads of iron and steel and transporting them to waiting flat cars.

Attach one wire from each of the two binding posts on the base of the Crane to transformer posts that deliver 12-16 volts either fixed or variable. Operating voltage of 12 to 16 volts may be required when the accessory is new. After the Crane has been in operation for a few hours and the various moving parts have been broken in, this voltage can be decreased to 12 or 14 volts.

HOW No. 165C CONTROLLER OPERATES

The No. 165C Controller, which is attached to the Crane by cable, has four push-button controls and a rotary knob switch(see Figure to right)

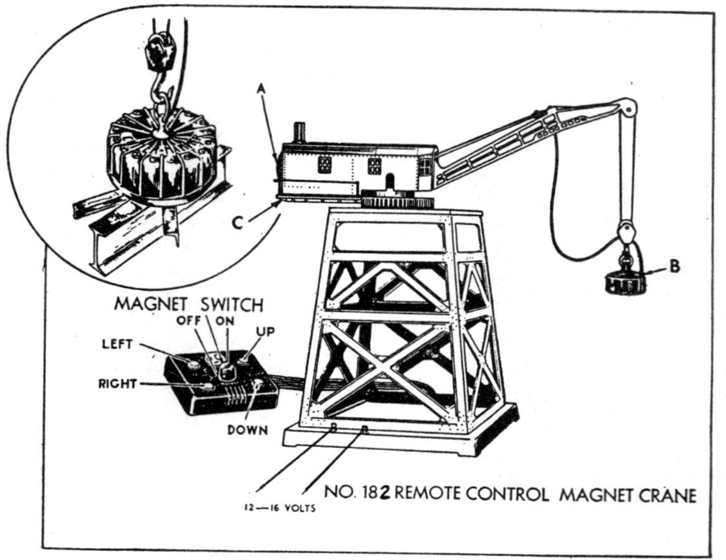

NO. 182 REMOTE CONTROL MAGNET CRANE

On the left side of the Controller, press and hold down on the upper button to rotate the cab and boom assembly in a counter-clockwise direction; similarly, the lower button will control the rotation in the opposite direction. The Crane, thus can be turned in a complete circle to either the right or left.

Turn the knob switch to "on" to energize the lifting magnet, indicated at "B" in the figure. A red light in the cab indicates that the magnet is energized. On the right side of the Controller, the upper button raises the magnet attached to the block and tackle and the bottom button lowers the magnet.

Note that the motor operates only when the buttons are pressed. Remove finger from any button and the motor stops immediately. You can also either raise or lower the boom by means of the hand-wheel at rear of cab as indicated by "A".

LAMP REPLACEMENT -- the cab must be removed before replacing lamp (No. 165-53, red, 18 V). To do this, unscrew boom control wheel at "A". Then remove two screws (which are indicated by "C") located under the rear part of the cab in opposite corners. Finally, lift the rear part of the cab slightly pulling it back about one-eighth of an inch and replace lamp.

A bag of Steel is supplied with each Crane to be used as loading material, but any other small, light-weight pieces of steel or iron commonly found around the house, such as nails may be substituted. To pick up a load, merely lower the magnet into the material, then energize the magnet by the rotary switch, lift and carry the load to its destination, turn switch "off" and load drops from magnet.

The Crane can be used also to carry other types of loads by removing the magnet from its hook. For example, you can construct your own bin or net in which to carry merchandise and attach it to the hook in place of the magnet.

IMPORTANT: Only the "Left" and "Up" buttons, or the "Right" and "Down" buttons may be pressed at the same time. Do not press any other two buttons simultaneously or the motor will stall.

If possible, fasten down base of Crane to your train platform using the holes provided in the base.

No. 192 RAILROAD CONTROL TOWER

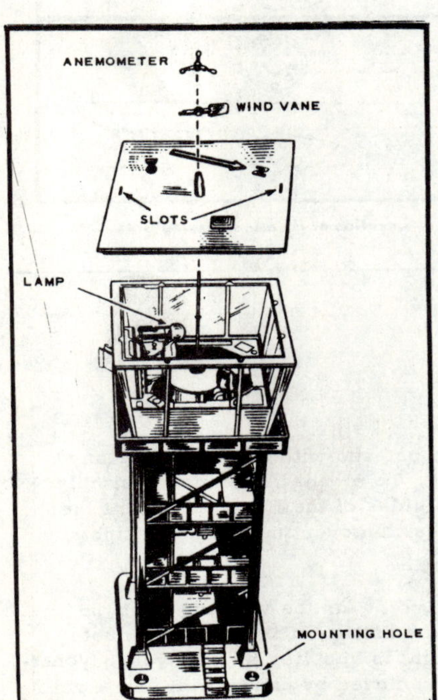

Power connections to the No. 192 Railroad Control Tower are made to the two springs clips under the base. The vibrator-type motor operates best in the 9 to 15 volt range; if possible, use a variable transformer outlet so that you can adjust the voltage to suit the individual characteristics of your motor.

NOTE: The Tower can be mounted on a permanent layout by wood screws passing through the rubber grommets in the base. Don't tighten the screws too firmly -- let the grommets keep some cushioning effect.

LAMP CHANGE: Access to a burnt-out lamp is gained by first removing the anemometer and wind indicator from the shaft. Then press in on the windows just below the two small slots in the roof to free the retaining claws. Use bayonet-base lamp # L53.

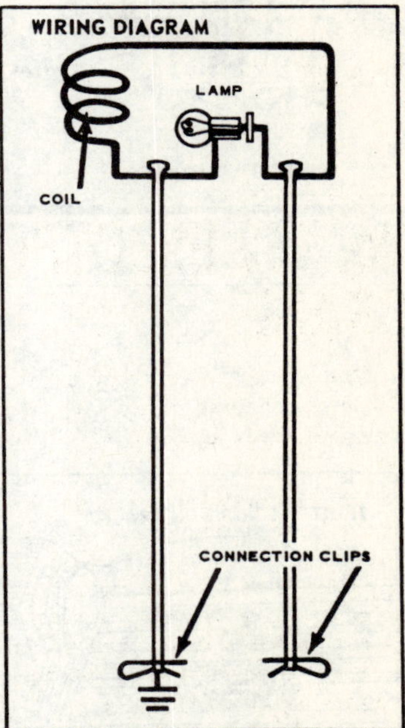

No. 252 CROSSING GATE

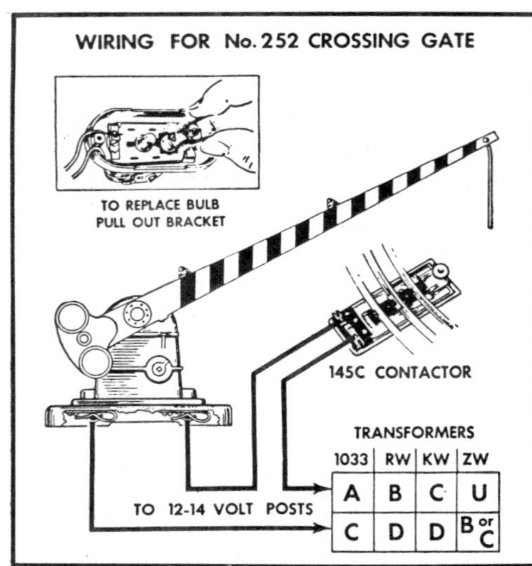

OPERATION: Normally the gate is up and the light is out. As train passes over contactor, current flows into solenoid pulling down gate and illuminating the lamp

No. 252 Crossing Gate, first made in 1950, is activated by a solenoid-and-plunger mechanism which is usually energized automatically by a train passing over a track contactor. Normally the solenoid plunger is at the bottom of its tube and the Gate is held in upright position by a pair of counterweights riveted to the rear of the Gate assembly. When the coil is energized the plunger moves upward and lowers the Gate by pushing against the fibre cam mounted in the center of the Crossing Gate shaft.

A lamp, mounted in a removable snap-in bracket, is connected in parallel with the coil and lights up simultaneously with the lowering of the Gate. A lucite bar in the Gate assembly is provided to transmit the lights to the two red 'lanterns' on top of the Crossing Gate. The operating voltage of the Crossing Gate is 10-14 volts.

SERVICE NOTES -- Except for physical breakage due to careless handling, No. 252 Crossing Gate is usually quite trouble free. After overheating or a long period of operation, the Gate may have a tendency to stick. This can generally be remedied by thorough cleaning of the plunger and the plunger hole in the coil spool. However, if the spool has been distorted by heat, the entire coil should be replaced. When reassembling, be sure to replace the insulating paper strip under the 'high' contact clip.

To improve operation Gates made in 1951 were molded with square hole for the shaft rotated 45° off horizontal. Similar change was made in the fibre cam -- therefore, make sure cam and Gate holes match.

Diagram of No. 252 Crossing Gate

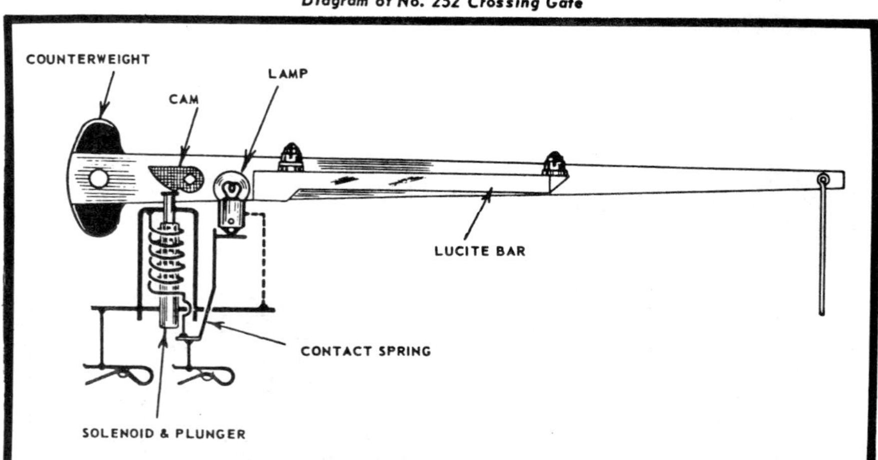

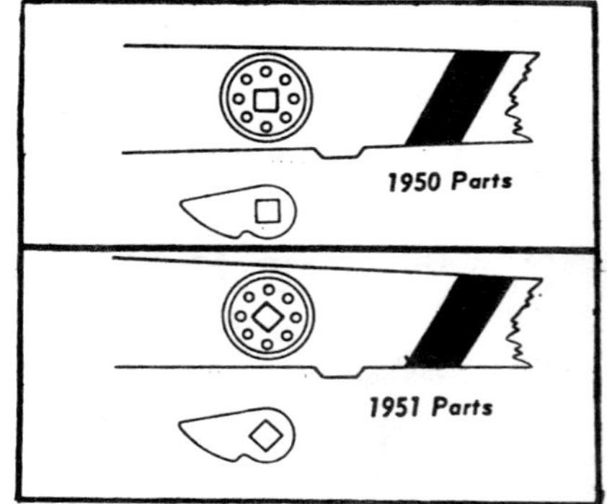

Location of Hole in Crossing Gate

No. 260 BUMPER

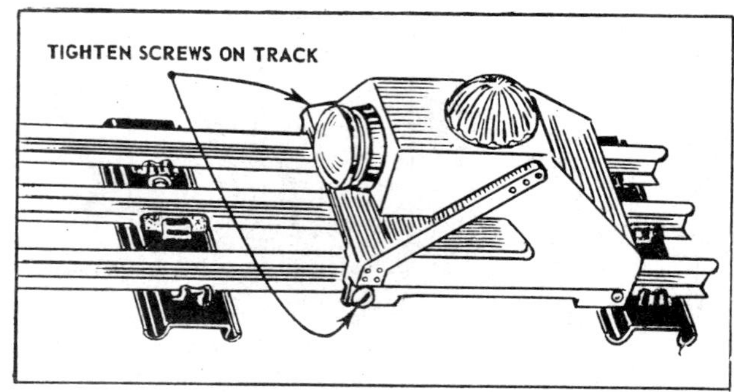

No. 260 Bumper can be used with any Lionel or any other "O" or "O27" track. To mount the Bumper, simply loosen the screws on the sides of the Bumper, mount the Bumper in the desired position over the track and tighten the screws.

In order to supply current for the warning light the brass spring contact on the bottom of the Bumper must touch the center rail. Light is supplied by a 14-volt bayonet-base bulb, which can be removed by unscrewing the jewel cap. For replacement, use lamp No. L53.

No. 262 CROSSING GATE

To be realistic every minature railroad should have street crossings. Naturally, all crossings must be properly protected by automatic gates.

No. 262 Crossing Gate automatically flashes the red lights and lowers its crossing gate as a train approaches. After the train has passed, the gate will rise to allow traffic to pass through the crossing.

Connect the Crossing Gate as shown in the diagram below. Be sure to use transformer binding posts which supply 12-14 volts. The No. 262 Crossing Gate is controlled by a No. 145C Contactor, which is an "ON-OFF" electrical switch (see 145C CONTACTOR). Note that on "Super-O" track the 145C Contactor must be engaged in the slots under the plastic ties.

WIRE CONNECTIONS

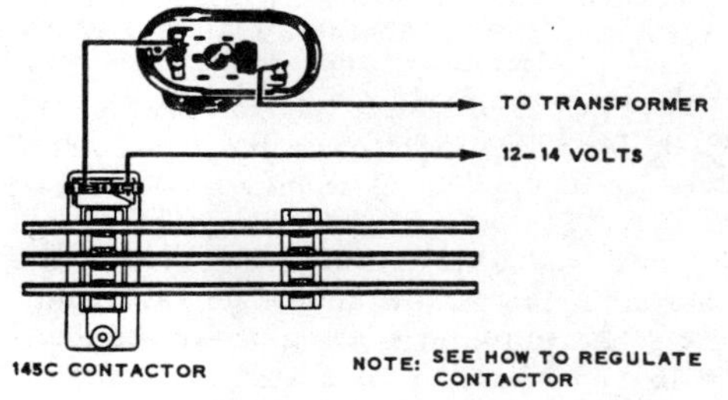

The Crossing Gate may be operated without the use of a 145C Contactor when a specially insulated track is substituted(see INSULATED TRACK SECTIONS). In this application, the metal wheels of the engine entering the insulated track section completes the electrical circuit and activates the Gate.

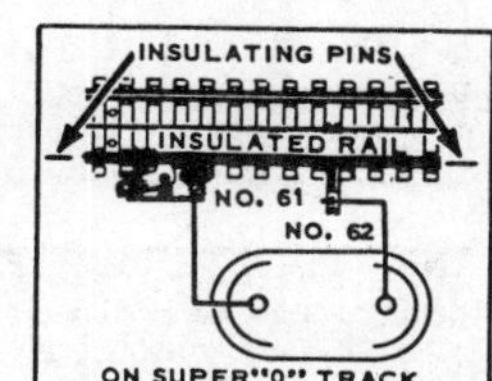

For "Super-O" track insulated track sections No. 48 Straight or No. 49 Curved may be used.

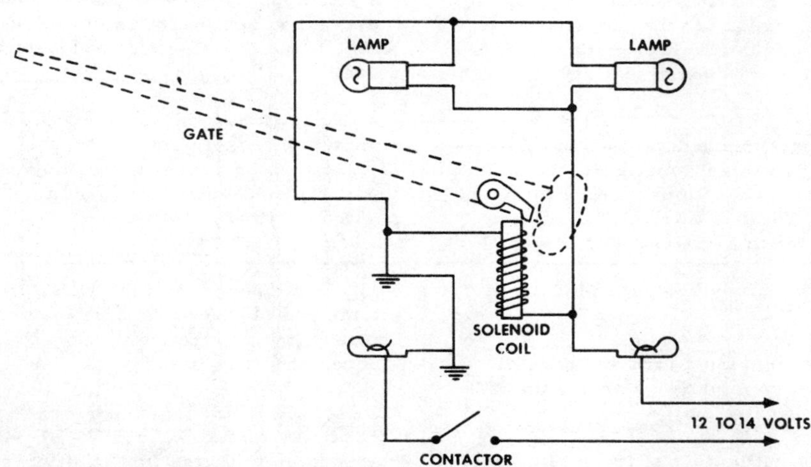

No. 264 FORK LIFT SET

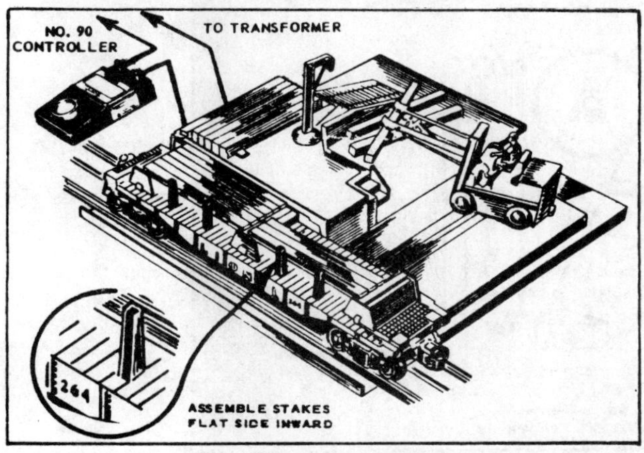

No. 264 Fork Lift Platform in Operating Position

No. 6264 FLAT CAR with TIMBERS

To prevent the timbers from "riding up" over the side of the car as they are picked up by the lift truck, the stakes along the side of the flat car shoud be assembled with the flat sides inward, toward the load, as shown below.

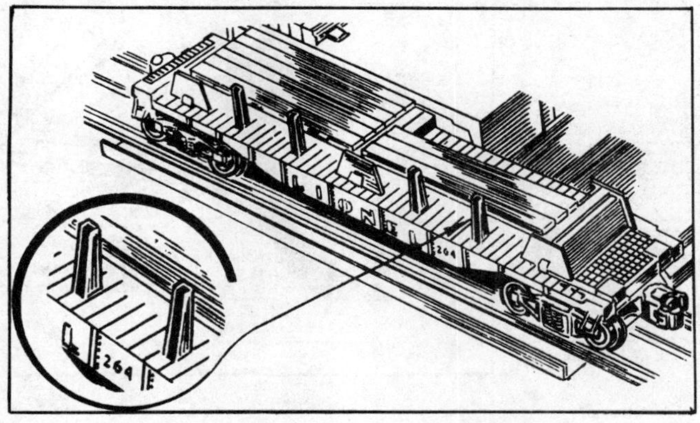

No. 264 Fork Lift Set consists of the platform equipped with a minature fork lift truck and one No. 6264 Flat Car loaded with timbers. The platform can be installed along any straight stretch of track at least two sections in length. The track should lie in the channel or track bed provided for it by the platform.

Electrical connections are made to the two binding posts located on the side of the platform. Since the operating range of the Fork Lift is 10-14 volts, the connections are made to any pair of transformer posts which furnish approximately this voltage. A No. 90 Controller is inserted in one of the electrical connections to provide control.

HOW TO OPERATE THE FORK LIFT

To unload the flat car, the car must be brought into position so that the slot which guides the lift truck is opposite the center of one set of timbers. (The metal stakes on the side of the car facing the platform should be removed.)

As the No. 90 Controller button is depressed, the lift truck will lift one timber from the flat car and deliver it to the unloading platform. The action is repeated until all of the timbers on one side of the flat car are unloaded. The car is then moved over until the second stack of timbers is in line with the motion of the lift truck and ready to be unloaded.

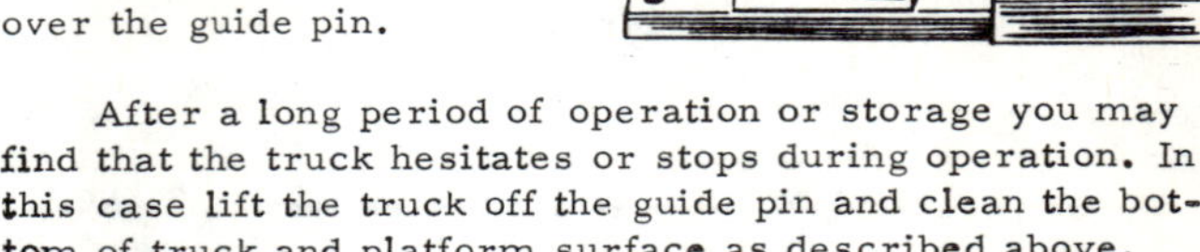

The Fork Lift Truck supplied is packed separately for safety in transit. Before assembling it to the platform wipe the bottom of the truck and the surface of the platform clean with a dry paper towel or napkin. Then lower the truck into position so that the hole in the bottom fits over the guide pin.

After a long period of operation or storage you may find that the truck hesitates or stops during operation. In this case lift the truck off the guide pin and clean the bottom of truck and platform surface as described above.

SERVICE NOTES

No. 264 Operating Fork Lift Platform is powered by a vibrator motor, similar in operation to the motor used in the No. 464 Lumber Mill (see No. 464 LUMBER MILL for detailed description).

The driving motor is connêcted to the lift truck through a series of gears, as illustrated in the schematic diagram on the following page. As the truck reaches the proper position on the front of the truck platform, it grips and lifts a piece of timber from a flat car, and carries it back to the main platform.

The drive line used in this mechanism is a special dewaxed 12 lb. test braided nylon line (Lionel part No. 345-80 in 4-foot lengths). The required length of the line is given in the schematic diagram. To install drive line, tie the proper length of line to the tension spring, wind it 1-1/2 times around the drive pulley, and thread it through the eyelet attached to the armature. Stretch the spring until it measures approximately 3/4 of an inch and crimp the eyelet to hold the line securely in place.

If it becomes necessary to use a new elelet do not attempt to rivet it in place because the eyelet must be perfectly tight and requires special riveting tools. Instead, solder it in place using acid core solder.

To reduce or increase spring tension, adjust the armature bracket with a pair of pliers, leaving a gap of .075 to .085 between armature and coil. When properly adjusted the motor should operate at 9 volts and begin to buzz at 14 volts.

Sluggish operation of the truck may be caused by any of the following:

1. Excessive friction between drive arm and base of unloader -- Bend drive arm up slightly by prying up with screwdriver at stud side of arm.

2. Cam slide rubbing against bottom of truck platform -- Lower the bent part of the drive arm with a pair of pliers.

3. Improper tension of buffer spring -- Run truck to the end of truck platform. Loosen string, holding buffer spring, stretch spring to approximately 1-7/16 inches and retighten.

4. If the truck does not reach the end of travel at track side of the platform -- Shorten the motor link by bending to dotted line position as shown below.

Make sure there are no burrs along slot edges by polishing with emery cloth. Lubricate flat surfaces with "Molycote" or graphite powder.

Schematic Diagram of No. 264 Fork Lift Platform

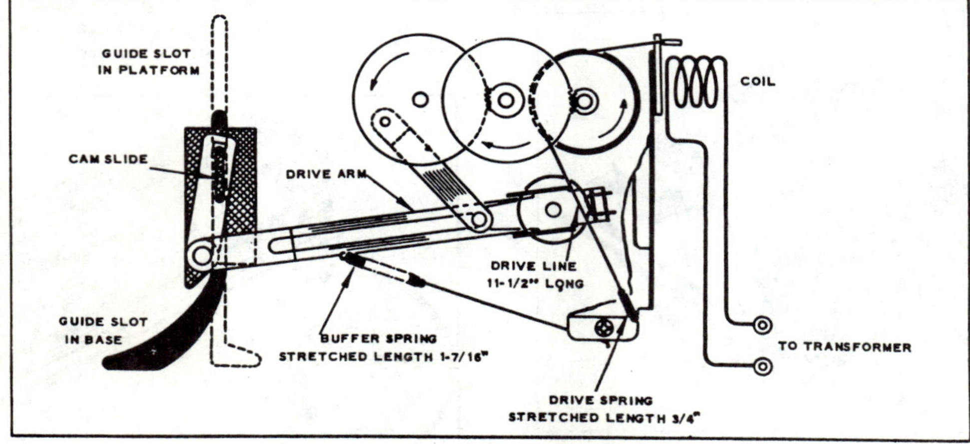

No. 282 PORTAL GANTRY CRANE

No. 282 Portal Gantry Crane performs all of the operations of a real railroad crane. It is equipped with an electromagnet which can load and unload iron and steel. If you want to use the "big hook" alone to lift freight slings and other non-magnetic loads, take off the electro-magnet and hang it out of the way on the cross-bar at the center of the boom. To facilitate operations in a busy dock or steel yard, the crane is provided with wheels so that it can be moved from place to place on its own rails. The legs of the crane are designed to span a single line of regular "O" or "O27" track and to give clearance to all Lionel rolling stock. To get greater "reach" the position of the boom can be adjusted by turning the hand wheel in the back of the cab.

The operating voltage of No. 282 Gantry Crane is 12 to 16 volts. Electrical connections are made as shown in Figure 1.

A properly functioning crane should be able to hoist a weight of approximately four (4) ounces.

OPERATION OF THE CRANE

Just as with a real crane, accurate spotting of the hook requires practice. To operate the Crane two hands must be used, with the left hand controlling the crane motor and the right hand controlling the kind of motion desired -- either rotation of the cab, or hoisting of the hook.

The center lever operates a mechanism which shifts the motor from the cab to the "big hook. To change the action from rotation to hoisting move the center lever up.

To raise the hook move the first and second levers up.

To lower the hook move the first lever down and the second lever up.

Here's a useful hint: When you are raising or lowering the hook and want to stop it accurately, first let go of the motor lever, then let go the hoisting lever. If you do this in reverse order the "coasting" of the motor will move the cab out of the desired position.

NOTE: If you continue the downward motion of the hook past its lowest point, the string lowering the hook will first unwind to its full length and then begin to rewind on its spool in the opposite direction. This will have the effect of reversing the "UP" and "DOWN" designations on the controller panel.

The lever on the right controls the electro-magnet. In the normal central position of this lever, the electro-magnet is off. When the lever is moved up and to the right -- into its "hold" slot -- the electromagnet will become energized and will pick up its steel or iron. The electromagnet lever does not snap back into its "off" position automatically, but must be moved back by hand. DO NOT ALLOW the electromagnet to remain on for too long a time or it will overheat.

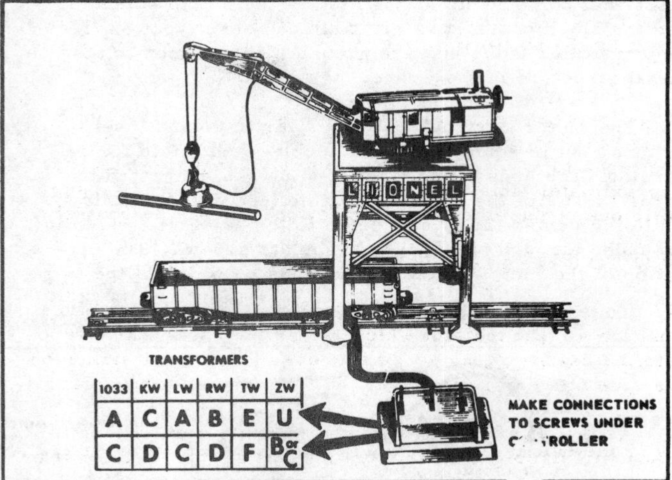

Figure - 1 - Operating Position of the No. 282 Crane

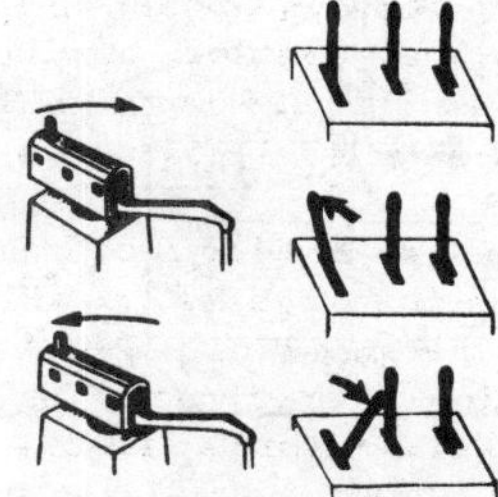

The lever on the left is the motor control. At the normal center position the motor is off.

To turn cab to the right move the first lever up.

To turn cab to the left move the first lever down.

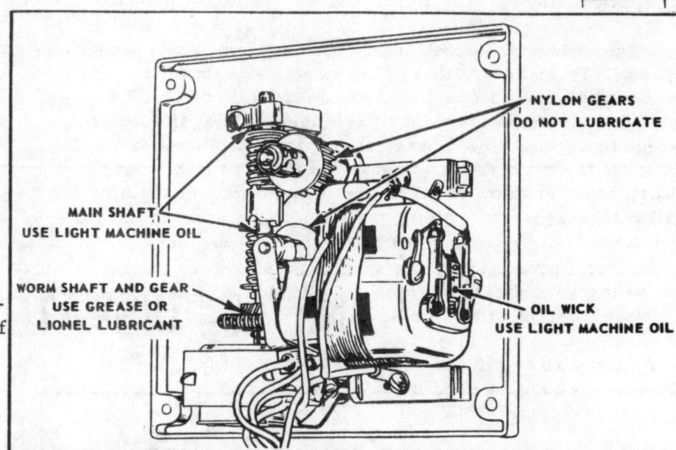

Figure 3 - How to Lubricate No. 282 Gantry Crane. In This Illustration the Mechanism Has Been Removed from the Structure for Clarity.

As with all mechanical equipment, No. 282 Portal Gantry Crane should be cleaned and lubricated periodically according to illustration in Figure 3 above. Do not over-lubricate -- a dab of grease or a drop of oil, properly applied, is all that is necessary.

Lubricant should be used on the worm shaft of the motor and its mating gear. The main shaft should receive a fine coat of light machine oil. The nylon gears should not be lubricated at all. The motor brushes and commutator should be cleaned and lubricated when necessary. In order to get at the motor the entire mechanism must be removed from the tower structure by removing four screws in the corners of the base.

No. 282 Portal Gantry Crane has three separate electrical components -- the motor, the clutch solenoid, and the electromagnet -- all of which receive power from the controller cable and are grounded in common to the metal structure of the Crane.

The motor is structurally similar to most Lionel motors, but is equipped with a double-would field for reversing. The ends of the field winding are connected to wires 1 and 2 of the controller cable (see diagram below), while the center tap is connected to the armature which is grounded through one of the brushplate screws. The direction of the motor's rotation depends on which of the two field winding ends is connected to the source of power by the position of the first controller lever.

The clutch solenoid, which applies the motor either to rotation of the cab or to hoisting of the hook, receives power from cable wire 3 and is grounded through the solder lug held by one of the motor mounting screws. In its normal position the clutch is engaged to the gear train which rotates the Crane cab, being held there by the tension of the clutch spring. When the clutch solenoid is energized by means of the second controller lever, the clutch shaft is pulled into the solenoid coil and engages the gear train which winds up the hoisting

Pictorial Wiring Diagram of No. 282 Portal Gantry Crane

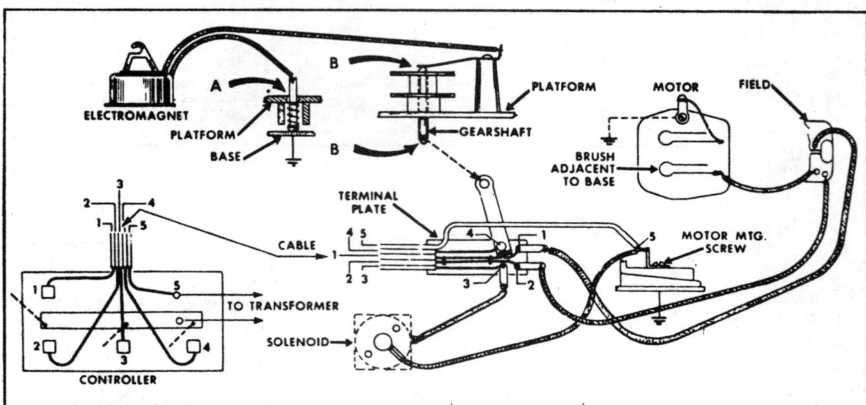

The electromagnet receives its power through cable wire 4 and through the two flat springs which make sliding contact with the two ends of the metal gear shaft at points "B". The electromagnet coil is grounded through the spring-loaded rectangular pin "A", which fits through the plastic platform and rides on the metal base of the crane. The electromagnet is energized by the third lever of the controller. Any failures of the electromagnet would most usually be due to poor electrical contacts at points "B" or by the binding of the grounding pin at point "A".

Most of the service problems encountered with the Gantry Crane are due to the failure of the clutch to stay in engagement with either the rotating gear or the hoisting hear. To correct, first check the position of the clutch on the clutch shaft by moving the clutch shaft by hand. The clutch should be fully engaged with the hoist-gear at the same point where the shaft bottoms in the solenoid. To make sure of this, it might be necessary first to tap the clutch away from the hoisting gear in order to allow the shaft to bottom; then tap the clutch back into place while holding the shaft down in the solenoid.

After the clutch is correctly located, it might be necessary to adjust the tension of the clutch spring. If the spring is too weak there is a tendency for the clutch to pop out of engagement with the rotating gear. If the spring is too strong, it will push the clutch out of engagement with the hoisting gear. One way to adjust spring tension is to tap the worm wheel along the clutch shaft in order to increase or decrease spring pressure against it. Another is to weaken or strengthen the spring itself, either by stretching it or by cutting off a turn.

No. 334 DISPATCHING BOARD

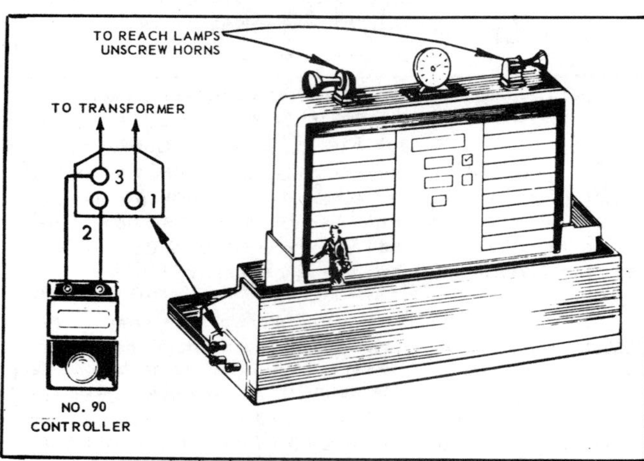

Figure 1 - Installation of No. 334 Dispatching Board

No. 334 Dispatching Board is a good piece of equipment for a passenger railroad terminal. It has a ticket office on one side and a huge illuminated dispatching board on the other.

The Dispatching Board has an operating voltage of 10-14 volts a-c and is connected to the transformer through a No. 90 Controller as illustrated in the figure to the left.

OPERATION OF DISPATCHING BOARD

When the controller button is pressed the attendant hurries across the catwalk in front of the Board and the information on the Board changes automatically. The button has to be pressed for an instant only.

Once the action is started it will continue automatically until the attendant returns to his post. Additional train information can be chalked in on the special "blackboard" surface of the dispatching board.

No. 334 Operating Dispatching Board is powered by a vibrator motor of the type described in section on No. 464 Lumber Mill. As illustrated in the schematic diagram below, the mylar drive belt moved by the motor is coupled to a carriage frame which rolls on its track carrying the worm and pinion fastened to the figure of the attendant.

Schematic Diagram of No. 334 Dispatching Board

As the carriage reaches the end of its travel on either side of the track, the worm shaft is pushed from one side to the other, rotating the pinion shaft and causing the attendant to swivel.

As the carriage reaches the midpoint of its travel from right to left, the pin which connects it to the drive belt engages one of the teeth of the plastic train arrival indicator, causing it to index to the next position.

To start the operation of the motor a push button controller connects terminal post 1 to post 2. As soon as the carriage has moved far enough to allow the internal switch to close, the controller button can be released and the action will continue automatically until the carriage completes its cycle of operation and returns to the starting position where it opens the internal switch and stops operation of the motor.

The proper operating range of the motor is between 10 and 14 volts. Excessively high voltage will cause the mechanism to clatter as the vibrating armature strikes the coil and may also throw the drive line off its pulley.

The drive line used in this mechanism is a special de-waxed braided nylon spinning line. It is Lionel part No. 345-80 in four foot lengths. The required length of line is given in the illustration above. To install drive line, tie the proper length of line to the drive spring, wind it 1-1/2 times around the drive pulley, and thread it through the eyelet attached to the armature. Stretch the spring until it measures 1-1/2 inches in length and crimp the eyelet to hold the line securely in place. To decrease or increase spring tension, bend the lug or tab, located on the armature, with a pair of pliers. If it becomes necessary to replace the drive line eyelet solder it in place using acid core solder.

No. 342 CULVERT LOADER

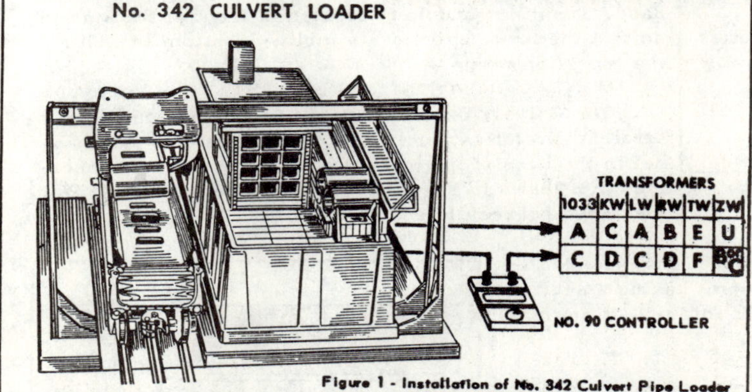

Figure 1 - Installation of No. 342 Culvert Pipe Loader

The Culvert Loader can be installed along any straight section of track. The track is laid in the channel of the base of the loader. The electrical connections for the loader are shown in Figure 1 above. The loader operates in the range of 12-16 volts.

No. 342 Culvert Pipe Loader Set consists of No. 342 Culvert Loader, a special No. 6342 Gondola with 7 sections of culvert pipe, and a No. 90 Controller.

The Loader can be used by itself, or in conjunction with No. 345 Culvert Unloader as illustrated below (see Figure 2). If the Loader is used by itself, the sections of culvert pipe are loaded on to the station rack by hand. Then No. 6342 Gondola is located in front of the station so that the highest part of its inclined bottom is under its traveling crane. The tilted bottom of the gondola allows each pipe section to roll forward and make room for the next section.

When the loader motor is started by pushing No. 90 Controller button, the traveling crane will run back and forth along its bean, taking a section of culvert pipe each time from the station and depositing it into the gondola.

CONTINUED

The Loader is powered by a vibrator similar in operating principle to the motor used in No. 464 Lumber Mill. The vibration of the vibrator coil armature is converted to rotation of the drive pulley by means of the nylon drive line and spring. The traveling crane or conveyor is linked to the motor, as illustrated in the schematic diagram below.

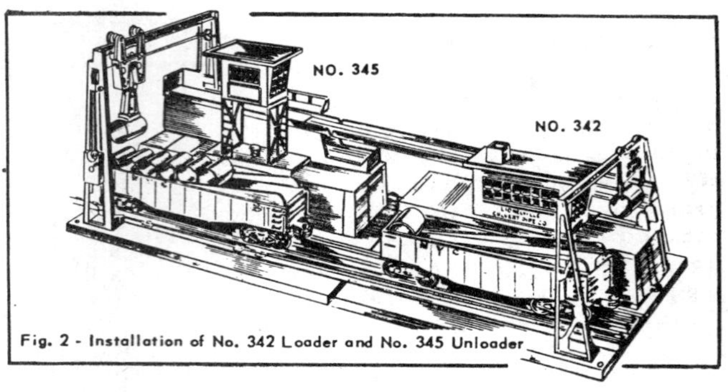

Fig. 2 - Installation of No. 342 Loader and No. 345 Unloader

ADJUSTING THE CONVEYOR TRAVEL

If the traveling conveyor does not reach the end of the travel at the platform or the track, first check the base at the points where it is bent to provide track channel. Correcting the bend over the edge of a work bench will adjust the position and alignment of the vertical supports of the traveling conveyor structure. An additional adjustment of the conveyor travel is provided by bending the center of the sweep are bracket.

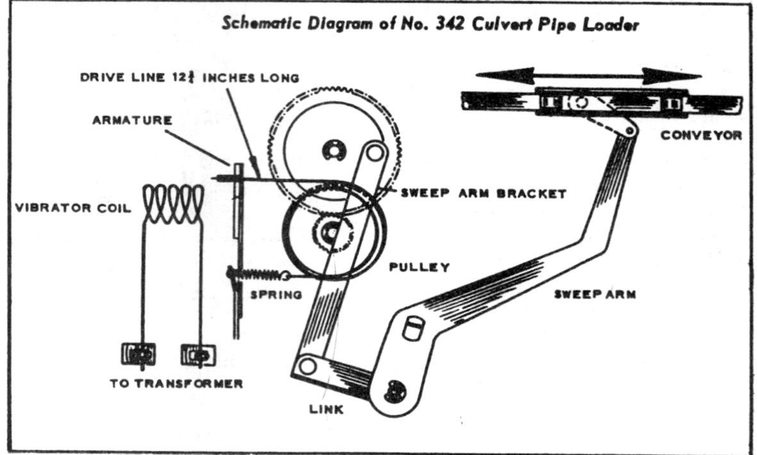

Schematic Diagram of No. 342 Culvert Pipe Loader

INSTALLING NEW DRIVE LINE

The drive line used in this mechanism is a special de-waxed 12-lb. test braided nylon spinning line (Lionel No. 345-80, four feet long). The required length of the line is given in the schematic diagram. To install drive line, tie the proper length of line to the drive spring, wind it 1-1/2 times around the drive pulley, and thread it through the eyelet attached to the armature. Stretch the spring until it measures 5/8 of an inch in length and crimp the eyelet to hold the line securely in place. To reduce or increase spring tension, adjust the tab to which the spring is attached with a pair of pliers.

NOTE: Excessive tightening of the nut on roof may cause the motor to slow down or to stop.

Sharp edges or burrs on the edge of the culvert section may cause it not to fall into the car properly.

No. 345 CULVERT UNLOADER

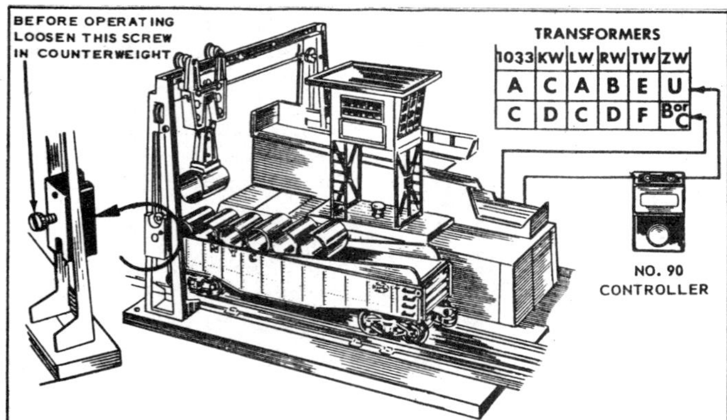

1033	KW	LW	RW	TW	ZW
A	C	A	B	E	U
C	D	C	D	F	B or C

Fig. 1 - Installation of No. 345 Culvert Pipe Unloader

No. 345 Culvert Pipe Unloader Set consists of No. 345 Culvert Unloader, a special No. 6342 Gondola with 7 sections of culvert pipe and a No. 90 Controller.

The Unloader can be used either by itself, or in conjunction with No. 342 Culvert Loader, as illustrated on the previous page on No. 342 Culvert Loader (Figure 2 on that page). If the Unloader is used by itself, the sections of culvert pipe are loaded on to the gondola by hand. Then the gondola is located in front of the station so that the lowest part of its inclined bottom is under the traveling crane.

The Culvert Unloader can be installed along any straight stretch of track. The track is laid in the channel in the base of the unloader. The electrical connections are shown in Figure 1. The unloader operates in the the range between 10 and 14 volts.

When the loader motor is started by pushing No. 90C Controller button the traveling crane will run back and forth along its beam, taking a section of culvert pipe each time from the car and depositing it into the station.

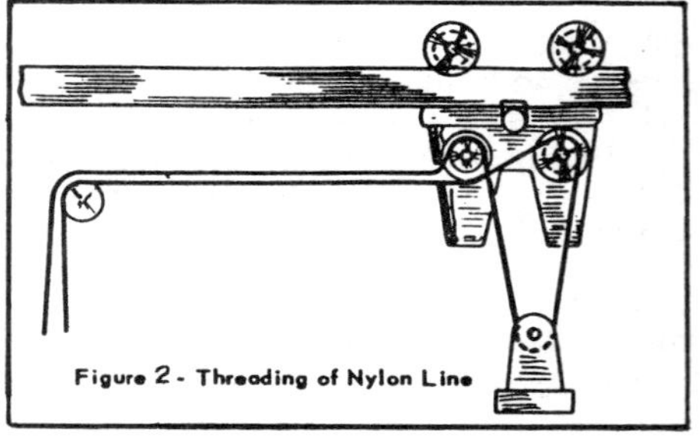
Figure 2 - Threading of Nylon Line

IMPORTANT

For safety in shipment the counterweight riding on the front post of the station is locked tightly against the post by means of a thumb screw. Before you can operate the unloader, loosen the screw to free the counterweight. Make sure that the nylon line is properly set in all the pulleys.

If the nylon line which moves the crane mechanism should become dislodged, do not untie it, but thread it back into place according to Figure 2.

No. 345 Culvert Unloader is powered by a vibrator motor described in detail in the section on No. 464 Lumber Mill. The moving belt is connected to the magnetic lift through a series of pulleys, as shown at left. As the traveling crane reaches proper position over the track, the magnetic lift drops to pick up a culvert section. After the crane reaches the unloading platform, the cluvert is "brushed off" the magnet by the edge of the platform.

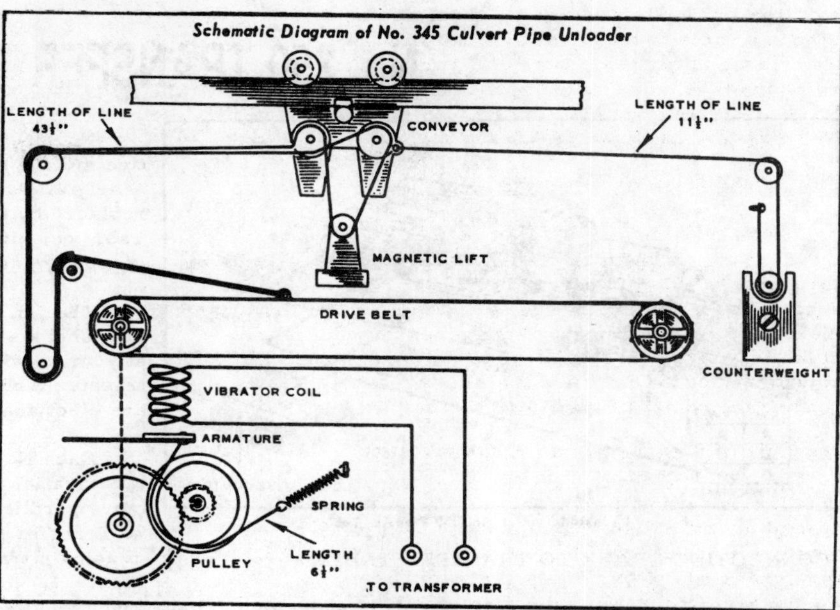

Excessively high voltage will cause the mechanism to clatter and may also throw the drive line off its pulley.

ADJUSTING CRANE TRAVEL

If the traveling crane does not reach the end of its travel at either the platform end or the track end, first check the base at the points where it is bent to provide track channel. Correcting the bend over the edge of a work bench will adjust the position and alignment of the vertical supports of the traveling crane structure. An additional adjustment for locating the position of the crane over the track is provided by bending the finger or tab on the beam.

INSTALLING DRIVE LINE

Method is same as described in section on No. 342 Culvert Loader with ONE EXCEPTION: stretch the spring until it measures 7/8 of an inch (not 5/8 of an inch).

ADJUSTING THE MAGNETIC LIFT

The magnetic lift must be strong enough to pick the culvert sections and yet allow them to be brushed off by the edge of the platform. The strength of the magnetic field is adjusted by adding or removing pieces of tape to the face of the magnet.

No. 348 MANUAL CULVERT PIPE UNLOADER

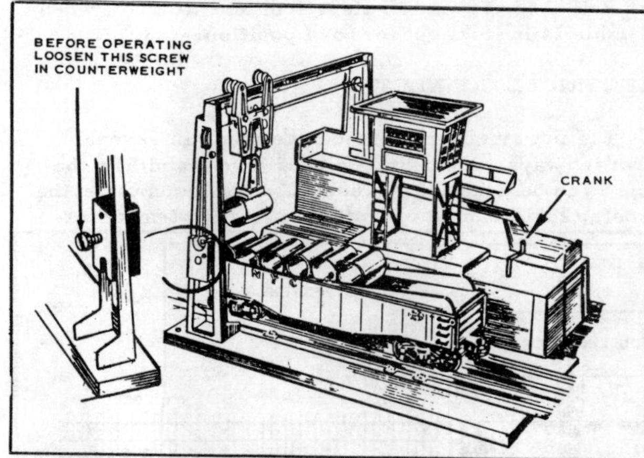

Figure 1–Installation of Culvert Pipe Unloader

No. 348 Culvert Pipe Unloader Set consists of No. 348 Culvert Unloader, a special No. 6342 Gondola and 7 sections of culvert pipe.

The sections of culvert pipe are loaded on to the Gondola by hand. Then the Gondola is located in front of the station so that the lowest part of its inclined bottom is under the traveling crane.

The Culvert Unloader can be installed along any straight stretch of track. The track is laid in the channel in the base of the Unloader.

When the crank is turned, the traveling crane will run back and forth along its beam, taking a section of culvert pipe each time from the car and depositing it into the station.

IMPORTANT

For safety in shipment the counterweight riding on the front post of the station is locked tightly against the post by means of a thumb screw. Before you can operate the Unloader, loosen the screw to free the counterweight. Make sure that the nylon line is properly set in all the pulleys.

If the nylon line which moves the crane mechanism should become dislodged, do not untie it, but thread it back into place according to the diagram at right (Figure 2).

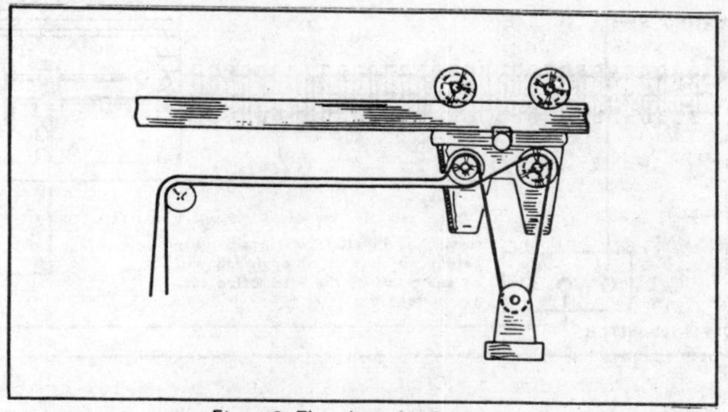

Figure 2–Threading of Nylon Line

No. 350 TRANSFER TABLE

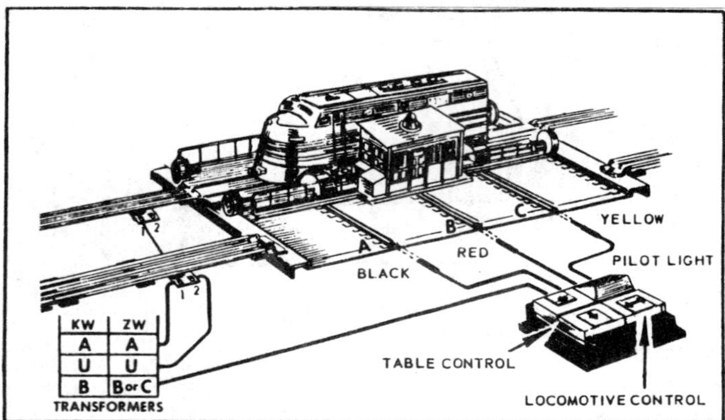

Figure 1 - Installation of No. 350 Transfer Table

No. 350 Transfer Table is a replica of the locomotive moving equipment which has replaced turntables on nearly all American railroads as steam locomotives are replaced by diesel and electric power. The Transfer Table permits a more compact maintenance yard and is generally easier to install and maintain.

The No. 350 Transfer Table is used for transferring engines and rolling stock between parallel tracks at your repair depot or freight terminal. Like real-life transfer tables, all functions of No. 350 Transfer Table are electrically controlled by the operator.

Each No. 350 Transfer Table is designed to service two parallel tracks about 5-3/4 inches apart. Four or more parallel tracks can be serviced by adding No. 350-50 Transfer Table Extensions. Several interesting ways of using a transfer table are shown in typical layouts in Figure 4.

CONNECTING TRACK TO TRANSFER TABLE

Select the track-mating adapter wires which match your track and mount them on the table bed with rail adapter brackets and screws as shown in Figure 2. Remove the rail pins from the rails which are to be attached to the bed of the transfer table. On "Super-O" Track you will also have to clip off the projections on the track bed so that the track rails can be brought as close as possible to the transfer table. Attach the approach track to the bed of the transfer table by inserting the ends of the adapter wires into the rail openings.

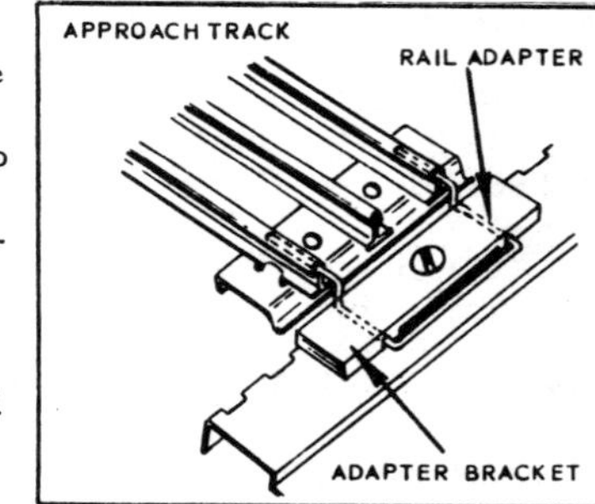

Figure 2 - Connecting Approach Track

Place the transfer table on its bed and move it back and forth by hand to see that there is no interference. Also check alignment by rolling a locomotive back and forth from the table to the approach track.

MASTER CONTROL CONNECTIONS

The far ends of the transfer bed rails are equipped with pins for attaching an extension. The front ends of the rails are marked A, B, and C to correspond to the terminals on the underside of the master control. The connecting wires supplied with the table are color coded to correspond with the wiring of the table.

Connect the wires to the master control terminals as follows: Black to A, red to B, and yellow to C. Plug in the pin ends of the wires into the corresponding rails.

NOTE: The sleeve on the yellow wire must be flush with rail C to prevent an electrical short circuit when the table is in its most forward position.

ELECTRICAL CONNECTIONS

The power connections can be made in several different ways, depending on your layout and how the table is to be used. If you use only one locomotive, the transfer table can be operated on regular track volt-

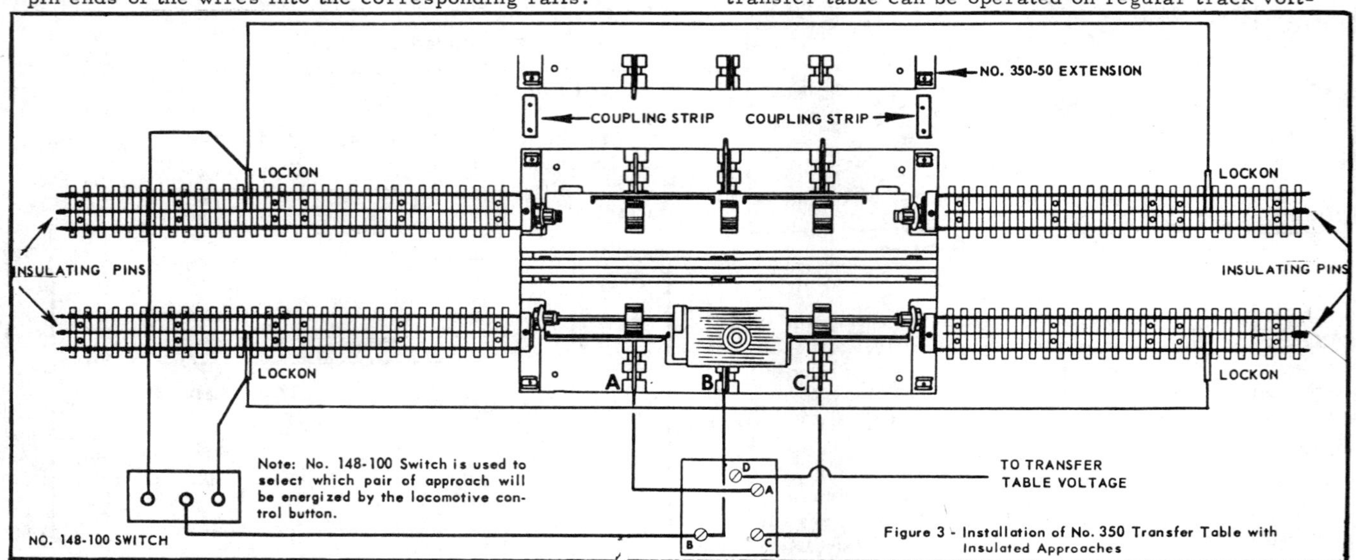

Figure 3 - Installation of No. 350 Transfer Table with Insulated Approaches

age. This is accomplished by connecting terminal D of the master controller to No. 1 terminal of the track lockon. If you have this hook-up, you will have to stop your locomotove in "neutral" position while you move your transfer table into alignment with the desired track. Once the transfer table is in alignment, you can move your locomotive and proceed with the transfer.

If you have more than one locomotive and wish to keep your main line in operation while a second locomotive is being transferred, you will have to use separate variable voltages for the transfer table and for the main line. This hook-up is shown in Figure 1. Note that this hook-up is possible only with transformers "KW" and "ZW" and that it is basically a two-train hook-up enabling you to operate your main line at one speed while the locomotive being transferred is operated at a much lower speed.

An adaptation of this second method, which simplifies control and operation of the transfer table and the locomotive being transferred, is illustrated in Figure 3. Here two sections of each approach track are insulated from the rest of the layout and wired to the same voltage as the transfer table, through terminal B of the master control. A No. 148-100 switch is installed so that power can be applied only to the insulated sections in alignment with the transfer table.

OPERATING THE TRANSFER TABLE

Position the transfer table on the transfer table bed with the engine house toward the front (see Figure 1). Make sure that the table wheels roll freely and that the table clears the approach track sections on both sides.

Depress forward or reverse table controls, as necessary, until the transfer table is aligned with the track desired. With no locomotive on the table track, the red light in the engine house and the light in the master switch will both go on at alignment. With a locomotive on the transfer table, only the light in the master switch will go on at alignment, indicating the table can be energized by pushing the locomotive control button on the master switch. In the hook-up in Figure 3 the approach tracks are also energized by the same control. This provides an added safety feature which makes it impossible for the locomotive to move off the approach track unless the transfer table is in position to receive it.

ADDING NO. 350-50 TRANSFER TABLE EXTENSION

One or more No. 350-50 Transfer Table Extensions may be added to extend the operating range of your transfer table. Push the open rail ends of the extension over the track pins in the far end of the transfer table. Insert a coupling strip, supplied with the extension, into each end of the mating edge to provide continuity of ground as shown in Figure 3. Connect the approach tracks as instructed for the transfer table.

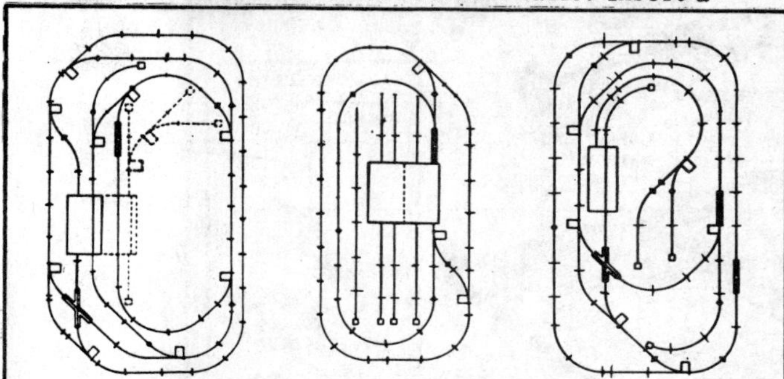

Figure 4 - Layouts Showing Use of No. 350 Transfer Tables

REPLACING LAMPS

To check the lamps, align the table with any of the approach tracks with no equipment on the table track. Both lamps should light. Replace the engine house lamp which is readily accessible, with a No. L19(R), 14-volt minature 2-pin base lamp.

To replace the master switch lamp, push in the two lips of the plastic lamp housing, on the underside of the master switch, and remove the housing. Replace the lamp with No. L12, 6-8 volt, minature 2-pin base lamp.

SCHEMATIC WIRING DIAGRAM

The electrical schematic diagram on the following page shows the relationship of the motor, the controller switches, and the lamps. In the diagram, all the power is supplied through terminal D on the controller. The two outer rails of the track bed supply power to the double-wound field of the motor. The left-hand rail, connected by the black lead to terminal A on the controller, supplies power through the sliding contact shoe to move the table forward. The right-hand rail, connected to terminal C by a yellow lead, is the power source for rearward movement. The sliding contactors are located so that they run off their rails and break the electrical connection if the table is allowed to overrun the approach tracks. The two-button switch which controls table travel is shaped so that both circuits cannot be actuated simultaneously with disastrous results for the motor. The button can be rocked, however, to achieve quick stops and reversals for fine adjustments.

The center rail of the track bed is connected by the red lead terminal B of the controller. The rail is carried in an insulating strip which has a raised flange extending above the rail. The contactor can only touch the rail at the two locations where it drops into the notches in the insulating strip. Thus, neither of the pilot lamps will light, and the center power rail of the table is dead, until the table is aligned with one of the approach tracks. When the circuit is completed, the current passes through the controller pilot lamp to terminal B, and thence to the center contactor. If no locomotive is on the table, the lamp on top of the housing goes on. If, however, there is a locomotive on the table, its motor circuit acts as a comparatively low parallel resistance and the lamp dims or goes out. The locomotive cannot draw enough current through the controller lamp to run. Pressing the train control button shorts out the controller lamp and puts full track voltage to the motor.

SERVICE NOTES

The table and controller are both sturdy and trouble-free. The railbed should be kept flat and level, preferably permanently fixed to the table top to assure uniform traction for both table drive wheels.

The table is scaled to the 70-foot average length

of the tables used in most railroad yards and will accomodate the largest single power unit made by Lionel as well as short industrial swithcers handling one car. To handle double units it is possible to connect two transfer tables end to end and operate them simultaneously by means of a single controller. The beds are mounted on a common platform or table so that the ends of the tables almost touch. Because the two motors usually vary slightly in performance, the tables must be connected rigidly together with a pair of "fishplates" made from aluminum, copper, or steelsheet. They are fastened down with #6 self-tapping screws.

If the motors do not synchronize closely enough the faster one can be slowed by placing a small resistance in series with the brush leads, that is the A and C power rails. A No. 1033-103 resistor may do the job, but an adjustable 3-ohm, 10 watt resistor should prove more flexible.

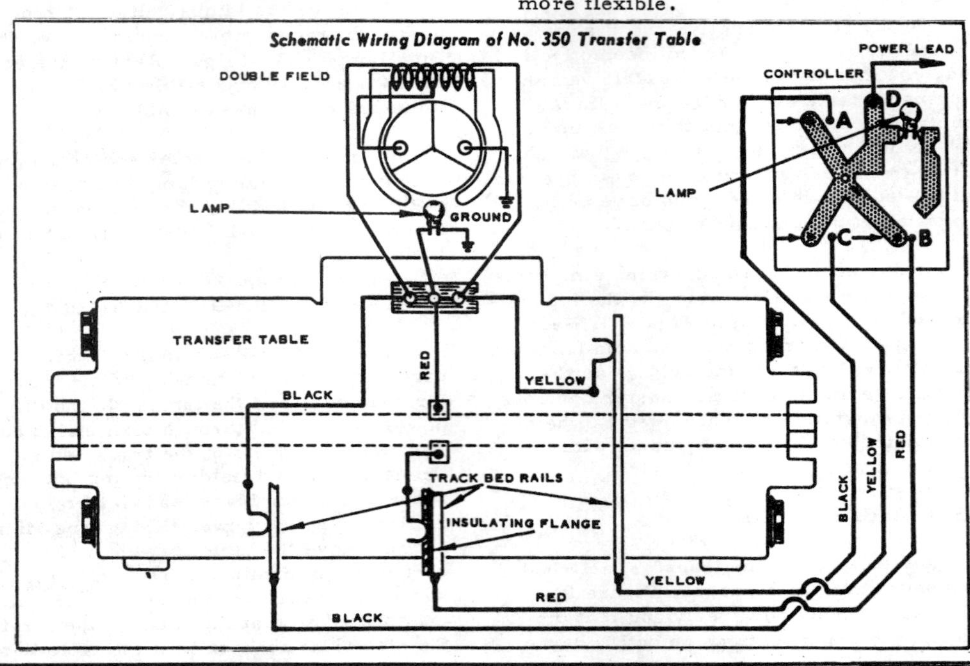

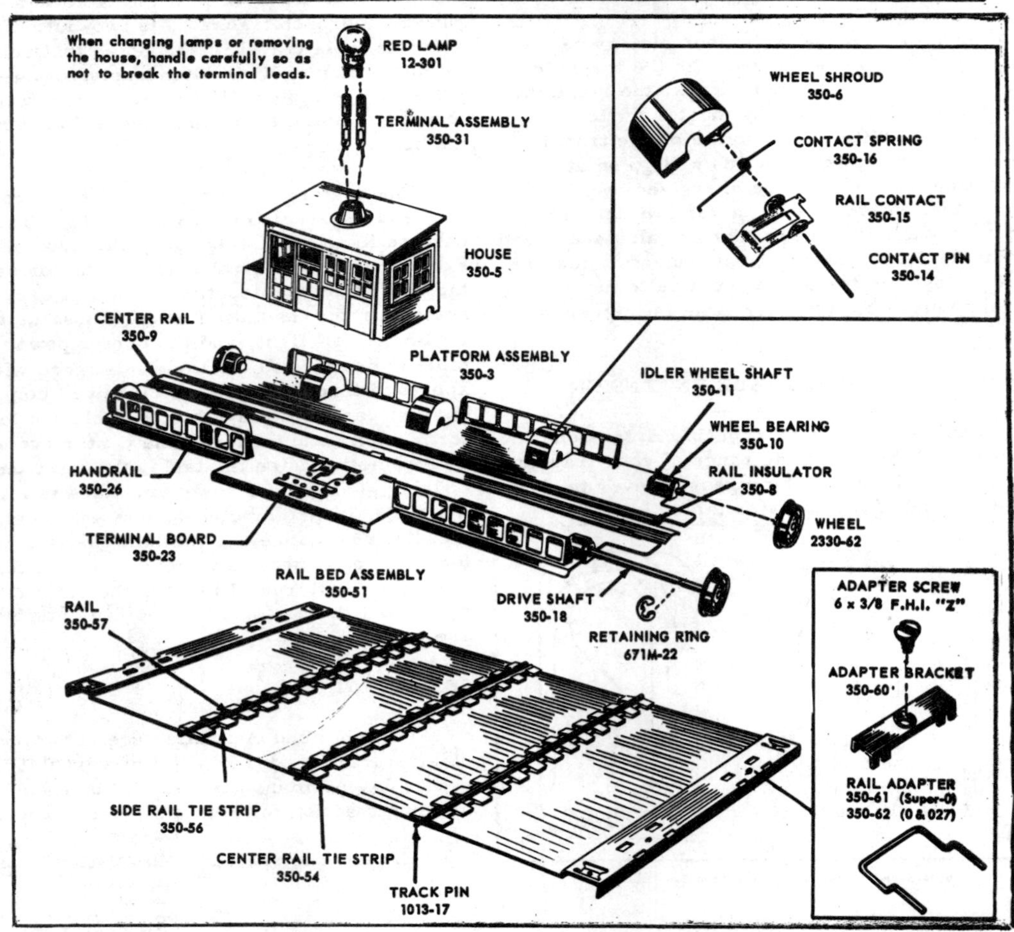

No. 352 ICING STATION

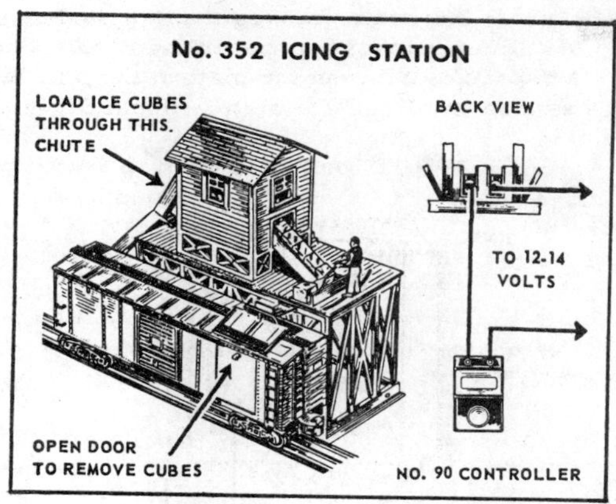

No. 352 Icing Station set consists of No. 352 Icing Station, 3652 Refrigerator car with five ice cubes, and a No. 90 Controller button. The Station operates in the range of 12-14 volts and is connected to the proper transformer terminals as shown in the figure to the left.

To operate the Icing Station, stop the car in front of the Station so that its icing hatch lines up with the ice delivery chute. When the No. 90 Controller button is pushed, the station slide opens the icing hatch of the car and the workman pushes a block of ice into the car. One block of ice is loaded into the car every time the controller button is pushed.

The ice blocks are removed from the car by swinging down the side panel of the car where indicated by the arrow in the installation figure. Ice blocks are loaded into the station by pushing them into the shack through the long chute on the end of the Icing Station.

Movement of the solenoid plunger actuates the two levers which move the figure of the iceman and, at the same time, open the ice hatch in the roof of the car so that the block of ice pushed by the iceman drops into the car. To control the speed of operation, the mechanism is equipped with a cylinder-and-piston pneumatic dash pot or shock-absorber similar to that used in No. 3662 Automatic Milk Car.

The effectiveness of the dash pot depends on the air seal between the cylinder and piston which is maintained by means of a mixture of oil and "Molykote" applied to the edge of the piston. Other parts of the mechanism, however, such as the two moving levers, should be lubricated only with Molykote powder.

Schematic Diagram of No. 352 Icing Station Mechanism

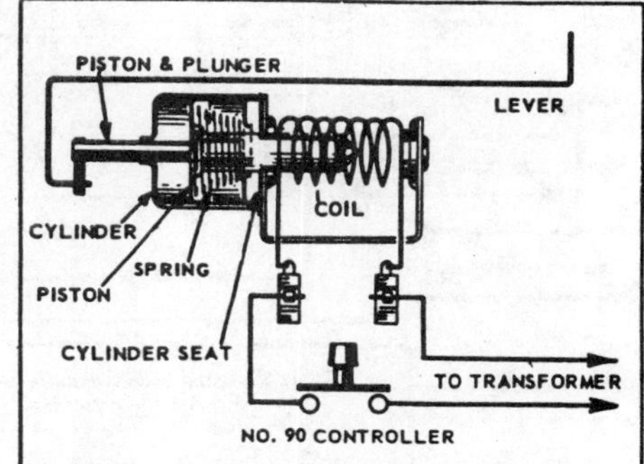

No. 356 FREIGHT STATION

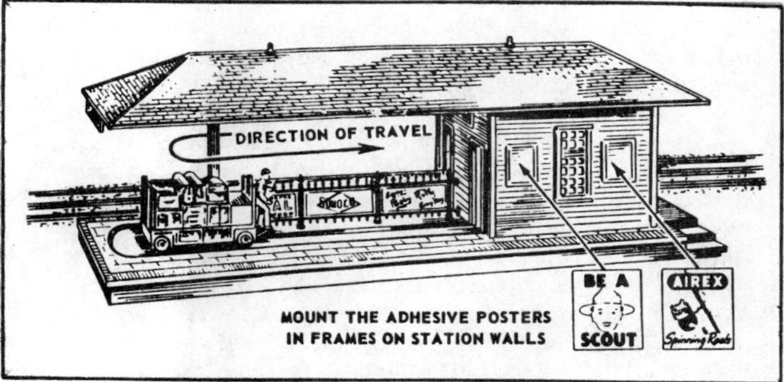

Figure 1 - Location of No. 356 Freight Station

No. 356 Freight Station can be located along any straight portion of track in your layout. If you have a permanent layout mounted on a board or platform, the Station can be fastened to the board by means of screws through the holes in the Station base. In this case, however, it is advisable to insert a rubber washer underneath the screw heads in order not to clamp the Station too rigidly.

The six adhesive posters furnished with the Station should be mounted in their frames on the side of the Station house. Peel back the paper backing from the posters and press them into position. No cement or water is necessary.

The Electrical connections for the Station is shown in Figure 2. A 364C Controller is connected between clips A and B. Clips B and C are connected to transformer posts. Normally 12-14 volts are used, as shown in the diagram, but since the Station has a very wide operating range, connections can also be made to variable voltage posts.

Two minature luggage trucks, one with luggage and one empty were furnished with the Stations made during the initial production. This was done to simulate loading and unloading of the trucks as they moved in and out of the station house. However, the greater weight of the loaded truck caused sufficient difference in the speed of the two trucks to affect the operation of the Station. Therefore, the baggage was abandoned in later production of No. 356 Freight Station.

CONTINUED

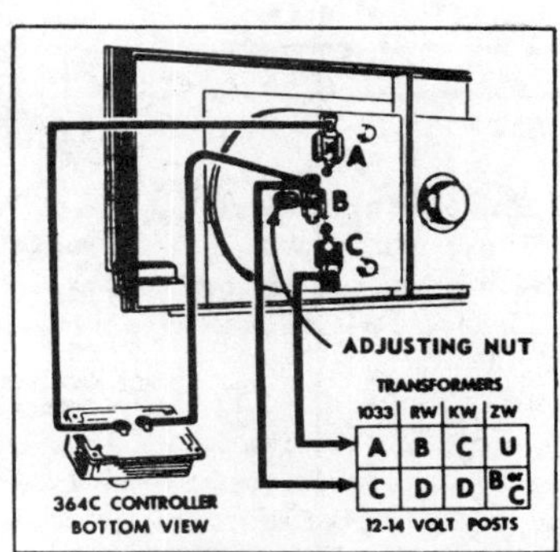

Figure 2 - Bottom View of Station Showing Wiring Connections

After all the electrical connections are made and the controller button switched on, the floor of the Station will beginto vibrate. If you then place a truck on the runway, in the direction of teh arrow, the little "fingers" on the bottom of the truck will cause the truck to move around the platform and into the station house. Once a truck has entered the station house, it is held there until a second truck enters the house and trips a release mechanism to permit the first truck to leave the house. Because of the location of the tripping mechanism, the trucks must travel in counter-clockwise direction.

Only one truck can be seen on the platform at any time. The idea of this operation is to make it appear as if one truck is being alternately loaded and unloaded inside the station house. If both trucks happen to enter the station house at the same time, you will have to trip the release mechanism with your finger to permit a truck to come out.

The vibration of the platform and the speed of the trucks depends on voltage applied and the setting of the two adjustment nuts on the bottom of the Station. These nuts are set at the factory, but if they do need adjusting, they should be set to allow some freedom for the station platform to move up and down when squeed by hand and also to allow a little space between the platform and the bottom of the station house.

The Station will buzz somewhat when in operation, but excessive noise or rattle may be caused by a loose roof, loose house, too high voltage, or a too tight setting of the adjustment nut.

The lamp should remain on at all times. It can be reached by removing the Station roof and is replaced with lamp No. 315-20.

The operation of the Station may also be affected somewhat by excessive tightness of the roof finials and also if the Station is permanently mounted to a platform by means of screws which bear too tightly on the station platform. When mounted in this way it is advisable to leave a little space between the platform and the screwhead.

The schematic wiring diagram to the left may be helpful in doing any repairs or adjustments on the No. 356 Freight Station.

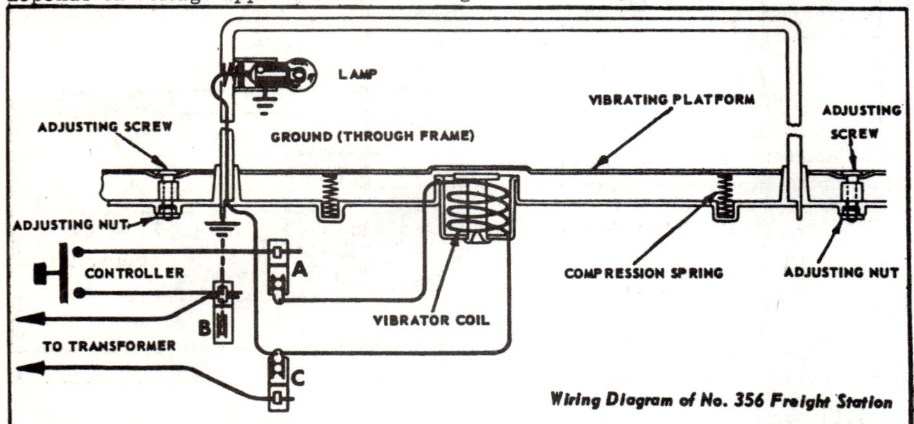

Wiring Diagram of No. 356 Freight Station

No. 362 BARREL LOADER

NO. 364C CONTROLLER

TO TRANSFORMER

ENLARGED VIEW OF TRACK CLIP

No. 362 Barrel Loader can be installed along any straight stretch of track. If desired, a remote control section may be located in front of its unloading chute so that an empty car can be uncoupled at that point and left there for loading. For use with Operating Barrel Car see No. 3562 OPERATING BARREL CAR.

If your layout is mounted on a board or platform, the Barrel Loader should be screwed to the platform through the holes in the rubber grommets on which the base rests. If your layout is not mounted permanently, the loader should be held to the track by means of the two metal clips supplied with it. The clips are pushed onto the edge of the base and the track located so that the track ties rest in the metal clips. This is done to keep the loader from vibrating away from the track during its operation.

ELECTRICAL CONNECTIONS

The loader operates on 12-14 volts and is connected to any pair of transformer terminals which give approximately that voltage. The connecting clips are located on the bottom of the loader base. To enable you to stop and start the Loader at will, a No. 364C Controller is inserted into one of the wire leads.

In operation the barrels are loaded one the loader platform by hand. When the controller is switched on, the loader mechanism sets up a vibration which moves the barrels toward the conveyor, tips them down on their side, and moves them to the top of the conveyor where they roll off intó a waiting 'empty'.

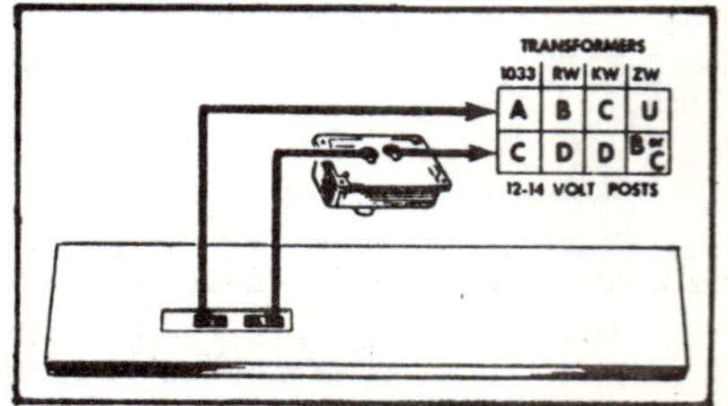

Wiring Diagram (Bottom View)

The operation of No. 362 Barrel Loader depends on the vibration of its spring-mounted ramp. The vibration is induced by an electro-magnetic coil, or vibrator, acting on the armature plate attached to the ramp.

As illustrated in the circuit diagram below, a copper oxide rectifier is placed in series with the coil circuit in order to cut off half of each 60-cycle alternation. This reduces the frequency of vibration from 120 to 60 per second and allows the springs holding the ramp to restore the ramp to its normal position between successive pulls of the electro-magnet.

The air gap between the vibrator and the armature is set at approximately 1/32", but varies from one piece to another and is adjusted for best performance individually. A coarse adjustment can be made by loosening the screw holding the coil bracket. Fine adjustment to close the gap is made by putting pressure on the ramp in the proper direction. To close the gap place a screwdriver against the base of the spring as shown in the sketch below left, and rap sharply with a hammer.

Because the vibration depends on the relative motion between the ramp and the base the loader's performance may vary considerably depending on whether the accessory is simply held to the track by means of the track clips provided, or is screwed down to the train board or platform. Rigid mounting of the Barrel Loader to the train platform should be avoided.

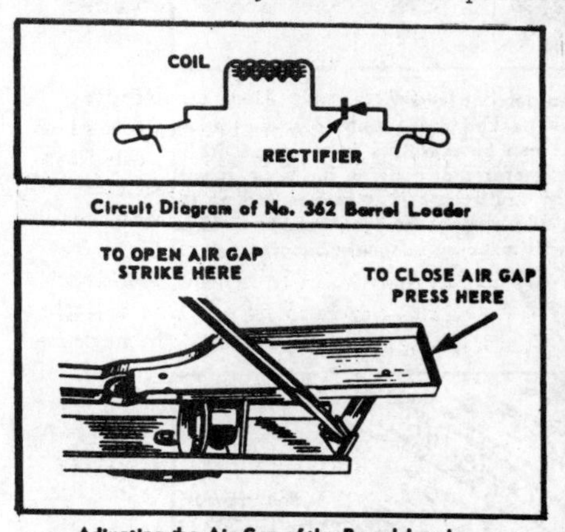

Circuit Diagram of No. 362 Barrel Loader

Adjusting the Air Gap of the Barrel Loader

Schematic Diagram of No. 362 Barrel Loader

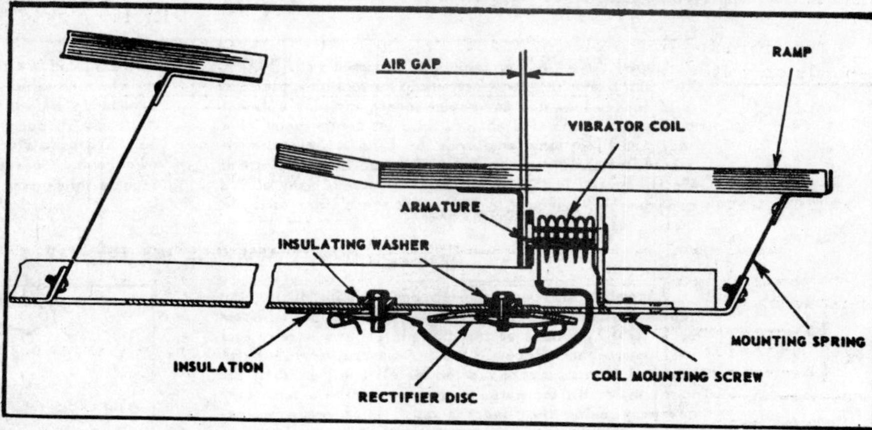

No. 364 LUMBER LOADER

No. 364 Lumber Loader can be installed along any straight stretch of track at least three sections in length. Since the loading and unloading are done along the same line of track, no special layout or spur line is necessary. A remote control section should be placed in the track layout in front of the loader receiving platform with the Lumber Loader positioned so that its receiving platform is in the center of the remote control section. The Loader should be set away from the track by approximately the thickness of a log, and as nearly level as possible.

HOW TO OPERATE LUMBER LOADER

The Lumber Loader is used most effectively with Lionel or other operating lumber cars. After a loaded lumber car is positioned on the remote control section, the logs are dumped into the receiving platform by pressing the "Unload" button of remote track controller. The logs are then moved automatically by a motorized conveyor belt to the unloading platform and reloaded into empty lumber cars stationed underneath the chute, as shown in the illustration below.

HOW TO CONNECT LUMBER LOADER

The Lumber Loader is connected to a transformer and to its controller by means of the three binding posts on the rear panel of the Loader (see below). Post "A" and "C" are connected to any pair of transformer terminals furnishing between 12 and 14 volts. Post "B" is connected through the No. 364C Controller to the same transformer terminal as post "C".

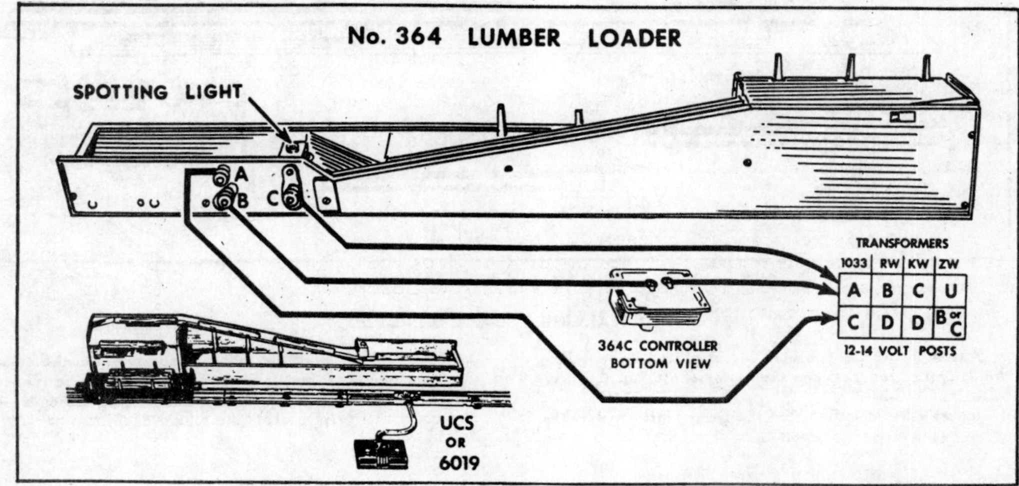

LIONEL No. 375 TURNTABLE

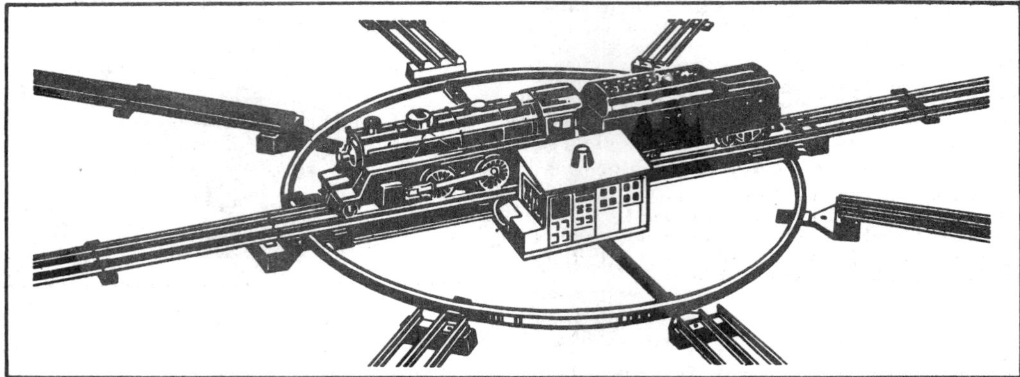

Lionel No. 375 Turntable can be used with "027", "0" and Super"0" track layouts. The turntable platform is 20 inches long and can accommodate any single diesel or electric locomotive as well as most steam locomotive and tender combinations made by Lionel. Several suggested turntable layouts in "027" and Super"0" track are illustrated in this folder and, of course, many others are possible. Layouts in "0" track are similar to those in "027" but are ten percent larger.

The turntable is packed disassembled and must be assembled before it can be installed in a layout. While the turntable can be operated directly on the floor, it will be much more sturdy and secure if it is mounted on its own base. A piece of plywood two feet square, ¼ of an inch in thickness, will make an adequate base.

HOW TO ASSEMBLE THE TURNTABLE

Assemble the two semi-circular rails by fitting the pin in one half in the rail opening of the other half. Fasten each joint by means of two fish-plates, two screws and two square nuts. Because the screws are very short (to avoid interference with the turntable) it may be difficult to fit them into the nuts. In this case make a temporary assembly using the longer screws which are supplied. Then take out the long screws, one at a time, and replace them with the short screws.

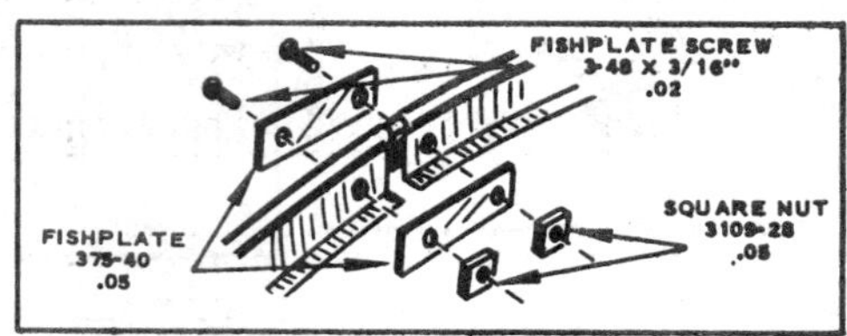

How to Assemble Turntable Rail

TRACK ADAPTER SCREW
6-32 X 3/16"
.02

WASHER
282-215
.02

#3 X 3/8" WOOD SCREW
0922-110
12 FOR .25

TRACK ADAPTER

CROSS BAR

HEX NUT
3104-13
.05

IF PLYWOOD BASE IS USED FASTEN THE CROSS-BARS AND TRACK ADAPTERS WITH WOOD SCREWS WHICH ARE SUPPLIED.

Open the cross-bars and set them at right angles to each other. Fasten the bars to the circular rail by means of screws, washers and plastic track adapters. Four of the adapters are used for this purpose. The four extra track adapters are placed between the points where the cross-bars are attached to the circular rail and are fastened to the rail by means of screws, washers and hex nuts.

The main purpose of these extra adapters is to support the turntable but they can also be used for mounting additional turntable sidings.

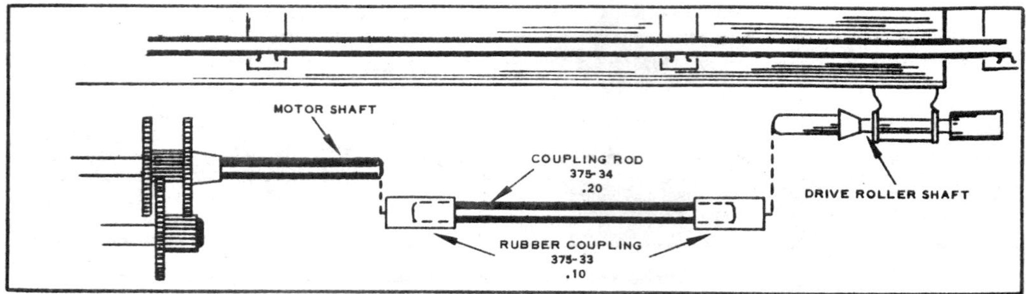

How to Assemble the Coupling Rod

INSTALLING THE COUPLING ROD

Assembly of the turntable is completed by installing the coupling rod between the motor shaft and the drive roller shaft.

Insert the coupling rod half-way into two rubber couplings. Then work the rubber couplings onto the ends of the motor shaft and the drive roller shaft. The rubber couplings should fit very tightly, but wetting the ends of the shaft will help to slide the rubber couplings on.

CONNECTING THE SIDINGS

The track sidings leading to the turntable can be fastened to any of the track adapters by means of track clips and special screw, or, if a wooden base is used, by wood screws. Four track clips and screws are supplied with the turntable but additional parts can be obtained from the Lionel Service Department.

NOTE: Before attempting to use the track clips turn the special screw into the track clip holes so that the screws will tap (cut grooves in) the metal of the clips.

The track must be positioned as close as possible to the ends of the track mounted on the turntable platform but without interfering with the movement of the table. If you use Super"0" track, you will have to cut off the projecting interlocks from the track base.

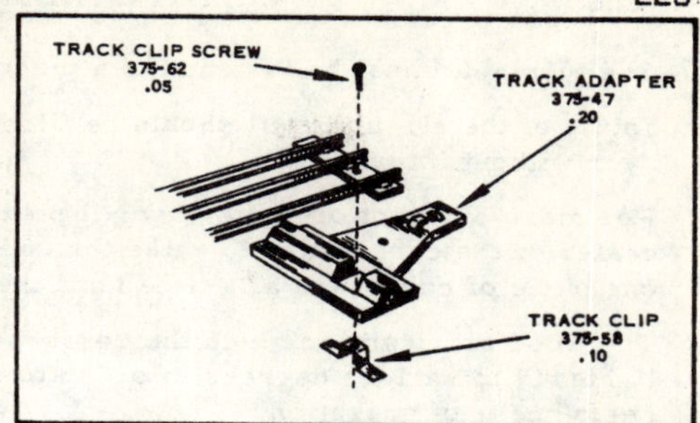

WIRING THE TURNTABLE

The turntable motor operates on direct current (D.C.) which is supplied by two "D" size flashlight batteries inserted into the turntable controller. The batteries are not supplied but can be obtained in any local hardware or stationery store.

The turntable track should receive power from your regular train transformer which supplies low voltage alternating current (A.C.).

Lay the four-wire cable attached to the bottom of the turntable flat and even underneath one of the cross-bars to keep it from getting in the way of the turntable platform. Remove the insulation from the ends of the four wires and spread them apart.

The green and blue wires are attached to the terminals of the turntable controller.

The brown and red wires are connected to transformer

How to Insert Batteries into Controller Box

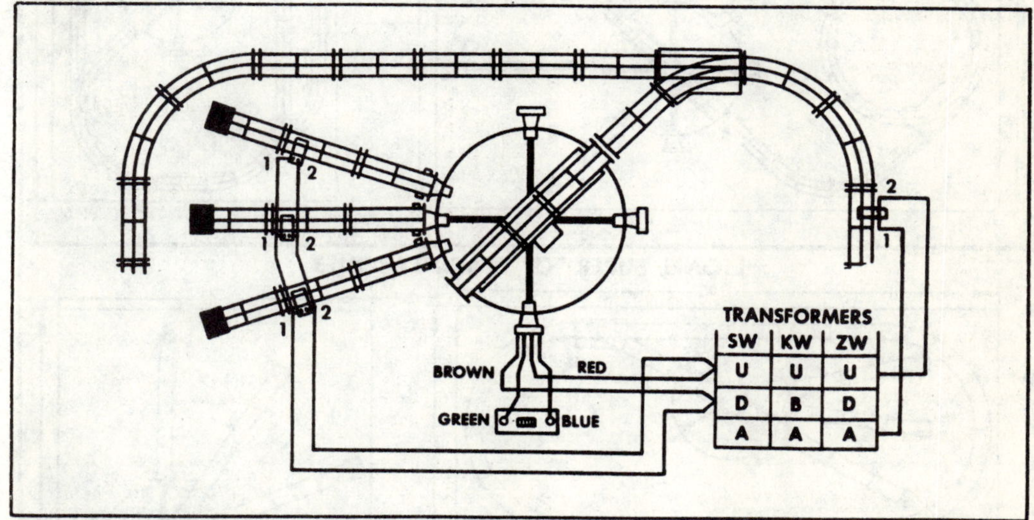

Wiring Diagram for a Typical Turntable Installation

WIRING THE TURNTABLE (cont'd.)

terminals as shown in the diagram. Note that it is advisable to use a transformer which can supply two independently variable track voltages so that one variable voltage post can supply power to the main line while the other variable voltage post can supply the turntable and the turntable sidings. In this way you can carry on the operations of the turntable without interfering with the traffic on the main line.

It is, of course, also possible to use two smaller transformers, one for the main line and the other for the turntable, but in this case you should be careful to "phase" the two transformers properly to keep from developing a short circuit as the locomotive moves from the main line to the turntable. If such a short circuit develops invert the plug of one of the transformers.

OPERATION OF THE TURNTABLE

After the turntable is assembled and properly wired, you can run the locomotive slowly onto the turntable, turn the table and then run the locomotive onto another siding. To avoid derailment, the turntable platform must be perfectly aligned with the adjacent siding. The movement of the turntable is controlled by the slide switch on the controller. With a little practice you will learn how to control it very accurately, by moving the switch off and on rapidly.

Note that the turntable is driven by a rubber roller turning against the turntable rail. To keep it from slipping, keep the rail dry and clean.

The turntable must be fastened to a piece of 1/4" plywood measuring 24" square.

Joints of the circular rail should be filed absolutely smooth so that the rollers will ride over without interference.

For more efficient operation, small pieces of cardboard should be inserted under the center of the cross-bars to raise the center of the structure from 1/16" to 1/4". Try one piece of cardboard at a time until the maximum efficiency is achieved.

The wood screws which hold the corss-bars to the plywood must be loosened and/or tightened to various degrees in order to relieve stresses and strains. This will improve smoothness of operation.

A small amount of <u>vaseline</u> applied to the center pivot will help. <u>DO NOT USE GREASE.</u>

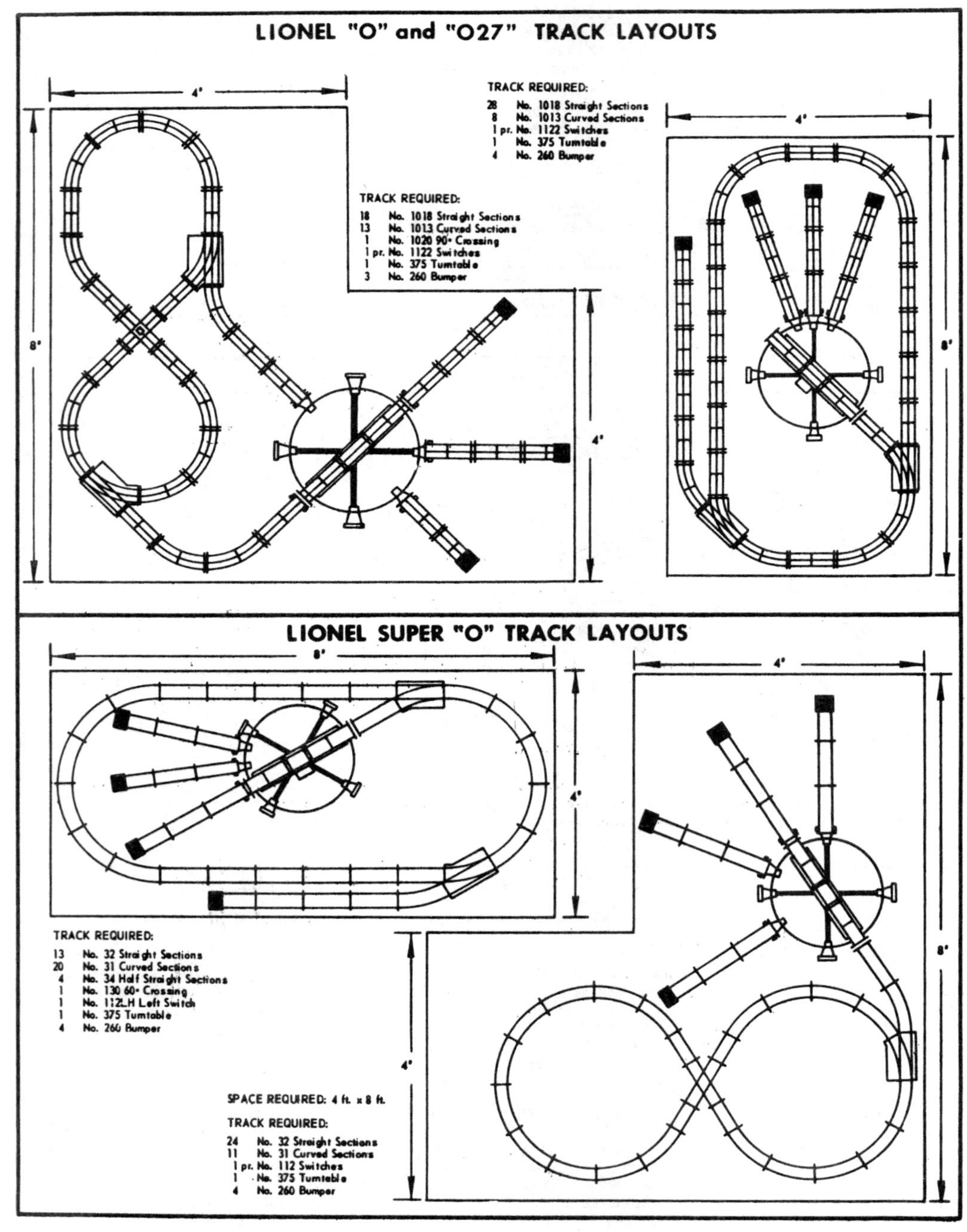

No. 394 ROTARY BEACON

Figure 1—Installation of No. 394 Rotary Beacon

No. 394 Rotary Beacon consists of a metal lattice work tower, a special lamp, and a rotating lens housing. Install the beacon as follows:

1. Clean the insulation off the two wires and connect to the beacon and the transformer as shown in Figure 1.

2. Unpack the lens housing carefully and gently lower it over the lamp so that the steel pivot inside the housing rests in the cup on top of the lamp (see upper inset in Figure 1.) Handle the housing carefully. It is very delicate.

After a minute or two of operation the lamp will heat the air inside the housing and this warm air streaming through the vanes in the top of the housing will cause it to turn slowly. If you wish you can start it off by spinning it gently in a clockwise direction. If rotation of the housing stops, move the pivot slightly to a different spot in the lamp cup.

IMPORTANT -- to make sure that the beacon operates at its normal speed, keep it out of drafts. The housing is so light that a slight air current will interfere with the motion considerably.

LAMP REPLACEMENT -- use lamp No. 394-10 with depressed center.

Tower Assembly 394-5 and Tower Assembly 395-5 are identical with the exception of the fingers which are lanced at the diamond-shaped holes in the 394-6 Platform in order to retain the Light Base casting. While the 394 Tower and Platform can be used for 395 Floodlight Tower the reverse is not true. The tower structure and its component parts have been made in various colors. The available color will be shipped.

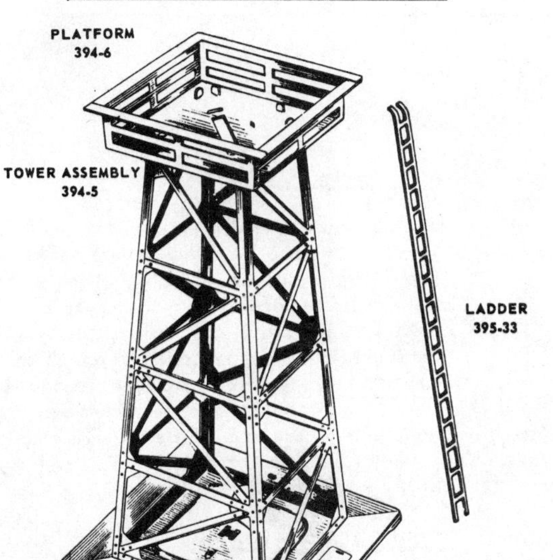

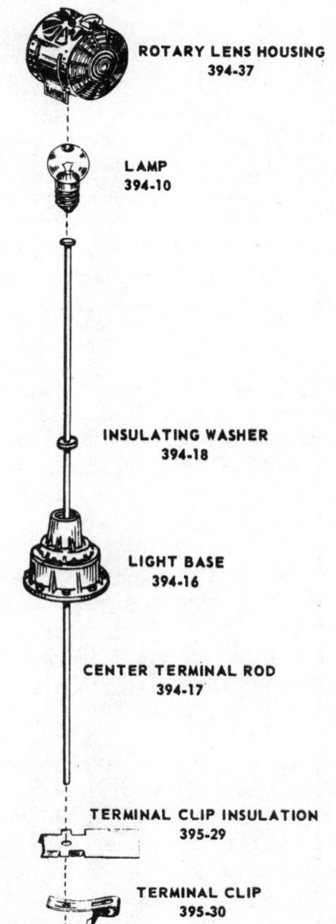

No. 397 COAL LOADER

No. 397 Coal Loader can be installed anywhere in the layout. No special sidings or spur lines are necessary since the loading and unloading are done at the same point in the track -- in front of hte Loader. A Remote Control Section should be located in front of the Loader so that coal dump cars can be unloaded into the Loader bin. Because it is difficult to couple cars on a curve, it is advisable to have at least one straight track section on both sides of the Remote Control Section.

The Loader operates on 12-14 volts and can be connected to any pair of transformer binding posts which deliver approximately this voltage. To start and stop the action, a No. 364C Controller is inserted in one of the connecting wires.

HOW TO OPERATE COAL LOADER

The Coal Loader can be used with any of the coal and ore dump cars made for "O" and "O27" track, but only Lionel Artificial Coal is recommended for use. Any other material such as gravel, sand, etc., will tend to clog up the conveyor mechanism. For this reason also the conveyor mechanism should not be lubricated -- you may dust occasionally with corn starch .

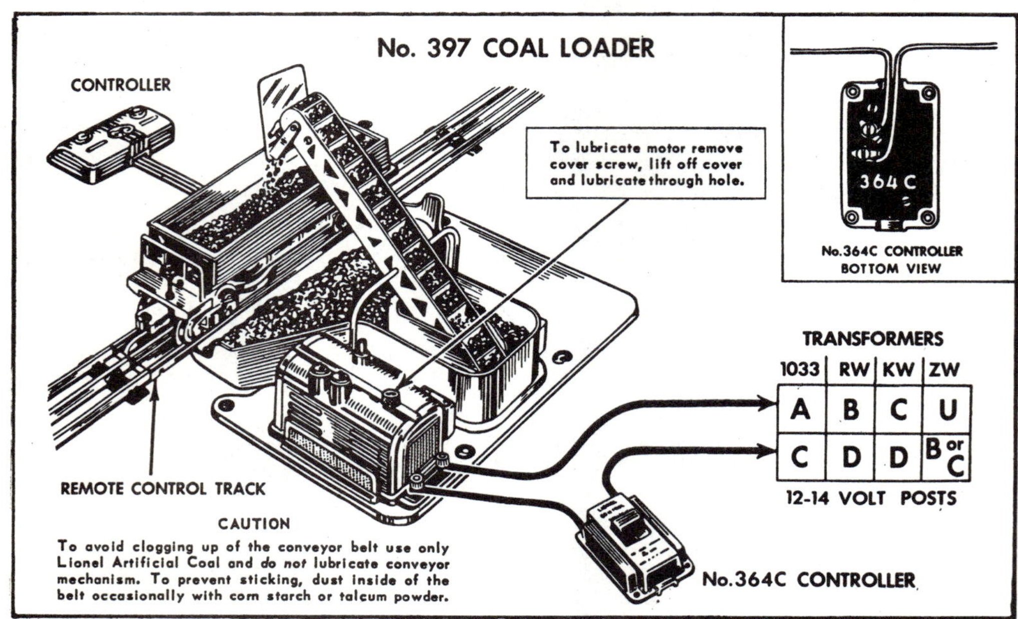

No. 397 Coal Loader consists of a coal receiving scoop and the loading conveyor belt, powered by a motor and gear box assembly and mounted on a metal die cast base.

In operation, a pair of cam mounted on a transverse extension of the motor shaft give the scoop a snapping reciprocating motion which 'kicks' the coal up the incline of the scoop into a storage well from where the coal is picked up by the moving conveyor belt and carried up for reloading into a waiting coal car.

A small number of the early 1948 models of No. 397 Coal Loader were also equipped with No. 70 lamp post mounted on the metal base. This lamp post was subsequently eliminated, and other changes were made in the details of the scoop, conveyor boom and motor to improve operation of the loader.

The Coal Loader operates on either a-c or d-c voltage ranging from 12 to 14 volts, with the lowest possible voltage giving the most satisfactory operation. Any power source may be used for the loader, but when the same transformer is used for both the track and the loader, it is important that the outside track rails and the loader binding post which is grounded to the metal post be connected to the same post of the transformer. Otherwise, a short circuit may result when the coal loader base touches the track.

SERVICE HINTS

1. Motor Servicing

The motor and gear box of the Loader are reached by removing the knurled cover screw and lifting off the diesel engine cover. They are quite trouble-free and require little attention besides an occasional cleaning of the commutator and replacement of brushes. Gear box libricant may be added through the motor cover screw hole. Note that in later models the motor brush plate using tubular brush holder and coil brush springs has been replaced by a brush plate using open brush holders and flat springs for better performance and easier servicing.

2. Sticky Conveyor Belt

Occasionally, particularly in older models, trouble may be caused by pieces of coal accumulating under the conveyor belt. This may be avoided by wrapping a length of smooth masking tape or scotch tape around the conveyor beam spacers, as shown at the top of the next page. Alternatively, the beam may be replaced

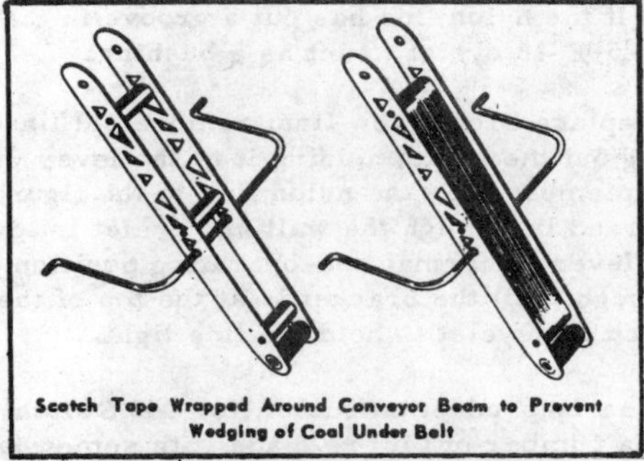
Scotch Tape Wrapped Around Conveyor Beam to Prevent Wedging of Coal Under Belt

with one of later design. In later models a cover clip (No. 397-77) was added to prevent coal particles from jamming between the conveyor and the scoop. Also, proper operation is aided by using large particled coal (Lionel No. 206 Artificial Coal is acceptable).

3. Sticky Conveyor Belt

In some cases after continued use the inside surface of the conveyor belt may become sticky or tacky. This condition may cause uneven conveyor motion so that particles of coal bounce off the conveyor ridges, and in some cases may even cause the belt to stick and jam between the driving roller and the conveyor beam webbing. To eliminate this difficulty simply coat the inside of the belt and the beam surfaces against which it rubs with ordinary corn starch.

4. Uneven Action of Coal Scoop

If the two cam followers do not strike their cams simultaneously, the vibrating action of the scoop will be uneven, causing the coal to pile up on one side of the scoop. This can be corrected without dismantling the loader by raising the front of the scoop, placing a screwdriver or other long tool against the bottom of the cam follower located on the opposite to where the piling occurs, and tapping it sharply to bring the follower closer to its cam. See diagram below.

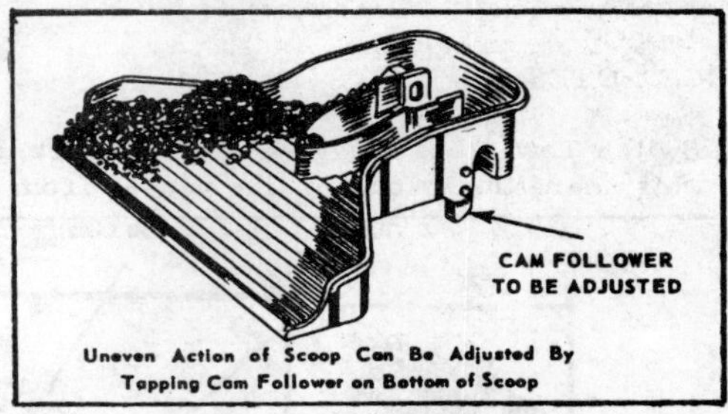

Uneven Action of Scoop Can Be Adjusted By Tapping Cam Follower on Bottom of Scoop

COAL LOADER AND No. 456 COAL RAMP

No. 397 Coal Loader may be used in conjunction with No. 456 Coal Ramp for continuous loading and unloading operation. For details and typical layout suggestions see NO. 456 COAL RAMP.

No. 445 SWITCH TOWER

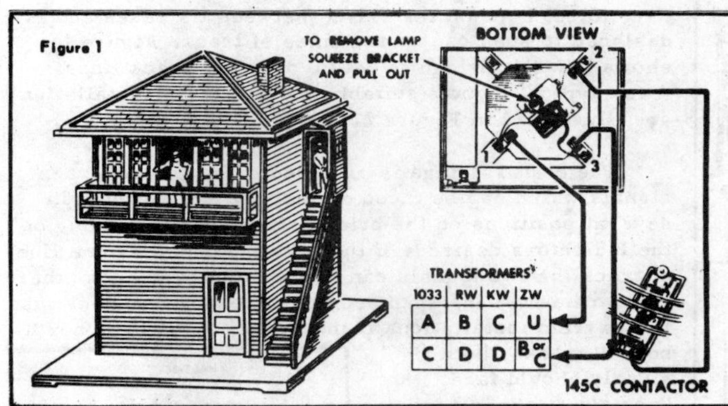

Wiring Diagram for No. 445 Switch Tower

No. 445 Switch Tower can be located anywhere on the layout. A good place for it is on the right hand side of the track near a switch track, so that the engineer who rides in his cab on the right side of the locomotive can see the signals.

The Switch Tower operates on approximately 12-14 volts. See the chart in Figure for combinations of binding posts which furnish approximately this voltage in Lionel transformers.

HOW TO CONNECT SWITCH TOWER TO CONTACTOR

In order to operate automatically the Switch Tower must be connected to a 145C Contactor. For details see 145C CONTACTOR.

HOW TO CONNECT TOWER TO No. 022 SWITCHES

If you have No. 022 switches, which are equipped with a non-derailing mechanism, and a fixed voltage plug you can operate the No. 445 Switch Tower by connecting it directly to the switch posts, as shown in Figure 2. By connecting No. 1 clip to either of the outside switch posts, you can make the tower operate either when the train is passing over the curved branch of the switch, or while it is passing over the straight section. By combining the various posts, you can get any action you want.

No. 445 Switch Tower is quite similar in operation to No. 145 Gateman and No. 151 Semaphore. A solenoid-and-plunger mechanism is linked to a forked lever arm so that the motion of the plunger causes one minature figure to emerge from the tower onto the tower balcony, while another figure, which is connected to the lever end by means of a nylon string, is caused to slide down the tower stairs.

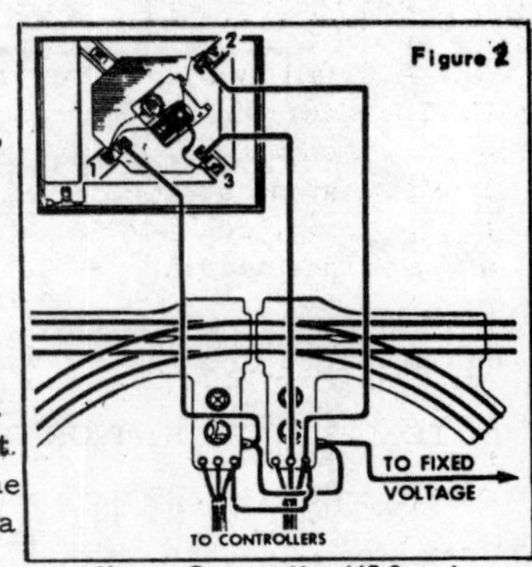

How to Connect No. 445 Switch Tower to No. 022 Switches

CONTINUED

The solenoid circuit is usually closed by the weight of a train passing over a track contactor, although other means, such as an insulated track rail, can be used. The return movement of the mechanism is accomplished by means of a coil spring attached to the lever arm.

Both the lamp and the solenoid are grounded through the metal base of the coil to the mounting post which serves as a pivot for the movement of the lever arm ending with terminal No.1. The high side of the lamp is connected to the mounting post ending at terminal No. 3, while the high side of the solenoid is connected to mounting post at terminal No. 2.

SERVICE NOTES

If Switch Tower has sluggish action, check the hole in the wall where the nylon tow line passes from lever assembly to the figure bracket. If the nylon line has cut a groove in the wall, insert a 259E-18 eyelet to act as a bushing.

To replace broken tow line: remove old line by spreading out the eyelet holding it to the lever with a sharp implement. Tie the nylon line to the figure bracket and thread it through the wall and eyelet in lever arm. With the lever in normal non-operating position pull the cord through until the bracket is at the top of the stairs. Then pinch the eyelet to hold the line tight.

The early production run of No. 445 Switch Tower included a number of towers made with somewhat undersized plunger links which did not permit the plunger to enter far enough into the coil and thus caused the coil to overheat when used continuously for long periods of time. To prevent possible trouble the undersized link should be replaced whenever found. The old link measures approximately 13/16" and was generally nickel plated. The correct link is about 3/32" longer and is brass-colored.

The tower is illuminated by means of a steadily burning 14-volt bayonet-base lamp mounted in a removeable lamp socket.

K-LINE®
Available from MDK, INC.
K-121 SWITCHMAN'S TOWER

TOW LINE
SPRING
LAMP
COIL
TRANSFORMER
145C CONTACTOR

Schematic Diagram of No. 445 Switch Tower

No. 450 SIGNAL BRIDGE

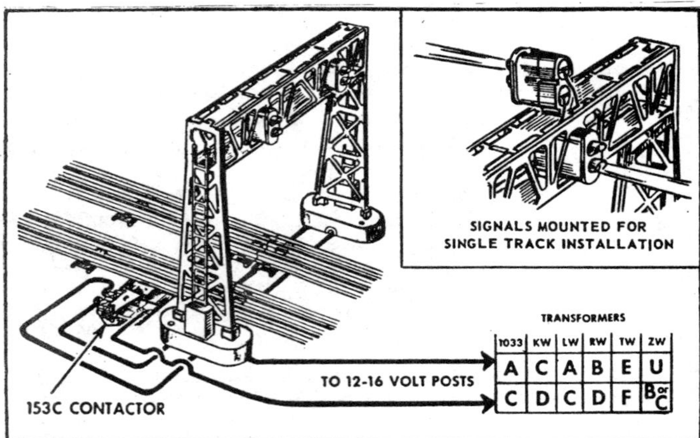

Figure 1 - Signal Bridge Installed over Two Lines of Track.

No. 450 measures 7-1/2" between its bases and is designed to span one or two lines of track. Figure 1 shows how the bridge is set up over two track lines. A few typical layouts suitable for two-track installation are illustrated in Figure 2.

The Signal Bridge is provided with two red-green signals which can be faced either way and mounted in several positions on the bridge structure, depending on the indicators desired. If the bridge spans only one line of track the two signals can be mounted over each other in the center of the span and face in opposite directions. In two train installations if the bridge spans two "northbound" tracks, both signals should face "south". If one of the tracks is "southbound", the signal over it should face "north".

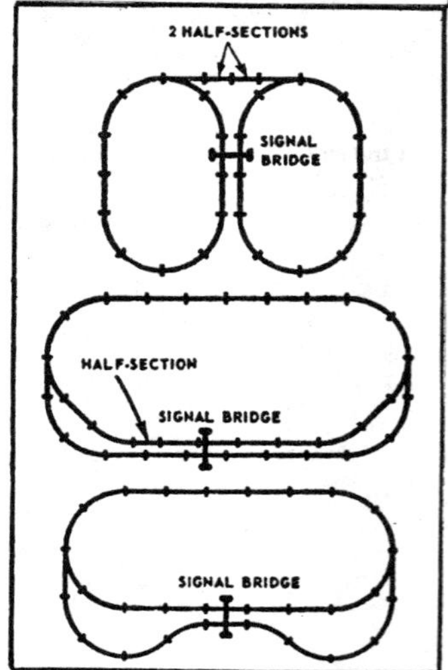

Figure 2 - Typical 'O' Layouts Suitable for Two-Track Installation of Signal Bridge.

Each of the signals is provided with a set of contact clips located on the bottom of the bridge base so that the signals can be wired to operate either independently or together.

For more complicated operations, additional signals No. 450L can be mounted on the bridge to give four-way indication.

AUTOMATIC OPERATION OF No. 450 SIGNAL BRIDGE

In order for the signal to be operated automatically by a passing train, a 153C Contactor is needed. The 153C Contactor is an electrical switch of the 'single-pole, double-throw' type designed to be operated by the weight of a passing train (see section on 153C CONTACTOR).

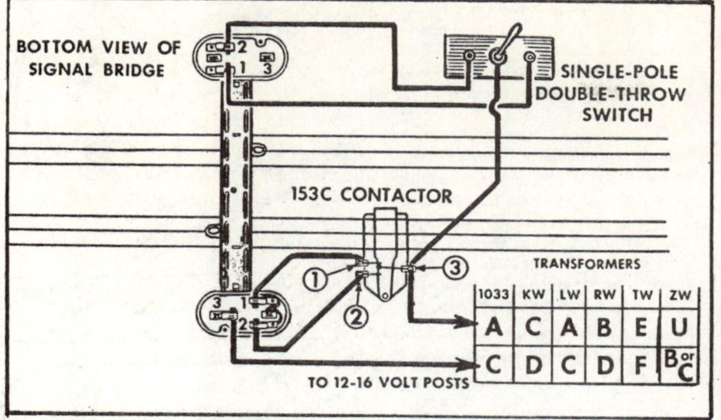

Figure 3 - Installation for One Automatic and One Manual Operation of the Two Signals.

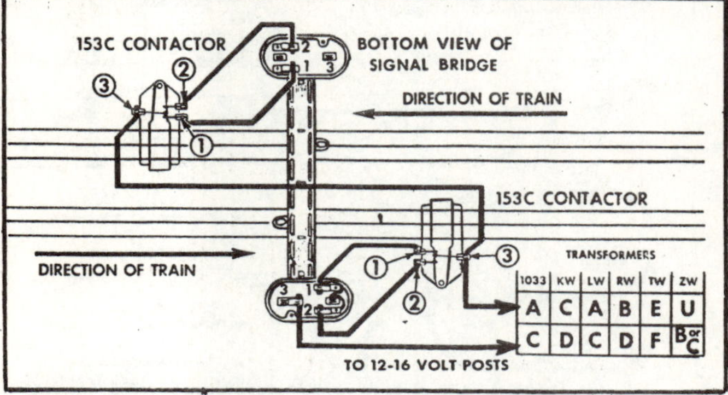

Figure 5 - Installation for Independent Automatic Operation of Both Bridge Signals.

Available from MDK, INC.
K-120 OVERHEAD DOUBLE TRACK SIGNAL BRIDGE

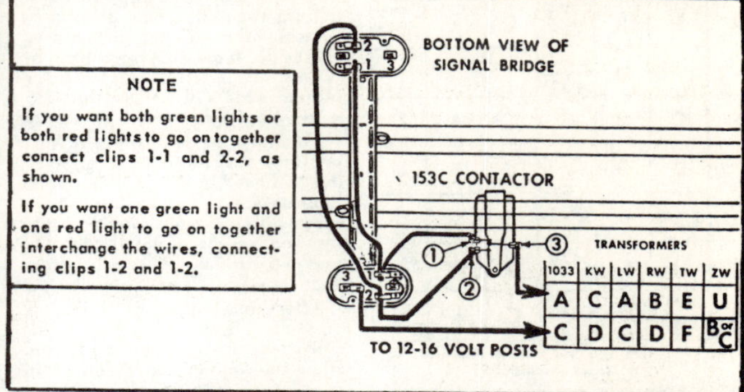

NOTE

If you want both green lights or both red lights to go on together connect clips 1-1 and 2-2, as shown.

If you want one green light and one red light to go on together interchange the wires, connecting clips 1-2 and 1-2.

Figure 4 - Wiring Diagram for Simultaneous Operation of Both Bridge Signals.

No. 456 COAL RAMP SET

WITH SPECIAL HOPPER CAR No. 3456

Lionel No. 456 Coal Ramp is patterned on elevated track structures commonly seen in large coal yards which are serviced by a railroad siding. The bumper on top of the ramp is equipped with an operating coupler which is used to anchor a coal hopper car on top of the ramp. Two electro-magnets built into the top of the ramp are used to operate the hopper's unloading mechanism and to uncouple the car from the rest of the train.

No. 456 Coal Ramp Set includes the elevated ramp together with its controller, a special No. 3456 operating hopper car, a bag of Lionel artificial coal and a pair of 3-inch steel rods which are used only if you choose to operate the 456 Coal Ramp in conjunction with Lionel No. 397 Coal Loader, as described later.

The Coal Ramp can be used with either "O" or "027" track layouts. The ramp is installed at the end of a siding, and is fastened to the track by means of two screws. When installing "027" track, set the track tie on top of the step in the ramp base and fasten it by means of two center screws. ("A" in Figure 1). Fasten screws firmly but not too tightly, or you will bend the track tie.

When installing "O" track fit the track tie *over* the step and fasten it by means of two outside screws marked "B" in Figure 2. The best way to assemble "O" track to the ramp is to raise the ramp, fit the track on the edge of the ramp step, as shown in Figure 3, and "roll" the track into place.

If your layout is not fastened down permanently to a table or base, track clips or rubber bands should be used to hold together the track sections in the siding. Otherwise, the train running up the ramp will tend to push the track sections apart.

Fig. 1—Connecting Ramp to "027" Track

Fig. 2—Connecting Ramp to "O" Track

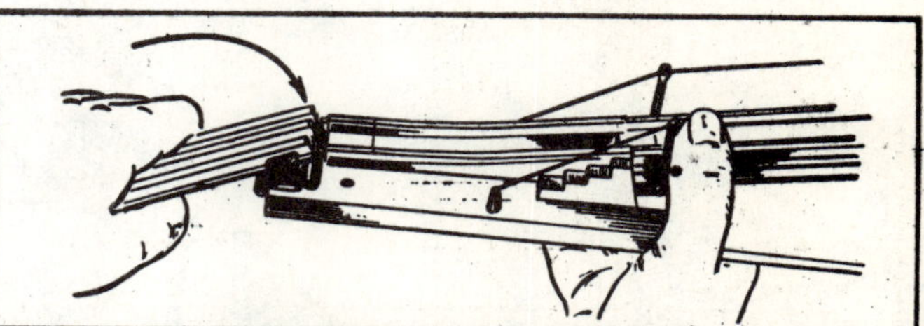

Figure 3—How to Assemble "O" Track to Coal Ramp Base

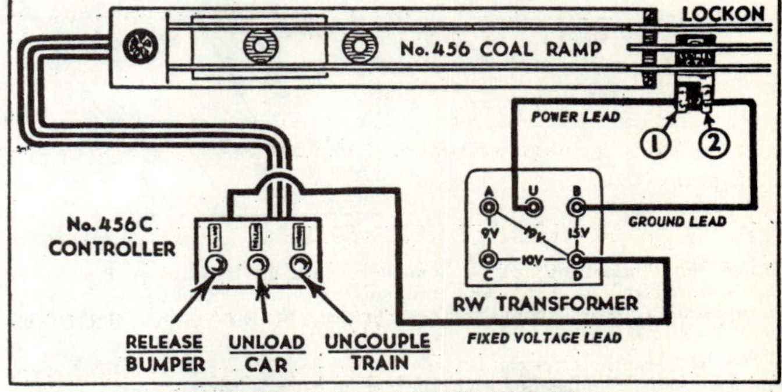

Figure 4—Electrical Connections of No. 456 Coal Ramp

The ramp is controlled by means of the three-button No. 456C Controller connected to the ramp by a three-wire cable. The fourth single wire coming out

CONTINUED

of the controller should be connected to the fixed voltage post on the transformer, as shown in Figure 4. While Type RW Transformer is shown in illustration, the chart in Figure 5 shows fixed voltage connections for other modern Lionel transformers.

HOW TO OPERATE COAL RAMP SET

To operate the coal ramp, load the hopper car with Lionel artificial coal. Couple the hopper car to the end of the train at least three cars long. The train must be long enough to keep the locomotive off the ramp. Then back the train slowly up the ramp. If the train tends to stall as it starts going up the ramp, raise the track voltage just enough to keep it moving slowly until the hopper car reaches the top of the ramp and couples to the bumper. Coupling is easiest when bumper coupler is open and car coupler is closed.

TRANSFORMER	TRANSFORMER CONNECTIONS					
	LOW TRACK VOLTAGE			HIGH TRACK VOLTAGE		
	FIXED VOLTAGE	GROUND RAILS LOCKON CLIP No. 2	POWER RAIL LOCKON CLIP No. 1	FIXED VOLTAGE	GROUND RAILS LOCKON CLIP No. 2	POWER RAIL LOCKON CLIP No. 1
A & Q	LOW VOLTAGE NOT USED			C	A	U THROUGH 167
R	E	B	C OR F THROUGH 167	D	A	C OR F THROUGH 167
V & Z	A OR B	U	C OR D THROUGH 167			
S	C	B	U	C	A	U
RW	D	B	U	D	A	U
VW & ZW	B OR C	U	A OR D			
KW	D	C	A OR B	D	U	A OR B
No. 1033	NOT USED	B	U	C	A	U

Figure 5—Fixed Voltage Posts on Lionel Transformers

After the hopper car is in position on top of the ramp, uncouple it from the train. This is done by pressing the "Uncouple" button and at the same time operating the "Direction" control on the transformer. This will reverse the locomotive and allow train to depart.

To dump the coal from the hopper into the receiving bin, press the "Unload" button as many times as necessary to unload the hopper completely. If you don't empty the hopper car, a small piece of coal might jam in the hopper doors and keep them from closing.

After the hopper is unloaded, press the "Release" button. This will open the bumper coupler and allow the hopper car to roll down the ramp. If your floor or platform is not level, insert a small spacer under the ramp to help the car roll down easier.

Note: As in real-life railroading, this operation requires skillful handling of the train. So don't expect to do it perfectly without a little practice.

OPERATING THE COAL RAMP WITH THE COAL LOADER

If desired, the Coal Ramp can be operated in conjunction with No. 397 Coal Loader so that the coal unloaded on the ramp will spill back into the tray of the Coal Loader from where it can be loaded back into an empty hopper car, as shown in Figure 6. Figures 7 and 8 illustrate typical layouts using the Coal Loader and the Coal Ramp. For this type of operation mount the coal bin on the two 3-inch metal rods which are inserted into the rubber grommets in the base of the Coal Loader. The distance between the ramp and the Remote Control Section should be approximately 7¾" to allow room for the Coal Loader. In some layouts you may have to cut a regular piece of track to proper size to align the Remote Control Section and the top of the Coal Ramp.

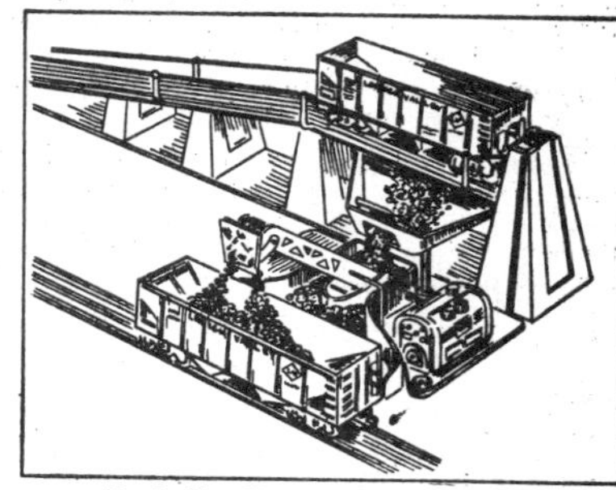

Fig. 6—How No. 456 Coal Ramp Can Be Used With No. 397 Coal Loader

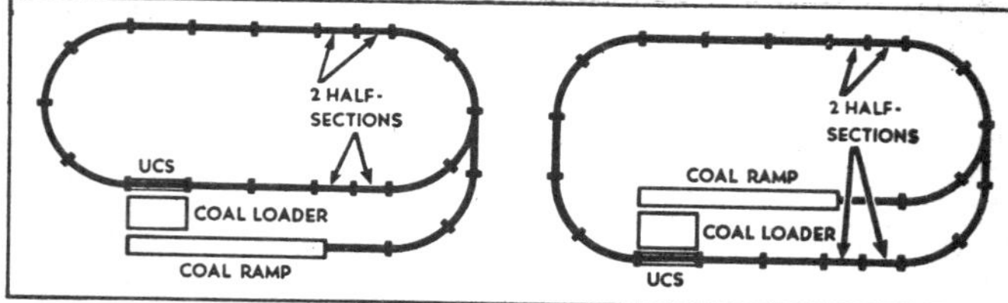

Figure 7—Simple "O" Layouts Showing Installation of No. 456 Coal Ramp and No. 397 Coal Loader

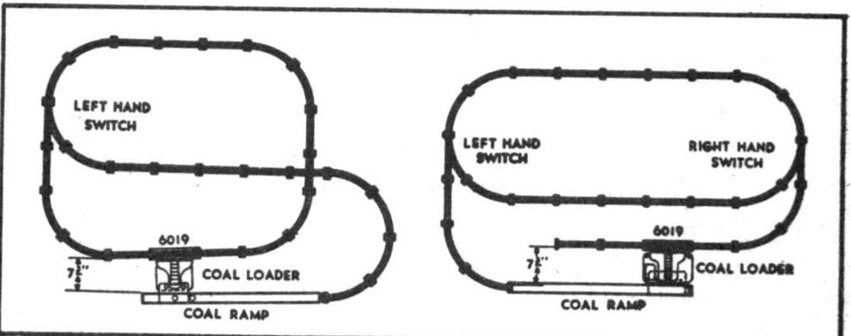

Figure 8—Typical "027" Layouts Showing Installation of No. 456 Coal Ramp and No. 397 Coal Loader. Note that the Layout Using a Crossing Is Not Strictly Symmetrical

No. 460 TRUCK TRANSPORT SET

FOR "O" AND "027" TRACK

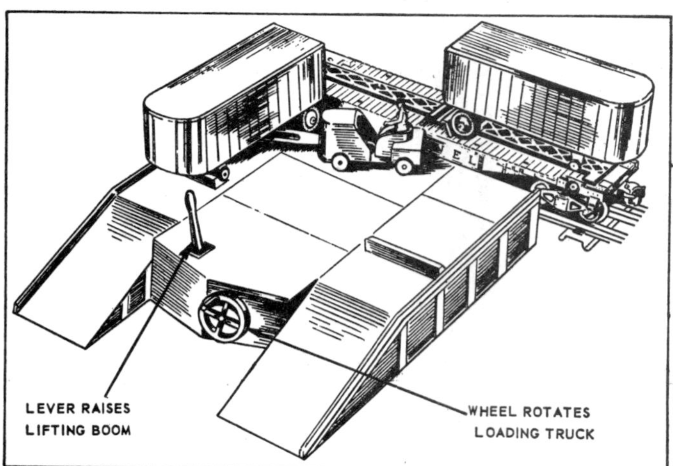

Figure 1—No. 460 Truck Transport Set

No. 460 Truck Transport Set is modeled on a new type of equipment recently introduced by many large railroads to provide "door-to-door" freight transportation service and in this way to meet the competition of the long haul truck lines.

No. 460 Transport Set consists of a special flat car, a pair of truck trailers and a loading and unloading platform. For an extended point-to-point delivery service on your railroad extra platforms, flat cars and trailers are available from your Lionel dealer.

INSTALLATION OF THE PLATFORM

The platform can be located along side of any straight stretch of track or siding within the reeach of the operator. To maintain the proper distance between the platform and the track a track rail must fit into the slots of the two locating arms which swivel from the platform base.

The platform does not have any electrical connections but is operated manually. The side of the platform facing the operator has two controls. The hand wheel on the right controls the pivoting action of the lift truck in the center of the platform. The hand lever on the left raises and lowers the lifting boom. Combined action of these two controls can lift and swing the trailers from the loading platform to the flat car.

No.497 COALING STATION

FOR " O " AND " 027 " TRACK

Figure 1 - How to Adjust Station Base for "0" Track

No. 497 Coaling Station can be installed along any stretch of track. In larger layouts a good location for a coaling station is on a service siding near a terminal. The station can be used with either "0" or "027" track. As it comes from the Factory the station base is prepared for use with "027" track. To convert it for use with "0" track, which is 1/4" higher than "027" track, remove the "027" power blade and replace it with the larger "0" blade. If the blade is tight in its casing, push it out from the bottom with a screwdriver. Also put on the extra "ground" clip to increase the height of the ground blade.

After making sure that the station base is ready for use with your track you can install it in your layout. First join two straight track sections and set them on the station base so that the joint between the two sections is in the center of the base. A set of notches is provided in the base to lock the track firmly in place. The flange of the "027" track will fit under the bottom notches. "0" track will fit under the top notches.

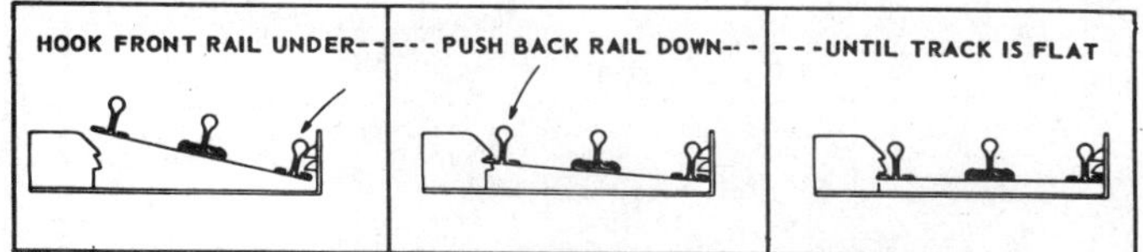

Figure 2 - How to Set Track into Place on Base of Station

The station is operated by means of its controller which is connected to the station with a four-conductor cable. The single wire coming out of the controller is connected either to No. 1 clip of a track lockon, as illustrated in Figure 3, or to a fixed voltage post of your transformer, as shown in Figure 4. If connected to the track lockon the station will operate on track voltage. If connected to a fixed voltage post the operation of the station will be independent of track voltage.

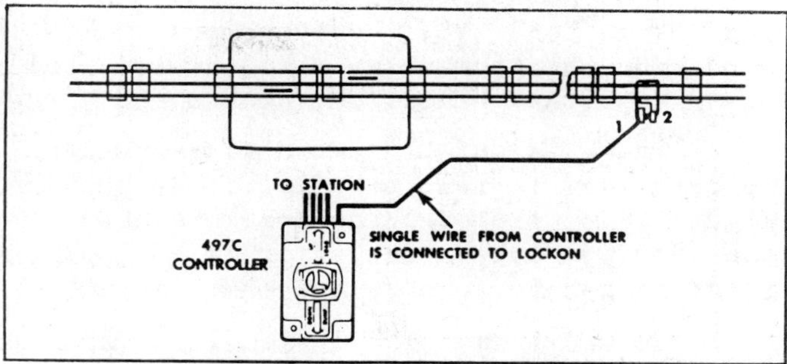

Figure 3 - Installation No. 497 Coaling Station

HOW TO OPERATE THE STATION

A train with a coal dump car is taken into the station and stopped so that the dump car is right in the center of the station. The car must be positioned accurately, and you may have to move it over by hand to make sure that the sliding contact shoes on the car trucks rest on the power and ground blades in the station base. The car should face the front of the station so that it can dump its load into the receiving tray.

When the dump car is in position, move the appropriate controller lever to "DUMP". This will tilt the dump car and empty its contents into the receiving bin. Do not use too much coal, or it will spill over and also make the tray difficult to raise. To raise the tray move the other lever to "UP" and keep it there

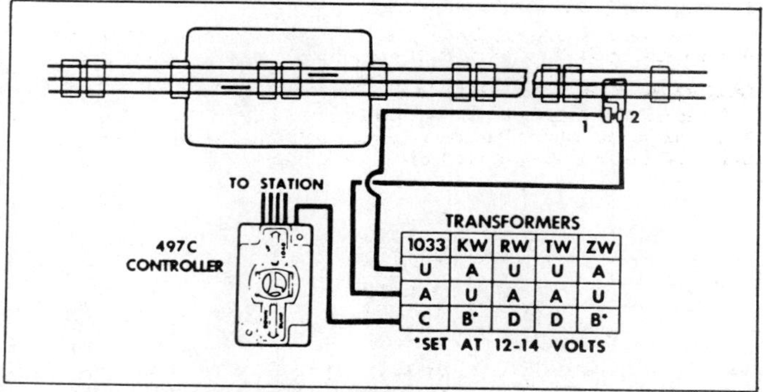

1033	KW	RW	TW	ZW
U	A	U	U	A
A	U	A	A	U
C	B*	D	D	B*

Figure 4 - Fixed Voltage Connection for Coaling Station

until the tray rises to the top of the station and pours the coal into the storage bin. Moving the lever to "DOWN" will reverse the station motor and lower the tray to its normal position. To load an empty car, set it under the storage bin and move lever to "LOAD".

NOTE: Because of the small amount of clearance between the locomotive and the receiving tray, it is best to wait until the tray is all the way down before running the train through the station.

ABOUT TRACK

TRACK SIZES

For years we have been restricted with sectional track as shown in this section and in the next two. However, now with K-LINE track, you can build your layout and expand your thinking to be like the real railroads. K-LINE offers, in addition to the standard Lionel selection, double and three foot straights, 42" and 72" curves.

Track is made in two different sizes: "O" Gauge and the lighter O-27 Gauge, The quickest way to tell the difference between them is by the shape of the track ties (see Figure 24). Although the track "gauge" of the distance between the running rails is the same for both types of track -- 1¼ inches -- "O" and O-27 track cannot be easily interchanged for use on the same layout.

To aid in automatic signalling and operation of accessories K-LINE also makes special insulated straight sections matching O-27 (K-233) and "O" Gauge (K-333) track

O-27 Gauge Track

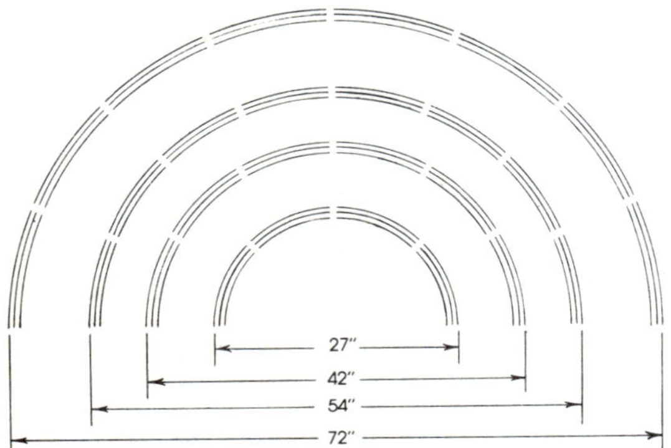

O-27 WIDE RADIUS TRACK
Compatible with our regular O-27 track in three diameters, 42", 54" and 72". Twelve sections of K-212 form a 42" circle, while sixteen sections of K-222 make a circle 54" in diameter. Our high speed, super-wide K-226's form a 72" circle with sixteen sections.

O-27 EXTRA LONG STRAIGHTS
Longer straights save time and money, conduct electricity better, and the fewer track connections make for quieter train travel. Both DOUBLE STRAIGHTS (K-252) and 3' EXTRA LONG STRAIGHTS (K-256) are available.

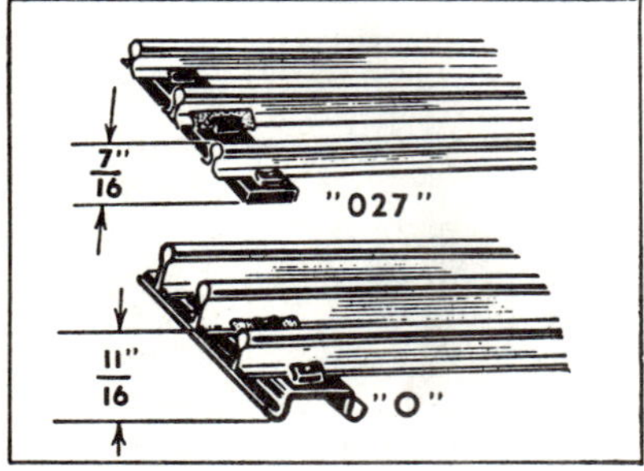

Figure 24—"O" and "027" Track

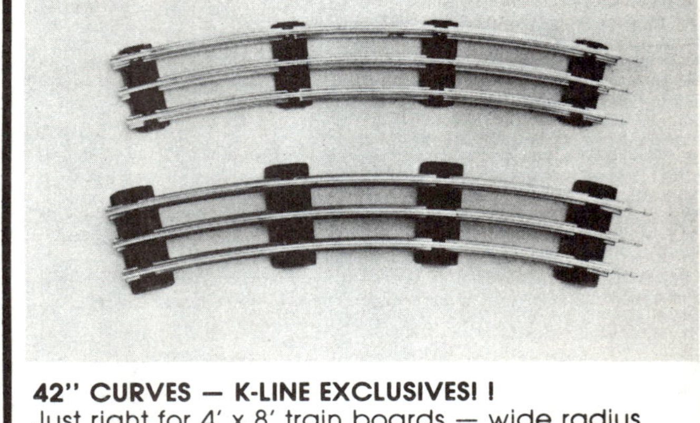

42" CURVES — K-LINE EXCLUSIVES! !
Just right for 4' x 8' train boards — wide radius curves that still fit the layout. Available in both O-27 (K-212) and "O" Gauge (K-312).

"O" Gauge Track

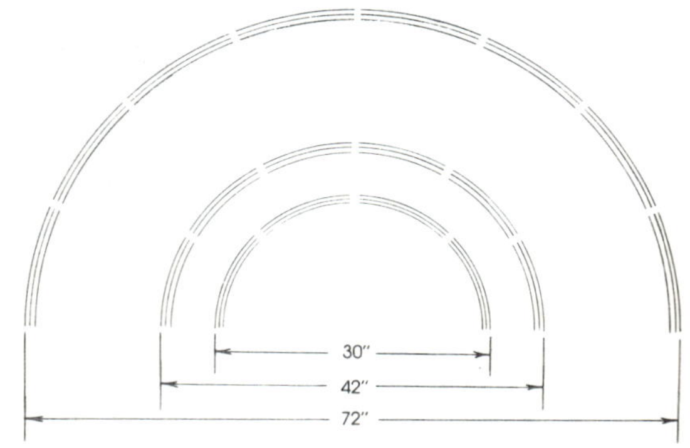

"O" GAUGE WIDE RADIUS CURVES
Twelve sections of K-312 Curves make a 42" circle, while sixteen K-322's form a circle 72" in diameter.

"O" GAUGE STRAIGHTS
Layouts grow quickly and economically with our K-342 O-72 STRAIGHTS and especially with our 3' EXTRA LONG STRAIGHTS (K-352).

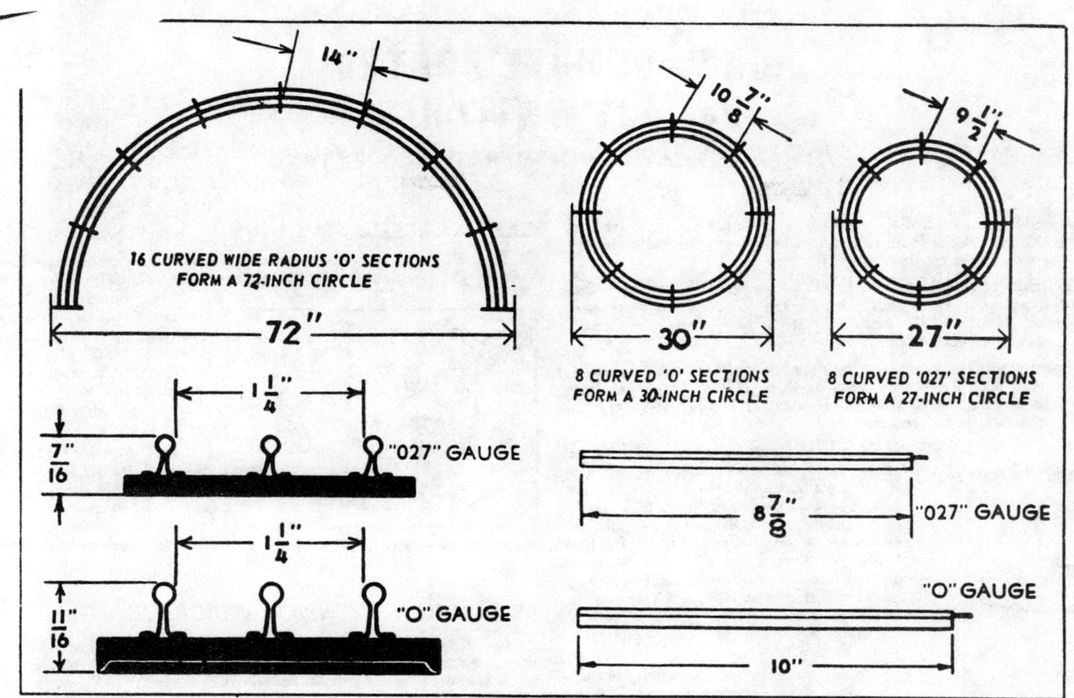

Figure 25—Comparison of Three Types of Track

LAYING THE TRACK

Track is flexible so that it is possible to construct layouts which are not strictly symmetrical. However, be careful not to bend or distort the track too much or you will cause your train to derail. If you fasten your track to a wooden base it will be more secure and will insure better train operation. Small screws are best for this purpose, since they are easier to remove than nails. Don't screw down the track too tightly. Track should be fastened merely to prevent shifting—not to clamp it down to the base. If you attempt to screw it down tightly, you will distort the track and cause the train to operate badly.

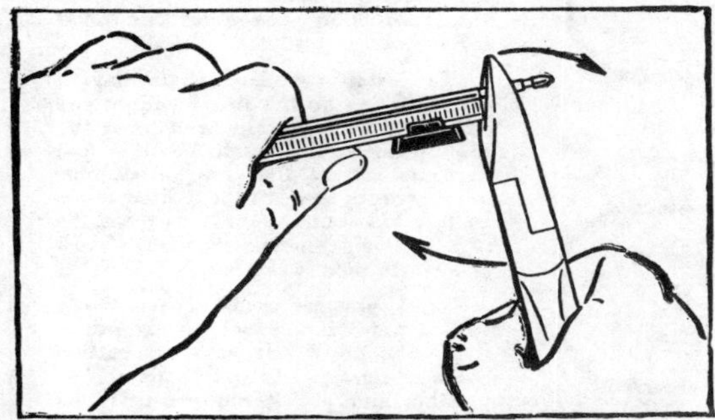
Figure 26—Removing Track Pins

Where special irregular lengths of track are needed cut the regular track section to proper size using a fine-toothed hack saw. Smooth the cut edges with a fine file.

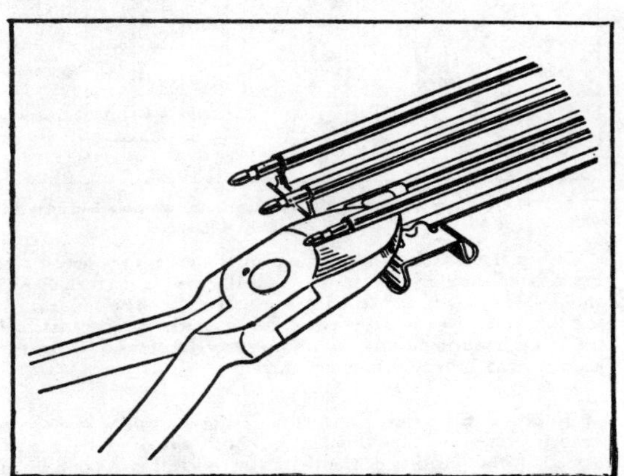
Figure 27—How to Tighten Pins in Track

REMOVING TRACK PINS

In many cases you may find it necessary to remove the steel pins from a track rail, either to place them into the opposite end of the rail or to replace them with fibre insulating pins. This can be done most easily with a pair of diagonal pliers, as shown in Figure 26. Use the rail flanges as a lever point and work the pin out gradually. Try not to distort the rail. To tighten pins in the track, or to reshape distorted or enlarged rail openings apply the pliers as shown in Figure 27. Many model railroaders make their own special track pliers by filing a round groove the size of a rail in a pair of flat nose pliers.

LIONEL REMOTE CONTROL No. 022 SWITCHES

WITH AUTOMATIC NON-DERAILING FEATURE

Railroad track switches, also known to railroaders as 'turnouts', are used to connect two lines of track so that the train can switch over from the main line to a siding, a spur line or to a different line entirely.

Lionel No. 022 switches are made to match 'O' gauge track. They have the same length and radius as ordinary straight and curved 'O' track sections and are installed in the track layout in the same way, with each switch replacing one straight and one curved track section.

Switches are generally sold in pairs, consisting of a right-hand and a left-hand switch. An easy way to tell the difference is this: If a train proceeding along the main line has to turn out to the left, it uses a left-hand switch; one turning out to the right uses a right-hand switch.

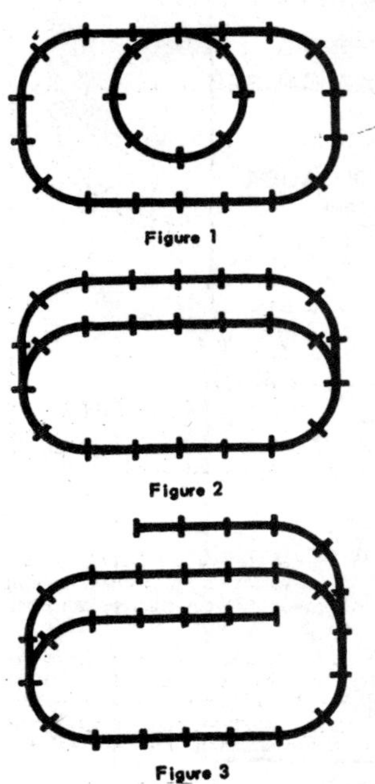

Track switches can be used in a great variety of ways some of which are illustrated in the simple layouts on the left. Except when used to enter a dead-end siding, as in Figure 3, a pair of switches is generally required in the layout so that a train has a way of getting back on the main track without backing out of the siding. The pairs of switches can be installed in a layout together, as in Figure 1, or separately, as in Figure 2.

These layouts, of course, merely illustrate how switches may be used. Innumerable other layouts can be developed through the use of crossings and additional track and switches. See your instruction booklet for additional layout ideas.

To install switches in the layout carefully line up the switch pins to the adjoining track sections and press the track firmly to the switch. You may find in some layouts that the switch pins interfere with those in the regular track. In this case remove the pins *from the regular track if possible; don't disturb any of the pins in the switch.*

Track pins are removed most easily with a pair of diagonal cutting pliers. Grasp the pin firmly with the cutting edges as close to the end of the rail as possible and pry it out gradually by using the rail flange as a lever point.

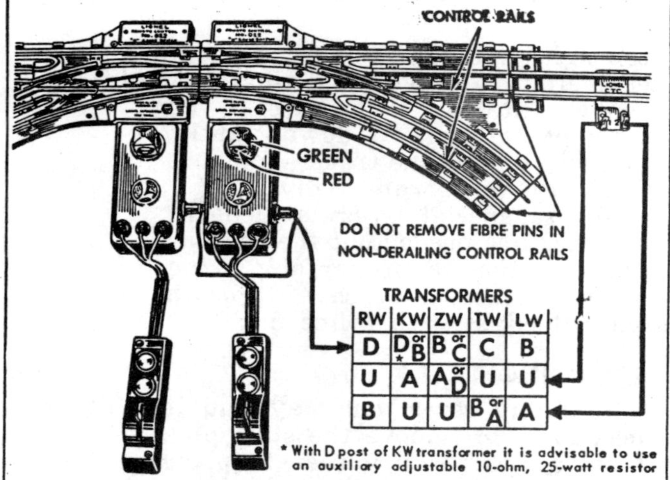

Figure 4—How to Connect 022 Switches to Modern Lionel Transformers.

SWITCH POWER CONNECTIONS

When the switch is installed in the layout, its power connections are made automatically so that it gets the regular track voltage. In most smaller layouts this arrangement is quite satisfactory. However, in larger layouts, it is frequently desirable to supply the switch mechanism with *fixed* voltage directly from the transformer. With fixed voltage supply the switch is independent of the variable track voltage and operates with a snap even though track voltage is reduced to slow down the train or is turned off entirely.

FIXED VOLTAGE PLUGS

To make fixed voltage connections No. 022 switch is provided with a Fixed Voltage Plug which fits into a socket located on the side of the switch box. Connect the wire leading from the Fixed Voltage Plug to the proper transformer binding post. See Figures 4, 5 and 6. Then centering the plug carefully push it firmly into the socket until the edge of the plug is flush with the switch cover. The plug should fit over the slotted pin which can be seen inside the switch.

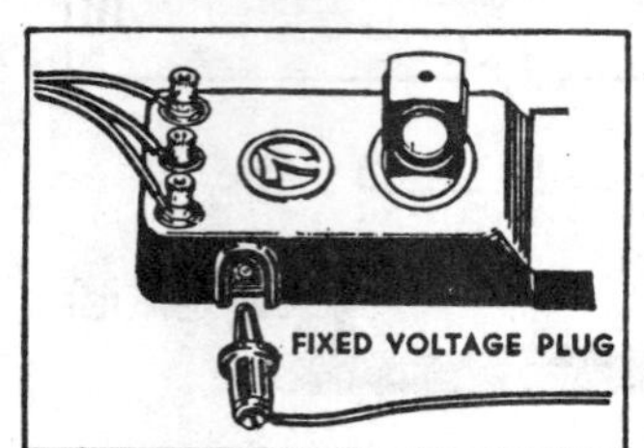

Figure 5—Fixed Voltage Plug.

The Fixed Voltage feature is optional, but when it is not used the plug should be removed from the socket because its insertion automatically disconnects the switch mechanism from its normal track power supply.

ADJUSTING THE SWITCH INDICATOR LIGHTS

No. 022 Switch is operated by means of its controller which is connected to the three binding posts by a 3-wire cable. After the switch is installed in the track layout, connect the center controller wire to the center post of the switch. Then connect the outside wires to the outside posts, and turn on the power. The lamp in the switch and one of the two lamps in the controller will light. Now, as the controller lever is moved forward or backward one of the indicator lamps in the controller will go out and the other will light instead. At the same time, the swivel rail of the switch will snap from one side to the other causing the lamp hood on the switch housing to rotate.

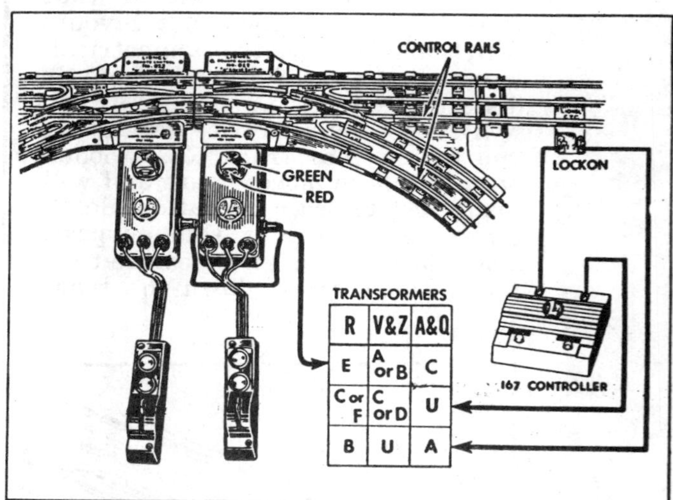

Figure 6—How to Connect 022 Switches to Transformers Requiring Separate No. 167 Whistle Controllers.

When the switch is in position for the train to proceed along the main line, green lamp should be on in the controller and the green light in the lamp hood should shine along the straight track. If red controller lamp is on, interchange the two outside wires connecting the controller to the switch. If the red side of the lamp hood is pointed along the straight track, lift up the lamp hood and snap it back into the ring correctly.

Note that no action takes place if the controller lever is moved more than once in the same direction. If, however, the lever is pressed in the reverse direction, the position of the switch swivel rail and lamp hood will change and the corresponding lamp in the controller will go on instead. By connecting and adjusting the controller in this way, you will know the position of the switch swivel rail even though it may be concealed, by merely noting whether the red or green controller indicator is on.

HOW TO REVERSE POSITION OF MOTOR UNIT

If you are constructing a layout in which you find the motor unit of the switch projecting too far from the side of the switch, and if you have room for

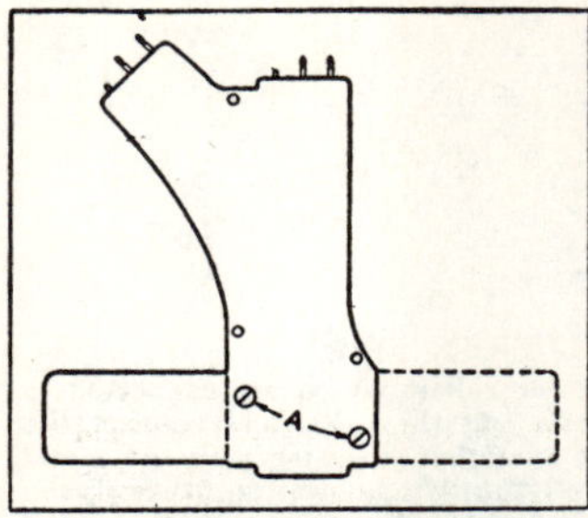

Figure 7—How to Change Position of Switch Motor Unit.

the motor unit on the other side, you may change the position of the motor unit as follows: Remove the two mounting screws indicated by letters "A" in Figure 7 and detach the motor unit from the switch. Insert the motor unit in position on the opposite side of the switch as indicated by dotted lines. Be sure that the driving pin is inserted in slot of swivel rail and replace the mounting screws. (If the lamps in the controller are adjusted to conform with the position of the switch as described in a previous section it will be necesary to interchange the lamps when reversing the position of the motor.)

NON-DERAILING FEATURE

Note that two of the rails of the 022 switch end with fibre pins, instead of regular steel pins. These pins insulate the control portions of the switch rails from the regular grounded outside rails and are part of the automatic non-derailing feature. The control rails are connected internally to the switch coils. As a locomotive approaches an 'open' switch its wheels and axles bridge one of the control rails to the opposite outside rail. This action completes the electrical circuit of the proper switch coil and throws the swivel rails of the switch to the correct position for the train to pass through. For good operation keep the control rails clean and free of rust or grease.

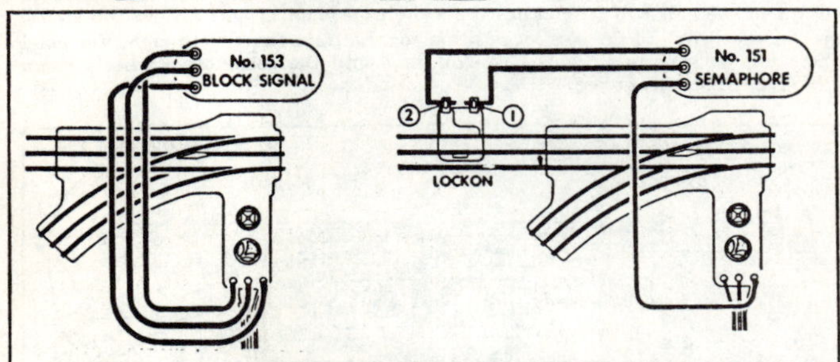

Figure 8—Left: How to Connect 153 Block Signal to 022 Switches.
Right: How to Connect 151 Semaphore to 022 Switches.

SPECIAL USES OF THE NON-DERAILING FEATURE

If desired, various track signals and accessories such as No. 153 Block Signal, No. 151 Semaphore, No. 145 Gateman, No. 445 Switch Tower and others can be connected to the outside binding posts of the switch boxes so that these accessories are controlled by the control rails of the switches. The wiring diagrams for such installations are shown in Figure 8 and 9 on this and following page. In some cases accessories connected to the switch will cause both lights in the switch controller to remain on continuously.

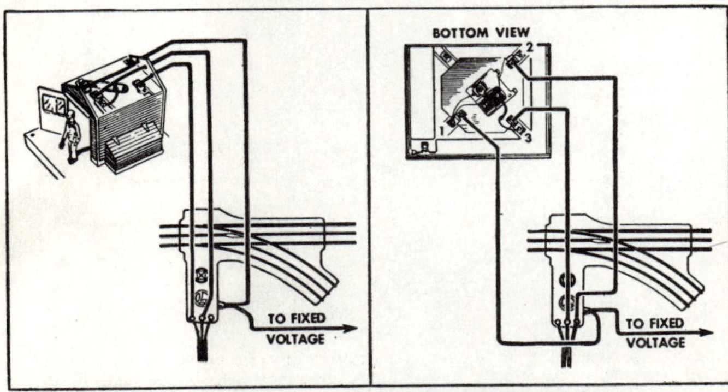

Figure 9—Left: How to Connect 145 Gateman to 022 Switches.
Right: How to Connect 445 Switch Tower to 022 Switches.

In Figure 9 the accessories are shown connected to fixed voltage through the switch fixed voltage plug. If this voltage is too high, track voltage can be used instead by connecting the power wire to No. 1 clip of a track lockon instead of the fixed voltage plug.

The control rails and mechanism of No. 022 switches can be used for several other insteresting applications. If the outside posts of the switches are interconnected as shown in Figure 10, the switches will control each other. Train leaving track section 'A' operates the non-derailing device in the 'exit' switch, throwing it to the position which allows the train to proceed onto the single track. Simultaneously the 'entry' switch is thrown to the position to allow the train to enter track section 'B'. As the train leaves section 'B' it will again throw both switches, but this time to the opposite direction, thus enabling it to go back into section 'A' on the next circuit of the track.

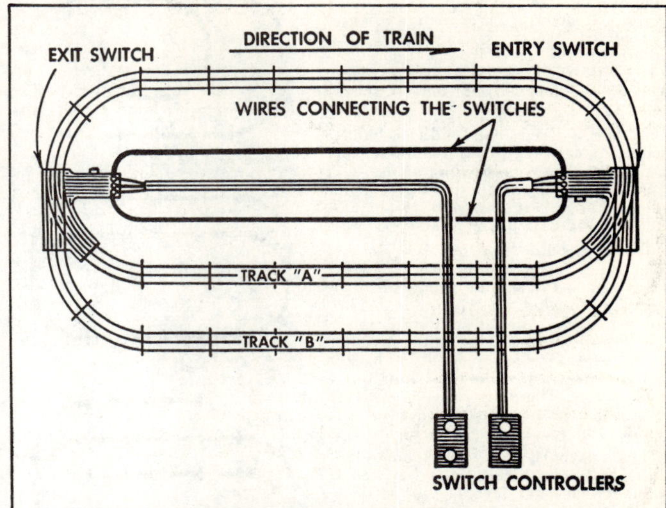

Figure 10—How to Inter-Connect Two Switches to Control Each Other.

MAINTENANCE OF SWITCHES

Lionel switches have been designed to be as simple and foolproof as possible. Keep the switches clean and free from interfering particles, paying particular attention to the non-derailing control rails. Do not remove the fibre pins in the switch.

To take out a burned-out lamp on the switch remove the lamp hood by grasping firmly and pulling upward. Remove lamp by pushing it in and then turning it slightly to the left. Replace with lamp No. L1445. Be sure to replace the lamp hood in correct position as described on previous page. In replacing the lamps in the controller, use No. L432(R) for the red lamp and No. L432(G) for the green lamp.

Remote Control Non-Derailing No. 1122(E) Switches

FOR '027' TRACK

Railroad track switches, also known to railroaders as 'turnouts', are used to connect two lines of track so that the train can cross over from the main line to a siding, a spur line or to a different line entirely.

Lionel No. 1122 switches are made to match '027' track. They have the same length and curvature as ordinary straight and curved '027' track sections and are installed in the track layout in the same way, with each switch replacing one straight and one curved track section.

Switches are generally sold in pairs, consisting of a right-hand and a left-hand switch. An easy way to tell the difference is this: If a train proceeding along the main line has to turn out to the left, it uses a left-hand switch; one turning out to the right uses a right-hand switch.

Track switches can be used in a great variety of ways some of which are illustrated in the simple layouts on the right. Except when used to enter a dead-end siding, or spur, as in Figure 3, a pair of switches is needed in the layout so that a train has a way of getting back on the main track without backing out of the siding. The pairs of switches can be installed in a layout together, as in Figure 1, or separately, as in Figure 2.

These layouts, of course, merely illustrate how switches may be used. Innumerable other layouts can be developed through the use of crossings and additional track and switches. See your instruction booklet for additional layout ideas.

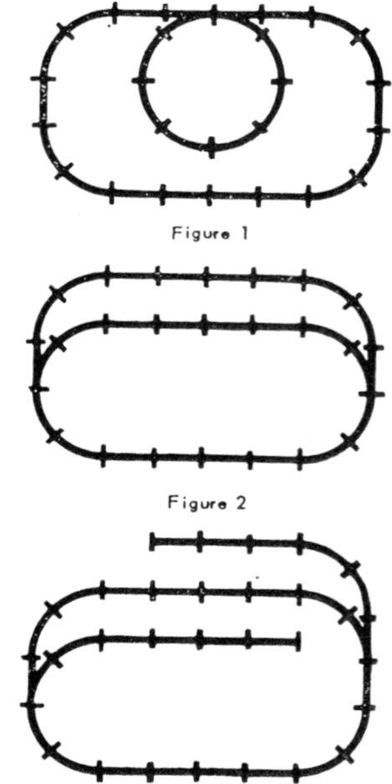

Figure 1

Figure 2

Figure 3

Switches are inserted in a track layout in the same manner as a piece of curved or straight track. Carefully line up the pins to the adjacent track section and press the track firmly to the switch. You may find in some layouts that the switch pins interfere with those in the track. In such cases remove the pins from the regular track; don't disturb any of the pins of the switch. Track pins are removed most easily with a pair of diagonal cutting pliers, as shown in Figure 4. Grasp the pin firmly with the cutting edges as close to the rail as possible and pry it out gradually by using the rail flange as a lever point. No separate electrical connections are necessary since the switch mechanism draws its power directly from the track.

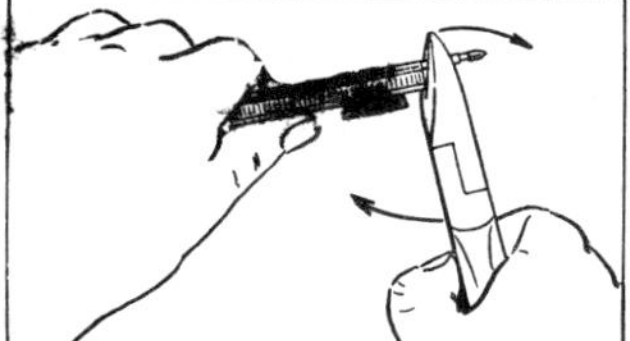

Figure 4—How to Remove Track Pins.

CONNECTING SWITCH CONTROLLERS

The switches are operated by means of controllers which are connected to the switches by 3-wire flat cables. Straighten out the cable and connect the wires to the switch posts in order, making sure that the wire with the metal lug is connected to the binding post nearest the switch box. To "throw" the switch move the controller lever and the swivel rails will snap over. If the action of the two levers does not correspond, reverse the connections of the two wires leading to the two posts farthest from the switch box.

When the switches are set for the train to travel along the straight-away, the green lens of the switch lantern should face in the direction of the straight-away. If the lantern does not give correct indication simply turn it around in its socket.

HOW THE NON-DERAILING FEATURE WORKS

Note that the two inner rails of the switch end with insulating track pins. These are the non-derailing control rails. As a locomotive approaches an 'open' switch along either one of the branches of the switch, its wheels bridge the control rail to the opposite outside rail. This action completes the electrical circuit to the coil which operates the switch mechanism and throws the swivel rails of the switch to the correct position for the train to pass through. For good operation be sure to keep the control rails and the locomotive wheels clean and free of rust or grease.

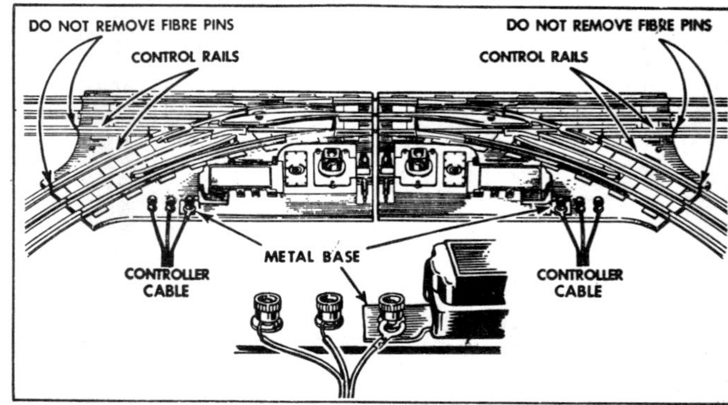

Figure 5—How to Connect Controller to No. 1122 Switches. Note that the Wire with the Metal Lug is Connected to the Post with a Metal Base.

POWER SUPPLY

HOUSEHOLD POWER LINES

Lionel electric trains and accessories operate on low voltage ranging from 8 volts to 18 volts, depending on the type and size of the locomotive and train and on the rated voltage of the lamps used in illuminated accessories. This low voltage is generally stepped down from the regular house power lines by means of a Lionel transformer.

While the house power supply used in this country is usually 110 to 125 volts, 60-cycle alternating current (AC), there are a number of exceptions. Some parts of California use 50-cycle current; some areas in Canada employ 25-cycle current, while some downtown areas in New York City still use 110-volt direct current (DC) with which a transformer cannot be used without a special DC-to-AC *inverter*.

Figure 60—Transformer Rating

The regular Lionel transformers are designed to work on 110 to 125-volt, 60-cycle, alternating current. Other combinations of voltage and frequency (cycles) require special transformers which are available although they may not be listed in the general catalogue. The voltage and frequency ratings of transformers always appear on the transformer panel. They must correspond to the rating of your power line, or the transformer may be severely damaged. In case of doubt always ask your electric company about the type of power you have before buying or installing any equipment which is to be plugged into your wall outlets. If you have a special problem consult your Lionel Dealer

VOLTAGES SUPPLIED BY LIONEL TRANSFORMERS

The following chart lists all nominal voltages supplied by the most popular Lionel transformers.

	Watts	Posts	Voltage Fixed	Voltage Variable
1033 1044 4090	90	A-B	5	
		B-C	11	
		A-C	16	
		A-U		5-16
		B-U		0-11
*1034	75	A-B	6	
		B-C	14	
		A-C	20	
		A-U		10-20
		B-U		4-14
RW	110	A-C	9	
		A-D	19	
		B-D	15	
		C-D	10	

	Watts	Posts	Voltage Fixed	Voltage Variable
		A-U		9-19
		B-U		6-16
KW	190	C-D	14	
		C-U	6	
		D-U	20	
		A-U		6-20
		B-U		6-20
		A-C		0-14
		B-C		0-14
ZW	275	A-U		6-20
		B-U		6-20
		C-U	None	6-20
		D-U		6-20

* This transformer has no built-in whistle controller.

HOW TRANSFORMERS OPERATE

A transformer consists essentially of two coils of insulated copper wire wound on a common iron core. Although the two coils are completely insulated from one another, an alternating voltage imposed on one of the coils (which is then termed the *primary* coil) electro-magnetically induces a voltage in the other, or *secondary*, coil. The relation between the two voltages depends on the ratio of the number of turns in the two coils. In *step-down* transformers the secondary winding has fewer turns than the primary winding and, consequently, the secondary voltage is lower than the primary or line voltage in the same ratio.

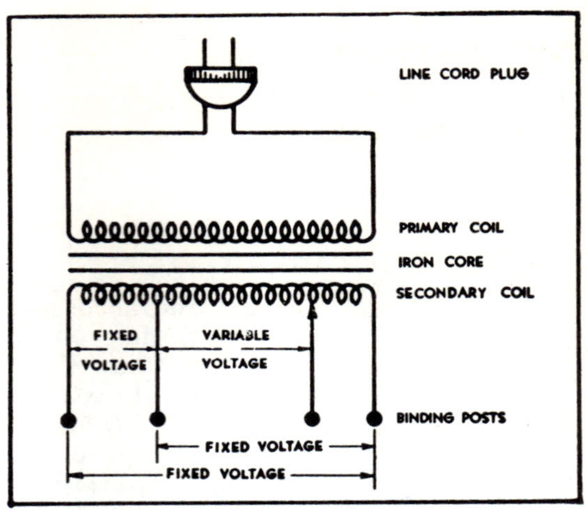

Schematic Diagram of a Lionel Transformer

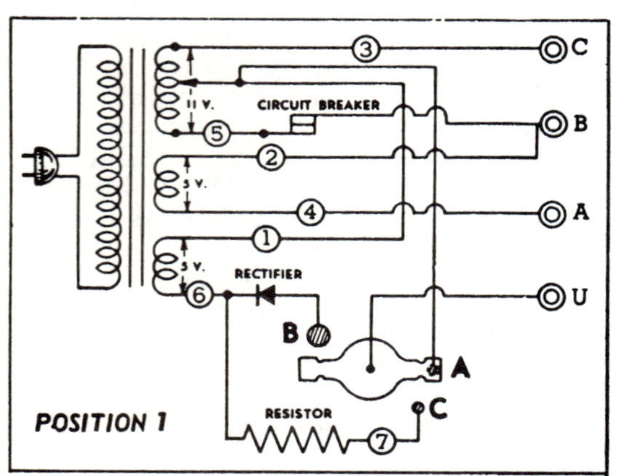

Diagram of "Multi-Control" Transformer No. 1033

POSITION 1. In the normal position the spring contact of the whistle control switch connects the variable voltage winding at contact rivet "A" to the transformer output binding post.

POSITION 2. As the switch is rotated clockwise, the contact spring makes contact with rivet "B". This produces the momentary high d.c. "pickup" surge to close the whistle relay.

POSITION 3. At the end of the swing the contact spring makes contact with rivet "C" thus connecting the resistor wire in parallel with the rectifier. In this position most of transformer current by-passes the rectifier leaving enough d.c. "holding" voltage to keep the relay closed.

Turning the control arm in counterclockwise direction, shown in POSITION 4, disconnects the transformer output from the output binding post causing the locomotive reversing unit to operate.

MULTI-CONTROL TRANSFORMERS

The name "Multi-Control" is applied to those Lionel transformers which are equipped with built-in controls for operating the train whistle and for reversing the direction of the train.

The built-in whistle controller converts a portion of the transformer a.c. output into d.c. voltage to operate the whistle relay in the tender.

An important feature of "Multi-Control' transformers is a compensating winding which is switched into the circuit automatically to make up for the voltage drop in the rectifier and for the load of the whistle motor.

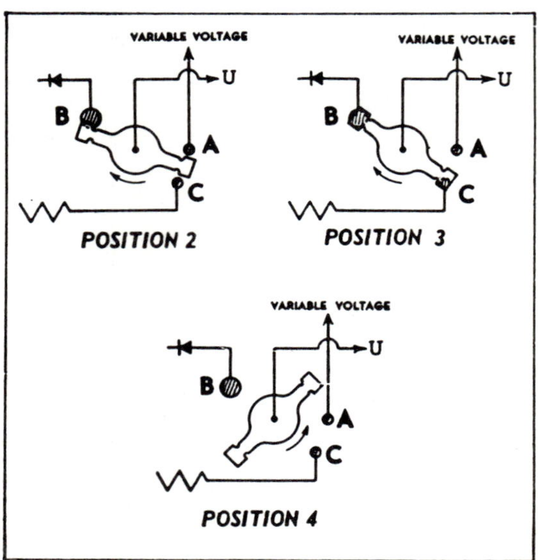

Diagram Showing the Operation of Whistle and Reverse Control in "Multi-Control" Transfarmers

ABOUT WATTAGE

In addition to their voltage and frequency rating, all transformers also bear a wattage rating. The wattage of a transformer corresponds to its *capacity,* or ability to furnish power. While the voltage and frequency of the transformer you must use are determined by the available power line, the selection of its wattage is guided by the size of your outfit and the number of lights and operating accessories. In planning to expand your railroad always estimate the power you will need to find out if your transformer will be adequate. *It is always wisest to get a transformer larger than the one you require for your immediate needs to provide power for future expansion.*

As a transformer becomes warm when in use its output normally diminishes. Because of this fact not more than three-quarters of its rated wattage should be drawn from a transformer continuously.

POWER REQUIREMENTS

The following table lists the power in watts used by various model railroad components:

"027" locomotive	25-35*
"O" locomotive	30-40*
Smoke generator	5
Operating accessories	10-40
Automatic track signals	10-15
Each 6-volt lamp	1.5
Each 14-volt lamp (small)	2.
Each 14-volt lamp (large)	3.
Each 18-volt lamp	5.

* These wattages are drawn by locomotives when pulling the regular number of cars and include the power used by the whistle. However, you must add the power used by lamps in illuminated cars.

Power requirements of automatic couplers and operating cars need not be added in the total since couplers draw current only for an instant and operating cars only when the train is not running. For the same reason do not add the power used by such accessories as the Lumber and Coal Loaders, Automatic Lift Bridges, and others. All such accessories can be generally used even with the smallest transformers, provided that they are operated when the train is standing still.

Accessory lights and equipment containing steadily burning lamps, such as switches and switch controllers, use a considerable amount of power and should be added in the total power requirements.

The following table can be used as a guide for the selection of additional accessories for your outfit or for a more adequate transformer for your railroad system.

Transformer	Capacity	Recommended for Operating the Following
1033 1044 4090	90 watts	One "027" outfit with smoke and whistle; few track or signal accessories.
RW	110 watts	Any "O" outfit with smoke and whistle; few switches and other accessories.
KW	190 watts	Two "O" outfits with smoke, whistle, switches and other accessories.
ZW	275 watts	Any practical railroad system with two or more trains, etc.

ABOUT VOLTAGE

A few words about voltage may help you understand the operation of your transformer so that you can use it to the best advantage. The "fixed" voltages marked on your transformer panel or the voltages indicated by your transformer voltage control at any particular setting are almost never the actual voltages delivered to your track or your accessories. The reasons for this variation are several. The voltages marked on your transformers are "nominal". That is, they are accurate only under certain specified conditions: when the line voltage fed into your transformer is just 115 volts and when *no current is drawn* from the transformer. Actually, the line voltages may vary from 125 to 110 volts, or even lower, depending on the standards in your locality and on how much electricity is being used at a particular time. This variation, naturally, results in a comparable variation in the output voltage of the transformer. If your train seems to run slower during a sudden storm it's probably because hundreds of people in your neighborhood had switched on their lights and so depressed the line voltage.

In the same way that a heavy demand for power may lower the voltage in your neighborhood, a heavy load on your transformer lowers *its* output voltage as well. For example, the fixed binding posts which are marked 14 volts may, under actual operating conditions deliver only 12 volts, or even less. In the case of a short circuit so much current is drawn from the transformer that its voltage drops to 2 or 3 volts—too low to operate the train or even light the lamps.

In addition to the voltage loss in the transformer itself, commonly called the "regulation" of the transformer, still further voltage losses occur in connecting wires. For this reason wiring of a large layout should be carefully planned. If a platform is used, the wiring is best located on the under surface of the platform. All wires should be as short as possible. To keep your wiring to a minimum, accessories which require the same voltage, should be ganged up in "parallel." This "feeder" system can be used for wiring operating accessories as well.

USING AUXILIARY LOCKONS

In operating large layouts it is frequently found that the train slows down when running on the portion of track farthest from the Lockon. This is due to voltage losses in the track itself and can be remedied by attaching additional Lockons at the points on the track where the train slows down. See Figure 61. Be careful to connect the No. 1 and No. 2 clips of the auxiliary Lockons to similarly numbered clips of the Lockon connected to the transformer or else a short circuit will result. Ordinary lamp cord is well suited to these connections as well as for "feeders" described above.

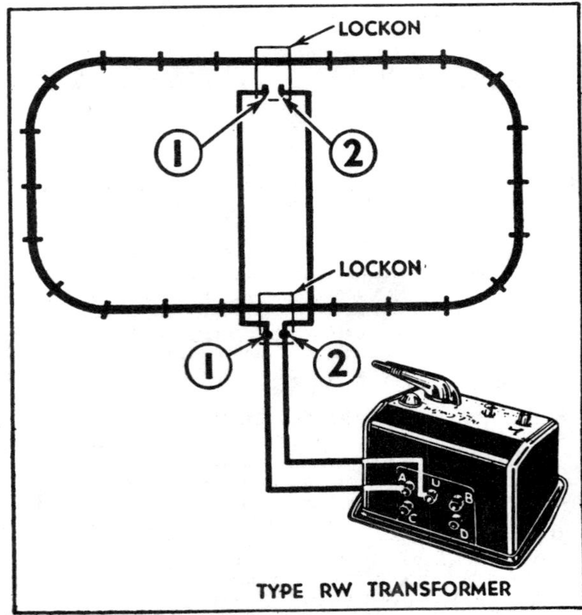

Figure 61—Using Voltage Lockons to Offset Voltage Losses

The main part of voltage losses in the track is due to loose track pins. These loose connections can be frequently detected by the heating effect of poor electrical contacts. After the layout has been in operation for a half hour or so, run your finger down the rails. Loose rail joints will then become apparent as hot spots on the track.

LIONEL TYPE KW "MULTI-CONTROL" TRAINmaster TRANSFORMER

115 Volts 60 Cycles 190 Watts Alternating Current Only

Lionel electric trains operate on low voltage, ranging from 8 to 18 volts, depending on the size and type of the locomotive and the number of cars and accessories used. Lionel transformers reduce, or *transform*, the available house voltage to the low voltage required. The plug at the end of the transformer cord is plugged into any convenient wall outlet and the low voltage is then obtained from the output terminals at the rear of the transformer.

Type "KW" Multi-Control transformers are made to operate on 115-volt 60-cycle alternating current, which is the normal house power supply used in the United States. The wattage rating of the "KW" transformer is 190 watts, and it is powerful enough to operate a railroad system with two trains and several switches and accessories. The wattage of a transformer is a measure of its capacity, or ability to furnish power. While your house current determines the rated *voltage* and *frequency*, in cycles, of the transformer, the *wattage* of the transformer you need is governed by the kind and number of trains and the number of lights and operating accessories in your model railroad system. The larger the train and the greater the number of accessories, the more power you need and the higher should be the wattage rating of your transformer. To assist you in planning your railroad system, the Instruction Booklet lists the power in watts required by each Lionel locomotive and railroad accessory.

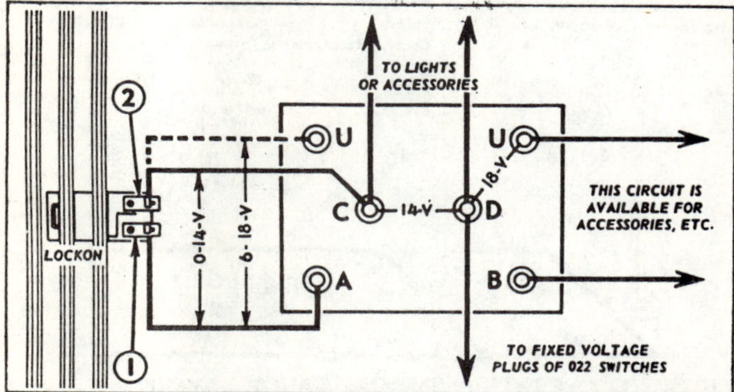

Figure 2—Connections for One-Train Layouts. If 0-14 Volt Range Is Too Low, You Can Use the 6-18 Volt Range by Connecting No. 2 Lockon Clip to Post U Instead of Post C, as Shown by Dotted Line.

HOW TO CONNECT TRANSFORMER TO TRACK

In order to get the electric current from the transformer to the track a pair of transformer posts supplying variable voltage must be connected to the track. The connection to the track is generally made by means of a track lockon. The lockon is clipped onto a convenient section of straight track and its terminals are connected to the transformer posts by means of two lengths of insulated wire. Be sure to use the 18-gauge maroon-covered wire furnished with the transformer.

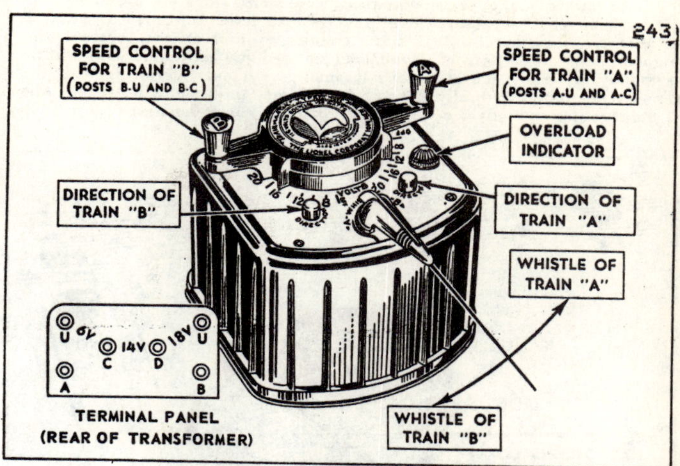

Figure 1—Type "KW" Multi-Control Transformer.

1. Strip the insulation from the ends of the two pieces of wire.
2. Wrap the end of one wire around one of the "U" posts and tighten the thumb nut. If you wrap the wire around the post in clockwise direction it will not slip out as you tighten the nut.
3. Connect the other end of this wire to No. 2 clip of the Lockon. This clip makes a connection to the outside or "ground" rails of the track. Push down the upper half of the clip until the metal loop projects through the slot on top. Insert bare end of the wire in the loop and release. Spring tension will hold the wire tight.
4. In the same manner connect either the "A" or the "B" transformer post to No. 1 clip of the lockon. No. 1 clip makes connection to center or "power" rail of the track.

CONTROLLING LOCOMOTIVE SPEED

"KW" transformers are designed to operate and control two separate train layouts. Train speed is regulated by varying the voltage delivered to the track. This voltage control is accomplished by the two throttles on top of the transformer. Each throttle controls two different voltage ranges.

Throttle "A" controls the voltage of either the A-U (6-18 volts) or the A-C (0-14 volts) circuit.

Throttle "B" controls the voltage of either the B-U (6-18 volts) or the B-C (0-14 volts) circuit.

In most cases, the 6-18 volt range is the best to use.

Note: Although the lettering on the transformer case indicates 20 volts as the maximum voltage available from the "KW" transformer this voltage has actually been reduced to 18 volts in order to improve the performance of No. 022 switches and other equipment connected to the "D" post of the transformer.

LIONEL TYPE ZW "MULTI-CONTROL" TRAINmaster TRANSFORMER

115 Volts 60 Cycles 275 Watts

Alternating Current Only

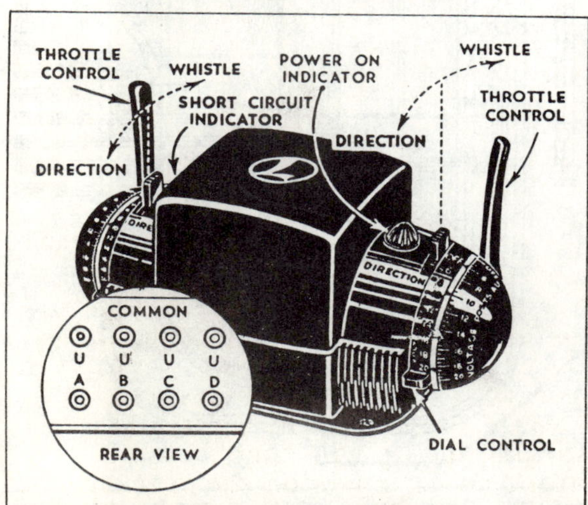

Figure 1—Type ZW "Multi-Control" Transformer.

Lionel electric trains operate on low voltage, ranging from 8 to 18 volts, depending on the size and type of the locomotive and the number of cars and accessories used. Lionel Transformers reduce, or *transform*, the available house voltage to the low voltage required. The plug at the end of the transformer cord is plugged into any convenient wall outlet of required voltage and frequency and the low voltage is then obtained from the output terminals at the rear of the transformer.

Type "ZW" Multi-Control Transformers are made to operate on 115-volt 60-cycle alternating current, which is the normal house power supply used in the United States. The wattage rating of the "ZW" Transformer is 275 watts, making it the most powerful model railroad transformer manufactured by Lionel. The wattage of a transformer is a measure of its *capacity*, or ability to furnish power. While your house current determines the rated voltage and frequency in cycles of the transformer, the wattage of the transformer you need is governed by the kind and number of trains and the number of lights and operating accessories in your model railroad system. The larger the train and the greater the number of accessories, the more power you need and the higher should be the wattage rating of the transformer. To assist you in planning your railroad system, the Instruction Booklet lists the power in watts required by each Lionel locomotive and accessory.

MULTI-CONTROL TRANSFORMERS

"ZW" Transformers have been given the name of "Multi-Control" transformers. This means that all the controls necessary for operating your locomotive and whistle are built into the transformer itself.

"ZW" Transformers are so designed that two trains can be operated and controlled independently of each other without any additional equipment. A method for operating two or more trains will be described later. On each end of the transformer there is a long throttle-type lever. This is the speed control. By moving this throttle you can regulate the voltage supplied to the track so that the train can be gradually accelerated or retarded in a realistic fashion. In Figure 2 the left-hand throttle controls the voltage supplied by the output binding posts labeled "A-U", while the right-hand throttle controls the pair labeled "D-U".

Next to each of the throttles you will find a short lever. This is a combination whistle and reversing control for that circuit. Moving the lever away from you, toward the side marked "Whistle", blows the train whistle. Moving the lever toward you, to the side marked "Direction", stops, starts and reverses the locomotive. A separate whistle and reverse lever is provided for each of the two throttle-controlled train circuits so that if you operate two trains on separate sections of your model railroad you can sound each whistle separately and start and stop each locomotive without interfering with the action of the other. Naturally, if you have only one train you will use only one of the throttles and only the whistle and direction controller next to it.

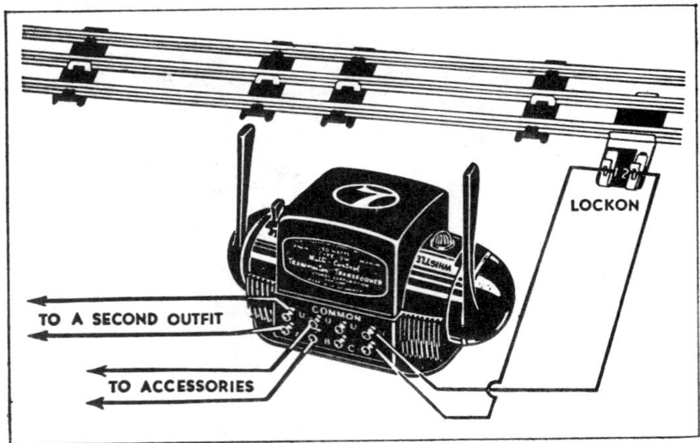

Figure 2—How to Connect the Transformer to Track.

CONNECTING TRANSFORMER TO TRACK

"ZW" Multi-Control Transformers have four pairs of binding posts located on the rear wall of the transformer case. Each pair of these posts provides a separate power source which can be controlled independently of the other three. *Of these the "A-U" and the "D-U" combinations are controlled by the throttles as described above and should be used for the main track supply.* The two center combinations, "B-U" and "C-U", are reserved for accessories as described in a later section.

In order to get current from a transformer to the track a pair of transformer binding posts must be connected to the track. This connection is generally made by means of a track Lockon, although in permanent installations the wires are sometimes soldered in place. The Lockon is clipped onto a convenient section of straight track and its terminals are connected to the binding posts by means of two lengths of insulated wire.

1. Strip the rubber insulation from the ends of two pieces of wire.
2. Wrap the end of one wire around one of the "U" binding posts of transformer and tighten thumb nut. Wire should be wrapped around post in clockwise direction.
3. Connect other end of this wire to No. 2 Lockon clip. Push down upper half of clip until metal loop projects through the slot on top. Insert bare end of wire into this loop and release clip.
4. In the same manner connect No. 1 Lockon clip to either "A" or "D" binding post and tighten thumb nut.

After the transformer is properly connected to the track, push the plug at the end of your transformer cord into a wall outlet. The green pilot light on the transformer should now go on. This indicates that the power is flowing into the transformer and that you have no "short circuits."

HOW THE CIRCUIT BREAKER OPERATES

To protect the transformer from overheating and damage due to short circuits "ZW" Transformers are equipped with built-in automatic circuit breakers. Whenever the current drawn from the transformer exceeds a certain limit the red warning light flashes on and the circuit breaker opens, cutting off power to the track. In a few seconds the circuit breaker automatically closes and the red light goes off. If, however, the short circuit which caused the overload still exists, the red light will go on again and the circuit breaker will reopen. This sequence will continue without damage to the transformer until the cause of the short circuit has been removed.

A short circuit is an excessive load on the transformer caused by a direct connection between the center rail and one of the outside rails. A derailed car or locomotive is the most frequent cause of short circuit so make sure that all the wheels of locomotive and cars are properly set on the rails. If your transformer shows a short circuit even after all the rolling stock has been removed from the rails it is probably due either to incorrect wire connections or to broken insulation on the power rail.

It is important to understand that the purpose of the circuit breaker is to protect the transformer itself. It operates only if the transformer is overloaded. It is possible, therefore, particularly in very large layouts, for the track to be "shorted" without causing the circuit breaker to operate or the red light to flash. In this case, although the transformer voltage may drop below the operating point of the trains, the transformer will not be injured because it is not being overloaded beyond its safe limit.

NOTE: After your transformer has been operating for a while you will find it warm to the touch. It is the nature of all electrical power equipment to become warm when in use.

WARNING: Do not attempt to blow the whistle while there is a short circuit or you may damage the whistle controller.

HOW TO CONNECT ACCESSORIES

While transformer binding posts "A-U" and "D-U" are reserved for train control, "B-U" and "C-U" are intended to supply power for lights, switches and other accessory equipment. The voltage supplied by these two combinations is regulated by the two dials located next to the throttle controls and may be set to any figure indicated on the dial. Most illuminated accessories operate on 12-14 volts, while operating accessories work on voltage ranging from 10 to 16 volts depending on the condition of the accessory, the higher voltage being frequently necessary when the accessory is new and its working parts stiff.

To determine the proper voltage for your accessories connect the accessory terminals to "B-U" or "C-U" posts of your transformer and slowly move the corresponding dial control from zero to the point where you get the desired brightness of illumination or satisfactory operation of the mechanism. Be careful, particularly in the case of illuminated accessories, not to set the voltage too high, or you will burn out the lamps. If you operate with the lowest voltage possible you will greatly extend the life of your lamps and other equipment. In the event that you have several accessories requiring the same voltage, it is possible to use the same transformer binding posts for all. A simple method for wiring a number of lights, etc. in "parallel" is shown in Figure 4. Two "feeders" to the transformer and individual leads from the feeder to each accessory eliminate unnecessary wiring. If your railroad is operated on a table or platform, the feeders may be concealed by attaching them underneath the platform and boring small holes for leads to each accessory. Remember that if two or more 12-volt accessories are wired together in "parallel", the voltage required is still 12 volts regardless of whether two, three or more accessories are so connected.

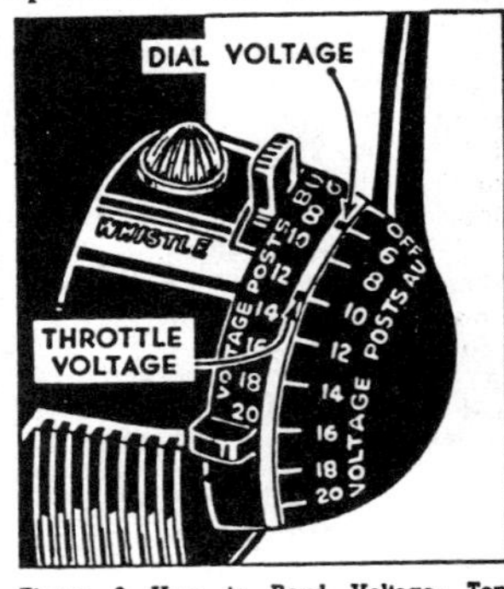

Figure 3—How to Read Voltage. Top Line Indicates Dial Voltage; Bottom Line Throttle Voltage. In this case the Accessory Voltage is Set at 8 Volts While the Track Voltage is 10 Volts.

Figure 4—How to Connect Accessories in "Parallel."

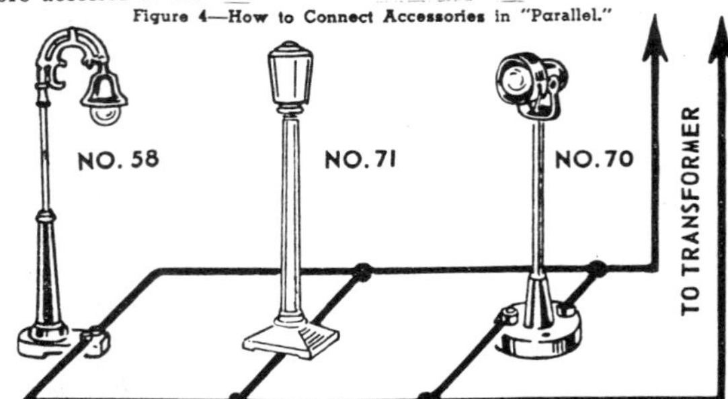

HOW TO OPERATE A TYPICAL LARGE LAYOUT

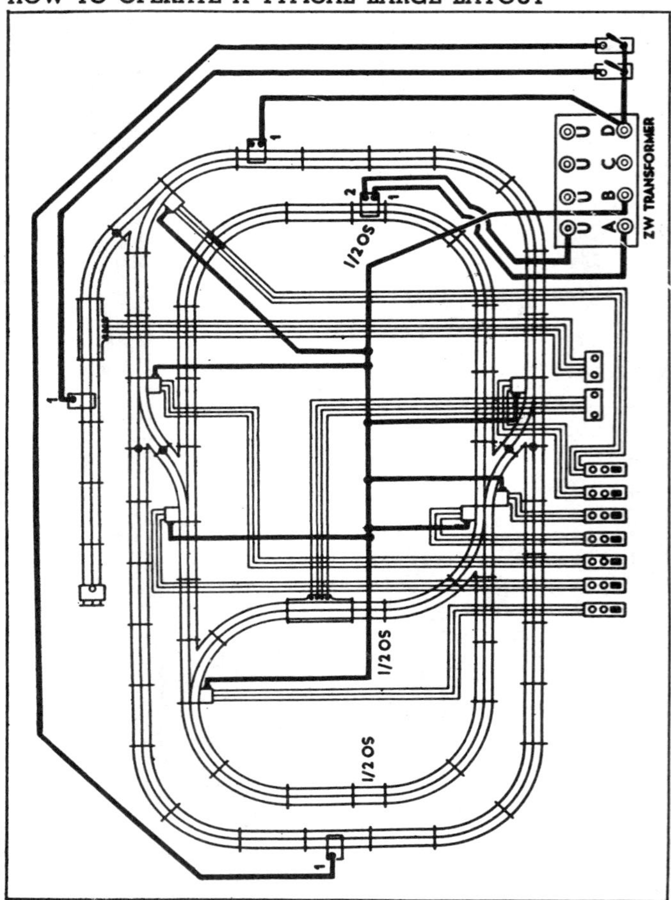

Figure 5—A Typical "O" Gauge Layout for Operating Two Trains. Track needed: 33 sections straight track, 3 half-sections straight track, 18 sections curved track, 4 right hand switches, 3 left hand switches, 2 remote control sections, 1 bumper.

Figure 5 shows an "O" Gauge layout for running two trains independently. In order to operate two trains in this manner, the layout must be "sectionalized", that is, one loop insulated from the other loop by fibre pins at each of the points indicated by dots. Each loop is controlled by a separate throttle lever, while the accessory binding posts are used for switches and other accessories which may be in the railroad system. Although this layout shows seven switches, three of these may be eliminated by leaving off the siding in the upper right of the diagram, and the connecting track in the center of the inside loop. Each switch has its own controller. For convenience all controllers should be mounted on a centrally located panel board. Two sections of Remote Control track used for uncoupling and for unloading are also shown on the layout.

When crossing from one loop to another it is important that the voltages supplied to the inner and the outer loops are approximately equal. This is done by setting both throttles at the same point. Unless this is done, the contact rollers of the locomotive crossing the insulating pins which separate the two circuits will bridge two dissimilar voltages causing a short circuit and stopping the train.

In the lower right hand corner of the diagram are shown two switches. The purpose of the left hand switch is to cut the current in or out of the siding, as desired. The other switch sectionalizes the left half of the outside loop. It will be convenient when you desire to stop a train on the left half of the outside loop while a second train crosses over from the inside loop to the right half of the outside loop.

OPERATING ADDITIONAL TRAINS

Since "ZW" Transformers have four independently variable circuits, as many as four trains can be operated independently of each other with a proper layout. However, in order to control the whistles and direction of the two additional trains, external No. 167 Whistle Controllers have to be added to the "B-U" and "C-U" circuits, since these two circuits do not have built-in controls. For directions on connecting and operating the 167 Whistle Controller see the Instruction Booklet or the leaflet supplied with controllers.